Active Directory Cookbook™

Other Microsoft .NET resources from O'Reilly

Related titles

Active Directory

Windows Server Cookbook™

Windows Server Hacks™

Windows Server 2003
  Network Administration

Learning Windows Server
  2003

**.NET Books
Resource Center**

dotnet.oreilly.com is a complete catalog of O'Reilly's books on .NET and related technologies, including sample chapters and code examples.

ONDotnet.com provides independent coverage of fundamental, interoperable, and emerging Microsoft .NET programming and web services technologies.

Conferences

O'Reilly brings diverse innovators together to nurture the ideas that spark revolutionary industries. We specialize in documenting the latest tools and systems, translating the innovator's knowledge into useful skills for those in the trenches. Visit *conferences.oreilly.com* for our upcoming events.

Safari Bookshelf (*safari.oreilly.com*) is the premier online reference library for programmers and IT professionals. Conduct searches across more than 1,000 books. Subscribers can zero in on answers to time-critical questions in a matter of seconds. Read the books on your Bookshelf from cover to cover or simply flip to the page you need. Try it today for free.

SECOND EDITION

Active Directory Cookbook™

Robbie Allen and Laura E. Hunter

O'REILLY®

Beijing · Cambridge · Farnham · Köln · Paris · Sebastopol · Taipei · Tokyo

Active Directory Cookbook™, Second Edition
by Robbie Allen and Laura E. Hunter

Published by O'Reilly Media, Inc., 1005 Gravenstein Highway North, Sebastopol, CA 95472.

O'Reilly books may be purchased for educational, business, or sales promotional use. Online editions are also available for most titles (*safari.oreilly.com*). For more information, contact our corporate/institutional sales department: (800) 998-9938 or *corporate@oreilly.com*.

Editor: Jeff Pepper

Production Editor: Laurel R.T. Ruma

Copyeditor: Derek Di Matteo

Proofreaders: Laurel R.T. Ruma and Sanders Kleinfeld

Indexer: Ellen Troutman

Cover Designer: Karen Montgomery

Interior Designer: David Futato

Illustrators: Robert Romano and Jessamyn Read

Printing History:

September 2003:   First Edition.

June 2006:   Second Edition.

ISBN: 0-596-10202-X

[M]

Table of Contents

Preface

In 1998 when Robbie first became involved with the Microsoft Windows 2000 Joint Development Program (JDP), there was very little data available on Active Directory. In the following months and even after the initial release of Windows 2000, there were very few books or white papers to help early adopters of Active Directory get started. And some of the information that had been published was often inaccurate or misleading. Many early deployers had to learn by trial and error. As time passed, more and more informative books were published, which helped fill the information gap.

By the end of the second year of its release, there was an explosion of information on Active Directory. Not only were there more than 50 books published, but Microsoft also cleaned up their documentation on MSDN (*http://msdn.microsoft.com*) and their AD web site (*http://www.microsoft.com/ad*). Now those sites have numerous white papers, many of which could serve as mini booklets. Other web sites have popped up as well that contain a great deal of information on Active Directory. With Windows Server 2003, Microsoft has taken their level of documentation a step higher. Extensive information on Active Directory is available directly from any Windows Server 2003 computer in the form of the Help and Support Center (available from the Start Menu). So with all this data available on Active Directory in the form of published books, white papers, web sites, and even from within the operating system, why would you want to purchase this one?

In the summer of 2002, Robbie was thumbing through the *Perl Cookbook* from O'Reilly, looking for help with an automation script that he was writing for Active Directory. It just so happened that there was a recipe that addressed the specific task he was trying to perform. In Cookbook parlance, a recipe provides instructions on how to solve a particular problem. We thought that since Active Directory is such a task-oriented environment, the Cookbook approach might be a very good format. After a little research, we found there were books (often multiple) on nearly every facet of Active Directory, including introductory books, design guides, books that focused on migration, programming books, and reference books. The one type of book that we didn't see was a task-oriented "how to" book, which is exactly what the Cookbook format provides.

Based on our experience, hours of research, and years of hanging out on Active Directory newsgroups and mailing lists, we've compiled more than 500 recipes that should answer the majority of "How do I do X" questions one could pose about Active Directory. And just as in the Perl community where the *Perl Cookbook* was a great addition that sells well even today, we believe the *Active Directory Cookbook*, Second Edition, will also be a great addition to any Active Directory library.

Who Should Read This Book?

As with many of the books in the Cookbook series, the *Active Directory Cookbook*, Second Edition, can be useful to anyone who has to deploy, administer, or automate Active Directory. This book can serve as a great reference for those who have to work with Active Directory on a day-to-day basis. And because of all the programming samples, this book can be really beneficial to programmers who want to get a jump-start on performing certain tasks in an application. For those without much programming background, the VBScript and Perl solutions are straightforward and should be pretty easy to follow and expand on.

The companion to this book, *Active Directory*, Third Edition, Joe Richards et al. (O'Reilly), is a great choice for those wanting a thorough description of the core concepts behind Active Directory, how to design an Active Directory infrastructure, and how to automate that infrastructure using Active Directory Service Interfaces (ADSI) and Windows Management Instrumentation (WMI). *Active Directory*, Third Edition, does not describe how to accomplish every possible task within Active Directory; that is the purpose of this book. These two books, along with the supplemental information should be sufficient to answer most questions you have about Active Directory.

What's in This Book?

This book consists of 23 chapters. Here is a brief overview of each chapter:

Chapter 1, *Getting Started*
> Sets the stage for the book by covering where you can find the tools used in the book, VBScript and Perl issues to consider, and where to find additional information.

Chapter 2, *Forests, Domains, and Trusts*
> Covers how to create and remove forests and domains, update the domain mode or functional levels, create different types of trusts, and other administrative trust tasks.

Chapter 3, *Domain Controllers, Global Catalogs, and FSMOs*
> Covers promoting and demoting domain controllers, finding domain controllers, enabling the global catalog, and finding and managing Flexible Single Master Operations (FSMO) roles.

Chapter 4, *Searching and Manipulating Objects*

Covers the basics of searching Active Directory: creating, modifying, and deleting objects, using LDAP controls, and importing and exporting data using LDAP Data Interchange Format (LDIF) and comma-separated variable (CSV) files.

Chapter 5, *Organizational Units*

Covers creating, moving, and deleting Organizational Units, and managing the objects contained within them.

Chapter 6, *Users*

Covers all aspects of managing user objects, including creating, renaming, moving, resetting passwords, unlocking, modifying the profile attributes, and locating users that have certain criteria (e.g., password is about to expire).

Chapter 7, *Groups*

Covers how to create groups, modify group scope, and type and manage membership.

Chapter 8, *Computers*

Covers creating computers, joining computers to a domain, resetting computers, and locating computers that match certain criteria (e.g., have been inactive for a number of weeks).

Chapter 9, *Printers and Shared Folders*

Covers new features that are available in the File Server Resource Manager and Print Manager in Windows Server 2003 R2, including new disk quota management capabilities and information on creating file screens to control what types of data can be saved to a shared folder.

Chapter 10, *Group Policy Objects*

Covers how to create, modify, link, copy, import, back up, restore, and delete GPOs using the Group Policy Management Console and scripting interface.

Chapter 11, *Schema*

Covers basic schema administration tasks, such as generating object identifiers (OIDs) and schemaIDGUIDs, how to use LDIF to extend the schema, and how to locate attributes or classes that match certain criteria (e.g., all attributes that are indexed).

Chapter 12, *Site Topology*

Covers how to manage sites, subnets, site links, and connection objects.

Chapter 13, *Replication*

Covers how to trigger and disable the Knowledge Consistency Checker (KCC), how to query metadata, force replication, and determine what changes have yet to replicate between domain controllers.

Chapter 14, *DNS and DHCP*

Covers creating zones and resource records, modifying DNS server configuration, querying DNS, and customizing the resource records a domain controller dynamically registers.

Chapter 15, *Security and Authentication*
> Covers how to delegate control, view and modify permissions, view effective permissions, and manage Kerberos tickets.

Chapter 16, *Logging, Monitoring, and Quotas*
> Covers how to enable auditing, diagnostics, DNS, NetLogon, Kerberos and GPO logging, obtain LDAP query statistics, and manage quotas.

Chapter 17, *Backup, Recovery, DIT Maintenance, and Deleted Objects*
> Covers how to back up Active Directory, perform authoritative and nonauthoritative restores, check DIT file integrity, perform online and offline defrags, and search for deleted objects.

Chapter 18, *Application Partitions*
> Covers creating and managing application partitions.

Chapter 19, *Active Directory Application Mode*
> Covers the new Active Directory Application Mode (ADAM) functionality that's available with R2.

Chapter 20, *Interoperability and Integration*
> Covers how to integrate Active Directory with various applications, services, and programming languages.

Chapter 21, *Active Directory Federation Services*
> Covers the new Active Directory Federation Services (ADFS) that's included with Windows Server 2003 R2.

Chapter 22, *Exchange Server 2003*
> Covers common administrative tasks for Exchange Server 2003.

Chapter 23, *Microsoft Identity Integration Server*
> Provides an introduction to Microsoft's Identity Integration Server (MIIS), a service that can be used to synchronize multiple directories or enforce data integrity within a single or multiple stores.

Conventions Used in This Book

The following typographical conventions are used in this book:

Constant width
> Indicates command-line elements, computer output, and code examples.

Constant width italic
> Indicates placeholders (for which you substitute an actual name) in examples and in registry keys

Constant width bold
> Indicates user input

Italic

> Introduces new terms and example URLs, commands, file extensions, filenames, directory or folder names, and UNC pathnames

 Indicates a tip, suggestion, or general note. For example, we'll tell you if you need to use a particular version or if an operation requires certain privileges.

 Indicates a warning or caution. For example, we'll tell you if Active Directory does not behave as you'd expect or if a particular operation has a negative impact on performance.

Using Code Examples

This book is here to help you get your job done. In general, you may use the code in this book in your programs and documentation. You do not need to contact us for permission unless you're reproducing a significant portion of the code. For example, writing a program that uses several chunks of code from this book does not require permission. Selling or distributing a CD-ROM of examples from O'Reilly books *does* require permission. Answering a question by citing this book and quoting example code does not require permission. Incorporating a significant amount of example code from this book into your product's documentation *does* require permission.

We appreciate, but do not require, attribution. An attribution usually includes the title, author, publisher, and ISBN. For example: *Active Directory Cookbook*, Second Edition, by Robbie Allen and Laura E. Hunter. Copyright 2006 O'Reilly Media, Inc., 0-596-10202-X.

If you feel your use of code examples falls outside fair use or the permission given above, feel free to contact us at *permissions@oreilly.com*.

We'd Like Your Feedback!

We at O'Reilly have tested and verified the information in this book to the best of our ability, but mistakes and oversights do occur. Please let us know about errors you may find, as well as your suggestions for future editions, by writing to:

O'Reilly Media, Inc.
1005 Gravenstein Highway North
Sebastopol, CA 95472
800-998-9938 (in the U.S. or Canada)
707-829-0515 (international or local)
707-829-0104 (fax)

We have a web page for the book where we list errata, examples, or any additional information. You can access this page at:

> http://www.oreilly.com/catalog/activedckbk2/

Examples can also be found at the author's web site:

> http://www.rallenhome.com/books/adcookbook2

To comment or ask technical questions about this book, send email to:

> bookquestions@oreilly.com

For more information about our books, conferences, software, Resource Centers, and the O'Reilly Network, see our web site at:

> http://www.oreilly.com

Safari® Enabled

 When you see a Safari® Enabled icon on the cover of your favorite technology book, that means the book is available online through the O'Reilly Network Safari Bookshelf.

Safari offers a solution that's better than e-books. It's a virtual library that lets you easily search thousands of top tech books, cut and paste code samples, download chapters, and find quick answers when you need the most accurate, current information. Try it for free at *http://safari.oreilly.com*.

Acknowledgments

Robbie Allen, from the First Edition

The people at O'Reilly were a joy to work with. I would like to thank Robert Denn for helping me get this book off the ground. I am especially grateful for Andy Oram's insightful and thought-provoking feedback.

I was very fortunate to have an all-star group of technical reviewers. If there was ever a need to assemble a panel of the top Active Directory experts, you would be hard pressed to find a more knowledgeable group of guys. Here they are in alphabetical order:

Rick Kingslan is a Senior Systems Engineer and Microsoft Windows Server MVP. If you've ever posted a question to an Active Directory newsgroup or discussion forum, odds are Rick participated in the thread. His uncanny ability to provide useful feedback on just about any Active Directory problem helped ensure I covered all the angles with each recipe.

Gil Kirkpatrick is the Executive Vice President & CTO of NetPro (*http://www.netpro.com*). Gil is also the author of *Active Directory Programming* from MacMillan. His extensive knowledge of the underpinnings of Active Directory helped clarify several issues I did not address adequately the first time through.

Tony Murray is the maintainer of the *www.ActiveDir.org* web site and mailing list, which is one of the premier Active Directory discussion forums. The myriad of questions posed to the list served as inspiration for this book. Tony's comments and suggestions throughout the book helped tremendously.

Todd Myrick has a unique perspective on Active Directory from his experience inside the government. Todd contributed several outside the-box ideas to the book that only a creative person, such as he, could have done.

Joe Richards is the creator of the *http://www.joeware.net* web site, which contains many must-have Active Directory tools, such as AdFind, Unlock, and much more. Joe is one of the most experienced Active Directory administrators and programmers I've met. He's had to do most of the tasks in this book at one point or another, so his contributions were significant.

Kevin Sullivan is the Project Manager for Enterprise Directory Management at Aelita. Kevin has as much experience with Active Directory as anyone you'll find. He is a frequent contributor to Active Directory discussion forums, and he provided numerous suggestions and clarifications throughout the book.

Last, but certainly not least, I would like to thank my wife Janet. Her love, support, and bright smile are constant reminders of how lucky I am. Did I mention she cooks, too?!

Laura E. Hunter, from the Second Edition

Like Robbie, I find that the O'Reilly staff always manage to make the writing and reviewing process a smooth one, and this project was no exception. I'd like to thank Robbie himself for tapping me to update this wonderful book to the Second Edition. The original incarnation of the *Active Directory Cookbook* remains one of the most well-read books on my AD bookshelf, so undertaking this project with Robbie was quite exciting.

I'd also like to thank Robbie for assembling yet another team of amazing technical reviewers, a number of whom have made a return engagement from reviewing the first edition of the book: Robert Buike, Rick Kingslan, Al Mulnick, Tony Murray, and Joe Richards.

Throughout the writing and editing process, my technical reviewers have helped me, challenged me, encouraged me, kept me honest, and occasionally even made me laugh out loud (which is quite a blessing when you're plugging away at an extensive project such as this one). I can't imagine completing this project without their advice, assistance, and input.

In addition to my technical reviewers, I would like to thank Brian Puhl of Microsoft for his assistance with the ADFS chapter, Gil Kirkpatrick of NetPro and Steven Plank of Microsoft for their outstanding work on the MIIS content, and Dean Wells of MSE Technology for being a generally outstanding resource for all things Active Directory. (He's not half-bad at karaoke, either.)

Finally, many thanks are due to my family for tolerating the continuous game of "Where's Laura?" during the weeks that I hid away in my office to complete this project, as well as my extended family within the Microsoft MVP program: Mark Arnold, Suzanna Moran (my running buddy from 3,000 miles away), Rafael Munoz, Sean O'Driscoll, Susan Leiter, Thomas Lee, Jimmy Andersson, Don Wells, Gary Wilson, Stuart Kwan, and Candice Pedersen.

## CHAPTER 1

Getting Started

1.0 Approach to the Book

If you are familiar with the O'Reilly Cookbook format that can be seen in other popular books, such as the *Perl Cookbook*, *Java Cookbook*, and *DNS and BIND Cookbook*, then the layout of this book will be familiar to you. The book is composed of 23 chapters, each containing 10 to 30 recipes for performing a specific Active Directory task. Within each recipe are four sections: Problem, Solution, Discussion, and See Also. The Problem section briefly describes the task that the recipe focuses on. The Solution section contains step-by-step instructions on how to accomplish the task. The Discussion section contains detailed information about the problem or solution. The See Also section contains references to additional sources of information that can be useful if you still need more information after reading the discussion. The See Also section may reference other recipes, MS Knowledge Base (*http:// support.microsoft.com*) articles, or documentation from the Microsoft Developers Network (MSDN; *http://msdn.microsoft.com*).

At Least Three Ways to Do It!

When we first began developing the content for the book, we struggled with how to capture the fact that you can do things multiple ways with Active Directory. You may be familiar with the famous Perl motto: There Is More Than One Way To Do It; well with Active Directory, there are often At Least Three Ways To Do It. You can perform a task with a graphical user interface (GUI), such as ADSI Edit, LDP, or the Active Directory Users and Computers snap-in; you can use a command-line interface (CLI), such as the *ds* utilities (i.e., *dsadd*, *dsmod*, *dsrm*, *dsquery*, *dsget*), *nltest*, *netdom*, *ldifde*, or freeware tools such as *adfind* and *admod* from *http://www.joeware. net*; and, finally, you can perform the same task using a scripting language, such as VBScript or Perl.

Since people prefer different methods, and no single method is necessarily better than another, we decided to write solutions to the recipes using one of each. That means instead of just a single solution per recipe, we include up to three solutions using GUI, CLI, and programmatic examples; in some cases you'll find more than one option for a given solution, as in the case where there is more than one command-line utility to perform a particular task. However, in cases where one of the methods cannot be used or would be too difficult to use to accomplish a given recipe, only the applicable methods are covered.

We also took this approach with the programmatic solutions; we use VBScript for the programming language, primarily because it is widely used among Windows administrators and is the most straightforward from a code perspective when using Active Directory Service Interface (ADSI) and Windows Script Host (WSH). For those familiar with other languages, such as Visual Basic, Perl, and JScript, it is very easy to convert code from VBScript.

The downside to using VBScript is that it does not have all of the facilities necessary to accomplish some complicated tasks. Therefore, we use Perl in a few recipes that require a complicated programmatic solution. For those of you who wish that all of the solutions were written with Perl instead of VBScript, you are in luck. On the book's web site, we've posted companion Perl solutions for every recipe that had a VBScript solution. Go to *http://www.rallenhome.com/books/adcookbook2/code.html* to download the code.

Windows 2000 Versus Windows Server 2003

Another challenge with writing this book is there are now three versions of Active Directory deployed on most corporate networks. The initial version released with Windows 2000 was followed by Windows Server 2003, and recently Microsoft released Windows Server 2003 R2, which provides a lot of updates and new features. We've decided to go with the approach of making everything work under the most recent version of Active Directory first, and earlier versions of Windows second. In fact, the majority of the solutions will work unchanged with Windows 2000 or 2003. For the recipes or solutions that are specific to a particular version, we include a note mentioning the version it is targeted for. Most GUI and programmatic solutions will work unchanged with all three versions, but Microsoft introduced several new CLIs with Windows Server 2003 and R2, most of which cannot be run on the Windows 2000 operating system. Typically, you can still use these newer tools on a Windows XP or Windows Server 2003 computer to manage Windows 2000 Active Directory.

1.1   Where to Find the Tools

For the GUI and CLI solutions to mean much to you, you need access to the tools that are used in the examples. The Windows 2000 Server Resource Kit and Windows Server 2003 Resource Kit are invaluable sources of information, along with providing numerous tools that aid administrators in daily tasks. More information on the Resource Kits can be found at the following web site: *http://www.microsoft.com/windows/reskits/*. The Windows 2000 Support Tools package, which in Windows Server 2003 is called the Windows Support Tools package, contains many essential tools for people that work with Active Directory. The Microsoft installer (MSI) for the Windows Support Tools can be found on a Windows 2000 Server, Windows Server 2003, or Windows Server 2003 R2 CD in the *\support\tools* directory. You can also use the Tool Finder feature available on the ActiveDir web site, located at *http://www.activedir.org/TF/Default.aspx*.

You'll also find a number of references to third-party command-line tools such as *adfind*, *admod*, *oldcmp*, *findexpacc*, and *memberof*. These tools were developed by Microsoft Directory Services MVP Joe Richards, and he has made them available for free download from his web site at *http://www.joeware.net*. While these tools are not native to the Windows operating system, they have become an invaluable addition to many Active Directory system administrators' toolkits, and we include them here to showcase their capabilities.

Once you have the tools at your disposal, there are a couple other issues to be aware of while trying to apply the solutions in your environment, which we'll now describe.

Running Tools with Alternate Credentials

A best practice for managing Active Directory is to create separate administrator accounts that you grant elevated privileges, instead of letting administrators use their normal user account that they use to access other Network Operating System (NOS) resources. This is beneficial because an administrator who wants to use elevated privileges has to log on with his administrative account explicitly instead of having the rights implicitly, which could lead to accidental changes in Active Directory. Assuming you employ this method, then you must provide alternate credentials when using tools to administer Active Directory unless you log on to a machine, such as a domain controller, with the administrative credentials.

There are several options for specifying alternate credentials. Many GUI and CLI tools have an option to specify a user and password to authenticate with. If the tool you want to use does not have that option, you can use the runas command instead. The following command would run the enumprop command from the Resource Kit under the credentials of the administrator account in the *rallencorp.com* domain:

```
> runas /user:administrator@rallencorp.com
/netonly "enumprop "LDAP://dc1/dc=rallencorp,dc=com""
```

To run a Microsoft Management Console (MMC) console with alternate credentials, simply use mmc as the command to run from runas:

```
> runas /user:administrator@rallencorp.com /netonly "mmc"
```

This will create an empty MMC console from which you can add consoles for any snap-ins that have been installed on the local computer.

The /netonly switch is necessary if the user you are authenticating with does not have local logon rights on the machine you are running the command from.

There is another option for running MMC snap-ins with alternate credentials. Click on the Start menu and browse to the tool you want to open, hold down the Shift key, and then right-click on the tool. If you select Run As, you will be prompted to enter credentials to run the tool under.

Targeting Specific Domain Controllers

Another issue to be aware of when following the instructions in the recipes is whether you need to target a specific domain controller. In the solutions in this book, we typically do not target a specific domain controller. When you don't specify a domain controller, you are using a *serverless bind* and there is no guarantee as to which server you will be hitting. Depending on your environment and the task you need to do, you may want to target a specific domain controller so that you know where the query or change will be taking place. Also, serverless binding can work only if the DNS for the Active Directory forest is configured properly and your client can query it. If you have a standalone Active Directory environment that has no ties to your corporate DNS, you may need to target a specific domain controller for the tools to work.

1.2   Getting Familiar with LDIF

Even with the new utilities available with Windows Server 2003, native support for modifying data within Active Directory using a command-line tool is relatively weak. The *dsmod* tool can modify attributes on a limited set of object classes, but it does not allow you to modify every object type.

One reason for the lack of native command-line tools to do this is that the command line is not well suited for manipulating objects, for example, that have multivalued attributes. If you want to specify more than just one or two values, a single command could get quite long. It would be easier to use a GUI editor, such as ADSI Edit, to do the task instead.

The LDAP Data Interchange Format (LDIF) was designed to address this issue. Defined in RFC 2849, LDIF allows you to represent directory additions, modifications, and deletions in a text-based file, which you can import into a directory using an LDIF-capable tool.

The *ldifde* utility has been available since Windows 2000 and it allows you to import and export Active Directory content in LDIF format. LDIF files are composed of blocks of entries. An entry can add, modify, or delete an object. The first line of an entry is the distinguished name. The second line contains a changetype, which can be add, modify, or delete. If it is an object addition, the rest of the entry contains the attributes that should be initially set on the object (one per line). For object deletions, you do not need to specify any other attributes. And for object modifications, you need to specify at least three more lines. The first should contain the type of modification you want to perform on the object. This can be add (to set a previously unset attribute or to add a new value to a multivalued attribute), replace (to replace an existing value), or delete (to remove a value). The modification type should be followed by a colon and the attribute you want to perform the modification on. The next line should contain the name of the attribute followed by a colon, and the value for the attribute. For example, to replace the last name attribute with the value Smith, you'd use the following LDIF:

```
dn: cn=jsmith,cn=users,dc=rallencorp,dc=com
changetype: modify
replace: sn
sn: Smith
-
```

Modification entries must be followed by a line that only contains a hyphen (-). You can put additional modification actions following the hyphen, each separated by another hyphen. Here is a complete LDIF example that adds a jsmith user object and then modifies the givenName and sn attributes for that object:

```
dn: cn=jsmith,cn=users,dc=rallencorp,dc=com
changetype: add
objectClass: user
samaccountname: jsmith
sn: JSmith

dn: cn=jsmith,cn=users,dc=rallencorp,dc=com
changetype: modify
add: givenName
givenName: Jim
-
replace: sn
sn: Smith
-
```

See Recipes 4.28 and 4.29 for more details on how to use the *ldifde* utility to import and export LDIF files.

1.3 Programming Notes

In the VBScript solutions, our intention was to provide the answer in as few lines of code as necessary. Since this book is not a pure programming book, we did not want to provide a detailed explanation of how to use ADSI or WMI. If you are looking for that, we recommend Part III of *Active Directory*, Third Edition, by Joe Richards et al. (O'Reilly).

The intent of the VBScript code is to provide you the basics for how a task can be automated and let you run with it. Most examples only take some minor tweaking to make them do something useful for you.

Just as with the GUI and CLI solutions, there are some important issues to be aware of when looking at the VBScript solutions.

Serverless Binds

We mentioned earlier that in the GUI and CLI examples we did not provide instructions for targeting a specific domain controller to perform a task. Instead, we rely on serverless binds in most cases. The same applies to the API solutions. A serverless bind for the RootDSE looks like the following in VBScript:

```
set objRootDSE = GetObject("LDAP://RootDSE")
```

That code will query the RootDSE for a domain controller in the domain of the currently logged on user. You can target a specific domain instead by simply specifying the domain name in the ADsPath:

```
set objRootDSE = GetObject("LDAP://apac.rallencorp.com/RootDSE")
```

And similarly, you can target a specific domain controller by including the server name in the ADsPath:

```
set objRootDSE = GetObject("LDAP://dc1/RootDSE")
```

So depending on how your environment is set up and what forest you want to query, you may or may not need to specify a domain or server name in the code.

Running Scripts Using Alternate Credentials

Just as you might need to run the GUI and CLI tools with alternate credentials, you may also need to run your scripts and programs with alternate credentials. One way is to use the runas method described earlier when invoking the script. A better option would be to use the Scheduled Tasks service to run the script under credentials you specify when creating the task. And yet another option is to hardcode the credentials in the script. Obviously, this is not very appealing in some scenarios because credentials can change over time, and as a security best practice you do not want the username and password contained in a script to be easily viewable by others. Nevertheless, it is a necessary evil, especially when developing against multiple forests, and we'll describe how it can be done with ADSI and ADO. As an alternative, you can configure a script to prompt you for the username and password during the actual running of the script.

With ADSI, you can use the IADsOpenDSObject::OpenDSObject method to specify alternate credentials. You can quickly turn any ADSI-based example in this book into one that authenticates as a particular user.

For example, a solution to print out the description of a domain might look like the following:

```
set objDomain = GetObject("LDAP://dc=apac,dc=rallencorp,dc=com")
WScript.Echo "Description: " & objDomain.Get("description")
```

Using `OpenDSObject`, it takes only one additional statement to make the same code authenticate as the administrator in the domain:

```
set objLDAP = GetObject("LDAP:")
set objDomain = objLDAP.OpenDSObject( _
    "LDAP://dc=apac,dc=rallencorp,dc=com", _
    "administrator@apac.rallencorp.com", _
    "MyPassword", _
    0)
WScript.Echo "Description: " & objDomain.Get("description")
```

It is just as easy to authenticate in ADO code as well. Take the following example, which queries all computer objects in the *apac.rallencorp.com* domain:

```
strBase    = "<LDAP://dc=apac,dc=rallencorp,dc=com>;"
strFilter  = "(&(objectclass=computer)(objectcategory=computer));"
strAttrs   = "cn;"
strScope   = "subtree"

set objConn = CreateObject("ADODB.Connection")
objConn.Provider = "ADsDSOObject"
objConn.Open "Active Directory Provider"
set objRS = objConn.Execute(strBase & strFilter & strAttrs & strScope)
objRS.MoveFirst
while Not objRS.EOF
    Wscript.Echo objRS.Fields(0).Value
    objRS.MoveNext
wend
```

Now, by adding two lines (shown in bold), we can authenticate with the administrator account:

```
strBaseDN  = "<LDAP://dc=apac,dc=rallencorp,dc=com>;"
strFilter  = "(&(objectclass=computer)(objectcategory=computer));"
strAttrs   = "cn;"
strScope   = "subtree"

set objConn = CreateObject("ADODB.Connection")
objConn.Provider = "ADsDSOObject"
objConn.Properties("User ID")  = "administrator@apac.rallencorp.com"
objConn.Properties("Password") = "MyPassword"
objConn.Open "Active Directory Provider"
set objRS = objConn.Execute(strBaseDN & strFilter & strAttrs & strScope)
objRS.MoveFirst
while Not objRS.EOF
    Wscript.Echo objRS.Fields(0).Value
    objRS.MoveNext
wend
```

To authenticate with ADO, you need to set the User ID and Password properties of the ADO connection object. We used the UPN of the administrator for the user ID. With ADSI and ADO, you can use a UPN, NT 4.0 style account name (e.g., APAC\ Administrator), or distinguished name for the user ID.

Defining Variables and Error Checking

An important part of any script is error checking. Error checking allows your programs to gracefully identify any issues that arise during execution and take the appropriate action. Another best practice is to define variables before you use them and clean them up after you are done with them. In this book, most of the programmatic solutions do not include any error checking, predefined variables, or variable clean up. Admittedly, this is not setting a good example, but if we included extensive error checking and variable management, it would have made this book considerably longer with little added value to the reader. Again, the goal is to provide you with a code snippet that shows you how to accomplish a task, not provide robust scripts that include all the trimmings.

Error checking with VBScript is pretty straightforward. At the beginning of the script include the following declaration:

```
On Error Resume Next
```

This tells the script interpreter to continue even if errors occur. Without that declaration, anytime an error is encountered the script will abort. When you use On Error Resume Next, you need to use the Err object to check for errors after any step where a fatal error could occur. The following example shows how to use the Err object.

```
On Error Resume Next
set objDomain = GetObject("LDAP://dc=rallencorp,dc=com")
if Err.Number <> 0 then
    Wscript.Echo "An error occured getting the domain object: " & Err.Description
    Wscript.Quit
end if
```

Two important properties of the Err object are Number, which if nonzero signifies an error, and Description, which will contain the error message.

As far as variable management goes, it is always a good practice to include the following at the beginning of every script:

```
Option Explicit
```

When this is used, every variable in the script must be declared or an exception will be generated when you attempt to run the script. Variables are declared in VBScript using the Dim keyword. After you are done with a variable, it is a good practice to set it to Nothing so you release any resources bound to the variable, and don't accidentally re-use the variable with its previous value. The following code shows a complete example for printing the display name for a domain with error checking and variable management included:

```
Option Explicit
On Error Resume Next

Dim objDomain
set objDomain = GetObject("LDAP://cn=users,dc=rallencorp,dc=com")
if Err.Number <> 0 then
   Wscript.Echo "An error occured getting the domain object: " & Err.Description
   Wscript.Quit
end if

Dim strDescr
strDescr = objDomain.Get("description")
if Err.Number <> 0 then
   Wscript.Echo "An error occured getting the description: " & Err.Description
   Wscript.Quit
end if

WScript.Echo "Description: " & strDescr

objDomain = Nothing
strDescr  = Nothing
```

1.4   Replaceable Text

This book is filled with examples. Every recipe consists of one or more examples that show how to accomplish a task. Most CLI- and VBScript-based solutions use parameters that are based on the domain, forest, OU, user, etc, that is being added, modified, queried, and so on. Instead of using fictitious names, in most cases, we use replaceable text. This text should be easily recognizable because it is in italics and surrounded by angle brackets (<>). Instead of describing what each replaceable element represents every time we use it, we've included a list of some of the commonly used ones here:

<DomainDN>
  Distinguished name of domain (e.g., *dc=amer,dc=rallencorp,dc=com*)

<ForestRootDN>
  Distinguished name of the forest root domain (e.g., *dc=rallencorp,dc=com*)

<DomainDNSName>
  Fully qualified DNS name of domain (e.g., *amer.rallencorp.com*)

<ForestDNSName>
  Fully qualified DNS name of forest root domain (e.g., *rallencorp.com*)

<DomainControllerName>
  Single label or fully qualified DNS hostname of domain controller (e.g., *dc01.rallencorp.com*)

<UserDN>
  Distinguished name of user (e.g., *cn=administrator,cn=users,dc=rallencorp,dc=com*)

<GroupDN>
> Distinguished name of group (e.g., *cn=DomainAdmins,cn=users,dc=rallencorp,
> dc=com*)

<ComputerName>
> Single label DNS hostname of computer (e.g., *rallen-xp*)

1.5   Where to Find More Information

While it is our hope that this book provides you with enough information to perform most of the tasks you need to do to maintain your Active Directory environment, it is not realistic to think every possible task has been covered. In fact, working on this book has made us realize just how much Active Directory administrators need to know.

Now that Active Directory has been around for a few years, a significant user base has been built, which has led to other great resources of information. This section contains some of the useful sources of information that we use on a regular basis.

Command-Line Tools

If you have any questions about the complete syntax or usage information for any of the command-line tools we use, you should first take a look at the help information for the tools. The vast majority of CLI tools provide syntax information by simply passing /? as a parameter. For example:

```
> dsquery /?
```

Microsoft Knowledge Base

The Microsoft Support web site is a great source of information and is home of the Microsoft Knowledge Base (MS KB) articles. Throughout the book, we include references to pertinent MS KB articles where you can find more information on the topic. You can find the complete text for a KB article by searching on the KB number at the following web site: *http://support.microsoft.com/default.aspx*. You can also append the KB article number to the end of this URL to go directly to the article: *http://support.microsoft.com/?kbid=*.

If you look up Knowledge Base articles on a regular basis, you can even add a Registry entry to allow your workstation to go directly to a KB article in Internet Explorer. Open your Registry Editor and navigate to the `HKEY_CURRENT_USER\Software\Microsoft\Internet Explorer\SearchUrl` key. Create a new sub-key called `KB`. Underneath this subkey, create a `REG_SZ` value containing the following data:

```
http://support.microsoft.com/?kbid=%s
```

Now close the Registry Editor and open up Internet Explorer. In the address bar, type **KB 875357** (or any other KB number) and the associated page on the Microsoft web site will open.

Microsoft Developers Network

MSDN contains a ton of information on Active Directory and the programmatic interfaces to Active Directory, such as ADSI and LDAP. We sometimes reference MSDN pages in recipes. Unfortunately, there is no easy way to reference the exact page we're talking about unless we provided the URL or navigation to the page, which would more than likely change by the time the book was printed. Instead we provide the title of the page, which you can use to search on via the following site: *http://msdn.microsoft.com/library.*

Web Sites

Microsoft Active Directory Home Page (http://www.microsoft.com/ad)
> This site is the starting point for Active Directory information provided by Microsoft. It contains links to white papers, case studies, and tools.

Microsoft Webcasts (http://support.microsoft.com/default.aspx?scid=fh;EN-US;pwebcst)
> Webcasts are on-demand audio/video technical presentations that cover a wide range of Microsoft products. There are several Active Directory-related webcasts that cover such topics as disaster recovery, upgrading to Windows Server 2003 Active Directory, and Active Directory tools.

Google Search Engine (http://www.google.com)
> Google is our primary starting point for locating information on Active Directory. It is a powerful search engine and is often quicker and easier to use to search the Microsoft web sites than using the search engines provided on Microsoft's sites.

LabMice Active Directory (http://www.labmice.techtarget.com/Windows2003/ActiveDirectory2003/default.htm)
> The LabMice web site contains a large collection of links to information on Active Directory. It has links to MS KB articles, white papers, and other web sites.

Robbie Allen's Home Page (http://www.rallenhome.com)
> This is the author's personal web site, which has information about the Active Directory books he has written and links to download the code contained in each (including this book).

Joe Richards' Home Page (http://www.joeware.net)
> This is the home of the joeware utilities that you'll see referenced throughout this book; you can always download the latest version of *adfind*, *admod*, etc, from Joe's site, as well as browse FAQs and forums discussing each of the utilities.

Petri.co.il by Daniel Petri (http://www.petri.co.il/ad.htm)
> This is another site that's run by a Microsoft MVP that contains a number of valuable links and tutorials.

Newsgroups

microsoft.public.windows.server.active_directory
> This is a very active newsgroup where several top-notch Active Directory experts answer questions posed by users.

microsoft.public.windows.server.dns
> This is another good resource if you have a DNS question you've been unable to find an answer for; odds are someone on this newsgroup will have an answer.

microsoft.public.adsi.general
> If you have questions about ADSI, this is another very active newsgroup where you can find answers.

If you have a question about a particular topic, a good starting point is to search the newsgroups using Google's Groups search engine (*http://groups.google.com*). Just like its web search engine, the group search engine is very fast and is an invaluable resource when trying to locate information.

Mailing Lists

ActiveDir (http://www.activedir.org)
> The ActiveDir mailing list is where the most advanced Active Directory questions can get answered. The list owner, Tony Murray, does an excellent job of not allowing topics to get out of hand (as can sometimes happen on large mailing lists). The list is very active and it is rare for a question to go unanswered. Some of Microsoft's Active Directory Program Managers also participate on the list and are very helpful with the toughest questions. Keeping track of this list is a must-have for any serious Active Directory administrator.

15 Seconds (http://15seconds.com/focus/ADSI.htm)
> Just as the ActiveDir list is crucial for AD administrators, the 15 seconds list is extremely valuable for AD developers. It is also very active and the participants are good about responding to questions quickly.

Books

In addition to the Resource Kit books, the following books are good sources of information:

Active Directory, Third Edition, by Joe Richards et al. (O'Reilly)
> This is a good all-purpose book on Active Directory. A few of the topics the third edition covers include new Windows Server 2003 features, designing Active Directory, upgrading from Windows 2000, Active Directory Application Mode (ADAM), and Active Directory automation.edition,

Managing Enterprise Active Directory Services, by Robbie Allen and Richard Puckett (Addison-Wesley)

> This is a great resource for anyone who has to support a large-scale Active Directory environment. The book preaches the benefits of automation in large environments and includes more than 300 sample scripts written in Perl and VBScript.

Active Directory Programming, by Gil Kirkpatrick (MacMillan)

> This is a great book for those interested in learning the details of ADSI and LDAP programming. The author, Gil Kirkpatrick, is a noted expert in the field.

Magazines

Windows & .NET Magazine (http://www.winnetmag.com)

> This is a general-purpose monthly magazine for system administrators that support Microsoft products. The magazine isn't devoted to Active Directory, but generally there are related topics covered every month.

Windows Scripting Solutions (http://www.winscriptingsolutions.com)

> This is a useful monthly newsletter that discusses automation scripts on a wide variety of Microsoft products, including Active Directory.

CHAPTER 2
Forests, Domains, and Trusts

2.0   Introduction

To the layperson, the title of this chapter may seem like a hodgepodge of unrelated terms. For the seasoned Active Directory administrator, however, these terms represent the most fundamental and, perhaps, most important concepts within Active Directory. In simple terms, a *forest* is a collection of data partitions and domains; a *domain* is a hierarchy of objects that is replicated between one or more domain controllers; a *trust* is an agreement between two domains or forests to allow security principals (i.e., users, groups, and computers) to access resources in either domain.

Active Directory domains are named using the Domain Name Service (DNS) namespace. You can group domains that are part of the same contiguous DNS namespace within the same domain tree. For example, the *sales.rallencorp.com*, *marketing.rallencorp.com*, and *rallencorp.com* domains are part of the *rallencorp.com* domain tree. A single domain tree is sufficient for most implementations, but one example in which multiple domain trees might be necessary is with large conglomerate corporations. Conglomerates are made up of multiple individual companies in which each company typically wants to maintain its own identity and, therefore, its own namespace. If you need to support noncontiguous namespaces within a single forest, you will need to create multiple domain trees. For example, *rallencorp.com* and *mycompany.com* can form two separate domain trees within the same forest.

 For more information on configuring DNS namespaces, see *DNS on Windows Server 2003* by Cricket Liu et al (O'Reilly).

Assuming that each company within the conglomerate wants its Active Directory domain name to be based on its company name, you have two choices for setting up this type of environment. You could either make each company's domain(s) a domain tree within a single forest, or you could implement multiple forests. One of the biggest differences between the two options is that all the domains within the forest trust each other, whereas separate forests, by default, do not have any trust relationships set up between them. Without trust relationships, users from one forest cannot access resources located in the other forest. In our conglomerate scenario, if you want users in each company to be able to access resources within their own domain, as well as the domains belonging to other companies in the organization, using separate domain trees can create an easier approach than separate forests. (However, it's important to keep in mind when designing your network that forests form the *security boundary* for Active Directory, as we'll cover in the next section "The Anatomy of a Forest") This is because transitive trusts are established between the root domains of each domain tree within a forest. As a result, every domain within a forest, regardless of which domain tree it is in, is trusted by every other domain. Figure 2-1 illustrates an example with three domain trees in a forest called *rallencorp.com*.

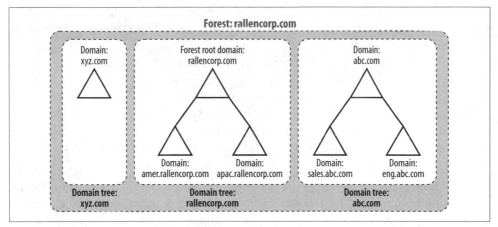

Figure 2-1. Multiple domain trees in a forest

Each domain increases the support costs of Active Directory due to the need for maintaining additional domain controllers, as well as the time you must spend configuring and maintaining the domain. When designing an Active Directory forest, your goal should be to keep the number of domains that you deploy to an absolute minimum. Since the forest constitutes the security boundary for an Active Directory environment, the minimalist approach towards the number of forests you use in an AD design becomes all the more sensible.

If you implement the alternative approach and create multiple Windows 2000 or Windows Server 2003 Active Directory forests, to create the fully trusted model you would have to create individual trusts between the domains in every forest. This can get out of hand pretty quickly if there are numerous domains. Fortunately, with Windows Server 2003 Active Directory, you can use the new trust type called a *forest trust* to create a single transitive trust between two forest root domains. This single trust allows all of the domains in both forests to fully trust each other.

There are many more issues to consider when deciding how many forests, domains, and domain trees to implement. For a thorough explanation of Active Directory design considerations, we recommend reading Part II of *Active Directory*, Third Edition, by Joe Richards et al. (O'Reilly).

In this chapter, we cover the most common tasks that you would need to do with forests, domains, and trusts. First, we're going to review how each item is represented within Active Directory.

The Anatomy of a Forest

A forest is a logical structure that is a collection of domains, plus the configuration and schema naming contexts, and application partitions. This means that all domains in a forest share a common configuration and schema between them. Forests are considered the primary security boundary in Active Directory. By this we mean that if you need to definitively restrict access to a resource within a particular domain so that administrators from other domains do not have any access to it whatsoever, you need to implement a separate forest, instead of using an additional domain within the current forest. This security concern is due to the transitive trust relationship that exists between all domains in a forest, the writeable naming contexts (NCs) that exist on all domain controllers in a forest, and the extensive rights and permissions that are granted to members of the Administrators group.

Active Directory relies on naming contexts to divide the AD database into separate partitions, each of which contain information that is replicated together as a logical unit. At a minimum, an Active Directory forest consists of three naming contexts: the Domain NC for the forest root domain, the Configuration NC, and the Schema NC. Here is a description of the type of partitions that can be part of a forest:

Configuration NC
> Contains data that is applicable across all domains and thus is replicated to all domain controllers in the forest. Some of this data includes the site topology, list of partitions, published services, display specifiers, and extended rights.

Schema NC
> Contains the objects that describe how data can be structured and stored in Active Directory. The classSchema objects in the Schema NC represent class definitions for objects. The attributeSchema objects describe what data can be stored with classes. The Schema NC is replicated to all domain controllers in a forest.

Domain NC
> A domain is a naming context that holds domain-specific data including user, group, and computer objects. This forms a collection of objects that is replicated between one or more domain controllers.

Application partitions
> Configurable partitions that can be rooted anywhere in the forest and can be replicated to any domain controller in the forest, or to a subset of domain controllers. These are not available with Windows 2000.

The Partitions container in the Configuration NC contains the complete list of all partitions that are associated with a particular forest, for example, LDAP:// dc=rallencorp,dc=com/.

The Anatomy of a Domain

Although forests constitute the security boundary in an Active Directory environment, you can split up your AD infrastructure into separate domains to create smaller administrative or replication boundaries within a large-scale network. Domains can also constitute a policy boundary, as certain Group Policy settings such as password policies and account lockout policies can only be applied at the domain level. Domains are represented in Active Directory by domainDNS objects. The distinguished name (DN) of a domainDNS object directly corresponds to the fully qualified DNS name of the domain. For example, the *amer.rallencorp.com* domain would have a DN of dc=amer,dc=rallencorp,dc=com. Table 2-1 contains a list of some of the interesting attributes that are available on domainDNS objects.

Table 2-1. Attributes of domainDNS objects

Attribute	Description
dc	The domain component of the domain distinguished name (e.g., *amer*).
fSMORoleOwner	The NTDS Settings object DN of the domain controller on which the schema can be modified. See Recipe 3.30 for more information.
gPLink	List of GPOs that have been applied to the domain. By default it will contain a reference to the Default Domain Policy GPO.
lockoutDuration	A 64-bit integer representing the time an account will be locked out before being automatically unlocked. See Recipe 6.15 for more information.
lockoutObservationWindow	A 64-bit integer representing the time after a failed logon attempt that the failed logon counter for the account will be reset to 0. See Recipe 6.15 for more information.
lockoutThreshold	Number of failed logon attempts after which an account will be locked. See Recipe 6.15 for more information.
masteredBy	A reference to the list of naming contexts hosted by a domain controller.
maxPwdAge	A 64-bit integer representing the maximum number of days a password can be used before a user must change it. See Recipe 6.15 for more information.
minPwdAge	A 64-bit integer representing the minimum number of days a password must be used before it can be changed. See Recipe 6.15 for more information.
minPwdLength	Minimum number of characters allowed in a password. See Recipe 6.15 for more information.
msDS-Behavior-Version	Number that represents the functional level of the domain. This attribute is new in Windows Server 2003. See Recipe 2.10 for more information.

Table 2-1. Attributes of domainDNS objects (continued)

Attribute	Description
ms-DS-MachineAccountQuota	The number of computer accounts a nonadministrator user account can join to the domain. See Recipe 8.11 for more information.
nTMixedDomain	Number that represents the mode of a domain. See Recipe 2.9 for more information.
pwdHistoryLength	Number of passwords to remember before a user can reuse a previous password. See Recipe 6.15 for more information.
pwdProperties	Bit flag that represents different options that can be configured for passwords used in the domain, including password complexity and storing passwords with reversible encryption. See Recipe 6.15 for more information.
subRefs	Multivalue attribute containing the list of subordinate naming contexts and application partitions, such as *DC=ForestDnsZones,DC=rallencorp,DC=com* within the *rallencorp.com* domain.
wellKnownObjects	GUIDs for well-known objects, such as the default computer container. See Recipe 8.14 for more information.
msDS-LogonTimeSyncInterval	Controls how often the lastLogonTimestamp attribute is replicated between domain controllers. Defaults to 14 days, which means that lastLogonTimestamp will replicate every 10 to 14 days to prevent excessive replication of lastLogonTimestamp.

In Active Directory, each domain is a naming context and is also represented under the Partitions container in the Configuration NC as a crossRef object, which allows each domain controller in a forest to be aware of every partition in the forest and not just those that are held by one particular DC. In this case, the relative distinguished name (RDN) of the crossRef object is the NetBIOS name of the domain as defined by the netBIOSName attribute of the domain object.

In our previous example of *amer.rallencorp.com*, the corresponding crossRef object for the domain (assuming the forest name was *rallencorp.com*) would be located at cn=AMER,cn=Partitions,cn=Configuration,dc=rallencorp,dc=com.

Table 2-2 contains some interesting attributes of crossRef objects.

 All naming contexts and application partitions have crossRef objects in the Partitions container, not just domain NCs.

Table 2-2. Attributes of crossRef objects

Attribute	Description
cn	Relative distinguished name of the object. If your forest is made up of a contiguous namespace, this value will be the NetBIOS name of the domain.
dnsRoot	Fully qualified DNS name of the domain.
nCName	Distinguished name of the corresponding domainDNS object.
netBIOSName	NetBIOS name of the domain. See Recipe 2.7 for more information.
trustParent	Distinguished name of the crossRef object representing the parent domain (if applicable).

The Anatomy of a Trust

Microsoft has relied on trust relationships to provide resource access across domain boundaries since the early days of Windows NT. Before Active Directory, all trust relationships were *one-way* and *nontransitive* in nature. A one-way trust relationship, as the name suggests, only enables resource access in a single direction: a single trust relationship will only enable resource access from DomainA to DomainB, but a separate trust would need to be created to enable access in the other direction. An nontransitive trust relationship means that if you create a trust from DomainA to DomainB and a second one from DomainB to DomainC, DomainA does *not* trust DomainC by default. This one-way nontransitive trust relationship was the only type that was available in Windows NT. Active Directory improved on this by automatically creating *two-way transitive* trust relationships between every domain in a domain tree, and between the root domains of all trees in every forest.

Trusts are stored as `trustedDomain` objects within the System container of a domain. Table 2-3 lists some of the important attributes of `trustedDomain` objects.

Table 2-3. Attributes of trustedDomain objects

Attribute	Description
cn	Relative distinguished name of the trust. This is the name of the target domain that is trusted. For Windows NT domains, it is the NetBIOS name. For Active Directory domains, it is the DNS name.
trustDirection	Flag that indicates whether the trust is disabled, inbound, outbound, or both inbound and out-bound. See Recipes 2.19 and 2.20 for more information.
trustType	Flag that indicates if the trust is to a down-level (NT4), up-level (Windows 2000 or above), or Kerberos (e.g., MIT) domain. See Recipe 2.19 for more information.
trustAttributes	Contain miscellaneous properties that can be enabled for a trust. See Recipe 2.19 for more information.
trustPartner	The name of the trust partner. See Recipe 2.19 for more information.

A trust also has a corresponding user object in the Users container of a domain. This is where the trust password is stored. The RDN of this user object is the same as the cn attribute for the corresponding `trustedDomain` object with a $ appended.

2.1   Creating a Forest

Problem

You want to create a new forest by creating a new forest root domain.

Solution

Using a graphical user interface

Run *dcpromo* from a command line or by clicking on Start → Run.

On a Windows 2000 domain controller:

1. Select "Domain controller for a new domain" and click Next.
2. Select "Create a new domain tree" and click Next.
3. Select "Create a new forest of domain trees" and click Next.
4. Follow the rest of the configuration steps to complete the wizard.

On a Windows Server 2003 domain controller:

1. Select "Domain controller for a new domain" and click Next.
2. Select "Domain in a new forest" and click Next.
3. Follow the rest of the configuration steps to complete the wizard.

Using a command-line interface

dcpromo can also be run in unattended mode. See Recipe 3.5 for more details.

Discussion

The act of creating a forest consists of creating a forest root domain. To do this, you need to use *dcpromo* to promote a Windows 2000 or Windows Server 2003 server to be a domain controller for a new domain. The *dcpromo* program has a wizard interface that requires you to answer several questions about the forest and domain you want to promote the server into. After *dcpromo* finishes, you will be asked to reboot the computer to complete the promotion process.

See Also

Recipe 2.3 for creating a domain, Recipe 3.1 for promoting a domain controller, Recipe 3.5 for automating the promotion of a domain controller, MS KB 238369 (How to Promote and Demote Domain Controllers in Windows 2000), and MS KB 324753 (How to Create an Active Directory Server in Windows Server 2003)

2.2   Removing a Forest

Problem

You want to tear down a forest and decommission any domains contained within it because you no longer need it.

Solution

To remove a forest, you need to demote (using *dcpromo*) all the domain controllers in the forest. When you run *dcpromo* on an existing domain controller, you will be given the option to demote the machine to a member server. After that is completed and depending on how your environment is configured, you may need to remove WINS and DNS entries that were associated with the domain controllers and domains unless they were automatically removed via WINS deregistration and dynamic DNS (DDNS) during demotion. The following commands can help determine if all entries have been removed:

```
> netsh wins server \\<WINSServerName> show name <DomainNetBiosName> 1b
> netsh wins server \\<WINSServerName> show name <DomainNetBiosName> 1c
> nslookup <DomainControllerDNSName>
> nslookup -type=SRV _ldap._tcp.gc._msdcs.<ForestDNSName>
> nslookup <ForestDNSName>
```

You should run the first two commands for every domain in the forest if the forest contained more than one.

You will also want to remove any trusts that have been established for the forest (see Recipe 2.22 for more details). For more information on how to demote a domain controller, see Recipe 3.4.

Discussion

The method described in this solution is the graceful way to tear down a forest. You can also use a brute force method to remove a forest by simply reinstalling the operating system on all domain controllers in the forest. This method is not recommended except in lab or test environments. The brute force method is not a clean way to do it because the domain controllers are unaware the forest is being removed and may generate errors until they are rebuilt. You'll also need to make sure any DNS resource records for the domain controllers are removed from your DNS servers since the domain controllers will not dynamically remove them like they do during the demotion process.

If you need to forcibly remove a single domain from an AD forest, you can also use the *ntdsutil* command-line utility; see Recipe 2.4 for more information.

See Also

Recipe 2.19 for viewing the trusts for a domain, Recipe 2.22 for removing a trust, and Recipe 3.4 for demoting a domain controller

2.3 Creating a Domain

Problem

You want to create a new domain that may be part of an existing domain tree or the root of a new domain tree.

Solution

Using a graphical user interface

Run *dcpromo* from a command line or Start → Run.

On a Windows 2000 domain controller, select "Domain controller for a new domain" and then you can select one of the following:

- Create a new domain tree → Place this new domain tree in an existing forest
- Create a new child domain in an existing domain tree

On a Windows Server 2003 domain controller, select "Domain controller for a new domain" and then you can select one of the following:

- Domain in a new forest
- Child domain in an existing domain tree
- Domain tree in an existing forest

Using a command-line interface

dcpromo can also be run in unattended mode. See Recipe 3.5 for more details.

Discussion

The two options *dcpromo* offers to create a new domain are adding the domain to an existing domain tree or starting a new domain tree. If you want to create a new domain that is a child domain of a parent domain (i.e., contained within the same contiguous namespace), then you are creating a domain in an existing domain tree. If you are creating the first domain in a forest or a domain that is outside the namespace of the forest root, then you are creating a domain in a new domain tree. For example, if you've already created the *rallenhome.corp* domain and then install the first DC in the *amer.rallenhome.corp* domain, then *amer.rallenhome.corp* is a *child domain*. Conversely, if you want to create a domain that is part of the *rallenhome.corp* forest but uses an entirely different naming convention (such as *rallenasia.corp*), then you are creating a new domain tree within an existing forest.

See Also

Recipe 3.1 for promoting a domain controller, Recipe 3.5 for automating the promotion of a domain controller, Designing the Active Directory Logical Structure from the Windows Server 2003 Deployment Guide, MS KB 238369 (How to Promote and Demote Domain Controllers in Windows 2000), and MS KB 255248 (How to Create a Child Domain in Active Directory and Delegate the DNS Namespace to the Child Domain)

2.4 Removing a Domain

Problem

You want to remove a domain from a forest. You may need to remove a domain during test scenarios or if you are collapsing or reducing the number of domains in a forest.

Solution

Removing a domain consists of demoting each domain controller in the domain, which is accomplished by running *dcpromo* on the domain controllers and following the steps to remove them. For the last domain controller in the domain, be sure to select "This server is the last domain controller in the domain" in the *dcpromo* wizard so that the objects associated with the domain get removed. If you do not select this option for the last domain controller in the domain, take a look at Recipe 2.5 for how to remove an orphaned domain.

 If the domain you want to remove has child domains, you have to remove these child domains before proceeding.

After all domain controllers have been demoted, depending on how your environment is configured you may need to remove any WINS and DNS entries that were associated with the domain controllers and domain that were automatically removed via WINS deregistration and DDNS during the demotion process. The following commands can help determine if all entries have been removed:

```
> netsh wins server \\<WINSServerName> show name <DomainNetBiosName> 1b
> netsh wins server \\<WINSServerName> show name <DomainNetBiosName> 1c
> nslookup <DomainControllerName>
> nslookup -type=SRV _ldap._tcp.dc._msdcs.<DomainDNSName>
> nslookup <DomainDNSName>
```

You will also want to remove any trusts that have been established for the domain (see Recipe 2.22 for more details). For more information on how to demote a domain controller, see Recipe 3.4.

Discussion

The "brute force" method for removing a forest as described in the "Discussion" for Recipe 2.2 is not a good method for removing a domain. Doing so will leave all of the domain controller and server objects, along with the domain object and associated domain naming context hanging around in the forest. If you used that approach, you would eventually see a bunch of replication and file replication service (FRS) errors in the event log caused by failed replication events from the nonexistent domain. You would need to remove the metadata associated with the removed domain using *ntdsutil* to correct these errors.

See Also

Recipe 2.2, Recipe 2.5, Recipe 2.19 for viewing the trusts for a domain, Recipe 2.22 for removing a trust, Recipe 3.4 for demoting a domain controller, MS KB 238369 (How to Promote and Demote Domain Controllers in Windows 2000), MS KB 255229 (Dcpromo Demotion of Last Domain Controller in Child Domain Does Not Succeed), and MS KB 332199 (Domain Controllers Do Not Demote Gracefully When You Use the Active Directory Installation Wizard to Force Demotion in Windows Server 2003 and in Windows 2000 Server)

2.5   Removing an Orphaned Domain

Problem

You want to completely remove a domain that was orphaned because the domain was forcibly removed, or the last domain controller in the domain failed or was otherwise decommissioned improperly.

Solution

Using a command-line interface

The following *ntdsutil* commands (in bold) would forcibly remove the *emea.rallencorp.com* domain from the *rallencorp.com* forest. Replace *<DomainControllerName>* with the hostname of the Domain Naming Flexible Single Master Operation (FSMO; pronounced *fiz-mo*) for the forest:

```
> ntdsutil "meta clean" "s o t" conn "con to server
  <DomainControllerName>" q q
metadata cleanup: "s o t" "list domains"
Found 4 domain(s)
0 - DC=rallencorp,DC=com
1 - DC=amer,DC=rallencorp,DC=com
2 - DC=emea,DC=rallencorp,DC=com
3 - DC=apac,DC=rallencorp,DC=com
select operation target: sel domain 2
```

```
No current site
Domain - DC=emea,DC=rallencorp,DC=com
No current server
No current Naming Context
select operation target: q
metadata cleanup: remove sel domain
```

You will receive a message indicating whether the removal was successful.

Discussion

Removing an orphaned domain consists of removing the domain object for the domain (e.g., dc-emea,dc=rallencorp,dc-com), all of its child objects, and the associated crossRef object in the Partitions container. You need to target the Domain Naming FSMO when using *ntdsutil* because that server is responsible for creation and removal of domains.

In the solution, shortcut parameters were used to reduce the amount of typing necessary. If each parameter were typed out fully, the commands would look as follows:

```
> ntdsutil "metadata cleanup" "select operation target" connections
  "connect to server <DomainControllerName>" quit quit
metadata cleanup: "select operation target" "list domains"
Found 4 domain(s)
0 - DC=rallencorp,DC=com
1 - DC=amer,DC=rallencorp,DC=com
2 - DC=emea,DC=rallencorp,DC=com
3 - DC=apac,DC=rallencorp,DC=com
select operation target: select domain 2
No current site
Domain - DC=emea,DC=rallencorp,DC=com
No current server
No current Naming Context
select operation target: quit
metadata cleanup: remove selected domain
```

See Also

Recipe 3.7 for removing an unsuccessfully demoted domain controller, MS KB 230306 (How to Remove Orphaned Domains from Active Directory), MS KB 251307 (How to Remove Orphaned Domains from Active Directory Without Demoting the Domain Controllers), and MS KB 255229 (Dcpromo Demotion of Last Domain Controller in Child Domain Does Not Succeed)

2.6 Finding the Domains in a Forest

Problem

You want a list of all domains in an Active Directory forest.

Solution

Using a graphical user interface

Open the Active Directory Domains and Trusts snap-in (*domain.msc*). The list of the domains in the default forest can be browsed in the left pane.

Using a command-line interface

You can retrieve this information using *ntdsutil*, *adfind*, or *dsquery*, as shown here:

```
> ntdsutil "d m" "sel op tar" c "co t s <DomainControllerName>"
  q "l d" q q q

> dsquery * -filter "objectcategory=domainDNS" -scope subtree

> adfind -root -s subtree -f "objectcategory=domainDNS" -dn
```

Using VBScript

```
' This code gets the list of the domains contained in the
' forest that the user running the script is logged into.

strForestRoot = "<ForestRootDN>" ' i.e., dc=rallencorp, dc=com
strADsPath = "<LDAP://cn=Partitions,cn=Configuration," & _
    strForestRoot & ">;"
strFilter   = "(netbiosname=*);"
strAttrs    = "dnsRoot;"
strScope    = "SubTree"

set objConn = CreateObject("ADODB.Connection") objConn.Provider = "ADsDSOObject"
objConn.Open "Active Directory Provider"
set objRS = objConn.Execute(strADsPath & strFilter & strAttrs & strScope)
objRS.MoveFirst while Not objRS.EOF
    For Each root in objRS.Fields("dnsRoot").Value
        WScript.Echo(root)
    Next
    objRS.MoveNext
wend
```

Discussion

Using a graphical user interface

If you want to view the domains for an alternate forest than the one you are logged into, right-click on "Active Directory Domains and Trusts" in the left pane and select "Connect to Domain Controller." Enter the forest name you want to browse in the Domain field. In the left pane, expand the forest root domain to see any subdomains.

Using a command-line interface

In the *ntdsutil* example, shortcut parameters were used to reduce the amount of typing needed. If each parameter were typed out fully, the command line would look like:

```
> ntdsutil "domain management" "select operation target" connections "connect
to server <DomainControllerName>" quit "List domains" quit quit quit
```

Using VBScript

In the VBScript solution, we use ADO to query the Partitions container for crossRef objects that refer to domain objects within the forest.

To find the list of domains for an alternate forest, include the name of the forest as part of the ADsPath used in the first line of code. The following would target the *othercorp.com* forest:

```
set objRootDSE = GetObject("LDAP://othercorp.com/" & "RootDSE")
```

See Also

Recipe 3.10 for finding the domain controllers for a domain

2.7   Finding the NetBIOS Name of a Domain

Problem

You want to find the NetBIOS name of a domain. Although Microsoft has moved to using DNS for its primary means of name resolution, the NetBIOS name of a domain is still important, especially with down-level clients that are still based on NetBIOS instead of DNS for name resolution.

Solution

Using a graphical user interface

1. Open the Active Directory Domains and Trusts snap-in (*domain.msc*).
2. Right-click the domain you want to view in the left pane and select Properties.

The NetBIOS name will be shown in the "Domain name (pre-Windows 2000)" field.

You can also retrieve this information using LDP, as follows:

1. Open LDP and from the menu, select Connection → Connect.
2. For Server, enter the name of a domain controller (or leave blank to do a server-less bind).

3. For Port, enter 389.

4. Click OK.

5. From the menu select Connection → Bind.

6. Enter credentials of a domain user.

7. Click OK.

8. From the menu, select Browse → Search.

9. For BaseDN, type the distinguished name of the Partitions container (e.g., cn=partitions,cn=configuration,dc=rallencorp, dc=com).

10. For Scope, select Subtree.

11. For Filter, enter:

    (&(objectcategory=crossref)(dnsHostName=*<DomainDNSName>*)(netbiosname=*))

12. Click Run.

Using a command-line interface

To find the NetBIOS name of a Windows domain, use the following command:

```
> dsquery * cn=partitions,cn=configuration,<ForestRootDN> -filter
"(&(objectcategory=crossref)(dnsroot=<DomainDNSName>)(netbiosname=*))" -attr
netbiosname
```

Or you can use the AdFind utility as follows:

```
> adfind -b cn=partitions,cn=configuration,<ForestRootDN>
-f "(&(objectcategory=crossref)(dnsroot=<DomainDNSName>))" cn netbiosname
```

Using VBScript

```
' This code prints the NetBIOS name for the specified domain
' ------ SCRIPT CONFIGURATION ------
strDomain = "<DomainDNSName>"  ' e.g. amer.rallencorp.com
' ------ END CONFIGURATION ---------

set objRootDSE = GetObject("LDAP://" & strDomain & "/RootDSE")
strADsPath =   "<LDAP://" & strDomain & "/cn=Partitions," & _
               objRootDSE.Get("configurationNamingContext") & ">;"
strFilter = "(&(objectcategory=Crossref)" & _
            "(dnsRoot=" & strDomain & ")(netBIOSName=*));"
strAttrs = "netbiosname;"
strScope = "Onelevel"
set objConn = CreateObject("ADODB.Connection")
objConn.Provider = "ADsDSOObject"
objConn.Open "Active Directory Provider"
set objRS = objConn.Execute(strADsPath & strFilter & strAttrs & strScope)
objRS.MoveFirst
WScript.Echo "NetBIOS name for " & strDomain & " is " & objRS.Fields(0).Value
```

Discussion

Each domain has a crossRef object that is used by Active Directory to generate *referrals* to other naming contexts within an Active Directory forest. Referrals are necessary when a client performs a query, and the domain controller handling the request does not have the matching object(s) in any naming contexts that it has stored locally. The NetBIOS name of a domain is stored in the domain's crossRef object in the Partitions container in the Configuration NC. Each crossRef object has a dnsRoot attribute, which is the fully qualified DNS name of the domain. The netBIOSName attribute contains the NetBIOS name for the domain.

2.8   Renaming a Domain

Problem

You want to rename a domain, for example due to organizational changes, legal restrictions, or because of a merger, acquisition, or divestiture. Renaming a domain is a very involved process and should be done only when absolutely necessary. Changing the name of a domain can have an impact on everything from DNS, replication, and GPOs to DFS and Certificate Services. A domain rename also requires rebooting all domain controllers, member servers, and client computers in the domain!

Solution

Under Windows 2000, there is no supported process to rename a domain. There is one workaround for mixed-mode domains in which you revert the domain and any of its child domains back to Windows NT domains. This can be done by demoting all Windows 2000 domain controllers and leaving the Windows NT domain controllers in place, or simply by rebuilding all of the 2000 DCs. You could then reintroduce Windows 2000 domain controllers and use the new domain name when setting up Active Directory. The process is not very clean and probably won't be suitable for most situations, but you can find out more about it in MS KB 292541.

A domain rename procedure is supported if a forest is running all Windows Server 2003 domain controllers and is at the Windows Server 2003 forest functional level. Microsoft provides a rename tool (*rendom.exe*) and detailed white paper describing the process at the following location: *http://www.microsoft.com/windowsserver2003/downloads/domainrename.mspx*.

Although the domain rename procedure is greatly simplified in Windows Server 2003, we highly recommend reading the entire white paper before attempting the procedure, as well as attempting the procedure in a test lab before performing it against a production environment.

Discussion

The domain rename process can accommodate very complex changes to your domain model. You can perform the following types of renames:

- Rename a domain to a new name without repositioning it in the domain tree.
- Reposition a domain within a domain tree.
- Create a new domain tree with a renamed domain.

One thing you cannot do with the domain rename procedure is reposition the forest root domain. You can rename the forest root domain, but you cannot change its status as the forest root domain. Another important limitation to note is that you cannot rename any domain in a forest that has had Exchange 2000 installed, though an Exchange Server 2003 is capable of handling domain renames. See the web site mentioned in the solution for more information on other limitations. The *random.exe* utility also includes the *gpfixup.exe* utility, which corrects references to Group Policy objects after the domain name changes. When working with Exchange 2003, you can also use the *xdr-fixup* tool to correct Exchange attributes to match the new domain name.

See Also

MS KB 292541 (How to Rename the DNS name of a Windows 2000 Domain) and *http://www.microsoft.com/windowsserver2003/downloads/domainrename.mspx*

2.9   Raising the Domain Functional Level to Windows 2000 Native Mode

Problem

You want to change the mode of a Windows 2000 Active Directory domain from mixed mode to native mode. You typically want to do this as soon as possible after installing a Windows 2000 domain to take advantage of features that aren't available with mixed-mode domains. (See this link for more information on the features available at the different functional levels: *http://technet2.microsoft.com/WindowsServer/en/Library/b3674c9b-fab9-4c1e-a8f6-7871264712711033.mspx*).

Solution

Using a graphical user interface

1. Open the Active Directory Domains and Trusts snap-in (*domain.msc*).
2. Browse to the domain you want to change in the left pane.

3. Right-click on the domain and select Properties. The current mode will be listed in the Domain Operation Mode box.

4. To change the mode, click the Change Mode button at the bottom.

Using a command-line interface

To change the mode to native mode, create an LDIF file called *change_domain_mode.ldf* with the following contents:

```
dn: <DomainDN>
changetype: modify
replace: ntMixedDomain
ntMixedDomain: 0
-
```

Then run *ldifde* to import the change.

```
> ldifde -i -f change_domain_mode.ldf
```

Alternately, you can use the AdMod utility to update your domain to native mode using the following syntax:

```
> admod -b dc=rallencorp,dc=com "ntMixedDomain::0"
```

Using VBScript

```
' This code changes the mode of the specified domain to native
' ------ SCRIPT CONFIGURATION ------
strDomain = "<DomainDNSName>"  ' e.g. amer.rallencorp.com
' ------ END CONFIGURATION ---------

set objDomain = GetObject("LDAP://" & strDomain)
if objDomain.Get("nTMixedDomain") > 0 Then
   Wscript.Echo "Changing mode to native . . . "
   objDomain.Put "nTMixedDomain", 0
   objDomain.SetInfo
else
   Wscript.Echo "Already a native mode domain"
end if
```

Discussion

The mode of a domain restricts the operating systems the domain controllers in the domain can run. In a mixed-mode domain, you can have Windows 2000 (and Windows Server 2003) and Windows NT domain controllers. In a native-mode domain, you can have only Windows 2000 (and Windows Server 2003) domain controllers. There are several important feature differences between mixed and native mode. Mixed mode imposes the following limitations:

- The domain cannot contain Universal security groups.

- Groups in the domain cannot have their scope or type changed.

- The domain cannot have nested groups (aside from global groups in domain local groups).
- Account modifications sent to Windows NT BDCs, including password changes, must go through PDC Emulator for the domain.
- The domain cannot use SID History.

The domain mode can be changed only from mixed to native mode. You cannot change it back from native to mixed mode without restoring your entire Active Directory environment from a previous backup. When a Windows 2000 domain is first created, it starts off in mixed mode even if all the domain controllers are running Windows 2000. The domain mode is stored in the `ntMixedDomain` attribute on the domain object (e.g., `dc=amer,dc=rallencorp,dc=com`). A value of 0 signifies a native-mode domain and 1 indicates a mixed-mode domain.

Windows Server 2003 Active Directory has a similar concept called *functional levels*. For more information on Windows Server 2003 functional levels, see Recipe 2.10 and Recipe 2.11.

See Also

Recipe 2.10 for raising the functional level of a Windows Server 2003 domain, Recipe 2.11 for raising the functional level of a Windows Server 2003 forest, MS KB 186153 (Modes Supported by Windows 2000 Domain Controllers)

2.10 Raising the Functional Level of a Windows Server 2003 Domain

Problem

You want to raise the functional level of a Windows Server 2003 domain. You should raise the functional level of a domain as soon as possible after installing a new Windows Server 2003 domain or upgrading from Windows 2000 to take advantage of the new features and enhancements.

Solution

Using a graphical user interface

1. Open the Active Directory Domains and Trusts snap-in (*domain.msc*).
2. In the left pane, browse to the domain you want to raise, right-click it, and select Raise Domain Functional Level.
3. Select the new functional level and click OK.

After a few seconds you should see a message stating whether the operation was successful.

Using a command-line interface

To retrieve the current functional level using DSQuery, use the following command:

```
> dsquery * <DomainDN> -scope base -attr msDS-Behavior-Version
```

DSQuery will return the following output in a mixed mode domain:

```
>  msDS-Behavior-Version
>  0
```

Or you can use the AdFind utility from *www.joeware.net* as follows:

```
> adfind -s Base -b <DomainDN> msDS-Behavior-Version
```

AdFind will return the following output in a mixed mode domain:

```
> AdFind V01.27.00cpp Joe Richards (joe@joeware.net) November 2005
>
> Using server: dc1.rallencorp.com:389
> Directory: Windows Server 2003
>
> dn:dc=rallencorp,dc=com
>> msDS-Behavior-Version: 0
>
>
> 1 Objects returned
```

To change the functional level to Windows Server 2003, create an LDIF file called *raise_domain_func_level.ldf* with the following contents:

```
dn: <DomainDN>
changetype: modify
replace: msDS-Behavior-Version
msDS-Behavior-Version: 2
-
```

Next, run *ldifde* to import the change.

```
> ldifde -i -f raise_domain_func_level.ldf
```

Alternately, you can use the AdMod utility to raise the domain functional level using the following syntax, with the output that follows:

```
> admod -b dc=rallencorp,dc=com "msDS-Behavior-Version::2"
>
> AdMod V01.06.00cpp Joe Richards (joe@joeware.net) June 2005
>
> DN Count: 1
> Using server: dc1.rallencorp.com
> Modifying specified objects...
>   DN: dc=rallencorp,dc=com...
>
> The command completed successfully
```

Using VBScript

```
' This code changes the functional level of the specified domain to
' the Windows Server 2003 domain functional level
' ------ SCRIPT CONFIGURATION ------
strDomain = "<DomainDNSName>"   ' e.g. amer.rallencorp.com
' ------ END CONFIGURATION ---------

set objDomain = GetObject("LDAP://" & strDomain)
objDomain.GetInfo
if objDomain.Get("msDS-Behavior-Version") < 2 then
   Wscript.Echo "Changing domain to Windows Server 2003 functional level . . . "
   objDomain.Put "msDS-Behavior-Version", 2
   objDomain.SetInfo
else
   Wscript.Echo "Domain already at Windows Server 2003 functional level "
end if
```

Discussion

In Windows Server 2003 Active Directory, functional levels have replaced the domain mode that was used in Windows 2000 to signify what operating systems are allowed to run on the domain controllers in the domain. With Windows Server 2003, there are functional levels for both domains and forests whereas with Windows 2000, the domain mode only applied to domains. The msDS-Behavior-Version attribute of the domainDNS object (e.g., dc=amer,dc=rallencorp,dc=com) holds the current domain functional level. Table 2-4 shows the three functional levels, their associated ms-DS-Behavior-Version value, and the operating systems that can be used on domain controllers in each.

Table 2-4. Windows Server 2003 domain functional levels

Functional level	ms-DS-Behavior-Version	Valid operating systems
Windows 2000	0	Windows 2000, Windows NT (when in mixed mode), Windows Server 2003
Windows Server 2003 Interim	1	Windows NT 4.0
		Windows Server 2003
Windows Server 2003	2	Windows Server 2003

When a domain is at the Windows 2000 functional level, the domain can be in mixed mode or native mode, as described in Recipe 2.9. Various new features of Windows Server 2003 Active Directory are enabled with each domain functional level. See Chapter 1 of *Active Directory*, Third Edition, by Joe Richards et al. (O'Reilly) for more details.

The value contained in ms-DS-Behavior-Version is mirrored in the domainFunctionality attribute of the RootDSE. That means you can perform anonymous queries against the RootDSE of a domain to quickly determine what functional level it is currently at.

One of the benefits of the GUI solution is that if a problem is encountered, you can save and view the output log, which will contain information on any errors that were encountered.

See Also

Recipe 2.9 for changing domain mode, Recipe 2.10 for raising the functional level of a Windows Server 2003 forest, Recipe 2.12 for preparing a forest with AdPrep, Chapter 1 of *Active Directory*, Third Edition, by Joe Richards et al. (O'Reilly), and MS KB 322692 (How to Raise the Domain Functional Level in Windows Server 2003)

2.11 Raising the Functional Level of a Windows Server 2003 Forest

Problem

You want to raise the functional level of a Windows Server 2003 forest. You should raise the functional level of a forest as soon as possible after installing a new Windows Server 2003 forest or upgrading from a Windows 2000 forest to take advantage of the new features and enhancements available in Windows Server 2003.

Solution

Using a graphical user interface

1. Open the Active Directory Domains and Trusts snap-in (*domain.msc*).
2. In the left pane, right-click on Active Directory Domains and Trusts and select Raise Forest Functional Level.
3. Select Windows Server 2003 Functional Level and click OK.

After a few seconds you should see a message stating whether the operation was successful.

Using a command-line interface

To retrieve the current forest functional level, use the following command:

```
> dsquery * <ForestRootDN> -scope base -attr msDS-Behavior-Version
```

Or you can use the AdFind utility found at *http://www.joeware.net*, producing the following output:

```
> adfind -b <ForestRootDN> -s base ms-DS-Behavior-Version
>
> AdFind V01.27.00cpp Joe Richards (joe@joeware.net) November 2005
>
> Using server: dc1.rallencorp.com:389
```

```
> Directory: Windows Server 2003
>
> dn:cn=Partitions,CN=Configuration,dc=rallencorp,dc=com
> >ms-DS-Behavior-Version: 0
>
>
> 1 Objects returned
```

To change the functional level to Windows Server 2003, create an LDIF file called *raise_forest_func_level.ldf* with the following contents:

```
dn: cn=partitions,cn=configuration,<ForestRootDN>
changetype: modify
replace: msDS-Behavior-Version
msDS-Behavior-Version: 2
-
```

Next, run *ldifde* to import the change.

```
> ldifde -i -f raise_forest_func_level.ldf
```

Or else you can use the AdMod utility as follows:

```
> admod -b <ForestDN> "msDS-Behavior-Version::2"
```

This will display results similar to the following:

```
> AdMod V01.06.00cpp Joe Richards (joe@joeware.net) June 2005
>
> DN Count: 1
> Using server: dc1.rallencorp.com
> Modifying specified objects...
>   DN: cn=Partitions,cn=Configuration,dc=rallencorp,dc=com...
>
> The command completed successfully
```

Using VBScript

```
' This code changes the functional level of the the forest the
' user running the script is logged into to Windows Server 2003.

set objRootDSE = GetObject("LDAP://RootDSE")
set objDomain = GetObject("LDAP://cn=partitions," & _
                          objRootDSE.Get("configurationNamingContext") )
if objDomain.Get("msDS-Behavior-Version") < 2 then
   Wscript.Echo "Attempting to change forest to " & _
                "Windows Server 2003 functional level . . . "
   objDomain.Put "msDS-Behavior-Version", 2
   objDomain.SetInfo
else
   Wscript.Echo "Forest already at Windows Server 2003 functional level"
end if
```

Discussion

Windows Server 2003 forest functional levels are very similar to domain functional levels. In fact, Table 2-4 applies to forest functional levels as well, except that the list of available operating systems applies to all domain controllers in the forest not just a single domain. So even if just one of the domains in the forest is at the Windows 2000 domain functional level, you cannot raise the forest above the Windows 2000 forest functional level. If you attempt to do so you will receive an error that the operation cannot be completed. After you raise the last Windows 2000 domain functional level to Windows Server 2003, you can then raise the forest functional level as well.

You may be wondering why there is a need to differentiate between forest and domain functional levels. The primary reason is new features. Some new features of Windows Server 2003 Active Directory require that all domain controllers in the forest are running Windows Server 2003. To ensure all domain controllers are running a certain operating system throughout a forest, Microsoft had to apply the functional level concept to forests as well as domains. For more information on the new features that are available with each functional level, see Chapter 1 of *Active Directory*, Third Edition, by Joe Richards et al. (O'Reilly).

The forest functional level is stored in the msDS-Behavior-Version attribute of the Partitions container in the Configuration NC. For example, in the *rallencorp.com* forest, it would be stored in cn=partitions,cn=configuration,dc=rallencorp,dc=com. The value contained in msDS-Behavior-Version is mirrored to the forestFunctionality attribute of the RootDSE, which means you can find the functional level of the forest by querying the RootDSE.

 One of the benefits of the GUI solution is that if a problem is encountered, you can save and view the output log, which will contain information on any errors that were encountered.

See Also

Recipe 2.9 for changing domain mode, Recipe 2.10 for raising the functional level of a Windows Server 2003 domain, Recipe 2.12 for preparing a forest with AdPrep, Chapter 1 of *Active Directory*, Third Edition, by Joe Richards et al. (O'Reilly), and MS KB 322692 (How to Raise the Domain Functional Level in Windows Server 2003)

2.12 Using AdPrep to Prepare a Domain or Forest for Windows Server 2003

Problem

You want to upgrade your existing Windows 2000 Active Directory domain controllers to Windows Server 2003. Before doing this, you must run the AdPrep tool, which extends the schema and adds several objects in Active Directory that are necessary for new features and enhancements.

Solution

First, run the following command on the Schema FSMO with the credentials of an account that is in both the Enterprise Admins and Schema Admins groups:

```
> adprep /forestprep
```

After the updates from /forestprep have replicated throughout the forest (see Recipe 2.11), run the following command on the Infrastructure FSMO in each domain with the credentials of an account in the Domain Admins group:

```
> adprep /domainprep
```

If the updates from /forestprep have not replicated to at least the Infrastructure FSMO servers in each domain, an error will be returned when running /domainprep. To debug any problems you encounter, see the AdPrep logfiles located at *%SystemRoot%\System32\Debug\Adprep\Logs*.

AdPrep can be found in the \i386 directory on the Windows Server 2003 CD. The tool relies on several files in that directory, so you cannot simply copy that file out to a server and run it. You must either run it from a CD or from a location where the entire directory has been copied.

Discussion

The adprep command prepares a Windows 2000 forest and domains for Windows Server 2003. Both /forestprep and /domainprep must be run before you can upgrade any domain controllers to Windows Server 2003 or install new Windows Server 2003 domain controllers.

The adprep command serves a similar function to the Exchange 2000 setup /forestprep and /domainprep commands, which prepare an Active Directory forest and domains for Exchange 2000. The adprep /forestprep command extends the schema and modifies some default security descriptors, which is why it must run on the Schema FSMO and under the credentials of someone in both the Schema Admins and Enterprise Admins groups. In addition, the adprep /forestprep and /domainprep commands add new objects throughout the forest, many of which are necessary for new features supported in Windows Server 2003 Active Directory.

Although not mandatory, it is helpful to run /domainprep from the server hosting the Infrastructure Master FSMO since this is the DC that controls the /domainprep process.

If you've installed Exchange 2000 or Services For Unix 2.0 in your forest prior to running AdPrep, there are schema conflicts with the AdPrep schema extensions that you'll need to fix first. MS KB 325379 and 314649 have a detailed list of compatibility issues and resolutions.

See Also

Recipe 2.11, Recipe 2.13 for determining if AdPrep has completed, Chapter 14 of *Active Directory*, Third Edition, by Joe Richards et al. (O'Reilly) for information on upgrading to Windows Server 2003, MS KB 331161 (List of Fixes to Use on Windows 2000 Domain Controllers Before You Run the Adprep/Forestprep Command), MS KB 314649 (Windows Server 2003 adprep /forestprep Command Causes Mangled Attributes in Windows 2000 Forests that Contain Exchange 2000 Servers), and MS KB 325379 (Upgrade Windows 2000 Domain Controllers to Windows Server 2003)

2.13   Determining Whether AdPrep Has Completed

Problem

You want to determine whether the AdPrep process, described in Recipe 2.12, has successfully prepared a Windows 2000 domain or forest for Windows Server 2003. After AdPrep has completed, you will then be ready to start promoting Windows Server 2003 domain controllers.

Solution

To determine whether adprep /domainprep completed, check for the existence of the following object where <DomainDN> is the distinguished name of the domain:

```
cn=Windows2003Update,cn=DomainUpdates,cn=System,<DomainDN>
```

To determine whether adprep /forestprep completed, check for the existence of the following object where <ForestRootDN> is the distinguished name of the forest root domain:

```
cn=Windows2003Update,cn=ForestUpdates,cn=Configuration,<ForestRootDN>
```

Discussion

As described in Recipe 2.12, the AdPrep utility is used to prepare a Windows 2000 forest for the upgrade to Windows Server 2003. One of the nice features of AdPrep is it stores its progress in Active Directory. For /domainprep, a container with a distinguished name of cn=DomainUpdates,cn=System,<DomainDN> is created that has child object containers cn=Operations and cn=Windows2003Update. After AdPrep completes a task, such as extending the schema, it creates an object under the cn=Operations container to signify its completion. Each object has a GUID for its name, which represents some internal operation for AdPrep.

For /domainprep, 52 of these objects are created. After all of the operations have completed successfully, the cn=Windows2003Update object is created to indicate /domainprep has completed (see Figure 2-2).

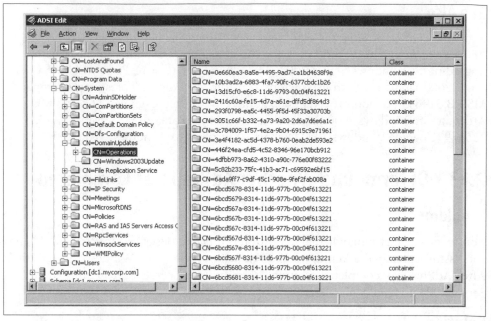

Figure 2-2. DomainPrep containers

For /forestprep, a container with the distinguished name of
cn=ForestUpdates,cn=Configuration,<*ForestRootDN*>, is created with child object
containers cn=Operations and cn=Windows2003Update.

The same principles apply as for /domainprep except that there will be 36 or more
operation objects stored within the cn=Operations container. After /forestprep completes, the cn=Windows2003Update object will be created that marks the successful
completion of /forestprep, and this object will have its Revision level set to 8.
Figure 2-3 shows an example of the container structure created by /forestprep.

See Also

Recipe 2.12 for running AdPrep, Chapter 13 for more on verifying Active Directory
replication, Chapter 14 of *Active Directory*, Third Edition, by Joe Richards et al.
(O'Reilly) for upgrading to Windows Server 2003, and MS KB 324392 (Enhancements to ADPrep.exe in Windows Server 2003 Service Pack 1)

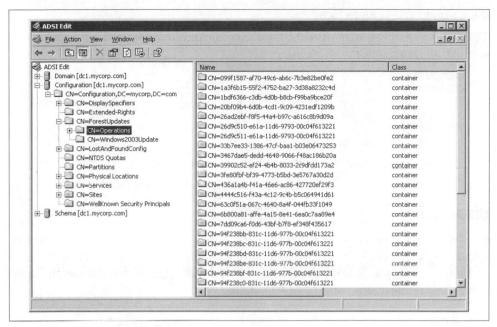

Figure 2-3. ForestPrep containers

2.14 Checking Whether a Windows 2000 Domain Controller Can Be Upgraded to Windows Server 2003

Problem

You want to determine whether a domain controller is ready to be upgraded to Windows Server 2003.

Solution

Using a graphical user interface

Insert a Windows Server 2003 CD into the Windows 2000 domain controller or map a drive to the files contained on the CD. Run the following command from the \i386 directory:

```
> winnt32 /checkupgradeonly
```

Using a command-line interface

To produce a compatibility report from the command line, first you need to create a text file containing the following information:

```
[Unattended]
Win9xUpgrade = Yes

[Win9xUpg]
ReportOnly = Yes
SaveReportTo = "\\server1\upgradereports\"
```

Save this file as *unattend.txt*, and then run the following from the command-line:

```
> winnt32 /checkupgradeonly /unattend:c:\unattend.txt
```

Discussion

The /checkupgradeonly switch simulates the initial steps for upgrading a server to Windows Server 2003. It verifies, among other things, that AdPrep has completed and checks any installed applications against a known list of compatible and non-compatible applications with the new operating system.

See Also

Recipe 2.13 for determining if AdPrep has completed and MS KB 331161 (List of Fixes to Use on Windows 2000 Domain Controllers Before You Run the Adprep/Forestprep Command)

2.15   Creating an External Trust

Problem

You want to create a one-way or two-way nontransitive trust from an AD domain to a Windows NT domain, or to a domain in an untrusted Active Directory forest.

Solution

Using a graphical user interface

1. Open the Active Directory Domains and Trusts snap-in (*domain.msc*).
2. In the left pane, right-click the domain you want to add a trust for and select Properties.
3. Click on the Trusts tab.
4. Click the New Trust button.
5. After the New Trust Wizard opens, click Next.
6. Type the NetBIOS name of the NT domain or the DNS name of the AD domain, and click Next.

---

7. Assuming the domain name was resolvable via its NetBIOS name or FQDN, the next screen will ask for the Direction of Trust. Select Two-way, One-way incoming, or One-way outgoing, and click Next.

8. If you selected Two-way or One-way Outgoing, you'll need to select the scope of authentication, which can be either Domain-wide or Selective, and click Next.

9. Enter and re-type the trust password and click Next.

10. Click Next twice to finish.

Using a command-line interface

```
> netdom trust TrustingDomainName/d:TrustedDomainName/add
```

For example, to create a trust from the NT4 domain RALLENCORP_NT4 to the AD domain RALLENCORP, use the following command:

```
> netdom trust RALLENCORP_NT4 /d:RALLENCORP /add
        /UserD:RALLENCORP\administrator /PasswordD:*
        /UserO:RALLENCORP_NT4\administrator /PasswordO:*
```

You can make the trust bidirectional, i.e., two-way, by adding a /TwoWay switch to the example.

Discussion

It is common when migrating from a Windows NT environment to Active Directory to set up trusts to down-level master account domains or resource domains, or to create a trust relationship with a single AD domain in a remote, untrusted forest. This allows AD users to access resources in the remote domain without providing alternate credentials. Windows NT does not support transitive trusts and, therefore, your only option is to create a nontransitive trust. That means you'll need to set up individual trusts between the NT domain in question and each Active Directory domain that contains users that need to access the resources within the AD domain.

See Also

MS KB 306733 (How to Create a Trust Between a Windows 2000 Domain and a Windows NT 4.0 Domain), MS KB 308195 (How to Establish Trusts with a Windows NT-Based Domain in Windows 2000), MS KB 309682 (How to Set Up a One-Way Nontransitive Trust in Windows 2000), MS KB 325874 (How to Establish Trusts with a Windows NT-Based Domain in Windows Server 2003), and MS KB 816301 (How to Create an External Trust in Windows Server 2003)

2.16 Creating a Transitive Trust Between Two AD Forests

 This recipe requires the Windows Server 2003 forest functional level in both forests.

Problem

You want to create a transitive trust between two AD forests. This causes all domains in both forests to trust each other without the need for additional trusts.

Solution

Using a graphical user interface

1. Open the Active Directory Domains and Trusts snap-in (*domain.msc*).
2. In the left pane, right click the forest root domain and select Properties.
3. Click on the Trusts tab.
4. Click the New Trust button.
5. After the New Trust Wizard opens, click Next.
6. Type the DNS name of the AD forest and click Next.
7. Select Forest trust and click Next.
8. Complete the wizard by stepping through the rest of the configuration screens.

Using a command-line interface

```
> netdom trust <Forest1DNSName> /Domain:<Forest2DNSName> /Twoway /Transitive /ADD
        [/UserD:<Forest2AdminUser> /PasswordD:*]
        [/UserO:<Forest1AdminUser> /PasswordO:*]
```

For example, to create a two-way forest trust from the AD forest *rallencorp.com* to the AD forest *othercorp.com*, use the following command:

```
> netdom trust rallencorp.com /Domain:othercorp.com /Twoway /Transitive /ADD
        /UserD:administrator@othercorp.com /PasswordD:*
        /UserO:administrator@rallencorp.com /PasswordO:*
```

Discussion

A new type of trust called a *forest trust* was introduced in Windows Server 2003. Under Windows 2000, if you wanted to create a fully trusted environment between two forests, you would have to set up individual external two-way trusts between every domain in both forests. If you have two forests with three domains each and wanted to set up a fully trusted model, you would need nine individual trusts. Figure 2-4 illustrates how this would look.

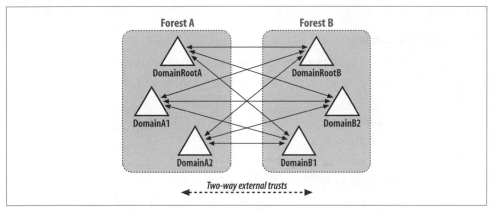

Figure 2-4. Trusts necessary for two Windows 2000 forests to fully trust each other

With a forest trust, you can define a single one-way or two-way transitive trust relationship that extends to all the domains in both forests. You may want to implement a forest trust if you merge or acquire a company and you want all of the new company's Active Directory resources to be accessible for users in your Active Directory environment and vice versa. Figure 2-5 shows a forest trust scenario. To create a forest trust, you need to use accounts from the `Enterprise Admins` group in each forest.

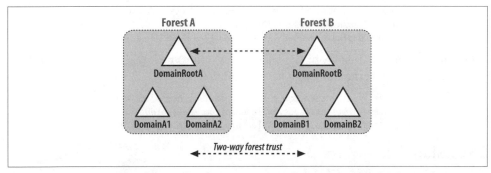

Figure 2-5. Trust necessary for two Windows Server 2003 forests to trust each other

2.17 Creating a Shortcut Trust Between Two AD Domains

Problem

You want to create a shortcut trust between two AD domains that are in the same forest or in two different forests. Shortcut trusts can make the authentication process more efficient between two domains in a forest.

Solution

Using a graphical user interface

1. Open the Active Directory Domains and Trusts snap-in (*domain.msc*).
2. In the left pane, right-click the domain you want to add a trust for, and select Properties.
3. Click on the Trusts tab.
4. Click the New Trust button.
5. After the New Trust Wizard opens, click Next.
6. Type the DNS name of the AD domain and click Next.
7. Assuming the AD domain was resolvable via DNS, the next screen will ask for the Direction of Trust. Select Two-way and click Next.
8. For the Outgoing Trust Properties, select all resources to be authenticated and click Next.
9. Enter and retype the trust password and click Next.
10. Click Next twice.

Using a command-line interface

```
> netdom trust <Domain1DNSName> /Domain:<Domain2DNSName> /Twoway /ADD
        [/UserD:<Domain2AdminUser> /PasswordD:*]
        [/UserO:<Domain1AdminUser> /PasswordO:*]
```

To create a shortcut trust from the *emea.rallencorp.com* domain to the *apac.rallencorp.com* domain, use the following netdom command:

```
> netdom trust emea.rallencorp.com /Domain:apac.rallencorp.com /Twoway /ADD
        /UserD:administrator@apac.rallencorp.com /PasswordD:*
        /UserO:administrator@emea.rallencorp.com /PasswordO:*
```

Discussion

Consider the forest in Figure 2-6. It has five domains in a single domain tree. For authentication requests for Domain 3 to be processed by Domain 5, the request must traverse the path from Domain 3 to Domain 2 to Domain 1 to Domain 4 to Domain 5. If you create a shortcut trust between Domain 3 and Domain 5, the authentication path is just a single hop from Domain 3 to Domain 5. To create a shortcut trust, you must be a member of the Domain Admins group in both domains, or a member of the Enterprise Admins group.

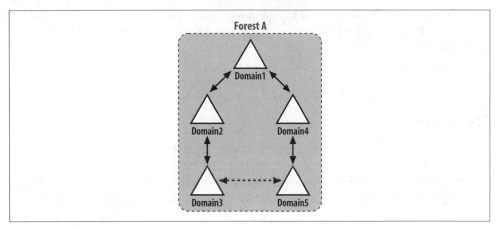

Figure 2-6. Shortcut trust

2.18   Creating a Trust to a Kerberos Realm

Problem

You want to create a trust to a Kerberos realm.

Solution

Using a graphical user interface

1. Open the Active Directory Domains and Trusts snap-in (*domain.msc*).
2. In the left pane, right-click the domain you want to add a trust for and select Properties.
3. Click on the Trusts tab.
4. Click the New Trust button.
5. After the New Trust Wizard opens, click Next.
6. Type the name of the Kerberos realm.
7. Select the radio button beside Realm Trust and click Next.
8. Select either Transitive or Nontransitive and click Next.
9. Select Two-way, One-way incoming, or One-way outgoing and click Next.
10. Enter and retype the trust password and click Next.
11. Click Next and click Finish.

Using a command-line interface

```
> netdom trust <ADDomainDNSName> /Domain:<KerberosRealmDNSName>
         /Realm /ADD /PasswordT:<TrustPassword>
         [/UserO:<ADDomainAdminUser> /PasswordO:*]
```

The *<TrustPassword>* has to match what was set on the Kerberos side. To create a realm trust from the *rallencorp.com* domain to the Kerberos realm called *kerb.rallencorp.com*, use the following command:

```
> netdom trust rallencorp.com /Domain:kerb.rallencorp.com
      /Realm /ADD /PasswordT:MyKerbRealmPassword
      /UserO:administrator@rallencorp.com /PasswordO:*
```

Discussion

You can create a Kerberos realm trust between an Active Directory domain and a non-Windows Kerberos v5 realm. A realm trust can be used to allow clients from the non-Windows Kerberos realm to access resources in Active Directory, and vice versa. See Recipe 16.5 for more information on MIT Kerberos interoperability with Active Directory.

See Also

Recipe 16.5, MS KB 260123 (Information on the Transitivity of a Kerberos Realm Trust), and MS KB 266080 (Answers to Frequently Asked Kerberos Questions)

2.19 Viewing the Trusts for a Domain

Problem

You want to view the trusts that have been configured for a domain.

Solution

Using a graphical user interface

1. Open the Active Directory Domains and Trusts snap-in (*domain.msc*).
2. In the left pane, right-click the domain you want to view and select Properties.
3. Click on the Trusts tab.

Using a command-line interface

To enumerate domain trusts using the *netdom* utility, use the following syntax:

```
> netdom query trust /Domain:<DomainDNSName>
```

You can also use *nltest*, available from the Windows Support Tools as follows:

```
> nltest /domain_trusts /All_Trusts
```

Using VBScript

```
strComputer = "."
Set objWMIService = GetObject("winmgmts:" _
    & "{impersonationLevel=impersonate}!\\" & _
```

```
        strComputer & "\root\MicrosoftActiveDirectory")

Set trustList = objWMIService.ExecQuery _
    ("Select * from Microsoft_DomainTrustStatus")

For each trust in trustList
    Wscript.Echo "Trusted domain: " & trust.TrustedDomain
    Wscript.Echo "Trust direction: " & trust.TrustDirection
    Wscript.Echo "(1: inbound, 2: outbound, 3: two-way)"
    Wscript.Echo "Trust type: " & trust.TrustType
    Wscript.Echo "(1: downlevel, 2: uplevel, 3: realm, 4: DCE)"
    Wscript.Echo "Trust attributes: " & trust.TrustAttributes
    Wscript.Echo "(1: nontransitive, 2: up-level clients only,"
    Wscript.Echo " 4: tree parent, 8: tree root)"
    Wscript.Echo "Trusted domain controller name: " & trust.TrustedDCName
Next
```

If the *rallencorp.com* domain is configured with a two-way external trust with the *barcelona.corp* domain, running this script from *dc1.rallencorp.com* would produce the following output:

```
Microsoft (R) Windows Script Host Version 5.6
Copyright (C) Microsoft Corporation 1996-2001. All rights reserved.

Trusted domain: barcelona.corp
Trust direction: 3
(1: inbound, 2: outbound, 3: two-way)
Trust type: 2
(1: downlevel, 2: uplevel, 3: realm, 4: DCE)
Trust attributes: 4
(1: nontransitive, 2: up-level clients only,
 4: tree parent, 8: tree root)
Trusted domain controller name: \\dc1.barcelona.corp
```

Discussion

Using a graphical user interface

You can view the properties of a particular trust by clicking on a trust and clicking the Properties button.

Using a command-line interface

You can include the /Direct switch with *netdom* if you want to view only direct-trust relationships. If you don't use /Direct, implicit trusts that occur due to transitive-trust relationships will also be listed.

The nltest command can take the following additional switches to modify the default behavior of the /domain_trusts switch:

/Primary

> Returns only the domain that the computer account you're running nltest from belongs to

`/Forest`
Returns domains that are in the same forest as the primary domain

`/Direct_Out`
Returns only those domains that are trusted by the primary domain

`/Direct_In`
Returns only those domains that trust the primary domain

`/v`
Displays domain SIDs and GUIDs

Using VBScript

The script listed in this recipe uses the TrustMon WMI provider, which is only available in Windows Server 2003. For Windows 2000 domain controllers, you can use the following script as an alternative:

```
' This code prints the trusts for the specified domain.
' ------ SCRIPT CONFIGURATION ------
strDomain = "<DomainDNSName>"    ' e.g. rallencorp.com
' ------ END CONFIGURATION ---------

' Trust Direction Constants taken from NTSecAPI.h
set objTrustDirectionHash = CreateObject("Scripting.Dictionary")
objTrustDirectionHash.Add "DIRECTION_DISABLED", 0
objTrustDirectionHash.Add "DIRECTION_INBOUND",  1
objTrustDirectionHash.Add "DIRECTION_OUTBOUND", 2
objTrustDirectionHash.Add "DIRECTION_BIDIRECTIONAL", 3

' Trust Type Constants - taken from NTSecAPI.h
set objTrustTypeHash = CreateObject("Scripting.Dictionary")
objTrustTypeHash.Add "TYPE_DOWNLEVEL", 1
objTrustTypeHash.Add "TYPE_UPLEVEL", 2
objTrustTypeHash.Add "TYPE_MIT", 3
objTrustTypeHash.Add "TYPE_DCE", 4

' Trust Attribute Constants - taken from NTSecAPI.h
set objTrustAttrHash = CreateObject("Scripting.Dictionary")
objTrustAttrHash.Add "ATTRIBUTES_NON_TRANSITIVE", 1
objTrustAttrHash.Add "ATTRIBUTES_UPLEVEL_ONLY", 2
objTrustAttrHash.Add "ATTRIBUTES_QUARANTINED_DOMAIN", 4
objTrustAttrHash.Add "ATTRIBUTES_FOREST_TRANSITIVE", 8
objTrustAttrHash.Add "ATTRIBUTES_CROSS_ORGANIZATION", 16
objTrustAttrHash.Add "ATTRIBUTES_WITHIN_FOREST", 32
objTrustAttrHash.Add "ATTRIBUTES_TREAT_AS_EXTERNAL", 64

set objRootDSE = GetObject("LDAP://" & strDomain & "/RootDSE")
set objTrusts  = GetObject("LDAP://cn=System," & _
                            objRootDSE.Get("defaultNamingContext") )
objTrusts.Filter = Array("trustedDomain")
Wscript.Echo "Trusts for " & strDomain & ":"

for each objTrust in objTrusts
```

```
        for each strFlag In objTrustDirectionHash.Keys
            if objTrustDirectionHash(strFlag) = objTrust.Get("trustDirection") then
                strTrustInfo = strTrustInfo & strFlag & " "
            end If
        next

        for each strFlag In objTrustTypeHash.Keys
            if objTrustTypeHash(strFlag) = objTrust.Get("trustType") then
                strTrustInfo = strTrustInfo & strFlag & " "
            end If
        next

        for each strFlag In objTrustAttrHash.Keys
            if objTrustAttrHash(strFlag) = objTrust.Get("trustAttributes") then
                strTrustInfo = strTrustInfo & strFlag & " "
            end If
        next

        WScript.Echo " " & objTrust.Get("trustPartner") & " : " & strTrustInfo
        strTrustInfo = ""
    next
```

See Also

The "Introduction" of this chapter for attributes of trustedDomain objects, Recipe 2.20 for another way to query trusts programmatically, MS KB 228477 (How to Determine Trust Relationship Configurations), and MSDN: TRUSTED_DOMAIN_INFORMATION_EX

2.20   Verifying a Trust

Problem

You want to verify that a trust is working correctly. This is the first diagnostics step to take if users notify you that authentication to a remote domain appears to be failing.

Solution

Using a graphical user interface

For the Windows 2000 version of the Active Directory Domains and Trusts snap-in (*domain.msc*):

1. In the left pane, right-click on the trusting domain and select Properties.
2. Click the Trusts tab.
3. Click the domain that is associated with the trust you want to verify.
4. Click the Edit button.
5. Click the Verify button.

For the Windows Server 2003 version of the Active Directory Domains and Trusts snap-in:

1. In the left pane, right-click on the trusting domain and select Properties.
2. Click the Trusts tab.
3. Click the domain that is associated with the trust you want to verify.
4. Click the Properties button.
5. Click the Validate button.

Using a command-line interface

```
> netdom trust <TrustingDomain> /Domain:<TrustedDomain> /Verify /verbose
  [/UserO:<TrustingDomainUser> /PasswordO:*]
  [/UserD:<TrustedDomainUser> /PasswordD:*]
```

Using VBScript

```
' The following code lists all of the trusts for the
' specified domain using the Trustmon WMI Provider.
' The Trustmon WMI Provider is only supported on Windows Server 2003.
' ------ SCRIPT CONFIGURATION ------
strDomain = "<DomainDNSName>"   ' e.g. amer.rallencorp.com
' ------ END CONFIGURATION ---------

set objWMI = GetObject("winmgmts:\\" & strDomain & _
                        "\root\MicrosoftActiveDirectory")
set objTrusts = objWMI.ExecQuery("Select * from Microsoft_DomainTrustStatus")
for each objTrust in objTrusts
    Wscript.Echo objTrust.TrustedDomain
    Wscript.Echo " TrustedAttributes: " & objTrust.TrustAttributes
    Wscript.Echo " TrustedDCName: "     & objTrust.TrustedDCName
    Wscript.Echo " TrustedDirection: "  & objTrust.TrustDirection
    Wscript.Echo " TrustIsOk: "         & objTrust.TrustIsOK
    Wscript.Echo " TrustStatus: "       & objTrust.TrustStatus
    Wscript.Echo " TrustStatusString: " & objTrust.TrustStatusString
    Wscript.Echo " TrustType: "         & objTrust.TrustType
    Wscript.Echo ""
next

' This code shows how to search specifically for trusts
' that have failed, which can be accomplished using a WQL query that
' contains the query: TrustIsOk = False
' ------ SCRIPT CONFIGURATION ------
strDomain = "<DomainDNSName>"   ' e.g. amer.rallencorp.com
' ------ END CONFIGURATION ---------

set objWMI = GetObject("winmgmts:\\" & strDomain & _
                        "\root\MicrosoftActiveDirectory")
set objTrusts = objWMI.ExecQuery("select * " _
                              & " from Microsoft_DomainTrustStatus " _
                              & " where TrustIsOk = False ")
```

```
if objTrusts.Count = 0 then
   Wscript.Echo "There are no trust failures"
else
   WScript.Echo "Trust Failures:"
   for each objTrust in objTrusts
      Wscript.Echo "  " & objTrust.TrustedDomain & " : " & _
                        objTrust.TrustStatusString
      Wscript.Echo ""
   next
end if
```

Discussion

Verifying a trust consists of checking connectivity between the domains and determining if the shared secrets of a trust are synchronized between the two domains.

Using a graphical user interface

The Active Directory Domains and Trusts screens have changed somewhat between Windows 2000 and Windows Server 2003. The Verify button has been renamed Validate.

Using a command-line interface

If you want to verify a Kerberos trust, use the /Kerberos switch with the netdom command.

Using VBScript

The WMI TrustMon Provider is new to Windows Server 2003. It provides a nice interface for querying and checking the health of trusts. One of the benefits of using WMI to access this kind of data is that you can use WQL, the WMI Query Language, to perform complex queries to find trusts that have certain properties. WQL is a subset of SQL, which is commonly used to query databases. In the second VBScript example, we used WQL to find all trusts that have a problem. You could expand the query to include additional criteria, such as trust direction and trust type.

See Also

MSDN: TrustMon Provider

2.21 Resetting a Trust

Problem

You want to reset a trust password. If you've determined a trust is broken, you need to reset it, which will allow users to authenticate across it again.

Solution

Using a graphical user interface

Follow the same directions as Recipe 2.20. The option to reset the trust will only be presented if the Verify/Validate did not succeed. In Windows Server 2003, if the trust validation process fails, you will be prompted to reset the trust password.

Using a command-line interface

```
> netdom trust <TrustingDomain> /Domain:<TrustedDomain> /Reset /verbose
  [/UserO:<TrustingDomainUser> /PasswordO:*]
  [/UserD:<TrustedDomainUser> /PasswordD:*]
```

Using VBScript

```
' This code resets the specified trust.
' ------ SCRIPT CONFIGURATION ------
' Set to the DNS or NetBIOS name for the Windows 2000,
' Windows NT domain or Kerberos realm you want to reset the trust for.
strTrustName = "<TrustToCheck>"

' Set to the DNS name of the source or trusting domain.
strDomain    = "<TrustingDomain>"
' ------ END CONFIGURATION ---------

' Enable SC_RESET during trust enumerations
set objTrustProv = GetObject("winmgmts:\\" & strDomain & _
              "\root\MicrosoftActiveDirectory:Microsoft_TrustProvider=@")
objTrustProv.TrustCheckLevel = 3   ' Enumerate with SC_RESET
objTrustProv.Put_

' Query the trust and print status information
set objWMI = GetObject("winmgmts:\\" & strDomain & _
              "\root\MicrosoftActiveDirectory")
set objTrusts = objWMI.ExecQuery("Select * " _
                    & " from Microsoft_DomainTrustStatus " _
                    & " where TrustedDomain = '" & strTrustName & "'" )
for each objTrust in objTrusts
    Wscript.Echo objTrust.TrustedDomain
    Wscript.Echo " TrustedAttributes: " & objTrust.TrustAttributes
    Wscript.Echo " TrustedDCName: "     & objTrust.TrustedDCName
    Wscript.Echo " TrustedDirection: "  & objTrust.TrustDirection
    Wscript.Echo " TrustIsOk: "         & objTrust.TrustIsOK
    Wscript.Echo " TrustStatus: "       & objTrust.TrustStatus
    Wscript.Echo " TrustStatusString: " & objTrust.TrustStatusString
    Wscript.Echo " TrustType: "         & objTrust.TrustType
    Wscript.Echo ""
next
```

Discussion

Resetting a trust synchronizes the shared secrets (i.e., passwords) for the trust. The PDC Emulators in both domains are used to synchronize the password, so they must be reachable.

Using a command-line interface

If you are resetting a Kerberos realm trust, you'll need to specify the `/PasswordT` option with `netdom`.

See Also

Recipe 2.20 for verifying a trust

2.22   Removing a Trust

Problem

You want to remove a trust. This is commonly done when the remote domain has been decommissioned or access to it is no longer required.

Solution

Using a graphical user interface

1. Open the Active Directory Domains and Trusts snap-in (*domain.msc*).

2. In the left pane, right-click on the trusting domain and select Properties.

3. Click the Trusts tab.

4. Click on the domain that is associated with the trust you want to remove.

5. Click the Remove button.

6. Click OK.

Using a command-line interface

To remove a trust relationship using the `netdom` utility, use the following syntax:

```
> netdom trust <TrustingDomain> /Domain:<TrustedDomain> /Remove /verbose
  [/UserO:<TrustingDomainUser> /PasswordO:*]
  [/UserD:<TrustedDomainUser> /PasswordD:*]
```

To remove a trust using a combination of AdFind and AdMod, issue the following two commands:

```
> adfind -b cn=<Trusted Domain>,cn=system,<Domain DN> -dsq | admod -rm
> adfind -b cn=<TrustName>$,cn=users,<Domain DN> -dsq | admod -rm
```

Both of these commands first use AdFind to return the object that needs to be deleted, then use the | operator to send that object to AdMod to perform the actual deletion.

Using VBScript

```
' This code deletes a trust in the specified domain.
' ------ SCRIPT CONFIGURATION ------
' Set to the DNS or NetBIOS name for the Windows 2000,
' Windows NT domain or Kerberos realm trust you want to delete.
strTrustName = "<TrustName>"
' Set to the DNS name of the source or trusting domain
strDomain    = "<DomainDNSName>"
' ------ END CONFIGURATION ---------

set objRootDSE = GetObject("LDAP://" & strDomain & "/RootDSE")
set objTrust = GetObject("LDAP://cn=System," & _
                            objRootDSE.Get("defaultNamingContext") )
objTrust.Delete "trustedDomain", "cn=" & strTrustName
set objTrustUser = GetObject("LDAP://cn=Users," & _
                            objRootDSE.Get("defaultNamingContext") )
objTrustUser.Delete "trustedDomain", "cn=" & strTrustName & "$"
WScript.Echo "Successfully deleted trust for " & strTrustName
```

Discussion

Trusts are stored in Active Directory as two objects; a trustedDomain object in the System container and a user object in the Users container. Both of these objects need to be removed when deleting a trust. The GUI and *netdom* solutions take care of that in one step, but in the VBScript and AdMod examples both objects needed to be explicitly deleted. It is also worth noting that each solution only deleted one side of the trust. If the trust was to a remote AD forest or NT 4.0 domain, you also need to delete the trust in that domain.

2.23   Enabling SID Filtering for a Trust

Problem

You want to enable Security Identifier (SID) filtering for a trust. By enabling SID filtering you can keep a hacker from spoofing a SID across a trust.

Solution

Using a command-line interface

```
> netdom trust <TrustingDomain> /Domain:<TrustedDomain> /EnableSIDHistory:No
   [/UserO:<TrustingDomainUser> /PasswordO:*]
   [/UserD:<TrustedDomainUser> /PasswordD:*]
```

Discussion

A security vulnerability exists with the use of SID history, which is described in detail in MS KB 289243. An administrator in a trusted domain can modify the SID history for a user, which could grant her elevated privileges in the trusting domain. The risk of this exploit is relatively low due to the complexity of forging an SID, but nevertheless, you should be aware of it. To prevent this from happening you can enable SID Filtering for a trust. When SID filtering is enabled, the only SIDs that are used as part of a user's token are from those domains in the trust path of the trusted domain—so if the trusted domain is *rallencorp.com* which has a child domain called *emea.rallencorp.com*, SID Filtering would accept SIDs from both the *rallencorp.com* domain and its child domain *emea*. SIDs that are not a part of the trusted domain's trust path are not included, so an SID from the *barcelona.corp* would be stripped from the user's access token. SID filtering makes things more secure, but prevents the use of SID history and can cause problems with transitive trusts and domain migrations. For example, if we migrated a user from *barcelona.corp* to *rallencorp.com*, that user's *barcelona.corp* SID history entry would be ignored as long as SID filtering was in place. You would need to update the Access Control Lists (ACLs) on resources in *barcelona.corp* to point to the migrated user's *rallencorp.com* SID, which would allow the user to access them with SID filtering in place.

SID Filtering is enabled by default on all trust relationships created in Windows 2000 Service Pack 4 and later. This can cause unexpected behavior if you created a trust relationship under an earlier Service Pack version, but then deleted and re-created the trust under SP4 or later. You can disable SID filtering by running the netdom command with the /EnableSIDHistory:Yes switch.

See Also

MS KB 289243 (MS02-001: Forged SID Could Result in Elevated Privileges in Windows 2000)

2.24   Enabling Quarantine for a Trust

Problem

You want to enable Quarantine for a trust. By enabling Quarantine, you can greatly restrict the acceptable domain SIDs in a trust relationship.

Solution

Using a command-line interface

```
> netdom trust <TrustingDomain> /Domain:<TrustedDomain> /Quarantine:Yes
   [/UserO:<TrustingDomainUser> /PasswordO:*]
   [/UserD:<TrustedDomainUser> /PasswordD:*]
```

Discussion

A security vulnerability exists with the use of SID history, which is described in detail in MS KB 289243. An administrator in a trusted domain can modify the SID history for a user, which could grant her elevated privileges in the trusting domain. The risk of this exploit is relatively low due to the complexity in forging a SID, but nevertheless, you should be aware of it. You can put strong restrictions in order to minimize the risk of privilege elevation by enabling Quarantine for a trust. When Quarantine is enabled, the only SIDs that are used as part of a user's token are from those domains in the trusted domain itself. So if the trusted domain is *rallencorp.com*, which has a child domain called *emea.rallencorp.com*, Quarantine will only accept SIDs from the *rallencorp.com* itself. Even domain SIDs that are a part of the trusted domain's trust path are not included, so a SID from the *emea.rallencorp.com* would be stripped from the user's access token. Enabling Quarantine for a trust effectively removes the transitivity of a forest trust relationship, restricting the trust relationship to only the domain that you specified when you created the trust. (This causes a forest trust to emulate the default behavior of an external trust instead.)

You can disable quarantine on a trust relationship by running the `netdom` command again and specifying the `/Quarantine:No` switch.

2.25 Managing Selective Authentication for a Trust

Problem

You want to enable or disable Selective Authentication for a trust. By enabling Selective Authentication, you can control which computers in a trusting domain can be accessed by users in a trusted domain. Disabling Selective Authentication will allow users in the trusted domain to authenticate to any computer in the trusting domain.

Solution

Using a graphical user interface

To enable Selective Authentication:

1. Open the Active Directory Domains and Trusts snap-in (*domain.msc*).
2. To enable selective authentication for a forest trust, right-click on the forest root domain and select Properties. To enable selective authentication for an external trust, right-click on the domain you wish to configure and select Properties.
3. On the Trusts tab, right-click on the trust that you wish to administer, and select Properties.
4. On the Authentication tab, click Selective Authentication.
5. Click OK to finish.

To disable Selective Authentication:

1. Open the Active Directory Domains and Trusts snap-in.

2. To enable forest-wide authentication for a forest trust, right-click on the forest root domain and select Properties. To enable domain-wide authentication for an external trust, right-click on the domain you wish to configure and select Properties.

3. On the Trusts tab, right-click on the trust that you wish to administer, and select Properties.

4. In the case of a forest trust, on the Authentication tab click Forest-Wide Authentication. For an external trust, on the Authentication tab click Domain-Wide Authentication.

5. Click OK to finish.

To grant permissions on individual computers in the trusted domain:

1. Open the Active Directory Users and Computers snap-in (*dsa.msc*).

2. Right-click on the computer object that you wish to grant permissions on, and select Properties.

3. On the Security tab, select the user or group that you want to authorize, select the Allow check-box next to the Allowed to Authenticate permission.

4. Click OK to finish.

Using a command-line interface

To enable selective authentication, use the following syntax:

```
> netdom trust <TrustingDomain> /Domain:<TrustedDomain> /SelectiveAUTH:Yes
  [/UserO:<TrustingDomainUser> /PasswordO:*]
  [/UserD:<TrustedDomainUser> /PasswordD:*]
```

Use the /SelectiveAUTH:No switch to enable domain- or forest-wide authentication.

Discussion

Trust relationships in Windows Server 2003 forests, by default, allow users in a trusting domain to authenticate to and access shared resources on any computer in the trusted domain. Selective Authentication, also known as the Authentication Firewall, will restrict access to only those computers in the trusted domain that you specifically designate. This level of increased security is particularly useful when you need to grant access to shared resources in your forest, but you need to restrict that access to only a limited set of users in the remote forest.

For users in a trusted Windows Server 2003 domain or forest to be able to access resources in a trusting Windows Server 2003 domain or forest, where the trust authentication setting has been set to selective authentication, each user must be explicitly granted the Allowed to Authenticate permission on the security descriptor of the computer objects (resource computers) that reside in the trusting domain or forest. By default, only members of the *Account Operators*, *Administrators*, *Domain Admins*, *Enterprise Admins*, and *SYSTEM* groups in the trusting domain have the ability to modify this permission.

 Enabling Selective Authentication has the potential to create a huge increase in your AD administrative overhead, and should only be enabled when the security risks outweigh the downside.

2.26   Finding Duplicate SIDs in a Domain

Problem

You want to find any duplicate SIDs in a domain. Generally, you should never find duplicate SIDs in a domain, but it is possible in some situations, such as when the relative identifier (RID) FSMO role owner has to be seized or you are migrating users from Windows NT domains.

Solution

Using a command-line interface

To find duplicate SIDs run the following command, replacing *<DomainControllerName>* with a domain controller or domain name:

```
> ntdsutil "sec acc man" "co to se <DomainControllerName>" "check dup sid" q q
```

The following message will be returned:

```
Duplicate SID check completed successfully. Check dupsid.log for any duplicates
```

The *dupsid.log* file will be in the directory where you started *ntdsutil*.

If you want to delete any objects that have duplicate SIDs, you can use the following command:

```
> ntdsutil "sec acc man" "co to se <DomainControllerName>" "clean dup sid" q q
```

Like the check command, the clean command will generate a message like the following upon completion:

```
Duplicate SID cleanup completed successfully. Check dupsid.log for any duplicate
```

Discussion

All security principals in Active Directory have an SID, which is used to uniquely identify the object in the Windows security system. There are two parts of an SID, the domain identifier and the RID. Domain controllers are allocated a RID pool from the RID FSMO for the domain. When a new security principal (user, group, or computer) is created, the domain controller takes an RID from its pool to generate an SID for the account.

In some rare circumstances, such as when the RID master role is seized, overlapping RID pools can be allocated, which can ultimately lead to duplicate SIDs. Having duplicate SIDs is a potentially hazardous problem because a user, group, or computer could gain access to sensitive data they were never intended to have access to.

See Also

MS KB 315062 (How to Find and Clean Up Duplicate Security Identifiers with Ntdsutil in Windows 2000) and MS KB 816099 (How to Find and Clean Up Duplicate Security Identifiers with Ntdsutil in Windows Server 2003)

2.27 Adding Additional Fields to Active Directory Users and Computers

Problem

You want to add to the list of attributes that you can search and sort records by within the ADUC MMC snap-in (*dsa.msc*).

Solution

Using a graphical user interface

In this example, we will add the operating system service pack level attributes of computer objects to ADUC to allow you to search and sort by these fields.

1. Open ADSI Edit from the Windows Support Tools.
2. If an entry for the Configuration NC is not already displayed, do the following:
3. Right-click on ADSI Edit in the right pane and click "Connect to...."
4. Under "Select a well-known naming context," select Configuration. Click Advanced if you need to specify alternate credentials, then click OK to create the connection.
5. In the left pane, click on CN=DisplaySpecifiers, then CN=409. Right-click on the container and select Properties.

If you are using a locale other than US English, specify the appropriate local number in place of CN=409.

6. Right-click on cn=computerDisplay and select Properties.

7. Double-click on attributeDisplayNames. Type **operatingSystemServicePack, Operating System Service Pack**, and click Add.

8. Click Apply, followed by OK.

Using a command-line interface

First create an LDIF file containing the following information. Save it as *modify_display_specifiers.ldif*:

```
dn: cn=computer-display,cn=409,cn=DisplaySpecifiers,
    cn=Configuration,<ForestRootDN>
changetype: modify
add: attributeDisplayNames
attributeDisplayNames: operatingSystemServicePack,Operating System Service Pack
-
```

Then run the following command:

```
> ldifde -v -i -f modify_display_specifiers.ldf
```

You can also modify this information using a combination of AdFind and AdMod, as follows:

```
> adfind –config –rb cn=computer-display,cn=409,cn=DisplaySpecifiers | admod
"attributeDisplayNames:+:operatingSystemServicePack,Operating System Service Pack"
```

Using VBScript

```
' The following script will append a new value to the
' US English display specifiers
'---------- SCRIPT CONFIGURATION ------------------
  Const ADS_PROPERTY_APPEND = 3
  strForestRoot = "<ForestRootDN>" ' i.e., "dc=rallencorp,dc=com"
' --------- END CONFIGURATION --------------------

strObjectDN = "cn=computer-display,cn=409,cn=displayspecifiers," & _
              "cn=configuration," & strForestRoot
set objObject = GetObject("LDAP://" & strObjectDN)
objObject.PutEx ADS_PROPERTY_APPEND, _
  "attributeDisplayNames", Array("operatingSystemServicePackLevel, " & _
  "Operating System Service Pack Level")
objObject.setInfo

WScript.Echo "Script completed successfully!"
```

Discussion

When working within the Active Directory Users and Computers MMC snap-in, there are a number of default attributes for each type of object that you can use to either search or sort on. Computer objects, for example, allow you to search and sort by the computer name, description, manager, operating system, and pre-Windows 2000 computer name. Once you add a new attribute to the display specifiers, you can access it by opening ADUC, right-clicking on a container and clicking on Find. Select Computers in the drop-down box next to Find, and click on Advanced. When you click on Field, you'll see the new field that you just added; you can now use it to search for objects within the ADUC snap-in.

Using VBScript

Because the attributeDisplayNames attribute is multivalued, we need to use the PutEx method to add a value to an existing list of values. If you accidentally use Put to update a multivalued attribute, you will overwrite the list of values with the single value you specify in the script.

See Also

Recipe 4.14 for more on modifying an object, MSDN: Attribute-Display-Names [AD Schema], and MSDN: PutEx method [ADSI]

## CHAPTER 3

Domain Controllers, Global Catalogs, and FSMOs

3.0 Introduction

Domain controllers are servers that host an Active Directory domain and provide authentication and directory services to clients. A domain controller can only be authoritative (i.e., it can only process authentication requests) for a single domain, but it can store partial read-only copies of objects in other domains in the forest if it is enabled as a global catalog server. All domain controllers in a forest also host a copy of the Configuration and Schema Naming Contexts, which are replicated to all domain controllers in a forest.

Active Directory is a multimaster directory, meaning that updates can be issued to any domain controller. However, some tasks are sensitive enough that they cannot be distributed to all servers due to potential issues arising from more than one DC performing the same update simultaneously. For example, if two different domain controllers made conflicting updates to the schema, the impact could be severe and could result in data loss or an unusable directory. For this reason, Active Directory supports FSMO roles. For each FSMO role, there is only one domain controller that acts as the role owner and performs the tasks associated with the role. These roles are termed "single master" because only a single DC can hold a role at any one time, but "flexible" because a single physical server can host multiple FSMOs, and a FSMO role can be transferred from one DC to another, largely without repercussion. See Recipe 3.30 for more information on FSMO roles.

The Anatomy of a Domain Controller

Each domain controller is represented in Active Directory by several objects; the two main ones are a computer object and an nTDSDSA object. The computer object is necessary because a domain controller needs to be represented as a security principal just like any other type of computer in Active Directory. The default location in a domain for domain controller computer objects is the Domain Controllers Organizational Unit (OU) at the root of the domain. They can be moved to a different OU, but it is highly recommended that you don't unless you know what you are doing and have a good reason for doing so; this is because any DCs that you move outside of the Domain Controller's OU will not receive the same Group Policy Object settings as those within the OU, which can lead to unpredictable behavior on your network. Table 3-1 contains some useful attributes of domain controller computer objects.

Table 3-1. Attributes of domain controller computer objects

Attribute	Description
dnsHostName	Fully qualified DNS name of the DC.
msDS-AdditionalDnsHostName	Contains the old DNS name of a renamed DC. This is new in Windows Server 2003.
msDS-AdditionalSamAccountName	Contains the old NetBIOS name of a renamed DC. This is new in Windows Server 2003.
operatingSystem	Textual description of the operating system running on the DC.
operatingSystemHotFix	Currently not being used, but will hopefully be populated with the installed hotfixes at some point.
operatingSystemServicePack	Service pack version installed on the DC.
operatingSystemVersion	Numeric version of the operating system installed on the DC.
sAMAccountName	NetBIOS style name of the DC.
serverReferenceBL	DN of the DC's server object contained under the Sites container in the Configuration NC.
servicePrincipalName	List of SPNs supported by the DC.

Domain controllers are also represented by several objects under the Sites container in the Configuration NC. The Sites container stores objects that are needed to create a site topology, including site, subnet, sitelink, and server objects. The site topology is necessary so that domain controllers, DFS file shares, and site-specific Group Policy Objects can replicate data efficiently around the network. Because a single site can span multiple domains, this is one reason why the Configuration NC is replicated throughout the entire Active Directory forest. See Chapter 11 for more information on sites and replication.

Each domain controller has an nTDSDSA object that is subordinate to the domain controller's server object in the site it is a member of. For example, if the DC1 domain controller were part of the RTP site, its nTDSDSA object would be located here:

    cn=NTDS Settings,cn=DC1,cn=RTP,cn=sites,cn=configuration,dc=rallencorp,dc=com

Table 3-2 lists some of the interesting attributes that are stored with nTDSDSA objects.

Table 3-2. Attributes of domain controller nTDSDSA objects

Attribute	Description
hasMasterNCs	List of DNs for the naming contexts the DC is authoritative for. This does not include application partitions.
hasPartialReplicaNCs	List of DNs for the naming contexts the DC has a partial read-only copy of.
msDS-HasDomainNCs	The DN of the domain the DC is authoritative for. This is new in Windows Server 2003.
msDS-HasMasterNCs	List of DNs for the naming contexts (domain, configuration, and schema) and application partitions the DC is authoritative for. This is new in Windows Server 2003.
options	If the low-order bit of this attribute is set, the domain controller stores a copy of the global catalog.
invocationID	GUID that is assigned to the Active Directory database itself when the domain controller is first installed. When the DC is first installed, the invocationID value is the same as the objectGUID for the DC itself; however, the invocationID changes whenever a restore operation is performed or when the DC is configured to host an application partition.

3.1 Promoting a Domain Controller

Problem

You want to promote a server to a domain controller. You may need to promote a domain controller to initially create a domain in an Active Directory forest, or to add additional domain controllers to the domain for load balancing and fault tolerance.

Solution

Run *dcpromo.exe* from a command line or via Start → Run and answer the questions according to the forest and domain you want to promote the server into.

Discussion

Promoting a server to a domain controller is the process where the server becomes authoritative for an Active Directory domain. When you run the *dcpromo* program, a wizard interface walks you through a series of screens that collects information about the forest and domain to promote the server into. There are several options for promoting a server:

- Promoting into a new forest (see Recipe 2.1)
- Promoting into a new domain tree or child domain (see Recipe 2.3)
- Promoting into an existing domain

You can automate the promotion process by running *dcpromo* during an unattended installation. See Recipe 3.5 for more details.

See Also

Recipe 2.1 for creating a new forest, Recipe 2.3 for creating a new domain, Recipe 3. 5, and MS KB 238369 (How to Promote and Demote Domain Controllers in Windows 2000)

3.2 Promoting a Domain Controller from Media

 This recipe requires that the server being promoted run Windows Server 2003.

Problem

You want to promote a new domain controller using a backup from another domain controller as the initial source of the Active Directory database instead of replicating the entire *NTDS.DIT* file over the network.

Solution

1. You first need to back up the system state of an existing domain controller in the domain the new server will go in. This can be accomplished by running the MS Backup utility found at Start → Programs → Accessories → System Tools → Backup.

2. Once you have a good backup, you then need to restore it to the new server, which can also be done using MS Backup. You should restore the files to an alternate location, not to their original location.

3. Next, run dcpromo with the /adv switch from a command line or by clicking Start → Run, as follows:

       dcpromo /adv

4. After the *dcpromo* wizard starts, select Additional Domain Controller for an existing domain and click Next.

5. Under Copy Domain Information, select From these restored backup files. Browse to the files that you restored in Step 2, and then click Next.

6. Enter credentials of a user in the Domain Admins group in the domain you are promoting the domain controller into and click Next.

7. Choose the folders to store the Active Directory database and log files and click Next.

8. Choose the folder to store SYSVOL and click Next.

9. Enter a Restore Mode password and click Next.

10. Click Next to start the promotion.

Discussion

The ability to promote a domain controller using the System State backup of another domain controller is a new feature in Windows Server 2003. With Windows 2000, a new domain controller had to replicate the entire *NTDS.DIT* Active Directory database file over a network connection from an existing domain controller. For organizations with a sizable Active Directory DIT file and/or very poor network connectivity to a remote site, replicating the full contents over the network presented challenges. Under these conditions, the promotion process could take a prohibitively long time to complete. Now with the new "Install from Media" option, the initial domain controller promotion process can be substantially quicker. After you've done the initial installation from media (i.e., backup tape or CD/DVD), the new domain controller will replicate any changes that have been made to the Active Directory database since the backup media was created.

 Be sure that the backup files you are using are much less than your AD forest's tombstone lifetime. If you install a domain controller using backup files that are older than this value, you could run into issues with deleted objects being re-injected into the Active Directory database after their tombstone lifetime has expired. In Windows Server 2003, the default tombstone lifetime is 60 days, or 180 days for a domain that has been newly installed with Windows Server 2003 Service Pack 1.

See Also

Recipe 17.1 for backing up Active Directory, Recipe 17.21 for modifying the tombstone lifetime of a domain, MS KB 240363 (How to Use the Backup Program to Back Up and Restore the System State in Windows 2000), MS KB 216993 (Useful Shelf Life of a System-State Backup of Active Directory), and MS KB 311078 (How to Use the Install from Media Feature to Promote Windows Server 2003-based Domain Controllers)

3.3   Verifying the Promotion of a Domain Controller

Problem

You want to verify that a domain controller has been successfully promoted within an Active Directory domain.

Solution

Using a command-line interface

```
> netdiag /test:dns
> netdiag /test:member
> netdiag /test:dsgetdc
```

```
> dcdiag /test:replications
> dcdiag /s:<DCName> /test:knowsofroleholders
> dcdiag /s:<DCName> /test:fsmocheck
```

Discussion

Once you've installed a domain controller using the *dcpromo* process, there are several steps that you can take to ensure that the promotion process has completed successfully. *dcdiag* and *netdiag* are two utilities that come with the Windows Support tools, and can perform a number of diagnostic tests, including the following:

- Verify that all necessary DNS records have been registered and are present on the DNS server.
- Check the domain membership for the newly-promoted computer.
- Confirm that the new DC can communicate with other DCs in the domain.
- Confirm that the new DC is replicating with other DCs.
- Verify that the new DC can communicate with all of the FSMO role holders.

See Also

MS KB 839880 (How to Troubleshoot RPC Endpoint Mapper Errors), MS KB 250842 (Troubleshooting Group Policy Application Problems), and MS KB 321708 (How to Use the Network Diagnostics Tool (Netdiag.exe) in Windows 2000)

3.4   Demoting a Domain Controller

Problem

You want to demote a domain controller from a domain. If you want to decommission a domain controller due to lack of use or change in architecture, you'll need to follow these demotion procedures.

Solution

Using a graphical user interface

1. Run the dcpromo command from a command line or Start → Run.
2. Click Next.
3. If the server is the last domain controller in the domain, check the box beside "This server is the last domain controller in the domain."
4. Click Next.
5. Type and confirm the password for the local Administrator account.
6. Click Next twice to begin the demotion.

Discussion

Before demoting a domain controller, you first need to ensure that all of the FSMO roles have been transferred to other servers; otherwise, they will be transferred to random domain controllers that may not be optimal for your installation. (Managing FSMO role holders is discussed in Recipe 3.30.) Also, if the DC is a global catalog server or running a service such as DNS, WINS, DHCP, etc., ensure that you have sufficient GCs and other infrastructure servers elsewhere in your forest that can handle the increased load.

It is important to demote a domain controller before decommissioning or rebuilding it so that its associated objects in Active Directory are removed, its DNS locator resource records are dynamically removed, and replication with the other domain controllers is not interrupted. If a domain controller does not successfully demote, or if you do not get the chance to demote it because of some type of hardware failure, see Recipe 2.4 for removing a domain from Active Directory, and Recipe 3.4 for instructions on manually removing a domain controller from Active Directory.

See Also

Recipe 2.4, Recipe 3.4, Recipe 3.7 for removing an unsuccessfully demoted domain controller, Recipe 3.22 for disabling the global catalog, Recipe 3.30, Recipe 3.31 for transferring FSMO roles, and MS KB 238369 (How to Promote and Demote Domain Controllers in Windows 2000)

3.5 Automating the Promotion or Demotion of a Domain Controller

Problem

You want to automate the installation or removal of a domain controller. You can make the promotion process part of your standard build process by incorporating the necessary configuration lines in your answer file(s).

Solution

You can automate the promotion of a domain controller by using the unattended process when building the server or by manually running *dcpromo* after the system has been built. Pass an answer file containing the necessary lines to promote the server to dcpromo by specifying a /answer switch. Here is an example:

```
> dcpromo /answer:<path_to_answer_file>
```

If you want to run *dcpromo* as part of an unattended setup, you need to add a [GUIRunOnce] section in your unattended setup file that calls the *dcpromo* process.

You can promote a domain controller only after setup has completed and someone logs in for the first time. That is why it is necessary to use a [GUIRunOnce] section, which sets the RunOnce registry key to kick off *dcpromo* on the first user logon, either at the console or via Terminal Services. Here is an example:

```
[GUIRunOnce]
"dcpromo /answer:%systemroot%\system32\$winnt$.inf"
```

The *dcpromo* answer section starts with [DCInstall]. Here is an example answer file for adding a domain controller to an existing domain in the *rallencorp.com* forest:

```
[DCINSTALL]
UserName=administrator
Password=RAllencorpAdminPassword
UserDomain=rallencorp.com
DatabasePath=%systemroot%\ntds
LogPath=%systemroot%\ntds
SYSVOLPath=%systemroot%\sysvol
SafeModeAdminPassword=DSrestoreModePassword
CriticalReplicationOnly=no
ReplicaOrNewDomain=Replica
ReplicaDomainDNSName=rallencorp.com
RebootOnSuccess=yes
CreateOrJoin=Join
```

Discussion

For a complete list of Windows Server 2003 [DCInstall] settings, see the *ref.chm* help file in *\support\tools\deploy.cab* that can be found on the Windows Server 2003 CD. For Windows 2000, the settings can be found in the *unattend.doc* file in *\support\tools\ deploy.cab* on the Windows Server 2003 CD. You'll specify each parameter using the following syntax: Parameter = Value. A portion of an unattended installation file that creates a new AD forest might look something like this:

```
[DCInstall]
CreateOrJoin = Create
AllowAnonymousAccess = No
AutoConfigDNS = Yes
```

See Also

MS KB 223757 (Unattended Promotion and Demotion of Windows 2000 Domain Controllers), MS KB 224390 (How to Automate Windows 2000 Setup and Domain Controller Setup), and Planning for Unattended Setup in the Windows Server 2003 Help and Support Center

3.6 Troubleshooting Domain Controller Promotion or Demotion Problems

Problem

You are having problems promoting or demoting a domain controller and you want to troubleshoot it.

Solution

The best source of information about the status of promotion or demotion problems are the *Dcpromo.log* and *Dcpromoui.log* files contained in the *%SystemRoot%\Debug* folder on the server. The *Dcpromo.log* captures the input entered into *dcpromo* and logs the information that is displayed as *dcpromo* progresses. The *Dcpromoui.log* file is much more detailed and captures discrete actions that occur during *dcpromo* processing, including any user input. A sample *dcpromoui.log* file might look something like this:

```
dcpromoui D38.A65 0000 opening log file C:\WINDOWS\debug\dcpromoui.log
dcpromoui D38.A65 0001 C:\WINDOWS\system32\dcpromo.exe
dcpromoui D38.A65 0002 file timestamp 11/19/2005 07:02:35.000
dcpromoui D38.A65 0003 local time 11/19/2005 07:03:45.406
dcpromoui D38.A65 0004 running Windows NT 5.2 build 3718
(BuildLab:3718.dnsrv.021114-1947) i386
...
dcpromoui D38.A65 00E3 Enter ControlSubclasser::UnhookWindowProc
dcpromoui D38.A65 00E4 exitCode = 0
dcpromoui D38.A65 00E5 closing log
```

Additionally, the Windows Server 2003 version of *dcdiag* contains two new tests that can aid in troubleshooting promotion problems. The dcpromo test reports anything it finds that could impede the promotion process. The RegisterInDNS test checks if the server can register records in DNS. Here is an example of running both commands to test against the rallencorp.com domain:

```
> dcdiag /test:dcpromo /DnsDomain:rallencorp.com /ReplicaDC /test:RegisterInDNS
```

Discussion

In most cases, the level of detail provided by *Dcpromoui.log* should be sufficient to pinpoint any problems, but you can increase logging if necessary. To enable the highest level of logging available, set the following registry value to FF0003: HKLM\Software\Microsoft\Windows\CurrentVersion\AdminDebug. You can confirm that this mask took effect by running *dcpromo* again, checking the *Dcpromoui.log*, and searching for "logging mask." For more information on the various logging settings, see MS KB 221254.

If *dcdiag* does not return sufficient information, the Network Monitor (*netmon*) program is very handy for getting a detailed understanding of the network traffic that is being generated and any errors that are being returned; this is part of the optional Network Monitoring and Management Tools that you can install via the Add/Remove Programs Control Panel applet. You can identify what other servers it is talking to or if it is timing out when attempting to perform certain queries or updates.

See Also

MS KB 221254 (Registry Settings for Event Detail in the Dcpromoui.log File) and MS KB 260371 (Troubleshooting Common Active Directory Setup Issues in Windows 2000)

3.7   Removing an Unsuccessfully Demoted Domain Controller

Problem

You want to manually remove a domain Controller from Active Directory if the *dcpromo* process was unsuccessful or you are unable to bring a domain controller back online after a hardware or software failure.

Solution

The first step in the removal process is to run the following *ntdsutil* command, where *<DomainControllerName>* is a domain controller in the same domain as the one you want to forcibly remove.

 The following *ntdsutil* syntax is applicable to Windows 2000 and Windows Server 2003 installations without Service Pack 1 installed. Windows Server 2003 Service Pack 1 greatly simplifies the syntax involved; we will cover the new syntax later.

```
> ntdsutil "meta clean" conn "co to ser <DomainControllerName>"
  q "s o t" "l d"
Found 2 domain(s)
0 - DC=rallencorp,DC=com
1 - DC=emea,DC=rallencorp,DC=com
```

Select the domain of the domain controller you want to remove. In this case, we'll select the *emea.rallencorp.com* domain:

```
select operation target: sel domain 1
```

Now, list the sites and select the site the domain controller is in (Use 1 for MySite1):

```
select operation target: list sites
Found 4 site(s)
0 - CN=Default-First-Site-Name,CN=Sites,CN=Configuration,DC=rallencorp,DC=com
1 - CN=MySite1,CN=Sites,CN=Configuration,DC=rallencorp,DC=com
2 - CN=MySite2,CN=Sites,CN=Configuration,DC=rallencorp,DC=com
3 - CN=MySite3,CN=Sites,CN=Configuration,DC=rallencorp,DC=com
select operation target: sel site 1
```

Next, select the server you want to remove; in this case, we're choosing 0 for DC5:

```
select operation target: list servers for domain in site
Found 2 server(s)
0 - CN=DC5,CN=Servers,CN=MySite1,CN=Sites,CN=Configuration,DC=rallencorp,DC=com
1 - CN=DC9,CN=Servers,CN=MySite1,CN=Sites,CN=Configuration,DC=rallencorp,DC=com
select operation target: sel server 0
```

Type quit to get back to the metadata cleanup menu.

```
select operation target: quit
metadata cleanup:
```

Finally, remove the server:

```
metadata cleanup: remove selected server
```

If successful, a message will state that the removal was complete. However, if you recieve an error message, check to see if the server's nTDSDSA object (e.g., CN=NTDSSettings,CN=DC5,CN=Servers,CN=MySite1,CN=Sites,CN=Configuration,DC=rall encorp,DC=com) is present. If so, *dcpromo* may have already removed it, and it will take time for the change to replicate. If it is still present, try the *ntdsutil* procedure again and if that doesn't work, manually remove that object and the parent object (e.g., CN=DC5) using ADSI Edit or another tool. (Deleting Active Directory objects is discussed in Recipe 4.24.)

In Windows Server 2003 Service Pack 1, the *ntdsutil* syntax for removing metadata from a failed server has been greatly simplified, as follows:

1. Go to the Windows command line and type ntdsutil.

2. From the *ntdsutil* menu, type metadata cleanup.

3. Type remove selected server cn=<*ServerName*>,cn=Servers,cn=SiteName, cn=Sites,cn=Configuration,dc=<*ForestRootDomain*> to remove the server meta-data associated with *dc1.rallencorp.com*.

Follow these additional steps to remove all traces of the domain controller:

1. Delete the CNAME record from DNS for <*GUID*>._msdcs.<*RootDomainDNSName*>, where <*GUID*> is the objectGUID for the server's nTDSDSA object. If scavenging is not enabled, you'll need to manually delete all associated SRV records. Delete any A and PTR records that exist for the server. When using Microsoft DNS, you can use the DNS MMC snap-in to accomplish these tasks.

2. Delete the computer object for the server under OU=DomainControllers,*<DomainDN>*. This can be done using the Active Directory Users and Computers snap-in or the AdMod utility.

3. Delete the FRS Member object for the computer contained under CN=DomainSystemVolume (SYSVOL share),CN=file replication service,CN=system,*<DomainDN>*. This can be done using the Active Directory Users and Computers snap-in when "Advanced Features" has been selected from the View menu (so the System container will be displayed), or with the AdMod tool.

4. Delete the server object associated with the failed domain controller in the Active Directory Sites and Services MMC.

Discussion

Forcibly removing a domain controller from a domain is not a task that should be undertaken lightly. If you need to replace a piece of server hardware quickly, consider giving the new hardware a different name just to ensure that nothing confuses the new server with the old one. If the domain controller that you're removing was the last one in the domain, you'll need to manually remove the domain from the forest as well. See Recipe 2.5 for more information on removing orphaned domains.

Here are some additional issues to consider when you forcibly remove a domain controller:

- Seize any FSMO roles the DC may have had to another domain controller.
- If the DC was a global catalog server, ensure there is another global catalog server configured in the site that can handle the increased workload.
- If the DC was a DNS server, ensure there is another DNS server that can handle the additional name resolution queries, and be sure that your clients are configured to use the correct nameserver.
- If the DC was the RID FSMO master, check to make sure duplicate SIDs have not been issued (see Recipe 2.24).
- Check to see if the DC hosted any application partitions and if so, consider making another server a replica server for those application partitions (see Recipe 17.5).

If the (former) domain controller that you forcibly removed is still active or otherwise returns to your network, you should strongly consider reinstalling the operating sytem to avoid potential conflicts from the server trying to re-insert itself back into Active Directory. To remove Active Directory from a server without reinstalling the operating system, you can run dcpromo /forceremoval from a command line to forcibly remove Active Directory from a server. See MS KB 332199 for more information.

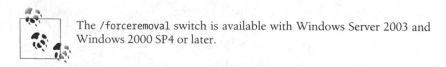 The /forceremoval switch is available with Windows Server 2003 and Windows 2000 SP4 or later.

Alternately, you can try this option to force the server to not recognize itself as a domain controller:

1. Change the `ProductOptions` value under the `HKLM\System\CurrentControlSet\Control` key from `LanmanNT` to `ServerNT`.

2. Reboot the server.

3. Delete the NTDS folder.

See Also

Recipe 2.5 for removing an orphaned domain, Recipe 2.24, Recipe 3.32 for seizing FSMO roles, Recipe 4.24, Recipe 17.5, MS KB 216498 (How to Remove Data in Active Directory After an Unsuccessful Domain Controller Demotion), and MS KB 332199 (Domain Controllers Do Not Demote Gracefully When You Use the Active Directory Installation Wizard to Force Demotion in Windows Server 2003 and in Windows 2000 Server)

3.8   Renaming a Domain Controller

Problem

You want to rename a domain controller.

Solution

Windows 2000 Active Directory

To rename a domain controller, you must first demote it to a member server. You can then rename it and then promote it back to a domain controller.

Windows Server 2003 Active Directory

Your first step in renaming a Windows Server 2003 domain controller is as follows, where <NewName> is a fully qualified domain name (FQDN):

```
> netdom computername <CurrentName> /Add:<NewName>
```

The new name will be automatically replicated throughout Active Directory and DNS. Once you've verified that the new name has replicated (which may take some time depending on your replication topology), you can designate it as the domain controller's primary name as follows, and then reboot the domain controller:

```
> netdom computername <CurrentName> /MakePrimary:<NewName>
```

See Chapter 13 for information on verifying Active Directory replication.

Once you're satisfied that your clients are accessing the domain controller using its new name, you can remove the old computer name using the following syntax:

```
> netdom computername <NewName> /remove:<OldName>
```

 To use the domain controller rename functionality, you must be running at the Windows Server 2003 domain functional level.

Discussion

There is no supported means to rename a Windows 2000 domain controller, which is why the only way you can approximate the process is by demoting the server before performing the rename, and then promoting the server to DC status using the new name. Before you demote the domain controller, you should transfer any FSMO roles it holds to other servers in your domain or forest. You can allow *dcpromo* to transfer the roles during the demotion process, but you should check afterward to verify which server(s) the role(s) were transferred to to ensure that they are placed appropriately for your environment. Likewise, if the domain controller is a global catalog server, ensure that another global catalog server is available to take its place.

Renaming a domain controller without needing to demote it is a new feature of Windows Server 2003. A new option has been added to the *netdom* utility to allow an alternate computer name to be associated with a computer in Active Directory. Once you've added a new name, you can then set that name to be the primary name, thereby renaming the computer.

The old name effectively remains with the domain controller until you remove it, which can be done using the `netdom computername /Remove:<Name>` command. You should reboot the server before removing the old name. The old names are stored in the `msDS-AdditionalDnsHostName` and `msDS-AdditionalSamAccountName` attributes on the domain controller's computer object.

 If you are in a domain that only contains one domain controller, the domain controller rename function will not be available to you. You will need to bring a second 2003 domain controller online, transfer all FSMO roles to the new server, and then demote the old server to rename it. For more invormation, see *http://www.microsoft.com/ technet/prodtechnol/windowsserver2003/library/ServerHelp/aad1169a-f0d2-47d5-b0ea-989081ce62be.mspx*.

See Also

MS KB 195242 (Cannot Change Computer Name of a Domain Controller), MS KB 296592 (How to Rename a Windows 2000 Domain Controller)

3.9 Creating an NT 4.0 BDC Object

Problem

You want to create a computer account for an NT 4.0 BDC within an Active Directory domain.

Solution

Using a graphical user interface

1. Open the Active Directory Users and Computers snap-in (*dsa.msc*).

2. If you need to change domains, right-click on Active Directory Users and Computers in the left pane, select Connect to Domain, enter the domain name and click OK.

3. In the left pane, browse to the parent container for the computer, right-click on it, and select New → Computer.

4. Enter the name of the computer. Place a check mark next to "Assign this computer as a pre-Windows 2000 computer" and "Assign this computer as a backup domain controller." Click Next to continue.

5. If you will be using this computer account as part of an RIS deployment, place a check mark next to "This is a managed computer" and enter the GUID that it should use, and then click Next. Otherwise, just click Next to continue.

6. Click Finish.

Using a command-line interface

```
> admod -b <ObjectDN> objectClass::computer
  userAccountControl::8224 sAMAccountName::<ComputerName>$ -add
```

Using VBScript

```
' This code creates a computer object.
' ------ SCRIPT CONFIGURATION ------
strBase = "<ParentComputerDN>"  ' e.g. cn=Computers,dc=rallencorp,dc=com
strComp = "<ComputerName>"      ' e.g. joe-xp
strDescr = "<Description>"       ' e.g. Joe's Windows XP workstation
' ------ END CONFIGURATION ---------
Const NT4 = &h2020

set objCont = GetObject("LDAP://" & strBase)
```

```
set objComp = objCont.Create("computer", "cn=" & strComp)
objComp.Put "sAMAccountName", strComp & "$"
objComp.Put "description", strDesc
objComp.Put "userAccountControl", NT4
objComp.SetInfo
Wscript.Echo "Computer account for " & strComp & " created"
```

Discussion

When a Windows Server 2003 domain is operating in either the Windows 2000 mixed or Windows Server 2003 interim domain functionality level, it can support domain controllers running Windows NT 4.0. In the Windows 2000 mixed mode, it will support NT4, Windows 2000, and Windows Server 2003, while in the interim mode it will only support NT4 and 2003. The Active Directory Users & Computers MMC snap-in now allows you to precreate a computer account for an NT 4.0 BDC; otherwise, you can create one at the command line or in a VBScript by ORing together the hexadecimal values of 0x2000 and 0x0020 in the userAccountControl attribute.

See Also

MS KB 242432 (Cannot add Windows NT 4.0 BDC to a Windows 2000 Domain) and MS KB 296480 (How to Upgrade a Windows NT 4.0 PDC to a Windows 2000-Based Domain Controller)

3.10   Finding the Domain Controllers for a Domain

Problem

You want to find the domain controllers in a domain.

Solution

Using a graphical user interface

1. Open the Active Directory Users and Computers snap-in (*dsa.msc*).
2. Right-click on the target domain and select Find.
3. In the Find drop-down box, select "Computers."
4. In the Role drop-down box, select "Domain controller."
5. Click Find Now. The list of domain controllers for the domain will be present in the right pane.

Using a command-line interface

To list all DCs in a domain, you can use *netdom*, *dsquery*, or *adfind* as follows:

```
> netdom query dc /Domain:<DomainDNSName>
```

```
> dsquery * cn=configuration,<ForestRootDN> -filter (objectclass=ntdsdsa)

> adfind –config –f objectclass=ntdsdsa -dn
```

Using VBScript

```
' This code displays the domain controllers for the specified domain.
' ------ SCRIPT CONFIGURATION ------
strDomain = "<DomainDNSName>"  ' e.g. emea.rallencorp.com
' ------ END CONFIGURATION ---------

set objRootDSE = GetObject("LDAP://" & strDomain & "/RootDSE")
set objDomain = GetObject("LDAP://" & objRootDSE.Get("defaultNamingContext"))
strMasteredBy = objDomain.GetEx("masteredBy")
for each strNTDSDN in strMasteredBy
   set objNTDS = GetObject("LDAP://" & strNTDSDN)
   set objServer = GetObject(objNTDS.Parent)
   Wscript.echo objServer.Get("dNSHostName")
next
```

Discussion

There are several ways to get a list of domain controllers for a domain. The GUI solution simply uses the built-in "Find" functionality of the Active Directory Users & Computers MMC. The CLI and VBScript solutions take a slightly different approach by looking at the masteredBy attribute on the domain object (e.g., dc=emea,dc=rallencorp,dc=com) of the domain. The masteredBy attribute contains a list of distinguished names of the nTDSDSA objects of all the domain controllers for that domain. The parent object of the nTDSDSA object, which is the server object of the domain controller, has a distinguishedName attribute that contains the distinguished name of the server.

And for yet another solution, see Recipe 3.26 to find out how to query DNS to get the list of domain controllers for a domain.

See Also

Recipe 3.26 for finding domain controllers via DNS

3.11 Finding the Closest Domain Controller

Problem

You want to find the closest domain controller for a particular domain.

Solution

Using a command-line interface

The following command finds the closest domain controller in the specified domain (*<DomainDNSName>*); that is, a domain controller that is located in the same site or in the closest site if a local DC is not available. By default, it will return the closest DC for the computer *nltest* is being run from, but you can optionally use the /server option to target a remote host. If you are interested in finding a DC within a particular site regardless of whether it is the closest DC to you, you can also optionally specify the /site option to find a domain controller that belongs to a particular site.

```
> nltest /dsgetdc:<DomainDNSName> [/site:<SiteName>] [/server:<ClientName>]
```

Using VBScript

```
' This code finds the closest domain controller in the domain
' that the computer running the script is in.
' ------ SCRIPT CONFIGURATION ------
strDomain = "<DomainDNSName>"   ' e.g. emea.rallencorp.com
' ------ END CONFIGURATION ---------

set objIadsTools = CreateObject("IADsTools.DCFunctions")
objIadsTools.DsGetDcName( Cstr(strDomain) )
Wscript.Echo "DC: " & objIadsTools.DCName
Wscript.Echo "DC Site: " & objIadsTools.DCSiteName
Wscript.Echo "Client Site: " & objIadsTools.ClientSiteName
```

Discussion

The DC locator process as described in MS KB 314861 and MS KB 247811 defines how clients find the closest domain controller. The process uses the site topology stored in Active Directory to calculate the site a particular client is in. After the client site has been identified, then it is a matter of finding a domain controller that is either a member of that same site or that is covering for that site.

The Microsoft DsGetDcName Directory Services API method implements the DC Locator process, but unfortunately cannot be used directly from a scripting language, such as VBScript. The IADsTools interface provides a wrapper around DsGetDcName, which is what we used. The nltest /dsgetdc command is also a wrapper around the DsGetDcName method, and is a handy tool when troubleshooting client issues related to finding an optimal domain controller.

Using a command-line interface

You can use *nltest* to return the closest domain controller that is serving a particular function. Some of the available functions include a global catalog server (/GC switch), time server (/TIMESERV switch), KDC (/KDC switch), and PDC (/PDC switch). Run nltest /? from a command line for the complete list.

Using VBScript

Similar to *nltest*, you can specify additional criteria for finding a domain controller by calling the `SetDsGetDcNameFlags` method before calling `DsGetDcName`. `SetDsGetDcNameFlags` accepts a comma-delimited string of the following flags:

```
DS_FORCE_REDISCOVERY
DS_DIRECTORY_SERVICE_REQUIRED
DS_DIRECTORY_SERVICE_PREFERRED
DS_GC_SERVER_REQUIRED
DS_PDC_REQUIRED
DS_IP_REQUIRED
DS_KDC_REQUIRED
DS_TIMESERV_REQUIRED
DS_WRITABLE_REQUIRED
DS_GOOD_TIMESERV_PREFERRED
DS_AVOID_SELF
DS_IS_FLAT_NAME
DS_IS_DNS_NAME
DS_RETURN_DNS_NAME
DS_RETURN_FLAT_NAME
```

See Also

For more information on the `IADsTools` interface see *IadsTools.doc* in the Support Tools, MS KB 247811 (How Domain Controllers Are Located in Windows), MS KB 314861 (How Domain Controllers Are Located in Windows XP), MSDN: DsGetDc-Name, and MSDN: MicrosoftDNS

3.12   Finding a Domain Controller's Site

Problem

You need to determine the site of which a domain controller is a member.

Solution

Using a graphical user interface

1. Open LDP and from the menu, select Connection → Connect.
2. For Server, enter the name of a domain controller (or leave blank to do a server-less bind).
3. For Port, enter 389.
4. Click OK.
5. From the menu select Connection → Bind.

---

6. Enter credentials of a domain user.

7. Click OK.

8. From the menu, select Browse → Search.

9. For BaseDN, type the distinguished name of the Sites container (for example, cn=sites,cn=configuration,dc=rallencorp, dc=com).

10. For Scope, select Subtree.

11. For Filter, enter:

    (&(objectcategory=server)(dnsHostName=<DomainControllerName>))

12. Click Run.

Using a command-line interface

To retrieve the site for a particular DC, use the following command syntax:

```
> nltest /dsgetsite /server:<DomainControllerName>
```

 The nltest /dsgetsite command is a wrapper around the DsGetSiteName method.

You can also use the AdFind utility as follows:

```
> adfind -config -rb cn=sites -f
"(&(objectcategory=server)(cn=<DomainConfrollerName>))" distinguishedName
```

For example, to find the site containing the server *dc1* in the *rallencorp.com* domain, you would see the following output:

```
> adfind -config -rb cn=sites -f "(&(objectcategory=server)(cn=dc1))"
distinguishedName
>
> AdFind V01.27.00cpp Joe Richards (joe@joeware.net) November 2005
>
> Using server: dc1.rallencorp.com:389
> Directory: Windows Server 2003
> Base DN: cn=sites,CN=Configuration,DC=rallencorp,DC=com
>
> dn:CN=dc1,CN=Servers,CN=Raleigh,CN=Sites,CN=Configuration,DC=rallencorp,DC=com
> distinguishedName: CN=dc1,CN=Servers,CN=Raleigh,CN=Sites,CN=Configuration,
DC=rallencorp,DC=com
>
> 1 Objects returned
```

 You can also specify the FQDN of the DC in question by using (&(objectcategory=server)(dnsHostName=dc1.rallencorp.com)).

Using VBScript

```
' This code prints the site the specified domain controller is in
' ------ SCRIPT CONFIGURATION ------
strDC = "<DomainControllerName>"  ' e.g. dc1.rallencorp.com
' ------ END CONFIGURATION ---------

set objRootDSE = GetObject("LDAP://" & strDC & "/RootDSE")
set objNTDS = GetObject("LDAP://" & objRootDSE.Get("dsServiceName"))
set objSite = GetObject(GetObject(GetObject(objNTDS.Parent).Parent).Parent)
WScript.Echo objSite.Get("cn")
```

Discussion

Domain controllers are represented in the site topology by a server object and a child nTDSDSA object. Actually, any type of server can conceivably have a server object; it is the nTDSDSA object that differentiates domain controllers from other types of servers. You'll often see the nTDSDSA object of a domain controller used to refer to that domain controller elsewhere in Active Directory. For example, the fSMORoleOwner attribute that represents the FSMO owners contains the distinguished name of the nTDSDSA object of the domain controller that is holding the role.

Using VBScript

Since we cannot use the DsGetSiteName method directly in VBScript, we need to take a more indirect approach. By querying the RootDSE of the target server, we can retrieve the dsServiceName attribute.

That attribute contains the DN of the nTDSDSA object for the domain controller, e.g., cn=NTDSSettings,cn=dc1,cn=MySite,cn=Sites,cn=Configuration,dc=rallencorp,dc=com. Then, by calling the Parent method three consecutive times, we can retrieve the object for cn=MySite,cn=Sites,cn=Configuration,dc=rallencorp,dc=com.

See Also

MSDN: DsGetSiteName

3.13   Moving a Domain Controller to a Different Site

Problem

You want to move a domain controller to a different site.

Solution

Using a graphical user interface

1. Open the Active Directory Sites and Services snap-in (*dssite.msc*).
2. In the left pane, expand the site that contains the domain controller.

3. Expand the Servers container.

4. Right-click on the domain controller you want to move and select Move.

5. In the Move Server box, select the site to which the domain controller will be moved and click OK.

Using a command-line interface

When using DSMove, you must specify the DN of the object you want to move. In this case, it needs to be the distinguished name of the server object for the domain controller. The value for the -newparent option is the distinguished name of the Servers container you want to move the domain controller to.

```
> dsmove "<ServerDN>" -newparent "<NewServersContainerDN>"
```

For example, the following command would move *dc2* from the Default-First-Site-Name site to the Raleigh site.

```
> dsmove "cn=dc2,cn=servers,cn=Default-First-Site-Name,cn=sites,cn=configuration,cn=
Rallencorp,dc=com" -newparent
"cn=servers,cn=Raleigh,cn=sites,cn=configuration,cn=rallencorp,dc=com"
```

You can also move an object using AdMod, as follows:

```
> admod -b cn=<ServerName>,cn=servers,cn=<OldSite>,cn=sites,cn=confi
guration,<ForestRootDN> -move cn=servers,cn=<NewSite>,cn=sites,cn=configurat
ion,<ForestRootDN>
```

Using VBScript

```
' This code moves a domain controller to a different site
' ------ SCRIPT CONFIGURATION ------
strDCName      = "<DomainControllerName>"  ' e.g. dc2
strCurrentSite = "<CurrentSiteName>"       ' e.g. Default-First-Site-Name
strNewSite     = "<NewSiteName>"           ' e.g. Raleigh
' ------ END CONFIGURATION ---------

strConfigDN = GetObject("LDAP://RootDSE").Get("configurationNamingContext")
strServerDN = "LDAP://cn=" & strDCName & ",cn=servers,cn=" & _
                  strCurrentSite & ",cn=sites," & strConfigDN
strNewParentDN = "LDAP://cn=servers,cn=" & strNewSite & ",cn=sites," & _
                  strConfigDN

set objCont = GetObject(strNewParentDN)
objCont.MoveHere strServerDN, "cn=" & strDCName
WScript.Echo "Successfully moved " & strDCName & " to " & strNewSite
```

Discussion

When you install a new domain controller, a server object and nTDSDSA object for the domain controller get added to the site topology. The Knowledge Consistency Checker (KCC) and Intersite Topology Generator (ISTG) use these objects to determine whom the domain controller should replicate with.

A domain controller is assigned to the site that has been mapped to the subnet it is located on. If there is no subnet object that has an address range that contains the domain controller's IP address, the server object is added to the Default-First-Site-Name site. If the domain controller should be in a different site, you'll then need to manually move it. It is a good practice to ensure that a subnet object that matches the domain controller's subnet is already in Active Directory before promoting the server into the forest. That way you do not need to worry about moving it after the fact.

 When moving a server object, remember that it has to be moved to a Servers container within a site, not directly under the site itself.

Using a command-line interface

In the solution provided, you need to know the current site of the domain controller you want to move. If you do not know the site it is currently in, you can use DSQuery to find it. In fact, you can use DSQuery in combination with DSMove in a single command line:

```
> for /F "usebackq" %i in (`dsquery server
  -name"<DomainControllerName>"`) do dsmove -newparent "cn=servers,
  cn=Default-First-Site,cn=sites, cn=configuration,<ForestDN>" %i
```

This command is long so we'll break it up into three parts to clarify it. The first part contains the for command extension that is built into the *cmd.exe* shell. When the /F "usebackq" syntax is specified, it is typically used to iterate over output from a command and perform certain functions on the output.

```
for /F "usebackq" %i in
```

The next part of the for loop contains the data to iterate over. In this case, we use DSQuery to return the distinguished name of the server object for *dc2*.

```
(`dsquery server -name "<DomainControllerName>"`)
```

The last part executes a command for each result returned from DSQuery. In this case, there should only be one result, so this command will only run once.

```
do dsmove -newparent "cn=servers,cn=Default-First-
Site,cn=sites,cn=configuration,<ForestDN>" %i
```

Using VBScript

Just as with the CLI solution, in the VBScript solution you need to specify which site the server is currently in. If you prefer, you can programmatically query for the current site, as shown in Recipe 3.12.

See Also

Recipe 3.12 for finding a domain controller's site and Recipe 4.20 for moving objects to different containers

3.14 Finding the Services a Domain Controller Is Advertising

Problem

You want to find the services that a domain controller is advertising.

Solution

The following command will display the list of services a domain controller is advertising:

```
> dcdiag /v /s:<DomainControllerName> /test:advertising
```

Running this command on a typical domain controller will produce the following output:

```
Starting test: Advertising
   The DC dc1 is advertising itself as a DC and having a DS.
   The DC dc1 is advertising as an LDAP server
   The DC dc1 is advertising as having a writeable directory
   The DC dc1 is advertising as a Key Distribution Center
   The DC dc1 is advertising as a time server
   The DS dc1 is advertising as a GC.
```

You can also use *nltest* to get similar information:

```
> nltest /server:<DomainControllerName> /dsgetdc:<DomainName>
```

Running this command on a domain controller in the *rallencorp.com* domain will produce the following output:

```
         DC: \\dc1.rallencorp.com
    Address: \\10.0.0.1
   Dom Guid: ac0e4884-cf79-4c9d-8cd9-817e3bfdab54
   Dom Name: rallencorp.com
Forest Name: rallencorp.com
Dc Site Name: Raleigh
Our Site Name: Raleigh
      Flags: PDC GC DS LDAP KDC TIMESERV GTIMESERV WRITABLE DNS_DC DNS_DOMAIN
DNS_FOREST CLOSE_SITE
```

In the previous example, GTIMESERV denotes a DC that is a master time server. WRITABLE denotes a DC that holds a writeable copy of the Active Directory database. Only NT 4.0 BDCs would not possess this flag.

Discussion

The dcdiag /test:advertising command is a wrapper around the DsGetDcName method. DsGetDcName returns a structure called DOMAIN_CONTROLLER_INFO that contains the list of services a domain controller provides. Table 3-3 contains the possible values returned from this call.

Table 3-3. DOMAIN_CONTROLLER_INFO flags

Value	Description
DS_DS_FLAG	Directory server for the domain
DS_GC_FLAG	Global catalog server for the forest
DS_KDC_FLAG	Kerberos Key Distribution Center for the domain
DS_PDC_FLAG	Primary domain controller of the domain
DS_TIMESERV_FLAG	Time server for the domain
DS_WRITABLE_FLAG	Hosts a writable directory service

See Also

MSDN: DsGetDcName and MSDN: DOMAIN_CONTROLLER_INFO

3.15   Restoring a Deleted Domain Controller

Problem

You want to restore the computer account of a domain controller that has been accidentally deleted.

Using a graphical user interface

1. Reboot a domain controller that is currently functioning correctly into Directory Services Restore Mode.

2. Perform a System State restore.

3. Before rebooting the server, perform the steps listed in the following section.

Using a command-line interface

To restore the computer account, use the following sequence of commands:

```
> ntdsutil
> authoritative restore
> restore subtree <ComputerDN>
> quit
> exit
```

Restart the domain controller after running these commands.

Discussion

When you restore a deleted object within Active Directory, you have the option of performing an *authoritative* or a *nonauthoritative* restore. In both cases, any changes that have been made to the AD database subsequent to the time that the backup was taken will be replicated back to the restored DC. With an authoritative restore, the version number of the object(s) being restored is incremented so that the restored objects will "win" in the case of any replication collisions. In a case where you want to restore an object that has been inadvertently deleted, you need to perform an authoritative restore to prevent the deletion from re-propagating to the restored domain controller. You can mark an entire restore as authoritative, or any subtree of your AD environment down to a single object. (In this case, the computer object for the DC that was deleted.)

See Also

Chapter 17 for more on recovering and restoring Active Directory and MS KB 216993 (Useful Shelf Life of a System-State Backup of Active Directory)

3.16 Resetting the TCP/IP Stack on a Domain Controller

Problem

You want to uninstall and re-install the TCP/IP protocol on a domain controller as part of a disaster recovery or troubleshooting operation.

Solution

Using a command-line interface

```
> netsh ip reset <Log_File_Name>
```

Discussion

Beginning in Windows 2000, the TCP/IP protocol has been installed as the default network protocol for Windows server and client products. In Windows 2000 in particular, uninstalling TCP/IP was a fairly laborious process involving numerous registry changes. This was greatly improved in Windows Server 2003 with the addition of the reset commands within *netsh*. Resetting the TCP/IP stack using *netsh* will remove all configuration information, including the default gateway and any configured DNS and WINS servers. This procedure might be necessary during a disaster recovery situation where you're restoring System State data to a server with a dissimilar hardware configuration, for example, as the restore process might corrupt the TCP/IP stack on the destination computer.

Using a command-line interface

In addition to resetting the TCP/IP stack, you can also reset Winsock using the following command:

```
> netsh winsock reset
```

Use this command with care, though, as resetting Winsock can cause network applications such as antivirus scanners to malfunction and require re-installation.

See Also

MS KB 317518 (How to Reset "Internet Protocol" (TCP/IP) in Windows Server 2003), MS KB 325356 (How to Remove and Reinstall TCP/IP on a Windows Server 2003 Domain Controller, and MS KB 299451 (How to Remove and Reinstall TCP/IP on a Windows 2000 Domain Controller)

3.17 Configuring a Domain Controller to Use an External Time Source

Problem

You want to set the reliable time source for a domain controller.

Solution

Using a command-line interface

Run the following commands from the command line on the domain controller that is serving as the PDC Emulator in your forest root domain:

```
> w32tm /config /syncfromflags:manual /manualpeerlist:<PeerList>
> w32tm /config /update
```

To then configure time synchronization for the other DCs in your environment, run the following command:

```
> w32tm /resync
```

Using the Registry

To configure your Windows Server 2003 PDC Emulator to sync to an external time provider, set the following Registry keys:

```
[HKLM\System\CurrentControlSet\Services\W32Time\Parameters\]
Type: REG_SZ - "NTP"

[HKLM\System\CurrentControlSet\Services\W32Time\Config\]
AnnounceFlags: REG_DWORD - 5

[HKLM\System\CurrentControlSet\Services\W32Time\TimeProviders\]
NTPServer: REG_DWORD - 1

[HKEY_LOCAL_MACHINE\SYSTEM\CurrentControlSet\Services\W32Time\Parameters\]
NTPServer: REG_SZ - <Peer1>,0x1,<Peer2>,0x1,<Peer3>,0x1
```

 <Peers> in this case refers to a comma-separated list of FQDNs of external time servers. Each DNS name must be followed by ",0x1" for the rest of these settings to take effect.

```
[HKEY_LOCAL_MACHINE\SYSTEM\CurrentControlSet\Services\W32Time\TimeProviders\
NtpClient\]
SpecialPollInterval: REG_DWORD - <TimeBetweenPollsInSeconds>

[HKEY_LOCAL_MACHINE\SYSTEM\CurrentControlSet\Services\W32Time\Config\]
MaxPosPhaseCorrection: REG_DWORD - <MaximumForwardOffsetInSeconds>

[HKEY_LOCAL_MACHINE\SYSTEM\CurrentControlSet\Services\W32Time\Config\]
MaxNegPhaseCorrection: REG_DWORD - <MaximumBackwardOffsetInSeconds>
```

Once you have made these changes to the Registry, stop and restart the W32time service by issuing the following commands:

```
> net stop w32time
> net start w32time
```

Using VBScript

```
' This codes configures a reliable time source on a domain controller
' ------ SCRIPT CONFIGURATION ------
strPDC = "<DomainControllerName>"        ' e.g. dc01.rallencorp.com
strTimeServer = "<TimeServerNameOrIP>"   ' e.g. ntp01.rallencorp.com
' ------ END CONFIGURATION ---------

strTimeServerReg = "SYSTEM\CurrentControlSet\Services\W32Time\Parameters"
const HKLM = &H80000002
set objReg = GetObject("winmgmts:\\" & strPDC & "\root\default:StdRegProv")
```

```
objReg.GetStringValue HKLM, strTimeServerReg, "ntpserver", strCurrentServer
WScript.Echo "Current Value: " & strCurrentServer
objReg.SetStringValue HKLM, strTimeServerReg, "ntpserver", strTimeServer
objReg.SetStringValue HKLM, strTimeServerReg, "type", "NTP"
strCurrentServer = ""
objReg.GetStringValue HKLM, strTimeServerReg, "ntpserver", strCurrentServer
WScript.Echo "New Value: " & strCurrentServer

' Restart Time Service
set objService = GetObject("winmgmts://" & strPDC & _
                           "/root/cimv2:Win32_Service='W32Time'")
WScript.Echo "Stopping " & objService.Name
objService.StopService( )

Wscript.Sleep 2000  ' Sleep for 2 seconds to give service time to stop

WScript.Echo "Starting " & objService.Name
objService.StartService( )
```

Discussion

You need to set a reliable time source on the PDC Emulator FSMO for only the forest root domain. All other domain controllers sync their time either from that server or from a PDC (or designated time server) within their own domain. The list of external time servers is stored in the registry under the W32Time Service registry key: HKLM\SYSTEM\CurrentControlSet\Services\W32Time\Parameters\ntpserver.

If you want a domain controller such as the PDC to use an external time source, you have to set the ntpserver registry value along with the type value. The default value for type on a domain controller is Nt5DS, which means that the domain controller will use the Active Directory domain hierarchy to find a time source. You can override this behavior and have a domain controller contact a non-DC time source by setting type to NTP. In the CLI example, the /setsntp switch automatically sets the type value to NTP. In the VBScript solution, we had to set it in the code.

After setting the time server, the W32Time service should be restarted for the change to take effect. You can check that the server was set properly by running the following command:

```
> net time /querysntp
```

Since the PDC Emulator is the time source for the other domain controllers, you should also make sure that it is advertising the time service, which you can do with the following command:

```
> nltest /server:<DomainControllerName> /dsgetdc:<DomainDNSName> /TIMESERV
```

 To configure the PDC Emulator to use its own internal clock as a time source instead of relying on an external clock, modify the HKLM\SYSTEM\CurrentControlSet\Services\W32Time\Config\AnnounceFlags DWORD value to contain a value of A.

See Also

MS KB 216734 (How to Configure an Authoritative Time Server in Windows 2000), MS KB 223184 (Registry Entries for the W32Time Service), MS KB 224799 (Basic Operation of the Windows Time Service), MS KB 816042 (How to Configure An Authoritative Time Server In Windows Server 2003), and MSDN: StdRegProv, and MSDN: Win32_Service

3.18 Finding the Number of Logon Attempts Made Against a Domain Controller

Problem

You want to find the number of logon requests a domain controller has processed.

Solution

The following query returns the number of logon requests processed:

```
> nltest /server:<DomainControllerName> /LOGON_QUERY
```

This will produce output similar to the following:

```
Number of attempted logons: 1054
```

Discussion

The nltest /LOGON_QUERY command is a wrapper around the I_NetLogonControl2 method, and can be useful to determine how many logon requests are being processed by a server. Viewing the results of the command over a period of time and comparing them against another DC in the same domain can also tell you if one domain controller is being used significantly more or less than the others.

See Also

MSDN: I_NetLogonControl2

3.19 Enabling the /3GB Switch to Increase the LSASS Cache

Problem

You have installed more than 1 GB of memory on your domain controllers and want to enable the /3GB switch so that the LSASS process can use more memory.

Solution

Using a command-line interface

```
> bootcfg /raw /"3GB" /ID <BootID>
```

 If you do not know the Boot ID of the partition you wish to modify, simply run bootcfg from a command prompt without any switches.

Alternately, you can edit the *boot.ini* file on the domain controller to contain the /3GB switch:

```
[boot loader]
timeout=30
default=multi(0)disk(0)rdisk(0)partition(2)\WINDOWS
[operating systems]
multi(0)disk(0)rdisk(0)partition(2)\WINDOWS="Windows Server 2003" /3GB
```

Restart the computer.

 On Windows Server 2003, you can edit the *boot.ini* file by opening the System applet in the Control Panel. Click the Startup and Recovery tab and click the Edit button, or else use the built-in msconfig utility.

On Windows 2000, the process involves a few more steps. You need to open an Explorer window, select Tools → Folder Options, and click the View tab. Uncheck "Hide protected operating system files (Recommended)," and check "Show hidden files and folders." Now browse to the root of your operating system partition (e.g., *C:*) and edit the *boot.ini* file with a text editor.

Discussion

When computers are referred to as 32- or 64-bit computers it means they support memory addresses that are 32 or 64 bits long. This is the total available memory (virtual and real) that can be processed by the system. Since the days of Windows NT, Microsoft has split memory allocation in half by giving applications up to 2 GB and the Windows kernel 2 GB of memory to use (32 bits of address space = 2^{32} = 4 GB). In many cases, administrators would rather allocate more memory to applications than to the kernel. For this reason, Microsoft developed the /3GB switch to allow applications to use up to 3 GB of memory, leaving the kernel with 1 GB.

The /3GB switch is supported on Windows 2000 Advanced Server, Windows 2000 Datacenter Server, and Windows Server 2003 Standard, Enterprise, and Data Center Edition; it should be used only if the computer has more than 1 GB of physical memory. As a rule, in Windows 2000 you should enable this switch if you have more than 512 MB of RAM installed, and more than 1.5 GB in Windows Server 2003. However, if you have more than 16 GB of RAM in a Windows Server 2003 computer, the extra RAM will not be utilized unless you manually remove the /3GB switch from the *boot.ini* file. For a good description of how LSASS uses memory, see MS KB 308356.

See Also

MS KB 99743 (Purpose of the BOOT.INI File in Windows 2000 or Windows NT), MS KB 291988 (A Description of the 4 GB RAM Tuning Feature and the Physical Address Extension Switch), and MS KB 308356 (Memory Usage By the Lsass.exe Process on Windows 2000-Based Domain Controllers)

3.20 Enabling the /PAE switch to Increase the Amount of Addressable RAM

You want to use the /PAE switch in the *boot.ini* file to enable Windows to address large amounts of physical RAM.

Solution

Using a command-line interface

```
> bootcfg /raw /"PAE" /ID <BootID>
```

Alternately, you can edit the *boot.ini* file on the domain controller to contain the /PAE switch:

```
[boot loader]
timeout=30
default=multi(0)disk(0)rdisk(0)partition(2)\WINDOWS
[operating systems]
multi(0)disk(0)rdisk(0)partition(2)\WINDOWS="Windows Server 2003" /PAE
```

Restart the computer.

> On Windows Server 2003, you can edit the *boot.ini* file by opening the System applet in the Control Panel. Click the Startup and Recovery tab and click the Edit button.
>
> On Windows 2000, the process involves a few more steps. You need to open an Explorer window, select Tools → Folder Options, and click the View tab. Uncheck "Hide protected operating system files (Recommended)" and check "Show hidden files and folders." Now browse to the root of your operating system partition (e.g., C:\) and edit the *boot.ini* file with a text editor.

Discussion

Because of the limitations of 32-bit addressing, the maximum amount of memory that a Windows 2000 or Windows Server 2003 computer can address, by default, is

4 GB. However, Windows 2000 Advanced Server and Windows Server 2003 Enterprise Edition can support larger amounts of RAM (8 GB and 32 GB, respectively) by enabling the /PAE switch in the *boot.ini* file. The /PAE switch is only available on 32-bit hardware; it should not be configured on 64-bit computers.

See Also

Memory Support and Windows Operating Systems: *http://www.microsoft.com/whdc/ system/platform/server/PAE/PAEmem.mspx*

3.21   Cleaning Up Distributed Link Tracking Objects

Problem

You want to make sure the Distributed Link Tracking (DLT) service is disabled and all DLT objects are removed from Active Directory. The Distributed Link Tracking Server service is used to track links to files on NTFS partitions. If a file that has a shortcut to it is renamed or moved, Windows uses the DLT service to find the file when the shortcut is opened. Most organizations are unaware this service even exists, yet it can populate thousands of objects in Active Directory. Unless you are actively using the functionality of the DLT service, it is recommended that you disable it.

Solution

If you upgrade a Windows 2000 domain controller to Windows Server 2003, the DLT Server service is stopped and set to disabled. A new install of Windows Server 2003 also has the service stopped and set to disabled. But the DLT Server service on Windows 2000 domain controllers is enabled by default. Unless you need it, you should stop the service and disable it on all of your domain controllers.

Next, remove any DLT objects (linkTrackVolEntry and linkTrackOMTEntry) from Active Directory. Since there can be hundreds of thousands of DLT objects, you will probably want to stagger the deletion of those objects. (This is not so much because of the delete operation itself, but because the scavenging process that occurs afterwards can be quite memory-intensive.) The script in MS KB 315229 (*dltpurge.vbs*) can delete DLT objects over a period of time instead of all at once. Here is an example of running the *dltpurge.vbs* script against the *dc1* domain controller in the *rallencorp.com* domain:

```
> cscript dltpurge.vbs -s dc1 -d dc=rallencorp,dc=com
```

Once you've run the DLT Purge process and the AD tombstone and garbage collection process has completed, it's also recommended that you perform an offline defragmentation of the Active Directory database if you are low on disk space and need to reduce the size of the AD database file (*NTDS.DIT*).

Discussion

DLT consists of a client and server service. The server service runs on domain controllers and the client service can run on any Windows 2000 or later machine. The server service stores data in Active Directory in the form of linkTrackVolEntry and linkTrackOMTEntry objects, which are used to track the names and locations of files on NTFS partitions. The cn=ObjectMoveTable,cn=FileLinks,cn=System,<DomainDN> container stores linkTrackOMTEntry objects containing information about files moved on computers in the domain.

While the cn=VolumeTable,cn=FileLinks,cn=System,<DomainDN> container stores linkTrackVolEntry objects that represent NTFS volumes on computers in the domain.

Over time, the number of DLT objects can grow substantially. Even though those objects do not take up much space (in fact, they will take up more space while waiting to be scavenged post-deletion than they will as active objects within the directory), if you are not actively taking advantage of this service, you should consider disabling it and removing all DLT objects from Active Directory.

See Also

Recipe 17.14 for more on performing an offline defragmentation of the AD database, MS KB 232122 (Performing Offline Defragmentation of the Active Directory Database), MS KB 312403 (Distributed Link Tracking on Windows-Based Domain Controllers), and MS KB 315229 (Text Version of Dltpurge.vbs for Microsoft Knowledge Base Article Q312403)

3.22 Enabling and Disabling the Global Catalog

Problem

You want to enable or disable the global catalog on a particular server.

Solution

Using a graphical user interface

1. Open the Active Directory Sites and Services snap-in (*dssite.msc*).
2. Browse to the nTDSDSA object (NTDS Settings) underneath the server object for the domain controller you want to enable or disable the global catalog for.
3. Right-click on NTDS Settings and select Properties.
4. Under the General tab, check (to enable) or uncheck (to disable) the box beside Global Catalog.
5. Click OK.

Using a command-line interface

In the following command, *<ServerObjectDN>* should be the server object DN, not the DN of the nTDSDSA object.

```
> dsmod server "<ServerObjectDN>" -isgc yes|no
```

For example, the following command will enable the global catalog on *dc1* in the Raleigh site:

```
> dsmod server
"cn=DC1,cn=servers,cn=Raleigh,cn=sites,cn=configuration,dc=rallencorp,dc=com" -isgc
Yes
```

You can also use AdMod with the following syntax and output:

```
> admod -b cn="NTDS Settings,cn=dc1,cn=Servers,cn=Raleigh,cn=Sites,cn=Configur
ation,dc=rallencorp,dc=com" "options::0"

> AdMod V01.06.00cpp Joe Richards (joe@joeware.net) June 2005

> DN Count: 1
> Using server: dc1.rallencorp.com
> Modifying specified objects...
>    DN: cn=NTDS Settings,cn=dc1,cn=Servers,cn=Raleigh,cn=Sites,cn=Configuration,d
c=rallencorp,dc=com...

> The command completed successfully
```

 Because options is a bitwise attribute, AdMod will summarily overwrite the value stored in the attribute, which may have unintended effects. See Chapter 4 for information on safely modifying bitwise operators.

Using VBScript

```
' This code enables or disables the GC for the specified DC
' ------ SCRIPT CONFIGURATION ------
strDC = "<DomainControllerName>"   ' e.g. dc01.rallencorp.com
strGCEnable = 1                    ' 1 = enable, 0 = disable
' ------ END CONFIGURATION ---------

set objRootDSE = GetObject("LDAP://" & strDC & "/RootDSE")
objNTDS = GetObject("LDAP://" & strDC & "/" & _
                    objRootDSE.Get("dSServiceName"))
objNTDS.Put "options", strGCEnable
objNTDS.SetInfo
```

Discussion

The first domain controller promoted into a forest is also made a global catalog (GC) server by default. If you want additional servers to have the global catalog, you have to enable it manually. In a single-domain environment, the global catalog server incurs no memory or bandwidth overhead beyond that of a domain controller, so you could conceivably configure each DC in a single-domain forest as a GC without any ill effects. In a multidomain environment, however, each global catalog server will require additional disk space to store a partial replica of other domains in the forest, and will require additional network bandwidth to replicate with other GCs. For more details on DC and GC placement planning, see *Active Directory*, Third Edition, by Joe Richards et al. (O'Reilly).

The global catalog on a domain controller becomes enabled when the low-order bit on the options attribute on the nTDSDSA object under the server object for the domain controller is set to 1, or disabled when it is set to 0. The DN of this object for *dc1* in the Default-First-Site-Name site looks like this:

```
cn=NTDSSettings,cn=DC1,cn=Default-First-Site-
Name,cn=Sites,cn=Configuration,dc=rallencorp,dc=com
```

After enabling the global catalog, it can take some time before the domain controller can start serving as a global catalog server. The length of time is based on the amount of data that needs to replicate and the type of connectivity between the domain controller's replication partners. This is also dependent on the Global Catalog Partition Occupancy setting, which is set in the HKLM\System\CurrentControlSet\Services\NTDS\Parameters key on the GC itself, which specifies how many directory partitions must be fully replicated to the GC before it is considered ready; this can range from no occupancy requirement whatsoever, to requiring that all partitions be fully synchronized before the GC can begin servicing requests. After replication is complete, you should see Event 1119 in the Directory Services log stating the server is advertising itself as a global catalog. At that point you should also be able to perform LDAP queries against port 3268 on that server. See Recipe 3.23 for more information on how to determine if global catalog promotion is complete.

See Also

Recipe 3.23 for determining if global catalog promotion is complete and MS KB 313994 (How to Create or Move a Global Catalog in Windows 2000)

3.23 Determining Whether Global Catalog Promotion Is Complete

Problem

You want to determine whether a domain controller is a global catalog server. After you initially enable the global catalog on a domain controller, it can take some time for all of the read-only naming contexts to replicate to it, depending on the number of domains, the volume of directory data, and the underlying network topology.

Solution

Query the isGlobalCatalogReady attribute on the RootDSE for the domain controller. A TRUE value means the server is a global catalog and a FALSE value indicates it is not.

For more information on how to query the RootDSE, see Recipe 4.1.

You can also check the Directory Services Event Log in the Event Viewer MMC for the presence of Event ID 1119, whose text reads as follows:

```
"This Windows Domain Controller is now a Global Catalog Server"
```

Using the Registry

To confirm that GC promotion has completed, check the value of the following Registry key:

```
> HKLM\System\CurrentControlSet\Services\NTDS\Parameters\
> Global Catalog Promotion Complete: REG_DWORD - "1" if complete, "0" if not.
```

Using a command-line interface

To confirm that a domain controller in the *rallencorp.com* domain is functioning as a global catalog server, use *nltest* with the following syntax:

```
> nltest /dsgetdc:rallencorp.com
```

If the DC in question is functioning as a GC, you'll see output similar to the following:

```
> C:\>nltest /dsgetdc:rallencorp.com
>           DC: \\dc1.rallencorp.com
>      Address: \\10.0.0.1
>     Dom Guid: ac0e4884-cf79-4c9d-8cd9-817e3bfdab54
>     Dom Name: rallencorp.com
>  Forest Name: rallencorp.com
> Dc Site Name: Raleigh
> Our Site Name: Raleigh
>        Flags: PDC GC DS LDAP KDC TIMESERV GTIMESERV WRITABLE DNS_DC DNS_DOMAIN
> DNS
>_FOREST CLOSE_SITE
> The command completed successfully
```

Discussion

Once a server has completed initial replication of the global catalog, the isGlobalCatalogReady attribute in the RootDSE will be marked TRUE. Another way to determine if a domain controller has been at least flagged to become a global catalog is by checking if the options attribute on the nTDSDSA object for the server has been set to 1. (Note that this does not necessarily mean the server is accepting requests as a global catalog.) An additional query to the RootDSE as described in the Solution, or directly to port 3268 (the global catalog port) could also confirm that the appropriate flag has been set.

See Also

Recipe 4.1 for viewing the RootDSE

3.24 Finding the Global Catalog Servers in a Forest

Problem

You want a list of the global catalog servers in a forest.

Solution

Using a graphical user interface

1. Open LDP and from the menu select Connection → Connect.
2. For Server, enter the name of a DC.
3. For Port, enter 389.
4. Click OK.
5. From the menu select Connection → Bind.
6. Enter the credentials of a domain user.
7. Click OK.
8. From the menu select Browse → Search.
9. For BaseDN, type the DN of the Sites container, for example, cn=sites,cn=configuration,dc=rallencorp,dc=com.
10. For Scope, select Subtree.
11. For Filter, enter (&(objectcategory=ntdsdsa)(options=1)).
12. Click Run.

Using a command-line interface

To enumerate all GCs in a forest using DSQuery, use the following syntax:

```
> dsquery server -forest –isgc
```

You can also use AdFind as follows:

```
> adfind -config -rb cn=sites -f "(&(objectcategory=ntdsdsa)
(options:AND:=1))" -bit distinguishedName
```

Using VBScript

```
' This code prints the global catalog servers for the specified forest.
```

```
' ------ SCRIPT CONFIGURATION ------
strForestName = "<ForestDNSName>"  ' e.g. rallencorp.com
' ------ END CONFIGURATION ---------

set objRootDSE = GetObject("LDAP://" & strForestName & "/" & "RootDSE")
strADsPath = "<LDAP://" & objRootDSE.Get("configurationNamingContext") & ">;"
strFilter  = "(&(objectcategory=ntdsdsa)(options=1));"
strAttrs   = "distinguishedname;"
strScope   = "SubTree"

set objConn = CreateObject("ADODB.Connection")
objConn.Provider = "ADsDSOObject"
objConn.Open "Active Directory Provider"
set objRS = objConn.Execute(strADsPath & strFilter & strAttrs & strScope)
objRS.MoveFirst
while not objRS.EOF
    set objNTDS = GetObject("LDAP://" & objRS.Fields(0).Value)
    set objServer = GetObject( objNTDS.Parent )
    Wscript.Echo objServer.Get("dNSHostName")
    objRS.MoveNext
wend
```

Discussion

To find the global catalog servers in a forest, you need to query for NTDS Settings
objects that have the low-order bit of the options attribute equal to 1 under the sites
container in the Configuration Naming Context. That attribute determines if a
domain controller should be a global catalog server, but it does not necessarily mean
it is a global catalog server yet. See Recipe 3.23 for more information on how to tell if
a server marked as a global catalog is ready to accept requests as one.

Another option for locating global catalogs is DNS, which is described in Recipe 3.26.

See Also

Recipe 3.23 for determining if global catalog promotion is complete and Recipe 3.26
to locate global catalogs using DNS

3.25 Finding the Domain Controllers or Global Catalog Servers in a Site

Problem

You want a list of the domain controllers or global catalog servers in a specific site.

Solution

Using a graphical user interface

1. Open the Active Directory Sites and Services snap-in (*dssite.msc*).
2. In the right pane, expand the site that contains the domain controller.
3. For the list of domain controllers, expand the Servers container.
4. To find the global catalog servers, expand each domain controller, right-click on NTDS Settings, and select Properties.
5. Global catalog servers will have the appropriate box checked beside Global Catalog.

Using a command-line interface

The following query finds all domain controllers in the specified site:

```
> adfind -config -rb cn=<SiteName>,cn=Sites -f (objectcategory=ntdsdsa)
```

To find only the global catalog servers in a site, use the same command with the -bit filter enabled to perform a bitwise search for a 1 in the options attribute:

```
adfind -config -rb cn=<SiteName>,cn=Sites -f
"(&(objectcategory=ntdsdsa)(options:AND:=1))" -bit
```

Using VBScript

```
' This code prints the domain controllers in a site and then
' prints the global catalog servers in the site
' ------ SCRIPT CONFIGURATION ------
strSite   = "<SiteName>"        ' e.g. Default-First-Site-Name
strForest = "<ForestDNSName>"   ' e.g. rallencorp.com
' ------ END CONFIGURATION ---------

set objRootDSE = GetObject("LDAP://" & strForest & "/RootDSE")
strADsPath = "<LDAP://cn=servers,cn=" & strSite & ",cn=sites," & _
             objRootDSE.Get("configurationNamingContext") & ">;"
strFilter  = "(objectcategory=ntdsdsa);"
strAttrs   = "distinguishedName;"
strScope   = "SubTree"

WScript.Echo "Domain controllers in " & strSite & ":"
set objConn = CreateObject("ADODB.Connection")
objConn.Provider = "ADsDSOObject"
objConn.Open "Active Directory Provider"
set objRS = objConn.Execute(strADsPath & strFilter & strAttrs & strScope)
objRS.MoveFirst
while not objRS.EOF
    Set objNTDS = GetObject("LDAP://" & objRS.Fields(0).Value)
    Set objServer = GetObject( objNTDS.Parent )
    Wscript.Echo " " & objServer.Get("dNSHostName")
```

```
    objRS.MoveNext
wend

' Global Catalog filter
strFilter  = "(&(objectcategory=ntdsdsa)(options=1));"
WScript.Echo ""
WScript.Echo "Global Catalogs in " & strSite & ":"
set objRS = objConn.Execute(strADsPath & strFilter & strAttrs & strScope)
objRS.MoveFirst
while not objRS.EOF
    set objNTDS = GetObject("LDAP://" & objRS.Fields(0).Value)
    set objServer = GetObject( objNTDS.Parent )
    Wscript.Echo "  " & objServer.Get("dNSHostName")
    objRS.MoveNext
wend
```

Discussion

Each domain controller has a server object within the Servers container for the site it is a member of (e.g., cn=DC1,cn=Servers,cn=MySite,cn=site,cn=configuration, dc=rallencorp,dc=com). Since other types of servers can have server objects in a site's Servers container, domain controllers are differentiated by the nTDSDSA object that is a child of the server object (e.g., cn=NTDSSettings,cn=DC1,cn=Servers, cn=MySite, cn=site, cn=confiugration, dc=rallencorp, dc=com). Querying for this nTDSDSA object will return a list of domain controllers in the site. Locating global catalog servers consists of the same query, except where the low-order bit of the options attribute of the nTDSDSA object is equal to 1. Note that this may not be available if replication has not completed after enabling the GC.

3.26 Finding Domain Controllers and Global Catalogs via DNS

Problem

You want to find domain controllers or global catalogs using DNS lookups.

Solution

Domain controllers and global catalog servers are represented in DNS as SRV records. You can query SRV records using *nslookup* by setting the type=SRV, such as the following:

```
> nslookup
Default Server: dns01.rallencorp.com
Address:  10.1.2.3

> set type=SRV
```

You then need to issue the following query to retrieve all domain controllers for the specified domain.

> _ldap._tcp.<DomainDNSName>

You can issue a similar query to retrieve global catalogs, but since they are forest-wide, the query is based on the forest name.

> _gc._tcp.<ForestDNSName>

 An alternate query to find Global Catalogs via *nslookup* would be to query for _gc._msdcs.<ForestDNSName>.

You can even find the domain controllers or global catalogs that are in a particular site or that *cover* a particular site by querying the following:

> _ldap._tcp.<SiteName>._sites.<DomainDNSName>
> _gc._tcp.<SiteName>._sites.<ForestDNSName>

See Recipe 12.20 for more information on site coverage.

Discussion

One of the benefits of Active Directory over its predecessor Windows NT is that it relies on DNS for name resolution, which is the standard for name resolution on the Internet and on most TCP/IP-based networks. Active Directory uses DNS to locate servers that serve a particular function, such as a domain controller for a domain, global catalog server, PDC Emulator, or KDC. It also uses the site topology information stored in Active Directory to populate site-specific records for domain controllers.

The DC locator process relies on this information in DNS to direct clients to the most optimal server when logging in. Reliance on DNS makes it easy to troubleshoot problems related to clients finding domain controllers. If you know the site a client is in, you can make a few DNS queries to determine which domain controller they should be using to authenticate.

The resource records that a domain controller registers in DNS can be restricted, if you have a lag site configured, for example, so querying DNS may return only a subset of the actual domain controllers that are available. See Recipes 13.14 and 13.15 for more information.

See Also

Recipe 13.14, Recipe 13.15, and Recipe 3.33 for finding the PDC Emulator via DNS, MS KB 267855 (Problems with Many Domain Controllers with Active Directory Integrated DNS Zones), and RFC 2782, A DNS RR for Specifying the Location of Services (DNS SRV)

3.27   Changing the Preference for a Domain Controller

Problem

You want a particular domain controller to be used less frequently for client requests or not at all. This may be necessary if a particular domain controller is overloaded, perhaps due to numerous application requests.

Solution

You can modify the Priority or Weight fields in SRV resource records by modifying the registry on the domain controller. Open *regedit* or *regedt32* on the domain controller and browse to the following key: HKLM\SYSTEM\CurrentControlSet\Services\Netlogon\Parameters. To configure the Priority, add a REG_DWORD with the name LdapSrvPriority. To configure the weight, add a REG_DWORD with the name LdapSrvWeight.

After you make the change, the *%SystemRoot%\System32\Config\netlogon.dns* file should be updated and the DDNS updates sent to the DNS server within an hour. You can also restart the NetLogon service to expedite the process.

Discussion

Each domain controller registers several SRV records that clients use as part of the DC locator process to find the closest domain controller. Two fields of the SRV record let clients determine which server to use when multiple possibilities are returned. The Priority field is used to dictate if a specific server or set of servers should always be contacted over others unless otherwise unavailable. A server with a higher priority (i.e., lower priority field value) will always be contacted before a server with a lower priority. For example, if DC1 has a SRV priority of 5 and DC2 has a SRV priority of 10, DC1 will always be used unless it is unavailable.

The Weight field, on the other hand, determines the percentage of time clients should use a particular server. You can easily calculate the percentage by dividing the weight by the sum of all Weights for servers with the same Priority. If servers DC1, DC2, and DC3 have Weights of 1, 2, and 3, respectively, then DC1 will be contacted one out of six times or (1 / (3 + 2 + 1)), DC2 will be contacted two out of every six times or 1/3 (2 / (3 + 2 + 1)), and DC3 will be contacted three out of every six times or 1/2 (3 / (3 + 2 + 1)). Here is an example of how the SRV records look with these weights:

```
C:\> nslookup -type=SRV _ldap._tcp.dc._msdcs.rallencorp.com
Server:  dns01.rallencorp.com
Address:  171.70.168.183

_ldap._tcp.dc._msdcs.rallencorp.com  SRV service location:
        priority     = 0
        weight       = 1
```

```
        port         = 389
        svr hostname = dc1.rallencorp.com
_ldap._tcp.dc._msdcs.rallencorp.com  SRV service location:
        priority     = 0
        weight       = 2
        port         = 389
        svr hostname = dc2.rallencorp.com
_ldap._tcp.dc._msdcs.rallencorp.com  SRV service location:
        priority     = 0
        weight       = 3
        port         = 389
        svr hostname = dc3.rallencorp.com
```

In certain situations, having this capability can come in handy. For example, the server acting as the PDC FSMO role owner typically receives more traffic from clients simply because of the nature of tasks that the PDC FSMO has to handle. If you find a certain server like the PDC FSMO has considerably higher load than the rest of the servers, you could change the priority or weight of the SRV records so that it is used less often during the DC locator process. You can increase the Priority to eliminate its use unless all other domain controllers fail, or modify the Weight to reduce how often it will be used.

You can modify this information manually within the DNS Management Console, or for multiple DCs using Group Policy Objects in the `Computer Configuration\ Administrative Templates\System\Net Logon\DC Locator DNS Records` GPO node.

See Also

MS KB 232025 (Description of the DNS SRV Resource Record Type)

3.28 Disabling the Global Catalog Requirement During a Windows 2000 or Windows Server 2003 Domain Login

Problem

You want to disable the requirement for a global catalog server to be reachable when a user logs into a Windows 2000 domain.

Solution

Using a graphical user interface

1. Open the Registry Editor (*regedit*).

2. In the left pane, expand HKEY_LOCAL_MACHINE → System → Current-ControlSet → Control.

3. Right-click on LSA and select New → Key.

4. Enter IgnoreGCFailures for the key name and hit Enter.

5. Restart the server.

Using a command-line interface

```
> reg add HKLM\SYSTEM\CurrentControlSet\Control\LSA\IgnoreGCFailures /ve
> shutdown /r
```

Using VBScript

```
' This code enables the IgnoreGCFailres registry setting and reboots
strLSA = "HKLM\SYSTEM\CurrentControlSet\Control\LSA\IgnoreGCFailures\"
Set objWSHShell = WScript.CreateObject("WScript.Shell")
objWSHShell.RegWrite strLSA, ""
WScript.Echo "Successfully created key"
WScript.Echo "Rebooting server . . . "
objWSHShell.Run "rundll32 shell32.dll,SHExitWindowsEx 2"
```

Discussion

With Windows 2000, a global catalog server must be contacted for every login attempt; otherwise, the login will fail (unless there is no network connectivity, which would result in a user being logged on with cached credentials). This is necessary to process all universal groups a user may be a member of. When a client attempts to authenticate with a domain controller, that domain controller contacts a global catalog server behind the scenes to enumerate the user's universal groups. (See Recipe 7.13 for more details.) If you have domain controllers in remote sites and they are not enabled as global catalog servers, you may run into a situation where users cannot log in if the network connection to the network with the closest global catalog server fails.

The only option you have available with Windows 2000 is to have the domain controllers ignore GC lookup failures ("Enabling Universal Group Caching in Windows Server 2003" provides a different solution for Windows Server 2003).

You can do this by adding an IgnoreGCFailures registry key under HKLM\SYSTEM\CurrentControlSet\Control\LSA on the domain controller(s) you want this to apply to. If you use universal groups in any capacity, having the domain controllers ignore GC failures can be very problematic because a user's token may not get updated with his universal group memberships. It may be useful, though, if you have branch office sites where you cannot deploy global catalog servers.

See Also

Recipe 3.29 for disabling the global catalog requirement for Windows Server 2003, Recipe 7.13 for enabling universal group caching, MS KB 216970 (Global Catalog

Server Requirement for User and Computer Logon), and MS KB 241789 (How to Disable the Requirement that a Global Catalog Server Be Available to Validate User Logons)

3.29 Enabling Universal Group Caching in Windows Server 2003

Problem

You want to disable the requirement for a global catalog server to be reachable when a user logs into a Windows 2003 domain.

 This recipe requires the Windows Server 2003 forest functional level.

Solution

See Recipe 7.13 for information on enabling universal group caching, which can reduce the need to contact a global catalog server during logon for universal group expansion.

3.30 Finding the FSMO Role Holders

Problem

You want to find the domain controllers that are acting as one of the FSMO roles.

Solution

Using a graphical user interface

For the Schema Master:

1. Open the Active Directory Schema snap-in.
2. Right-click on Active Directory Schema in the left pane and select Operations Master.

For the Domain Naming Master:

1. Open the Active Directory Domains and Trusts snap-in (*domain.msc*).
2. Right-click on Active Directory Domains and Trusts in the left pane and select Operations Master.

For the PDC Emulator, RID Master, and Infrastructure Master:

1. Open the Active Directory Users and Computers snap-in (*dsa.msc*).
2. Make sure you've targeted the correct domain.
3. Right-click on Active Directory Users and Computers in the left pane and select Operations Master.
4. There are individual tabs for the PDC, RID, and Infrastructure roles.

Using a command-line interface

In the following command, you can leave out the /Domain *<DomainDNSName>* option to query the domain you are currently logged into.

```
> netdom query fsmo /Domain:<DomainDNSName>
```

To query the owner of an individual FSMO role, you can use the dsquery server command shown here, where *<Role>* can be schema, name, infr, pdc, or rid:

```
> dsquery server -hasfsmo <Role>
```

Using VBScript

```
' This code prints the FSMO role owners for the specified domain.
' ------ SCRIPT CONFIGURATION ------
strDomain = "<DomainDNSName>"  ' e.g. emea.rallencorp.com
' ------ END CONFIGURATION ---------

set objRootDSE = GetObject("LDAP://" & strDomain & "/RootDSE")
strDomainDN  = objRootDSE.Get("defaultNamingContext")
strSchemaDN = objRootDSE.Get("schemaNamingContext")
strConfigDN = objRootDSE.Get("configurationNamingContext")

' PDC Emulator
set objPDCFsmo = GetObject("LDAP://" & strDomainDN)
Wscript.Echo "PDC Emulator: " & objPDCFsmo.fsmoroleowner

' RID Master
set objRIDFsmo = GetObject("LDAP://cn=RID Manager$,cn=system," & strDomainDN)
Wscript.Echo "RID Master: " & objRIDFsmo.fsmoroleowner

' Schema Master
set objSchemaFsmo = GetObject("LDAP://" & strSchemaDN)
Wscript.Echo "Schema Master: " & objSchemaFsmo.fsmoroleowner

' Infrastructure Master
set objInfraFsmo = GetObject("LDAP://cn=Infrastructure," & strDomainDN)
Wscript.Echo "Infrastructure Master: " & objInfraFsmo.fsmoroleowner

' Domain Naming Master
set objDNFsmo = GetObject("LDAP://cn=Partitions," & strConfigDN)
Wscript.Echo "Domain Naming Master: " & objDNFsmo.fsmoroleowner
```

Discussion

Several Active Directory operations are sensitive, such as updating the schema, and therefore need to be restricted to a single domain controller to prevent corruption of the AD database. This is because Active Directory cannot guarantee the proper evaluation of these functions in a situation where they may be invoked from more than one DC. The FSMO mechanism is used to limit these functions to a single DC.

There are five designated FSMO roles that correspond to these sensitive functions. A FSMO role can apply either to an entire forest or to a specific domain. Each role is stored in the fSMORoleOwner attribute on various objects in Active Directory depending on the role. Table 3-4 contains a list of FSMO roles.

Table 3-4. FSMO roles

Role	Description	fSMORoleOwner location	Domain or forest-wide?
Schema	Processes schema updates	CN=Schema,CN=Configuration,< *ForestDN*>	Forest
Domain Naming	Processes the addition, removal, and renaming of domains	CN=Partitions, CN=Configuration,*<ForestDN>*	Forest
Infrastructure	Maintains references to objects in other domains	CN=Infrastructure,*<DomainDN>*	Domain
RID	Handles RID pool allocation for the domain controllers in a domain	CN=RidManager$,CN=System, *<DomainDN>*	Domain
PDC Emulator	Acts as the Windows NT master browser and also as the PDC for downlevel clients and Backup Domain Controllers (BDCs)	*<DomainDN>*	Domain

Using VBScript

If you want to get the DNS name for each FSMO, you'll need to get the parent object of the nTDSDSA object and use the dNSHostName attribute, similar to Recipe 3.11. The code for getting the Schema Master could be changed to the following to retrieve the DNS name of the DC:

```
set objSchemaFsmo = GetObject("LDAP://cn=Schema,cn=Configuration," & strForestDN)
set objSchemaFsmoNTDS = GetObject("LDAP://" & objSchemaFsmo.fsmoroleowner)
set objSchemaFsmoServer = GetObject(objSchemaFsmoNTDS.Parent)
Wscript.Echo "Schema Master: " & objSchemaFsmoServer.Get("dNSHostName")
```

See Also

Recipe 3.11, MS KB 197132 (Windows 2000 Active Directory FSMO Roles), MS KB 223346 (FSMO Placement and Optimization on Windows 2000 Domain Controllers), MS KB 234790 (How to Find Servers That Hold Flexible Single Master

Operations Roles), and MS KB 324801 (How to View and Transfer FSMO Roles in Windows Server 2003)

3.31 Transferring a FSMO Role

Problem

You want to transfer a FSMO role to a different domain controller. This may be necessary if you need to take a current FSMO role holder down for maintenance.

Solution

Using a graphical user interface

1. Use the same directions as described in Recipe 3.30 for viewing a specific FSMO, except target (i.e., right-click and select Connect to Domain Controller) the domain controller you want to transfer the FSMO *to* before selecting Operations Master.

2. Click the Change button.

3. Click OK twice.

4. You should then see a message stating whether the transfer was successful.

Using a command-line interface

The following would transfer the PDC Emulator role to *<NewRoleOwner>*. See the discussion to see about transferring the other roles.

```
> ntdsutil roles conn "co t s <NewRoleOwner>" q "transfer PDC" q q
```

Using VBScript

```
' This code transfers the PDC Emulator role to the specified owner.
' See the discussion to see about transferring the other roles.
' ------ SCRIPT CONFIGURATION ------
strNewOwner = "<NewRoleOwner>"  ' e.g. dc2.rallencorp.com
' ------ END CONFIGURATION ---------

Set objRootDSE = GetObject("LDAP://" & strNewOwner & "/RootDSE")
Set domainNC = GetObject("LDAP://" & objRootDSE.get("defaultNamingContext"))
domainSID = domainNC.objectSid
objRootDSE.Put "becomePDC", domainSID
objRootDSE.SetInfo
```

Discussion

The first domain controller in a new forest is assigned the two forest-wide FSMO roles (schema and domain naming). The first domain controller in a new domain gets the other three domain-wide roles. It is very likely you'll need to move the roles around to different domain controllers at some point. Also, when you need to decommission a domain controller that is currently a FSMO role owner (either permanently or for a significant period of time), you'll want to transfer the role beforehand.

If you plan to install a hotfix or do some other type of maintenance that only necessitates a quick reboot, you may not want to go to the trouble of transferring the FSMO role. This is because some FSMO roles are more time-critical than others, and some come into use on a far more frequent basis. For example, the PDC Emulator role is used extensively (and therefore should be transferred to a domain controller of equal or better capacity as a best practice), but the Schema Master is needed only when you are extending the schema by installing a new software package, such as Microsoft Exchange. If a FSMO role owner becomes unavailable before you can transfer it, you'll need to seize the role (see Recipe 3.32).

Using a command-line interface

Any role can be transferred using *ntdsutil* by replacing "transfer PDC" in the solution with one of the following:

- "transfer domain naming master"
- "transfer infrastructure master"
- "transfer RID master"
- "transfer schema master"

Using VBScript

FSMO roles can be transferred programmatically by setting the become<*FSMORole*> operational attribute on the RootDSE of the domain controller to transfer the role to. The following are the available attributes that can be set that correspond to each FSMO role:

- becomeDomainMaster
- becomeInfrastructureMaster
- becomePDC
- becomeRidMaster
- becomeSchemaMaster

See Also

Recipe 3.30 for finding FSMO role holders, Recipe 3.32 for seizing a FSMO role, MS KB 223787 (Flexible Single Master Operation Transfer and Seizure Process), MS KB 255504 (Using Ntdsutil.exe to Seize or Transfer FSMO Roles to a Domain Controller), and MS KB 324801 (How to View and Transfer FSMO Roles in Windows Server 2003)

3.32   Seizing a FSMO Role

Problem

You need to seize a FSMO role because the current role holder is down and will not be restored.

Solution

Using a command-line interface

The following would seize the PDC Emulator role to <NewRoleOwner>:

```
> ntdsutil roles conn "co t s <NewRoleOwner>" q "seize PDC" q q
```

Any of the other roles can be transferred as well using *ntdsutil* by replacing "seize PDC" in the previous solution with one of the following:

- "seize domain naming master"
- "seize infrastructure master"
- "seize RID master"
- "seize schema master"

Using VBScript

Seizing a FSMO role is typically not something you would want to do programmatically, but you could. All you need to do is set the fSMORoleOwner attribute for the object that represents the FSMO role as described in Recipe 3.30 with the distinguished name of nTDSDSA object of the new role owner. However, this can be an extremely dangerous operation in the case of the RID Master FSMO since it maintains extensive information that needs to be gracefully moved from one DC to another to avoid corruption of the AD database. In the case of the RID master, you should use *ntdsutil* to transfer or seize the role whenever possible.

Discussion

Seizing a FSMO role should not be done lightly. The general recommendation is to seize a FSMO role only when you cannot possibly bring the previous role holder back online. One reason that seizing a role is problematic is that you could possibly lose data. For example, let's say that you extended the schema and immediately after it was extended the Schema FSMO went down. If you could not bring that server back online, those extensions may have not replicated before the server went down. You would need to determine if the any of the schema extensions replicated and, if not, re-extend the schema. Other issues can result from losing the RID FSMO, where duplicate RID pools may be allocated. See Recipe 3.30 for more information.

See Also

Recipe 3.30 for finding FSMO role holders, Recipe 3.31 for transferring a FSMO role, MS KB 223787 (Flexible Single Master Operation Transfer and Seizure Process), and MS KB 255504 (Using Ntdsutil.exe to Seize or Transfer FSMO Roles to a Domain Controller)

3.33 Finding the PDC Emulator FSMO Role Owner via DNS

Problem

You want to find the PDC Emulator for a domain using DNS.

Solution

Using a command-line interface

```
> nslookup -type=SRV _ldap._tcp.pdc._msdcs.<DomainDNSName>
```

Discussion

The PDC Emulator FSMO role is the only FSMO role that is stored in DNS. Like many of the other Active Directory-related DNS records, the PDC record is stored as an SRV record under *_ldap._tcp.pdc._msdcs.<DomainDNSName>* where *<DomainDNSName>* is the domain the PDC is in. This allows your Active Directory clients to use normal DNS name resolution to locate the PDC Emulator for their domain.

See Also

Recipe 3.26 for finding domain controllers via DNS

3.34 Finding the PDC Emulator FSMO Role Owner via WINS

Problem

You want to find the PDC Emulator for a domain using WINS.

Solution

Using a command-line interface

```
> netsh wins server \\<WINS server> show name netbiosname 1b
```

Discussion

In addition to registering a record with DNS, the PDC Emulator FSMO role will also register a record with a WINS server if it is configured to point to one. The PDC Emulator will register a record called "<*DomainName*>1b" to allow any down-level clients to locate the PDCe using NetBIOS name resolution.

See Also

Recipe 3.33 for finding the PDC Emulator via DNS

## CHAPTER 4

Searching and Manipulating Objects

4.0 Introduction

Active Directory is based on the Lightweight Directory Access Protocol (LDAP) and supports the LDAP version 3 specification defined in RFC 2251. And while many of the AD tools and interfaces, such as ADSI, abstract and streamline LDAP operations to make things easier, any good AD administrator or developer must have a thorough understanding of LDAP to fully utilize Active Directory. This chapter will cover some of the LDAP-related tasks you may need to perform when working with Active Directory, along with other tasks related to searching and manipulating objects within the directory.

The Anatomy of an Object

The Active Directory schema is composed of a hierarchy of classes that define the types of objects that can be created within Active Directory, as well as the different attributes that they can possess. These classes support *inheritance*, which enables developers to reuse existing class definitions for more than one type of object; for example, the description attribute is available with every type of AD object, but the attribute itself is only defined *once* within the schema. At the top of the inheritance tree is the top class, from which every class in the schema is derived. Table 4-1 contains a list of some of the attributes that are available from the top class, and subsequently are defined on every object that is created in Active Directory.

Table 4-1. Common attributes of objects

Attribute	Description
cn	RDN attribute for most object classes, also referred to as the *common name*.
whenCreated	Timestamp when the object was created. See Recipe 4.27 for more information.
description	Multivalued attribute that can be used as a generic field for storing a description of the object. Although this attribute is multivalued, objects such as users and groups can only have one value populated due to legacy support requirements.

Table 4-1. Common attributes of objects (continued)

Attribute	Description
displayName	Name of the object displayed in administrative interfaces.
distinguishedName	Distinguished name of the object.
whenChanged	Timestamp when the object was last changed by the local server. See Recipe 4.27 for more information
name	RDN of the object. The value of this attribute will mirror the naming attribute (e.g., cn, ou, dc).
nTSecurityDescriptor	Security descriptor assigned to the object.
objectCategory	Used as a grouping mechanism for objects with a similar purpose (e.g., Person).
objectClass	List of classes from which the object's class was derived.
objectGUID	Globally unique identifier for the object.
uSNChanged	Update sequence number (USN) assigned by the local server after the last change to the object (can include creation).
uSNCreated	USN assigned by the local server when the object was created.

4.1   Viewing the RootDSE

Problem

You want to view attributes of the RootDSE, which can be useful for discovering basic information about a forest, domain, or domain controller without hardcoding the name of a particular naming context into a query.

Solution

Using a graphical user interface

1. Open LDP from the Windows Support Tools.
2. From the menu, select Connection → Connect.
3. For Server, enter a domain controller, domain name, or leave blank to do a serverless bind.
4. For Port, enter 389.
5. Click OK.
6. The contents of the RootDSE will be shown in the right pane.

Using a command-line interface

To display the RootDSE of a domain controller using AdFind, use the following syntax:

```
> adfind -b -s base
```

You'll see results similar to the following (truncated for readability):

```
>currentTime: 20051130204431.0Z
>subschemaSubentry: CN=Aggregate,CN=Schema,CN=Configuration,DC=rallenhome,DC=com
>dsServiceName: CN=NTDS Settings,CN=2K3-SP1-R2,CN=Servers,CN=Default-First-Site-
Name,CN=Sites,CN=Configuration,DC=rallenhome,DC=com
>namingContexts: DC=rallenhome,DC=com
>namingContexts: CN=Configuration,DC=rallenhome,DC=com
>namingContexts: CN=Schema,CN=Configuration,DC=rallenhome,DC=com
>namingContexts: DC=DomainDnsZones,DC=rallenhome,DC=com
>namingContexts: DC=ForestDnsZones,DC=rallenhome,DC=com
>defaultNamingContext: DC=rallenhome,DC=com
>schemaNamingContext: CN=Schema,CN=Configuration,DC=rallenhome,DC=com
>configurationNamingContext: CN=Configuration,DC=rallenhome,DC=com
>rootDomainNamingContext: DC=rallenhome,DC=com
>serverName: CN=2K3-SP1-R2,CN=Servers,CN=Default-First-Site-Name,CN=Sites,CN=Con
figuration,DC=rallenhome,DC=com
>supportedCapabilities: 1.2.840.113556.1.4.800
>supportedCapabilities: 1.2.840.113556.1.4.1670
>supportedCapabilities: 1.2.840.113556.1.4.1791
>isSynchronized: TRUE
>isGlobalCatalogReady: TRUE
>domainFunctionality: 0
>forestFunctionality: 0
>domainControllerFunctionality: 2
```

Using VBScript

```
' This code prints the attributes of the RootDSE
set objRootDSE = GetObject("LDAP://RootDSE")
objRootDSE.GetInfo
for i = 0 to objRootDSE.PropertyCount - 1
    set strProp = objRootDSE.Item(i)
    WScript.Echo strProp.Name & " "
    for each strPropval in strProp.Values
        WScript.Echo "  " &  strPropval.CaseIgnoreString
    next
next
```

Discussion

The RootDSE was originally defined in RFC 2251 as part of the LDAPv3 specification. It is not part of the Active Directory namespace per se. It is a synthetic object that is maintained separately by each domain controller.

The RootDSE can be accessed anonymously using LDP; the command-line and VBScript solutions use the credentials of the currently logged-on user unless you specify an alternate username and password. In the CLI and VBScript solutions, serverless binds were ysed against the RootDSE. In that case, the DC Locator process is used to find a domain controller in the domain you authenticate against. This can also be accomplished with LDP by not entering a server name from the Connect dialog box.

The RootDSE is key to writing portable AD-enabled applications. It provides a mechanism to programmatically determine the distinguished names of the various naming contexts (among other things), which means that you do not need to hard-code that information in scripts and programs. Here is an example from LDP when run against a Windows Server 2003–based domain controller:

```
ld = ldap_open("dc01", 389);
Established connection to dc01.
Retrieving base DSA information . . .
Result <0>: (null)
Matched DNs:
Getting 1 entries:
>> Dn:
1> currentTime: 05/26/2003 15:29:42 Pacific Standard Time Pacific Daylight Time;

1> subschemaSubentry:CN=Aggregate,CN=Schema,CN=Configuration,DC=rallencorp,DC=com;

1> dsServiceName: CN=NTDS Settings,CN=DC01,CN=Servers,CN=Default-First-Site-
Name,CN=Sites,CN=Configuration,DC=rallencorp,DC=com;

5> namingContexts: DC=rallencorp,DC=com; CN=Configuration,DC=rallencorp,DC=com;
CN=Schema,CN=Configuration,DC=rallencorp,DC=com;
DC=DomainDnsZones,DC=rallencorp,DC=com; DC=ForestDnsZones,DC=rallencorp,DC=com;

1> defaultNamingContext: DC=rallencorp,DC=com;

1> schemaNamingContext: CN=Schema,CN=Configuration,DC=rallencorp,DC=com;

1> configurationNamingContext: CN=Configuration,DC=rallencorp,DC=com;

1> rootDomainNamingContext: DC=rallencorp,DC=com;

21> supportedControl: 1.2.840.113556.1.4.319; 1.2.840.113556.1.4.801; 1.2.840.113556.
1.4.473; 1.2.840.113556.1.4.528; 1.2.840.113556.1.4.417; 1.2.840.113556.1.4.619; 1.2.
840.113556.1.4.841; 1.2.840.113556.1.4.529; 1.2.840.113556.1.4.805; 1.2.840.113556.1.
4.521; 1.2.840.113556.1.4.970; 1.2.840.113556.1.4.1338; 1.2.840.113556.1.4.474; 1.2.
840.113556.1.4.1339; 1.2.840.113556.1.4.1340; 1.2.840.113556.1.4.1413; 2.16.840.1.
113730.3.4.9; 2.16.840.1.113730.3.4.10; 1.2.840.113556.1.4.1504; 1.2.840.113556.1.4.
1852; 1.2.840.113556.1.4.802;

2> supportedLDAPVersion: 3; 2;

12> supportedLDAPPolicies: MaxPoolThreads; MaxDatagramRecv; MaxReceiveBuffer;
InitRecvTimeout; MaxConnections; MaxConnIdleTime; MaxPageSize; MaxQueryDuration;
MaxTempTableSize; MaxResultSetSize; MaxNotificationPerConn; MaxValRange;

1> highestCommittedUSN: 53242;

4> supportedSASLMechanisms: GSSAPI; GSS-SPNEGO; EXTERNAL; DIGEST-MD5;

1> dnsHostName: dc01.rallencorp.com;

1> ldapServiceName: rallencorp.com:dc01$@RALLENCORP.COM;
```

```
1> serverName: CN=DC01,CN=Servers,CN=Default-First-Site-
Name,CN=Sites,CN=Configuration,DC=rallencorp,DC=com;

3> supportedCapabilities: 1.2.840.113556.1.4.800; 1.2.840.113556.1.4.1670; 1.2.840.
113556.1.4.1791;

1> isSynchronized: TRUE;

1> isGlobalCatalogReady: TRUE;

1> domainFunctionality: 0 = ( DS_BEHAVIOR_WIN2000 );

1> forestFunctionality: 0 = ( DS_BEHAVIOR_WIN2000 );

1> domainControllerFunctionality: 2 = ( DS_BEHAVIOR_WIN2003 );
```

Using VBScript

All attributes of the RootDSE were retrieved and displayed. Typically, you will need only a few of the attributes, in which case you'll want to use Get or GetEx as in the following example:

```
strDefaultNC = objRootDSE.Get("defaultNamingContext")
```

Or if want to get an object based on the DN of one of the naming contexts, you can call GetObject using an ADsPath:

```
set objUser = GetObject("LDAP://cn=administrator,cn=users," & _
                         objRootDSE.Get("defaultNamingContext") )
```

See Also

RFC 2251, MS KB 219005 (Windows 2000: LDAPv3 RootDSE), MSDN: IADsPropertyEntry, MSDN: IADsProperty Value, MSDN: IADs::Get, and MSDN: IADs:: GetEx

4.2   Viewing the Attributes of an Object

Problem

You want to view one or more attributes of an object.

Solution

Using a graphical user interface

1. Open LDP from the Windows Support Tools.
2. From the menu, select Connection → Connect.
3. For Server, enter the name or IP address of a domain controller or domain that contains the object.

4. For Port, enter 389.

5. Click OK.

6. From the menu, select Connection → Bind.

7. Enter credentials of a user that can view the object (if necessary).

8. Click OK.

9. From the menu, select View → Tree.

10. For BaseDN, type the DN of the object you want to view.

11. For Scope, select Base.

12. Click OK.

Using a command-line interface

To obtain a list of attributes for a particular object using DSQuery, use the following syntax:

```
> dsquery * "<ObjectDN>" -scope base -attr *
```

For Windows 2000, use this command:

```
> enumprop "LDAP://<ObjectDN>"
```

To query for an object using AdFind, use the following syntax:

```
> adfind -b <Parent Container DN> -f <Object CN>
```

For example, querying for the administrator user object would product the following output:

```
C:\>adfind -b dc=rallenhome,dc=com -f cn=administrator

AdFind V01.27.00cpp Joe Richards (joe@joeware.net) November 2005

Using server: 2k3-sp1-r2.rallenhome.com:389
Directory: Windows Server 2003

dn:CN=Administrator,CN=Users,DC=rallenhome,DC=com
>objectClass: top
>objectClass: person
>objectClass: organizationalPerson
>objectClass: user
>cn: Administrator
>description: Built-in account for administering the computer/domain
>distinguishedName: CN=Administrator,CN=Users,DC=rallenhome,DC=com
>instanceType: 4
>whenCreated: 20051130122215.0Z
>whenChanged: 20051130195130.0Z
>uSNCreated: 8194
>memberOf: CN=Group Policy Creator Owners,CN=Users,DC=rallenhome,DC=com
>memberOf: CN=Domain Admins,CN=Users,DC=rallenhome,DC=com
>memberOf: CN=Enterprise Admins,CN=Users,DC=rallenhome,DC=com
>memberOf: CN=Schema Admins,CN=Users,DC=rallenhome,DC=com
```

```
>memberOf: CN=Administrators,CN=Builtin,DC=rallenhome,DC=com
>uSNChanged: 13905
>name: Administrator
>objectGUID: {A5C30B01-535C-4BCF-83C1-ABA5D445B9F6}
>userAccountControl: 66048
>badPwdCount: 0
>codePage: 0
>countryCode: 0
>badPasswordTime: 0
>lastLogoff: 0
>lastLogon: 127778606063352544
>pwdLastSet: 127777249491195376
>primaryGroupID: 513
>objectSid: S-1-5-21-751427308-4037830757-4109730475-500
>adminCount: 1
>accountExpires: 9223372036854775807
>logonCount: 7
>sAMAccountName: Administrator
>sAMAccountType: 805306368
>objectCategory: CN=Person,CN=Schema,CN=Configuration,DC=rallenhome,DC=com
>isCriticalSystemObject: TRUE


1 Objects returned
```

Using VBScript

```
' This code prints all default attributes for the specified object.
' ------ SCRIPT CONFIGURATION ------
strObjectDN = "<ObjectDN>" ' e.g. cn=jsmith,cn=users,dc=rallencorp,dc=com
' ------ END CONFIGURATION ---------

DisplayAttributes("LDAP://" & strObjectDN)

Function DisplayAttributes( strObjectADsPath )

    set objObject = GetObject(strObjectADsPath)
    objObject.GetInfo

    'Declare the hash (dictionary), constants and variables
    'Values taken from ADSTYPEENUM
    set dicADsType = CreateObject("Scripting.Dictionary")
    dicADsType.Add 0, "INVALID"
    dicADsType.Add 1, "DN_STRING"
    dicADsType.Add 2, "CASE_EXACT_STRING"
    dicADsType.Add 3, "CASE_IGNORE_STRING"
    dicADsType.Add 4, "PRINTABLE_STRING"
    dicADsType.Add 5, "NUMERIC_STRING"
    dicADsType.Add 6, "BOOLEAN"
    dicADsType.Add 7, "INTEGER"
    dicADsType.Add 8, "OCTET_STRING"
    dicADsType.Add 9, "UTC_TIME"
    dicADsType.Add 10, "LARGE_INTEGER"
    dicADsType.Add 11, "PROV_SPECIFIC"
```

```
dicADsType.Add 12, "OBJECT_CLASS"
dicADsType.Add 13, "CASEIGNORE_LIST"
dicADsType.Add 14, "OCTET_LIST"
dicADsType.Add 15, "PATH"
dicADsType.Add 16, "POSTALADDRESS"
dicADsType.Add 17, "TIMESTAMP"
dicADsType.Add 18, "BACKLINK"
dicADsType.Add 19, "TYPEDNAME"
dicADsType.Add 20, "HOLD"
dicADsType.Add 21, "NETADDRESS"
dicADsType.Add 22, "REPLICAPOINTER"
dicADsType.Add 23, "FAXNUMBER"
dicADsType.Add 24, "EMAIL"
dicADsType.Add 25, "NT_SECURITY_DESCRIPTOR"
dicADsType.Add 26, "UNKNOWN"
dicADsType.Add 27, "DN_WITH_BINARY"
dicADsType.Add 28, "DN_WITH_STRING"

for intIndex = 0 To (objObject.PropertyCount - 1)
    set objPropEntry = objObject.Item(intIndex)
    for Each objPropValue In objPropEntry.Values
        value = ""

        if (dicADsType(objPropValue.ADsType) = "DN_STRING") then
            value = objPropValue.DNString

        elseIf (dicADsType(objPropValue.ADsType) = "CASE_EXACT_STRING") then
            value = objPropValue.CaseExactString

        elseIf (dicADsType(objPropValue.ADsType) = "CASE_IGNORE_STRING") then
            value = objPropValue.CaseIgnoreString

        elseIf (dicADsType(objPropValue.ADsType) = "PRINTABLE_STRING") then
            value = objPropValue.PrintableString

        elseIf (dicADsType(objPropValue.ADsType) = "NUMERIC_STRING") then
            value = objPropValue.NumericString

        elseIf (dicADsType(objPropValue.ADsType) = "BOOLEAN") then
            value = CStr(objPropValue.Boolean)

        elseIf (dicADsType(objPropValue.ADsType) = "INTEGER") then
            value = objPropValue.Integer

        elseIf (dicADsType(objPropValue.ADsType) = "LARGE_INTEGER") then
            set objLargeInt = objPropValue.LargeInteger
            value = objLargeInt.HighPart * 2^32 + objLargeInt.LowPart

        elseIf (dicADsType(objPropValue.ADsType) = "UTC_TIME") then
            value = objPropValue.UTCTime

        else
```

```
            value = "<" & dicADsType.Item(objPropEntry.ADsType) & ">"

        end if
        WScript.Echo objPropEntry.Name & " : " & value
      next
   next
End Function
```

Discussion

Objects in Active Directory are made up of a collection of attributes. Attributes can be single- or multivalued. Each attribute also has an associated syntax that is defined in the schema. See Recipe 11.8 for a complete list of syntaxes.

Using a graphical user interface

You can customize the list of attributes returned from a search with LDP by modifying the Attributes: field under Options → Search. To include all attributes enter an asterisk (*). To modify the default subset of attributes that are returned, enter a semicolon-separated list of attributes. You can also use the numeric attribute ID instead of the attribute name, such as using 1.1 in place of distinguishedName.

Using a command-line interface

The -attr option for the dsquery command accepts a whitespace-separated list of attributes to display. Using an asterisk (*) will return all default attributes.

For the enumprop command, you can use the /ATTR option and a comma-separated list of attributes to return. In the following example, only the name and whenCreated attributes would be returned:

```
> enumprop /ATTR:name,whenCreated "LDAP://<ObjectDN>"
```

When using AdFind, you have several shortcut switches to reduce the amount of typing you need to do. If you are searching for an object in the default container, you can use the –default switch rather than something like –b dc=rallenhome,dc=com. Likewise, if you are querying the Configuration NC, you can use the -config switch, -root for the root partition, or -schema for the Schema partition. If you want to query a subcontainer of one of these partitions, you can add the –rb switch, which stands for *Relative Base*.

Using VBScript

The DisplayAttributes function prints the attributes that contain values for the object passed in. After using GetObject to bind to the object, the IADs::GetInfo method was used to populate the local property cache with all of the object's attributes from AD. To print each value of a property, you have to know its type or syntax. The ADsType method returns an integer from the ADSTYPEENUM enumeration that corresponds with a particular syntax (e.g., Boolean). Based on the syntax, you call a specific method (e.g., `Boolean`) that can properly print the value. If you didn't incorporate this logic and tried to print all values using the `CaseIgnoreString` method for example, an error would get generated when the script encountered an octet string because octet strings (i.e., binary data) do not have a `CaseIgnoreString` representation.

The values from the `ADSTYPEENUM` enumeration are stored in key/value pairs in a dictionary object (i.e., `Scripting.Dictionary`). In the dictionary object, the key for the dictionary is the `ADSTYPEENUM` integer and the value is a textual version of the syntax. The dictionary object was used to print the textual syntax of each attribute. You iterated over all the properties in the property cache using `IADsPropertyList` and `IADsPropertyEntry` objects, which are instantiated with the `IADsPropertyList::Item` method.

 The `DisplayAttributes` function is used throughout the book in examples where the attributes for a given type of object are displayed.

See Also

Recipe 11.8, MSDN: IADsPropertyEntry, MSDN: IADsPropertyList, MSDN: ADSTYPEENUM, MSDN: IADs::GetInfo, and Chapter 20 from *Active Directory, Third Edition,* by Joe Richards et al. (O'Reilly)

4.3   Counting Objects in Active Directory

Problem

You want to retrieve the number of directory objects that meet the result of an LDAP query.

Solution

Using a graphical user interface

1. Open LDP from the Windows Support Tools.
2. From the menu, select Connection → Connect.
3. For Server, enter the name or IP address of a domain controller or domain that contains the object.
4. For Port, enter 389.
5. Click OK.
6. From the menu, select Connection → Bind.
7. Enter credentials of a user that can view the object (if necessary).

8. Click OK.

9. From the menu, select Browse → Search.

10. Enter the base DN, scope, and the LDAP filter of the objects that you're looking for.

11. Click on Options and remove the check mark next to Display Results. This will display the number of objects returned by the query without displaying the details of the items that are returned.

12. Click OK and then click Run to perform the query.

Using a command-line interface

To retrieve a count of objects that match a particular query, use the following syntax:

```
> adfind -b <Search Base> -s <Scope> -f <Search Filter> -c
```

For example, retrieving the number of user objects in the *rallencorp.com* domain would use the following syntax:

```
> adfind -default -f "(&(objectclass=user)(objectcategory=person))" -c
>
> AdFind V01.27.00cpp Joe Richards (joe@joeware.net) November 2005
>
> Using server: 2k3-sp1-r2.rallencorp.com:389
> Directory: Windows Server 2003
> Base DN: DC=rallencorp,DC=com
>
> 5 Objects returned
```

Using VBScript

```
' This code lists the number of objects
' returned based on the specified criteria.
' ------ SCRIPT CONFIGURATION ------
strBase   = "<LDAP://<BaseDN>>;" ' BaseDN should be the search base
strFilter = "<Filter>;"          ' Valid LDAP search filter
strAttrs  = "<AttrList>;"         ' Comma-seperated list
strScope  = "<Scope>"            ' Should be on of Subtree, Onelevel, or Base
' ------ END CONFIGURATION ---------

set objConn = CreateObject("ADODB.Connection")
objConn.Provider = "ADsDSOObject"
objConn.Open "Active Directory Provider"
set objRS = objConn.Execute(strBase & strFilter & strAttrs & strScope)
Wscript.Echo(objRS.RecordCount & " objects returned.")
```

Discussion

Using VBScript

The VBScript solution uses the RecordCount property of an ADO Recordset, which contains the number of records that were returned by a particular query. The script listed here does not enable paging, so it will not work if more than 1,000 records will be returned by a query unless you specify the "Page size" property of the connection object, similar to the following:

```
objConn.Properties("Page size") = <PageSize>
```

4.4   Using LDAP Controls

Problem

You want to use an LDAP control as part of an LDAP operation.

Solution

Using a graphical user interface

1. Open LDP from the Windows Support Tools.

2. From the menu, select Options → Controls.

3. For the Windows Server 2003 version of LDP, select the control you want to use under Load Predefined. The control should automatically be added to the list of Active Controls.

   For the Windows 2000 version of LDP, you'll need to type the object identifier (OID) of the control under Object Identifier.

4. Enter the value for the control under Value.

5. Select whether the control is server- or client-side under Control Type.

6. Check the box beside Critical if the control is critical.

7. Click the Check-in button.

8. Click OK.

9. At this point, you will need to invoke the LDAP operation (e.g., Search) that will use the control. In the dialog box for any operation, be sure that the "Extended" option is checked before initiating the operation.

Using a command-line interface

The AdMod utility will enable a number of LDAP controls, either by default or through the use of various command-line switches. For example, the -showdel switch will invoke the Show Deleted Objects LDAP control and -stats will invoke the Show Stats control.

Using VBScript

None of the ADSI automation interfaces directly expose LDAP controls. That means they cannot be utilized from VBScript. On the other hand, many of the controls such as paged searching or deleting a subtree are wrapped within their own ADSI methods that can be used within VBScript.

Any LDAP-based API, such as the Perl Net::LDAP modules, can be used to set controls as part of LDAP operations.

Discussion

LDAP controls were defined in the LDAPv3 specification as a way to extend LDAP and its operations without breaking the protocol. Many controls have been implemented, some of which are used when searching the directory (e.g., paged searching, Virtual List View (VLV), finding deleted objects, and attribute scoped query), and some are needed to do certain modifications to the directory (e.g., cross-domain object moves, tree delete, and permissive modify). Controls can be marked as critical, which means they must be processed with the request or an error is returned. If an unsupported control is not flagged as critical, the server can continue to process the request and ignore the control.

The complete list of controls supported by Active Directory is included in Table 4-2.

Table 4-2. LDAP controls supported by Active Directory

Name	OID	Description
Paged Results	1.2.840.113556.1.4.319	Instructs the server to return search results in "pages."
Cross Domain Move	1.2.840.113556.1.4.521	Used to move objects between domains.
DIRSYNC	1.2.840.113556.1.4.841	Used to find objects that have changed over a period of time.
Domain Scope	1.2.840.113556.1.4.1339	Informs the server to not generate any referrals in a search response.
Extended DN	1.2.840.113556.1.4.529	Used to return an object's GUID and SID (for security principals) as part of its distinguished name.
Lazy Commit	1.2.840.113556.1.4.619	Informs the server to return after directory modifications have been written to memory, but before they have been written to disk. This can speed up processing of a lot of modifications.
Change Notification	1.2.840.113556.1.4.528	Used by clients to register for notification of when changes occur in the directory.
Permissive Modify	1.2.840.113556.1.4.1413	Allows duplicate adds of the same value for an attribute or deletion of an attribute that has no values to succeed (normally, it would fail in that situation).
SD Flags	1.2.840.113556.1.4.801	Used to pass flags to the server to control certain security descriptor options.
Search Options	1.2.840.113556.1.4.1340	Used to pass flags to the server to control search options.
Show Deleted Objects	1.2.840.113556.1.4.417	Used to inform the server to return any deleted objects that matched the search criteria.
Server-side Sort Request	1.2.840.113556.1.4.473	Used to inform the server to sort the results of a search.

Table 4-2. LDAP controls supported by Active Directory (continued)

Name	OID	Description
Server-side Sort Response	1.2.840.113556.1.4.474	Returned by the server in response to a sort request.
Tree Delete	1.2.840.113556.1.4.805	Used to delete portions of the directory tree, including any child objects.
Verify Name	1.2.840.113556.1.4.1338	Used to target a specific GC server that is used to verify DN-valued attributes that are processed during addition or modification operations.
VLV Request	2.16.840.1.113730.3.4.9	Used to request a virtual list view of results from a search. This control is new to Windows Server 2003.
VLV Response	2.16.840.1.113730.3.4.10	Response from server returning a virtual list view of results from a search. This control is new to Windows Server 2003.
Attribute Scoped Query	1.2.840.113556.1.4.1504	Used to force a query to be based on a specific DN-valued attribute. This control is new to Windows Server 2003. See Recipe 4.8 for an example.
Search Stats	1.2.840.113556.1.4.970	Used to return statistics about an LDAP query. See Recipe 16.10 for an example.

See Also

Recipe 4.8, Recipe 16.10, RFC 2251 (Lightweight Directory Access Protocol (v3)) for a description of LDAP controls, MSDN: Extended Controls, and MSDN: Using Controls

4.5   Using a Fast or Concurrent Bind

Problem

You want to perform an LDAP bind using a concurrent bind, also known as a fast bind. Concurrent binds are typically used in situations where you need to authenticate a lot of users, and those users either do not need to directly access the directory or else the directory access is done with another account.

Solution

 This works only on a Windows Server 2003 domain controller.

Using a graphical user interface

1. Open LDP from the Windows Support Tools.
2. From the menu, select Connection → Connect.
3. For Server, enter the name of a DC.

4. For Port, enter 389.

5. Click OK.

6. From the menu, select Options → Connection Options.

7. Under Option Name: select LDAP_OPT_F*_CONCURRENT_BIND.

8. Click the Set button.

9. From the menu, select Connection → Bind.

10. Enter credentials of a user.

11. Click OK.

Using VBScript

```
const ADS_F*_BIND = 32
set objLDAP = GetObject("LDAP:")
set objUser = objLDAP.OpenDSObject("LDAP://<ObjectDN>", _
                                   "<UserUPN>", _
                                   "<UserPassword>", _
                                   ADS_F*_BIND)
```

Discussion

Unlike simple binding, concurrent binding does not generate a security token or determine a user's group memberships during the authentication process. It only determines if the authenticating user has a valid enabled account and password, which makes it much faster than a typical bind. This is usually used programmatically for AD-enabled applications to improve the speed of AD authentication; it's not something that you'll typically do on the fly. Concurrent binding is implemented as a session option that is set after you establish a connection to a domain controller, but before any bind attempts are made. After the option has been set, any bind attempt made with the connection will be a concurrent bind.

There are a couple of caveats when using concurrent binds. First, you cannot enable signing or encryption, which means that all data for concurrent binds will be sent over the network in clear text. Secondly, because the user's security token is not generated, access to the directory is done anonymously and access restrictions are based on the ANONYMOUS LOGON principal.

It is worth mentioning that there is another type of bind—a fast bind—which has been available since Windows 2000, but it is completely different from the procedure just described. This fast bind is implemented within ADSI, and simply means that when you fast bind to an object, the objectClass attribute for the object is not retrieved; therefore, the object-specific IADs class interfaces are not available. For example, if you bound to a user object using an ADSI fast bind, then only the basic IADs interfaces would be available, not the IADsUser interfaces.

This is the complete list of interfaces that are available for objects retrieved with fast binds:

- `IADs`
- `IADsContainer`
- `IDirectoryObject`
- `IDirectorySearch`
- `IADsPropertyList`
- `IADsObjectOptions`
- `ISupportErrorInfo`
- `IADsDeleteOps`

You must use the `IADsOpenDSObject::OpenDSObject` interface to enable fast binds. If you call `IADsContainer::GetObject` on a child object of a parent you used a fast bind with, the same fast bind behavior applies. Unlike concurrent binds, ADSI fast binds do not impose any restrictions on the authenticating user. This means that the object-specific `IADs` interfaces will not be available. Also, no check is done to verify the object exists when you call `OpenDSObject`.

ADSI fast binds are useful when you need to make a lot of updates to objects that you know exist (perhaps from an ADO query that returned a list of DNs) and you do not need any IADs-specific interfaces. Instead of two trips over the network per object binding, there would only be one.

See Also

MSDN: Using Concurrent Binding and MSDN: ADS_AUTHENTICATION_ENUM

4.6 Connecting to an Object GUID

Problem

You want to bind to a container using its Globally Unique Identifier (GUID)

Solution

Using a graphical user interface

1. Open LDP from the Windows Support Tools.
2. From the menu, select Connection → Connect.
3. For Server, enter the name of a domain controller (or leave blank to do a server-less bind).
4. For Port, enter 389.
5. Click OK.

6. From the menu, select Connection → Bind.

7. Enter credentials of a user.

8. Click OK.

9. From the menu, select Browse → Search.

10. For BaseDN, enter the GUID in the following format:

    `<GUID=758A39F4A44A0C48A16016457C1AE9E9>`

11. For Scope, select the appropriate scope.

12. For Filter, enter an LDAP filter.

13. Click Run.

Using a command-line interface

```
> adfind -b "<GUID=ObjectGUID>"
```

Using VBScript

```
' This code illustrates how to bind to an object GUID.
' ------ SCRIPT CONFIGURATION ------
strDomain = "<DomainDNSName>"   ' e.g. apac.rallencorp.com
strGUID = "<GUID>" ' e.g. "aa312825768811d1aded00c04fd8d5cd"
                      ' for the default Computers container
' ------ END CONFIGURATION ---------

set objRootDSE = GetObject("LDAP://" & strDomain & "/RootDSE")
set objContainer = GetObject("LDAP://<GUID=" & _
                             strGUID & "," & _
                             objRootDSE.Get("defaultNamingContext") & ">" )
WScript.Echo objContainer.Get("distinguishedName")
```

Discussion

Each object in Active Directory has a GUID associated with it, stored in the objectGUID attribute. The GUID is for most purposes a unique identifier that retains its value even if an object is updated, renamed, or moved. This makes the GUID the preferable means of binding to an object, rather than hardcoding a reference to an object name that might change or by using a potentially complex LDAP query.

See Also

For a more in-depth discussion of the objectGUID attribute, see "GUIDs, or Having Unique in the Name Doesn't Make It So" (*http://blog.joeware.net/2005/06/19/42/*), MSDN: IADs.GUID, MSDN: Using objectGUID to Bind to an Object, and "Connecting to a Well-Known GUID."

4.7   Connecting to a Well-Known GUID

Problem

You want to connect to LDAP using one of the well-known GUIDs in Active Directory.

Solution

Using a graphical user interface

1. Open LDP.

2. From the menu, select Connection → Connect.

3. For Server, enter the name of a domain controller (or leave blank to do a server-less bind).

4. For Port, enter 389.

5. Click OK.

6. From the menu, select Connection → Bind.

7. Enter credentials of a domain user.

8. Click OK.

9. From the menu, select View → Tree.

10. For the DN, enter:

    ```
    <WKGUID=<WKGUID>,<DomainDN>>
    ```

    where `<WKGUID>` is the well-known GUID that you want to connect to, and `<DomainDN>` is the distinguished name of a domain.

11. Click OK. In the left-hand menu, you can now browse the container corresponding to the well-known GUID that you specified.

Using a command-line interface

To enumerate the well-known GUIDs in the Domain NC, use the following syntax:

```
> adfind -default -s base wellknownObjects
```

To display the WKGUIDs in the Configuration NC, replace -default with –config in the previous syntax.

To connect to a well-known GUID using AdFind, use the following syntax:

```
> adfind -b "<WKGUID=<WKGUID>,<DomainDN>>" -s base -dn
```

 Because of additional security settings attached to the Deleted Objects container, if you specify this GUID you must also use the –showdel switch in adfind.

Using VBScript

```
' This code illustrates how to bind to the default computers container.
' ------ SCRIPT CONFIGURATION ------
strDomain = "<DomainDNSName>"    ' e.g. apac.rallencorp.com
strWKGUID = "<WKGUID>" ' e.g. "aa312825768811d1aded00c04fd8d5cd"
                       ' for the default Computers container
' ------ END CONFIGURATION ---------

set objRootDSE = GetObject("LDAP://" & strDomain & "/RootDSE")
set objCompContainer = GetObject("LDAP://<WKGUID=" & _
                       strWKGUID & "," & _
                       objRootDSE.Get("defaultNamingContext") & ">" )
WScript.Echo objCompContainer.Get("distinguishedName")
```

Discussion

The domain NC in Active Directory contains a number of well-known GUIDs that correspond to containers that exist in every AD implementation. These GUIDs are stored as wellKnownObjects attributes within the <DomainDN> object, and allow administrators and developers to consistently connect to critical containers even if they are moved or renamed. The <DomainDN> container possesses the following objects that correspond to well-known GUIDs:

- CN=NTDS Quotas,<DomainDN>
- CN=Microsoft,CN=Program Data,<DomainDN>
- CN=Program Data,<DomainDN>
- CN=ForeignSecurityPrincipals,<DomainDN>
- CN=Deleted Objects,<DomainDN>
- CN=Infrastructure,<DomainDN>
- CN=LostAndFound,<DomainDN>
- CN=System,<DomainDN>
- OU=Domain Controllers,<DomainDN>
- CN=Computers,<DomainDN>
- CN=Users,<DomainDN>

The Configuration NC adds these additional WKGUIDs:

- CN=NTDS Quotas,CN=Configuration,<ForestRootDN>
- CN=LostAndFoundConfig,CN=Configuration,<ForestRootDN>
- CN=Deleted Objects,CN=Configuration,<ForestRootDN>

See Also

MSDN: Binding to Well-Known Objects Using WKGUID

4.8 Searching for Objects in a Domain

Problem

You want to find objects in a domain that match certain criteria.

Solution

Using a graphical user interface

1. Open LDP from the Windows Support Tools.
2. From the menu, select Connection → Connect.
3. For Server, enter the name of a domain controller (or leave blank to do a server-less bind).
4. For Port, enter 389.
5. Click OK.
6. From the menu, select Connection → Bind.
7. Enter credentials of a user.
8. Click OK.
9. From the menu, select Browse → Search.
10. For BaseDN, type the base distinguished name where the search will start. (You can leave this blank if you wish to connect to the domain NC as the base DN.)
11. For Scope, select the appropriate scope.
12. For Filter, enter an LDAP filter.
13. Click Run.

Using a command-line interface

To run a query using the built-in DSQuery tool, use the following syntax:

```
> dsquery * <BaseDN> -scope <Scope> -filter "<Filter>" -attr "<AttrList>"
```

To retrieve the SAM account name for all user objects within the *rallencorp.com* domain, for example, use the following syntax:

```
> dsquery * dc=rallencorp,dc=com -filter
"(&(objectclass=user)(objectcategory=person))" -attr sAMAccountName
```

To run a query using adfind, use the following syntax:

```
> adfind -b <BaseDN> -s <Scope> -f <Filter> <Attributes>
```

Querying for SAM account names of user objects with adfind takes the following syntax:

```
> adfind -b dc=rallencorp,dc=com -f "(&(objectclass=user)(objectcategory=person))"
sAMAccountName
```

Both DSQuery and AdFind assume a default search scope of subtree; you only need to specify the search scope if you want to use a different one.

Using VBScript

```
' This code searches for objects based on the specified criteria.
' ------ SCRIPT CONFIGURATION ------
strBase   = "<LDAP://<BaseDN>>;" ' BaseDN should be the search base
strFilter - "<Filter>;"          ' Valid LDAP search filter
strAttrs  = "<AttrList>;"        ' Comma-seperated list
strScope  = "<Scope>"           ' Should be on of Subtree, Onelevel, or Base
' ------ END CONFIGURATION ---------

set objConn = CreateObject("ADODB.Connection")
objConn.Provider = "ADsDSOObject"
objConn.Open "Active Directory Provider"
set objRS = objConn.Execute(strBase & strFilter & strAttrs & strScope)
objRS.MoveFirst
While Not objRS.EOF
    Wscript.Echo objRS.Fields(0).Value
    objRS.MoveNext
Wend
WScript.Echo("Search complete!")
```

Discussion

Most tools that can be used to search Active Directory require a basic understanding of how to perform LDAP searches using a base DN, search scope, and search filter as described in RFC 2251 and 2254. The base DN is where the search begins in the directory tree. The search scope defines how far down in the tree to search from the base DN. The search filter is a prefix notation string that contains equality comparisons of attribute and value pairs.

The scope can be base, onelevel (or one), or subtree (or sub). A base scope will only match the base DN, onelevel will only match objects that are contained directly under the base DN, and subtree will match everything from the base DN and any objects beneath it.

There are no LDAP query scopes that will walk backward "up" the tree.

The search filter syntax is a powerful way to represent simple and complex queries. For example, a filter that matches all of the user objects would be (&(objectclass=user)(objectcategory=Person)). For more information on filters, see RFC 2254.

Using a graphical user interface

To customize the list of attributes returned for each matching object, look at the GUI discussion in Recipe 4.2.

Using a command-line interface

<AttrList> should be a space-separated list of attributes to return. To return all attributes that have been populated with a value, leave this field blank or use an asterisk (*).

Using VBScript

The VBScript solution used ADO to perform the search. When using ADO, you must first create a connection object with the following three lines:

```
set objConn = CreateObject("ADODB.Connection")
objConn.Provider = "ADsDSOObject"
objConn.Open "Active Directory Provider"
```

At this point you can pass parameters to the Execute method, which will return a ResultSet object. You can iterate over the ResultSet by using the MoveFirst and MoveNext methods.

See Recipe 4.9 for more information on specifying advanced options in ADO like the page size.

See Also

Recipe 4.2 for viewing attributes of objects, Recipe 4.9 for setting advanced ADO options, RFC 2251 (Lightweight Directory Access Protocol (v3)), RFC 2254 (Lightweight Directory Access Protocol (v3)), MSDN: Searching with ActiveX Data Objects (ADO), and for a good white paper on performing queries with LDAP see: *http://www.microsoft.com/windows2000/techinfo/howitworks/activedirectory/ldap.asp*

4.9   Searching the Global Catalog

Problem

You want to perform a forest-wide search using the global catalog.

Solution

Using a graphical user interface

1. Open LDP from the Windows Support Tools.
2. From the menu, select Connection → Connect.
3. For Server, enter the name of a global catalog server.

4. For Port, enter 3268.

5. Click OK.

6. From the menu, select Connection → Bind.

7. Enter the credentials of a user.

8. Click OK.

9. From the menu, select Browse → Search.

10. For BaseDN, type the base distinguished name of where to start the search.

11. For Scope, select the appropriate scope.

12. For Filter, enter an LDAP filter.

13. Click Run.

Using a command-line interface

To query the global catalog using DSQuery, use the following syntax:

```
> dsquery * <BaseDN> -gc -scope <Scope> -filter "<Filter>" -attr "<AttrList>"
```

To run a query using AdFind, use the following syntax:

```
> adfind –gc –b <BaseDN> -s <Scope> –f <Filter> <Attributes>
```

Using VBScript

```
' This code searches the global catalog
' ------ SCRIPT CONFIGURATION ------
strBase   = "<GC://<BaseDN>>;"
strFilter = "<Filter>;"
strAttrs  = "<AttrList>;"
strScope  = "<Scope>"
' ------ END CONFIGURATION ---------

set objConn = CreateObject("ADODB.Connection")
objConn.Provider = "ADsDSOObject"
objConn.Open "Active Directory Provider"
set objRS = objConn.Execute(strBase & strFilter & strAttrs & strScope)
objRS.MoveFirst
while Not objRS.EOF
    Wscript.Echo objRS.Fields(0).Value
    objRS.MoveNext
wend
```

Discussion

The global catalog facilitates forest-wide searches. When you perform a normal LDAP search over port 389, you are searching against a particular partition within Active Directory, whether that is the Domain naming context, Configuration naming context, Schema naming context, or an application partition. If you have multiple domains in your forest, this type of search will not search against all domains but only the domain that you specify.

The global catalog, by contrast, contains a subset of the attributes for all objects in the forest (excluding objects in application partitions). Think of it as a subset of all the naming contexts combined. Every object in the directory will be contained in the global catalog (except for objects contained within application partitions), but only some of the attributes of those objects will be available. For that reason, if you perform a global catalog search and do not get values for attributes you were expecting to, make sure those attributes are included in the global catalog, also known as the partial attribute set (PAS). See Recipe 11.11 for more information on adding information to the PAS. As an alternative, you can query a DC within the domain containing the object to return a list of all attributes configured for that object.

Using a graphical user interface

The only difference between this solution and Recipe 4.8 is that the "Port" has changed to 3268, which is the standard GC port.

Using a command-line interface

The only difference between this solution and Recipe 4.8, both for DSQuery and AdFind, is the addition of the -gc flag.

Using VBScript

The only difference between this solution and Recipe 4.8 is that strBase variable changed to use the GC: progID:

```
strBase = "<GC://<BaseDN>>;"
```

See Also

Recipe 11.11, Recipe 4.8 for searching for objects and MSDN: Searching with ActiveX Data Objects (ADO)

4.10 Searching for a Large Number of Objects

Problem

Your search is returning exactly 1,000 objects, which is only a subset of the objects you expected, and you want it to return all matching objects.

Solution

You might notice that searches with large numbers of matches stop displaying after 1,000. Domain controllers return only a maximum of 1,000 entries from a search unless paging is enabled. This is done to prevent queries from consuming a lot of resources on domain controllers by retrieving the results all at once instead of in pages or batches. The following examples are variations of Recipe 4.8, which will show how to enable paging and return all matching entries.

Using a graphical user interface

1. Open LDP from the Windows Support Tools.
2. From the menu, select Connection → Connect.
3. For Server, enter the name of a domain controller (or leave blank to do a server-less bind).
4. For Port, enter 389.
5. Click OK.
6. From the menu, select Connection → Bind.
7. Enter the credentials of a user.
8. Click OK.
9. From the menu, select Browse → Search.
10. For BaseDN, type the base distinguished name of where the search will start. (You can leave this blank if you wish to connect to the domain NC as the base DN.)
11. For Scope, select the appropriate scope.
12. For Filter, enter an LDAP filter.
13. Click Options to customize the options for this query.
14. For Timeout (s), enter a value such as 10.
15. For Page size, enter the number of objects to be returned with each page (e.g., 1,000).
16. Under Search Call Type, select Paged.
17. Click OK and then Run to perform the query. A page of results (i.e., 1,000 entries) will be displayed each time you click Run until all results have been returned.

Using a command-line interface

```
> dsquery * <BaseDN> -limit 0 -scope <Scope> -filter "<Filter>" -attr "<AttrList>"
```

Using VBScript

```
' This code enables paged searching
' ------ SCRIPT CONFIGURATION ------
strBase   = "<LDAP://<BaseDN>>;"
strFilter = "<Filter>;"
strAttrs  = "<AttrList>;"
strScope  = "<Scope>"
' ------ END CONFIGURATION ---------
```

```
set objConn = CreateObject("ADODB.Connection")
objConn.Provider = "ADsDSOObject"
objConn.Open "Active Directory Provider"
set objComm = CreateObject("ADODB.Command")
objComm.ActiveConnection = objConn
objComm.Properties("Page Size") = 1000
objComm.CommandText = strBase & strFilter & strAttrs & strScope
set objRS = objComm.Execute
objRS.MoveFirst
while Not objRS.EOF
    Wscript.Echo objRS.Fields(0).Value
    objRS.MoveNext
wend
```

Discussion

Paged searching support is implemented via an LDAP control. LDAP controls were defined in RFC 2251 and the Paged control in RFC 2696. Controls are extensions to LDAP that were not built into the protocol, so not all directory vendors support the same ones.

In Active Directory, you can change the default maximum page size of 1,000 by modifying the LDAP query policy. See Recipe 4.27 for more information.

If you need searches to return hundreds of thousands of entries, Active Directory will return a maximum of only 262,144 entries even when paged searching is enabled. This value is defined in the LDAP query policy and can be modified like the maximum page size (see Recipe 4.27).

Using a graphical user interface

A word of caution when using LDAP to display a large number of entries—by default, only 2,048 lines will be displayed in the right pane. To change that value, go to Options → General and change the Line Value under Buffer Size to a larger number.

Using a command-line interface

The only difference between this solution and Recipe 4.8 is the addition of the -limit 0 flag. With -limit set to 0, paging will be enabled according to the default LDAP query policy; matching objects will be returned within those parameters. If -limit is not specified, a maximum of 100 entries will be returned.

AdFind will return a large number of objects from a query without any modification.

Using VBScript

To enable paged searching in ADO, you must instantiate an ADO Command object. A Command object allows for various properties of a query to be set, such as size limit, time limit, and page size. See MSDN for the complete list.

See Also

Recipe 4.8 for searching for objects, Recipe 4.27 for viewing the default LDAP policy, RFC 2251 (Lightweight Directory Access Protocol (v3)), RFC 2696 (LDAP Control Extension for Simple Paged Results Manipulation), and MSDN: Searching with ActiveX Data Objects (ADO)

4.11 Searching with an Attribute-Scoped Query

 This recipe requires the Windows Server 2003 forest functional level.

Problem

You want to perform a search using an individual value within a multivalued attribute as part of the search criteria. An attribute-scoped query can do this in a single query, instead of the previous method, which required multiple queries.

Solution

Using a graphical user interface

1. Follow the steps in Recipe 4.4 to enable an LDAP control.
2. Select the Attribute Scoped Query control (you can select controls by name with the Windows Server 2003 version of LDAP). For the Windows 2000 version of LDAP, add a control with an OID of 1.2.840.113556.1.4.1504.
3. For Value, enter the multivalued attribute name (e.g., member).
4. Click the Check in button.
5. Click OK.
6. From the menu, select Browse → Search.
7. For BaseDN, type the DN of the object that contains the multivalued attributes.
8. For Scope, select Base.
9. For Filter, enter an LDAP filter to match against the objects that are part of the multivalued DN attribute.
10. Click Run.

Attribute-scoped queries can only be performed using a Base scope.

Using a command-line interface

AdFind has recently been updated to permit attribute-scoped queries by using the `<Code>-asq</Code>` switch.

Using VBScript

At the time of publication of this book, you cannot use attribute-scoped queries with ADSI, ADO, and VBScript. In an ADO search, you can use the `ADSI Flags` property as part of a `Connection` object to set the search preference, but there is no way to set the attribute that should be matched, which must be included as part of the LDAP control.

Discussion

When dealing with group objects, you may have encountered the problem where you wanted to search against the members of a group to find a subset or to retrieve certain attributes about each member. This normally involved performing a query to retrieve all of the members, and additional queries to retrieve whatever attributes you needed for each member. This was less than ideal, so an alternative was developed for Windows Server 2003.

With an attribute-scoped query, you can perform a single query against the `group` object and return whatever properties you need from the member's object, or return only a subset of the members based on certain criteria. Let's look at the LDAP search parameters for an attribute-scoped query:

Attribute Scoped Query Control Value
>   The value to set for this control should be the multivalued DN attribute that you want to iterate over (e.g., `member`).

Base DN
>   This must be the DN of the object that contains the multivalued DN attribute (e. g., `cn=DomainAdmins,cn=users,dc=rallencorp,dc=com`).

Scope
>   This must be set to `Base` to query only the group object itself.

Filter
>   The filter will match against objects defined in the Control Value. For example, a filter of `(&(objectclass=user)(objectcategory=Person))` would match user objects only. You can also use any other attributes that are available with those objects. The following filter would match all user objects that have a `department` attribute equal to "Sales":

>   `(&(objectclass=user)(objectcategory=Person)(department=Sales))`

Attributes
   This should contain the list of attributes to return for object matched in the multivalued DN.

See Also

Recipe 4.4, MSDN: Performing an Attribute Scoped Query and MSDN: Searching with ActiveX Data Objects (ADO)

4.12   Searching with a Bitwise Filter

Problem

You want to search against an attribute that contains a *bit flag*, which requires you to use a bitwise filter to perform the search.

Solution

Using a graphical user interface

1. Open LDP from the Windows Support Tools.
2. From the menu, select Connection → Connect.
3. For Server, enter the name of a domain controller (or leave blank to do a server-less bind).
4. For Port, enter 389.
5. Click OK.
6. From the menu, select Connection → Bind.
7. Enter credentials of a user.
8. Click OK.
9. From the menu, select Browse → Search.
10. For BaseDN, type the base distinguished name of where the search will start. (You can leave this blank if you wish to connect to the domain NC as the base DN.)
11. For Scope, select the appropriate scope.
12. For the Filter, enter the bitwise expression, such as the following, which will find all universal groups:

    ```
    (&(objectclass=group)(objectCategory=group)(groupType:1.2.840.113556.1.4.804:=8))
    ```
13. Click Run.

Using a command-line interface

The following query finds universal groups in the *rallencorp.com* domain by using a bitwise OR filter:

```
> dsquery * dc=rallencorp,dc=com -scope subtree -attr "name" -filter
"(&(objectclass=group)(objectCategory=group)
(groupType:1.2.840.113556.1.4.804:=8) )"
```

The following query finds disabled user accounts in the *rallencorp.com* domain by using a bitwise AND filter:

```
> dsquery * dc=rallencorp,dc=com -attr name -scope subtree -filter
"(&(objectclass=user)(objectcategory=person)(useraccountcontrol:1.2.840.113556.1.4.
803:=514))"
```

You can also perform queries that use bitwise filters using AdFind. The following will find all disabled user accounts in the *rallencorp.com* domain:

```
> adfind -default -bit -f useraccountcontrol:AND:=2
```

Similarly, the following will return all universal groups in the *rallencorp.com* domain using a bitwise filter:

```
> adfind -default -bit -f groupType:AND:=8
```

Using VBScript

```
' The following query finds all disabled user accounts in the
' rallencorp.com domain
strBase   = "<LDAP://dc=rallencorp,dc=com>;"
strFilter = "(&(objectclass=user)(objectcategory=person)" & _
            "(useraccountcontrol:1.2.840.113556.1.4.803:=2));"
strAttrs  = "name;"
strScope  = "subtree"

set objConn = CreateObject("ADODB.Connection")
objConn.Provider = "ADsDSOObject"
objConn.Open "Active Directory Provider"
set objRS = objConn.Execute(strBase & strFilter & strAttrs & strScope)
objRS.MoveFirst
while Not objRS.EOF
    Wscript.Echo objRS.Fields(0).Value
    objRS.MoveNext
wend
```

Discussion

Many attributes in Active Directory are composed of bit flags. A bit flag is often used to encode properties about an object into a single attribute. For example, the groupType attribute on group objects is a bit flag that is used to determine the group scope and type.

The userAccountControl attribute on user and computer objects is used to describe a whole series of properties, including account status (i.e., enabled or disabled), account lockout, password not required, smartcard authentication required, etc.

The searchFlags and systemFlags attributes on attributeSchema objects define, among other things, whether an attribute is constructed, indexed, and included as part of Ambiguous Name Resolution (ANR).

To search against these types of attributes, you need to use bitwise search filters. There are two types of bitwise search filters you can use, one that represents a logical OR and one that represents logical AND. This is implemented within a search filter as a *matching rule*. A matching rule is simply a way to inform the LDAP server (in this case, a domain controller) to treat part of the filter differently. Here is an example of what a matching rule looks like:

```
(userAccountControl:1.2.840.113556.1.4.803:=514)
```

The format is (*attributename*:*MatchingRuleOID*:=*value*), though AdFind allows you to use an easier syntax for bitwise queries. As mentioned, there are two bitwise matching rules, which are defined by OIDs. The logical AND matching rule OID is 1.2.840.113556.1.4.803 and the logical OR matching rule OID is 1.2.840.113556.1.4.804. These OIDs instruct the server to perform special processing on the filter. A logical OR filter will return success if any bit specified by *value* is stored in *attributename*. Alternatively, the logical AND filter will return success if all bits specified by *value* match the value of *attributename*. Perhaps an example will help clarify this.

To create a normal user account, you have to set userAccountControl to 514. The number 514 was calculated by adding the normal user account flag of 512 together with the disabled account flag of 2 (512 + 2 = 514). If you use the following logical OR matching rule against the 514 value, as shown here:

```
(useraccountcontrol:1.2.840.113556.1.4.804:=514)
```

then all normal user accounts (flag 512) OR disabled accounts (flag 2) would be returned. This would include enabled user accounts (from flag 512), disabled computer accounts (from flag 2), and disabled user accounts (from flag 2). In the case of userAccountControl, flag 2 can apply to both user and computer accounts, which is why both would be included in the returned entries.

One way to see the benefits of bitwise matching rules is that they allow you to combine a bunch of comparisons into a single filter. In fact, it may help to think that the OR filter could also be written using two expressions:

```
(|(useraccountcontrol:1.2.840.113556.1.4.804:=2)
(useraccountcontrol:1.2.840.113556.
1.4.804:=512))
```

Just as before, this will match userAccountControl attributes that contain either the 2 or 512 flags; we're performing two OR operations against the same value, first ORing the value against 2, then against 512.

For the logical AND operator, similar principles apply. Instead of any of the bits in the flag being a possible match, ALL of the bits in the flag must match for it to return a success. If the userAccountControl example was changed to use logical AND, it would look like this:

```
(useraccountcontrol:1.2.840.113556.1.4.803:=514)
```

In this case, only normal user accounts that are also disabled would be returned. The same filter could be rewritten using the & operator instead of | as in the following:

```
(&(useraccountcontrol:1.2.840.113556.1.4.803:=2)
(useraccountcontrol:1.2.840.113556.1.4.803:=512))
```

An important subtlety to note is that when you are comparing only a single bit flag value, the logical OR and logical AND matching rule would return the same result. So if you wanted to find any normal user accounts you could search on the single bit flag of 512 using either of the following:

```
(useraccountcontrol:1.2.840.113556.1.4.803:=512)
```

```
(useraccountcontrol:1.2.840.113556.1.4.804:=512)
```

See Also

MSDN: Enumerating Groups by Scope or Type in a Domain, MSDN: Determining Which Properties Are Non-Replicated, Constructed, Global Catalog, and Indexed, and MS KB 305144 (How to Use the UserAccountControl Flags to Manipulate User Account Properties)

4.13   Creating an Object

Problem

You want to create an object.

Solution

In each solution below, an example of adding a user object is shown. Modify the examples as needed to include whatever class and attributes you need to create.

Using a graphical user interface

1. Open ADSI Edit from the Windows Support Tools.
2. If an entry for the naming context you want to browse is not already displayed, do the following:
   a. Right-click on ADSI Edit in the right pane and click "Connect to…."

b. Fill in the information for the naming context, container, or OU you want to add an object to. Click on the Advanced button if you need to enter alternate credentials.

3. In the left pane, browse to the container or OU you want to add the object to. Once you've found the parent container, right-click on it and select New → Object.

4. Under Select a Class, select user.

5. For the cn, enter jsmith and click Next.

6. For sAMAccountName, enter jsmith and click Next.

7. Click the More Attributes button to enter additional attributes.

8. Click Finish.

You can also create an object using LDP as follows:

1. Open LDP from the Windows Support Tools.

2. From the menu, select Connection → Connect.

3. For Server, enter the name of a domain controller (or leave blank to do a serverless bind).

4. For Port, enter 389.

5. Click OK.

6. From the menu, select Connection → Bind.

7. Enter credentials of a user.

8. Click OK.

9. Click Browse → Add Child. For DN, enter the Distinguished Name of the object that you want to create.

10. Under Attribute and Values, enter the name of any attribute that you want to populate along with its associated value, and then click Enter. Repeat this until you've added all of the required attributes for the type of object you are creating, as well as any optional attributes that you want to populate.

11. Click Run to create the object.

Using a command-line interface

Create an LDIF file called *create_object.ldf* with the following contents:

```
dn: cn=jsmith,cn=users,dc=rallencorp,dc=com
changetype: add
objectClass: user
samaccountname: jsmith
```

Then run the following command:

```
> ldifde -v -i -f create_object.ldf
```

It is also worth noting that you can add a limited number of object types with the dsadd command. Run dsadd /? from a command line for more details.

You can also create objects using AdMod; to create a new user object in the *rallencorp.com* domain use the following syntax:

```
> C:\>admod -b "cn=Joe Smith,cn=users,dc=rallencorp,dc=com"
     objectclass::user samaccountname::jsmith -add
```

Using VBScript

```
set objUsersCont = GetObject("LDAP://cn=users,dc=rallencorp,dc=com")
set objUser = objUsersCont.Create("user", "CN=jsmith")
objUser.Put "sAMAccountName", "jsmith" ' mandatory in Windows 2000
objUser.SetInfo
```

Discussion

To create an object in Active Directory, you have to specify the objectClass, RDN value, and any other mandatory attributes that are not automatically set by Active Directory. Some of the automatically generated attributes include objectGUID, instanceType, and objectCategory.

In the jsmith example, the object class was user, the RDN value was jsmith, and the only other attribute set was sAMAccountName; this attribute is only mandatory in Windows 2000, is it optional in Windows Server 2003, and cannot be set at all in ADAM. Admittedly, this user object is unusable in its current state because it will be disabled by default and no password was set, but it should give you an idea of how to create an object. In the case of a user object, you'll need to configure a password that meets any existing password complexity requirements before enabling the user.

Using a graphical user interface

Other tools, such as AD Users and Computers, could be used to do the same thing, but ADSI Edit is useful as a generic object editor.

One attribute that you will not be able to set via ADSI Edit is the password (unicodePwd attribute). It is stored in binary form and needs to be edited using a secure connection. If you want to set the password for a user through a GUI, you can do it with the AD Users and Computers snap-in.

Using a command-line interface

For more on *ldifde*, see Recipe 4.28.

With DSAdd, you can set numerous attributes when creating an object. The downside is that as of the publication of this book, you can create only these object types: computer, contact, group, OU, quota, and user.

Using VBScript

The first step to create an object is to call `GetObject` on the parent container. Then call the `Create` method on that object and specify the `objectClass` and RDN for the new object. The `sAMAccountName` attribute is then set by using the `Put` method. Finally, `SetInfo` commits the change. If `SetInfo` is not called, the creation will not get committed to the domain controller.

See Also

Recipe 4.28, Recipe 4.29 for importing objects using LDIF, MSDN: IADsContainer:: GetObject, MSDN: IADsContainer::Create, MSDN: IADs::Put, and MSDN: IADs:: SetInfo

4.14 Modifying an Object

Problem

You want to modify one or more attributes of an object.

Solution

The following examples set the last name (sn) attribute for the `jsmith` user object.

Using a graphical user interface

1. Open ADSI Edit.
2. If an entry for the naming context you want to browse is not already displayed, do the following:
   a. Right-click on ADSI Edit in the right pane and click "Connect to…."
   b. Fill in the information for the naming context, container, or OU you want to add an object to. Click on the Advanced button if you need to enter alternate credentials.
3. In the left pane, browse to the container or OU that contains the object you want to modify. Once you've found the object, right-click on it and select Properties.
4. Right-click the sn attribute and select Edit.
5. Enter Smith and click OK.
6. Click Apply, followed by OK.

You can also modify an object using LDP as follows:

1. Open LDP from the Windows Support Tools.
2. From the menu, select Connection → Connect.

3. For Server, enter the name of a domain controller (or leave blank to do a server-less bind).

4. For Port, enter 389.

5. Click OK.

6. From the menu, select Connection → Bind.

7. Enter credentials of a user.

8. Click OK.

9. Click Browse → Modify. For DN, enter the Distinguished Name of the object that you want to modify.

10. Under Attribute and Values, enter the name of any attribute that you want to modify along with its associated value, and then click Enter. Repeat this until you've added all of the attributes that you want to modify.

11. Click Run to modify the object.

Using a command-line interface

Create an LDIF file called *modify_object.ldf* with the following contents:

```
dn: cn=jsmith,cn=users,dc=rallencorp,dc=com
changetype: modify
replace: givenName
givenName: Jim
-
```

Then run the following command:

```
> ldifde -v -i -f modify_object.ldf
```

To modify an object using AdMod, you'll use the following general syntax:

```
> admod -b <ObjectDN> <attribute>:<operation>:<value>
```

For example, you can add a description to a user object using the following syntax:

```
> C:\>admod -b cn="Joe Smith,cn=Users,dc=rallencorp,dc=com"
        description::Consultant
```

You can modify a limited number of object types with the dsmod command. Run dsmod /? from a command line for more details.

Using VBScript

```
strObjectDN = "cn=jsmith,cn=users,dc=rallencorp,dc=com"
set objUser = GetObject("LDAP://" & strObjectDN)
objUser.Put "sn", "Smith"
objUser.SetInfo
```

Discussion

Using a graphical user interface

If the parent container of the object you want to modify has a lot of objects in it, you may want to add a new connection entry for the DN of the target object. This will be easier than trying to hunt through a container full of objects. You can do this by right-clicking ADSI Edit and selecting "Connect to…." Under Connection Point, select Distinguished Name and enter the DN of the object.

Using a command-line interface

For more on *ldifde*, see Recipe 4.28.

As of the publication of this book, the only types of objects you can modify with DSMod are computer, contact, group, ou, server, quota and user.

As you saw in the recipe, the basic format of the AdMod command when used to modify an attribute is as follows:

```
> admod -b <ObjectDN> <attribute>:<operation>:<value>
```

The value used for *<operation>* can be any one of the following:

<blank>
: Updates the attribute with the new value. (In practical terms, this leads to a syntax of *<attribute>*::*<value>*, with nothing included between the two colons.)

+
: Adds a value to an attribute.

-
: Clears an attribute.

++
: Adds multiple values to an attribute.

--
: Removes multiple values from an attribute.

AdMod also has a special syntax to allow you to modify a password from the command-line, which cannot be performed from ADSI Edit since the password attribute is stored as a Registry BLOB that cannot be edited. To configure a new password using AdMod, simply use the following syntax:

```
> admod -b cn=joe,cn=marketing,dc=rallencorp,dc=com #setpwd#::newpass
```

 You can also modify the unicodepwd attribute directly by encrypting the AdMod connection using the -kerbenc switch.

Using VBScript

If you need to do anything more than simple assignment or replacement of a value for an attribute, you'll need to use the PutEx method instead of Put. PutEx allows for greater control of assigning multiple values, deleting specific values, and appending values.

PutEx requires three parameters: update flag, attribute name, and an array of values to set or unset. The update flags are defined by the ADS_PROPERTY_OPERATION_ENUM collection and listed in Table 4-3. Finally, SetInfo commits the change. If SetInfo is not called, the creation will not get committed to the domain controller.

Table 4-3. ADS_PROPERTY_OPERATION_ENUM

Name	Value	Description
ADS_PROPERTY_CLEAR	1	Remove all value(s) of the attribute.
ADS_PROPERTY_UPDATE	2	Replace the current values of the attribute with the ones passed in. This will clear any previously set values.
ADS_PROPERTY_APPEND	3	Add the values passed into the set of existing values of the attribute.
ADS_PROPERTY_DELETE	4	Delete the values passed in.

In the sample below, each update flag is used while setting the otherTelephoneNumber attribute:

```
strObjectDN = "cn=jsmith,cn=users,dc=rallencorp,dc=com"

const ADS_PROPERTY_CLEAR  = 1
const ADS_PROPERTY_UPDATE = 2
const ADS_PROPERTY_APPEND = 3
const ADS_PROPERTY_DELETE = 4

set objUser = GetObject("LDAP://" & strObjectDN)

' Add/Append two values
objUser.PutEx ADS_PROPERTY_APPEND, "otherTelephoneNumber", _
            Array("555-1212", "555-1213")
objUser.SetInfo
' Now otherTelephoneNumber = 555-1212, 555-1213

' Delete one of the values
objUser.PutEx ADS_PROPERTY_DELETE, "otherTelephoneNumber", Array("555-1213")
objUser.SetInfo
' Now otherTelephoneNumber = 555-1212

' Change values
objUser.PutEx ADS_PROPERTY_UPDATE, "otherTelephoneNumber", Array("555-1214")
objUser.SetInfo
' Now otherTelephoneNumber = 555-1214

' Clear all values
```

```
objUser.PutEx ADS_PROPERTY_CLEAR, "otherTelephoneNumber",  vbNullString
objUser.SetInfo
' Now otherTelephoneNumber = <empty>
```

See Also

MSDN: IADs::Put, MSDN: IADs::PutEx, MSDN: IADs::SetInfo, and MSDN: ADS_
PROPERTY_OPERATION_ENUM

4.15   Modifying a Bit Flag Attribute

Problem

You want to modify an attribute that contains a bit flag.

Solution

Using VBScript

```
' This code safely modifies a bit flag attribute
' ------ SCRIPT CONFIGURATION ------
strObject = "<ObjectDN>"        ' e.g. cn=jsmith,cn=users,dc=rallencorp,dc=com
strAttr = "<AttrName>"          ' e.g. rallencorp-UserProperties
boolEnableBit = <TRUEorFALSE>   ' e.g. FALSE
intBit = <BitValue>             ' e.g. 16
' ------ END CONFIGURATION ---------

set objObject = GetObject("LDAP://" & strObject)
intBitsOrig = objObject.Get(strAttr)
intBitsCalc = CalcBit(intBitsOrig, intBit, boolEnableBit)

if intBitsOrig <> intBitsCalc then
   objObject.Put strAttr, intBitsCalc
   objObject.SetInfo
   WScript.Echo "Changed " & strAttr & " from " & intBitsOrig & " to " & intBitsCalc
else
   WScript.Echo "Did not need to change " & strAttr & " (" & intBitsOrig & ")"
end if


Function CalcBit(intValue, intBit, boolEnable)

   CalcBit = intValue

   if boolEnable = TRUE then
      CalcBit = intValue Or intBit
   else
      if intValue And intBit then
         CalcBit = intValue Xor intBit
      end if
   end if

End Function
```

Discussion

Recipe 4.12 described how to search against attributes that contain a bit flag, which are used to encode various settings about an object in a single attribute. As a quick recap, you need to use a logical OR operation to match any bits being searched against, and a logical AND to match a specific set of bits. If you want to set an attribute that is a bit flag, you need to take special precautions to ensure you don't overwrite an existing bit. Let's consider an example. RAllenCorp wants to secretly store some politically incorrect information about its users, including things like whether the user is really old or has big feet. They don't want to create attributes such as rallencorp-UserHasBigFeet, so they decide to encode the properties in a single bit flag attribute. They decide to call the attribute rallencorp-UserProperties with the possible bit values shown in Table 4-4.

Table 4-4. Sample bit flag attribute values

Value	Description
1	User is overweight
2	User is very tall
4	User has big feet
8	User is very old

After they extend the schema to include the new attribute, RAllenCorp needs to initially populate the attribute for all their users. To do so they can simply logically OR the values together that apply to each user. So if settings 4 and 8 apply to the *jsmith* user, his rallencorp-UserProperties would be set to 12 (4 OR 8). No big deal so far. The issue comes in when they need to modify the attribute in the future.

 You will, however, find that searching for information based on a bit flag attribute is not terribly efficient. This is because bit flags cannot be indexed; you need to calculate the value for every object populated with the bit flag attribute in question.

They later find out that *jsmith* was a former basketball player and is 6'8". They need to set the 2 bit (for being tall) in his rallencorp-UserProperties attribute. To set the 2 bit they need to first determine if it has already been set. If it has already been set, then there is nothing to do. If the 2 bit hasn't been set, they need to logical OR 2 with the existing value of *jsmith*'s rallencorp-UserProperties attribute. If they simply set the attribute to 2, it would overwrite the 4 and 8 bits that had been set previously. In the VBScript solution, they could use the CalcBit function to determine the new value:

```
intBitsCalc = CalcBit(intBitsOrig, 2, TRUE)
```

The result would be 14 (12 OR 2).

The same logic applies if they want to remove a bit, except the XOR logical operator is used.

 Active Directory contains numerous bit flag attributes, most notably options (which is used on several different object classes) and userAccountControl (which is used on user objects). We do not recommend blindly setting those attributes unless you know what you are doing. It is preferable to use a script from this recipe so that it calculates the new value based on the existing value.

You should note that it's certainly possible to modify bitwise attributes using a GUI tool like ADSI Edit or a command-line tool like DsMod or AdMod. However, it will require a certain amount of manual effort as you'll first need to make note of the existing attribute value and then calculate the new value using a calculator or some other method. The VBScript solution presented here simply automated that process by performing the lookup and calculations for you.

See Also

Recipe 4.12 for searching with a bitwise filter

4.16 Dynamically Linking an Auxiliary Class

 This recipe requires the Windows Server 2003 forest functional level.

Problem

You want to dynamically link an auxiliary class to an existing object instance.

Solution

In each solution below, an example of adding the custom rallencorp-SalesUser auxiliary class to the jsmith user object will be described.

Using a graphical user interface

1. Open ADSI Edit.
2. If an entry for the naming context you want to browse is not already displayed, do the following:
   a. Right-click on ADSI Edit in the right pane and click "Connect to...."
   b. Fill in the information for the naming context, container, or OU you want to add an object to. Click on the Advanced button if you need to enter alternate credentials.

3. In the left pane, browse to the container or OU that contains the object you want to modify. Once you've found the object, right-click on it and select Properties.

4. Right-click the sn attribute and select Edit.

5. Click the More Attributes button to enter additional attributes.

6. Edit the values for the objectClass attribute.

7. For "Value to add," enter rallencorp-SalesUser.

8. Click Add.

9. Click OK twice.

Using a command-line interface

Create an LDIF file called *dynamically_link_class.ldf* with the following contents:

```
dn: cn=jsmith,cn=users,dc=rallencorp,dc=com
changetype: modify
add: objectClass
objectClass: rallencorp-SalesUser
-
```

Then run the following command:

```
> ldifde -v -i -f dynamically_link_class.ldf
```

Alternately, you can use AdMod as follows:

```
> admod –b <ObjectDN> objectClass:+:<Dynamic Object Class>
```

Using VBScript

```
const ADS_PROPERTY_APPEND = 3
set objUser = GetObject("LDAP://cn=jsmith,cn=users,dc=rallencorp,dc=com")
objUser.PutEx ADS_PROPERTY_APPEND,"objectClass",Array("rallencorp-SalesUser")
objUser.SetInfo
```

Discussion

Dynamically linking an auxiliary class to an object is an easy way to use new attributes without modifying the object class definition in the schema directly. In Windows 2000, auxiliary classes could only be statically linked in the schema. With Windows Server 2003, you can dynamically link them by appending the auxiliary class name to the objectClass attribute of an object.

A situation in which it makes more sense to dynamically link auxiliary classes rather than link them statically is when several organizations or divisions within a company maintain their own user objects and want to add new attributes to the user class. Under Windows 2000, each organization would need to create their new attributes and auxiliary class in the schema, and then modify the user class to include the new auxiliary class. If you have 10 organizations that want to do the same thing, user objects in the forest could end up with a lot of attributes that would go unused. In Windows Server 2003, each division can instead create the new attributes and auxiliary class, and then dynamically link the auxiliary class with the specific objects that they want to have the new attributes. This eliminates the step of modifying the user class in the schema to contain the new auxiliary classes.

It is also worth mentioning that extensive use of dynamically linked auxiliary classes can lead to problems. If several groups are using different auxiliary classes, it might become hard to determine what attributes you can expect on your user objects. Essentially, you could end up with many variations of a user class that each group has implemented through the use of dynamic auxiliary classes. For this reason, use of dynamic auxiliary classes should be closely monitored. In addition, some tools that access Active Directory may not work properly with auxiliary classes.

See Also

Recipe 4.14 for modifying an object

4.17   Creating a Dynamic Object

 This recipe requires the Windows Server 2003 forest functional level.

Problem

You want to create an object that is automatically deleted after a period of time unless it is refreshed.

Solution

Using a graphical user interface

At the time of publication of this book, neither ADSI Edit nor LDP supported creating dynamic objects.

Using a command-line interface

Create an LDIF file called *create_dynamic_object.ldf* with the following contents:

```
dn: cn=jsmith,cn=users,dc=rallencorp,dc=com
changetype: add
objectClass: user
objectClass: dynamicObject
entryTTL: 1800
sAMAccountName: jsmith
```

Then run the following command:

```
> ldifde -v -i -f create_dynamic_object.ldf
```

Using VBScript

```
' This code creates a dynamic user object with a TTL of 30 minutes (1800 secs)
set objUsersCont = GetObject("LDAP://cn=users,dc=rallencorp,dc=com")
set objUser = objUsersCont.Create("user", "CN=jsmith")
objUser.Put "objectClass", "dynamicObject"
objUser.Put "entryTTL", 1800
objUser.Put "sAMAccountName", "jsmith" ' mandatory attribute
objUser.SetInfo
```

Discussion

The ability to create dynamic objects is a new feature in Windows Server 2003, which you can use to create objects that only have a limited lifespan before they are automatically removed from the directory. To create a dynamic object, you simply need to specify the objectClass to have a value of dynamicObject in addition to its structural objectClass (e.g., user) value when instantiating the object. The entryTTL attribute can also be set to the number of seconds before the object is automatically deleted. If entryTTL is not set, the object will use the dynamicObjectDefaultTTL attribute specified in the domain. The entryTTL cannot be lower than the dynamicObjectMinTTL for the domain. See Recipe 4.19 for more information on how to view and modify these default values.

Dynamic objects have a few special properties worth noting:

- A static object cannot be turned into a dynamic object. The object must be marked as dynamic when it is created.
- Dynamic objects cannot be created in the Configuration NC and Schema NC.
- Dynamic objects do not leave behind tombstone objects.
- Dynamic objects that are containers cannot have static child objects.

See Also

Recipe 4.18 for refreshing a dynamic object and Recipe 4.19 for modifying the default dynamic object properties

4.18 Refreshing a Dynamic Object

 This recipe requires the Windows Server 2003 forest functional level.

Problem

You want to refresh a dynamic object to keep it from expiring and getting deleted from Active Directory.

Solution

In each solution below, an example of adding a user object is used. Modify the examples as needed to refresh whatever object is needed.

Using a graphical user interface

1. Open LDP.
2. From the menu, select Connection → Connect.
3. For Server, enter the name of a domain controller (or leave it blank to do a serverless bind).
4. For Port, enter 389.
5. Click OK.
6. From the menu, select Connection → Bind.
7. Enter credentials of a user that can modify the object.
8. Click OK.
9. Select Browse → Modify.
10. For DN, enter the DN of the dynamic object you want to refresh.
11. For Attribute, enter entryTTL.
12. For Values, enter the new time to live (TTL) for the object in seconds.
13. Under Operation, select Replace.
14. Click Enter.
15. Click Run.

Using a command-line interface

Create an LDIF file called *refresh_dynamic_object.ldf* with the following contents:

```
dn: cn=jsmith,cn=users,dc=rallencorp,dc=com
changetype: modify
replace: entryTTL
entryTTL: 1800
-
```

Then run the following command:

```
> ldifde -v -i -f refresh_dynamic_object.ldf
```

You can also use AdMod with the following syntax:

```
> admod -b <ObjectDN> entryTTL::<TTL in Seconds>
```

Using VBScript

```
set objUser = GetObject("LDAP://cn=jsmith,cn=users,dc=rallencorp,dc=com")
objUser.Put "entryTTL", "1800"
objUser.SetInfo
```

Discussion

Dynamic objects expire after their TTL becomes 0. You can determine when a dynamic object will expire by looking at the current value of an object's entryTTL attribute or by querying msDS-Entry-Time-To-Die, which contains the seconds remaining until expiration. If you've created a dynamic object and need to refresh it so that it will not get deleted, you must reset the entryTTL attribute to a new value. There is no limit to the number of times you can refresh a dynamic object. As long as the entryTTL value does not reach 0, the object will remain in Active Directory.

See Also

Recipe 4.14 for modifying an object and Recipe 4.17 for creating a dynamic object

4.19   Modifying the Default TTL Settings for Dynamic Objects

Problem

You want to modify the minimum and default TTLs for dynamic objects.

Solution

In each solution below, we'll show how to set the DynamicObjectDefaultTTL setting to 172800. Modifying the DynamicObjectMinTTL can be done in the same manner.

Using a graphical user interface

1. Open ADSI Edit.
2. If an entry for the Configuration naming context is not already displayed, do the following:
   a. Right-click on ADSI Edit in the right pane and click "Connect to…."
   b. Fill in the information for the naming context for your forest. Click on the Advanced button if you need to enter alternate credentials.
3. In the left pane, browse to the following path under the Configuration naming context: Services → Windows NT → Directory Service.
4. Right-click cn=Directory Service and select Properties.
5. Edit the msDS-Other-Settings attribute.
6. Click on DynamicObjectDefaultTTL=<xxxxx> and click Remove.
7. The attribute/value pair should have been populated in the "Value to add" field.
8. Edit the number part of the value to be 172800.
9. Click Add.
10. Click OK twice.

Using a command-line interface

The following `ntdsutil` command connects to *<DomainControllerName>*, displays the current values for the dynamic object TTL settings, sets the DynamicObjectDefaultTTL to 172800, commits the change, and displays the results:

```
> ntdsutil "config settings" connections "connect to server <DomainControllerName>"
  q "show values" "set DynamicObjectDefaultTTL to 172800" "commit changes"
  "show values" q q
```

Using VBScript

```
' This code modifies the default TTL setting for dynamic objects in a forest
' ------ SCRIPT CONFIGURATION ------
strNewValue    = 172800

'Could be DynamicObjectMinTTL instead if you wanted to set that instead
strTTLSetting = "DynamicObjectDefaultTTL"
' ------ END CONFIGURATION ---------

const ADS_PROPERTY_APPEND = 3
const ADS_PROPERTY_DELETE = 4

set objRootDSE = GetObject("LDAP://RootDSE")
set objDS = GetObject("LDAP://CN=Directory Service,CN=Windows NT," & _
                      "CN=Services,CN=Configuration," & _
                      objRootDSE.Get("rootDomainNamingContext"))
for each strVal in objDS.Get("msDS-Other-Settings")
    Set objRegEx = New RegExp
    objRegEx.Pattern = strTTLSetting & "="
    objRegEx.IgnoreCase = True
    Set colMatches = objRegEx.Execute(strVal)
    For Each objMatch in colMatches
        Wscript.Echo "Deleting " & strVal
        objDS.PutEx ADS_PROPERTY_DELETE, "msDS-Other-Settings", Array(strVal)
        objDS.SetInfo
    Next
Next

Wscript.Echo "Setting " & strTTLSetting & "=" & strNewValue
objDS.PutEx ADS_PROPERTY_APPEND, _
         "msDS-Other-Settings", _
         Array(strTTLSetting & "=" & strNewValue)
objDS.SetInfo
```

Discussion

Two configuration settings apply to dynamic objects:

dynamicObjectDefaultTTL
: Defines the default TTL that is set for a dynamic object at creation time unless another one is set via entryTTL.

dynamicObjectMinTTL
: Defines the smallest TTL that can be configured for a dynamic object.

Unfortunately, these two settings are not stored as discrete attributes. Instead, they are stored as attribute-value-assertions (AVA) in the msDS-Other-Settings attribute on the cn=DirectoryServices,cn=WindowsNT,cn=Configuration,<ForestRootDN> object. AVAs are used occasionally in Active Directory on multivalued attributes, in which the values take the form of Setting1=Value1, Setting2=Value2, etc.

For this reason, you cannot simply manipulate AVA attributes as you would another attribute. You have to be sure to add or replace values with the same format, as they existed previously.

Using a command-line interface

You can use *ntdsutil* in interactive mode or in single-command mode. In this solution, we've included all the necessary commands on a single line. You can, of course, step through each command by simply running *ntdsutil* in interactive mode and entering each command one by one.

Using VBScript

Because you are dealing with AVAs, the VBScript solution is not very straightforward. Getting a pointer to the Directory Service object is easy, but then you must step through each value of the mSDS-Other-Settings attribute until you find the one you are looking for. The reason it is not straightforward is that you do not know the exact value of the setting you are looking for. All you know is that it begins with DynamicObjectDefaultTTL=. That is why it is necessary to resort to regular expressions. With a regular expression, you can compare each value against DefaultObjectDefaultTTL= and if you find a match, delete that value only. After you've iterated through all of the values and hopefully deleted the one you are looking for, you append the new setting using PutEx. Simple as that!

See Also

Recipe 4.14 for modifying an object and MSDN: Regular Expression (RegExp) Object

4.20   Moving an Object to a Different OU or Container

Problem

You want to move an object to a different container or OU.

Solution

Using a graphical user interface

1. Open ADSI Edit.

2. If an entry for the naming context you want to browse is not already displayed, do the following:

   a. Right-click on ADSI Edit in the right pane and click "Connect to...."

   b. Fill in the information for the naming context, container, or OU containing the object. Click on the Advanced button if you need to enter alternate credentials.

3. In the left pane, browse to the container, or OU that contains the object you want to modify. Once you've found the object, right-click on it and select Move.

4. Browse to the new parent of the object, select it, and click OK.

 You can also move most objects within the Active Directory Users and Computers MMC snap-in (*dsa.msc*) by navigating to the object in question, right-clicking on it, and selecting Move. In Windows Server 2003, you can also drag-and-drop the object to its new location.

Using a command-line interface

To move an object to a new parent container within the same domain, you can use either dsmove or admod, as follows:

```
> dsmove "<ObjectDN>" -newparent "<NewParentDN>"
```

Or:

```
> admod –b <ObjectDN> -move <NewParentDN>
```

Using VBScript

```
' This code moves an object from one location to another in the same domain.
' ------ SCRIPT CONFIGURATION ------
strNewParentDN = "LDAP://<NewParentDN>"
strObjectDN    = "LDAP://cn=jsmith,<OldParentDN>"
strObjectRDN   = "cn=jsmith"
' ------ END CONFIGURATION ---------

set objCont = GetObject(strNewParentDN)
objCont.MoveHere strObjectDN, strObjectRDN
```

Discussion

Using a graphical user interface

If the parent container of the object you want to move has a lot of objects in it, you may want to add a new connection entry for the DN of the object you want to move. This may save you time searching through the list of objects in the container. You can do this by right clicking ADSI Edit and selecting "Connect to...." Under Connection Point, select Distinguished Name and enter the DN of the object you want to move.

Using a command-line interface

The DSMove utility can work against any type of object (no limitations as with DSAdd and DSMod). The first parameter is the DN of the object to be moved. The second parameter is the new parent container of the object. The -s parameter can additionally be used to specify a specific server to work against.

Using VBScript

The MoveHere method can be tricky, so an explanation of how to use it to move objects is in order. First, you need to call GetObject on the new parent container. Then call MoveHere on the parent container object with the ADsPath of the object to move as the first parameter and the RDN of the object to move as the second.

The reason for the apparent duplication of cn=jsmith in the MoveHere method is that the same method can also be used for renaming objects within the same container (see Recipe 4.23).

 Regardless of the method you use to move objects, you need to ensure that the user who is performing the move has the appropriate permissions to create objects in the destination container.

See Also

Recipe 4.23, MS KB 313066 (How to Move Users, Groups, and Organizational Units Within a Domain in Windows 2000), and MSDN: IADsContainer::MoveHere

4.21 Moving an Object to a Different Domain

Problem

You want to move an object to a different domain.

Solution

Using a graphical user interface

To migrate user, computer, group, or OU objects between domains in the same forest, use the following steps:

1. Open the Active Directory Migration Tool (ADMT) MMC snap-in.
2. Right-click on the Active Directory Migration Tool folder, and select one of the following:
   - User Account Migration Wizard
   - Group Account Migration Wizard
   - Computer Migration Wizard

Using a command-line interface

To migrate objects from the command-line using the ADMT utility, use the following syntax:

```
> ADMT [ USER | GROUP | COMPUTER | SECURITY | SERVICE |
        REPORT | KEY | PASSWORD | CONFIG | TASK ] <Options>
```

For example, to migrate a computer object, you would use the following syntax:

```
> ADMT COMPUTER /N <ComputerName> /SD:<Source Domain> /TD:<Target Domain>
/TO:<Target OU>
```

To move an object using the movetree Resource Kit utility, use the following syntax:

```
> movetree /start /s SourceDC /d TargetDC /sdn SourceDN /ddn TargetDN
```

In the following example, the cn=jsmith object in the *amer.rallencorp.com* domain will be moved to the *emea.rallencorp.com* domain.

```
> movetree /start /s dc-amer1 /d dc-emea1\
  /ddn cn=jsmith,cn=users,dc=amer,dc=rallencorp,dc=com\
  /sdn cn=jsmith,cn=users,dc=emea,dc=rallencorp,dc=com\
```

 Movetree should only be used to migrate objects such as contacts that cannot currently be migrated by ADMT. In all other cases, Microsoft recommends using ADMT to move objects between domains.

Using VBScript

```
set objObject = GetObject("LDAP://TargetDC/TargetParentDN")
objObject.MoveHere "LDAP://SourceDC/SourceDN", vbNullString
```

In the following example, the cn=jsmith object in the *amer.rallencorp.com* domain will be moved to the *emea.rallencorp.com* domain.

```
set objObject = GetObject( _
    "LDAP://dc-amer1/cn=users,dc=amer,dc=rallencorp,dc=com")
objObject.MoveHere _
    "LDAP://dc-emea1/cn=jsmith,cn=users,dc=emea,dc=rallencorp,dc=com", _
    vbNullString
```

Discussion

You can move objects between domains assuming you follow a few guidelines:

- The user performing the move operation must have permission to modify objects in the parent container of both domains.
- You need to explicitly specify the target DC (serverless binds usually do not work). This is necessary because the "Cross Domain Move" LDAP control is being used behind the scenes. For more information on controls, see "Using LDAP Controls."
- The move operation must be performed against the RID master for both domains.

- Both domains must be in native mode.

- When you move a user object to a different domain, its objectSID is replaced with a new SID (based on the new domain), and the old SID is optionally added to the sIDHistory attribute.

See Also

Recipe 4.4 for more on LDAP controls, MS KB 238394 (How to Use the MoveTree Utility to Move Objects Between Domains in a Single Forest), MSDN: IADsContainer::MoveHere, and MS KB 326480 (How to Use Active Directory Migration Tool version 2 to migrate from Windows 2000 to Windows Server 2003)

4.22 Referencing an External Domain

Problem

You need to create a reference to an external Active Directory domain.

Solution

Using a graphical user interface

1. Open ADSI Edit from the Windows Support Tools.

2. If an entry for the naming context you want to browse is not already displayed, do the following:

   a. Right-click on ADSI Edit in the right pane and click "Connect to...."

   b. Fill in the information for the naming context, container, or OU you want to add an object to. Click on the Advanced button if you need to enter alternate credentials.

3. Right-click on the top-level node and open a connection to the Configuration NC.

4. Right-click on the Partitions container and select New → Object. Click Next.

5. For the cn attribute, enter the FQDN of the external domain, *othercorp.com* for example. Click Next.

6. For the nCName attribute, enter the DN of the external domain, such as dc=othercorp,dc=com. Click Next.

7. For the dnsRoot attribute, enter the DNS name of a server that can respond to LDAP queries about the domain in question, such as *dc1.othercorp.com*.

8. Click Next and then Finish to create the crossRef object.

Using a command-line interface

Create an LDIF file called *create_crossref.ldf* with the following contents:

```
dn: cn=othercorp.com,cn=partitions,cn=configuration,dc=rallencorp,dc=com
```

```
changetype: add
objectClass: crossRef
cn: othercorp.com
nCName: dc=othercorp,dc=com
dnsRoot: dc1.othercorp.com
```

Then run the following command:

```
> ldifde -v -i -f create_crossref.ldf
```

You can also create a `crossRef` using AdMod as follows:

```
> admod -b cn=othercorp.com,cn=partitions,cn=configuration,<ForestRootDN>
objectClass::crossRef cn::othercorp.com nCName::dc=othercorp,dc=com
dnsRoot::dc1.othercorp.com -add
```

Using VBScript

```
set objPartitions =
GetObject("LDAP://cn=partitions,cn=configuration,dc=rallencorp,dc=com")
set objCrossRef = objPartitions.Create("crossRef", "CN=othercorp.com")
objCrossRef.Put "cn", "othercorp.com" ' mandatory attribute
objCrossRef.Put "nCName", "dc=othercorp,dc=com" ' mandatory attribute
objCrossRef.Put "dnsRoot", "dc1.othercorp.com" ' mandatory attribute
objCrossRef.SetInfo
```

Discussion

Similar to the way in which DNS servers use iterative queries to resolve hostnames that can only be resolved by remote servers, LDAP uses *referrals* to resolve queries for objects contained in naming contexts that are not hosted by the local DC. When a DC receives any query, it will search the Partitions container for a `crossRef` object containing the DN that's being used as the Base DN of the query. If the DC locates a `crossRef` that matches the search base of the query, and that `crossRef` indicates a naming context that's hosted by the domain controller itself, then the DC will perform the search locally. If the `crossRef` refers to a NC that's hosted on a remote server, the DC generates a *referral* to the server that is pointed to by the `crossRef` object. If the DC can't locate a relevant `crossRef` object, it will use DNS to attempt to generate an additional location to refer the client to.

In most cases, Active Directory will generate LDAP referrals automatically. However, you should manually create a `crossRef` object to generate LDAP referrals for an external domain, such as referrals to *othercorp.com* that are generated by the *rallencorp.com* domain.

See Also

MS KB 241737 (How to Create a Cross-Reference to an External Domain in Active Directory), MS KB 817872 (How to Create crossRef Objects for a DNS Namespace Subordinate of an Existing Active Directory Forest), MSDN: Referrals [Active Directory], and MSDN: When Referrals Are Generated [Active Directory]

4.23 Renaming an Object

Problem

You want to rename an object and keep it in its current container or OU.

Solution

Using a graphical user interface

1. Open ADSI Edit.
2. If an entry for the naming context you want to browse is not already displayed, do the following:
   a. Right-click on ADSI Edit in the right pane and click "Connect to…."
   b. Fill in the information for the naming context, container, or OU that contains the object you want to rename. Click on the Advanced button if you need to enter alternate credentials.
3. In the left pane, browse to the container or OU that contains the object you want to modify. Once you've found the object, right-click on it and select Rename.
4. Enter the new name and click OK.

You can also rename a leaf object by using LDP as follows:

1. Open LDP from the Windows Support Tools.
2. From the menu, select Connection → Connect.
3. For Server, enter the name of a domain controller (or leave blank for a serverless bind).
4. For Port, enter 389.
5. Click OK.
6. From the menu, select Connection → Bind.
7. Enter credentials of a user.
8. Click OK.
9. Click Browse → Modify RDN. For Old DN, enter the Distinguished Name of the object that you want to rename. For New DN, enter the object's new name.
10. Click Run to rename the object.

Using a command-line interface

To rename an object using the built-in DSMove utility, use the following syntax:

```
> dsmove "<ObjectDN>" -newname "<NewName>"
```

To use AdMod, use the following:

```
> admod -b "<ObjectDN>" -rename "<NewName>"
```

Using VBScript

```
' This code renames an object and leaves it in the same location.
' ------ SCRIPT CONFIGURATION ------
strCurrentParentDN = "<CurrentParentDN>"
strObjectOldName   = "cn=<OldName>"
strObjectNewName   = "cn=<NewName>"
'      -- END CONFIGURATION ---------

set objCont = GetObject("LDAP://" & strCurrentParentDN)
objCont.MoveHere "LDAP://" & strObjectOldName & "," & _
               strCurrentParentDN, strObjectNewName
```

Discussion

Before you rename an object, you should ensure that no applications reference it by name. You can make objects rename-safe by requiring all applications that must store a reference to objects to use the GUID of the object, rather than the name.

The GUID (stored in the objectGUID attribute) is effectively unique and does not change when an object is renamed.

 Keep in mind that you may wish to perform other cleanup tasks when renaming an object. In the case of a user who is changing his name, you may wish to update his Display Name and sn attributes to match his new CN.

Using a graphical user interface

If the parent container of the object you want to rename has a lot of objects in it, you may want to add a new connection entry for the DN of the object you want to rename. This may save you time searching through the list of objects in the container. You can do this by right-clicking ADSI Edit and selecting "Connect to..." under Connection Point, select Distinguished Name and enter the DN of the object you want to rename.

You can also rename most objects within the Active Directory Users and Computers MMC snap-in (*dsa.msc*) by navigating to the object in question, right-clicking on it and selecting Rename.

Using a command-line interface

The two parameters that are needed to rename an object are the original DN of the object and the new RDN (-newname). The -s option can also be used to specify a server name to work against.

Using VBScript

The MoveHere method can be tricky to use, so an explanation of how to use it to rename objects is in order. First, you need to call GetObject on the parent container of the object you want to rename. Then call MoveHere on the parent container object and specify the ADsPath of the object to rename as the first parameter. The new RDN including prefix (e.g., cn=) of the object should be the second parameter.

See Also

MSDN: IADsContainer::MoveHere

4.24   Deleting an Object

Problem

You want to delete an individual object.

Solution

Using a graphical user interface

1. Open ADSI Edit.
2. If an entry for the naming context you want to browse is not already displayed, do the following:
   a. Right-click on ADSI Edit in the right pane and click "Connect to...."
   b. Fill in the information for the naming context, container, or OU that contains the object you want to delete. Click on the Advanced button if you need to enter alternate credentials.
3. In the left pane, browse to the object you want to delete.
4. Right-click on the object and select Delete.
5. Click Yes to confirm.

You can also delete an object using LDP, as follows:

1. Open LDP from the Windows Support Tools.
2. From the menu, select Connection → Connect.
3. For Server, enter the name of a domain controller (or leave blank for a serverless bind).
4. For Port, enter 389.
5. Click OK.
6. From the menu, select Connection → Bind.
7. Enter credentials of a user.
8. Click OK.

---

9. Click Browse → Delete. For DN, enter the Distinguished Name of the object that you want to delete.

10. Click Run to delete the object.

Using a command-line interface

You can delete an object using the built-in *dsrm* utility, as well as ADMod. For *dsrm*, use the following syntax:

```
> dsrm "<ObjectDN>"
```

For AdMod, enter the following:

```
> admod -b "<ObjectDN>" -del
```

Using VBScript

```
strObjectDN = "<ObjectDN>"
set objUser = GetObject("LDAP://" & strObjectDN)
objUser.DeleteObject(0)
```

Discussion

This recipe covers deleting individual objects. If you want to delete a container or OU and all the objects in it, take a look at Recipe 4.25.

Using a graphical user interface

If the parent container of the object you want to delete has a lot of objects in it, you may want to add a new connection entry for the DN of the object you want to delete. This may save you time searching through the list of objects in the container and could help avoid accidental deletions. You can do this by right-clicking ADSI Edit and selecting "Connect to...." Under Connection Point, select Distinguished Name and enter the DN of the object you want to delete.

You can also delete most objects within the Active Directory Users and Computers MMC snap-in (*dsa.msc*) by navigating to the object in question, right-clicking on it, and selecting Delete.

Using a command-line interface

The dsrm utility can be used to delete any type of object (no limitations based on object type as with dsadd and dsmod). The only required parameter is the DN of the object to delete. You can also specify -noprompt to keep it from asking for confirmation before deleting. The -s parameter can be used as well to specify a specific server to target. AdMod will not prompt you in this manner.

Using VBScript

Using the DeleteObject method is straightforward. Passing 0 as a parameter is required, but does not have any significance at present.

An alternate and perhaps safer way to delete objects is to use the `IADsContainer::`
`Delete` method. To use this method, you must first bind to the parent container of
the object. You can then call `Delete` by passing the object class and RDN of the
object you want to delete. Here is an example for deleting a user object:

```
set objCont = GetObject("LDAP://ou=Sales,dc=rallencorp,dc=com")
objCont.Delete "user", "cn=rallen"
```

`Delete` is safer than `DeleteObject` because you have to be more explicit about what
you are deleting. With `DeleteObject` you only need to specify a distinguished name
and it will delete it. If you happen to mistype the DN or the user input to a web page
that uses this method is mistyped, the result could be disastrous.

See Also

Recipe 4.25 for deleting a container, MS KB 258310 (Viewing Deleted Objects in
Active Directory), MSDN: IADsContainer::Delete, and MSDN: IADsDeleteOps::
DeleteObject

4.25   Deleting a Container That Has Child Objects

Problem

You want to delete a container or organizational unit and all child objects contained
within.

Solution

Using a graphical user interface

Open ADSI Edit and follow the same steps as in Recipe 4.24. The only difference is
that you'll be prompted to confirm twice instead of once before the deletion occurs.

Using a command-line interface

You can delete a container and its child objects using the built-in *dsrm* utility, as well
as AdMod. For *dsrm*, use the following syntax:

```
> dsrm "<ObjectDN>" -subtree
```

For AdMod, enter the following:

```
> admod -b "<ObjectDN>" -del -treedelete
```

Using VBScript

The same code from Recipe 4.24 will also delete containers and objects contained
within them.

Discussion

As you can see from the solutions, there is not much difference between deleting a leaf node versus deleting a container that has child objects. However, there is a distinction in what is happening in the background.

Deleting an object that has no children can be done with a simple LDAP delete operation. On the other hand, to delete a container and its children, the tree-delete LDAP control has to be used. If you were to do the deletion from an LDAP-based tool like LDP (the Active Directory Administration Tool), you would first need to enable the Subtree Delete control, which has an OID of 1.2.840.113556.1.4.805. LDP provides another option to do a Recursive Delete from the client side. That will essentially iterate through all the objects in the container, deleting them one by one. The Subtree Delete is much more efficient, especially when dealing with large containers.

As with the other operations we've discussed in this chapter (create, rename, move, etc), the user performing the delete operation needs to have the necessary permissions to delete the object or objects in question. Active Directory permissions is discussed more extensively in Chapter 15.

See Also

Recipe 4.24 for deleting objects, Chapter 15, and MSDN: IADsDeleteOps::DeleteObject

4.26 Viewing the Created and Last Modified Timestamp of an Object

Problem

You want to determine when an object was either created or last updated.

Solution

Using a graphical user interface

1. Follow the steps in Recipe 4.2.
2. Ensure that createTimestamp and modifyTimestamp are included in the list of attributes to be returned by looking at Attributes under Options → Search.

Using a command-line interface

You can view the created and modified timestamps using the built-in DSQuery utility, as well as AdFind. For DSQuery, use the following syntax:

```
> dsquery * "<ObjectDN>" -attr name createTimestamp modifyTimestamp
```

For AdFind, use the following:

```
> adfind -default -rb cn=Users -f "cn=Joe Smith" createTimestamp
  modifyTimestamp
```

Using VBScript

```
' This code prints the created and last modified timestamp
' for the specified object.
' ------ SCRIPT CONFIGURATION ------
strObjectDN = "<ObjectDN>"
' ------ END CONFIGURATION ---------

set objEntry = GetObject("LDAP://" & strObjectDN)
Wscript.Echo "Object Name:  " & objEntry.Get("name")
Wscript.Echo " Created: " & objEntry.Get("createTimestamp")
Wscript.Echo " Changed: " & objEntry.Get("modifyTimestamp")
```

Discussion

When an object is created or modified in Active Directory, the createTimestamp and modifyTimestamp attributes get set with the current time. The createTimestamp attribute is replicated between domain controllers, so assuming the latest modification of the object in question has replicated to all domain controllers, they will all contain the timestamp when the object was created. (modifyTimestamp is not replicated.)

See Also

Recipe 4.2 for viewing the attributes of an object, Chapter 13 for a more detailed description of the Active Directory replication process, and *Active Directory*, Third Edition, by Joe Richards et al. (O'Reilly)

4.27 Modifying the Default LDAP Query Policy

Problem

You want to view or modify the default LDAP query policy of a forest. The query policy contains settings that restrict search behavior, such as the maximum number of entries that can be returned from a search.

Solution

Using a graphical user interface

1. Open ADSI Edit.
2. In the Configuration partition, browse to Services → Windows NT → Directory Service → Query Policies.
3. In the left pane, click on the Query Policies container, then right-click on the Default Query Policy object in the right pane, and select Properties.

4. Double-click on the lDAPAdminLimits attribute.

5. Click on the attribute you want to modify and click Remove.

6. Modify the value in the "Value to add" box and click Add.

7. Click OK twice.

Using a command-line interface

To view the current settings, use the following command:

```
> ntdsutil "ldap pol" conn "con to server <DomainControllerName>" q "show values"
```

To change the MaxPageSize value to 2000, you can do the following:

```
> ntdsutil "ldap pol" conn "con to server <DomainControllerName>" q
ldap policy: set MaxPageSize to 2000
ldap policy: Commit Changes
```

Using VBScript

```
' This code modifies a setting of the default query policy for a forest
' ------ SCRIPT CONFIGURATION ------
pol_attr  = "MaxPageSize" ' Set to the name of the setting you want to modify
new_value = 1000          ' Set to the value of the setting you want modify
' ------ END CONFIGURATION ---------

Const ADS_PROPERTY_APPEND = 3
Const ADS_PROPERTY_DELETE = 4

set rootDSE = GetObject("LDAP://RootDSE")
set ldapPol = GetObject("LDAP://cn=Default Query Policy,cn=Query-Policies," & _
                "cn=Directory Service,cn=Windows NT,cn=Services," & _
                rootDSE.Get("configurationNamingContext") )
set regex = new regexp
regex.IgnoreCase = true
regex.Pattern = pol_attr & "="
for Each prop In ldapPol.GetEx("ldapAdminLimits")
   if regex.Test(prop) then
      if prop - pol_attr & "=" & new_value then
         WScript.Echo pol_attr & " already equal to " & new_value
      else
         ldapPol.PutEx ADS_PROPERTY_APPEND, "lDAPAdminLimits", _
                   Array( pol_attr & "=" & new_value )
         ldapPol.SetInfo
         ldapPol.PutEx ADS_PROPERTY_DELETE, "lDAPAdminLimits", Array(prop)
         ldapPol.SetInfo
         WScript.Echo "Set " & pol_attr & " to " & new_value
      end if
      Exit For
   end if
next
```

Discussion

The LDAP query policy contains several settings that control how domain controllers handle searches. By default, one query policy is defined for all domain controllers in a forest, but you can create additional ones and apply them to a specific domain controller or even at the site level (so that all domain controllers in the site use that policy).

Query policies are stored in the Configuration NC as queryPolicy objects. The default query policy is located at: cn=Default Query Policy,cn=Query-Policies, cn=Directory Service, cn=Windows NT, cn=Services, *<ConfigurationPartitionDN>*. The lDAPAdminLimits attribute of a queryPolicy object is multivalued and contains each setting for the policy in name-value pairs. Table 4-5 contains the available settings.

Table 4-5. LDAP query policy settings

Name	Default value	Description
MaxPoolThreads	4 per proc	Maximum number of threads that are created by the DC for query execution.
MaxDatagramRecv	4096	Maximum number of datagrams that can be simultaneously processed by the DC.
MaxReceiveBuffer	10485760	Maximum size in bytes for an LDAP request that the server will attempt to process. If the server receives a request that is larger then this value, it will close the connection.
InitRecvTimeout	120 secs	Initial receive time-out.
MaxConnections	5000	Maximum number of open connections.
MaxConnIdleTime	900 secs	Maximum amount of time a connection can be idle.
MaxActiveQueries	20	Maximum number of queries that can be active at one time.
MaxPageSize	1000	Maximum number of records that will be returned by LDAP responses.
MaxQueryDuration	120 secs	Maximum length of time the domain controller can execute a query.
MaxTempTableSize	10000	Maximum size of temporary storage that is allocated to execute queries.
MaxResultSetSize	262144	Controls the total amount of data that the domain controller stores for this kind of search. When this limit is reached, the domain controller discards the oldest of these intermediate results to make room to store new intermediate results.
MaxNotificationPerConn	5	Maximum number of notifications that a client can request for a given connection.

Since the settings are stored as name/value pairs inside a single attribute, also referred to as AVAs, the VBScript solution has to iterate over each value and use a regular expression to determine when the target setting has been found. It does this by matching *<SettingName>*= at the beginning of the string. See Recipe 4.19 for more on AVAs.

You should not change the default query policy in production unless you've done plenty of testing. Changing some of the settings may result in unexpected application or domain controller behavior.

Instead of modifying the default LDAP query policy, you can create a new one from scratch. In the Query Policies container (where the default query policy object is located), create a new queryPolicy object and set the lDAPAdminLimits attribute as just described based on the settings you want configured. Then modify the queryPolicyObject attribute on the nTDSDSA object of a domain controller you want to apply the new policy to. This can be done via the Active Directory Sites and Services snap-in by browsing to the nTDSDSA object of a domain controller (cn=NTDS Settings), right-clicking on it, and selecting Properties. You can then select the new policy from a drop-down menu beside Query Policy. Click OK to apply the new policy.

See Also

Recipe 4.19, MS KB 315071 (How to View and Set LDAP Policy in Active Directory by Using Ntdsutil.exe)

4.28   Exporting Objects to an LDIF File

Problem

You want to export objects to an LDAP Data Interchange Format (LDIF) file.

Solution

Using a graphical user interface

None of the standard Microsoft tools support exporting LDIF from a GUI.

Using a command-line interface

```
> ldifde -f output.ldf -l <AttrList> -p <Scope> -r "<Filter>" -d "<BaseDN>"
```

Using VBScript

There are no COM or VBScript-based interfaces to LDIF. With Perl you can use the Net::LDAP::LDIF module, which supports reading and writing LDIF files.

Discussion

The LDIF specification defined in RFC 2849 describes a well-defined file-based format for representing directory entries. The format is intended to be both human and machine parseable, which adds to its usefulness. LDIF is the de facto standard for importing and exporting a large number of objects in a directory and is supported by virtually every directory vendor including Microsoft.

Using a command-line interface

The -f switch specifies the name of the file to use to save the entries to, -s is the DC to query, -l is the comma-separated list of attributes to include, -p is the search scope, -r is the search filter, and -d is the base DN. If you encounter any problems using ldifde, the -v switch enables verbose mode and can help identify problems.

See Also

Recipe 4.29 for importing objects using LDIF, RFC 2849 (The LDAP Data Interchange Format (LDIF)—Technical Specification), and MS KB 237677 (Using LDIFDE to Import and Export Directory Objects to Active Directory)

4.29   Importing Objects Using an LDIF File

Problem

You want to import objects into Active Directory using an LDIF file. The file could contain object additions, modifications, and deletions.

Solution

Using a command-line interface

To import objects using the *ldifde* utility, you must first create an LDIF file with the objects to add, modify, or delete. Here is an example LDIF file that adds a user, modifies the user twice, and then deletes the user:

```
dn: cn=jsmith,cn=users,dc=rallencorp,dc=com
changetype: add
objectClass: user
samaccountname: jsmith
sn: JSmith

dn: cn=jsmith,cn=users,dc=rallencorp,dc=com
changetype: modify
add: givenName
givenName: Jim
-
replace: sn
sn: Smith
-

dn: cn=jsmith,cn=users,dc=rallencorp,dc=com
changetype: delete
```

Once you've created the LDIF file, you just need to run the ldifde command to import the new objects.

```
> ldifde -i -f input.ldf
```

Discussion

For more information on the LDIF format, check RFC 2849.

Using a command-line interface

To import with *ldifde*, simply specify the -i switch to turn on import mode and -f *<filename>* for the file. It can also be beneficial to use the -v switch to turn on verbose mode to get more information in case of errors. The Windows Server 2003 version of *ldifde* also includes the -j switch that will create a logfile for troubleshooting purposes.

See Also

Recipe 4.28 for information on LDIF, RFC 2849 (The LDAP Data Interchange Format (LDIF)—Technical Specification), and MS KB 237677 (Using LDIFDE to Import and Export Directory Objects to Active Directory)

4.30   Exporting Objects to a CSV File

Problem

You want to export objects to a comma-separated variable (CSV) file. The CSV file can then be opened and manipulated from a spreadsheet application or with a text editor.

Solution

Using a command-line interface

You can export objects to a CSV file using the built-in *csvde* utility, as well as AdFind. For *csvde*, use the following syntax:

```
> csvde -f output.csv -l <AttrList> -p <Scope> -r "<Filter>" -d "<BuseDN>"
```

For AdFind, use the *adcsv.pl* script that comes with the AdFind download to convert AdFind output into a CSV file.

Discussion

Once you have a CSV file containing entries, you can use a spreadsheet application such as Excel to view, sort, and manipulate the data.

Using a command-line interface

The parameters used by *cvsde* are nearly identical to those used by *ldifde*. The -f switch specifies the name of the file to use to save the entries to, -s is the DC to query,

-l is the comma-separated list of attributes to include, -p is the search scope (base, onelevel, or subtree), -r is the search filter, and -d is the base DN. If you encounter any issues, the -v switch enables verbose mode and can help identify problems.

AdFind offers a number of additional switches to customize the behavior of CSV file output, including the following:

-csv *xxx*
> CSV output. *xxx* is an optional string that specifies value to use for empty attributes.

-csvdelim *x*
> Delimiter to use for separating attributes in CSV output. The default is (,).

-csvmvdelim *x*
> Delimiter to use for separating multiple values in output. The default is (;).

-csvq *x*
> Character to use for quoting attributes. The default is (").

See Also

Recipe 4.31 for importing objects using a CSV file

4.31 Importing Objects Using a CSV File

Problem

You want to import objects into Active Directory using a CSV file.

Solution

Using a command-line interface

To import objects using the *csvde* utility, you must first create a CSV file containing the objects to add. The first line of the file should contain a comma-separated list of attributes you want to set, with DN being the first attribute. Here is an example:

```
DN,objectClass,cn,sn,userAccountControl,sAMAccountName,userPrincipalName
```

The rest of the lines should contain entries to add. If you want to leave one of the attributes unset, then leave the value blank (followed by a comma). Here is a sample CSV file that would add two user objects:

```
DN,objectClass,sn,userAccountControl,sAMAccountName,userPrincipalName
"cn=jim,cn=users,dc=rallencorp,dc=com",user,Smith,512,jim,jim@rallencorp.com
"cn=john,cn=users,dc=rallencorp,dc=com",user,,512,john,john@rallencorp.com
```

Once you've created the CSV file, you just need to run *cvsde* to import the new objects:

```
> csvde -i -f input.csv
```

Discussion

The major difference between *csvde* and *ldifde* is that you can only use *csvde* to import objects; unlike *ldifde*, you can't use it to modify existing objects. Note that each line of the CSV import file, except the header, should contain entries to add objects. You cannot modify attributes of an object or delete objects using *csvde*. If you have a spreadsheet containing objects you want to import, first save it as a CSV file and use *csvde* to import it.

Using a command-line interface

To import with *csvde*, simply specify the -i switch to turn on import mode and -f <filename> for the file. It can also be beneficial to use the -v switch to turn on verbose mode to get more information in case of errors.

See Also

Recipe 4.30 for exporting objects in CSV format and MS KB 327620 (How to Use Csvde to Import Contacts and User Objects into Active Directory)

## CHAPTER 5

Organizational Units

5.0 Introduction

An LDAP directory such as Active Directory stores data in a hierarchy of *containers* and *leaf nodes* called the directory information tree (DIT). Leaf nodes are end points in the tree, while containers can store other containers and leaf nodes. In Active Directory, the two most common types of containers are organizational units (OUs) and container objects. The *container objects* are generic containers that do not have any special properties about them other than that they can contain objects. *Organizational units*, on the other hand, have some special properties, such as the ability to link a Group Policy Object (GPO) to an OU. In most cases when designing a hierarchy of objects in Active Directory, especially users and computers, you should use OUs instead of containers. There is nothing you can do with a container that you can't do with an OU, but the reverse is certainly not the case.

The Anatomy of an Organizational Unit

Organizational units can be created as a child of a domain object or another OU; by default, OUs cannot be added as a child of a container object. (See Recipe 5.13 for more on how to work around this.) OUs themselves are represented in Active Directory by organizationalUnit objects. Table 5-1 contains a list of some interesting attributes that are available on organizationalUnit objects.

Table 5-1. Attributes of organizationalUnit objects

Attribute	Description
description	Textual description of the OU.
gPLink	List of GPOs that have been linked to the OU. See Recipe 5.14 for more information.
gpOptions	Contains 1 if GPO inheritance is blocked and 0 otherwise.
msDS-Approx-Immed-Subordinates	Approximate number of direct child objects in the OU. See Recipe 5.11 for more information.

Table 5-1. Attributes of organizationalUnit objects (continued)

Attribute	Description
managedBy	DN bitwise of user or group that is in charge of managing the OU.
ou	Relative distinguished name of the OU.
modifyTimestamp	Timestamp of when the OU was last modified.
createTimestamp	Timestamp of when the OU was created.

5.1   Creating an OU

Problem

You want to create an OU.

Solution

Using a graphical user interface

1. Open the ADUC snap-in.
2. If you need to change domains, right-click on the Active Directory Users and Computers label in the left pane, select Connect to Domain, enter the domain name, and click OK.
3. In the left pane, browse to the parent container of the new OU, right-click on it, and select New → Organizational Unit.
4. Enter the name of the OU and click OK.
5. To enter a description for the new OU, right-click on the OU in the left pane and select Properties.
6. Click OK after you are done.

Using a command-line interface

You can create a new OU using the built-in DSAdd utility, as well as AdMod. To create an OU using DSAdd, use the following syntax:

```
> dsadd ou "<OrgUnitDN>" -desc "<Description>"
```

To create an OU with AdMod, use the following syntax:

```
> admod -b <OrgUnitDN> objectclass::organizationalUnit
  description::"<Description>" -add
```

For example, creating the Finance OU with the description of "Finance OU" in the *rallencorp.com* domain would look like this:

```
> C:\>admod -b ou=Finance,dc=rallencorp,dc=com
  objectclass::organizationalUnit
  description::"Finance OU" -add
>
```

```
> AdMod V01.06.00cpp Joe Richards (joe@joeware.net) June 2005
>
> DN Count: 1
> Using server: 2k3-sp1-r2.rallencorp.com
> Adding specified objects...
>    DN: ou=Finance,dc=rallencorp,dc=com...
>
> The command completed successfully
```

Using VBScript

```
' This code creates an OU
' ------ SCRIPT CONFIGURATION ------
strOrgUnit       = "<OUName>"       ' e.g. Tools
strOrgUnitParent = "<ParentDN>"     ' e.g. ou=Engineering,dc=rallencorp,dc=com
strOrgUnitDescr  = "<Description>" ' e.g. Tools Users
' ------ END CONFIGURATION ---------

set objDomain = GetObject("LDAP://" & strOrgUnitParent)
set objOU = objDomain.Create("organizationalUnit", "OU=" & strOrgUnit)
objOU.Put "description", strOrgUnitDescr
objOU.SetInfo
WScript.Echo "Successfully created " & objOU.Name
```

Discussion

OUs are used to structure data within Active Directory. Typically, there are four reasons why you would need to create an OU:

Segregate objects
> It is common practice to group related data into an OU. For example, user objects and computer objects are typically stored in separate containers (in fact, this is the default configuration with Active Directory). One reason for this is to make searching the directory easier.

Delegate administration
> Perhaps the most often used reason for creating an OU is to delegate administration. With OUs you can give a person or group of people rights to perform certain administrative functions on objects within the OU.

Apply a GPO
> An OU is the smallest container object that a GPO can be applied to. If you have different types of users within your organization that need to apply different GPOs, the easiest way to set that up is to store the users in different OUs and apply GPOs accordingly.

Controlling visibility of objects
> You can use OUs as a way to restrict what users can see in the directory.

In each solution in this recipe, the `description` attribute of the new OU was set. This is not a mandatory attribute, but it is good practice to set it so that others browsing the directory have a general understanding of the purpose of the OU. Also, consider setting the managedBy attribute to reference a user or group that is the owner of the OU.

See Also

MS KB 308194 (How to How to Create Organizational Units in a Windows 2000 Domain)

5.2   Enumerating the OUs in a Domain

Problem

You want to enumerate all containers and OUs in a domain, which effectively displays the structure of the domain.

Solution

Using a graphical user interface

1. Open the Active Directory Users and Computers snap-in.
2. If you need to change domains, right-click on "Active Directory Users and Computers" in the left pane, select Connect to Domain, enter the domain name, and click OK.
3. In the left pane, you can browse the directory structure.

Using a command-line interface

The following command will enumerate all OUs in the domain of the user running the command using the built-in DSQuery utility:

```
> dsquery ou domainroot
```

You can also retrieve this information using AdFind, using the following syntax:

```
> adfind -default -f "objectcategory=organizationalUnit" -dn
```

Output from the adfind command will resemble the following:

```
> adfind -default -f "objectcategory=organizationalUnit" -dn
>
> AdFind V01.27.00cpp Joe Richards (joe@joeware.net) November 2005
>
> Using server: dc1.rallencorp.com:389
> Directory: Windows Server 2003
> Base DN: DC=rallencorp,DC=com
>
> dn:OU=Domain Controllers,DC=rallencorp,DC=com
> dn:OU=Finance,DC=rallencorp,DC=com
> dn:OU=FinanceTemps,OU=Finance,DC=rallencorp,DC=com
>
> 3 Objects returned
```

Using VBScript

```
' This code recursively displays all container and organizationalUnit
' objects under a specified base.  Using "" for the second parameter means
' that there will be no indention for the first level of objects displayed.
DisplayOUs(LDAP://<DomainDN>", "")

' DisplayOUs takes the ADsPath of the object to display
' child objects for and the number of spaces (indention) to
' use when printing the first parameter
Function DisplayOUs( strADsPath, strSpace)
   set objObject = GetObject(strADsPath)
   Wscript.Echo strSpace & strADsPath
   objObject.Filter = Array("container","organizationalUnit")
   for each objChildObject in objObject
      DisplayObjects objChildObject.ADsPath, strSpace & " "
   next
End Function
```

Discussion

Using a graphical user interface

If you want to expand all containers and OUs within an OU, you have to manually expand each one within ADUC; there is no "expand all" option.

Using a command-line interface

To enumerate both OUs and containers, you have to a use a more generic dsquery command. The following command will display all containers and OUs in the domain of the user running the command:

```
> dsquery * domainroot -filter
"(|(objectcategory=container)(objectcategory=organizationalunit))" -scope subtree
-limit 0
```

Using VBScript

When iterating over the contents of an OU using a for each loop, paging will be enabled so that all child objects will be returned (instead of only 1,000 per the administrative limit). To display all child container objects regardless of depth, use a recursive function called DisplayOUs.

5.3   Finding an OU

Problem

You want to find a specific OU within an Active Directory domain.

Solution

Using a graphical user interface

1. Open the ADUC snap-in.
2. If you need to change domains, right-click on the Active Directory Users and Computers label in the left pane, select Connect to Domain, enter the domain name, and click OK.
3. Right-click on the domain node and select Find.
4. In the Find drop-down box, select Organizational Unit. In the Named: text box, enter the name of the OU.
5. Click Find Now.

Using a command-line interface

```
> adfind -default -f "ou=<OU Name>"
```

Using VBScript

```
Set objCommand = CreateObject("ADODB.Command")
Set objConnection = CreateObject("ADODB.Connection")
objConnection.Provider = "ADsDSOObject"
objConnection.Open "Active Directory Provider"
objCommand.ActiveConnection = objConnection

strBase = "<LDAP://<DomainDN>>"
strOUName = "Finance"
strFilter = "(&(objectCategory=organizationalUnit)" _
  "&(name=" & strOUName & "))"
strAttributes = "distinguishedName"
strQuery = strBase & ";" & strFilter & ";" & strAttributes & ";subtree"

objCommand.CommandText = strQuery
objCommand.Properties("Page Size") = 100
objCommand.Properties("Timeout") = 30
objCommand.Properties("Cache Results") = False
Set objRecordSet = objCommand.Execute

While Not objRecordSet.EOF
  strName = objRecordSet.Fields("distinguishedName").Value
  Wscript.Echo "Distinguished Name: " & strName
  objRecordSet.MoveNext
Wend

objConnection.Close
```

Discussion

In a heavily nested environment, you may need to locate an OU based on its name when you don't necessarily know its location. By using the ADUC GUI or a command-line tool with a search scope of subtree, you can easily recurse through the entire domain structure to find an OU based on its name, description, or any other attributes. In VBScript, you can use an ADO query to find objects that possess the specific attributes that you're looking for.

 When designing your Active Directory structure, you should try to keep OU nesting from becoming too deep, since processing many levels of Group Policy Objects can greatly increase the logon times for your clients. In the interests of keeping things simple, it's often a good idea to keep your OU structure shallow whenever possible.

See Also

Recipe 5.2, Recipe 5.4, and MSDN: VBScript ADO Programming

5.4   Enumerating the Objects in an OU

Problem

You want to enumerate all the objects in an OU.

Solution

The following solutions will enumerate all the objects directly under an OU. Look at the Discussion section for more on how to display all objects under an OU regardless of the number of objects involved.

Using a graphical user interface

1. Open the ADUC snap-in.
2. If you need to change domains, right-click on "Active Directory Users and Computers" in the left pane, select Connect to Domain, enter the domain name, and click OK.
3. In the left pane, browse to the OU you want to view.
4. The contents of the OU will be displayed in the right pane.

Using a command-line interface

To list the contents of an OU using the built-in DSQuery utility, use the following syntax:

```
> dsquery * "<OrgUnitDN>" -limit 0 -scope onelevel
```

You can also use AdFind, as follows:

```
> adfind -b "<OrgUnitDN>" -s one -dn
```

Using VBScript

```
set objOU = GetObject("LDAP://<OrgUnitDN>")
for each objChildObject in objOU
    Wscript.Echo objChildObject.ADSPath
next
```

Discussion

Using a graphical user interface

By default, ADUC will display only 2,000 objects. To view more than 2,000 objects, select View → Filter Options. Then modify the maximum number of items displayed per folder.

Using a command-line interface

Using -limit 0, all objects under the OU will be displayed. If -limit is not specified, 100 will be shown by default. You can also specify your own number if you want to only display a limited number of objects.

The -scope onelevel or -s onelevel (for AdFind) option causes only direct child objects of the OU to be displayed. Displaying all objects regardless of depth is referred to as the subtree scope, which is the default search scope for AdFind and DSQuery.

To save on typing, you can use the -default switch with AdFind, which automatically uses the Domain DN as its search base. You can use this in combination with the -rb (Relative Base) switch, which will only require you to type in the relative DN of the OU that you want to search. So to list the objects in the cn=Finance,dc=rallencorp,dc=com OU, you can use the following abbreviated AdFind syntax:

```
> adfind -default -rb ou=Finance -s one -dn
```

Another option would be to use the -incldn switch that will return objects that contain a particular search string anywhere within the Distinguished Name. So specifying -incldn "ou=Finance" would return the cn=Finance,dc=rallencorp,dc=com OU, as well as the cn=FinanceTemps,cn=Finance,dc=rallencorp,dc=com OU.

Using VBScript

When a for each loop iterates over the contents of an OU, paging will be enabled so that all child objects will be returned regardless of how many there are. If you want to display all child objects and objects contained in any child OUs, you need to implement a recursive function such as the following:

```
' Using "" for the second parameter means that the there will be no
' indention for the first level of objects displayed.
DisplayNestedOUs "LDAP://<OrgUnitDN>", "")
```

```
' DisplayObjects takes the ADsPath of the object to display child
' objects for and the second is the number of spaces (indention)
' to use when printing the first parameter
Function DisplayNestedOUs( strADsPath, strSpace)
    set objObject = GetObject(strADsPath)
    Wscript.Echo strSpace & strADsPath
    for each objChildObject in objObject
        DisplayObjects objChildObject.ADsPath, strSpace & " "
    next
End Function
```

This code is nearly identical to that shown in Recipe 5.2. The only difference is that the Filter method to restrict the type of objects displayed was not used.

See Also

Recipe 5.2

5.5   Deleting the Objects in an OU

Problem

You want to delete all child objects in an OU, but not the OU itself.

Solution

Using a graphical user interface

1. Open the ADUC snap-in.
2. If you need to change domains, right-click on "Active Directory Users and Computers" in the left pane, select Connect to Domain, enter the domain name, and click OK.
3. In the left pane, browse to and select the OU that contains the objects you want to delete.
4. Highlight all the objects in the right pane and press the Delete key on your keyboard.
5. Press F5 to refresh the contents of the OU. If objects still exist, repeat the previous step.

Using a command-line interface

To delete all objects within an OU, but not the OU itself, you need to use the -subtree and -exclude options with the dsrm command:

```
> dsrm "<OrgUnitDN>" -subtree -exclude
```

You can also perform this task by piping the results of an `adfind` query into `admod`, as follows:

```
>adfind -default -rb ou=<OU Name> -s one -dsq | admod -unsafe -del
```

Using VBScript

```
' This code deletes the objects in an OU, but not the OU itself
set objOU = GetObject("LDAP://<OrgUnitDN>")
for each objChildObject in objOU
    Wscript.Echo "Deleting " & objChildObject.ADSPath
    objChildObject.DeleteObject(0)
next
```

Discussion

If you want to delete the objects in an OU and recreate the OU, you can either delete the OU itself, which will delete all child objects, or you could just delete the child objects. The benefit to the latter approach is that you do not need to reconfigure the ACL on the OU or re-link any Group Policy Objects after you've re-created the OU.

See Also

Recipe 5.4 for enumerating objects in an OU, Recipe 5.6 for deleting an OU, and MSDN: IADsDeleteOps::DeleteObject

5.6 Deleting an OU

Problem

You want to delete an OU and all objects in it.

Solution

Using a graphical user interface

1. Open the ADUC snap-in.
2. If you need to change domains, right-click on "Active Directory Users and Computers" in the left pane, select Connect to Domain, enter the domain name, and click OK.
3. In the left pane, browse to the OU you want to delete, right-click on it, and select Delete.
4. Click Yes.
5. If the OU contains child objects, you will be asked for confirmation again before deleting it. Click Yes to continue.

Using a command-line interface

To delete an OU and all objects contained within, use the `-subtree` option with the `dsrm` command. If you don't use `-subtree` and the object you are trying to delete has child objects, the deletion will fail.

```
> dsrm "<OrgUnitDN>" -subtree
```

You can also delete an OU and all of its contents using the following `admod` command:

```
> admod -b "<OrgUnitDN>" -del -treedelete
```

Using VBScript

```
' This code deletes an OU and all child objects of the OU
set objOU = GetObject("LDAP://<OrgUnitDN>")
objOU.DeleteObject(0)
```

Discussion

Deleting OUs that do not contain objects is just like deleting any other type of object. Deleting an OU that contains objects, however, requires a special type of delete operation. The Tree Delete LDAP control (OID: 1.2.840.113556.1.4.805) must be used by the application or script to inform AD to delete everything contained in the OU. All three solutions in this case use the control behind the scenes, but if you were going to perform the operation via an LDAP utility such as LDP, you would need to enable the control first.

See Also

Recipe 4.4 for using LDAP controls and MSDN: IADsDeleteOps::DeleteObject

5.7   Moving the Objects in an OU to a Different OU

Problem

You want to move some or all of the objects in an OU to a different OU. You may need to do this as part of a domain restructuring effort.

Solution

Using a graphical user interface

1. Open the ADUC snap-in.
2. If you need to change domains, right-click on the Active Directory Users and Computers node in the lefthand pane, select Connect to Domain, enter the domain name, and click OK.

3. In the left pane, browse to and select the OU that contains the objects you want to move.

4. Highlight the objects in the right pane you want to move, right-click on them, and select Move.

5. Browse to and select the parent container you want to move the objects to, and then click OK.

6. Press F5 to refresh the contents of the OU. If objects still exist, repeat the previous three steps.

Using a command line interface

To move each object from one OU to another, you can use dsquery as part of a for-do loop as follows:

```
> for /F "usebackq delims=""" %i in (`dsquery * "<OldOrgUnitDN>" -scope
  Onelevel') do dsmove -newparent "<NewOrgUnitDN>" %i
```

An alternative is to pipe the results of an adfind query into admod using the following syntax:

```
> C:\>adfind -b "<OldOrgUnitDN>" -s one -dsq |
      admod -move "<NewOrgUnitDN>"
```

Using VBScript

```
' This code moves objects from the "old" OU to the "new" OU
' ------ SCRIPT CONFIGURATION ------
strOldOrgUnit = "<OldOrgUnitDN>" ' e.g. ou=Eng Tools,dc=rallencorp,dc=com
strNewOrgUnit = "<NewOrgUnitDN>" ' e.g. ou=Tools,dc=rallencorp,dc=com
' ------ END CONFIGURATION ---------

set objOldOU = GetObject("LDAP://" & strOldOrgUnit)
set objNewOU = GetObject("LDAP://" & strNewOrgUnit)
for each objChildObject in objOldOU
    Wscript.Echo "Moving " & objChildObject.Name
    objNewOU.MoveHere objChildObject.ADsPath, objChildObject.Name
next
```

Discussion

When you move objects from one OU to another, you need to be aware of two significant Active Directory design factors that can affect the behavior of the objects that you're moving: delegation and Group Policy Object inheritance.

The first factor to be aware of is *delegation*. As an administrator, you can delegate permissions at the OU level so that specific users and groups can (or cannot) access or modify information concerning the objects contained within that OU. When you move an object from one OU to another, that object inherits the delegation settings from its new parent OU. This means that a user or group who had rights to an object before it was moved may no longer have rights to it afterwards, and a user or group who did not have rights to the object before may have been delegated rights to the destination OU. You need to be aware of this setting to be sure that you do not allow or prevent object access unintentionally. Active Directory security and delegation is discussed further in Chapter 15.

The second factor to keep in mind is that of GPO inheritance. You can link a GPO at the site, domain, or OU level; any child objects that you move to a new OU will cease to receive the GPO settings that were applied to the old OU and will receive those settings associated with the new OU instead.

The one exception to this would be if you were moving an object from a parent OU to its child OU, for example moving from ou=Finance,dc=rallencorp,dc=com to ou=FinanceTemps,ou=Finance,dc=rallencorp,dc=com. In this example, the rules of GPO inheritance would cause the moved objects to receive any GPO settings linked to the Finance OU, followed by any GPO settings linked to the Finance Temps OU. Again, you need to be certain that moving an object from one OU to another does not create any unintended effects.

 You can use the Group Policy Management Console's Resultant Set of Policy (Modeling) wizard to simulate the effect that the move will have on objects within the originating OU before you actually perform the move.

Using a graphical user interface

If you want to move more than 2,000 objects at one time, you will need to modify the default number of objects displayed as described in the Discussion section of Recipe 5.4.

Using a command-line interface

Since dsmove can move only one object at a time, you need to use a for-do loop to iterate over each child object returned. Also note that if you want to move more than 100 objects, you'll need to specify the -limit xx option with dsquery, where xx is the maximum number of objects to move (use 0 for all).

Similarly, AdMod will only move 10 objects at a time by default. To move more objects than this, you need to either specify the –safety xx option where xx is the maximum number of objects to modify, or else use –unsafe to move an unlimited number of objects.

Using VBScript

For more information on the MoveHere method, see Recipe 5.8.

See Also

Recipe 4.20 for moving objects, Recipe 5.4 for enumerating objects in an OU, and MSDN: IADsContainer::MoveHere

5.8   Moving an OU

Problem

You want to move an OU and all its child objects to a different location in the directory tree.

Solution

Using a graphical user interface

1. Open the ADUC snap-in.
2. If you need to change domains, right-click on "Active Directory Users and Computers" in the left pane, select Connect to Domain, enter the domain name, and click OK.
3. In the left pane, browse to the OU you want to move.
4. Right-click on the OU and select Move.
5. Select the new parent container for the OU and click OK.

Using a command-line interface

You can move an OU from one location to another by using either DSMove or AdMod. The DSMove syntax is as follows:

```
> dsmove "<OrgUnitDN>" -newparent "<NewParentDN>"
```

If you wish to move an OU with AdMod, use the following syntax:

```
> C:\>admod -b "<OrgUnitDN>" -move "<NewParentDN>"
```

Using VBScript

```
set objOU = GetObject("LDAP://<NewParentDN>")
objOU.MoveHere "LDAP://<OrgUnitDN>", "<OrgUnitRDN>"
```

Discussion

One of the benefits of Active Directory is the ability to structure and restructure data easily. Moving an OU, even one that contains a complex hierarchy of other OUs and objects, can be done without impacting the child objects.

If any applications have a dependency on the location of specific objects, you need to ensure they are either updated with the new location or preferably reference the objects by GUID, not by distinguished name.

You should also be mindful of the impact of inherited ACLs and the effect of any new GPOs that are linked to the new parent OU. Keep in mind that any GPOs that were already linked to the OU will stay intact and the link will follow the OU to its new location in the directory structure.

See Also

MS KB 313066 (How to Move Users, Groups, and Organizational Units Within a Domain in Windows 2000) and MSDN: IADsContainer::MoveHere

5.9   Renaming an OU

Problem

You want to rename an organizational unit in your domain.

Solution

Using a graphical user interface

1. Open the ADUC snap-in.
2. If you need to change domains, right-click on "Active Directory Users and Computers" in the left pane, select Connect to Domain, enter the domain name, and click OK.
3. In the left pane, browse to the OU you want to move.
4. Right-click on the OU and select Rename.
5. Type in the new name for the OU and press Enter.

Using a command-line interface

To rename an object using the built-in DSMove utility, use the following syntax:

```
> dsmove "<ObjectDN>" -newname "<NewName>"
```

To use admod, use the following:

```
> admod -b "<ObjectDN>" –rename "<New Object RDN>"
```

Using VBScript

```
' This code renames an object and leaves it in the same location.
' ------ SCRIPT CONFIGURATION ------
strCurrentParentDN = "<CurrentParentDN>"
strObjectOldName   = "ou=<OldName>"
strObjectNewName   = "ou=<NewName>"
```

```
' ------ END CONFIGURATION ---------
      set objCont = GetObject("LDAP://" & strCurrentParentDN)
      objCont.MoveHere "LDAP://" & strObjectOldName & "," & _
                   strCurrentParentDN, strObjectNewName
```

Discussion

Before you rename an OU, you should ensure that none of your production applications reference it by name. You can make objects rename safe by requiring all applications that must store a reference to an object to use the GUID of the object, rather than the name. The GUID (stored in the objectGUID attribute) is effectively unique within a forest and does not change when an object is renamed.

Using a command-line interface

The two parameters needed to rename an object are the original DN of the object and the new RDN (-newname). The -s option can also be used to specify a server name to work against.

Using VBScript

The MoveHere method can be tricky to use, so an explanation of how to use it to rename objects is in order. First, you need to call GetObject on the parent container of the object you want to rename. Then call MoveHere on the parent container object and specify the ADsPath of the object to rename as the first parameter. The new RDN including prefix (e.g., ou=) of the object should be the second parameter.

See Also

Recipe 4.23 and MSDN: IADsContainer::MoveHere

5.10   Modifying an OU

Problem

You want to modify one or more attributes of an OU.

Solution

The following examples set the description (description) attribute for the Finance Organizational Unit.

Using a graphical user interface

1. Open ADSI Edit.
2. If an entry for the naming context you want to browse is not already displayed, do the following:

a. Right-click on ADSI Edit in the right pane and click "Connect to...."

b. Fill in the information for the naming context, container, or OU you want to add an object to. Click on the Advanced button if you need to enter alternate credentials.

3. In the left pane, browse to the container or OU that contains the object you want to modify. Once you've found the object, right-click on it and select Properties.

4. Right-click the description attribute and select Edit.

5. Enter Finance Department and click OK.

6. Click Apply, followed by OK.

Using a command-line interface

To modify an object using AdMod, you'll use the following general syntax:

```
> admod -b <ObjectDN> <attribute>:<operation>:<value>
```

For example, you can add a description to an OU object using the following syntax:

```
> admod -b cn="ou=Finance,dc=rallencorp,dc=com"
  description::"Finance Department"
```

You can modify a limited number of object types with DSMod. Run dsmod /? from a command line for more details.

Using VBScript

```
strObjectDN = "ou=Finance,dc=rallencorp,dc=com"
set objUser = GetObject("LDAP://" & strObjectDN)
objUser.Put "description", "Finance Department"
objUser.SetInfo
```

Discussion

Modifying the attributes of an OU is a relatively straightforward process that's similar to modifying other types of objects within Active Directory. You can modify most attributes of an OU using the Active Directory Computers and Users MMC snap-in, but some attributes will be available for editing only by using ADSI Edit or a command-line or scripting utility.

Using VBScript

To simply view some common properties of an OU, use the following code:

```
strOUDN = ou="<OU DN>" ' i.e. "ou=Finance,dc=rallencorp,dc=com"
Set objContainer = GetObject("LDAP://" & strOUDN)

For Each strValue in objContainer.description
  WScript.Echo "Description: " & strValue
Next

Wscript.Echo "Street Address: " & strStreetAddress
```

```
Wscript.Echo "Province/State: " & objContainer.st
Wscript.Echo "Postal/ZIP Code: " & objContainer.postalCode
Wscript.Echo "Country: " & objContainer.c
```

To clear a property of an OU, you need to use the `PutEx` method in combination with the `ADS_PROPERTY_CLEAR` value, as follows:

```
Const ADS_PROPERTY_CLEAR = 1
strOUDN = ou="<OU DN>" ' i.e. "ou=Finance,dc=rallencorp,dc=com"

Set objContainer = GetObject("LDAP://" & strOUDN)

objContainer.PutEx ADS_PROPERTY_CLEAR, "description", 0
objContainer.PutEx ADS_PROPERTY_CLEAR, "street", 0
objContainer.PutEx ADS_PROPERTY_CLEAR, "st", 0
objContainer.PutEx ADS_PROPERTY_CLEAR, "postalCode", 0
objContainer.PutEx ADS_PROPERTY_CLEAR, "c", 0
objContainer.SetInfo
```

See Also

MSDN: IADs::Put, MSDN: IADs::PutEx, MSDN: IADs::SetInfo, and MSDN: ADS_PROPERTY_OPERATION_ENUM

5.11 Determining Approximately How Many Child Objects an OU Has

Problem

You want to quickly determine a rough approximation of how many child objects, if any, an OU contains.

Solution

Using a graphical user interface

1. Open LDP.
2. From the Menu, select Browse → Search.
3. For Base DN, enter `<OrgUnitDN>`.
4. For Filter, enter (objectclass=*).
5. For Scope, select Base.
6. Click the Options button and enter `msDS-Approx-Immed-Subordinates` for Attributes.
7. Click OK and then Run.
8. The results will be displayed in the right-hand pane.

Another option would be to run a search using the onelevel scope and count the number of objects returned by the query. In LDP you can suppress the display of results so that it only displays the number of objects returned rather than displaying the specifics of each item.

Using a command-line interface

You can retrieve the number of child objects that are contained in an OU using either DSQuery or AdFind. To perform this task using DSQuery, use the following syntax:

```
> dsquery * "<OrgUnitDN>" -scope base -attr msDS-Approx-Immed-Subordinates
```

The syntax for AdFind is as follows:

```
> adfind -b "<OrgUnitDN>" -s base msDS-Approx-Immed-Subordinates
```

Using VBScript

```
' This code displays the approximate number of child objects for an OU
set objOU = GetObject("LDAP://<OrgUnitDN>")
objOU.GetInfoEx Array("msDS-Approx-Immed-Subordinates"), 0
WScript.Echo "Number of child objects: " & _
            objOU.Get("msDS-Approx-Immed-Subordinates")
```

Discussion

The msDS-Approx-Immed-Subordinates attribute is new to Windows Server 2003. It contains the approximate number of direct child objects in a container or organizational unit. Note that this is an approximation and can be off by 10 percent or more of the actual total for large containers. (For instance, we ran this query for a container with 2,008 objects in it that reported a value of 1306 for the msDS-Appox-Immed-Subordinates attribute.) The main reason for adding this attribute was to give applications an idea of how many objects a container has so that it can display them accordingly.

msDS-Approx-Immed-Subordinates is a constructed attribute, i.e., the value is not actually stored in Active Directory like other attributes. Rather, Active Directory computes the value when an application asks for it. In the VBScript solution, the GetInfoEx method needs to be called because some constructed attributes, such as this one, are not retrieved when GetInfo or Get is called.

You can accomplish similar functionality with Windows 2000 Active Directory, but you need to perform a onelevel search against the OU and then count the number of objects returned. This method is by no means as quick as using msDS-Approx-Immed-Subordinates in Windows Server 2003, but it produces more accurate results.

See Also

MSDN: GetInfoEx

5.12 Delegating Control of an OU

Problem

You want to delegate administrative access of an OU to allow a group of users to manage objects in the OU.

Solution

Using a graphical user interface

1. Open the ADUC snap-in.

2. If you need to change domains, right-click on "Active Directory Users and Computers" in the left pane, select Connect to Domain, enter the domain name, and click OK.

3. In the left pane, browse to and select the target OU, and then select Delegate Control.

4. Select the users and/or groups to delegate control to by using the Add button, and then click Next.

5. Select the type of privilege to grant to the users or groups you selected in Step 4, and then click Next.

6. Click Finish.

Using a command-line interface

ACLs can be set via a command-line with the *dsacls* utility from the Support Tools. See Recipe 15.14 for more information.

Discussion

Although you can delegate control of an OU to a particular user, it is almost universally a better practice to use a group instead. Even if there is only one user to delegate control to, you should create a group, add that user as a member, and use that group in the ACL. That way in the future when you have to replace that user with someone else, you can simply make sure the new person is in the correct group instead of modifying ACLs again. The Delegation of Control wizard is discussed further in Recipe 15.7.

See Also

Recipe 15.14 for changing the ACL on an object and Recipe 15.7

5.13 Assigning or Removing a Manager for an OU

Problem

You want to assign or remove a manager for an OU.

Solution

Using a graphical user interface

1. Open the ADUC snap-in.
2. If you need to change domains, right-click on Active Directory Users and Computers in the left pane, select Connect to Domain, enter the domain name, and click OK.
3. In the left pane, right-click on the domain and select Find.
4. Right-click on the OU and select Properties.
5. Select the Managed By tab.
6. Click the Change button.
7. Locate the group or user to delegate control to and click OK.
8. To remove a manager from an OU, return to the Managed By tab and click Clear.

Using a command line interface

To add a manager for an OU, use the following syntax:

```
> admod -b <ObjectDN> managedBy::<ManagerDN>
```

To clear the managedBy attribute, use the following:

```
> admod -b <ObjectDN> managedBy:-
```

Using VBScript

```
strObjectDN = "ou=Finance,dc=rallencorp,dc=com"
strUserDN = "cn=Joe Smith,ou=Finance,dc=rallencorp,dc=com"
set objUser = GetObject("LDAP://" & strObjectDN)
objUser.Put "managedBy", strUserDN
objUser.SetInfo
```

Discussion

In the case of an OU, specifying a user, group, computer, or another OU in the Managed By tab does not confer any particular rights onto the manager; this is used as a strictly informational field. When you configure a manager for an OU, the manager's DN is placed in the OU's managedBy attribute, and the OU's DN is placed in the managers managedObjects attribute. managedObjects is a multivalued attribute to allow a single object to manage multiple objects simultaneously.

See Also

MSDN: Managed-by attribute [AD Schema] and MSDN: Managed-Objects [AD Schema]

5.14   Allowing OUs to Be Created Within Containers

Problem

You want to create an OU within a container. By default, you cannot create OUs within container objects due to restrictions in the Active Directory Schema.

Solution

Using a graphical user interface

1. Open the Active Directory Schema snap-in as a user that is a member of the *Schema Admins* group. See Recipe 11.1 for more on using the Schema snap-in.
2. Expand the *Classes* folder, right-click on the organizationalUnit class, and select Properties.
3. Select the Relationship tab and, next to Possible Superior, click Add Superior (Windows Server 2003) or Add (Windows 2000).
4. Select container and click OK.
5. Click OK.

Using a command-line interface

Create an LDIF file called *ou_in_container.ldf* with the following contents:

```
dn: cn=organizational-unit,cn=schema,cn=configuration,<ForestRootDN>
changetype: modify
add: possSuperiors
possSuperiors: container
-
```

Then run the ldifde command to import the change:

```
> ldifde -i -f ou_in_container.ldf
```

You can also modify this attribute using AdMod, as follows:

```
> admod –b cn=organizational-unit,cn=schema,cn=configuration,<ForestRootDN>
possSuperiors:+:container
```

Using VBScript

```
' This code modifies the schema so that OUs can be created within containers
Const ADS_PROPERTY_APPEND = 3
set objRootDSE = GetObject("LDAP://RootDSE")
set objOUClass = GetObject("LDAP://cn=organizational-unit," & _
```

```
                    objRootDSE.Get("schemaNamingContext") )
    objOUClass.PutEx ADS_PROPERTY_APPEND, "possSuperiors", Array("container")
    objOUClass.SetInfo
```

Discussion

Allowing OUs to be created within containers requires a simple modification to the schema. You have to make the container class one of the possible superiors (possSuperiors attribute) for the organizationalUnit class. This might be necessary if you have a script or tool that is specifically looking for organizationalUnit objects to perform specific actions; if a container object contains child OUs, they would be bypassed by such a tool. However, it's not the default configuration since most AD designs will be more likely to leverage OUs rather than container objects.

See Also

Recipe 11.1 for using the Schema snap-in and MS KB 224377 (Configuring Different Containers to Hold Organizational Units)

5.15   Linking a GPO to an OU

Problem

You want to apply the settings in a GPO to the users and/or computers within an OU, also known as linking the GPO to the OU.

Solution

Using a graphical user interface

1. Open the GPMC snap-in.

2. Expand Forest in the left pane.

3. Expand Domain and navigate down to the OU in the domain you want to link the GPO to.

4. Right-click on the OU and select either "Create and Link a GPO Here" (if the GPO does not already exist) or "Link an Existing GPO" (if you have already created the GPO).

5. To unlink a GPO, right-click on an existing link and remove the check mark next to Link Enabled.

Using VBScript

```
' This code links a GPO to an OU in the specified domain
' ------ SCRIPT CONFIGURATION ------
strDomainDN = "<DomainDN>"   ' e.g. dc=rallencorp,dc=com
strGPO      = "<GPOName>"     ' e.g. WorkstationsGPO
strOUDN     = "<OrgUnitDN>"   ' e.g. ou=Workstations,dc=rallencorp,dc=com
```

```
' ------ END CONFIGURATION ---------

strBaseDN    = "<LDAP://cn=policies,cn=system,dc=" & strDomainDN & ">;"
strFilter    = "(&(objectcategory=grouppolicycontainer)" & _
               "(objectclass=grouppolicycontainer)" & _
               "(displayname=" & strGPO & "));"
strAttrs     = "ADsPath;"
strScope     = "OneLevel"

set objConn = CreateObject("ADODB.Connection")
objConn.Provider = "ADsDSOObject"
objConn.Open "Active Directory Provider"
set objRS = objConn.Execute(strBaseDN & strFilter & strAttrs & strScope)
if objRS.EOF <> TRUE then
   objRS.MoveFirst
end if

if objRS.RecordCount = 1 then
   strGPOADsPath = objRS.Fields(0).Value
   WScript.Echo "GPO Found: " & strGPOADsPath
elseif objRS.RecordCount = 0 then
   WScript.Echo "Did not founding matching GPO for: " & strGPO
   Wscript.Quit
elseif objRS.RecordCount > 1 then
   WScript.Echo "More than 1 GPO found matching: " & strGPO
   Wscript.Quit
end if

set objOU = GetObject("LDAP://" & strOUDN)

on error resume next
strGPLink = objOU.Get("gpLink")
if Err.Number then
   if Err.Number <> -2147463155 then
      WScript.Echo "Fatal error while retrieving gpLink attribute: " & _
                   Err.Description
      Wscript.Quit
   end if
end if
on error goto 0

objOU.Put "gpLink", strGPLink & "[" & strGPOADsPath & ";0]"
objOU.SetInfo
WScript.Echo "GPO successfully linked"

' The following code segment will remove any GPOs that
' are linked to an OU

Const ADS_PROPERTY_CLEAR = 1

Set objContainer = GetObject _
   ("LDAP://<OU DN>") ' i.e. "ou=Finance,dc=rallencorp,dc=com"
objContainer.PutEx ADS_PROPERTY_CLEAR, "gPLink", 0
objContainer.PutEx ADS_PROPERTY_CLEAR, "gPOptions", 0
objContainer.SetInfo
```

Discussion

The GPOs that are linked to an OU are stored in the gpLink attribute of the OU. The format of the gpLink attribute is kind of strange, so you have to be careful when programmatically or manually setting that attribute. Since multiple GPOs can be linked to an OU, the gpLink attribute has to store multiple values; unfortunately, it does not store them as you might expect in a multivalued attribute. Instead, the links are stored as part of the single-valued gpLink attribute. The ADsPath of each linked GPO is concatenated into a string, with each enclosed in square brackets. The ADsPath for each GPO is followed by ;0 to signify the link is enabled or ;1 to signify the link is disabled. Here is an example gpLink with two GPOs linked:

```
[LDAP://cn={6491389E-C302-418C-8D9D-
BB24E65E7507},cn=policies,cn=system,DC=rallencorp,DC=com;0]
[LDAP://cn={6AC1786C-016F-
11D2-945F-00C04fB984F9},cn=policies,cn=system,DC=rallencorp,DC=com;0]
```

A much better VBScript solution for linking GPOs is described in Recipe 10.14, which uses the GPMC APIs.

See Also

Recipe 10.14 for more information on GPMC and MS KB 248392 (Scripting the Addition of Group Policy Links)

## CHAPTER 6

Users

6.0   Introduction

User accounts are some of the most frequently used objects in Active Directory; they create the means of authenticating and authorizing someone to access resources on your network. Because Windows 2000 and Windows Server 2003 systems manage users through Active Directory, many key issues that system administrators deal with are covered in this chapter. In particular, Active Directory manages information regarding user passwords; group membership; enabling, disabling or expiring user accounts, and keeping track of when users have logged on to your network.

The Anatomy of a User

The default location for user objects in a domain is the cn=Users container directly off the domain root. You can, of course, create user objects in other containers and organizational units in a domain, or move them to these containers after they've been created. Table 6-1 contains a list of some of the interesting attributes that are available on user objects. This is by no means a complete list. There are many other informational attributes that we haven't included.

Table 6-1. Attributes of user objects

Attribute	Description
accountExpires	Large integer representing when the user's account is going to expire. See Recipe 6.29 for more information.
cn	Relative distinguished name of user objects. This is commonly the username of the user.
displayName	Typically the full name of a user. This attribute is used in administrative tools to display a user's descriptive name.
givenName	First name of the user.
homeDirectory	Local or UNC path of user's home directory. See Recipe 6.29 for more information.
homeDrive	Defines the drive letter to map the user's home directory to. See Recipe 6.29 for more information.

Table 6-1. Attributes of user objects (continued)

Attribute	Description
lastLogon	The last time that a user logged onto a particular DC. This information is not replicated among domain controllers.
lastLogonTimestamp	Approximate last logon timestamp, which is replicated among domain controllers. This attribute is new in Windows Server 2003. See Recipe 6.30 for more information.
managedObjects	Multivalued, linked attribute (with managedBy) that contains a list of DNs of objects the user manages.
lockoutTime	Large integer representation of the timestamp for when a user was locked out. See Recipe 6.12 for more information.
memberOf	List of DNs of the groups the user is a member of. See Recipe 6.18 for more information.
objectSID	Octet string representing the SID of the user.
primaryGroupID	ID of the primary group for the user. See Recipe 6.20 for more information.
profilePath	UNC path to profile directory. See Recipe 6.29 for more information.
pwdLastSet	Large integer denoting the last time the user's password was set. See Recipe 6.26 for more information.
sAMAccountName	NetBIOS style name of the user. This is limited to 20 characters to support legacy applications.
sIDHistory	Multivalued attribute that contains a list of SIDs that is associated with the user.
scriptPath	Path and filename of logon script. See Recipe 6.32 for more information.
sn	Last name of user.
tokenGroups	List of SIDs for the groups in the domain the user is a member of (both directly and via nesting).
unicodePwd	Octet string that contains a hash of a user's password. This attribute cannot be directly queried.
userAccountControl	Account flags that define such things as account status and password change status.
userPrincipalName	Internet-style account name for user, which a user can use to logon to a computer. In most cases this should map to the user's email address, but this does not always need to be the case, particularly in ADAM.
userWorkstations	List of computers a user can log on to, stored as a Unicode string.

6.1 Modifying the Default Display Name Used When Creating Users in ADUC

Problem

You want to modify how the default display name gets generated when you create a new user through the ADUC snap-in.

Solution

Using a graphical user interface

1. Open ADSI Edit.

2. In the Configuration Naming Context browse to DisplaySpecifiers → *<Locale>* where *<Locale>* is the locale for your language (e.g., the U.S. English locale is 409).

3. Double-click on cn=user-Display.

4. Edit the createDialog attribute with the value you want the new default to be (e.g., %<sn>, %<givenName>).

5. Click OK.

Using a command-line interface

```
> admod -b cn=user-Display,cn=409,cn=DisplaySpecifiers,cn=Configuration,
  <ForestRootDN> createDialog::"%<sn>, %<givenName>"
```

Using VBScript

```
' This code modifies the default ADUC display name.
' ------ SCRIPT CONFIGURATION ------
strNewDefault = "%<sn>, %<givenName>"
strForestName = "<ForestDNSName>"      ' e.g. rallencorp.com
' ------ END CONFIGURATION ---------

Set objRootDSE = GetObject("LDAP://" & strForestName & "/RootDSE")
Set objDispSpec = GetObject("LDAP://cn=User-Display,cn=409," & _
                            "cn=DisplaySpecifiers," & _
                            objRootDSE.Get("ConfigurationNamingContext"))
objDispSpec.Put "createDialog", strNewDefault
objDispSpec.SetInfo
WScript.Echo "New default for user's display name has been set to: " & _
             strNewDefault
```

Discussion

When you create a new user object in the Active Directory Users and Computers snap-in, it will automatically fill in the Full Name field as you type in the First Name, Initials, and Last Name fields. As a convenience, you may want to alter that behavior so that it automatically fills in a different value. To do that, you need to modify the User-Display display specifier, which has the following distinguished name:

cn=user-Display,cn=*<Locale>*,cn=DisplaySpecifiers,cn=Configuration,*<ForestRootDN>*

<Locale> should be replaced with your language specific locale and *<ForestRootDN>* should contain the distinguished name for your forest root domain. You need to modify the createDialog attribute, which by default has no value. Replacement variables are presented by %*<attribute>*, where *attribute* is an attribute name. For example, if you wanted to make the default be "LastName, FirstName" you would use the following value:

%<sn>, %<givenName>

See Also

MS KB 250455 (XADM: How to Change Display Names of Active Directory Users)

6.2   Creating a User

Problem

You want to create a user object.

Solution

Using a graphical user interface

1. Open the ADUC snap-in.

2. If you need to change domains, right-click on "Active Directory Users and Computers" in the left pane, select Connect to Domain, enter the domain name, and click OK.

3. In the left pane, browse to and select the container where the new user should be located and select New → User.

4. Enter the values for the first name, last name, full name, and user logon name fields as appropriate and click Next.

5. Enter and confirm password, set any of the password flags, and click Next.

6. Click Finish.

Using a command-line interface

You can create a user with the built-in DSAdd utility or by using AdMod. Using DSAdd requires the following syntax:

```
> dsadd user "<UserDN>" -upn <UserUPN> -fn "<UserFirstName>"
-ln "<UserLastName>" -display "<UserDisplayName>" -pwd <UserPasswd>
```

To create a user account with AdMod, use the following syntax:

```
> admod -b "<UserDN>" -add objectClass::user
  sAMAccountName::<SAMAccount> unicodepwd::<password> userAccountControl::512 -
kerbenc
```

Using VBScript

```
' Taken from ADS_USER_FLAG_ENUM
Const ADS_UF_NORMAL_ACCOUNT = 512

set objParent = GetObject("LDAP://<ParentDN>")
set objUser   = objParent.Create("user", "cn=<UserName>") ' e.g. joes
objUser.Put "sAMAccountName", "<UserName>"   ' e.g. joes
objUser.Put "userPrincipalName", "<UserUPN>" ' e.g. joes@rallencorp.com
objUser.Put "givenName", "<UserFirstName>"   ' e.g. Joe
```

```
objUser.Put "sn", "<UserLastName>"              ' e.g. Smith
objUser.Put "displayName", "<UserFirstName> <UserLastName>" ' e.g. Joe Smith
objUser.SetInfo
objUser.SetPassword("<Password>")
objUser.AccountDisabled = FALSE
objUser.SetInfo
objUser.Put "userAccountControl", ADS_UF_NORMAL_ACCOUNT
objUser.SetInfo
```

Discussion

The only mandatory attribute that must be set when creating a user is
sAMAccountName, which is the account name that is used to interoperate with down-
level domains—and even this attribute is only mandatory in Windows Server 2003.
To make the account immediately available for a user to use, you'll need to make
sure the account is enabled, which is accomplished by setting userAccountControl to
512 after you've set a password that follows any password complexity rules in place
for the domain (order is important in this case). If you only set the sAMAccountName
when creating a user object, the account will be disabled by default.

With Windows Server 2003, you can also create user accounts using the
inetOrgPerson class, which is described in Recipe 6.3. inetOrgPerson objects can be
used for user authentication and restricting access to resources in much the same
way as user objects.

Using a graphical user interface

To set additional attributes, double-click on the user account after it has been created. There are several tabs to choose from that contain attributes that are grouped
together based on function (e.g., Profile).

Using a command-line interface

Several additional attributes can be set with the dsadd user command. Run dsadd
user /? for the complete list. When creating a user with AdMod, you must specify
the userClass, objectCategory, and sAMAccount attributes as a minimum. You can
add additional attributes with the admod command by using the <attributename>::
<value> syntax.

Using VBScript

Take a look at Recipe 6.29 for more information on the userAccountControl attribute
and the various flags that can be set for it.

See Also

Recipe 6.3 for creating users in bulk, Recipe 6.4 for creating an inetOrgPerson user,
Recipe 6.29, and MSDN: ADS_USER_FLAG_ENUM

6.3 Creating a Large Number of Users

Problem

You want to create a large number of user objects, either for testing purposes or to initially populate Active Directory with your employee, customer, or student user accounts.

Solution

Using a command-line interface

The following example uses a for-do loop in combination with dsadd to create 1,000 users under the bulk OU in the *rallencorp.com* domain with usernames such as User1, User2, User3, etc. The password is set, but no other attributes are configured. You can modify the dsadd syntax to populate additional attributes, as well.

```
> for /L %i in (1,1,1000) do dsadd user cn=User%i,ou=bulk,dc=rallencorp,dc=com
-pwd User%i
```

You can also use the *ldifde* utility to perform a bulk import of unique usernames. Create an *.LDF* file using the following syntax (separate multiple entries with a blank line in-between):

```
dn: CN=Robbie Allen, OU=Training, DC=rallencorp, DC=com
changetype: add
cn: Robbie Allen
objectClass: user
samAccountName: rallen
```

Once you've created the LDIF file containing your user records, import the file using the following command:

```
> ldifde -i -f <filename.ldf> -s <servername>
```

You may notice that the LDIF file does not specify the user's password; this attribute must be modified after the user object has been created.

Using VBScript

```
' This code creates a large number of users with incremented user names
' e.g. User1, User2, User3, ....
' ------ SCRIPT CONFIGURATION ------
intNumUsers = 1000          ' Number of users to create
strParentDN = "<ParentDN>" ' e.g. ou=bulk,dc=emea,dc=rallencorp,dc=com
' ------ END CONFIGURATION ---------

' Taken from ADS_USER_FLAG_ENUM
Const ADS_UF_NORMAL_ACCOUNT = 512

set objParent = GetObject("LDAP://" & strParentDN)
```

```
for i = 1 to intNumUsers
    strUser = "User" & i
    Set objUser = objParent.Create("user", "cn=" & strUser)
    objUser.Put "sAMAccountName", strUser
    objUser.SetInfo
    objUser.SetPassword(strUser)
    objUser.SetInfo
    objUser.Put "userAccountControl", ADS_UF_NORMAL_ACCOUNT
    objUser.AccountDisabled=FALSE
    objUser.SetInfo
    WScript.Echo "Created " & strUser
next
WScript.Echo ""
WScript.Echo "Created " & intNumUsers & " users"
```

Discussion

Using ADSI and even the new DS command-line utilities on Windows Server 2003, you can create hundreds and even thousands of users easily and quickly. We ran both the CLI and VBScript solutions in a test domain on a single processor machine. The VBScript solution took less than 1.5 minutes and the CLI solution took less than 5 minutes to create 1,000 user objects. Admittedly, they are not populating very many attributes, but it shows that you can quickly populate Active Directory with user accounts very easily. You can also modify the examples to pull real data from a data source, such as an employee database.

See Also

Recipe 6.2 for creating a user and MS KB 263911 (How to Set a User's Password using LDIFDE)

6.4   Creating an inetOrgPerson User

Problem

You want to create an inetOrgPerson object, which is the standard LDAP object class to represent users.

Solution

Using a graphical user interface

1. Open the ADUC snap-in.
2. If you need to change domains, right-click on "Active Directory Users and Computers" in the left pane, select Connect to Domain, enter the domain name, and click OK.
3. In the left pane, browse to the parent container of the new user, right-click on it, and select New → InetOrgPerson.

4. Enter first name, last name, and user logon name fields as appropriate and click Next.

5. Enter and confirm the password, set any of the password flags, and click Next.

6. Click Finish.

Using a command-line interface

DSAdd does not support creating inetOrgPerson objects, so use *ldifde* instead. First, you need to create an LDIF file called *create_inetorgperson.ldf* with the following contents:

```
dn: <UserDN>
changetype: add
objectclass: inetorgperson
sAMAccountName: <UserName>

dn: <UserDN>
changetype: modify
add: userAccountControl
userAccountControl: 512
```

Be sure to replace *<UserDN>* with the distinguished name of the user you want to add and *<UserName>* with the user's username. Then run the following command:

```
> ldifde -i -f create_inetorgperson.ldf
```

You can also use the AdMod utility to create an inetOrgPerson object, as follows:

```
> admod -b "cn=inetOrgPerson,cn=Users,dc=rallencorp,dc=com"
  objectclass::inetOrgPerson sAMAccountName::InetOrg -add
```

Using VBScript

```
' This code creates an inetOrgPerson object

set objParent = GetObject("LDAP://<ParentDN>")
set objUser   = objParent.Create("inetorgperson", "cn=<UserName>")

' Taken from ADS_USER_FLAG_ENUM
Const ADS_UF_NORMAL_ACCOUNT = 512

objUser.Put "sAMAccountName", "<UserName>"
objUser.Put "userPrincipalName", "<UserUPN>"
objUser.Put "givenName", "<UserFirstName>"
objUser.Put "sn", "<UserLastName>"
objUser.Put "displayName", "<UserFirstName> <UserLastName>"
objUser.SetInfo
objUser.SetPassword("<Password>")
objUser.SetInfo
objUser.Put "userAccountControl", ADS_UF_NORMAL_ACCOUNT
objUser.AccountDisabled = FALSE
objUser.SetInfo
```

Discussion

The inetOrgPerson object class was defined in RFC 2798. It is the closest thing in the LDAP world to a standard representation of a user, and most LDAP vendors support the inetOrgPerson class. Unfortunately, Microsoft did not support inetOrgPerson with the initial release of Active Directory. Even though they provided an add-on later to extend the schema to support it, the damage had been done. Most Active Directory implementations were already using the user object class and were unlikely to convert, which required vendors to build in support for the user class.

> You can download the InetOrgPerson Kit for Windows 2000 from the following web site: *http://msdn.microsoft.com/library/en-us/dnactdir/html/inetopkit.asp*. This requires that you extend the schema to support an additional object class and new attributes. It also creates a schema conflict with Windows Server 2003. See MS KB 314649 for more information.

In Windows Server 2003 Active Directory, inetOrgPerson is supported natively. You can create inetOrgPerson objects for your users, who can use them to authenticate just as they would accounts of the user object class. If you haven't deployed Active Directory yet and you plan on integrating a lot of third party LDAP-based applications that rely on inetOrgPerson, you may want to consider using it over user. You won't be losing any information or functionality because the inetOrgPerson class inherits directly from the user class. For this reason, the inetOrgPerson class has even more attributes than the Microsoft user class.

The one potential downside is that some of the Microsoft tools, such as the DS utilities, do not support modifying inetOrgPerson objects. (You can, however, use AdMod to perform these modifications.)

See Also

Recipe 6.2 for creating a user, MS KB 314649, and RFC 2798 (Definition of the InetOrgPerson LDAP Object Class)

6.5   Converting a user Object to an inetOrgPerson Object (or Vice Versa)

Problem

You want to convert one or more user objects to inetOrgPerson objects to improve interoperability in a heterogeneous environment.

Using a graphical user interface

 This requires the Windows Server 2003 forest functional level.

1. Open ADSI Edit.
2. If an entry for the naming context you want to browse is not already displayed, do the following:
   a. Right-click on ADSI Edit in the right pane and click "Connect to…."
   b. Fill in the information for the domain naming context, container, or OU that contains the object you want to modify. Click on the Advanced button if you need to enter alternate credentials.
3. In the left pane, browse to the naming context, container, or OU containing the user object that you want to view. Once you've found the object, right-click on it and select Properties.
4. Scroll to `objectClass` and select Edit.
5. Under Value to add, enter `inetOrgPerson` and click Add.
6. Click OK twice to save your changes.

Using a command-line interface

To convert a user object to an `inetOrgPerson`, use the following syntax:

```
> admod -b "<UserDN>" objectClass:+:inetOrgPerson
```

 To revert the object back to a regular user, replace + with - in the previous syntax.

Using VBScript

```
' This code will convert a user object to inetOrgPerson.

' ------ SCRIPT CONFIGURATION ------
strUserDN = "<UserDN>" ' e.g. cn=jsmith,cn=Users,dc=rallencorp,dc=com
strClass = "inetOrgPerson"
' ------ END CONFIGURATION ---------

set objUser = GetObject("LDAP://" & strUserDN)
objUsr.PutEx ADS_PROPERTY_APPEND,"objectClass",Array(strClass)
objUsr.SetInfo
```

Discussion

In a heterogeneous environment, you may wish to convert one or more Active Directory user objects to `inetOrgPerson` objects. Since the `inetOrgPerson` class inherits from the user class, making this modification is a simple matter of adding the "inetOrgPerson" value to an object's objectClass attribute. It's important to note that this is the only instance in which you can modify structural classes in this manner; you can't simply modify a user object with whatever class you wish, even if that class inherits from the user class.

See Also

MS KB 307998 (Changing the Naming Attribute of the InetOrgPerson Class)

6.6   Modifying an Attribute for Several Users at Once

Problem

You want to modify an attribute for several users at once.

Solution

Using a graphical user interface

 This requires the Windows Server 2003 version of the ADUC snap-in.

1. Open the ADUC snap-in.
2. If you need to change domains, right-click on "Active Directory Users and Computers" in the left pane, select Connect to Domain, enter the domain name, and click OK.
3. In the left pane, browse to the parent container of the objects you want to modify.
4. In the right pane, highlight each object you want to modify, right-click, and select Properties.
5. Check the box beside the attribute(s) you want to modify and edit the fields for the attributes.
6. Click OK.

Using a command-line interface

The following command sets the home directory of all users under a parent container (*<ParentDN>*) to be on a particular file server (*<FileServer>*). The user (i.e., $username$) is automatically replaced with the sAMAccountName for the user.

```
> dsquery user "<ParentDN>" -limit 0 -scope onelevel | dsmod user -hmdir
"\\<FileServerName>\$username$"
```

Using VBScript

```
' This code sets the home drive of all users under a container
' to be on a file server where the share name is the same as the user's
' sAMAccountName.
set objParent = GetObject("LDAP://<ParentDN>")
objParent.Filter = Array("user")
for each objUser in objParent
    strSAM = objUser.Get("sAMAccountName")
    Wscript.Echo "Modifying " & strSAM
    objUser.HomeDirectory = "\\<FileServerName>\" & _
                            strSAM
    objUser.SetInfo
next
```

Discussion

It is often necessary to update several users at once due to an organizational, geographic, or file server change. In each solution, we showed how to modify all users within a parent container, but you may need to use different criteria for locating the users.

With ADUC, you are limited to modifying multiple users that belong to the same container. However, with the Windows Server 2003 version of ADUC you can create a Saved Query that returns users based on any criteria you specify. You can then highlight those users and modify them as described in the GUI solution.

With the CLI solution, you can modify the dsquery user command to search on whatever criteria you want. The same applies in the VBScript solution, but you'll need to use an ADO query instead of the Filter method if you want to do anything more complex.

See Also

Recipe 4.8 for more information on searching with ADO

6.7   Setting a User's Profile Attributes

Problem

You want to set one or more of the user profile attributes.

Solution

Using a graphical user interface

1. Open the ADUC snap-in.
2. In the left pane, right-click on the domain and select Find.
3. Select the appropriate domain beside In.

4. Beside Name, type the name of the user and click Find Now.

5. In the Search Results window, double-click on the user.

6. Click the Profile tab.

7. Modify the various profile settings as necessary.

8. Click OK.

Using a command-line interface

You can update a user's profile attributes using either DSMod or AdMod. DSMod uses the following syntax:

```
> dsmod user "<UserDN>" -loscr <ScriptPath> -profile <ProfilePath>
-hmdir <HomeDir> -hmdrv <DriveLetter>
```

AdMod uses the following syntax:

```
> admod -b "<UserDN>" <attribute>::<NewValue>
```

Using VBScript

```
' This code sets the various profile related attributes for a user.
strUserDN = "<UserDN>"    ' e.g. cn=jsmith,cn=Users,dc=rallencorp,dc=com
set objUser = GetObject("LDAP://" & strUserDN)
objUser.Put "homeDirectory", "\\fileserver\" & objUser.Get("sAMAccountName")
objUser.Put "homeDrive", "z:"
objUser.Put "profilePath", "\\fileserver\" & _
            objUser.Get("sAMAccountName") & "\profile"
objUser.Put "scriptPath", "login.vbs"
objUser.SetInfo
Wscript.Echo "Profile info for " & objUser.Get("sAMAccountName") & " updated"
```

Discussion

The four attributes that make up a user's profile settings include the following:

homeDirectory
UNC path to home directory

homeDrive
Drive letter (e.g., Z:) to map home directory

profilePath
UNC path to profile directory

scriptPath
Path to logon script

When you set the homeDirectory attribute, the folder being referenced needs to already exist. For an example on creating shares for users, see MS KB 234746.

See Also

MS KB 234746 (How to Create User Shares for All Users in a Domain with ADSI), MS KB 271657 (Scripted Home Directory Paths Require That Folders Exist), and MS KB 320043 (How to Assign a Home Directory to a User)

6.8   Moving a User

Problem

You want to move a user object to a different container or OU.

Solution

Using a graphical user interface

1. Open the ADUC snap-in.
2. If you need to change domains, right-click on "Active Directory Users and Computers" in the left pane, select Connect to Domain, enter the domain name, and click OK.
3. In the left pane, right-click on the domain and select Find.
4. Type the name of the user and click Find Now.
5. In the Search Results window, right-click on the user and select Move.
6. Browse to and select the new parent container or OU.
7. Click OK.

 In Windows Server 2003 and above, you can also drag and drop objects from one container or OU into another.

Using a command-line interface

You can move an object using either the built-in DSMove utility or AdMod. DSMove takes the following syntax:

```
> dsmove "<UserDN>" -newparent "<NewParentDN>"
```

To move an object using AdMod, do the following:

```
> admod -b "<Current User DN>" -move "<New Parent DN>"
```

Using VBScript

```
' This code moves a user from one container to another.
' ------ SCRIPT CONFIGURATION ------
strUserDN = "<UserDN>"        ' e.g. cn=rallen,cn=users,dc=rallencorp,dc=com
strOUDN = "<NewParentDN>"     ' e.g. ou=Sales,dc=rallencorp,dc=com
```

```
' ------ END CONFIGURATION ---------

Set objUser = GetObject("LDAP://" & strUserDN)
Set objOU = GetObject("LDAP://" & strOUDN)
objOU.MoveHere objUser.ADsPath, objUser.Name
```

Discussion

Moving a user object between OUs in the same domain has no direct impact on the actual user in terms of any security or distribution groups that the user is a member of. The only thing to be cautious of is the impact of moving the user to a new OU that may have different security settings or GPOs applied to it.

See Also

Recipe 4.20 for moving objects between OUs

6.9   Redirecting Users to an Alternative OU

 This solution requires the Windows Server 2003 domain functional level.

Problem

You want to redirect all new users from the default OU (i.e., cn=Users) into the destination OU that you specify.

Using a graphical user interface

1. Open LDP.
2. From the menu, select Connection → Connect.
3. For Server, enter the name of a domain controller (or leave blank to do a serverless bind).
4. For Port, enter 389.
5. Click OK.
6. From the menu, select Connection → Bind.
7. Enter credentials of a domain user.
8. Click OK.
9. From the menu, select Browse → Modify.
10. For DN, enter the distinguished name of the domainDNS object of the domain you want to modify.
11. For Attribute, enter wellKnownObjects.

12. For Values, enter the following:

```
B:32:A9D1CA15768811D1ADED00C04FD8D5CD:CN=Users,<DomainDN>
```

where *<DomainDN>* is the same as the DN you enter for the DN field.

13. Select Delete for the Operation and click the Enter button.

14. Go back to the Values field and enter the following:

```
B:32:A9D1CA15768811D1ADED00C04FD8D5CD:<NewUsersParent>,<DomainDN>
```

where *<NewUsersParent>* is the new parent container for new computer objects (e.g., ou=RAllenCorp Users).

15. Select Add for the Operation and click the Enter button.

16. Click the Run button.

17. The result of the operations will be displayed in the right pane of the main LDP window.

Using the command-line interface

To redirect the default OU that new users will be created into, use the following syntax:

```
> redirusr "<DestinationDN>"
```

Discussion

Most modern methods for creating user accounts, including the ADUC MMC snap-in, AdFind, and DSAdd, allow you to specify which OU a new user should be created in. However, some utilities such as net user or the WinNT ADSI provider still rely on a legacy API that will create a user only in its default location until it is manually moved to another OU by an administrator. The default location in Windows Server 2003 is the cn=Users container; this can create issues applying Group Policy to new user objects since the Users container cannot have a GPO linked to it. To ensure that all newly created users receive the necessary Group Policy settings as soon as they are created, use the *redirusr.exe* utility to redirect all new users that are not otherwise placed into a designated OU into the destination OU that you specify. You only need to run this utility once per domain, and the destination OU needs to exist before you run the utility.

See Also

MS KB 324949 (Redirecting the Users and Computers Containers in Windows Server 2003)

6.10 Renaming a User

Problem

You want to rename a user.

Solution

Using a graphical user interface

1. Open the ADUC snap-in.
2. In the left pane, right-click on the domain and select Find.
3. Type the name of the user and click Find Now.
4. In the Search Results window, right-click on the user and select Rename.
5. You can modify the Full Name, Last Name, First Name, Display Name, User Principal Name (logon name), and SAM Account Name (pre-Windows 2000).
6. Click OK after you are done.

Using a command-line interface

The following command will rename the RDN of the user:

```
> dsmove "<UserDN>" -newname "<NewUserName>"
```

You can modify the UPN (-upn), First Name (-fn), Last Name (-ln), and Display Name (-display) using the dsmod user command. For example, the following command would change the user's UPN and last name:

```
> dsmod user "<UserDN>" -upn "<NewUserUPN>" -ln "<NewUserLastName>"
```

You can also rename an object by using AdMod with the following syntax:

```
> admod -b "<UserDN>" -rename "<New UserName>"
```

Using VBScript

```
' This code renames the RDN of a user and the sAMAccountName attribute.
' ------ SCRIPT CONFIGURATION ------
strParentDN   = "<ParentDN>"     ' e.g. cn=Users,dc=rallencorp,dc=com
strUserOldName = "<OldUserName>" ' e.g. jsmith
strUserNewName = "<NewUserName>" ' e.g. jim
' ------ END CONFIGURATION -------

set objCont = GetObject("LDAP://" & strParentDN)
objCont.MoveHere "LDAP://cn=" & strUserOldName & "," & strParentDN, _
              "cn=" & strUserNewName
set objUser = GetObject("LDAP://cn=" & strUserNewName & "," & strParentDN)
objUser.Put "sAMAccountName", strUserNewName
objUser.SetInfo
WScript.Echo "Rename successful"
```

Discussion

Renaming a user object can have a couple different meanings in Active Directory. In the generic object sense, renaming an object consists of changing the RDN for the object to something else, as when cn=jsmith becomes cn=joe. Typically, though, you need to rename more than that with users. For example, let's say you had a username naming convention of FirstInitialLastName so Joe Smith's username would be jsmith. Let's pretend that Joe decides one day that Smith is way too common and he wants to be unique by changing his last name to Einstein. Now his username should be jeinstein. The following attributes would need to change to complete a rename of his object:

- His RDN should change from cn=jsmith to cn=jeinstein.
- His sAMAccountName should change to jeinstein.
- His userPrincipalName (UPN) should change to jeinstein@rallencorp.com.
- His mail (email address) attribute should change to jeinstein@rallencorp.com.
- His sn (last name) attribute should change to Einstein.

While this example may be contrived, it shows that renaming Joe Smith to Joe Einstein can take up to five attribute changes in Active Directory, or more if you include updates to proxy addresses and other attributes that are typically tied to the user's name. It is also important to note that if you change any of the first three in the bulleted list (RDN, UPN, or SAM Account Name), you should have the user log off and log back on after the changes have replicated. Since most applications and services rely on user GUID or SID, which doesn't change during a user rename, the person should not be impacted, but you want to have him or her log off and back on anyway, just in case.

See Also

Recipe 4.23 for renaming objects

6.11 Copying a User

Problem

You want to copy an existing user account, which may be serving as a template, to create a new account.

Solution

Using a graphical user interface

1. Open the ADUC snap-in.
2. In the left pane, browse to the parent container of the template user object.

3. In the right pane, right-click on the user and select Copy.

4. Enter the name information for the new user and click Next.

5. Enter a password, check any options you want enabled, and click Next.

6. Click Finish.

Using VBScript

```
' This code copies the attributes in the Attrs array from an
' existing object to a new one.
' ------ SCRIPT CONFIGURATION ------
arrAttrs       = Array("department","co","title","l", "c", "st")
strParentDN    = "<ParentContainer>"     ' e.g. cn=Users,dc=rallencorp,dc=com
strTemplateUser = "<TemplateUserName>"   ' e.g. template-user-sales
strNewUser     = "<NewUserName>"         ' e.g. jdoe
strPassword    = "<Password>"
' ------ END CONFIGURATION ---------

Const ADS_UF_NORMAL_ACCOUNT = 512   ' from ADS_USER_FLAG_ENUM

Set objTemplate = GetObject("LDAP://cn=" & strTemplateUser & _
                            "," & strParentDN)
Set objParent   = GetObject("LDAP://" & strParentDN)
Set objUser     = objParent.Create("user", "cn=" & strNewUser)

objUser.Put "sAMAccountName", strNewUser

for each strAttr in arrAttrs
   objUser.Put strAttr, objTemplate.Get(strAttr)
next

objUser.SetInfo
objUser.SetPassword(strPassword)
objUser.SetInfo

objUser.Put "userAccountControl", ADS_UF_NORMAL_ACCOUNT
objUser.AccountDisabled = FALSE
objUser.SetInfo

WScript.Echo "Successfully created user"
```

Discussion

Copying a user consists of copying the attributes that are common among a certain user base, which can include department, address, and perhaps even organizational information. ADUC actually uses attributes that are marked in the schema as "Copied when duplicating a user" to determine which attributes to copy. The VBScript solution just used a hard-coded set of attributes. If you are interested in finding the attributes that are configured in the schema to get copied, see Recipe 11.13.

Using a graphical user interface

To copy a user in ADUC, you have to browse to the user object. If you locate the user by using Find instead, the Copy option is not available when right-clicking a user in the search results window.

Using VBScript

ADSI has a CopyHere method, but it is available only for the NDS provider. It was not implemented for the LDAP provider and so copying a user via a single method is not supported.

See Also

Recipe 11.13 for finding the attributes that should be copied when duplicating a user

6.12   Finding Locked Out Users

Problem

You want to find users whose accounts are locked out.

Solution

Using a command-line interface

The following command finds all locked out users in the domain of the specified domain controller:

```
> unlock <DomainControllerName> *  -view
```

Discussion

Despite the deceptively simple command just shown, finding the accounts that are currently locked out is a surprisingly complicated task. You would imagine that you could run a query using DSQuery or AdFind (similar to the one to find disabled users in Recipe 6.17), but unfortunately it is not that easy.

The lockoutTime attribute is populated with a timestamp when a user is locked. One way to find locked out users would be to find all users that have something populated in lockoutTime (i.e., lockoutTime=*). That query would definitely find all the currently locked users, but it would also find all the users that subsequently became unlocked and have yet to log in since being unlocked; the lockoutTime attribute doesn't get reset until the next time the user logs on successfully. This is where the complexity comes into place.

To determine the users that are currently locked out, you have to query the lockoutDuration attribute stored on the domain object (e.g., dc=rallencorp,dc=com). This attribute defines the number of minutes that an account will stay locked before becoming automatically unlocked. You need to take this value and subtract it from the current time to derive a timestamp that would be the outer marker for which users could still be locked. You can then compare this timestamp with the `lockoutTime` attribute of the user object. The search filter to find all locked users once you've determined the locked timestamp would look something like this:

```
(&(objectcategory=Person)(objectclass=user)(lockoutTime>DerivedTimestamp))
```

For any users that have a `lockoutTime` that is less than the derived timestamp, their account has already been automatically unlocked per the `lockoutDuration` setting.

None of the current standard GUI or CLI tools incorporates this kind of logic, but fortunately Joe Richards wrote the *unlock.exe* utility, which does. And as its name implies, you can also unlock locked accounts with it. Thanks, Joe!

See Also

MS KB 813500 (Support WebCast: Microsoft Windows 2000 Server and Windows Server 2003: Password and Account Lockout Features)

6.13   Unlocking a User

Problem

You want to unlock a locked out user.

Solution

Using a graphical user interface

1. Open the ADUC snap-in.
2. In the left pane, right-click on the domain and select Find.
3. Select the appropriate domain beside In.
4. Type the name of the user beside Name and click Find Now.
5. In the Search Results window, right-click on the user and select Unlock.
6. Click OK.

Using a command-line interface

To unlock all locked user accounts in your domain, use *unlock.exe* with the following syntax:

```
> unlock . *
```

To unlock a specific user object, replace * with the user's `sAMAccountName` or `distinguished name`, as follows:

```
> unlock . joe.smith
```

Using VBScript

```
' This code unlocks a locked user.
' ------ SCRIPT CONFIGURATION ------
strUsername = "<UserName>"           ' e.g. jsmith
strDomain = "<NetBiosDomainName>" ' e.g. RALLENCORP
' ------ END CONFIGURATION ---------

set objUser = GetObject("WinNT://" & strDomain & "/" & strUsername)
if objUser.IsAccountLocked = TRUE then
   objUser.IsAccountLocked = FALSE
   objUser.SetInfo
   WScript.Echo "Account unlocked"
else
   WScript.Echo "Account not locked"
end if
```

Discussion

If you've enabled account lockouts in a domain (see Recipe 6.12), users will inevitably get locked out. A user can get locked out for a number of reasons, but generally it is because a user mistypes his password a number of times, changes his password and does not log off and log on again, or has mapped drives.

You can use ADSI's IADsUser::IsAccountLocked method to determine if a user is locked out. You can set IsAccountLocked to FALSE to unlock a user. Unfortunately, there is a bug with the LDAP provider version of this method, so you have to use the WinNT provider instead. See MS KB 250873 for more information on this bug. You can also query the msDS-User-Account-Control-Computed attribute of an object; however, you can only retrieve this using a base-level query.

See Also

Recipe 6.12 for finding locked out users, Recipe 6.14 for viewing the account lockout policy, MS KB 250873 (Programmatically Changing the Lockout Flag in Windows 2000), and MSDN: Account Lockout

6.14   Troubleshooting Account Lockout Problems

Problem

A user is having account lockout problems and you need to determine from where and how it is getting locked out.

Solution

Using a graphical user interface

LockoutStatus is a new program available for Windows 2000 or Windows Server 2003 that can help identify which domain controller's users are getting locked out. It works by querying the lockout status of a user against all domain controllers in the user's domain.

To determine the lockout status of a user:

1. Launch LockoutStatus and select File → Select Target from the menu.
2. Enter the target user name and the domain of the user.
3. Click OK.

At this point, each domain controller in the domain will be queried and the results will be displayed.

Discussion

The *lockoutstatus.exe* tool is just one of many that are available in the new "Account Lockout and Management" toolset provided by Microsoft. These new lockout tools are intended to help administrators with account lockout problems that were very difficult to troubleshoot given the tools available under Windows 2000. Along with the tool mentioned in the Solution section, here are a few others that are included in the set:

ALockout.dll
> A script that uses this DLL called *EnableKerbLog.vbs* (included with the toolset), can be used to enable logging of application authentication. This can help identify applications that are using bad credentials and causing account lockouts.

ALoInfo.exe
> Displays services and shares that are using a particular account name. It can also print all the users and their password age.

NLParse.exe
> A filter tool for the *netlogon.log* files. You can use it to extract just the lines that relate to account lockout information.

EventCombMT
> A utility to parse Event Logs from multiple servers, either to collect all entries together or to search for individual events across multiple computers. This is extremely useful when troubleshooting user account lockouts, for example, by determining which computer is causing the account lockout.

All of the new Account Lockout tools can be downloaded from:

> *http://microsoft.com/downloads/details.aspx?familyid=7AF2E69C-91F3-4E63-8629-B999ADDE0B9E&displaylang=en*

See Also

MS KB 813500 (Support WebCast: Microsoft Windows 2000 Server and Windows Server 2003: Password and Account Lockout Features)

6.15   Viewing the Account Lockout and Password Policies

Problem

You want to view the account lockout and password policies for a domain.

Solution

Using a graphical user interface

1. Open the Domain Security Policy snap-in.
2. In the left menu, expand Default Domain Policy → Computer Configuration → Windows Settings → Security Settings → Account Policies.
3. Click on Password Policy or Account Lockout Policy and double-click the property you want to set or view in the right frame.

Using a command-line interface

To view the account lockout and password properties of your domain, use the following AdFind query:

```
> adfind -default -s base  Lockoutduration lockoutthreshold lockoutobservationwindow
maxpwdage minpwdage minpwdlength pwdhistorylength pwdproperties
```

Using VBScript

```
' This code displays the current settings for the password
' and account lockout policies.
' ------ SCRIPT CONFIGURATION ------
strDomain = "<DomainDN>"   ' e.g. rallencorp.com
' ------ END CONFIGURATION ---------

set objRootDSE = GetObject("LDAP://" & strDomain & "/RootDSE")
set objDomain  = GetObject("LDAP://" & _
                           objRootDSE.Get("defaultNamingContext") )

' Hash containing the domain password and lockout policy attributes
' as keys and the units (e.g. minutes) as the values
set objDomAttrHash = CreateObject("Scripting.Dictionary")
objDomAttrHash.Add "lockoutDuration", "minutes"
objDomAttrHash.Add "lockoutThreshold", "attempts"
objDomAttrHash.Add "lockoutObservationWindow", "minutes"
objDomAttrHash.Add "maxPwdAge", "minutes"
```

```
objDomAttrHash.Add "minPwdAge", "minutes"
objDomAttrHash.Add "minPwdLength", "characters"
objDomAttrHash.Add "pwdHistoryLength", "remembered"
objDomAttrHash.Add "pwdProperties", " "

' Iterate over each attribute and print it
for each strAttr in objDomAttrHash.Keys
    if IsObject( objDomain.Get(strAttr) ) then
        set objLargeInt = objDomain.Get(strAttr)
        if objLargeInt.LowPart - 0 then
           value = 0
        else
           value = Abs(objLargeInt.HighPart * 2^32 + objLargeInt.LowPart)
           value = int ( value / 10000000 )
           value = int ( value / 60 )
        end if
    else
        value = objDomain.Get(strAttr)
    end if
    WScript.Echo strAttr & " = " & value & " " & objDomAttrHash(strAttr)
next

'Constants from DOMAIN_PASSWORD_INFORMATION
Set objDomPassHash = CreateObject("Scripting.Dictionary")
objDomPassHash.Add "DOMAIN_PASSWORD_COMPLEX", &h1
objDomPassHash.Add "DOMAIN_PASSWORD_NO_ANON_CHANGE", &h2
objDomPassHash.Add "DOMAIN_PASSWORD_NO_CLEAR_CHANGE", &h4
objDomPassHash.Add "DOMAIN_LOCKOUT_ADMINS", &h8
objDomPassHash.Add "DOMAIN_PASSWORD_STORE_CLEARTEXT", &h16
objDomPassHash.Add "DOMAIN_REFUSE_PASSWORD_CHANGE", &h32

' The PwdProperties attribute requires special processing because
' it is a flag that holds multiple settings.
for each strFlag In objDomPassHash.Keys
  if objDomPassHash(strFlag) and objDomain.Get("PwdProperties") then
    WScript.Echo "  " & strFlag & " is enabled"
  else
    WScript.Echo "  " & strFlag & " is disabled"
  end If
next
```

Discussion

Several parameters controlling account lockout and password complexity can be set on the Domain Security GPO. The properties that can be set for the "Account Lockout Policy" include:

Account lockout duration
Number of minutes an account will be locked before being automatically unlocked. A value of 0 indicates accounts will be locked out indefinitely, i.e., until an administrator manually unlocks them.

Account lockout threshold
> Number of failed logon attempts after which an account will be locked.

Reset account lockout counter after
> Number of minutes after a failed logon attempt that the failed logon counter for an account will be reset to 0.

The properties that can be set for the "Password Policy" include:

Enforce password history
> Number of passwords to remember before a user can reuse a previous password.

Maximum password age
> Maximum number of days a password can be used before a user must change it.

Minimum password age
> Minimum number of days a password must be used before it can be changed.

Minimum password length
> Minimum number of characters a password must be.

Password must meet complexity requirements
> If enabled, passwords must meet all of the following criteria:
> - Not contain all or part of the user's account name
> - Be at least six characters in length
> - Contain characters from three of the following four categories:
>   - English uppercase characters (A–Z)
>   - English lowercase characters (a–z)
>   - Base 10 digits (0–9)
>   - Nonalphanumeric characters (e.g., !, $, #, %)

Store passwords using reversible encryption
> If enabled, passwords are stored in such a way that they can be retrieved and decrypted. This is essentially the same as storing passwords in plain text, and should be avoided unless it is absolutely necessary.

Using a graphical user interface

On a domain controller or machine that has *adminpak.msi* installed, the Domain Security Policy snap-in is present from the Start menu under Administrative Tools. On a member server, you need to open the GPO snap-in and locate the Domain Security policy. See the "Introduction" to Chapter 10 for more information on GPOs.

Using a command-line interface

There is no standard CLI that can be used to modify a GPO, but you can use AdFind to view each of the attributes on the domain object that make up the account lockout and password policy settings.

Using VBScript

The VBScript solution required quite a bit of code to perform the simple task of printing out the account lockout and password policy settings. First, create a `Dictionary` object with each of the six attributes as the keys and the unit's designation for each key (e.g., minutes) as the value. Then iterate over each key, printing it along with the value retrieved from the domain object.

Some additional code was necessary to distinguish between the values returned from some of the attributes. In the case of the time-based attributes, such as `lockoutDuration`, an `IADsLargeInteger` object was returned from the `Get` method instead of a pure integer or string value. `IADsLargeInteger` objects represent 64-bit, also known as Integer8, numbers. 32-bit systems, which make up the majority of systems today, have to break 64-bit numbers into two parts (a high and low part) to store them. Unfortunately, VBScript cannot natively handle a 64-bit number and stores it as a double precision. To convert a 64-bit number into something VBScript can handle, you have to first multiply the high part by 4,294,967,296 (2^{32}) and then add the low part to the result.

```
value = Abs(objLargeInt.HighPart * 2^32 + objLargeInt.LowPart)
```

Then you divide by 10,000,000 or 10^7, which represents the number of 100 nanosecond intervals per second:

```
value = int ( value / 10000000 )
```

You then use the `int` function to discard any remainder and finally divided the result by 60 (number of seconds):

```
value = int ( value / 60 )
```

The last part of the code iterates over another `Dictionary` object that contains constants representing various flags that can be set as part of the `pwdProperties` attribute.

 Note that the result is only an approximation in minutes and can be off by several minutes, hours, or even days depending on the original value.

See Also

The "Introduction" to Chapter 10, MS KB 221930 (Domain Security Policy in Windows 2000), MS KB 255550 (Configuring Account Policies in Active Directory), MSDN: IADsLargeInteger, and MSDN: DOMAIN_PASSWORD_INFORMATION

6.16 Enabling and Disabling a User

Problem

You want to enable or disable a user account.

Solution

Using a graphical user interface

1. Open the ADUC snap-in.
2. In the left pane, right-click on the domain and select Find.
3. Select the appropriate domain beside In.
4. Type the name of the user beside Name and click Find Now.
5. In the Search Results window, right-click on the user and select Enable Account to enable or Disable Account to disable.
6. Click OK.

Using a command-line interface

To enable a user, use the following command:

```
> dsmod user <UserDN> -disabled no
```

To disable a user, use the following command:

```
> dsmod user <UserDN> -disabled yes
```

Using VBScript

```
' This code will enable or disable a user.
' ------ SCRIPT CONFIGURATION ------
' Set to FALSE to disable account or TRUE to enable account
strDisableAccount = FALSE
strUserDN = "<UserDN>" ' e.g. cn=jsmith,cn=Users,dc=rallencorp,dc=com
' ------ END CONFIGURATION ---------

set objUser = GetObject("LDAP://" & strUserDN)
if objUser.AccountDisabled = TRUE then
   WScript.Echo "Account for " & objUser.Get("cn") & " currently disabled"
   if strDisableAccount = FALSE then
      objUser.AccountDisabled = strDisableAccount
      objUser.SetInfo
      WScript.Echo "Account enabled"
   end if
else
   WScript.Echo "Account currently enabled"
   if strDisableAccount = TRUE then
      objUser.AccountDisabled = strDisableAccount
      objUser.SetInfo
      WScript.Echo "Account disabled"
   end if
end if
```

Discussion

Account status is used to control whether a user is allowed to log on or not. When an account is disabled, the user is not allowed to log on to her workstation with the account or to access AD controlled resources. Much like the lockout status, the account status is stored as a flag in the userAccountControl attribute (see Recipe 6.29).

There is an IADsUser::AccountDisabled property that allows you to determine and change the status. Set the method FALSE to enable the account or TRUE to disable.

See Also

Recipe 6.17 for finding disabled users and Recipe 6.29 for more on the userAccountControl attribute

6.17 Finding Disabled Users

Problem

You want to find disabled users in a domain.

Solution

Using a graphical user interface

1. Open the ADUC snap-in.
2. In the left pane, connect to the domain you want to query.
3. Right-click on the domain and select Find.
4. Beside Find, select Common Queries.
5. Check the box beside "disabled accounts."
6. Click the Find Now button.

Using a command-line interface

You can enumerate all disabled user objects in your domain by using the built-in DSQuery utility, as follows:

```
> dsquery user <DomainDN> -disabled
```

You can also use a bitwise query in AdFind to product the same output, using the following syntax:

```
> adfind -bit -b <DomainDN> -f
"&(objectcategory=person)(objectclass=user)(useraccountcontrol:AND:=2)"
```

You can replace *<DomainDN>* with the DN of a specific Organizational Unit if you wish to restrict the results of your AdFind query.

Using VBScript

```
' This code finds all disabled user accounts in a domain.
' ------ SCRIPT CONFIGURATION ------
strDomainDN = "<DomainDN>"     ' e.g. dc=rallencorp,dc=com
' ------ END CONFIGURATION ---------

strBase   = "<LDAP://" & strDomainDN & ">;"
strFilter = "(&(objectclass=user)(objectcategory=person)" & _
            "(useraccountcontrol:1.2.840.113556.1.4.803:=2));"
strAttrs  = "name;"
strScope  = "subtree"

set objConn = CreateObject("ADODB.Connection")
objConn.Provider = "ADsDSOObject"
objConn.Open "Active Directory Provider"
set objRS = objConn.Execute(strBase & strFilter & strAttrs & strScope)
objRS.MoveFirst
while Not objRS.EOF
    Wscript.Echo objRS.Fields(0).Value
    objRS.MoveNext
wend
```

Discussion

Users in Active Directory can either be enabled or disabled. A disabled user cannot log in to the domain. Unlike account lockout, which is an automatic process that is based on the number of times a user incorrectly enters a password, an account has to be manually enabled or disabled.

All disabled user accounts have the bit that represents 2 (0010) set in their userAccountControl attribute. This doesn't mean that the attribute will be equal to 2, it just means that the bit that equals 2 will be enabled—other bits may also be set. See Recipes 4.12 and 4.15 for a more detailed explanation of bit flags.

See Also

Recipes 4.12, 4.15, and 6.16 for enabling and disabling users

6.18   Viewing a User's Group Membership

Problem

You want to view the group membership of a user.

Solution

Using a graphical user interface

1. Open the ADUC snap-in.
2. In the left pane, right-click on the domain and select Find.
3. Select the appropriate domain beside In.
4. Type the name of the user beside Name and click Find Now.
5. In the Search Results window, double-click on the user.
6. Click the Member Of tab.
7. To view all indirect group membership (from nested groups), you'll need to double-click on each group.

Using a command-line interface

The following command displays the groups *<UserDN>* is a member of. Use the -expand switch to list nested group membership as well:

```
> dsget user <UserDN> -memberof [-expand]
```

You can also use the GetUserInfo tool (another tool available from *http://www.joeware.net*) with the following syntax:

```
> getuserinfo \\<Domain>\<Username>
```

A third option would be to use the *whoami* tool, as follows:

```
> whoami /groups
```

To round out the command-line options for viewing group memberships, you can use the MemberOf joeware utility with the following syntax:

```
> memberof -u <Domain>\<User>
```

 To query group membership from a specific domain controller using MemberOf, use the –s switch followed by the name of the DC.

Using VBScript

```
' This code displays the group membership of a user.
' It avoids infinite loops due to circular group nesting by
' keeping track of the groups that have already been seen.
' ------ SCRIPT CONFIGURATION ------
strUserDN = "<UserDN>"   ' e.g. cn=jsmith,cn=Users,dc=rallencorp,dc=com
' ------ END CONFIGURATION ---------

set objUser = GetObject("LDAP://" & strUserDN)
Wscript.Echo "Group membership for " & objUser.Get("cn") & ":"
strSpaces = ""
set dicSeenGroup = CreateObject("Scripting.Dictionary")
```

```
    DisplayGroups("LDAP://" & strUserDN, strSpaces, dicSeenGroup)

    Function DisplayGroups ( strObjectADsPath, strSpaces, dicSeenGroup)

        set objObject = GetObject(strObjectADsPath)
        WScript.Echo strSpaces & objObject.Name
        on error resume next ' Doing this to avoid an error when memberOf is empty
        if IsArray( objObject.Get("memberOf") ) then
            colGroups = objObject.Get("memberOf")
        else
            colGroups = Array( objObject.Get("memberOf") )
        end if

        for each strGroupDN In colGroups
            if Not dicSeenGroup.Exists(strGroupDN) then
                dicSeenGroup.Add strGroupDN, 1
                DisplayGroups "LDAP://" & strGroupDN, strSpaces & " ", dicSeenGroup
            end if
        next

    End Function
```

Discussion

The memberOf attribute on user objects is multivalued and contains the list of distinguished names for groups of which the user is a member. memberOf is actually linked with the member attribute on group objects, which holds the distinguished names of its members. For this reason, you cannot directly modify the memberOf attribute; you must instead modify the member attribute on the group.

The primary group of a user, which the user is technically a member of, will not be shown in either the CLI or VBScript solutions except in the case of the MemberOf utility. This is due to the fact that the primary group is not stored in the memberOf attribute like the rest of the groups. See Recipe 6.20 and Recipe 7.12 for more on finding the primary group of a user.

See Also

Recipe 6.20, Recipe 7.4 for more on viewing the nested members of a group, Recipe 7.12, Recipe 10.16 for more information on linked attributes, and MS KB 906208 (When You Try to Log Onto a Windows Server 2003-Based Domain by Using a Domain User Account, the Logon Request Fails)

6.19   Removing All Group Memberships from a User

Problem

You want to remove all group membership information from a user object.

Solution

Using a graphical user interface

1. Open the ADUC snap-in.
2. In the left pane, right-click on the domain and select Find.
3. Select the appropriate domain beside In.
4. Type the name of the user beside Name and click Find Now.
5. In the Search Results window, double-click on the user.
6. Click the Member Of tab.
7. Highlight each group listed in the Member Of tab and select Remove. Click Yes to confirm.
8. Click OK.

Using VBScript

```
Const ADS_PROPERTY_DELETE = 4
Const E_ADS_PROPERTY_NOT_FOUND  = &h8000500D

Set objUser = GetObject("LDAP://<UserDN>")
arrMemberOf = objUser.GetEx("memberOf")

If Err.Number = E_ADS_PROPERTY_NOT_FOUND Then
    WScript.Echo "No group memberships found."
    WScript.Quit
End If

For Each Group in arrMemberOf
    Set objGroup = GetObject("LDAP://" & Group)
    objGroup.PutEx ADS_PROPERTY_DELETE, _
        "member", Array("<UserDN>")
    objGroup.SetInfo
Next
```

Discussion

Using VBScript

A user's group membership is a constructed attribute, consisting of the contents of both the memberOf and primaryGroupID attributes; therefore, the code necessary to clear a user's group memberships actually involves modifying each group object in turn, rather than modifying the user object itself.

See Also

MSDN: Adding Members to Groups in a Domain [Active Directory] and MSDN: Group Objects [Active Directory]

6.20   Changing a User's Primary Group

Problem

You want to change the primary group of a user.

Solution

Using a graphical user interface

1. Open the ADUC snap-in.
2. In the left pane, right-click on the domain and select Find.
3. Select the appropriate domain beside In.
4. Type the name of the user beside Name and click Find Now.
5. In the Search Results window, double-click on the user.
6. Click the Member Of tab.
7. Click on the name of the group you want to set as the primary group.
8. Click the Set Primary Group button.
9. Click OK.

Using VBScript

```
' This code first checks to see if the user's primary group is already
' set to the specified group.  If not it will a) add the user to the group
' if not already a member and b) set the primary group id to the group.
' ------ SCRIPT CONFIGURATION ------
strUserDN  = "<UserDN>"     ' e.g. cn=rallen,ou=Sales,dc=rallencorp,dc=com
strGroupDN = "<GroupDN>"    ' e.g. cn=SalesGroup,ou=Sales,dc=rallencorp,dc=com
' ------ END CONFIGURATION ---------

Const ADS_PROPERTY_APPEND = 3

set objUser = GetObject("LDAP://" & strUserDN )
WScript.Echo

set objGroup = GetObject("LDAP://" & strGroupDN )
objGroup.GetInfoEx Array("primaryGroupToken"), 0
if objGroup.Get("primaryGroupToken") = objUser.Get("primaryGroupID") then
    WScript.Echo "Primary group for user already set to " & strGroupDN
    WScript.Quit
end if

intAddMember = 1
for each strMemberDN in objUser.GetEx("memberOf")
    if LCase(strMemberDN) = LCase(strGroupDN) then
        intAddMember = 0
        Exit for
    end if
```

```
next

if intAddMember > 0 then
    objGroup.PutEx ADS_PROPERTY_APPEND, "member", Array(strUserDN)
    objGroup.SetInfo
    WScript.Echo "Added " & strUserDN & " as member of " & strGroupDN
end if

objUser.Put "primaryGroupID", objGroup.Get("primaryGroupToken")
objUser.SetInfo
WScript.Echo "Changed primary group id of " & strUserDN & _
             " to " & objGroup.Get("primaryGroupToken")
```

Discussion

The primary group is a holdover from Windows NT that was used to support Macintosh and POSIX clients. That said, you might have some legacy applications that depend on the primary group and therefore you may have to change some users' primary group.

Changing the primary group is not difficult, but it is not straightforward either. The primary group is stored on user objects in the primaryGroupID attribute, which contains the RID of the primary group. You can obtain this value by querying the primaryGroupToken attribute on the target group object. Before you can set the primaryGroupID on the user object, you have to first make sure the user is a member of the group. If you try to set the primaryGroupID for a group in which the user is not a member, you will get an error.

The default primaryGroupID is set to 513 (Domain Users) for all users.

See Also

Recipe 7.12 for determining the group name given a group ID, MS KB 297951 (How to Use the PrimaryGroupID Attribute to Find the Primary Group for a User), MS KB 321360 (How to Use Native ADSI Components to Find the Primary Group), and MS KB 243330 (Well-Known Security Identifiers in Windows Operating Systems)

6.21 Transferring a User's Group Membership to Another User

Problem

You want to copy one user's group membership to another user.

Solution

Using a graphical user interface

1. Open the ADUC snap-in.
2. In the left pane, right-click on the domain and select Find.
3. Select the appropriate domain beside In.
4. Beside Name, type the name of the user you want to transfer groups from and click Find Now.
5. In the Search Results window, double-click on the user.
6. Click the Member Of tab.
7. For each group you want to add another user in, do the following:
   a. Double-click on the group.
   b. Click the Members tab.
   c. Click the Add button.
   d. Find the user you want to add in the object picker and click OK.
   e. Click OK.

Using a command-line interface

The following command line will add *<NewUserDN>* to all of the groups that *<CurrentUserDN>* is a member of:

```
> for /F "usebackq delims=""" %i in (`dsget user
"<CurrentUserDN>" -memberof`) do dsmod group %i -addmbr "<NewUserDN>"
```

If you want to get fancy and remove *<CurrentUserDN>* from each of the groups in the same operation, simply add an -rmmbr option on the end:

```
> for /F "usebackq delims=""" %i in (`dsget user
"<CurrentUserDN>" -memberof`) do dsmod group %i -addmbr "<NewUserDN>"
-rmmbr "<CurrentUserDN>"
```

Using VBScript

```
' This code adds the "new" user to the groups the "current"
' user is a member of
' ------ SCRIPT CONFIGURATION ------
strCurrentUserDN = "<CurrentUserDN>"
                    ' e.g. cn=jsmith,ou=Sales,dc=rallencorp,dc=com
strNewUserDN     = "<NewUserDN>"

' ------ SCRIPT CONFIGURATION ------

Const ADS_PROPERTY_APPEND = 3
```

```
set objCurrentUser = GetObject("LDAP://" & strCurrentUserDN )
set objNewUser = GetObject("LDAP://" & strNewUserDN )

on error resume next
WScript.Echo "Transfering groups from " & strCurrentUserDN & " to " & strNewUserDN
for each strGroupDN in objCurrentUser.GetEx("memberOf")
    set objGroup = GetObject("LDAP://" & strGroupDN)
    objGroup.PutEx ADS_PROPERTY_APPEND, "member", Array( strNewUserDN )
    objGroup.SetInfo
    if Err then
        WScript.Echo "Error adding user to group: " & strGroupDN
    else
        WScript.Echo "Added user to group: " & strGroupDN
    end if
next
```

Discussion

Employees come and go; people take on new responsibilities and move on to new jobs. It is common to have movement within an organization. When this happens, typically someone is replacing the person that is moving on. The new person needs to get up to speed as quickly as possible, including getting accounts set up and access to any necessary resources. A big part of this includes getting added to the correct groups. You can help facilitate this by using one of the processes outlined in the Solution section to help the user gain access to the exact same groups that the former employee was a member of.

One important issue to point out is that the memberOf attribute, which was used in the Solution section to determine a user's group membership, contains only the groups that are visible to the DC that's being queried; this can vary depending on whether the DC in question is a Global Catalog and whether the user belongs to any universal groups. Any groups the user is a member of outside of the user's domain will not be transferred. To transfer universal group membership outside of a domain, you will need to perform a query against the global catalog for all group objects that have a member attribute that contains the DN of the user. You can also search the Global Catalog for the memberOf attribute for a given user to determine a user's universal group memberships.

See Also

Recipe 7.5 for adding and removing members of a group

6.22   Setting a User's Password

Problem

You want to set the password for a user.

Solution

Using a graphical user interface

1. Open the ADUC snap-in.
2. In the left pane, right-click on the domain and select Find.
3. Select the appropriate domain beside In.
4. Type the name of the user beside Name and click Find Now.
5. In the Search Results window, right-click on the user and select Reset Password.
6. Enter and confirm the new password.
7. Click OK.

Using a command-line interface

This command changes the password for the user specified by *<UserDN>*. Using * after the -pwd option prompts you for the new password. You can replace * with the password you want to set, but it is not a good security practice since other users that are logged into the machine may be able to see it.

```
> dsmod user <UserDN> -pwd *
```

You can also use admod with the #setpwd# switch, as follows:

```
> admod -b "<UserDN>" #setpwd#::<NewPassword>
```

You can also modify the unicodepwd attribute directly by encrypting the admod connection using the –kerbenc switch, as follows:

```
> admod –b "<UserDN>" unicodepwd::<Password> -kerbenc
```

Using VBScript

```
' This code sets the password for a user.
' ------ SCRIPT CONFIGURATION ------
strUserDN = "<UserDN>"     ' e.g. cn=jsmith,cn=Users,dc=rallencorp,dc=com
strNewPasswd = "<NewPasword>"
' ------ END CONFIGURATION ---------

set objUser = GetObject("LDAP://" & strUserDN)
objUser.SetPassword(strNewPasswd)
Wscript.Echo "Password set for " & objUser.Get("cn")
```

Discussion

A one-way hash of a user's password is stored in the unicodePwd attribute. There are several supported methods to modify this attribute directly, or you can use one of the supported APIs to do so. See Recipe 6.23 to see how to set the password using native LDAP and Recipe 6.24 for changing the password via Kerberos.

With the VBScript solution, you can use the `IADsUser::SetPassword` method or `IADsUser::ChangePassword`. The latter requires the existing password to be known before setting it. This is the method you'd want to use if you've created a web page that accepts the previous password before allowing a user to change it.

See Also

Recipe 6.23 for setting the password via LDAP, Recipe 6.24 for setting the password via Kerberos, MS KB 225511 (New Password Change and Conflict Resolution Functionality in Windows), MS KB 264480 (Description of Password-Change Protocols in Windows 2000), MSDN: IADsUser::SetPassword, and MSDN: IADsUser::ChangePassword

6.23 Setting a User's Password via LDAP

Problem

You want to set the password for a user using LDAP.

Solution

You have to first enable 128-bit encryption in your Active Directory domain. See Recipe 15.1 for more on this.

You can then set the `unicodePwd` attribute of a user object using LDAP operations over an SSL or TLS connection.

The value for the `unicodePwd` attribute must be a Unicode string that is surrounded by quotes and is BER encoded. See Recipe 11.4 for more on encoding text with Base64.

Discussion

The `unicodePwd` attribute can be directly modified over a SSL or TLS connection, but it can never be read.

See Also

Recipe 11.4 for more on Base64 encoding, Recipe 15.1 for enabling SSL/TLS, MS KB 263991 (How to Set a User's Password with Ldifde), MS KB 264480 (Description of Password-Change Protocols in Windows 2000), and MS KB 269190 (How to Change a Windows 2000 User's Password Through LDAP)

6.24 Setting a User's Password from Unix

Problem

You want to change a password using Kerberos from a Unix machine.

Solution

If you have MIT Kerberos 5 client installed and configured properly, you can run the following commands, which will change your password in Active Directory:

```
$ kinit
Password for jsmith@RALLENCORP.COM: ****
$ kpasswd
Password for jsmith@RALLENCORP.COM: ****
Enter new password: ******
Enter it again: ******
Password changed.
```

Discussion

See Recipe 15.22 for more information on Kerberos.

See Also

MS KB 264480 (Description of Password-Change Protocols in Windows 2000), RFC 3244 (Microsoft Windows 2000 Kerberos Change Password and Set Password Protocols), and IETF *draft-ietf-cat-kerb-chg-password-02.txt*

6.25 Preventing a User from Changing Her Password

Problem

You want to disable a user's ability to change her password.

Solution

Using a graphical user interface

1. Open the ADUC snap-in.
2. In the left pane, right-click on the domain and select Find.
3. Select the appropriate domain beside In.
4. Beside Name, type the name of the user you want to modify and click Find Now.
5. In the Search Results window, double-click on the user.
6. Click the Account tab.
7. Under Account options, check the box beside "User cannot change password."
8. Click OK.

Using a command-line interface

```
> dsmod user <UserDN> -canchpwd no
```

Using VBScript

```
' This code disables a user's ability to change password
' ------ SCRIPT CONFIGURATION ------
strUserDN = "<UserDN>"      ' e.g. cn=rallen,ou=Sales,dc=rallencorp,dc=com
' ------ END CONFIGURATION ---------

Const ACETYPE_ACCESS_DENIED_OBJECT = 6
Const ACEFLAG_OBJECT_TYPE_PRESENT = 1
Const RIGHT_DS_CONTROL_ACCESS = 256
Const CHANGE_PASSWORD_GUID = "{ab721a53-1e2f-11d0-9819-00aa0040529b}"

set objUser = GetObject("LDAP://" & strUserDN)
set objSD = objUser.Get("ntSecurityDescriptor")
set objDACL = objSD.DiscretionaryAcl

' Add a deny ACE for Everyone
set objACE = CreateObject("AccessControlEntry")
objACE.Trustee = "Everyone"
objACE.AceFlags = 0
objACE.AceType = ACETYPE_ACCESS_DENIED_OBJECT
objACE.Flags = ACEFLAG_OBJECT_TYPE_PRESENT
objACE.ObjectType = CHANGE_PASSWORD_GUID
objACE.AccessMask = RIGHT_DS_CONTROL_ACCESS
objDACL.AddAce objACE

' Add a deny ACE for Self
' (This is only necessary to prevent a user from
'  changing their own password.)
set objACE = CreateObject("AccessControlEntry")
objACE.Trustee = "Self"
objACE.AceFlags = 0
objACE.AceType = ACETYPE_ACCESS_DENIED_OBJECT
objACE.Flags = ACEFLAG_OBJECT_TYPE_PRESENT
objACE.ObjectType = CHANGE_PASSWORD_GUID
objACE.AccessMask = RIGHT_DS_CONTROL_ACCESS
objDACL.AddAce objACE

objSD.DiscretionaryAcl = objDACL
objUser.Put "ntSecurityDescriptor", objSD
objUser.SetInfo
WScript.Echo "Enabled no password changing for " & strUserDN
```

Discussion

Even though in the GUI solution you check and uncheck the "User cannot change password" setting, actually making the change in Active Directory is a little more complicated as is evident in the VBScript solution. Not allowing a user to change her password consists of setting two deny Change Password ACEs on the target user object. One deny ACE is for the Everyone account and the other is for Self.

The VBScript solution should work as is, but it is not very robust in terms of checking to see if the ACEs already exist and making sure they are in the proper order. If you need to make the code more robust, we suggest checking out MS KB 269159 for more information on setting ACEs properly.

See Also

MS KB 269159 (How to Use Visual Basic and ADsSecurity.dll to Properly Order ACEs in an ACL)

6.26 Requiring a User to Change His Password at Next Logon

Problem

You want to require a user to change his password the next time he logs on to the domain.

Solution

Using a graphical user interface

1. Open the ADUC snap-in.
2. In the left pane, right-click on the domain and select Find.
3. Select the appropriate domain beside In.
4. Beside Name, type the name of the user you want to modify and click Find Now.
5. In the Search Results window, double-click on the user.
6. Click the Account tab.
7. Under Account options, check the box beside "User must change password at next logon."
8. Click OK.

Using a command-line interface

You can configure the "User must change password" using either DSMod or AdMod. To modify this setting using DSMod, use the following syntax:

```
> dsmod user "<UserDN>" -mustchpwd yes
```

For AdMod, do the following:

```
> admod -b "<UserDN>" pwdLastSet::0
```

Using VBScript

```
' This code sets the flag that requires a user to change their password
' ------ SCRIPT CONFIGURATION ------
strUserDN = "<UserDN>"  ' e.g. cn=rallen,ou=Sales,dc=rallencorp,dc=com
' ------ END CONFIGURATION ---------
set objUser = GetObject("LDAP://" & strUserDN)
objUser.Put "pwdLastSet", 0
objUser.SetInfo
WScript.Echo "User must change password at next logon: " & strUserDN
```

Discussion

When a user changes her password, a timestamp is written to the pwdLastSet attribute of the user object. When the user logs in to the domain, this timestamp is compared to the maximum password age that is defined by the Domain Security Policy to determine if the password has expired. To force a user to change her password at next logon, set the pwdLastSet attribute of the target user to zero, and verify that the user's account doesn't have the "password never expires" option enabled.

To disable this option so that a user does not have to change her password, set pwdLastSet to -1. These two values (0 and -1) are the only ones that can be set on the pwdLastSet attribute.

6.27   Preventing a User's Password from Expiring

Problem

You want to prevent a user's password from expiring.

Solution

Using a graphical user interface

1. Open the ADUC snap-in.
2. In the left pane, right-click on the domain and select Find.
3. Select the appropriate domain beside In.
4. Beside Name, type the name of the user you want to modify and click Find Now.
5. In the Search Results window, double-click on the user.
6. Click the Account tab.
7. Under Account options, check the box beside "Password never expires."
8. Click OK.

Using a command-line interface

```
> dsmod user "<UserDN>" -pwdneverexpires yes
```

Using VBScript

```
' This code sets a users password to never expire
' See Recipe 4.12 for the code for the CalcBit function
' ------ SCRIPT CONFIGURATION ------
strUserDN = "<UserDN>"   ' e.g. cn=rallen,ou=Sales,dc=rallencorp,dc=com
' ------ END CONFIGURATION ---------

intBit = 65536
strAttr = "userAccountControl"

set objUser = GetObject("LDAP://" & strUserDN)
intBitsOrig = objUser.Get(strAttr)
intBitsCalc = CalcBit(intBitsOrig, intBit, TRUE)
if intBitsOrig <> intBitsCalc then
    objUser.Put strAttr, intBitsCalc
    objUser.SetInfo
    WScript.Echo "Changed " & strAttr & " from " & _
                  intBitsOrig & " to " & intBitsCalc
else
    WScript.Echo "Did not need to change " & strAttr & " (" & _
                  intBitsOrig & ")"
end if
```

Discussion

Setting a user's password to never expire overrides any password aging policy you've defined in the domain. To disable password expiration, you need to set the bit equivalent of 65536 (i.e., 10000000000000000) in the userAccountControl attribute of the target user.

See Also

Recipe 4.15 for more on modifying a bit flag attribute and Recipe 6.29 for more on setting the userAccountControl attribute

6.28 Finding Users Whose Passwords Are About to Expire

Problem

You want to find the users whose passwords are about to expire.

Solution

Using a command-line interface

```
> dsquery user -stalepwd <NumDaysSinceLastPwdChange>
```

You can also use the FindExpAcc *joeware* tool with the following syntax:

```
> findexpacc -pwd
```

Using Perl

```perl
#!perl
# This code finds the user accounts whose password is about to expire
# ------ SCRIPT CONFIGURATION ------
# Domain and container/OU to check for accounts that are about to expire
my $domain   = '<DomainDNSName>';
my $cont     = ''; # set to empty string to query entire domain
                   # Or set to a relative path in the domain, e.g. cn=Users
# Days since password change
my $days_ago = <NumDaysSinceLastPwdChange>  # e.g. 60;
# ------ END CONFIGURATION ---------

use strict;
use Win32::OLE;
   $Win32::OLE::Warn = 3;
use Math::BigInt;

# Need to convert the number of seconds from $day_ago
# to a large integer for comparison against pwdLastSet
my $past_secs = time - 60*60*24*$days_ago;
my $intObj = Math::BigInt->new($past_secs);
   $intObj = Math::BigInt->new($intObj->bmul('10 000 000'));
my $past_largeint = Math::BigInt->new(
                                $intObj->badd('116 444 736 000 000 000'));
   $past_largeint =~ s/^[+-]//;

# Setup the ADO connections
my $connObj                         = Win32::OLE->new('ADODB.Connection');
$connObj->{Provider}                = "ADsDSOObject";
# Set these next two if you need to authenticate
# $connObj->Properties->{'User ID'}    = '<User>';
# $connObj->Properties->{'Password'}   = '<Password>';
$connObj->Open;
my $commObj                         = Win32::OLE->new('ADODB.Command');
$commObj->{ActiveConnection}        = $connObj;
$commObj->Properties->{'Page Size'} = 1000;
# Grab the default domain naming context
my $rootDSE = Win32::OLE->GetObject("LDAP://$domain/RootDSE");
my $rootNC = $rootDSE->Get("defaultNamingContext");
# Run ADO query and print results
$cont .= "," if $cont and not $cont =~ /,$/;
my $query   = "<LDAP://$domain/$cont$rootNC>;";
$query .=   "(&(objectclass=user)";
$query .=    "(objectcategory=Person)";
$query .=    "(!useraccountcontrol:1.2.840.113556.1.4.803:=2)";
$query .=    "(pwdLastSet<=$past_largeint)";
$query .=    "(!pwdLastSet=0));";
$query .=   "cn,distinguishedName;";
$query .= "subtree";
$commObj->{CommandText} = $query;
my $resObj = $commObj->Execute($query);
die "Could not query $domain: ",$Win32::OLE::LastError,"\n"
   unless ref $resObj;
```

```
print "\nUsers who haven't set their passwd in $days_ago days or longer:\n";
my $total = 0;
while (!($resObj->EOF)) {
    print "\t",$resObj->Fields("distinguishedName")->value,"\n";
    $total++;
    $resObj->MoveNext;
}
print "Total: $total\n";
```

Discussion

When a Windows-based client logs on to Active Directory, a check is done against the domain password policy and the user's pwdLastSet attribute to determine if the user's password has expired. If it has, the user is prompted to change it. In a pure Windows-based environment, this notification process may be adequate, but if you have a lot of non–Windows-based computers that are joined to an Active Directory domain (e.g., Kerberos-enabled Unix clients), or you have a lot of application and service accounts, you'll need to develop your own user password expiration notification process. Even in a pure Windows environment, cached logins present a problem because when a user logs into the domain with cached credentials (i.e., when the client is not able to reach a domain controller), this password expiration notification check is not done.

The process of finding users whose passwords are about to expire is a little complicated. Fortunately, the new dsquery user command helps by providing an option for searching for users that haven't changed their password for a number of days (-stalepwd). The downside to the dsquery user command is that it will not only find users whose password is about to expire, but also users that must change their password at next logon (i.e., pwdLastSet = 0). The Perl solution does not suffer from this limitation.

Using a command-line interface

You can use the FindExpAcc tool to query Active Directory for expired user or computer accounts, as well as active accounts with expired passwords. It also includes switches that are familiar from AdFind and AdMod, such as -b to specify the Base DN, -f to specify an LDAP filter, etc.

Using Perl

The Perl solution consists of a two-step process. First, you need to calculate a time in the past at which you would consider a password old or about to expire. The pwdLastSet attribute is a replicated attribute on user objects that contain the timestamp (as a large integer) of when the user last set her password. If today is May 31 and you want to find all users who have not set their password for 30 days, you need to query for users who have a pwdLastSet timestamp older than May 1.

First, a brief word on timestamps stored as large integers. It may seem odd, but large integer timestamps are represented as the number of 100-nanosecond intervals since January 1, 1601. To convert the current time to a large integer, you have to find the current time in seconds since the epoch (January 1, 1970), multiply that by 10,000,000, and then add 116,444,736,000,000,000 to it. This will give you an approximate time (in 100-nanosecond intervals) as a large integer. It is only an approximate time because when dealing with big numbers like this, a degree of accuracy is lost during the arithmetic.

 We chose to use Perl over VBScript because VBScript doesn't handle computing large integers given the current time and date very well. You can find an example of how to accomplish this task using VBScript at: *http://msdn.microsoft.com/library/default.asp?url=/library/ en-us/dnclinic/html/scripting09102002.asp.*

Now that you know how to calculate the current time, you need to calculate a time in the past as a large integer. Remember, you need to find the time at which passwords are considered close to expiring. In the Perl solution, you can configure the number of days since users changed their password. Once you've calculated this value, all you need to come up with is a search filter that you can use in ADO to find the matching users.

The first part of the filter will match all user objects.

```
$query .= "(&(objectclass=user)";
$query .= "(objectcategory=Person)";
```

But you really only want to find all enabled user objects (do you care if a disabled user object's password is about to expire?). This next bitwise filter will match only enabled user objects. See Recipe 6.17 for more information on finding disabled and enabled users.

```
$query .= "(!useraccountcontrol:1.2.840.113556.1.4.803:=2)";
```

The next part of the filter is the important part. This is where you use the derived last password change timestamp to compare against pwdLastSet.

```
$query .= "(pwdLastSet<=$past_largeint)";
```

Finally, you exclude all users that are required to change their password at next logon (pwdLastSet equal to zero).

```
$query .= "(!pwdLastSet=0));";
```

See Also

Recipe 6.15 for more on the password policy for a domain, Recipe 6.17, Recipe 6.22 for how to set a user's password, and Recipe 6.27 for how to set a user's password to never expire

6.29 Setting a User's Account Options (userAccountControl)

Problem

You want to view or update the userAccountControl attribute for a user. This attribute controls various account options, such as if the user must change his password at next logon and if the account is disabled.

Solution

Using a graphical user interface

1. Open the ADUC snap-in.
2. In the left pane, right-click on the domain and select Find.
3. Select the appropriate domain beside In.
4. Beside Name, type the name of the user and click Find Now.
5. In the Search Results window, double-click on the user.
6. Select the Account tab.
7. Many of the userAccountControl flags can be set under Account options.
8. Click OK after you're done.

Using a command-line interface

The dsmod user command has several options for setting various userAccountControl flags, as shown in Table 6-2. Each switch accepts yes or no as a parameter to either enable or disable the setting.

Table 6-2. dsmod user options for setting userAccountControl

dsmod user switch	Description
-mustchpwd	Sets whether the user must change password at next logon.
-canchpwd	Sets whether the user can change his or her password.
-disabled	Set account status to enabled or disabled.
-reversiblepwd	Sets whether the user's password is stored using reversible encryption.
-pwdneverexpires	Sets whether the user's password never expires.

Using VBScript

```
' This code enables or disables a bit value in the userAccountControl attr.
' See Recipe 4.12 for the code for the CalcBit function.
' ------ SCRIPT CONFIGURATION ------
strUserDN = "<UserDN>"        ' e.g. cn=rallen,ou=Sales,dc=rallencorp,dc=com
intBit = <BitValue>           ' e.g. 65536
```

```
boolEnable = <TrueOrFalse> ' e.g. TRUE
' ------ END CONFIGURATION ---------

strAttr = "userAccountControl"
set objUser = GetObject("LDAP://" & strUserDN)
intBitsOrig = objUser.Get(strAttr)
intBitsCalc = CalcBit(intBitsOrig, intBit, boolEnable)
if intBitsOrig <> intBitsCalc then
    objUser.Put strAttr, intBitsCalc
    objUser.SetInfo
    WScript.Echo "Changed " & strAttr & " from " & _
                intBitsOrig & " to " & intBitsCalc
else
    WScript.Echo "Did not need to change " & strAttr & " (" & _
                intBitsOrig & ")"
end if
```

Discussion

The userAccountControl attribute on user (and computer) objects could be considered the kitchen sink of miscellaneous and sometimes completely unrelated user account properties. If you have to work with creating and managing user objects very much, you'll need to become intimately familiar with this attribute.

The userAccountControl attribute is a bit flag, which means you have to take a couple extra steps to search against it or modify it. See Recipe 4.12 for more on searching with a bitwise filter and Recipe 4.15 for modifying a bit flag attribute.

The dsmod user command can be used to modify a subset of userAccountControl properties, as shown in Table 6-2. Table 6-3 contains the complete list of userAccountControl properties as defined in the ADS_USER_FLAG_ENUM enumeration.

Table 6-3. ADS_USER_FLAG_ENUM values

Name	Value	Description
ADS_UF_SCRIPT	1	Logon script is executed.
ADS_UF_ACCOUNTDISABLE	2	Account is disabled.
ADS_UF_HOMEDIR_REQUIRED	8	Home Directory is required.
ADS_UF_LOCKOUT	16	Account is locked out.
ADS_UF_PASSWD_NOTREQD	32	A password is not required.
ADS_UF_PASSWD_CANT_CHANGE	64	Read-only flag that indicates if the user cannot change his password.
ADS_UF_ENCRYPTED_TEXT_PASSWORD_ALLOWED	128	Store password using reversible encryption.
ADS_UF_TEMP_DUPLICATE_ACCOUNT	256	Account provides access to the domain, but no other domain that trusts the domain.
ADS_UF_NORMAL_ACCOUNT	512	Enabled user account.

Table 6-3. ADS_USER_FLAG_ENUM values (continued)

Name	Value	Description
ADS_UF_INTERDOMAIN_TRUST_ACCOUNT	2048	A permit to trust account for a system domain that trusts other domains.
ADS_UF_WORKSTATION_TRUST_ACCOUNT	4096	Enabled computer account.
ADS_UF_SERVER_TRUST_ACCOUNT	8192	Computer account for backup domain controller.
ADS_UF_DONT_EXPIRE_PASSWD	65536	Password will not expire.
ADS_UF_MNS_LOGON_ACCOUNT	131072	MNS logon account.
ADS_UF_SMARTCARD_REQUIRED	262144	Smart card is required for logon.
ADS_UF_TRUSTED_FOR_DELEGATION	524288	Allow Kerberos delegation.
ADS_UF_NOT_DELEGATED	1048576	Do not allow Kerberos delegation even if ADS_UF_TRUSTED_FOR_DELEGATION is enabled.
ADS_UF_USE_DES_KEY_ONLY	2097152	Requires DES encryption for keys.
ADS_UF_DONT_REQUIRE_PREAUTH	4194304	Account does not require Kerberos preauthentication for logon.
ADS_UF_PASSWORD_EXPIRED	8388608	Read-only flag indicating account's password has expired. Only used with the WinNT provider.
ADS_UF_TRUSTED_TO_AUTHENTICATE_FOR_DELEGATION	16777216	Account is enabled for delegation.

See Also

Recipe 4.12, Recipe 4.15 for setting a bit flag attribute, and MSDN: ADS_USER_FLAG_ENUM

6.30 Setting a User's Account to Expire

Problem

You want a user's account to expire at some point in the future.

Solution

Using a graphical user interface

1. Open the ADUC snap-in.
2. In the left pane, right-click on the domain and select Find.
3. Select the appropriate domain beside In.
4. Beside Name, type the name of the user you want to modify and click Find Now.
5. In the Search Results window, double-click on the user.
6. Click the Account tab.

7. Under Account expires, select the radio button beside End of.

8. Select the date the account should expire.

9. Click OK.

Using a command-line interface

Valid values for the -acctexpires flag include a positive number of days in the future when the account should expire, to expire the account at the end of the day, or to never expire the account.

```
> dsmod user "<UserDN>" -acctexpires <NumDays>
```

Using VBScript

```
' This code sets the account expiration date for a user.
' ------ SCRIPT CONFIGURATION ------
strExpireDate = "<Date>"    ' e.g. "07/10/2004"
strUserDN = "<UserDN>"      ' e.g. cn=rallen,ou=Sales,dc=rallencorp,dc=com
' ------ END CONFIGURATION --------

set objUser = GetObject("LDAP://" & strUserDN)
objUser.AccountExpirationDate = strExpireDate
objUser.SetInfo
WScript.Echo "Set user " & strUserDN & " to expire on " & strExpireDate

' These two lines would disable account expiration for the user
' objUser.Put "accountExpires", 0
' objUser.SetInfo
```

Discussion

User accounts can be configured to expire on a certain date. Account expiration is stored in the accountExpires attribute on a user object. This attribute contains a large integer representation of the date in which the account expires, expressed in 100 nanosecond intervals since January 1, 1601. If you set this attribute to 0, it disables account expiration for the user (i.e., the account will never expire). Note that this is different than the dsmod user command where a value of 0 with -acctexpires will cause the account to expire at the end of the day. Why does it differ from how the accountExpires attribute works? Great question. The accountExpires attribute itself will be updated whenever the existing expiration date passes.

See Also

MS KB 278359 (Account Expiration for a Migrated User Appears to be One Day Ahead of or Behind the Date in the Source Domain) and MSDN: Account Expiration

6.31 Finding Users Whose Accounts Are About to Expire

Problem

You want to find users whose accounts are about to expire.

Solution

Using Perl

```perl
# This code finds the user accounts that are about to expire.
# ------ SCRIPT CONFIGURATION ------
# Domain and container/OU to check for accounts that are about to expire
my $domain    = '<DomainDNSName>';   ' e.g. amer.rallencorp.com
my $cont      = '';  # set to empty string to query entire domain
                     # Or set to a relative path in the domain, e.g. cn=Users
# Number of weeks until a user will expire
my $weeks_ago = 4;
# ------ END CONFIGURATION ---------

use strict;
use Win32::OLE;
    $Win32::OLE::Warn = 3;
use Math::BigInt;

# Need to convert the number of seconds until $weeks_ago
# to a large integer for comparison against accountExpires
my $future_secs = time + 60*60*24*7*$weeks_ago;
my $intObj = Math::BigInt->new($future_secs);
    $intObj = Math::BigInt->new($intObj->bmul('10 000 000'));
my $future_largeint =
        Math::BigInt->new($intObj->badd('116 444 736 000 000 000'));
    $future_largeint =~ s/^[+-]//;

# Now need to convert the current time into a large integer
    $intObj = Math::BigInt->new( time );
    $intObj = Math::BigInt->new($intObj->bmul('10 000 000'));
my $current_largeint =
        Math::BigInt->new($intObj->badd('116 444 736 000 000 000'));
    $current_largeint =~ s/^[+-]//;

# Set up the ADO connections.
my $connObj                         = Win32::OLE->new('ADODB.Connection');
$connObj->{Provider}                = "ADsDSOObject";
# Set these next two if you need to authenticate
# $connObj->Properties->{'User ID'}   = '<User>';
# $connObj->Properties->{'Password'}  = '<Password>';
$connObj->Open;
my $commObj                         = Win32::OLE->new('ADODB.Command');
$commObj->{ActiveConnection}        = $connObj;
$commObj->Properties->{'Page Size'} = 1000;
```

```
# Grab the default domain name.
my $rootDSE = Win32::OLE->GetObject("LDAP://$domain/RootDSE");
my $rootNC = $rootDSE->Get("defaultNamingContext");

# Run ADO query and print results.
$cont .= "," if $cont and not $cont =~ /,$/;
my $query  = "<LDAP://$domain/$cont$rootNC>;";
$query .=   "(&(objectclass=user)";
$query .=      "(objectcategory=Person)";
$query .=      "(!useraccountcontrol:1.2.840.113556.1.4.803:=2)";
$query .=      "(accountExpires<=$future_largeint)";
$query .=      "(accountExpires>=$current_largeint)";
$query .=      "(!accountExpires=0));";
$query .=   "cn,distinguishedName;";
$query .= "subtree";
$commObj->{CommandText} = $query;
my $resObj = $commObj->Execute($query);
die "Could not query $domain: ",$Win32::OLE::LastError,"\n"
    unless ref $resObj;

print "\nUsers whose account will expire in $weeks_ago weeks or less:\n";
my $total = 0;
while (!($resObj->EOF)) {
    print "\t",$resObj->Fields("distinguishedName")->value,"\n";
    $total++;
    $resObj->MoveNext;
}
print "Total: $total\n";
```

Discussion

The code to find expiring user objects is very similar to that of Recipe 6.28 for finding expiring passwords. The main difference is that instead of querying the pwdLastSet attribute, you need to query accountExpires. Also, instead of setting accountExpires to a timestamp in the past as you did for pwdLastSet, it needs to contain a future timestamp for when accounts will expire. This makes the logic only slightly different. Let's break down the search filter and review the other differences.

This part of the filter finds all enabled user objects:

```
$query .=   "(&(objectclass=user)";
$query .=      "(objectcategory=Person)";
$query .=      "(!useraccountcontrol:1.2.840.113556.1.4.803:=2)";
```

This next part finds only the accounts that are going to expire. The second line prevents all currently expired accounts from being returned.

```
$query .=      "(accountExpires<=$future_largeint)";
$query .=      "(accountExpires>=$current_largeint)";
```

The last part of the filter excludes users that are marked to never expire:

```
$query .=      "(!accountExpires=0));";
```

See Also

Recipe 6.28 for more on large integer manipulation, Recipe 6.30 for setting a user's account to expire, and MS KB 318714 (How to Limit User Logon Time in a Domain in Windows 2000)

6.32 Determining a User's Last Logon Time

 This recipe requires the Windows Server 2003 forest functional level.

Problem

You want to determine the last time a user logged into a domain.

Solution

Using a graphical user interface

If you install the *AcctInfo.dll* extension to ADUC, you can view the last logon timestamp:

1. Open the ADUC snap-in.
2. In the left pane, right-click on the domain and select Find.
3. Select the appropriate domain beside In.
4. Beside Name, type the name of the user you want to modify and click Find Now.
5. In the Search Results window, double-click on the user.
6. Click the Additional Account Info tab.
7. View the value for Last-Logon-Timestamp.

 AcctInfo.dll can be downloaded from the Microsoft download site as a part of the Account Lockout and Management Tools:

> *http://microsoft.com/downloads/details.aspx?FamilyId=7AF2E69C-91F3-4E63-8629-B999ADDE0B9E&displaylang=en*

Using a command-line interface

```
> adfind -b <UserDN> lastLogonTimestamp -tdc
```

 The –tdc and –tdcs switches will display attributes such as `lastLogonTimestamp` in a human-readable format.

Using VBScript

```
' This code prints the last logon timestamp for a user.
' ------ SCRIPT CONFIGURATION ------
strUserDN = "<UserDN>"  ' e.g. cn=rallen,ou=Sales,dc=rallencorp,dc=com
' ------ END CONFIGURATION ---------

set objUser =  GetObject("LDAP://" & strUserDN)
set objLogon = objUser.Get("lastLogonTimestamp")
intLogonTime = objLogon.HighPart * (2^32) + objLogon.LowPart
intLogonTime = intLogonTime / (60 * 10000000)
intLogonTime = intLogonTime / 1440
WScript.Echo "Approx last logon timestamp: " & intLogonTime + #1/1/1601#
```

 Note that the result is only an approximation in minutes and can be off by several minutes, hours, or even days depending on the original value.

Discussion

Trying to determine when a user last logged on has always been a challenge in the Microsoft NOS environment. In Windows NT, you could retrieve a user's last logon timestamp from a PDC or BDC, but this timestamp was the last time the user logged on to the individual PDC or BDC itself. That means to determine the actual last logon, you'd have to query every domain controller in the domain. In large environments, this wasn't practical. With Windows 2000 Active Directory, things did not improve much. A lastLogon attribute is used to store the last logon timestamp, but unfortunately, this attribute isn't replicated. So again, to get an accurate picture, you'd have to query every domain controller in the domain for the user's last logon attribute and keep track of the most recent one.

Now with Windows Server 2003 there is finally a viable solution. A new attribute was added to the schema for user objects called lastLogonTimestamp. This attribute is similar to the lastLogon attribute that was available previously, with two distinct differences. First, and most importantly, this attribute is replicated. That means when a user logs in, the lastLogonTimestamp attribute will get populated and then replicate to all domain controllers in the domain.

The second difference is that since lastLogonTimestamp is replicated, special safeguards needed to be put in place so that users that logged in repeatedly over a short period of time did not cause unnecessary replication traffic. For this reason, the lastLogonTimestamp is updated only if the last update occurred a week or more ago by default. (This window is configurable by modifying the msDS-LogonTimeSyncInterval on the domain NC.) This means that the lastLogonTimestamp attribute could be up to a week off in terms of accuracy with a user's actual last logon. Ultimately, this shouldn't be a problem for most situations because lastLogonTimestamp is intended to address the common problem where administrators want to run a query and determine which users have not logged in over the past month or more.

See Also

Recipe 6.33 for finding users that have not logged on recently

6.33 Finding Users Who Have Not Logged On Recently

 This recipe requires the Windows Server 2003 domain functional level.

Problem

You want to determine which users have not logged on recently.

Solution

Using a graphical user interface

1. Open the ADUC snap-in.
2. In the left pane, right-click on the domain and select Find.
3. Beside Find, select Common Queries.
4. Select the number of days beside "Days since last logon."
5. Click the Find Now button.

Using a command-line interface

You can locate users who have not logged on for a certain amount of time using either the built-in DSQuery tool or the OldCmp utility from *http://www.joeware.net*:

```
> dsquery user -inactive <NumWeeks>
```

OldCmp can create a report of all user objects based on several criteria. To create a report of all users in the *rallencorp.com* domain whose passwords are more than 90 days old, for example, use the following syntax:

```
> oldcmp -report -users -b dc=rallencorp,dc=com -s subtree -llts -age 90
-sh
```

Using Perl

```
# This code finds the users that have not logged in over a period of time
# ------ SCRIPT CONFIGURATION ------
# Domain and container/OU to check for inactive accounts
my $domain    = '<DomainDNSName>'; # e.g. amer.rallencorp.com
my $cont      = 'cn=Users'; # set to empty string to query entire domain
                          # Or set to a relative path in the domain:
                          #    e.g. cn=Users
# Number of weeks a user needs to be inactive to be returned
```

```perl
my $weeks_ago = <NumWeeks>;   # e.g. 4
# ------ END CONFIGURATION ---------

use strict;
use Win32::OLE;
   $Win32::OLE::Warn = 3;
use Math::BigInt;

# Need to convert the number of seconds since $weeks_ago
# to a large integer for comparison against lastLogonTimestamp
my $past_secs = time - 60*60*24*7*$weeks_ago;
my $intObj = Math::BigInt->new($past_secs);
   $intObj = Math::BigInt->new($intObj->bmul('10 000 000'));
my $past_largeint = Math::BigInt->new(
                      $intObj->badd('116 444 736 000 000 000'));
   $past_largeint =~ s/^[+-]//;

# Setup the ADO connections
my $connObj                         = Win32::OLE->new('ADODB.Connection');
$connObj->{Provider}                = "ADsDSOObject";
# Set these next two if you need to authenticate
# $connObj->Properties->{'User ID'}   = '<UserUPNOrDN>';
# $connObj->Properties->{'Password'}  = '<Password>';
$connObj->Open;
my $commObj                         = Win32::OLE->new('ADODB.Command');
$commObj->{ActiveConnection}        = $connObj;
$commObj->Properties->{'Page Size'} = 1000;

# Grab the default domain name
my $rootDSE = Win32::OLE->GetObject("LDAP://$domain/RootDSE");
my $rootNC = $rootDSE->Get("defaultNamingContext");

# Run ADO query and print results
$cont .= "," if $cont and not $cont =~ /,$/;
my $query  = "<LDAP://$domain/$cont$rootNC>;";
$query .= "(&(objectclass=user)";
$query .=   "(objectcategory=Person)";
$query .=   "(!useraccountcontrol:1.2.840.113556.1.4.803:=2)";
$query .=   "(lastlogontimestamp<=$past_largeint));";
$query .= "cn,distinguishedName;";
$query .= "subtree";
$commObj->{CommandText} = $query;
my $resObj = $commObj->Execute($query);
die "Could not query $domain: ",$Win32::OLE::LastError,"\n"
   unless ref $resObj;

print "\nUsers that have been inactive for $weeks_ago weeks or more:\n";
my $total = 0;
while (!($resObj->EOF)) {
   my $cn  = $resObj->Fields(0)->value;
   print "\t",$resObj->Fields("distinguishedName")->value,"\n";
   $total++;
   $resObj->MoveNext;
}
print "Total: $total\n";
```

Discussion

As discussed in Recipe 6.32, in Windows Server 2003 a new attribute on user objects called `lastLogonTimestamp` contains the approximate last time the user logged on. Using this to find the users that have not logged on in a number of weeks is much easier than the option with Windows 2000, where we would need to query every domain controller in the domain. However, the `lastLogonTimestamp` attribute has a certain amount of latency associated with it to cut down on replication traffic; the date contained in this attribute can be anywhere from 10 to 14 days off in a default Windows Server 2003 domain. This latency can be made longer or shorter by modifying the `msDS-LogonTimeSyncInterval` attribute of the Domain NC.

The GUI and CLI solutions are straightforward, but the Perl solution is a little more complicated. The code is very similar to that of Recipe 6.32, and we suggest reading that if you are curious about the large integer conversions going on.

See Also

Recipe 6.28 for more on computing large integer timestamps and Recipe 6.32 for more on finding a user's last logon timestamp

6.34   Viewing a User's Permitted Logon Hours

Problem

You want to see the hours that a user is permitted to log onto the network.

Solution

Using a graphical user interface

1. Open the ADUC snap-in.
2. If you need to change domains, right-click on "Active Directory Users and Computers" in the left pane, select Connect to Domain, enter the domain name, and click OK.
3. Right-click on the user and select Properties. From the Account tab, click on Logon Hours.
4. Select the hours that you want to allow or disallow, and click Logon Permitted or Logon Denied. Click OK.
5. Click Apply, followed by OK.

Using VBScript

```
Days = Array _
    ("Sunday", "Monday", "Tuesday", "Wednesday", "Thursday", "Friday", "Saturday")
```

```
Set objUser = GetObject("LDAP://<UserDN>")
arrHours = objUser.Get("logonHours")

For i = 1 To LenB(arrHours)
    arrHoursBytes(i-1) = AscB(MidB(arrHours, i, 1))
    WScript.Echo "MidB returns: " & MidB(arrHours, i, 1)
    WScript.Echo "arrHoursBytes: " & arrHoursBytes(i-1)
    wscript.echo vbcrlf
Next

intCounter = 0
intLoopCounter = 0
WScript.echo "Day  Byte 1   Byte 2   Byte 3"
For Each HourByte In arrHoursBytes
    arrHourBits = DisplayLogonHourBits(HourByte)

    If intCounter = 0 Then
        WScript.STDOUT.Write Days(intLoopCounter) & Space(2)
        intLoopCounter = intLoopCounter + 1
    End If

    For Each HourBit In arrHourBits
        WScript.STDOUT.Write HourBit
        intCounter = 1 + intCounter

        If intCounter = 8 or intCounter = 16 Then
            Wscript.STDOUT.Write Space(1)
        End If

        If intCounter = 24 Then
            WScript.echo vbCr
            intCounter = 0
        End If
    Next
Next

Function DisplayLogonHourBits(x)
    Dim arrBits(7)
    For i = 7 to 0 Step -1
        If x And 2^i Then
            arrBits(i) = 1
        Else
            arrBits(i) = 0
        End If
    Next
    DisplayLogonHourBits = arrBits
End Function
```

Discussion

Using VBScript

The logonHours attribute of a user object is represented as a binary number, rather than a simple string like most of the other attributes we've discussed. Because of this, manipulating it directly is a bit trickier than simply inserting a new string in place of an old one. In the VBScript example shown in this recipe, we use a VBScript function that manipulates the various bits of the attribute to produce the correct values.

See Also

MS KB 816666 (How to Limit User Logon Time in a Domain in Windows Server 2003) and MSDN: Logon-Hours attribute [AD Schema]

6.35   Viewing a User's Managed Objects

Problem

You want to view the objects that are owned by a user.

Solution

Using a graphical user interface

1. Open ADSI Edit.
2. If an entry for the naming context you want to browse is not already displayed, do the following:
   a. Right-click on ADSI Edit in the right pane and click "Connect to...."
   b. Fill in the information for the naming context, container, or OU you want to add an object to. Click on the Advanced button if you need to enter alternate credentials.
3. In the left pane, browse to the naming context, container, or OU of the object you want to view. Once you've found the object, right-click on it and select Properties.
4. View the managedObjects attribute.

Using a command-line interface

```
> adfind -b "<UserDN>" managedObjects
```

Using VBScript

```
' This code displays the managed objects for a user
' ------ SCRIPT CONFIGURATION ------
strUserDN = "<UserDN>"  ' e.g. cn=jsmith,cn=Users,dc=rallencorp,dc=com
' ------ END CONFIGURATION ---------

on error resume next
set objUser = GetObject("LDAP://" & strUserDN)
Wscript.Echo objUser.Get("cn") & "'s Managed Objects:"
colObjects =  objUser.GetEx("managedObjects")
if Err.Number = -2147463155 then
```

```
    Wscript.Echo " none"
else
    for each strObjectDN in colObjects
        Wscript.Echo " " & strObjectDN
    next
end if
```

Discussion

The managedObjects attribute is linked to the managedBy attribute that can be set on certain objects in Active Directory like computers, OUs, and groups. Setting the managedBy attribute provides a quick way to define who owns an object. If you do use it, you can use the managedObjects attribute on user, contact, or group objects to get the list of objects for which the user has been configured in the managedBy attribute.

6.36   Creating a UPN Suffix for a Forest

Problem

You want users to have a different UPN suffix from the default provided by your forest.

Solution

Using a graphical user interface

1. Open the Active Directory Domains and Trusts snap-in.
2. In the left pane, right-click Active Directory Domains and Trusts and select Properties.
3. Under Alternative UPN suffixes, type the name of the suffix you want to add.
4. Click Add and OK.

Using a command-line interface

```
> admod –b cn=Partitions,cn=configuration,<ForestRootDN>
  uPNSuffixes:+:rallenhome.com
```

 The *attributeName:+:attributeValue* syntax will add an additional value to an existing list of values in a multivalued attribute. Using *attributeName::attributeValue* would add the value you specify and remove all other values.

Using VBScript

```
' This code adds a new UPN suffix.
' ------ SCRIPT CONFIGURATION ------
strNewSuffix = "<NewSuffix>"    ' e.g. othercorp.com
strDomain = "<DomainDNSName>"   ' e.g. rallencorp.com
```

```
'  ------ END CONFIGURATION ---------

set objRootDSE = GetObject("LDAP://" & strDomain & "/RootDSE")
set objPartitions = GetObject("LDAP://cn=Partitions," & _
                             objRootDSE.Get("ConfigurationNamingContext"))
objPartitions.PutEx ADS_PROPERTY_APPEND, "uPNSuffixes", Array(strNewSuffix)
objPartitions.SetInfo
```

Discussion

The UPN allows users to log on with a friendly name that may even correspond to their email address. UPN logons also do not require the domain to be known so that it can be abstracted away from the user. You may need to create an additional UPN suffix (e.g., *@rallencorp.com*) if you want UPNs to map to email addresses, but your AD forest is rooted at a different domain name (e.g., *ad.rallencorp.com*) than the domain name used in email addresses (e.g., *rallencorp.com*).

Using VBScript

UPN suffixes are stored in the multivalued uPNSuffixes attribute on the Partitions container in the Configuration naming context. The default forest UPN suffix is assumed and not stored in that attribute.

See Also

MS KB 243280 (Users Can Log On Using User Name or User Principal Name), MS KB 243629 (How to Add UPN Suffixes to a Forest), and MS KB 269441 (How to Use ADSI to List the UPN Suffixes that Are Defined in Active Directory)

## CHAPTER 7

Groups

7.0   Introduction

A group is a simple concept that has been used in many different types of standalone and networked systems over the years. In generic terms, a group is just a collection of objects. Groups are used most frequently in a security context, where you create a collection of users and assign certain permissions or rights to that group, rather than to each individual user within the group. When applying security settings, it's much easier to use a group rather than individual users, because you only need to apply the security setting once instead of once per user.

In Active Directory, groups are flexible objects that can contain virtually any other type of object as a member, although they'll generally only contain users, InetOrg-Persons, computers, and other groups. Active Directory groups can be used for many different purposes including controlling access to resources, defining a filter for the application of group policies, and as an email distribution list.

The ways in which a group can be used in an Active Directory forest are defined by the group's *scope* and *type*. The *type* of a group can be either *security* or *distribution*. Security groups can be used to restrict access to Windows resources, whereas distribution groups can be used only as a simple grouping mechanism for sending email messages or for some other non-Windows security-related function. Both security and distribution groups can be used as email lists, but only security groups can be used to assign access to resources.

The *scope* of a group determines where members of the group can be located within the forest and where in the forest you can use the group in an ACL. The supported group scopes include *universal*, *global*, and *domain local*. Universal groups and domain local groups can have members that are part of any domain in the same forest (or a separate forest if a cross-forest trust exists), whereas global groups can only have members that are part of the same domain that the group is contained in. When assigning permissions to group objects, universal and global groups can be assigned permissions to resources anywhere in the forest, whereas domain local groups can only be assigned permissions to resources in the same domain. (In this way, domain local and global groups are functional opposites of one another.)

The Anatomy of a Group

Groups are represented in Active Directory by group objects. Table 7-1 contains a list of some of the noteworthy attributes that are available on group objects.

Table 7-1. Attributes of group objects

Attribute	Description
cn	Relative distinguished name of group objects.
whenCreated	Timestamp of when the OU was created.
description	Textual description of the group.
groupType	Flag containing the group scope and type. See Recipe 7.8 for more information.
info	Additional notes about a group.
primaryGroupToken	Local RID for the group. This matches the primaryGroupID attribute that is set on user objects.
managedBy	DN of a user or group that is the owner of the group.
managedObjects	List of DNs of objects for which this group is listed in the managedBy attribute.
Member	List of DNs of members of the group.
memberOf	List of DNs of the groups this group is a member of.
whenChanged	Timestamp of when the OU was last modified.
sAMAccountName	Down-level account name for the group. Typically this is the same as the cn attribute.
wWWHomePage	URL of the home page for the group.
sAMAccountType	Describes the type of account that was created for an object, such as a domain object, a group object, a normal user account, etc.

7.1 Creating a Group

Problem

You want to create a group.

Solution

Using a graphical user interface

1. Open the ADUC snap-in.
2. If you need to change domains, right-click on Active Directory Users and Computers in the left pane, select Connect to Domain, enter the domain name, and click OK.

3. In the left pane, browse to the parent container of the new group, right-click on it, and select New → Group.

4. Enter the name of the group and select the group scope (global, domain local, or universal) and group type (security or distribution).

5. Click OK.

Using a command-line interface

In the following example, *<GroupDN>* should be replaced with the DN of the group to create, *<GroupScope>* should be l, g, or u for domain local, global, and universal groups, respectively, and -secgroup should be set to yes if the group is a security group or no otherwise. Another recommended option is to set -desc for specifying a group description.

```
> dsadd group "<GroupDN>" -scope <GroupScope> -secgrp yes|no -desc "<GroupDesc>"
```

You can also create a group object using admod, using the following syntax:

```
> admod -b "<GroupDN>" objectClass::group groupType::
"<GroupType>" sAMAccountName::"<Pre-Windows2000Name>" -add
```

For example, to create a global security group called "Finance Users" in the Finance OU of the *rallencorp.com* domain, you can use either of the following commands:

```
> dsadd group "cn=Finance Users,ou=Finance,dc=rallencorp,dc=com" -scope global -
secgrp yes
```

```
> admod -b "cn=Finance Users,ou=Finance,dc=rallencorp,dc=com" groupType::8
sAMAccountName::"Finance Users" -add
```

In the case of AdMod, you must specify the numeric value for the group type, which can be any one of those listed in Table 7-2.

Table 7-2. Numeric values for group types

Group type	Numeric value
Universal Distribution Group	8
Universal Security Group	−2147483640
Domain Local Distribution Group	4
Domain Local Security Group	−2147483644
Global Distribution Group	2
Global Security Group	−2147483646

These values are defined in the ADS_GROUP_TYPE_ENUM enumeration; see Recipe 7.8 for more information.

If you omit the sAMAccountName attribute when creating the group, it will be automatically populated with a random string.

Using VBScript

```
' The following code creates a global security group.
' ------ SCRIPT CONFIGURATION ------
strGroupParentDN = "<GroupParentDN>"   ' e.g. ou=Groups,dc=rallencorp,dc=com
strGroupName     = "<GroupName>"       ' e.g. ExecAdminsSales
strGroupDescr    = "<GroupDesc>"       ' e.g. Executive Admins for Sales group
' ------ END CONFIGURATION ---------

' Constants taken from ADS_GROUP_TYPE_ENUM
Const ADS_GROUP_TYPE_DOMAIN_LOCAL_GROUP = 4
Const ADS_GROUP_TYPE_GLOBAL_GROUP       = 2
Const ADS_GROUP_TYPE_LOCAL_GROUP        = 4
Const ADS_GROUP_TYPE_SECURITY_ENABLED   = -2147483648
Const ADS_GROUP_TYPE_UNIVERSAL_GROUP    = 8

set objOU = GetObject("LDAP://" & strGroupParentDN)
set objGroup = objOU.Create("group","cn=" & strGroupName)
objGroup.Put "groupType", ADS_GROUP_TYPE_GLOBAL_GROUP _
                     Or ADS_GROUP_TYPE_SECURITY_ENABLED
objGroup.Put "sAMAccountName", strGroupName
objGroup.Put "description", strGroupDescr
objGroup.SetInfo
```

Discussion

In each solution, a group was created with no members. For more information on how to add and remove members, see Recipe 7.5.

The groupType attribute contains a flag indicating both group scope and type. The available flag values are defined in the ADS_GROUP_TYPE_ENUM enumeration. Recipe 7.8 contains more information on setting the group scopes and types.

See Also

Recipe 7.5 for adding and removing group members, Recipe 7.8 for setting group scope and type, MS KB 231273 (Group Type and Scope Usage in Windows), MS KB 232241 (Group Management with ADSI in Windows 2000), MS KB 816302 (How to Manage Groups in Active Directory in Windows Server 2003), and MSDN: ADS_GROUP_TYPE_ENUM

7.2 Viewing the Permissions of a Group

Problem

You want to list the AD object permissions that have been assigned to a group object.

Solution

Using a graphical user interface

1. Open the Active Directory Users and Computers (ADUC) snap-in.
2. If you need to change domains, right-click on Active Directory Users and Computers in the left pane, select Connect to Domain, enter the domain name, and click OK.
3. In the left pane, right-click on the domain and select Find.
4. Enter the name of the group and click Find Now.
5. Double-click on the group in the bottom results pane.
6. Click on the Security tab. The users and groups that have been assigned permissions to the object are listed in the bottom pane; select each entry to view the permissions that have been assigned to it.
7. Click on Advanced to view the owner of the group, as well as any auditing that has been configured.

Using a command-line interface

```
> dsacls "<GroupDN>"
```

Using VBScript

```
Const SE_DACL_PROTECTED = &H1000

Set objGroup = GetObject("LDAP://<GroupDN>")

Set objNtSecurityDescriptor = objGroup.Get("nTSecurityDescriptor")

Control = objNtSecurityDescriptor.Control

WScript.Echo "Group Permissions"
If (intNtSecurityDescriptorControl And SE_DACL_PROTECTED) Then
    Wscript.Echo "Permission inheritance is disabled."
Else
    WScript.Echo "Permission inheritance is enabled."
End If
WScript.Echo

Set objDACL = objNtSecurityDescriptor.DiscretionaryAcl
DisplayAceInformation objDACL, "DACL"
```

```
Sub DisplayAceInformation(SecurityStructure, strType)
    Const ADS_ACETYPE_ACCESS_ALLOWED = &H0
    Const ADS_ACETYPE_ACCESS_DENIED = &H1
    Const ADS_ACETYPE_ACCESS_ALLOWED_OBJECT = &H5
    Const ADS_ACETYPE_ACCESS_DENIED_OBJECT = &H6
    intAceCount = 0
    For Each objAce In SecurityStructure
        strTrustee = Mid(objAce.Trustee,1,12)
        If StrComp(strTrustee, "NT AUTHORITY", 1) <> 0 Then
            intAceCount = intAceCount + 1
            WScript.Echo strType & " permission entry: " & intAceCount
            WScript.Echo "Name: " & objAce.Trustee

            intAceType = objAce.AceType
            If (intAceType = ADS_ACETYPE_ACCESS_ALLOWED Or _
                intAceType = ADS_ACETYPE_ACCESS_ALLOWED_OBJECT) Then
                WScript.Echo "Allow ACE"
            ElseIf (intAceType = ADS_ACETYPE_ACCESS_DENIED Or _
                intAceType = ADS_ACETYPE_ACCESS_DENIED_OBJECT) Then
                WScript.Echo "Deny ACE"
            Else
                WScript.Echo "Unknown ACE."
            End If
            ReadBitsInAccessMask(objAce.AccessMask)
            WScript.Echo VbCr
        End If
    Next
End Sub

Sub ReadBitsInAccessMask(AccessMask)
    Const ADS_RIGHT_DELETE = &H10000
    Const ADS_RIGHT_READ_CONTROL = &H20000
    Const ADS_RIGHT_WRITE_DAC = &H40000
    Const ADS_RIGHT_WRITE_OWNER = &H80000
    Const ADS_RIGHT_DS_CREATE_CHILD = &H1
    Const ADS_RIGHT_DS_DELETE_CHILD = &H2
    Const ADS_RIGHT_ACTRL_DS_LIST = &H4
    Const ADS_RIGHT_DS_SELF = &H8
    Const ADS_RIGHT_DS_READ_PROP = &H10
    Const ADS_RIGHT_DS_WRITE_PROP = &H20
    Const ADS_RIGHT_DS_DELETE_TREE = &H40
    Const ADS_RIGHT_DS_LIST_OBJECT = &H80
    Const ADS_RIGHT_DS_CONTROL_ACCESS = &H100

    WScript.Echo VbCrLf & "Standard Access Rights"
    If (AccessMask And ADS_RIGHT_DELETE) Then _
        WScript.Echo vbTab & "-Delete an object."
    If (AccessMask And ADS_RIGHT_READ_CONTROL) Then _
        WScript.Echo vbTab & "-Read permissions."
    If (AccessMask And ADS_RIGHT_WRITE_DAC) Then _
        WScript.Echo vbTab & "-Write permissions."
    If (AccessMask And ADS_RIGHT_WRITE_OWNER) Then _
        WScript.Echo vbTab & "-Modify owner."
```

```
    WScript.Echo VbCrLf & "Directory Service Specific Access Rights"
    If (AccessMask And ADS_RIGHT_DS_CREATE_CHILD) Then _
        WScript.Echo vbTab & "-Create child objects."
    If (AccessMask And ADS_RIGHT_DS_DELETE_CHILD) Then _
        WScript.Echo vbTab & "-Delete child objects."
    If (AccessMask And ADS_RIGHT_ACTRL_DS_LIST) Then _
        WScript.Echo vbTab & "-Enumerate an object."
    If (AccessMask And ADS_RIGHT_DS_READ_PROP) Then _
        WScript.Echo vbTab & "-Read the properties of an object."
    If (AccessMask And ADS_RIGHT_DS_WRITE_PROP) Then _
        WScript.Echo vbTab & "-Write the properties of an object."
    If (AccessMask And ADS_RIGHT_DS_DELETE_TREE) Then _
        WScript.Echo vbTab & "-Delete a tree of objects"
    If (AccessMask And ADS_RIGHT_DS_LIST_OBJECT) Then _
        WScript.Echo vbTab & "-List a tree of objects."

    WScript.Echo VbCrLf & "Control Access Rights"
    If (AccessMask And ADS_RIGHT_DS_CONTROL_ACCESS) + _
        (AccessMask And ADS_RIGHT_DS_SELF) = 0 Then
        WScript.Echo "-None"
    Else
        If (AccessMask And ADS_RIGHT_DS_CONTROL_ACCESS) Then _
            WScript.Echo vbTab & "-Extended access rights."
        If (AccessMask And ADS_RIGHT_DS_SELF) Then
            WScript.Echo vbTab & "-Active Directory must validate a property "
            WScript.Echo vbTab & " write operation beyond the schema " & _
                "definition "
            WScript.Echo vbTab & " for the attribute."
        End If
    End If
End Sub
```

Discussion

In an Active Directory environment, you can set permissions on an object within the directory in much the same way that you can set NTFS permissions on files and folders. Each AD object has a Security Descriptor (SD) associated with it that is made up of a Discretionary Access Control List (DACL) that dictates which users and groups can access an object, and a System Access Control List (SACL) that controls which users' or groups' activities should be audited. The DACL and SACL are each made up of one or more Access Control Entries (ACEs), one for each user or group and its associated permission.

See Also

MSDN: Creating a DACL [Security], MSDN: Order of ACEs in a DACL [Security], MSDN: SACL Access Right [Security], and MSDN: Retrieving an Object's SACL [Security]

7.3   Viewing the Direct Members of a Group

Problem

You want to view the direct members of a group.

Solution

Using a graphical user interface

1. Open the ADUC snap-in.
2. If you need to change domains, right-click on Active Directory Users and Computers in the left pane, select Connect to Domain, enter the domain name, and click OK.
3. In the left pane, right-click on the domain and select Find.
4. Enter the name of the group and click Find Now.
5. Double-click on the group in the bottom results pane.
6. Click the Members tab.

Using a command-line interface

You can enumerate the direct members of a group using the built-in DSGet utility, or AdFind. Using DSGet requires the following syntax:

```
> dsget group "<GroupDN>" -members
```

To list group members with AdFind, enter the following:

```
> adfind -b "<GroupDN>" members
```

Using VBScript

```
' This code prints the direct members of the specified group.
' ------ SCRIPT CONFIGURATION ------
strGroupDN = "<GroupDN>" ' e.g. cn=SalesGroup,ou=Groups,dc=rallencorp,dc=com
' ------ END CONFIGURATION ---------

set objGroup = GetObject("LDAP://" & strGroupDN)
Wscript.Echo "Members of " & objGroup.Name & ":"
for each objMember in objGroup.Members
    Wscript.Echo objMember.Name
next
```

Discussion

The member attribute of a group object contains the distinguished names of the direct members of the group. By direct members, we mean the members that have been directly added to the group. This is in contrast to indirect group members, which are members of the group due to nested group membership. See Recipe 7.4 for how to find the nested membership of a group.

The memberOf attribute is a *back-link* to member. This means that, for each group membership that's listed in a group's member attribute, the DN of the group itself appears in that user/computer/group's memberOf attribute. Think of it this way: if the FinanceUsers group has Jane as a *member*, then Jane is a *member of* the FinanceUsers group. In this way, Active Directory uses forward links and back-links to maintain consistency between groups and their membership.

See Also

Recipe 7.4 for viewing nested group membership

7.4   Viewing the Nested Members of a Group

Problem

You want to view the nested membership of a group.

Solution

Using a graphical user interface

1. Open the ADUC snap-in.
2. If you need to change domains, right-click on Active Directory Users and Computers in the left pane, select Connect to Domain, enter the domain name, and click OK.
3. In the left pane, right-click on the domain and select Find.
4. Enter the name of the group and click Find Now.
5. Double-click on the group in the bottom results pane.
6. Click the Members tab.
7. You must now double-click on each group member to view its membership.

Using a command-line interface

```
> dsget group "<GroupDN>" -members -expand
```

Using VBScript

```
' This code prints the nested membership of a group.
' ------ SCRIPT CONFIGURATION ------
strGroupDN = "<GroupDN>"  ' e.g. cn=SalesGroup,ou=Groups,dc=rallencorp,dc=com
' ------ END CONFIGURATION ---------

strSpaces  = " "
set dicSeenGroupMember = CreateObject("Scripting.Dictionary")
Wscript.Echo "Members of " & strGroupDN & ":"
DisplayMembers("LDAP://" & strGroupDN, strSpaces, dicSeenGroupMember)
```

```
Function DisplayMembers ( strGroupADsPath, strSpaces, dicSeenGroupMember)

    set objGroup = GetObject(strGroupADsPath)
    for each objMember In objGroup.Members
        Wscript.Echo strSpaces & objMember.Name
        if objMember.Class = "group" then
            if dicSeenGroupMember.Exists(objMember.ADsPath) then
                Wscript.Echo strSpaces & "   ^ already seen group member " & _
                                    "(stopping to avoid loop)"
            else
                dicSeenGroupMember.Add objMember.ADsPath, 1
                DisplayMembers objMember.ADsPath, strSpaces & " ", _
                                    dicSeenGroupMember
            end if
        end if
    next

End Function
```

Discussion

As described in Recipe 7.3, group membership is stored in the multivalued member attribute on group objects. But that attribute will not show the complete picture because group nesting is allowed in Active Directory after you've transitioned from mixed mode. To view the complete group membership, you have to recurse through each group's members.

In the VBScript example, we used a dictionary object (referred to as a hash or associative array in other languages) to ensure that we did not get in an infinite loop. The dictionary object stores each group member; before the DisplayMembers function is called a check is performed to determine if the group has already been evaluated. If so, a message is displayed indicating the group will not be processed again. If this type of checking was not employed and you had a situation where group A was a member of group B, group B was a member of group C, and group C was a member of group A, the loop would repeat without terminating.

See Also

Recipe 7.3 for viewing group membership and MSDN: IADsMember

7.5   Adding and Removing Members of a Group

Problem

You want to add or remove members of a group.

Solution

Using a graphical user interface

1. Open the ADUC snap-in.
2. If you need to change domains, right-click on Active Directory Users and Computers in the left pane, select Connect to Domain, enter the domain name, and click OK.
3. In the left pane, right-click on the domain and select Find.
4. Enter the name of the group and click Find Now.
5. Double-click on the group in the bottom results pane.
6. Click the Members tab.
7. To remove a member, click on the member name, click the Remove button, click Yes, and click OK.
8. To add a member, click on the Add button, enter the name of the member, and click OK twice.

Using a command-line interface

The -addmbr option in dsmod adds a member to a group:

```
> dsmod group "<GroupDN>" -addmbr "<MemberDN>"
```

To add a group member with admod, use the following syntax:

```
> admod -b "<GroupDN>" member:+:"<MemberDN>"
```

The -rmmbr option in dsmod removes a member from a group:

```
> dsmod group "<GroupDN>" -rmmbr "<MemberDN>"
```

To remove a group member with admod, use the following syntax:

```
> admod -b "<GroupDN>" member:-:"<MemberDN>"
```

The -chmbr option in dsmod replaces the complete membership list:

```
> dsmod group "<GroupDN>" -chmbr "<Member1DN Member2DN . . . >"
```

To replace the membership of a group with admod, use the following two commands:

```
> admod -b "<GroupDN>" :-
> admod -b "<GroupDN>" member:++:"<Member1DN>;<Member2DN>;<Member3DN>"
```

Using VBScript

```
' This code adds a member to a group.
' ------ SCRIPT CONFIGURATION ----
strGroupDN = "<GroupDN>"  ' e.g. cn=SalesGroup,ou=Groups,dc=rallencorp,dc=com
strMemberDN = "<MemberDN>" ' e.g. cn=jsmith,cn=users,dc=rallencorp,dc=com
' ------ END CONFIGURATION ---------

set objGroup = GetObject("LDAP://" & strGroupDN)
' Add a member
```

```
objGroup.Add("LDAP://" & strMemberDN)
' This code removes a member from a group.
' ------ SCRIPT CONFIGURATION ------
strGroupDN = "<GroupDN>"  ' e.g. cn=SalesGroup,ou=Groups,dc=rallencorp,dc=com
strMemberDN = "<MemberDN>" ' e.g. cn=jsmith,cn=users,dc=rallencorp,dc=com
' ------ END CONFIGURATION ---------

set objGroup = GetObject("LDAP://" & strGroupDN)
' Remove a member
objGroup.Remove("LDAP://" & strMemberDN)
```

Discussion

Since there are no restrictions on what distinguished names you put in the member attribute, you can essentially have any type of object as a member of a group. Although OUs are typically used to structure objects that share certain criteria, group objects can be used to create loose collections of objects.

The benefit of using group objects as a collection mechanism is that the same object can be a member of multiple groups, whereas an object can only be a part of a single OU. Another key difference is that you can assign permissions on resources to groups because they are considered security principals in Active Directory, whereas OUs are not. This is different from some other directories, such as Novell NetWare, where OUs act more like security principals.

See Also

Recipe 7.3 for viewing group membership, MSDN: IADsGroup::Add, and MSDN: IADsGroup::Remove

7.6   Moving a Group Within a Domain

Problem

You want to move a group to a different OU or container within the same domain.

Solution

Using a graphical user interface

1. Open ADSI Edit.
2. If an entry for the naming context you want to browse is not already displayed, do the following:
   a. Right-click on ADSI Edit in the right pane and click "Connect to…."
   b. Fill in the information for the naming context, container, or OU containing the object. Click on the Advanced button if you need to enter alternate credentials.

3. In the left pane, browse to the container or OU that contains the group you want to move. Once you've found the object, right-click on it and select Move.

4. Browse to the new parent of the object, select it, and click OK.

Using a command-line interface

To move an object to a new parent container within the same domain, you can use either DSMove or AdMod, as follows:

```
> dsmove "<GroupDN>" -newparent "<NewParentDN>"
```

Or:

```
> admod -b "<GroupDN>" -move "<NewParentDN>"
```

Using VBScript

```
' This code moves an object from one location to another in the same domain.
' ------ SCRIPT CONFIGURATION ------
strNewParentDN = "LDAP://<NewParentDN>"
strGroupRDN    = "<GroupRDN>" ' i.e. "cn=Finance"
strGroupDN     = "LDAP://cn=<GroupRDN>,<OldParentDN>"
' ------ END CONFIGURATION ---------

set objCont = GetObject(strNewParentDN)
objCont.MoveHere strGroupDN, strGroupRDN
```

Discussion

Using a command-line interface

The DSMove utility can work against any type of object, including groups. The first parameter is the DN of the group that you want to move. The second parameter is the new parent container of the group. The -s parameter can additionally be used to specify a specific server to work against.

Using VBScript

The MoveHere method can be tricky, so an explanation of how to use it to move objects is in order. First, you need to call GetObject on the new parent container. Then call MoveHere on the parent container object with the ADsPath of the object to move as the first parameter and the RDN of the group being moved as the second.

The reason for the apparent duplication of cn=<GroupName> in the MoveHere method is that the same method can also be used for renaming objects (including groups) within the same container (see Recipe 4.20).

See Also

Recipe 4.20 for moving an object to a different OU, Recipe 4.21 for moving an object to a different domain, Recipe 7.8 for changing group scope and type, MS KB 313066

(How to Move Users, Groups, and Organizational Units Within a Domain in Windows 2000), and MSDN: IADsContainer::MoveHere

7.7   Moving a Group to Another Domain

Problem

You want to move a group to a different domain.

Solution

Using a graphical user interface

To migrate user, computer, group, or OU objects between domains in the same forest, use the following steps:

1. Open the ADMT MMC snap-in.

2. Right-click on the Active Directory Migration Tool folder, and select the Group Account Migration Wizard.

3. On the Test or Migrate Changes screen, click Migrate Now?

4. On the Domain Selection screen, enter the DNS or NetBIOS name of the source and target domains and click Next.

5. On the Group Selection screen, select the group objects that you wish to migrate and click Next. (You cannot migrate built-in or well-known groups such as Domain Users or Domain Admins using this process.)

6. On the Organizational Unit Selection screen, enter the name of the target OU or select Browse to open up an object picker in the target domain. Click Next to continue.

7. On the Group Options screen, select one or more of the following and click Next:

   Update user rights
   > This will copy any user rights that are assigned in the source domain to the target domain.

   Copy group members
   > Specifies whether the user objects that belong to the group should be migrated along with the group. If you don't select this option, the group will be created in the target domain with no members.

   Update previously migrated objects
   > Supports migrations that take place over time by comparing the source and target groups and migrating any changes that have taken place.

   Fix membership of group
   > This will add any migrated user accounts to groups in the target domain if the user accounts were members of the source groups in the source domain.

Migrate group SIDs to target domain

> Adds the security identifiers (SID) of the migrated group accounts in the source domain to the SID history of the new group in the target domain.

8. On the Naming Conflicts screen, select whether you want to migrate group objects that conflict with objects in the target domain and click Next.

9. Follow the remainder of the wizard to complete the migration.

Using a command-line interface

To migrate a group from the command-line using the ADMT utility, use the following syntax:

```
> ADMT GROUP /N "<GroupName1>" "<GroupName2>" /IF:YES /SD:"<SourceDomainDN>"
/TD:"<TargetDomainDN>" /TO:"<TargetOUDN>"
```

Using VBScript

```
set objObject = GetObject("LDAP://TargetDC/TargetParentDN")
objObject.MoveHere "LDAP://SourceDC/SourceDN", vbNullString
```

In the following example, the "cn=Finance Users" group in the *amer.rallencorp.com* domain will be moved to the *emea.rallencorp.com* domain:

```
set objObject = GetObject( _
    "LDAP://dc-amer1/cn=Finance Users,dc=amer,dc=rallencorp,dc=com")
objObject.MoveHere _
    "LDAP://dc-emea1/cn=Finance Users,cn=users,dc=emea,dc=rallencorp,dc=com", _
    vbNullString
```

Discussion

The only types of group that can be moved between domains using the built-in operating system tools are universal groups. If you want to move a global or domain local group to a different domain, first convert it to a universal group, move the group, then convert it back to a global or domain local group.

When you convert a group between types, you may encounter problems because different groups have different membership restrictions. See the "Introduction" to this chapter for more information on group type membership restrictions.

Another way to accomplish inter-domain group moves is by using the ADMT, which might be quite useful if you need to move a large number of groups. With ADMT, you can move and restructure groups without needing to go to all the trouble of converting the group to a universal group and then modifying the group membership. For more information on the latest version of ADMT, see: *http://www.microsoft.com/windowsserver2003/technologies/directory/activedirectory/default.mspx*.

7.8 Changing the Scope or Type of a Group

Problem

You want to change the scope or type of a group.

Solution

Using a graphical user interface

1. Open the ADUC snap-in.
2. If you need to change domains, right-click on Active Directory Users and Computers in the left pane, select Connect to Domain, enter the domain name, and click OK.
3. In the left pane, right-click on the domain and select Find.
4. Enter the name of the group you want to modify and click Find Now.
5. Double-click on the group in the results pane.
6. In the group properties dialog box, select the new scope or type, and click OK.

Using a command-line interface

The following example changes the group scope for *<GroupDN>* to *<NewScope>*, which should be l for domain local group, g for global group, or u for universal group.

```
> dsmod group "<GroupDN>" -scope <NewScope>
```

The following example changes the group type for *<GroupDN>*. For the -secgrp switch, specify yes to change to a security group or no to make the group a distribution group.

```
> dsmod group "<GroupDN>" -secgrp yes|no
```

To change the scope and/or type of a group using AdMod, use the following syntax:

```
> admod -b <GroupDN> groupType::<GroupType>
```

Just as when you created a group using AdMod, you must specify the numeric value for the group type; refer back to Recipe 7.1 for more information.

Using VBScript

```
' This code sets the scope and type of the specified group
' to a universal security group.
' ------ SCRIPT CONFIGURATION ------
strGroupDN = "<GroupDN>"  ' e.g. cn=SalesGroup,ou=Groups,dc=rallencorp,dc=com
' ------ END CONFIGURATION ---------

' Constants taken from ADS_GROUP_TYPE_ENUM
ADS_GROUP_TYPE_DOMAIN_LOCAL_GROUP = 1
ADS_GROUP_TYPE_GLOBAL_GROUP       = 2
```

```
ADS_GROUP_TYPE_LOCAL_GROUP          = 4
ADS_GROUP_TYPE_SECURITY_ENABLED     = -2147483648
ADS_GROUP_TYPE_UNIVERSAL_GROUP      = 8

set objGroup = GetObject("LDAP://" & strGroupDN )
objGroup.Put "groupType", ADS_GROUP_TYPE_UNIVERSAL_GROUP _
                       Or ADS_GROUP_TYPE_SECURITY_ENABLED
objGroup.SetInfo
```

Discussion

Group scope and type are stored as a flag in the groupType attribute on group objects. To directly update groupType, you must logically OR the values associated with each type and scope, as shown in the API solution, or use the raw numeric values listed in Recipe 7.1 when using AdMod. Note that there is no specific value for the distribution list type. If you want to create a distribution list, just do not include the ADS_GROUP_TYPE_SECURITY_ENABLED flag when setting groupType. To convert a group from one scope to another, the domain must be at Windows 2000 native domain functional level or higher. There are also additional group types that are available through Authorization Manger, which is discussed in Recipe 7.10.

 For a good description of the usage scenarios for each group type, see Chapter 11 in *Active Directory*, Third Edition, by Joe Richards et al. (O'Reilly).

See Also

Recipe 7.1, Recipe 7.10, MS KB 231273 (Group Type and Scope Usage in Windows), MSDN: ADS_GROUP_TYPE_ENUM, and MSDN: What Type of Group to Use

7.9   Modifying Group Attributes

Problem

You want to modify one or more attributes of an object.

Solution

Set the last name (sn) attribute for the jsmith user object.

Using a graphical user interface

1. Open ADSI Edit.
2. If an entry for the naming context you want to browse is not already displayed, do the following:

a. Right-click on ADSI Edit in the right pane and click "Connect to...."

b. Fill in the information for the naming context, container, or OU containing the group that you want to modify. Click on the Advanced button if you need to enter alternate credentials.

3. In the left pane, browse to the container or OU that contains the group you want to modify. Once you've found the group, right-click on it and select Properties.

4. Right-click the attribute that you want to modify and select Edit.

5. Enter the new value that you want to use and click OK.

6. Click Apply, followed by OK.

Using a command-line interface

Create an LDIF file called *modify_object.ldf* with the following contents:

```
dn: cn=Finance Users,cn=users,dc=rallencorp,dc=com
changetype: modify
add: description
description: Members of the Finance Department
-
```

Then run the following command:

```
> ldifde -v -i -f modify_object.ldf
```

To modify a group using AdMod, you'll use the following general syntax:

```
> admod -b <GroupDN> <attribute>:<operation>:<value>
```

For example, you can add a description to a group object using the following syntax:

```
> C:\>admod -b cn="Finance Users,cn=Users,dc=rallencorp,dc=com"
  description::"Members of the Finance Department"
```

You can also modify group objects with the `dsmod group` command using the following syntax:

```
> dsmod group <GroupDN> <options>
```

The available options for `dsmod` include the following:

`-samid <NewSAMName>`
    Updates the `sAMAccountName` attribute of the group object

`-desc <NewDescription>`
    Updates the `description` attribute of the group object

`-secgrp {yes | no}`
    Configures the group object as a security group (yes) or a distribution group (no)

`-scope {l | g | u}`
    Configures the group scope as domain local (l), global (g), or universal (u)

```
{-addmbr | -rmmbr | -chmbr} <MemberDN1> <MemberDN2>
```
Adds the specified objects to the group (addmbr), removes the specified objects (rmmbr), or replaces the membership list wholesale with only the specified objects (chmbr)

Using VBScript

```
strGroupDN = "cn=Finance Users,cn=users,dc=rallencorp,dc=com"
set objGroup = GetObject("LDAP://" & strGroupDN)
objGroup.Put "description", "Members of the Finance Department"
objGroup.SetInfo
```

Discussion

Using a graphical user interface

If the parent container of the object you want to modify has a lot of objects in it, you may want to add a new connection entry for the DN of the target object. This will be easier than trying to hunt through a container full of objects. You can do this by right-clicking ADSI Edit and selecting "Connect to…" under Connection Point, then select Distinguished Name and enter the DN of the object.

Using a command-line interface

For more on *ldifde*, see Recipe 4.28.

Using VBScript

If you need to do anything more than simple assignment or replacement of a value for an attribute, you'll need to use the PutEx method instead of Put. PutEx allows for greater control of assigning multiple values, deleting specific values, and appending values.

PutEx requires three parameters: update flag, attribute name, and an array of values to set or unset. The update flags are defined by the ADS_PROPERTY_OPERATION_ENUM collection and listed in Recipe 4.14. Finally, SetInfo commits the change. If SetInfo is not called, the creation will not get committed to the domain controller.

See Also

Recipe 4.14, Recipe 4.28, MSDN: IADs::Put, MSDN: IADs::PutEx, MSDN: IADs::SetInfo, and MSDN: ADS_PROPERTY_OPERATION_ENUM

7.10   Creating a Dynamic Group

Problem

You want to create a dynamic group using the optional Authorization Manager (AZMan) component.

Solution

Using a graphical user interface

1. Install the Authorization Manager component through Add/Remove Programs, if it is not already present.

2. Open the Authorization Manager MMC snap-in.

3. Right-click on the Authorization Manager node and select Open Authorization Store.

4. Under "Select authorization store type," select one of the following:

   Active Directory
   > Enter the name of the application partition such as `cn=ERP,cn=Program Data,dc=rallencorp,dc=com`, or click Browse to select it from the Active Directory tree.

   XML file
   > Enter the path to the XML file, or click Browse to select it from the filesystem.

5. Drill down to Console Root → Authorization Manager → Authorization Share → Application Name → Groups.

6. Right-click on Groups and select New → Group.

 This will create a group that is scoped to the entire authorization store. You can drill down to an individual application to create a group that is only applicable within the app itself.

7. From the New Application Group screen, enter the name of the group and a description. Under Group Type, select LDAP query. Click OK to create the group.

8. Right-click on the group you just created and select Properties. From the LDAP tab, enter the LDAP attributes that will make up the group. For example, you can configure the group to include only Managers by entering (`title=Manager`).

9. Click OK to finish creating the group.

Using a command-line interface

The following syntax will create an application group that's based on an LDAP query:

```
> admod -b <GroupDN> groupType::32 sAMAccountType::1073741825 msDS-AzLDAPQuery::
"(&(objectcategory=person)(objectclass=user))" -add
```

Using VBScript

```
' The following code will create an application group
' that is scoped to an individual application rather than
' the entire authorization store

AzManStore = CreateObject("AzRoles.AzAuthorizationStore")

Set Application1 = AzManStore.OpenApplication("ERP")
Set AppGroup = _
  Application1.CreateApplicationGroup("HR Managers",VT_EMPTY)
AppGroup.Type = AZ_GROUPTYPE_LDAP_QUERY
AppGroup.Description = "Users with hiring authority"
AppGroup.LdapQuery = _
  "(memberOf= CN=HR Managers,OU=Distribution Lists,DC=enterprise,DC=com)"

'----- Persist the changes to the application group and then the app ------
AppGroup.Submit
Application1.Submit
```

Discussion

Authorization Manager is a new feature in Windows Server 2003 that allows application developers to create role-based authorization groups that are based on a company's organizational structure. Groups created through Authorization Manager are similar to the ones that you would create using Active Directory Users and Computers or a corresponding command-line utility or script, except that AzMan groups are created and maintained for use by a single application or a specific set of applications created by a developer. An application developer or administrator can create AzMan groups without having administrative rights to the domain as a whole, and group membership can be configured so that it is dynamically determined; that is, you can configure a group of users based on a dynamic set of criteria rather than needing to discretely specify each individual group member one at a time. Once a developer or administrator has created a group using Authorization Manager, these groups can be assigned specific roles within an application that allow them to perform certain tasks. These groups are not Windows Security enabled groups and although they have an SID, cannot currently be used to secure resources.

See Also

MSDN: Qualifying Access with Business Logic in Scripts, MSDN: Using Dynamic Business Rules in Windows Server 2003 Authorization Manager, MSDN: Authorization Manager Model [Security], MS KB 324470 (How to Install and Administer the Authorization Manager in Windows Server 2003), and MSDN: Dynamic Groups in Windows Server 2003 Authorization Manager

7.11 Delegating Control for Managing Membership of a Group

Problem

You want to delegate the ability to manage the membership of a group.

Solution

Using a graphical user interface

 This is a new feature of the Windows Server 2003 version of ADUC.

1. Open the ADUC snap-in.
2. If you need to change domains, right-click on Active Directory Users and Computers in the left pane, select Connect to Domain, enter the domain name, and click OK.
3. In the left pane, right-click on the domain and select Find.
4. Enter the name of the group and click Find Now.
5. Double-click on the group in the results pane.
6. Select the Managed By tab.
7. Click the Change button.
8. Locate the group or user to delegate control to and click OK.
9. Check the box beside "Manager can update membership list."
10. Click OK.

Using a command-line interface

```
> dsacls <GroupDN> /G <GroupName>@DomainName:WP;member;
```

In the following example, the SalesAdmin group will be given rights to modify membership of the PreSales group:

```
> dsacls cn=presales,ou=sales,dc=rallencorp,dc=com /G salesadmins@rallencorp.com:
WP;member;
```

Using VBScript

```
' This code grants write access to the member attribute of a group.
' ------ SCRIPT CONFIGURATION ------
strGroupDN = "<GroupDN>"  ' e.g. cn=SalesGroup,ou=Sales,dc=rallencorp,dc=com"
strUserOrGroup = "<UserOrGroup>"  ' e.g. joe@rallencorp.com or RALLENCORP\joe
' ------ END CONFIGURATION ---------

set objGroup = GetObject("LDAP://" & strGroupDN)
'###########################
' Constants
'###########################
' ADS_ACETYPE_ENUM
Const ADS_ACETYPE_ACCESS_ALLOWED_OBJECT = &h5
Const ADS_FLAG_OBJECT_TYPE_PRESENT = &h1
Const ADS_RIGHT_DS_WRITE_PROP = &h20

' From schemaIDGUID of member attribute
Const MEMBER_ATTRIBUTE = "{bf9679c0-0de6-11d0-a285-00aa003049e2}"

'###########################
' Create ACL
'###########################
set objSD = objGroup.Get("nTSecurityDescriptor")
set objDACL = objSD.DiscretionaryAcl

' Set WP for member attribute
set objACE = CreateObject("AccessControlEntry")
objACE.Trustee     = strUserOrGroup
objACE.AccessMask = ADS_RIGHT_DS_WRITE_PROP
objACE.AceFlags    = 0
objACE.Flags       = ADS_FLAG_OBJECT_TYPE_PRESENT
objACE.AceType     = ADS_ACETYPE_ACCESS_ALLOWED_OBJECT
objACE.ObjectType = MEMBER_ATTRIBUTE

objDACL.AddAce objACE

'###########################
' Set ACL
'###########################
objSD.DiscretionaryAcl = objDACL
objGroup.Put "nTSecurityDescriptor", objSD
objGroup.SetInfo
WScript.Echo "Delegated control of member attribute for " & _
             strGroupDN & " to " & strUserOrGroup
```

Discussion

To grant a user or group the ability to manage group membership, you have to grant
the write property (WP) permission on the member attribute of the target group. You

can add this ACE directly using dsacls, or more indirectly with ADUC. ADUC in Windows Server 2003 has a new feature that allows you to simply check a box to grant the ability to modify group membership to the object represented by the managedBy attribute.

If you want to configure additional permissions, such as the ability to modify the description attribute for the group, you will need to go to the Security tab in ADUC, or specify the appropriate attribute with the /G switch with dsacls. For example, this will grant write property on the description attribute:

```
/G <GroupName>@DomainDNSName:WP;description;
```

See Also

Recipe 15.7 for delegating control in Active Directory

7.12   Resolving a Primary Group ID

Problem

You want to find the name of a user's primary group.

Solution

Using a graphical user interface

1. Open the ADUC snap-in.
2. If you need to change domains, right-click on Active Directory Users and Computers in the left pane, select Connect to Domain, enter the domain name, and click OK.
3. In the left pane, right-click on the domain and select Find.
4. Type the name of the user and click Find Now.
5. In the Search Results window, double-click on the user.
6. Click the Member Of tab.
7. The Primary Group name is shown on the bottom half of the dialog box.

Using VBScript

```
' This code prints the group name of a user's primary group
'-----------SCRIPT CONFIGURATION----------------------------
strUserDN = "<UserDN>" ' i.e. "cn=jsmith,dc=rallencorp,dc=com"
strDomain = "<DomainNetBIOSName>" ' i.e. RALLENCORP
'----------------------------------------------------------

' Grab the primary group's RID from the user object
set objUser = GetObject("LDAP://" & strUserDN)
strGroupRID = objUser.Get("primaryGroupID")
```

```
' Grab the user's SID to obtain the domain SID
strUserName = objUser.sAMAccountName
Set WMIUser = GetObject("winmgmts:{impersonationlevel=impersonate}!" _
    & "/root/cimv2:Win32_UserAccount.Domain='" & strDomain & "'" _
    & ",Name='" & strUserName & "'")
strUserSID = WMIUser.SID
strDomainSID = mid(strUserSID,1,(InStrREV(strUserSID,"-")))

' Now construct the Primary Group SID
strGroupSID = strDomainSID & strGroupRID

' Bind to the primary group using its SID and echo its name
set objGroup = GetObject("LDAP://<SID=" & strGroupSID &">")
strGroupDN = objGroup.distinguishedName
WScript.Echo(strGroupDN)
```

Discussion

When trying to determine a user's group membership, you have to look at the user's
memberOf attribute, which contains a list of DNs for each group the user is a member
of, as well as the user's primary group. By default, all users are assigned Domain Users
as their primary group. Therefore, by default all users in a domain are implicitly
members of the Domain Users group. Unfortunately, a user's primary group will not
show up in the memberOf attribute unless explicitly added.

 Services for Macintosh and POSIX-based applications are the main
users of primary groups. If you don't use either of those, you don't
need to worry about changing a user's primary group.

The primary group is stored in the primaryGroupID attribute on user objects. Unfortunately, the information that's stored in that attribute is the relative identifier (RID) of
the group, not the DN or even sAMAccountName as you might expect. group objects
have a primaryGroupToken attribute, which contains the same value, but is a constructed attribute. Because Active Directory dynamically constructs it, you cannot
utilize it in search filters. So even if you have the primaryGroupID of a user (e.g., 513),
you cannot do a simple query to find out which group it is associated with. You can
find the name of a user's primary group relatively easily using the Active Directory
Users and Computers snap-in as described in the GUI solution.

Using VBScript

The VBScript solution uses a combination of WMI and ADSI to retrieve the distinguished name of the user's primary group by constructing and deconstructing various SIDs. Every user, computer, and group object in Active Directory possesses a SID
that is composed of two parts: the SID for the Active Directory domain, followed by
the RID for the object. The domain SID will be identical for all objects that exist in
the same AD domain; only the RID will differ. Because of this, you can retrieve the
user object's SID using the Win32_UserAccount WMI namespace, and then remove the

final -*xxxx* to obtain the domain SID. Once you have the domain SID, it's fairly simple to append the primary group RID to the end of it, thus creating a usable SID for the primary group itself.

See Also

MS KB 297951 (How to Use the PrimaryGroupID Attribute to Find the Primary Group for a User) and MS KB 321360 (How to Use Native ADSI Components to Find the Primary Group)

7.13   Enabling Universal Group Membership Caching

 This recipe requires the Windows Server 2003 forest functional level.

Problem

You want to enable universal group membership caching so that a global catalog server is not needed during most user logins.

Solution

Using a graphical user interface

1. Open the Active Directory Sites and Services snap-in.
2. In the left pane, browse to the site you want to enable group caching for and click on it.
3. In the right pane, double-click on the NTDS Site Settings object.
4. Under Universal Group Membership Caching, check the box beside Enable Universal Group Caching.
5. If you want to force the cache refresh from a particular site, select a site or else leave the default set to <Default>.
6. Click OK.

Using a command-line interface

You can use a combination of the dsquery site and dsget site commands to find if a site has group caching enabled:

```
> dsquery site -name <SiteName> | dsget site -dn -cachegroups -prefGCSite
```

You can use *ldifde* to enable group caching. Create a file called *enable_univ_cache.ldf* with the following contents, but change <SiteName> to the name of the site you want to enable, and *<ForestRootDN>* with the distinguished name of the forest root domain:

```
dn: cn=NTDS Site Settings,cn=<SiteName>,cn=sites,cn=configuration,<ForestRootDN>
changetype: modify
replace: options
options: 32
-
```

Then use the following command to import the change:

```
> ldifde -i -f enable_univ_cache.ldf
```

You can also perform this change by using AdMod with the following syntax:

```
> admod -b "cn=NTDS Site Settings,cn=<SiteName>,cn=sites,cn=
configuration,<ForestRootDN>" options::32
```

Using VBScript

```
' This code enables universal group caching for the specified site.
' ------ SCRIPT CONFIGURATION ------
strSiteName = "<SiteName>"   ' e.g. Default-First-Site-Name
' ------ END CONFIGURATION ---------

set objRootDSE = GetObject("LDAP://RootDSE")
set objSite = GetObject("LDAP://cn=NTDS Site Settings,cn=" & strSiteName & _
            ",cn=sites," & objRootDSE.Get("configurationNamingContext") )
objSite.Put "options", 32
objSite.SetInfo
WScript.Echo "Successfully enabled universal group caching for " & _
            strSiteName
```

Discussion

When a client logs on to a Windows 2000 Active Directory domain controller, the domain controller that authenticates the user needs to contact a global catalog server in order to fully authenticate the client. This is necessary because global catalogs are the only servers that store universal group information, which is necessary to completely determine a user's group memberships upon logon. (If the DC that authenticates the user is itself a GC, then it does not need to contact any other servers to complete the authentication process.)

Universal groups can be created and used anywhere in a forest. Objects located anywhere in a forest can be added as members of a universal group. Since a universal group could be created in a domain other than where the user object resides, it is necessary to store universal group membership in the global catalog. That way, during logon, domain controllers can query a global catalog to determine all universal groups a user is a member of. Microsoft's primary reason for making this a requirement during logon is that a user could be part of a universal group that has been explicitly denied access to certain resources. If universal groups aren't evaluated, a user could gain access to resources that were previously restricted.

To remove this limitation in Windows Server 2003 Active Directory, *universal group caching* was introduced. Universal group caching can be enabled on a per site basis and allows domain controllers to cache universal group information locally, thus removing the need to query the global catalog during client logon.

You can enable universal group caching manually by enabling the 10,000 bit (32 in decimal) on the options attribute of the NTDS Site Settings object. The CLI and VBScript solutions blindly wrote 32 to that attribute, which is not ideal. See Recipe 4.15 for more information on properly setting a bit flag attribute. The Sites and Services snap-in hides this logic and just requires you to check a box. Another setting can also be configured that relates to universal group caching. By default, domain controllers will use the site topology to determine the optimal site to use to query a global catalog server for universal group information. You can override this feature and explicitly set which site domain controllers should use by selecting the site in the Sites and Services snap-in or by setting the msDS-Preferred-GC-Site attribute on the NTDS Site Settings object to the DN of the target site.

See Also

Recipe 4.15

7.14 Restoring a Deleted Group

Problem

You want to restore a group object that has been inadvertently deleted, as well as restoring its members.

Solution

Using a graphical user interface

1. Reboot the domain controller in Directory Services Restore Mode.
2. Perform a System State restore.
3. Before rebooting the server, perform the steps listed in the following section.

Using a command line interface

1. To restore the user and group accounts, use the following sequence of commands (replace *<ContainerDN>* with the name of the container or OU containing the user and group objects that need to be restored):

   ```
   > ntdsutil
   > authoritative restore
   ```

```
> restore subtree <ContainerDN>
> quit
> exit
```

2. Reboot the domain controller into normal mode and wait for replication to complete.

3. Reboot the domain controller into Directory Services Restore Mode again. Perform the commands in Step 1 a second time. (It is only necessary to mark the restore as authoritative a second time; you do not need to perform the actual System State restore again.)

4. Restart the domain controller after running these commands.

Discussion

In most cases, it is sufficient when restoring a deleted object within Active Directory to simply perform an *authoritative* restore of the object or container. However, things get a bit more complicated when you're restoring group objects as well as the users who were members of those groups. Because you cannot easily control the order in which objects are restored to the AD database, you may run into a situation where a group object gets restored *before* the users who were members of that group. In this case, when Active Directory attempts to populate the restored group's member attribute, it can only populate it with user objects that already exist within the directory. Put another way, if some or all of the users or other groups that are referenced in the restored group's member attribute have not yet been restored, they will not be included in the restored group's member attribute. This will leave the restored group in an inconsistent state, since it will not possess all of the members that it had before it was deleted.

To correct this issue, it's necessary to perform the authoritative restore process *twice* when restoring groups and their members. The first authoritative restore will re-create all users that should be members of the group objects. The second pass will go back and correctly re-populate the member attribute of any restored groups, now that all of the needed user objects exist within Active Directory.

See Also

MS KB 216993 (Useful Shelf Life of a System-State Backup of Active Directory), MS KB 840001 (How to Restore Deleted User Accounts and Their Group Memberships in Active Directory), and Chapter 17 for more on recovering and restoring Active Directory

## CHAPTER 8

Computers

8.0   Introduction

As far as Active Directory is concerned, computers are very similar to users. In fact, computer objects inherit directly from the user object class, which is used to represent user accounts. That means that computer objects possess all of the attributes of user objects and then some. Computers need to be represented in Active Directory for many of the same reasons users do, including the need to access resources securely, utilize GPOs, and have permissions assigned to them.

To participate in a domain, computers need a *secure channel* to a domain controller. A secure channel is an authenticated connection that can transmit encrypted data. To set up the secure channel, a computer must present a password to a domain controller. Similar to the way in which it authenticates a user account, Active Directory will use Kerberos authentication to verify the identity of a computer account. Without the computer object and, by association, the password stored with it that is changed behind the scenes on a regular basis by the operating system, there would be no way for the domain controller to verify a computer is what it claims to be.

The Anatomy of a Computer

The default location for computer objects in a domain is the cn=Computers container located directly off the domain root. You can, however, create computer objects anywhere in a domain. And in Windows Server 2003, you can modify the default location for computer objects as described in Recipe 8.12. Table 8-1 contains a list of some of the interesting attributes that are available on computer objects.

Table 8-1. Attributes of computer objects

Attribute	Description
cn	Relative distinguished name of computer objects.
dnsHostName	Fully qualified DNS name of the computer.

Table 8-1. Attributes of computer objects (continued)

Attribute	Description
lastLogonTimestamp	The approximate timestamp of the last time the computer logged in to the domain. This is a new attribute in Windows Server 2003.
managedBy	The distinguished name (DN) of user or group that manages the computer.
memberOf	List of DNs of the groups the computer is a member of.
operatingSystem	Textual description of the operating system running on the computer. See Recipe 8.13 for more information.
operatingSystemHotFix	Currently not being used, but will hopefully be populated at some point.
operatingSystemServicePack	Service pack version installed on the computer. See Recipe 8.13 for more information.
operatingSystemVersion	Numeric version of the operating system installed on the computer. See Recipe 8.13 for more information.
pwdLastSet	Large integer that can be translated into the last time the computer's password was set. See Recipe 8.9 for more information.
sAMAccountName	NetBIOS-style name of the computer. This is typically the name of the computer with $ at the end.
userAccountControl	Account flag that defines various account properties. In the case of a computer object, this specifies whether the computer is a member computer or a domain controller.

8.1   Creating a Computer

Problem

You want to create a computer account.

Solution

Using a graphical user interface

1. Open the ADUC snap-in.

2. If you need to change domains, right-click on Active Directory Users and Computers in the left pane, select "Connect to Domain," enter the domain name, and click OK.

3. In the left pane, browse to the parent container for the computer, right-click on it, and select New → Computer.

4. Enter the name of the computer. If necessary, place a checkmark next to "Assign this computer as a pre-Windows 2000 computer" or "Assign this computer as a backup domain controller." Click Next to continue.

5. If you will be using this computer account as part of an RIS deployment, place a checkmark next to "This is a managed computer" and enter the GUID that it should use, and then click Next. Otherwise, just click Next to continue.

6. Click Finish.

Using a command-line interface

You can create a computer object using either the built-in DSAdd utility or AdMod. To create an account using DSAdd, use the following syntax:

```
> dsadd computer "<ComputerDN>" -desc "<Description>"
```

To create a computer account using AdMod, enter the following:

```
> admod -b "<ComputerDN>" objectclass::computer
  sAMAccountName::<ComputerName>$ userAccountControl::4096
  description::"<Description>" -add
```

Using VBScript

```
' This code creates a computer object.
' ------ SCRIPT CONFIGURATION ------
strBase = "<ParentComputerDN>"  ' e.g. cn=Computers,dc=rallencorp,dc=com
strComp = "<ComputerName>"      ' e.g. joe-xp
strDescr = "<Description>"       ' e.g. Joe's Windows XP workstation
' ------ END CONFIGURATION ---------

' ADS_USER_FLAG_ENUM
Const ADS_UF_WORKSTATION_TRUST_ACCOUNT = &h1000 ' 4096

set objCont = GetObject("LDAP://" & strBase)
set objComp = objCont.Create("computer", "cn=" & strComp)
objComp.Put "sAMAccountName", strComp & "$"
objComp.Put "description", strDesc
objComp.Put "userAccountControl", ADS_UF_WORKSTATION_TRUST_ACCOUNT
objComp.SetInfo
Wscript.Echo "Computer account for " & strComp & " created"
```

Discussion

Creating a computer object in Active Directory is not much different from creating a user object. We set the description attribute in the CLI and API solutions, but it is not a mandatory attribute. The only mandatory attribute is sAMAccountName, which should be set to the name of the computer with $ appended. Also note that these solutions simply create a computer object. This does not mean any user can join a computer to the domain with that computer account. For more information on creating a computer object and allowing a specific user or group to join the computer to the domain, see Recipe 8.2.

See Also

Recipe 8.2 for creating a computer for a user, MS KB 222525 (Automating the Creation of Computer Accounts), MS KB 283771 (How to Prestage Windows 2000 Computers in Active Directory), MS KB 315273 (Automating the Creation of Computer Accounts), MS KB 320187 (How to Manage Computer Accounts in Active Directory in Windows 2000), and MSDN: ADS_USER_FLAG_ENUM

8.2 Creating a Computer for a Specific User or Group

Problem

You want to create a computer account for a specific user or group to join to the domain. This requires setting permissions on the computer account so that the user or group can modify certain attributes.

Solution

Using a graphical user interface

1. Open the ADUC snap-in.
2. If you need to change domains, right-click on Active Directory Users and Computers in the left pane, select "Connect to Domain," enter the domain name, and click OK.
3. In the left pane, browse to the parent container for the computer, right-click on it, and select New → Computer.
4. Enter the name of the computer.
5. Under "The following user or group can join this computer to a domain," click the Change button.
6. Use the Object Picker to select a user or group to join the computer to the domain.
7. Click OK.

Using a command-line interface

In the following solution, replace <ComputerDN> with the distinguished name of the computer object and <UserOrGroup> with the user principal name or NT-style name of a user or group you want to manage the computer:

```
> dsadd computer <ComputerDN>
> dsacls <ComputerDN> /G <UserOrGroup>:CALCGRSDDTRC;;
> dsacls <ComputerDN> /G <UserOrGroup>:WP;description;
> dsacls <ComputerDN> /G <UserOrGroup>:WP;sAMAccountName;
> dsacls <ComputerDN> /G <UserOrGroup>:WP;displayName;
> dsacls <ComputerDN> /G <UserOrGroup>:WP;"userAccountControl;
> dsacls <ComputerDN> /G <UserOrGroup>:WS;"Validated write to service principal\
name";
> dsacls <ComputerDN> /G <UserOrGroup>:WS;"Validated write to DNS host name";
```

 You can replace the first line of this code with the AdMod code from Recipe 8.1 if you choose.

Using VBScript

```
' This code creates a computer object and grants a user/group rights over it.
' ------ SCRIPT CONFIGURATION ------
strComputer = "<ComputerName>"    ' e.g. joe-xp
strUser     = "<UserOrGroup>"     ' e.g. joe@rallencorp.com or RALLENCORP\joe
strDescr    = "<ComputerDescr>"   ' e.g. Joe's workstation
strDomain   = "<ComputerDomain>"  ' e.g. rallencorp.com
' ------ END CONFIGURATION ---------

'############################
' Constants
'############################

' ADS_USER_FLAG_ENUM
Const ADS_UF_PASSWD_NOTREQD            = &h0020
Const ADS_UF_WORKSTATION_TRUST_ACCOUNT = &h1000

' ADS_ACETYPE_ENUM
Const ADS_ACETYPE_ACCESS_ALLOWED        = &h0
Const ADS_ACETYPE_ACCESS_ALLOWED_OBJECT = &h5

' ADS_FLAGTYPE_ENUM
Const ADS_FLAG_OBJECT_TYPE_PRESENT = &h1

' ADS_RIGHTS_ENUM
Const ADS_RIGHT_DS_SELF         = &h8
Const ADS_RIGHT_DS_WRITE_PROP   = &h20
Const ADS_RIGHT_DS_CONTROL_ACCESS = &h100
Const ADS_RIGHT_ACTRL_DS_LIST   = &h4
Const ADS_RIGHT_GENERIC_READ    = &h80000000
Const ADS_RIGHT_DELETE          = &h10000
Const ADS_RIGHT_DS_DELETE_TREE  = &h40
Const ADS_RIGHT_READ_CONTROL    = &h20000

' schemaIDGUID values
Const DISPLAY_NAME      = "{bf967953-0de6-11d0-a285-00aa003049e2}"
Const SAM_ACCOUNT_NAME  = "{3e0abfd0-126a-11d0-a060-00aa006c33ed}"
Const DESCRIPTION       = "{bf967950-0de6-11d0-a285-00aa003049e2}"

' controlAccessRight rightsGUID values
Const USER_LOGON_INFORMATION      = "{5f202010-79a5-11d0-9020-00c04fc2d4cf}"
Const USER_ACCOUNT_RESTRICTIONS   = "{4C164200-20C0-11D0-A768-00AA006E0529}"
Const VALIDATED_DNS_HOST_NAME     = "{72E39547-7B18-11D1-ADEF-00C04FD8D5CD}"
Const VALIDATED_SPN               = "{F3A64788-5306-11D1-A9C5-0000F80367C1}"

'############################
' Create Computer
'############################

set objRootDSE = GetObject("LDAP://" & strDomain & "/RootDSE")
set objContainer = GetObject("LDAP://cn=Computers," & _
                             objRootDSE.Get("defaultNamingContext"))
set objComputer = objContainer.Create("Computer", "cn=" & strComputer)
```

```
objComputer.Put "sAMAccountName", strComputer & "$"
objComputer.Put "userAccountControl", _
                ADS_UF_PASSWD_NOTREQD Or ADS_UF_WORKSTATION_TRUST_ACCOUNT
objComputer.Put "description", strDescr
objComputer.SetInfo

'############################
' Create ACL
'############################

set objSD = objComputer.Get("nTSecurityDescriptor")
set objDACL = objSD.DiscretionaryAcl

' Special: Control Rights, List Children
'          Generic Read, Delete,
'          Delete Subtree, Read Permission
set objACE1 = CreateObject("AccessControlEntry")
objACE1.Trustee    = strUser
objACE1.AccessMask = ADS_RIGHT_DS_CONTROL_ACCESS Or _
                     ADS_RIGHT_ACTRL_DS_LIST Or _
                     ADS_RIGHT_GENERIC_READ Or _
                     ADS_RIGHT_DELETE Or _
                     ADS_RIGHT_DS_DELETE_TREE Or ADS_RIGHT_READ_CONTROL
objACE1.AceFlags   = 0
objACE1.AceType    = ADS_ACETYPE_ACCESS_ALLOWED

' Write Property: description
set objACE2 = CreateObject("AccessControlEntry")
objACE2.Trustee    = strUser
objACE2.AccessMask = ADS_RIGHT_DS_WRITE_PROP
objACE2.AceFlags   = 0
objACE2.Flags      = ADS_FLAG_OBJECT_TYPE_PRESENT
objACE2.AceType    = ADS_ACETYPE_ACCESS_ALLOWED_OBJECT
objACE2.ObjectType = DESCRIPTION

' Write Property: sAMAccountName
set objACE3 = CreateObject("AccessControlEntry")
objACE3.Trustee    = strUser
objACE3.AccessMask = ADS_RIGHT_DS_WRITE_PROP
objACE3.AceFlags   = 0
objACE3.Flags      = ADS_FLAG_OBJECT_TYPE_PRESENT
objACE3.AceType    = ADS_ACETYPE_ACCESS_ALLOWED_OBJECT
objACE3.ObjectType = SAM_ACCOUNT_NAME

' Write Property: displayName
set objACE4 = CreateObject("AccessControlEntry")
objACE4.Trustee    = strUser
objACE4.AccessMask = ADS_RIGHT_DS_WRITE_PROP
objACE4.AceFlags   = 0
objACE4.Flags      = ADS_FLAG_OBJECT_TYPE_PRESENT
objACE4.AceType    = ADS_ACETYPE_ACCESS_ALLOWED_OBJECT
objACE4.ObjectType = DISPLAY_NAME

' Write Property: Logon Information
```

```
set objACE5 = CreateObject("AccessControlEntry")
objACE5.Trustee    = strUser
objACE5.AccessMask = ADS_RIGHT_DS_WRITE_PROP
objACE5.AceFlags   = 0
objACE5.AceType    = ADS_ACETYPE_ACCESS_ALLOWED_OBJECT
objACE5.Flags      = ADS_FLAG_OBJECT_TYPE_PRESENT
objACE5.ObjectType = USER_LOGON_INFORMATION

' Write Property: Account Restrictions
set objACE6 = CreateObject("AccessControlEntry")
objACE6.Trustee    = strUser
objACE6.AccessMask = ADS_RIGHT_DS_WRITE_PROP
objACE6.AceFlags   = 0
objACE6.AceType    = ADS_ACETYPE_ACCESS_ALLOWED_OBJECT
objACE6.Flags      = ADS_FLAG_OBJECT_TYPE_PRESENT
objACE6.ObjectType = USER_ACCOUNT_RESTRICTIONS

' Write Self: Validated SPN
set objACE7 = CreateObject("AccessControlEntry")
objACE7.Trustee    = strUser
objACE7.AccessMask = ADS_RIGHT_DS_SELF
objACE7.AceFlags   = 0
objACE7.AceType    = ADS_ACETYPE_ACCESS_ALLOWED_OBJECT
objACE7.Flags      = ADS_FLAG_OBJECT_TYPE_PRESENT
objACE7.ObjectType = VALIDATED_SPN

' Write Self: Validated DNS Host Name
set objACE8 = CreateObject("AccessControlEntry")
objACE8.Trustee    = strUser
objACE8.AccessMask = ADS_RIGHT_DS_SELF
objACE8.AceFlags   = 0
objACE8.AceType    = ADS_ACETYPE_ACCESS_ALLOWED_OBJECT
objACE8.Flags      = ADS_FLAG_OBJECT_TYPE_PRESENT
objACE8.ObjectType = VALIDATED_DNS_HOST_NAME

objDACL.AddAce objACE1
objDACL.AddAce objACE2
objDACL.AddAce objACE3
objDACL.AddAce objACE4
objDACL.AddAce objACE5
objDACL.AddAce objACE6
objDACL.AddAce objACE7
objDACL.AddAce objACE8

'############################
' Set ACL
'############################
objSD.DiscretionaryAcl = objDACL
objComputer.Put "nTSecurityDescriptor", objSD
objComputer.SetInfo
WScript.Echo "Successfully created " & strComputer & _
             " and gave rights to " & strUser
```

Discussion

By default, members of the Authenticated Users group can join up to 10 computers to an Active Directory domain. If you've modified this default behavior or need to allow a user to add computers to the domain on a regular basis, you need to grant certain permissions so that the user has rights to modify the computer object. When you create a computer via the ADUC snap-in, you have the option to select a user or group to manage the computer object and join a computer to the domain using that object. When you use that method, eight ACEs are added to the ACL of the computer object. They are:

- List Contents, Read All Properties, Delete, Delete Subtree, Read Permissions, All Extended Rights (i.e., Allowed to Authenticate, Change Password, Send As, Receive As, Reset Password)
- Write Property for description
- Write Property for sAMAccountName
- Write Property for displayName
- Write Property for Logon Information
- Write Property for Account Restrictions
- Validate write to DNS hostname
- Validate write for service principal name

Using a graphical user interface

If you want to modify the default permissions that are applied when you select a user or group through the GUI, double-click on the computer object after you've created it and go to the Security tab. For the Security tab to be visible, you have to select View → Advanced Features.

Using a command-line interface

With the *dsacls* utility, you can specify either a UPN (*user@domain*) or down-level style (*DOMAIN\user*) account name when applying permissions. Also, *dsacls* requires that the displayName of the attribute, property set, or extended right you are setting the permission on be used instead of the lDAPDisplayName, as one might expect. That is why we had to use "Validated write to service principal name," which is the displayName for the Validated-SPN controlAccessRight object, with the ACE for the SPN-validated write. *dsacls* is also case sensitive, so be sure to specify the correct case for the words in the displayName.

Using VBScript

After creating the computer object, similar to Recipe 8.1, create an ACE object for each of the eight ACEs previously listed using the IADsAccessControlEntry interface.

To apply the ACEs, retrieve the current security descriptor for the computer object, which is stored in the nTSecurityDescriptor attribute, and then add the eight ACEs. Finally, call SetInfo to commit the change to Active Directory. For more information on setting ACEs and ACLs programmatically, see the IADsAccessControlEntry documentation in MSDN.

See Also

Recipe 8.1 for creating a computer account, MS KB 238793 (Enhanced Security Joining or Resetting Machine Account in Windows 2000 Domain), MS KB 283771 (How to Prestage Windows 2000 Computers in Active Directory), MS KB 320187 (How to Manage Computer Accounts in Active Directory in Windows 2000), MSDN: IADsAccessControlEntry, MSDN: ADS_ACETYPE_ENUM, and MSDN: ADS_ RIGHTS_ENUM, MSDN: ADS_FLAGTYPE_ENUM

8.3   Joining a Computer to a Domain

Problem

You want to join a computer to a domain after the computer object has already been created in Active Directory.

Solution

Using a graphical user interface

1. Log on to the computer you want to join to the domain and open the Control Panel.
2. Open the System applet.
3. Click the Computer Name tab.
4. Click the Change button.
5. Under "Member of," select Domain.
6. Enter the domain you want to join and click OK.
7. You may be prompted to enter credentials that grant permission to join the computer.
8. Reboot the computer.

   Note that the tabs in the System applet vary between Windows 2000, Windows XP, and Windows Server 2003.

Using a command-line interface

```
> netdom join <ComputerName> /Domain <DomainName> /UserD <DomainUserUPN>
/PasswordD * /UserO <ComputerAdminUser> /PasswordO * /Reboot
```

Using VBScript

```
' This code joins a computer to a domain.
' ------ SCRIPT CONFIGURATION ------
strComputer     = "<ComputerName>"        ' e.g. joe-xp
strDomain       = "<DomainName>"          ' e.g. rallencorp.com
strDomainUser   = "<DomainUserUPN>"       ' e.g. administrator@rallencorp.com
strDomainPasswd = "<DomainUserPasswd>"
strLocalUser    = "<ComputerAdminUser>"   ' e.g. administrator
strLocalPasswd  = "<ComputerUserPasswd>"
' ------ END CONFIGURATION ---------

'#########################
' Constants
'#########################
Const JOIN_DOMAIN              = 1
Const ACCT_CREATE             = 2
Const ACCT_DELETE             = 4
Const WIN9X_UPGRADE           = 16
Const DOMAIN_JOIN_IF_JOINED   = 32
Const JOIN_UNSECURE           = 64
Const MACHINE_PASSWORD_PASSED = 128
Const DEFERRED_SPN_SET        = 256
Const INSTALL_INVOCATION      = 262144

'#########################
' Connect to Computer
'#########################
set objWMILocator = CreateObject("WbemScripting.SWbemLocator")
objWMILocator.Security_.AuthenticationLevel = 6
set objWMIComputer = objWMILocator.ConnectServer(strComputer, _
                                                 "root\cimv2", _
                                                 strLocalUser, _
                                                 strLocalPasswd)
set objWMIComputerSystem = objWMIComputer.Get( _
                          "Win32_ComputerSystem.Name='" & _
                          strComputer & "'")

'#########################
' Join Computer
'#########################
rc = objWMIComputerSystem.JoinDomainOrWorkGroup(strDomain, _
                                                strDomainPasswd, _
                                                strDomainUser, _
                                                vbNullString, _
                                                JOIN_DOMAIN)
if rc <> 0 then
    WScript.Echo "Join failed with error: " & rc
else
    WScript.Echo "Successfully joined " & strComputer & " to " & strDomain
end if
```

Discussion

When trying to add a computer to Active Directory, you can either precreate the computer object as described in Recipes 8.1 and 8.2 before joining it to the domain, or you can perform both operations at the same time.

Using a graphical user interface

If you have the correct permissions in Active Directory, you can actually create a computer object at the same time as you join it to a domain via the instructions described in the GUI solution. Since the System applet doesn't allow you to specify an OU for the computer object, if it needs to create a computer object, it will do so in the default Computers container. See Recipe 8.15 for more information on the default computers container and how to change it.

Using a command-line interface

The netdom command will attempt to create a computer object for the computer during a join if one does not already exist. An optional /OU switch can be added to specify the OU in which to create the computer object. To do so, you'll need to have the necessary permissions to create and manage computer objects in the OU.

There are some restrictions on running the netdom join command remotely. If a Windows XP machine has the ForceGuest security policy setting enabled, you cannot join it remotely. Running the netdom command directly on the machine works regardless of the ForceGuest setting.

Using VBScript

In order for the Win32_ComputerSystem::JoinDomainOrWorkGroup method to work remotely, you have to use an AuthenticationLevel equal to 6 so that the traffic between the two machines (namely the passwords) is encrypted. You can also create computer objects using JoinDomainOrWorkGroup by using the ACCT_CREATE flag in combination with JOIN_DOMAIN.

 This function works only with Windows XP and Windows Server 2003 and is not available for Windows 2000 and earlier machines.

Just like with the *netdom* utility, you cannot run this script against a remote computer if that computer has the ForceGuest setting enabled.

See Also

More information on the ForceGuest setting can be found here: *http://www.microsoft. com/resources/documentation/Windows/XP/all/reskit/en-us/prde_ffs_ypuh.asp*, MS KB 238793 (Enhanced Security Joining or Resetting Machine Account in Windows 2000

Domain), MS KB 251335 (Domain Users Cannot Join Workstation or Server to a Domain), MS KB 290403 (How to Set Security in Windows XP Professional That Is Installed in a Workgroup), MSDN: Win32_ComputerSystem::JoinDomainOrWorkgroup, and MSDN: NetJoinDomain

8.4   Moving a Computer Within the Same Domain

Problem

You want to move a computer object to a different container or OU within the same domain.

Solution

Using a graphical user interface

1. Open the ADUC snap-in.
2. If you need to change domains, right-click on Active Directory Users and Computers in the left pane, select "Connect to Domain," enter the domain name, and click OK.
3. In the left pane, right-click on the domain and select Find.
4. Beside Find, select Computers.
5. Type the name of the computer and click Find Now.
6. In the Search Results window, right-click on the computer and select Move.
7. Browse to and select the new parent container or OU.
8. Click OK.

 With the Windows Server 2003 version of Active Directory Users and Computers, you can also use the new drag-and-drop functionality to move computers and other objects.

Using a command-line interface

You can move a computer object to a new container using the built-in DSMove utility or AdMod. To use DSMove, enter the following syntax:

```
> dsmove "<ComputerDN>" -newparent "<NewParentDN>"
```

To move a computer object using AdMod, use the following:

```
> admod -b "<ComputerDN>" -move "<NewParentDN>"
```

Using VBScript

```
' This code moves a computer to the specified container/OU.
' ------ SCRIPT CONFIGURATION ------
strCompDN = "<ComputerDN>"  ' e.g. cn=joe-xp,cn=Users,dc=rallencorp,dc=com
strOUDN = "<NewParentDN>"   ' e.g. ou=workstations,dc=rallencorp,dc=com
' ------ END CONFIGURATION ---------

set objComp = GetObject("LDAP://" & strCompDN)
set objOU = GetObject("LDAP://" & strOUDN)
objOU.MoveHere objComp.ADsPath, objComp.Name
```

Discussion

You can move computer objects around a domain without much impact on the computer itself. You just need to be cautious of the security settings on the new parent OU, which may impact a user's ability to manage the computer object in Active Directory. Also, if GPOs are used differently on the new parent, it could impact booting and logon times, and how the computer's operating system behaves after a user has logged on.

See Also

Recipe 4.20 for moving an object to a different OU, and Recipe 8.5 for moving a computer to a different domain

8.5 Moving a Computer to a New Domain

Problem

You want to move a computer object to a different domain.

Solution

Using a graphical user interface

To migrate a computer object between domains in the same forest, use the following steps:

1. Open the ADMT MMC snap-in.
2. Right-click on the Active Directory Migration Tool folder and select the Computer Account Migration Wizard.
3. On the Domain Selection page, enter the DNS or NetBIOS name of the source and target domains. Click Next.
4. On the Translate Objects screen, specify which objects should have new ACLs applied in the new domain. Select any, none, or all of the following, and then click Next to continue:

- Files and folders
- Local groups
- Printers
- Registry
- Shares
- User profiles
- User rights

5. On the Security Migration Options screen, select the following options to determine how local user accounts will be migrated into the new domain. Select one of the following and click Next to continue:

Replace
> This option will replace any references to objects from the source domain with references to objects in the target domain.

Add
> This option adds references to objects in the target domain while leaving the source domain objects intact.

Remove
> This option removes all references to source domain objects.

6. On the Naming Conflicts page, configure how the wizard should handle naming conflicts during the migration process. Select one of the following and click Next to continue:

- Ignore conflicting accounts and don't migrate.
- Replace conflicting accounts.
- Rename conflicting accounts by adding a designated prefix or suffix.

7. On the Options screen, select the amount of time the wizard should wait before rebooting the target computer into the new domain.

8. Click Next to review your choices and begin the migration process.

Using a command-line interface

The following command will migrate a computer object from the *rallencorp.com* domain to the *emea.rallencorp.com* domain. It will place the migrated object in the *Finance* OU and will wait two minutes before rebooting the target computer:

```
ADMT COMPUTER /N "FIN101-A" "FIN101-A" /SD:"emea.rallencorp.com"
/ID:"emea.rallencorp.com" /TO:"Finance" /RDL:2
```

Using VBScript

```
set objObject = GetObject("LDAP://TargetDC/TargetParentDN")
objObject.MoveHere "LDAP://SourceDC/SourceDN", vbNullString
```

Discussion

You can move objects between domains assuming you follow a few guidelines:

- The user requesting the move must have permission to modify objects in the parent container of both domains.

- You need to explicitly specify the target DC (serverless binds usually do not work). This is necessary because the Cross Domain Move LDAP control is being used behind the scenes. (For more information on controls, see Recipe 4.4.)

- The move operation must be performed against the RID master for both domains. This is done to ensure that two objects that are being moved simultaneously don't somehow get assigned the same RID.

- Both domains must be in native mode.

See Also

Recipe 4.4 for more on LDAP controls, MSDN: IADsContainer::MoveHere, and MS KB 326480 (How to Use Active Directory Migration Tool version 2 to migrate from Windows 2000 to Windows Server 2003)

8.6 Renaming a Computer

Problem

You want to rename a computer.

Solution

Using a graphical user interface

1. Log on to the computer either directly or with a remote console application such as Terminal Services.

2. Open the Control Panel and double-click on the System applet.

3. Select the Computer Name tab and click the Change button.

4. Under Computer Name, type the new name of the computer and click OK until you are out of the System applet.

5. Reboot the machine.

Using a command-line interface

You can rename a computer object by using the built-in *netdom* utility with the following syntax:

```
> netdom renamecomputer <ComputerName> /NewName <NewComputerName> /UserD
<DomainUserUPN> /PasswordD * /UserO <ComputerAdminUser> /PasswordO * /Reboot
```

Using VBScript

```
' This code renames a computer in AD and on the host itself.
' ------ SCRIPT CONFIGURATION ------
strComputer     = "<ComputerName>"        ' e.g. joe-xp
strNewComputer  = "<NewComputerName>"     ' e.g. joe-pc
strDomainUser   = "<DomainUserUPN>"       ' e.g. administrator@rallencorp.com
strDomainPasswd = "<DomainUserPasswd>"
strLocalUser    = "<ComputerAdminUser>"   'e.g. joe-xp\administrator
strLocalPasswd  = "<ComputerAdminPasswd>"
' ------ END CONFIGURATION ---------


'###########################
' Connect to Computer
'###########################
set objWMILocator = CreateObject("WbemScripting.SWbemLocator")
objWMILocator.Security_.AuthenticationLevel = 6
set objWMIComputer = objWMILocator.ConnectServer(strComputer, _
                                                 "root\cimv2", _
                                                 strLocalUser, _
                                                 strLocalPasswd)
set objWMIComputerSystem = objWMIComputer.Get( _
                            "Win32_ComputerSystem.Name='" & _
                            strComputer & "'")
'###########################
' Rename Computer
'###########################
rc = objWMIComputerSystem.Rename(strNewComputer, _
                                 strDomainPasswd, _
                                 strDomainUser)
if rc <> 0 then
    WScript.Echo "Rename failed with error: " & rc
else
    WScript.Echo "Successfully renamed " & strComputer & " to " & _
                 strNewComputer
end if

WScript.Echo "Rebooting . . . "
set objWSHShell = WScript.CreateObject("WScript.Shell")
objWSHShell.Run "rundll32 shell32.dll,SHExitWindowsEx 2"
```

Discussion

Renaming a computer consists of two operations: renaming the computer object in Active Directory and renaming the hostname on the machine itself. To do it in one step, which each of the three solutions offers, you must have permission in Active Directory to rename the account and administrator permissions on the target machine. For the rename operation to be complete, you must reboot the computer.

In some cases, renaming a computer can adversely affect services running on the computer. For example, you cannot rename a machine that is a domain controller, Exchange Server, or a Windows Certificate Authority without taking additional steps and precautions.

Using a graphical user interface

After you rename the computer, you will be prompted to reboot the machine. You can cancel if necessary, but you'll need to reboot at some point to complete the rename operation.

Using a command-line interface

The renamecomputer option in *netdom* is new to Windows Server 2003. It can run remotely and includes a /Reboot switch that allows you to automatically reboot the computer after the rename is complete.

Using VBScript

The Win32_ComputerSystem::Rename method must be run on the local machine unless the computer is a member of a domain. Unlike the GUI and CLI solutions, you cannot specify alternate credentials for the connection to the computer other than domain credentials. For this reason, the user and password you use with the Rename method must have administrative privileges on the target machine (i.e., part of the Administrators group) and on the computer object in Active Directory.

The Rename method is new in Windows XP and Windows Server 2003, and is not available on Windows 2000 and earlier machines.

See Also

Recipe 4.23 for renaming objects, MS KB 228544 (Changing Computer Name in Windows 2000 Requires Restart), MS KB 238793 (Enhanced Security Joining or Resetting Machine Account in Windows 2000 Domain), MS KB 260575 (How to Use Netdom.exe to Reset Machine Account Passwords of a Windows 2000 Domain Controller), MS KB 325354 (How to Use the Netdom.exe Utility to Rename a Computer in Windows Server 2003), and MSDN: Win32_ComputerSystem::Rename

---

8.7 Add or Remove a Computer Account from a Group

Problem

You want to add or remove a computer account from an Active Directory security group.

Solution

Using a graphical user interface

1. Open the ADUC snap-in.
2. If you need to change domains, right-click on "Active Directory Users and Computers" in the left pane, select "Connect to Domain," enter the domain name, and click OK.
3. In the left pane, browse to the parent container of the objects you want to modify.
4. In the right pane, highlight each object you want to modify, right-click, and select Properties.
5. On the Member of tab, click Add.
6. Click the group to which you want to add the computer, and then click Add. To add the computer to more than one group, press Ctrl while selecting the groups you want to add the computer to, and then click Add.
7. To remove a group, select the group object and click Remove.
8. Click OK to finish.

Using a command-line interface

To add a computer object to a group, use the following syntax:

```
> admod -b "<GroupDN>" member:+:"<ComputerDN>"
```

 To remove an object, replace :+: with :-: in the previous syntax.

Using VBScript

```
' This code adds and removes a computer object from a group.
' ------ SCRIPT CONFIGURATION ------
strGroupDN = "<GroupDN>"  ' e.g. cn=SalesGroup,ou=Groups,dc=rallencorp,dc=com
strComputerDN = "<ComputerDN>" ' e.g. cn=Fin101,cn=Computers,dc=rallencorp,dc=com
' ------ END CONFIGURATION ---------
```

```
set objGroup = GetObject("LDAP://" & strGroupDN)
' Add a member
objGroup.Add("LDAP://" & strComputerDN)

' Remove a member
objGroup.Remove("LDAP://" & strComputerDN)
```

Discussion

In Active Directory, both user and computer objects are security principals that can be assigned rights and permissions within a domain. As such, computer objects can be added to or removed from group objects to make for simpler resource administration. You can make this change through ADUC or ADSI Edit, or by manually editing the member attribute of the appropriate group object.

See Also

MSDN: NT-Group-Members attribute [AD Schema] and MSDN: Member Attribute [AD Schema]

8.8   Testing the Secure Channel for a Computer

Problem

You want to test the secure channel of a computer.

Solution

Using a command-line interface

```
> nltest /server:<ComputerName> /sc_query:<DomainName>
```

Discussion

Every member computer in an Active Directory domain establishes a secure channel with a domain controller. The computer's password is stored locally in the form of an LSA secret and in Active Directory. This password is used by the NetLogon service to establish the secure channel with a domain controller. If for some reason the LSA secret and computer password become out of sync, the computer will no longer be able to authenticate in the domain. The nltest /sc_query command can query a computer to verify its secure channel is working. Here is sample output from the command when things are working:

```
Flags: 30 HAS_IP  HAS_TIMESERV
Trusted DC Name \\dc1.rallencorp.com
Trusted DC Connection Status Status = 0 0x0 NERR_Success
The command completed successfully
```

If a secure channel is failing, you'll need to reset the computer as described in Recipe 8.9. Here is sample output when things are not working:

```
Flags: 0
Trusted DC Name
Trusted DC Connection Status Status = 1311 0x51f ERROR_NO_LOGON_SERVERS
The command completed successfully
```

See Also

Recipe 8.9 for resetting a computer and MS KB 216393 (Resetting Computer Accounts in Windows 2000 and Windows XP)

8.9   Resetting a Computer Account

Problem

You want to reset a computer because its secure channel is failing.

Solution

Using a graphical user interface

1. Open the ADUC snap-in.
2. If you need to change domains, right-click on Active Directory Users and Computers in the left pane, select "Connect to Domain," enter the domain name, and click OK.
3. In the left pane, right-click on the domain and select Find.
4. Beside Find, select Computers.
5. Type the name of the computer and click Find Now.
6. In the Search Results, right-click on the computer and select Reset Account.
7. Click Yes to verify.
8. Click OK.
9. Rejoin the computer to the domain.

Using a command-line interface

You can use the DSMod utility to reset a computer's password. You will need to rejoin the computer to the domain after doing this.

```
> dsmod computer "<ComputerDN>" -reset
```

Another option is to use the netdom command, which can reset the secure channel between the computer and the domain controller without affecting the computer's password, so that you do not need to rejoin it to the domain:

```
> netdom reset <ComputerName> /Domain <DomainName> /User0 <UserUPN> /Password0 *
```

You can also use the `nltest` command to reset a secure channel using the following syntax:

```
> nltest /sc_reset:<DomainName>\<DCName>
```

Using VBScript

```
' This resets an existing computer object's password to initial default.
' You'll need to rejoin the computer after doing this.
set objComputer = GetObject("LDAP://<ComputerDN>")
objComputer.SetPassword "<ComputerName>"
```

Discussion

When you've identified that a computer's secure channel has failed, you'll need to reset the computer object, which consists of setting the computer object password to the name of the computer. This is the default initial password for new computers. Every 30 days, Windows 2000 and newer systems automatically change their passwords in the domain. After you've set the password, you'll need to rejoin the computer to the domain since it will no longer be able to communicate with a domain controller due to unsynchronized passwords. However, the `netdom reset` command will try to reset the password on both the computer and in Active Directory, which will not necessitate rejoining it to the domain if successful.

From a practical standpoint, you should first attempt to reset the secure channel between the computer and the domain using the `netdom` or `nltest` syntaxes, since doing so will not require you to unjoin and rejoin the computer to the domain; in particular, this will save you from performing the associated reboots involved with rejoining the domain. If resetting the secure channel does not correct the issue you're facing, you can then resort to resetting the computer's password.

See Also

Recipe 8.3 for joining a computer to a domain, Recipe 8.8 for testing a secure channel, MS KB 216393 (Resetting Computer Accounts in Windows 2000 and Windows XP), and MS KB 325850 (How to Use Netdom.exe to Reset Machine Account Passwords of a Windows Server 2003 Domain Controller)

8.10 Finding Inactive or Unused Computers

Problem

You want to find inactive computer accounts in a domain.

Solution

These solutions might only apply to Windows-based machines. Other types of machines—e.g., Unix, Mac, Network Attached Storage (NAS)—that have accounts in Active Directory might not update their login timestamps or passwords, which are used to determine inactivity.

Using a command-line interface

The following query will locate all inactive computers in the current forest:

```
> dsquery computer forestroot -inactive <NumWeeks>
```

You can also use domainroot in combination with the -d option to query a specific domain:

```
> dsquery computer domainroot -d <DomainName> -inactive <NumWeeks>
```

or you can target your query at a specific container:

```
> dsquery computer ou=MyComputers,dc=rallencorp,dc=com -inactive <NumWeeks>
```

These commands can only be run against a Windows Server 2003 domain functional level or higher domain.

You can also use the OldCmp joeware utility to create a report of all computer accounts whose passwords are older than a certain number of days (90 by default) by using the following syntax:

```
> oldcmp -report
```

To specify an alternate password age with oldcmp, use the -age x switch. You can also use the -llts switch to use the lastLogonTimeStamp attribute to perform the age calculations. (Without this switch, oldcmp will use pwdLastSet by default.)

Using Perl

```perl
#!perl

#----------------------
# Script Configuration
#----------------------
# Domain and container/OU to check for inactive computer accounts
my $domain        = 'amer.rallencorp.com';

# set to empty string to query entire domain
my $computer_cont = 'cn=Computers,';
```

```perl
# Number of weeks used to find inactive computers
my $weeks_ago = 30;
#-----------------------
# End Configuration
#-----------------------

use strict;
use Win32::OLE;
    $Win32::OLE::Warn = 3;
use Math::BigInt;

# Must convert the number of seconds since $weeks_ago
# to a large integer for comparison against lastLogonTimestamp
my $sixmonth_secs = time - 60*60*24*7*$weeks_ago;
my $intObj = Math::BigInt->new($sixmonth_secs);
    $intObj = Math::BigInt->new($intObj->bmul('10 000 000'));
my $sixmonth_int = Math::BigInt->new(
                        $intObj->badd('116 444 736 000 000 000'));
    $sixmonth_int =~ s/^[+-]//;

# Set up the ADO connections
my $connObj                      = Win32::OLE->new('ADODB.Connection');
$connObj->{Provider}             = "ADsDSOObject";
$connObj->Open;
my $commObj                      = Win32::OLE->new('ADODB.Command');
$commObj->{ActiveConnection}     = $connObj;
$commObj->Properties->{'Page Size'} = 1000;

# Grab the default root domain name
my $rootDSE = Win32::OLE->GetObject("LDAP://$domain/RootDSE");
my $rootNC = $rootDSE->Get("defaultNamingContext");

# Run ADO query and print results
my $query  = "<LDAP://$domain/$computer_cont$rootNC>;";
$query .=  "(&(objectclass=computer)";
$query .=    "(objectcategory=computer)";
$query .=    "(lastlogontimestamp<=$sixmonth_int));";
$query .= "cn,distinguishedName;";
$query .= "subtree";
$commObj->{CommandText} = $query;
my $resObj = $commObj->Execute($query);
die "Could not query $domain: ",$Win32::OLE::LastError,"\n"
  unless ref $resObj;

print "\nComputers that have been inactive for $weeks_ago weeks or more:\n";
my $total = 0;
while (!($resObj->EOF)) {
   my $cn = $resObj->Fields(0)->value;
   print "\t",$resObj->Fields("distinguishedName")->value,"\n";
   $total++;
   $resObj->MoveNext;
}
print "Total: $total\n";
```

Discussion

Using a command-line interface

The `dsquery computer` command is very handy for finding inactive computers that have not logged in to the domain for a number of weeks or months. You can pipe the results of the query to the *dsrm* command-line utility if you want to remove the inactive computer objects from Active Directory in a single command. Here is an example that would delete all computers in the current domain that have been inactive for 12 weeks or longer:

```
> for /F "usebackq" %i in (`dsquery computer domainroot -inactive 12`) do dsrm %i
```

You can also use OldCmp to disable inactive accounts, and then either delete them or move them to an alternate OU. OldCmp has a number of safeties built into the utility to prevent you from deleting a large number of computer accounts without meaning to. For example, OldCmp will not delete an account unless it has first been disabled, it will not modify more than 10 objects at a time unless you manually specify a higher limit, and it simply will not do anything at all to a domain controller computer account under any circumstances. Unless you have a requirement for quickly removing unused computer objects, we'd recommend allowing them to remain inactive for at least three months before removing them. If you don't really care when the objects get removed, use a year (i.e., 52 weeks) to be on the safe side.

Using Perl

With Windows 2000 Active Directory, the only way you can determine if a computer is inactive is to query either the `pwdLastSet` or `lastLogon` attributes. The `pwdLastSet` attribute is a 64-bit integer that translates into the date and time the computer last updated its password. Since computers are supposed to change their password every 30 days, you could run a query that finds the computers that have not changed their password in several months. This is difficult with VBScript because it does not handle 64-bit integer manipulation very well. There are third-party add-ons that provide 64-bit functions, but none of the built-in VBScript functions can do it and it is nontrivial to implement without an add-on.

The `lastLogon` attribute can also be used to find inactive computers because that attribute contains a 64-bit integer representing the last time the computer logged into the domain. The problem with the `lastLogon` attribute is that it is *not replicated*. Since it is not replicated, you have to query every domain controller in the domain to find the most recent `lastLogon` value. As you can imagine, this is less than ideal, especially if you have a lot of domain controllers.

Fortunately, in Windows Server 2003, Microsoft added a new attribute called `lastLogonTimestamp` to user and computer objects. This attribute contains the approximate last logon timestamp (again in a 64-bit, large-integer format) for the user or computer and is replicated to all domain controllers. It is the approximate last logon because the domain controllers will update the value only if it hasn't been updated for a certain period of time (such as a week). This prevents the attribute from being updated constantly and causing a lot of unnecessary replication traffic.

Since VBScript was out of the question, we turned to our first love—Perl. It is very rare to find a problem that you can't solve with Perl and this is no exception. The biggest issue is manipulating a number to a 64-bit integer, which we can do with the `Math::BigInt` module.

First, we determine the time in seconds from 1970 for the date that we want to query computer inactivity against. That is, take the current time and subtract the number of weeks we want to go back. Then we have to convert that number to a big integer. The last step is simply to perform an ADO query for all computers that have a `lastLogonTimestamp` less than or equal to the value we just calculated.

See Also

Recipe 6.31 for finding users whose accounts are about to expire

8.11 Changing the Maximum Number of Computers a User Can Join to the Domain

Problem

You want to grant users the ability to join more or fewer than 10 computers to a domain. This limit is called the *machine account quota*.

Solution

Using a graphic al user interface

1. Open the ADSI Edit MMC snap-in and connect to the Domain Naming Context.
2. Right-click on the `domainDNS` object for the domain you want to change and select Properties.
3. Edit the `ms-DS-MachineAccountQuota` attribute and enter the new quota value.
4. Click OK twice.

Using a command-line interface

In the following LDIF code replace `<DomainDN>` with the distinguished name of the domain you want to change and replace `<Quota>` with the new machine account quota:

```
dn: <DomainDN>
changetype: modify
replace: ms-DS-MachineAccountQuota
ms-DS-MachineAccountQuota: <Quota>
-
```

If the LDIF file was named *change_computer_quota.ldf*, you would then run the following command:

```
> ldifde -v -i -f change_computer_quota.ldf
```

You can also make this change using AdMod, as follows:

```
> admod –b <DomainDN> ms-DS-MachineAccountQuota::<Quota>
```

Using VBScript

```
' This code sets the machine account quota for a domain.
' ------ SCRIPT CONFIGURATION ------
intQuota  = <Quota>
strDomain = "<DomainDNSName>"  ' e.g. emea.rallencorp.com
' ------ END CONFIGURATION ---------

set objRootDSE = GetObject("LDAP://" & strDomain & "/RootDSE")
set objDomain = GetObject("LDAP://" & objRootDSE.Get("defaultNamingContext"))
objDomain.Put "ms-DS-MachineAccountQuota", intQuota
objDomain.SetInfo
WScript.Echo "Updated user quota to " & intQuota
```

Discussion

In a default Active Directory installation, members of the Authenticated Users group can add and join up to 10 computer accounts in the default Computers container. The number of computer accounts that can be created is defined in the ms-DS-MachineAccountQuota attribute on the domainDNS object for a domain. The default setting is artificially set to 10, but you can easily change that to whatever number you want, including 0, via the methods described in the Solution section. If you set it to 0, users have to be granted explicit permissions in Active Directory to join computers; refer to Recipe 8.3 for instructions on granting these permissions.

Another method for granting users the right to add computer objects, although not recommended, is via Group Policy. If you grant the "Add workstation to domain" right via Computer Configuration → Windows Settings → Security Settings → Local Policies → User Rights Assignment on a GPO that's been linked to the Domain Controllers OU, then users will be able to create computer accounts even if they do not have create child permissions on the default Computers container. This is a holdover from Windows NT to maintain backward compatibility and should not be used unless absolutely necessary. In fact, a good security best practice would be to *remove* this user right from any user or group objects that do not require it.

See Also

Recipe 8.3 for permissions needed to join computers to a domain, MS KB 251335 (Domain Users Cannot Join Workstation or Server to a Domain), and MS KB 314462 ("You Have Exceeded the Maximum Number of Computer Accounts" Error Message When You Try to Join a Windows XP Computer to a Windows 2000 Domain)

8.12 Modifying the Attributes of a Computer Object

Problem

You want to modify one or more attributes of a computer object.

Solution

Using a graphical user interface

1. Open ADSI Edit.
2. If an entry for the naming context you want to browse is not already displayed, do the following:
    a. Right-click on ADSI Edit in the right pane and click "Connect to...."
    b. Fill in the information for the naming context, container, or OU you want to add an object to. Click on the Advanced button if you need to enter alternate credentials.
    c. In the left pane, browse to the container or OU that contains the computer object you want to modify. Once you've found the object, right-click on it and select Properties.
3. Right-click the attribute you want to modify and select Edit.
4. Enter the new value and click OK.
5. Click Apply, followed by OK.

Using a command-line interface

Create an LDIF file called *modify_object.ldf* with the following contents:

```
dn: <ComputerDN>
changetype: modify
add: <AttributeName>
<AttributeName>: <AttributeValue>
-
```

Then run the following command:

```
> ldifde -v -i -f modify_object.ldf
```

To modify an object using AdMod, you'll use the following general syntax:

```
> admod –b <ComputerDN> <attribute>:<operation>:<value>
```

For example, you can add a location to a computer object using the following syntax:

```
> admod -b cn="Fin101,cn=Computers,dc=rallencorp,dc=com"
  location::"Berlin, Germany"
```

Using VBScript

```
' The following code will modify the location attribute
' of a computer object.
```

```
Set objComputer = GetObject ("LDAP://<ComputerDN>")

objComputer.Put "Location" , "<NewLocationValue>"
objComputer.SetInfo
```

Discussion

Like all objects within Active Directory, computer objects have various attributes
that can be queried, modified, and deleted during the day-to day management of
your domain. Because computer objects inherit from the user class, they include similar informational attributes to the user objects, as well as attributes that are specific
to computer objects, including:

- Location
- Description
- operatingSystemVersion
- operatingSystemServicePack
- sAMAccountName
- pwdLastSet
- primaryGroupID

See Also

Recipe 8.10 for finding inactive or unused computers, Recipe 8.13 for finding computers with a particular OS, and MSDN: Computer System Hardware Classes [WMI]

8.13   Finding Computers with a Particular OS

Problem

You want to find computers that have a certain OS version, release, or service pack
in a domain.

Solution

Using a graphical user interface

1. Open LDP.
2. From the menu, select Connection → Connect.
3. For Server, enter the name of a domain controller (or leave blank to do a server-
   less bind).
4. For Port, enter 389.
5. Click OK.
6. From the menu, select Connection → Bind.

7. Enter credentials of a user to perform the search.

8. Click OK.

9. From the Menu, select Browse → Search.

10. For Base DN, enter the base of where you want your search to begin.

11. For Filter, enter a filter that contains the OS attribute you want to search on. For example, a query for all computers that are running Windows XP would be the following:

```
(&(objectclass=computer)(objectcategory=computer)(operatingSystem=Windows XP
Professional))
```

12. Select the appropriate Scope based on how deep you want to search.

13. Click the Options button if you want to customize the list of attributes returned for each matching object.

14. Click Run, and the results will be displayed in the right pane.

You can also perform this search using the Active Directory Users and Computers MMC snap-in (*dsa.msc*), as follows:

1. Open the ADUC MMC snap-in.

2. Right-click on the domain, OU, or container that you wish to search, and click Find.

3. In the Find drop-down box, select Computers.

4. Click on the Advanced tab. Click on Field and select Operating System.

5. Select the Condition that you want to search on from one of the following:
   - Starts with
   - Ends with
   - Is (exactly)
   - Is not
   - Present
   - Not present

6. In the Value field, enter the value that you want to search for, such as "Windows Server 2003."

7. Click Find Now.

Using a command-line interface

You can query for computer objects of a particular operating system using either DSQuery or AdFind. To perform the query with DSQuery, use the following syntax:

```
> dsquery * <DomainDN> -scope subtree -attr "*" -filter "(&(objectclass=
computer)(objectcategory=computer)(operatingSystem=Windows Server 2003))"
```

To use AdFind, enter the following:

```
> adfind -b <DomainDN> -s subtree -f
  "(&(objectclass=computer)(objectcategory=computer)
  (operatingSystem=Windows Server 2003))"
```

Using VBScript

```
' This code searches for computer objects that have Service Pack 1 installed.
' ------ SCRIPT CONFIGURATION ------
strBase    = "<LDAP://" & "<DomainDN>" & ">;"
' ------ END CONFIGURATION ---------

strFilter  = "(&(objectclass=computer)(objectcategory=computer)" & _
             "(operatingSystemServicePack=Service Pack 1));"
strAttrs   = "cn,operatingSystem,operatingSystemVersion," & _
             " operatingSystemServicePack;"
strScope   = "subtree"

set objConn = CreateObject("ADODB.Connection")
objConn.Provider = "ADsDSOObject"
objConn.Open "Active Directory Provider"
Set objRS = objConn.Execute(strBase & strFilter & strAttrs & strScope)
objRS.MoveFirst
while Not objRS.EOF
    Wscript.Echo objRS.Fields(0).Value
    Wscript.Echo objRS.Fields(1).Value
    Wscript.Echo objRS.Fields(2).Value
    Wscript.Echo objRS.Fields(3).Value
    Wscript.Echo objRS.Fields(4).Value
    WScript.Echo
    objRS.MoveNext
wend
```

Discussion

When a computer joins an Active Directory domain, the operating system attributes are updated for the computer object. There are four of these attributes, which can be used in queries to find computers that match certain OS-specific criteria, like service pack level.

These attributes include the following:

operatingSystem
> Descriptive name of the installed Operating System—e.g., Windows Server 2003, Windows 2000 Server, and Windows XP Professional

operatingSystemVersion
> Numerical representation of the operating system—e.g., 5.0 (2195) and 5.2 (3757)

`operatingSystemServicePack`

Current service pack level if one is installed—e.g., Service Pack 2 and Service Pack 3

 This recipe typically applies only to Windows-based machines. Other types of machines (e.g., Unix) that have accounts in Active Directory might not automatically update their OS attributes, though some newer Unix- or Linux-based NAS devices have been configured to do. Additionally, the `operatingSystem` attribute does not distinguish between Windows NT 4 server and Windows NT 4 workstation.

8.14   Binding to the Default Container for Computers

 This recipe requires the Windows Server 2003 domain functional level.

Problem

You want to bind to the default container that new computer objects are created in.

Solution

Using a graphical user interface

1. Open LDP.
2. From the menu, select Connection → Connect.
3. For Server, enter the name of a domain controller (or leave blank to do a server-less bind).
4. For Port, enter 389.
5. Click OK.
6. From the menu, select Connection → Bind.
7. Enter credentials of a domain user.
8. Click OK.
9. From the menu, select View → Tree.
10. For the DN, enter:

        <WKGUID=aa312825768811d1aded00c04fd8d5cd,<DomainDN>>

    where <DomainDN> is the distinguished name of a domain.
11. Click OK.
12. In the lefthand menu, you can now browse the default computers container for the domain.

Using a command-line interface

With tools like *netdom*, if there is an option to specify only the name of the computer and not its DN or parent container, the computer object will be created in the default Computers container by default. You can use the *redircmp* utility to change this default location, as we will discuss in Recipe 8.15.

Using VBScript

```
' This code illustrates how to bind to the default computers container.
' ------ SCRIPT CONFIGURATION -- ---
strDomain = "<DomainDNSName>"    ' e.g. apac.rallencorp.com
' ------ END CONFIGURATION ---------

' Computer GUID as defined in ntdsapi.h
Const ADS_GUID_COMPUTRS_CONTAINER = "aa312825768811d1aded00c04fd8d5cd"

set objRootDSE = GetObject("LDAP://" & strDomain & "/RootDSE")
set objCompContainer = GetObject("LDAP://<WKGUID=" & _
                          ADS_GUID_COMPUTRS_CONTAINER & "," & _
                          objRootDSE.Get("defaultNamingContext") & ">" )
WScript.Echo objCompContainer.Get("distinguishedName")
```

Discussion

In much the same way that the TCP/IP protocol defines a list of well-known ports that are commonly used by industry applications (TCP 20 and 21 for FTP, TCP port 80 for HTTP, etc.), Active Directory defines Well-Known GUIDs that map to container objects that are present in every AD installation. The Domain NC defines the following WKGUIDs:

- Users
- Computers
- System
- Domain Controllers
- Infrastructure
- Deleted Objects
- Lost and Found

The Configuration NC also defines its own Deleted Objects WKGUID.

For example, the default computers container has the following WKGUID:

```
aa312825768811d1aded00c04fd8d5cd
```

You can use the GUID to bind to the default computers container in the domain using the following ADsPath:

```
LDAP://<WKGUID=aa312825768811d1aded00c04fd8d5cd,dc=apac,dc=rallencorp,dc=com>
```

The list of well-known objects for a domain is contained in the wellKnownObjects attribute of the domainDNS object for the domain. The wellKnownObjects attribute is multivalued with DNWithBinary syntax. The following is an example of what that attribute looks like for the *rallencorp.com* domain:

```
B:32:AA312825768811D1ADED00C04FD8D5CD:CN=Computers,DC=rallencorp,DC=com;
B:32:F4BE92A4C777485E878E9421D53087DB:CN=Microsoft,CN=Program
Data,DC=rallencorp,DC=com;
B:32:09460C08AE1E4A4EA0F64AEE7DAA1E5A:CN=Program Data,DC=rallencorp,DC=com;
B:32:22B70C67D56E4EFB91E9300FCA3DC1AA:
CN=ForeignSecurityPrincipals,DC=rallencorp,DC=com;
B:32:18E2EA80684F11D2B9AA00C04F79F805:CN=Deleted Objects,DC=rallencorp,DC=com;
B:32:2FBAC1870ADE11D297C400C04FD8D5CD:CN=Infrastructure,DC=rallencorp,DC=com;
B:32:AB8153B7768811D1ADED00C04FD8D5CD:CN=LostAndFound,DC=rallencorp,DC=com;
B:32:AB1D30F3768811D1ADED00C04FD8D5CD:CN=System,DC=rallencorp,DC=com;
B:32:A361B2FFFFD211D1AA4B00C04FD7D83A:OU=Domain Controllers,DC=rallencorp,DC=com;
B:32:A9D1CA15768811D1ADED00C04FD8D5CD:CN=Users,DC=rallencorp,DC=com;
```

Each value has the format of:

```
B:NumberofBytes:GUID:DistinguishedName
```

As you can see, the GUID for the first value is the same as the one we used in the ADsPath above to bind to the default computers container.

See Also

Recipe 8.15 for changing the default computers container, and MSDN: Binding to Well-Known Objects Using WKGUID

8.15 Changing the Default Container for Computers

Problem

You want to change the container that computers are created in by default.

Solution

Using a graphical user interface

1. Open LDP.
2. From the menu, select Connection → Connect.
3. For Server, enter the name of a domain controller (or leave blank to do a server-less bind).
4. For Port, enter 389.
5. Click OK.
6. From the menu, select Connection → Bind.
7. Enter credentials of a domain user.
8. Click OK.

9. From the menu, select Browse → Modify.

10. For DN, enter the distinguished name of the domainDNS object of the domain you want to modify.

11. For Attribute, enter wellKnownObjects.

12. For Values, enter the following:

```
B:32:AA312825768811D1ADED00C04FD8D5CD:CN=Computers,<DomainDN>
```

where *<DomainDN>* is the same as the DN you enter for the DN field.

13. Select Delete for the Operation and click the Enter button.

14. Go back to the Values field and enter the following:

```
B:32:AA312825768811D1ADED00C04FD8D5CD:<NewComputersParent>,<DomainDN>
```

where *<NewComputersParent>* is the new parent container for new computer objects (e.g., ou=RAllenCorp Computers).

15. Select Add for the Operation and click the Enter button.

16. Click the Run button.

The result of the operations will be displayed in the right pane of the main LDP window.

Using a command-line interface

```
> redircmp "<NewParentDN>"
```

Using VBScript

```
' This code changes the default computers container.
' ------ SCRIPT CONFIGURATION ------
strNewComputersParent = "<NewComputersParent>" ' e.g. OU=RAllenCorp Computers
strDomain             = "<DomainDNSName>"       ' e.g. rallencorp.com
' ------ END CONFIGURATION ---------

Const COMPUTER_WKGUID = "B:32:AA312825768811D1ADED00C04FD8D5CD:"
' ADS_PROPERTY_OPERATION_ENUM
Const ADS_PROPERTY_APPEND = 3
Const ADS_PROPERTY_DELETE = 4

set objRootDSE = GetObject("LDAP://" & strDomain & "/RootDSE")
set objDomain = GetObject("LDAP://" & objRootDSE.Get("defaultNamingContext"))
set objCompWK = GetObject("LDAP://" & _
                      "<WKGUID=AA312825768811D1ADED00C04FD8D5CD," & _
                      objRootDSE.Get("defaultNamingContext") & ">")

objDomain.PutEx ADS_PROPERTY_DELETE, "wellKnownObjects", _
              Array( COMPUTER_WKGUID & objCompWK.Get("distinguishedName"))
objDomain.PutEx ADS_PROPERTY_APPEND, "wellKnownObjects", _
              Array( COMPUTER_WKGUID & strNewComputersParent & "," & _
                      objRootDSE.Get("defaultNamingContext") )
objDomain.SetInfo
WScript.Echo "New default Computers container set to " & _
              strNewComputersParent
```

Discussion

Most Active Directory administrators do not use the Computers container within the Domain naming context as their primary computer repository. One reason is that since it is a container and not an OU, you cannot apply Group Policy Objects to it. If you have another location where you store computer objects, you might want to consider changing the default container used to bind to the computers container by changing the well-known objects attribute, as shown in this recipe. This can be beneficial if you want to ensure computers cannot sneak into Active Directory without having the appropriate group policies applied to them. While you can also apply GPOs at the site or the domain level, forcing new computers into a particular Organizational Unit ensures that those computers receive the Group Policy settings that you want them to receive through GPOs linked at the OU level. However, this does not protect you from an administrator (whether intentionally or accidentally) explicitly creating a computer object in the incorrect OU; this only protects you from applications or utilities that do not allow or do not require you to specify an OU when creating the computer.

 See Recipe 8.14 for more information on how well-known objects are specified in Active Directory.

See Also

MS KB 324949 (Redirecting the Users and Computers Containers in Windows Server 2003 Domains)

8.16   Listing All the Computer Accounts in a Domain

Problem

You want to obtain a list of all computer accounts in an Active Directory domain.

Solution

Using a graphical user interface

1. Open the Active Directory Users and Computers MMC snap-in.
2. Right-click on the domain node and select Find.
3. In the Find drop-down box, select Computers and click Find Now.

   All computer objects in the domain will be displayed in the Search Results window.

Using a command-line interface

```
> adfind -default -f (objectCategory=computer)
```

Using VBScript

```
' The following script will enumerate all computer accounts
' within an Active Directory domain.

Const ADS_SCOPE_SUBTREE = 2
strDomain = "<DomainDN>"

Set objConnection = CreateObject("ADODB.Connection")
Set objCommand =   CreateObject("ADODB.Command")
objConnection.Provider = "ADsDSOObject"
objConnection.Open "Active Directory Provider"

Set objCOmmand.ActiveConnection = objConnection
objCommand.CommandText = _
    "Select Name, Location from 'LDAP://" & strDomain & "' " _
        & "Where objectCategory='computer'"
objCommand.Properties("Page Size") = 1000
objCommand.Properties("Searchscope") = ADS_SCOPE_SUBTREE
Set objRecordSet = objCommand.Execute
objRecordSet.MoveFirst

Do Until objRecordSet.EOF
    Wscript.Echo "Computer Name: " & objRecordSet.Fields("Name").Value
    Wscript.Echo "Location: " & objRecordSet.Fields("Location").Value
    objRecordSet.MoveNext
Loop
```

Discussion

Using VBScript

To obtain a list of domain controllers, rather than just computer objects, you should query the Configuration NC rather than the domain NC, and replace "where objectCategory=computer" with "where objectCategory=ntDSDSA".

See Also

MSDN: Object Class and Object Category [Active Directory] and MSDN: Object-Class Attribute [AD-Schema]

8.17   Identifying a Computer Role

Problem

You want to identify the role that a particular computer serves in an Active Directory domain.

Solution

Using a graphical user interface

1. Open the Active Directory Users and Computers MMC snap-in.
2. Right-click on the domain node and select Find.
3. In the Find drop-down box, select Computers and click Find Now.

   The role of each computer will be displayed in the Machine Role column in the Search Results window.

Using a command-line interface

```
> wmic computersystem get domainrole
```

For a domain controller that holds the PDC Emulator FSMO role, this will return the following output:

```
DomainRole
5
```

 For a DC that doesn't hold the PDCe FSMO, this command will return a value of 4.

Using VBScript

```
' The following code will return the domain role of the
' local computer.
strComputer = "."
Set objWMIService = GetObject("winmgmts:" _
    & "{impersonationLevel=impersonate}!\\" _
    & strComputer & "\root\cimv2")
Set colComputers = objWMIService.ExecQuery _
    ("Select DomainRole from Win32_ComputerSystem")
For Each objComputer in colComputers
    Select Case objComputer.DomainRole
        Case 0
            strComputerRole = "Standalone Workstation"
        Case 1
            strComputerRole = "Member Workstation"
        Case 2
            strComputerRole = "Standalone Server"
        Case 3
            strComputerRole = "Member Server"
        Case 4
            strComputerRole = "Backup Domain Controller"
        Case 5
            strComputerRole = "Primary Domain Controller"
    End Select
    Wscript.Echo strComputerRole
Next
```

Discussion

Using a command-line interface

WMIC is the command-line component of the Windows Management Instrumentation that uses aliases to enable you to easily access WMI namespaces from the command line. To run `wmic` against a remote computer, specify the /node:"`<ComputerFQDN>`" switch.

Using VBScript

Rather than relying on an `if...else` construct to produce output, this script uses `Select Case`. In situations where there are numerous possible outcomes for a conditional statement, `Select Case` can produce far more elegant code than using numerous `if...else` statements.

## CHAPTER 9

Printers and Shared Folders

9.0   Introduction

Some of the significant improvements in Windows Server 2003 R2 are upgrades to the file server and print server roles. Although both of these roles have been available since the early days of Windows NT and Active Directory, the R2 File Server Resource Manager and Print Management Console have enabled a number of new features and management capabilities.

> In this chapter, I've focused on those tasks that are new to Windows Server 2003 R2; for more information on file and print server management, take a look at the *Windows Server Cookbook* by Robbie Allen (O'Reilly).

The new File Server Resource Manager provides you with the ability to manage disk quotas (which should already be familiar to a Windows 2000 or 2003 administrator) as well as the new *file-screen* capability. File screening allows you to specify one or more file extensions that can or cannot be stored on a file server by your users. For example, you can create a file screen that will prevent users from storing audio and video files on a file server in order to prevent misuse of corporate resources. You can combine this with disk quotas to proactively manage the storage needs on your network. In the case of both disk quotas and file screens, you can set up a *hard quota* (or *active screen*) that will prevent users from exceeding their quota limits or saving unauthorized files, or a *soft quota* (or *passive screen*) that will simply monitor disk usage to help you in making reporting and capacity planning decisions.

You can standardize the configuration of both disk quotas and file screens by using templates. Just like other sorts of templates, these will allow you to apply the same disk quota or file-screen configuration to multiple folders or volumes; if you make a change to a template, you can have the change propagated out to any quota or template that receives its configuration from that template.

For both file screens and disk quotas, you can set up notifications to inform administrators or users when their quotas are filling up or if a file screen has been violated. In addition, you can configure scheduled or on-demand reports of overall disk usage, or usage for a particular group of users.

The new Print Management Console in R2 allows you to manage printers and printing-related tasks much more easily than in earlier versions of Windows. You can use the Print Management Console to manage all installed printers, drivers, and print queues from a single console.

9.1 Installing the Print Server Role

Problem

You want to add the print server role on a Windows Server 2003 server.

Solution

Using a graphical user interface

1. Open the Configure Your Server wizard.
2. Click Next to bypass the initial Welcome screen.
3. On the Server role screen, select Print Server and click Next.
4. On the Summary screen, click Next to begin the installation.
5. Specify the path to the second R2 disc if necessary, and then click Finish.

Using a command-line interface

To add the Print Server role from the command-line, first create an *unattend.txt* file containing the following:

```
[Networking]

[NetServices]
MS_Server = params.MS_Server

[Components]
PMCSnap = On
```

Once you've saved the file, use the following syntax to install the Print Server role:

```
> sysocmgr /i:c:\windows\inf\sysoc.inf /u:c:\unattend.txt
```

Using VBScript

```
' This code creates an unattended installation file,
' and then installs the Print Server Role
' ------ SCRIPT CONFIGURATION ------
strFile = "c:\unattend.txt"
```

```
constForWriting = 2
strComputer = "<ServerName>"     ' use "." for the local computer
' ------ END CONFIGURATION ---------


set objFSO = CreateObject("Scripting.FileSystemObject")
set objFile = objFSO.OpenTextFile(strFile, constForWriting, True)
objFile.WriteLine("[Networking]")
objFile.WriteLine("[NetServices]")
objFile.WriteLine("MS_Server = params.MS_Server
objFile.WriteLine("[Components]")
objFile.WriteLine("PMCSnap = ON")
objFile.Close

set objWshShell = WScript.CreateObject("WScript.Shell")
intRC = objWshShell.Run("sysocmgr /i:%windir%\inf\sysoc.inf /u:" & _
                        strFile, 0, TRUE)
if intRC <> 0 then
   WScript.Echo "Error returned from sysocmgr command: " & intRC
else
   WScript.Echo "Print Server role installed"
end if
```

Discussion

The Print Manager role is not installed by default in Windows Server 2003 R2; you need to add the role manually using Add/Remove programs or the Configure Your Server wizard. This role has been greatly improved in R2 by including the Print Management Console MMC snap-in, which provides a unified view of installed drivers and forms, printer ports, and the ability to deploy printers using Group Policy.

See Also

MS KB 222444 (How to Add or Remove Windows Components with Sysocmgr.exe)

9.2   Creating a Printer Filter

Problem

You want to create a printer filter to view only specific printers within the Print Management Console.

Solution

Using a graphical user interface

1. Open the Print Management Console MMC snap-in.
2. Right-click on Custom Printer Filters and select Add New Printer Filter.

3. Enter a name and description for the printer filter. Optionally, place a check-mark next to "Display the total number of printers." Click Next to continue.

4. On the "Define a printer filter" screen, you can specify up to three conditions for the filter.

5. In the Field drop-down box, select one of the following:
   - Printer Name
   - Queue Status
   - Jobs in Queue
   - Server Name
   - Comments
   - Driver Name
   - Is Shared
   - Location
   - Share Name

6. For the Condition drop-down, select one of the following:
   - is exactly
   - is not exactly
   - begins with
   - not begin with
   - ends with
   - not end with
   - contains
   - not contain

7. In the Value textbox, type a value that the condition should meet.

8. When you have entered all necessary information, click Next to continue.

9. On the Set Notifications (Optional) page, select one or both of the following:

   Send e-mail notification
   This will send an email whenever a printer that meets the criteria of the filter is found. Enter the recipient email address(es), sender email address, SMTP server, and message.

   Run script
   This will run a script whenever a printer that meets the criteria of the filter is found. Enter the path to the script and any command-line arguments.

10. Click Finish to create the filter.

Discussion

One of the new features of the Print Management Console is the ability to create one or more custom printer filters using WMI information. This provides you with an at-a-glance view of all the printers in your environment, as well as printers that meet one or more specific criteria. There are three default print filters available when you first launch the PMC: All Printers, Printers Not Ready, and Printers With Jobs. You can create additional filters based on the printer name, queue status, the number of jobs in a queue, etc.

See Also

Professor Windows January 2006 column: "R2 – Better than C-3PO" (*http://www. microsoft.com/technet/community/columns/profwin/pw0106.mspx*)

9.3 Managing Printer Drivers

Problem

You want to add or remove print drivers on a print server.

Solution

Using a graphical-user interface

To add a print driver to a print server, do the following:

1. Open the Print Management MMC snap-in.
2. Double-click on the Print Servers node, then the print server that you want to manage.
3. Right-click on the Drivers node and select Add Driver. Click Next to continue.
4. On the Processor and Operating System Selection screen, place a checkmark next to the processors and OSes that will be used by your client computers. Click Next to continue.
5. Select the manufacturer and model of the printer, or click Have Disk to use a manufacturer-supplied print driver.
6. Click Next and then Finish to add the driver.

To manage existing print drivers, do the following:

1. Open the Print Management MMC snap-in.
2. Double-click on the Print Servers node, then the print server that you want to manage.
3. Right-click on the Drivers node and select Manage Drivers.

---

4. To add a new driver, click Add and follow the instructions in the previous section. To delete an installed driver, click Remove. To reinstall a print driver from media, click Re-Install.

5. Click OK when you're finished.

Using a command-line interface

To add a printer driver, enter the following:

```
> cscript prndrvr.vbs -a -v 3 -e "Windows NT x86"
```

To delete a printer driver, use the following syntax:

```
> cscript prndrvr.vbs -d -m "<DriverName>" -v 3 -e "Windows NT x86"
```

To list the printer drivers that are installed on a print server, use the following:

```
> cscript prndrvr.vbs -l
```

 You can use the -s parameter to specify a remote computer, as well as -u and -p to specify an alternate username and password.

Using VBScript

```
' The following script will add a printer driver, and then
' list all the installed drivers on a particular computer.
'---------------- SCRIPT CONFIGURATION ---------------------
strComputer = "<ComputerName>" ' use "." for the local computer
strDriverName = "<DriverName>" ' i.e. "HP Laserjet 4050 TN"
strPlatform = "<PlatformName>" ' i.e. "Windows NT X66"
strVersion = "<VersionNumber>" ' i.e. "3" for XP/2000
'---------------- END CONFIGURATION -----------------------

Set objWMIService = GetObject("winmgmts:" _
    & "{impersonationLevel=impersonate}!\\" & strComputer & "\root\cimv2")

Set objDriver = objWMIService.Get("Win32_PrinterDriver")
objWMIService.Security_.Privileges.AddAsString "SeLoadDriverPrivilege", True

objDriver.Name = strDriverName
objDriver.SupportedPlatform = strPlatform
objDriver.Version = strVersion
errResult = objDriver.AddPrinterDriver(objDriver)

' Now list all installed printer drivers
Set installedPrinters =  objWMIService.ExecQuery _
    ("Select * from Win32_PrinterDriver")

For each printer in installedPrinters
    Wscript.Echo "Name: " & printer.Name
    Wscript.Echo "Description: " & printer.Description
```

```
        Wscript.Echo "Driver Path: " & printer.DriverPath
        Wscript.Echo "File Path: " & printer.FilePath
        Wscript.Echo "Version: " & printer.Version
    Next
```

Discussion

In previous versions of Windows, you needed to manage print drivers on a printer-by-printer basis using the *prndrvr.vbs* utility; there wasn't an intuitive way to manage all of the drivers that were installed on a particular print server from a graphical user interface. The Print Management Console in R2 allows you to view, add, update, and remove print drivers for an entire print server from a single management console. You can also manage drivers using the *prndrvr.vbs* utility that's built into Windows Server 2003, R2, and Windows XP, or by using the `Win32_PrinterDriver` WMI class through VBScript or another scripting language.

In the command-line solution, `-v 3` indicates that you are installing a driver that supports Windows XP and Windows 2000. Other available versions are version 0 to support Windows 95, 98, and ME; version 1 to support Windows NT 3.51; and version 2 to support Windows NT 4.0. The –e switch indicates the environment for the driver that you wish to install; your available options for –e are as follows:

```
"Windows NT x86"
"Windows NT Alpha_AXP"
"Windows IA64"
"Windows NT R4000"
"Windows NT PowerPC"
"Windows 4.0"
```

See Also

Network Printing Tools and Settings (*http://technet2.microsoft.com/WindowsServer/ en/Library/573e8381-1d1f-409f-9ec2-a1d5efb4315b1033.mspx*) and MSDN: Win32_ PrinterDriver class [WMI]

9.4   Deploying Printers Through Group Policy

Problem

You want to deploy printers to a group of users or computers using a GPO.

Solution

Using a graphical user interface

To deploy a printer using Group Policy, you must first push the printer installation settings to a GPO as follows:

---

1. Open the Print Management MMC snap-in. Double-click on the print server you want to manage and then click Printers.

2. Right-click the printer you want to manage and select "Deploy with Group Policy."

3. From the Deploy with Group Policy dialog box, click Browse to select a GPO and click OK.

4. Select one or both of the following:
   - The users that this GPO applies to (per user), to allow a printer connection to follow a user to multiple computers
   - The computers that this GPO applies to (per machine), to allow a printer connection to be available to any user who logs on to a particular computer

5. Select Add and then OK when you're finished.

 When deploying printers using Group Policy, Windows 2000 machines can support only per-user connections.

Using a command-line interface

After you've created the appropriate GPO, add the following to a startup script (for per-machine printer connections) or to a logon script (for per-user printer connections):

```
> pushprinterconnections.exe -log
```

Discussion

A common complaint with previous versions of the Windows Server operating system was the inability to easily push printer settings to clients using Group Policy. This has been greatly improved with the Print Management Console in R2, as you now have a "Deploy with Group Policy" option built right into the MMC console. You can deploy printers on a per-user or per-computer basis; the former is useful for users whose printer connections need to follow them from computer to computer, while the latter is useful in a branch office or lab setting where all users of a particular computer need access to the same printer.

See Also

Recipe 9.5 for more on displaying printers in Active Directory and Chapter 10 for more on Group Policy deployment

9.5 Publishing Printers in Active Directory

Problem

You want to publish a printer in Active Directory to make it easier for users to locate and access it.

Solution

Using a graphical user interface

1. Open the Print Management MMC snap-in. Double-click on the print server that you want to manage, and then select Printers.

2. Right-click on the printer that you want to list or remove, and then click "List in Directory" or "Remove from Directory."

Using a command-line interface

```
> cscript pubprn.vbs \\<ServerName>\<PrinterName> "<PrinterDN>"
```

Discussion

The idea of publishing printers in Active Directory has been around since its inception with Windows 2000; in fact, the "List in Directory" option is selected by default when you first share a printer object. By listing a printer in Active Directory, users on your network can easily search for printers that meet certain criteria such as name, location, or other identifying characteristics. Any changes that are made to the printer's attributes get automatically propagated to Active Directory.

See Also

MS KB 234619 (Publishing a Printer in Windows Active Directory)

9.6 Installing the File Server Resource Manager

Problem

You want to install the File Server Resource Manager on a Windows Server 2003 R2 computer.

Solution

Using a graphical user interface

1. Open the Configure Your Server wizard. Click Next to bypass the initial Welcome screen.

2. On the Server role screen, select File Server and click Next. Click Next twice to begin.

3. On the File Server environment screen, select one or more of the following optional components:

   Replicate data to and from this server
   Installs DFS Replication Service

   Manage a SAN (Storage Area Network)
   Installs Storage Manager for SANs

   Share files with UNIX systems
   Installs Microsoft Services for NFS

   Share files with Apple Macintosh computers
   Installs File Services for Macintosh

4. Click Next to continue. Reboot the server if prompted to do so.

Discussion

Installing the File Server role on a Windows Server 2003 R2 computer enables a number of mandatory components, as well as provides the options to configure optional pieces to enable additional functionality. At a minimum, the File Server role will install Storage Reporting, Disk Quotas, File Screening, and the DFS Management MMC snap-in.

See Also

Recipe 9.7 for more on creating disk quota templates and Recipe 9.8 for creating disk quotas

9.7   Managing Disk Quota Templates

Problem

You want to create and manage disk quota templates on a Windows file server.

Solution

Using a graphical user interface

1. Open the File Server Management MMC snap-in. Navigate to File Server Management → File Server Resource Manager → Quota Management.

2. Right-click on Quota Templates and select "Create quota template."

3. If you want to copy information from an existing template, select it in the "Copy properties from quota template (optional)" drop-down box and click Copy.

4. Under Settings, enter a Template Name and optional Label.

5. Under Space Limit, specify the disk space limit in KB, MB, GB, or TB. Select either "Hard quota: do not allow users to exceed limit" or "Soft quota: Allow users to exceed limit (used for monitoring)."

6. In the Notification Threshold section, you can specify one or more actions that Windows will take when a user reaches a certain percentage of her quota limit.

7. Click Add to create a new notification. Under "Generate notifications when usage reaches (%)," specify the percentage of the disk quota that should initiate the notification.

8. To send an email notification, on the E-mail Message tab, place a checkmark next to "Send e-mail to the following administrators" and/or "Send e-mail to the user who exceeds the threshold." On this tab you can also specify the subject and body of the email message to be sent to the user.

9. To generate a message in the Event Log, go to the Event Log tab and place a checkmark next to "Send Warning to Event Log." Under the Log Entry text box, specify the text of the message that should be logged.

10. To run a command when a threshold is generated, go to the Command tab and place a checkmark next to "Run this command or script." Under "Command settings," specify any command-line arguments and the working directory. Under "Command security," specify the account that the script should run as: Local Service, Network Service, or LocalSystem.

11. To generate one or more reports when a threshold is generated, go to the Report tab and place a checkmark next to "Generate reports." Select one or more of the following reports to be generated:
    - Duplicate files
    - File screening audit
    - Files by File Group
    - Files by Owner
    - Large Files
    - Least Recently Accessed Files
    - Most Recently Accessed Files
    - Quota Usage

12. To email the reports, place a checkmark next to "Send reports to the following administrators" and specify one or more email addresses separated by semicolons, and/or place a checkmark next to "Send reports to the user who exceeded the threshold."

13. Once you've created one or more notification thresholds, click OK to create the quota template.

Discussion

While you can create disk quotas manually, disk quota *templates* allow you to create consistent quota settings for multiple quotas on a single server as well as on multiple servers. In addition to the space limitation that's imposed by the quota, you can specify whether it is a hard or a soft quota—that is, whether a user is prohibited from saving files when they've gone over their quota (a hard quota), or just the OS makes note of the fact that a user has overrun his quota without preventing him from saving additional files. You can also specify what types of notifications (if any) will be generated when a user exceeds a defined quota threshold: sending an email to an administrator when a user exceeds 85 percent of her quota, generating an Event Viewer message when she exceeds 95 percent, etc. You can configure multiple notification thresholds for a single quota; no notifications are configured by default.

See Also

Recipe 9.8 for more on managing disk quotas

9.8 Managing Disk Quotas

Problem

You want to create a disk quota on a file server.

Solution

Using a graphical user interface

1. Open the File Server Management MMC snap-in. Navigate to File Server Management → File Server Resource Manager → Quota Management.

2. Right-click on Quotas and select "Create quota." Under "Quota path," specify the directory that this quota should apply to or click Browse to navigate to it using Windows Explorer. Select the radio button next to "Create quota on path."

3. To base the quota on a quota template, select the "Derive properties from this quota template (recommended)," and select the template from the drop-down box. To manually specify a quota, select the "Define custom quota properties" radio button. Click on Custom Properties to define the properties for this quota; the process is similar to the steps used in defining a quota template.

4. Click Create.

Using a command-line interface

The following command will create a 100 MB soft disk quota entry on the *D:* drive:

```
> dirquota quota add /path:d:\* /limit:100mb /type:soft
```

Using VBScript

```
'---------SCRIPT CONFIGURATION-----------------------
strComputer = "<ComputerName>"       ' Use "." for local computer
strDomain = "<DomainDN>"             ' e.g. RALLENCORP
strUser = "<UsersAMAccountName>"     ' e.g. jsmith
strDeviceID = "<DriveLetter>"        ' e.g. D:
'----------------------------------------------------

Set objWMIService = GetObject("winmgmts:" _
    & "{impersonationLevel=impersonate}!\\" & strComputer & "\root\cimv2")

Set objAccount = objWMIService.Get _
    ("Win32_Account.Domain=strDomain,Name=strUser")
Set objDisk = objWMIService.Get _
    ("Win32_LogicalDisk.DeviceID=strDeviceID")
Set objQuota = objWMIService.Get _
    ("Win32_DiskQuota").SpawnInstance_

objQuota.QuotaVolume = objDisk.Path_.RelPath
objQuota.User = objAccount.Path_.RelPath
objQuota.Limit = 10485760
objQuota.WarningLimit = 8388608
objQuota.Put_
```

Discussion

Once you've created one or more quota templates, you can specify actual disk quotas that apply to folders that reside on a particular hard drive. It's a good idea to create quotas based on templates rather than specifying them manually, since this will simplify the administration of your file server. (For example, if you need to change a quota template after it is initially created, you can specify that those template changes should be automatically propagated to any quotas that are based on that template.) Otherwise you can create a quota manually, specifying the same information as is required when creating a quota template.

See Also

Recipe 9.7 for more on creating quota templates, Recipe 9.9 for more on managing auto-quotas, and Recipe 9.10 for information on modifying quota templates

9.9   Managing Auto-Quotas

Problem

You want to create a quota that will apply to any new folders created on a file server.

Solution

Using a graphical user interface

1. Open the File Server Management MMC snap-in. Navigate to File Server Management → File Server Resource Manager → Quota Management.

2. Right-click on Quotas and select "Create quota." Under "Quota path," specify the directory that this quota should apply to or click Browse to navigate to it using Windows Explorer.

3. Select the radio button next to "Auto apply template and create quotas on existing and new subfolders."

4. Create the remainder of the quota as specified in Recipe 9.8.

Using a command-line interface

The following command will create an auto-quota on the D:\ drive based on the "DefaultAutoQuota" template:

```
> dirquota autoquota /path:d:\* /sourcetemplate:"DefaultAutoQuota"
```

Discussion

When you create a new disk quota, by default the quota will apply only to the individual folder that you specify. By using auto-templates, you can configure a quota that will automatically be applied to any subfolders that are created beneath the folder you named in the quota definition. This is a useful setting for many scenarios, such as specifying an auto-quota for a root folder that houses your users' home folders or roaming profiles so that any new user will receive the auto-quota by default. Every time a new subfolder is created to which an auto-quota applies, a new quota entry will be automatically created that can be viewed within the File Resource Manager.

See Also

Recipe 9.7 for more on managing disk quota templates, Recipe 9.8 for more on defining disk quotas, and Recipe 9.10 for information on modifying existing quotas

9.10   Modifying Quota Settings

Problem

You want to modify an existing quota template or auto-template. Modifying these items can affect new quotas that are created as well as existing quotas that are already in effect.

Solution

Using graphical user interface

To modify an existing quota template, do the following:

1. Open the File Server Management MMC snap-in. Navigate to File Server Management → File Server Resource Manager → Quota Management.

2. To modify a quota template, double-click on Quota Templates. Right-click on the quota you want to modify and select Edit Template Properties. Modify the template as described in Recipe 9.7 and click OK.

3. On the "Update Quotas Derived from Template" screen, select one of the following and click OK:

    Apply template only to derived quotas that match the original template
    This will apply the new template only to quota entries that haven't been customized or modified since the original template was applied.

    Apply template to all derived quotas
    This will apply the new template to all quota entries that were based on the original template. Any customizations that you've made will be lost.

    Do not apply template to derived quotas
    This will keep any existing quota entries unchanged.

To modify a quota entry, do the following:

1. Open the File Server Management MMC snap-in. Navigate to File Server Management → File Server Resource Manager → Quota Management.

2. To modify a quota, double-click on Quotas. Right-click on the quota you want to modify and select "Edit quota properties."

3. Under "Auto apply quota properties" select the new quota template that should be applied from the drop-down box and click OK.

4. On the Update Quotas Derived from Template screen, select one of the following and click OK:

    Apply quota only to derived quotas that match the original template
    This will apply the new quota only to quota entries that haven't been customized or modified since the original auto-quota was applied.

    Apply quota to all derived quotas
    This will apply the new template to all quota entries that were based on the original auto-quota. Any customizations that you've made will be lost.

    Do not apply quota to derived quotas
    This will keep any existing quota entries unchanged.

Using a command-line interface

The following command will modify a quota entry, changing the notification threshold from 90 percent to 80 percent:

```
> dirquota Quota Modify /Path:D:\home\* /Modify-Threshold:90,80
```

Discussion

The major advantage of using disk quota templates and auto-quotas is automation: any time you make a change to the template or the auto-quota, this change will automatically apply to any new quotas that are *derived* from the template. However, the question remains of what do to with any existing quotas that have already been created, particularly if you've modified any of those quotas from the original template definition. When you modify a template definition, you have three choices regarding existing quota entries: you can modify only those entries that match the original template definition (i.e., only quota entries that haven't been modified in any way); you can choose to apply the new template settings to *all* quota entries that are taken from the template, losing any modifications you've made to existing entries; or you can choose to apply the template changes to only *new* entries, leaving any existing quota entries unchanged. Likewise, when you modify an auto-quota definition, you can choose to push those changes to all existing subfolders, to only those subfolders whose quota definitions haven't changed, or to apply the change to new subfolders only.

See Also

Recipe 9.7 for more on managing disk quota templates, Recipe 9.8 for more on defining disk quotas, and Recipe 9.9 for information on auto-quotas

9.11   Defining File Groups

Problem

You want to create a file group to be used within Windows Server 2003 R2's File Screening capabilities.

Solution

Using a graphical user interface

1. Open the File Server Management MMC snap-in. Navigate to File Server Management → File Server Resource Manager → File Screening Management.

2. Right-click on File Groups and select "Create file group."

3. Under File group name, enter a display name for the file group.

4. Under Files to include, enter one or more files to include in the file group. You can specify individual filenames or use standard wildcard notation such as ? and *. Click Add to add one or more entries to the include list, or click Remove to delete an entry.

5. Under Files to exclude, enter one or more files to exclude from the file group. You can specify individual filenames or use standard wildcard notation such as ? and *. Click Add to add one or more entries to the exclude list, or click Remove to delete an entry.

6. Click OK to save the changes you've made to the file group.

Using a command-line interface

The following command will create a file group called Mailbox Files that contains four types of files:

```
> filescrn filegroup add /filegroup:"Mailbox Files"
/Member:"*.mbx|*.inbox|*.pst|*.ost"
```

Discussion

File groups are the building blocks for the file-screen capabilities that are built into the file server role in Windows Server 2003 R2. You'll use file groups to define a file screen, a file-screen exception, or a storage report for your file server. It's important to note that the file group itself does not define what should be *done* with those files: if you have a file group configured for *.mp3* files, a file screen using that group would prevent MP3 files from being saved to a particular directory, while configuring a file-screen exception using this group would *allow* MP3 files to be saved in the directory that you specify.

See Also

Recipe 9.12 for managing file-screen templates, Recipe 9.13 for managing file screens, and Recipe 9.14 for managing file-screen exceptions

9.12 Managing File-Screen Templates

Problem

You want to create a file-screen template to manage the file-screen process on a Windows Server 2003 R2 server.

Solution

Using a graphical user interface

1. Open the file server Management MMC snap-in. Navigate to File Server Management → File Server Resource Manager → File Screening Management.

2. Right-click on File Screen Templates and select Create File Screen Template.

3. If you want to copy information from an existing template, select it in the "Copy properties from template (optional)" drop-down box and click Copy.

4. On the Settings tab, enter a name for the file-screen template. Under Screening type, select either "Active screening: do not allow users to save unauthorized files" or "Passive screening: allow users to save unauthorized files (use for monitoring)."

5. Under File Groups, select one or more file groups to monitor using this file-screen template. Place checkmarks next to a pre-existing group, or click Create or Edit to create or modify existing file groups.

> If you make changes to an existing file group here, the changes will affect all file screens, file-screen exceptions, file-screen templates, and storage reports that use this file group. Be sure to understand the implications of this before editing an existing file group during this process.

6. To send an email notification when a user violates (or attempts to violate) the conditions of a file screen, on the E-mail Message tab, place a checkmark next to "Send e-mail to the following administrators" and/or "Send e-mail to the user who attempted to save an unauthorized file." On this tab, you can also specify the subject and body of the email message to be sent to the user.

7. To generate a message in the Event Log, go to the Event Log tab and place a checkmark next to Send Warning to Event Log. Under the Log Entry text box, specify the text of the message that should be logged.

8. To run a command when a user attempts to save an unauthorized file, go to the Command tab and place a checkmark next to "Run this command or script." Under Command settings, specify any command-line arguments and the working directory of the command or script. Under Command security, specify the account that the script should run as: Local Service, Network Service, or Local-System.

9. To generate one or more reports when a threshold is exceeded, go to the Report tab and place a checkmark next to Generate reports. Select one or more of the following reports to be generated:
   - Duplicate files
   - File screening audit

- Files by File Group
- Files by Owner
- Large Files
- Least Recently Accessed Files
- Most Recently Accessed Files
- Quota Usage

10. To email the reports, place a checkmark next to "Send reports to the following administrators" and specify one or more email addresses separated by semicolons, and/or place a checkmark next to "Send reports to the user who attempted to save the unauthorized file."

11. Once you've specified these settings, click OK to create the file-screen template.

Using a command-line interface

The following command will configure an active file-screen template based on the Music Files template:

```
> filescrn template add /template:"Prevent Saving Music File"
    /SourceTemplate:"Music Files" /Type:Active
```

Discussion

Similar to creating disk quota templates, you can create file-screen templates to ensure a consistent configuration of file screens on your file server, and to ensure that you need to make any configuration changes only from a single central location. By default, you have the following file-screen templates available out of the box:

Block Audio and Video Files
    Performs active screening of most common A/V file extensions, including *.aac*, *.mp3*, *.md4*, *.midi*, *.wmv*, and many others.

Block Executable Files
    Performs active screening of most common executable file extensions, such as *.bat*, *.cmd*, and *.exe*.

Block Image Files
    Performs active screening of image files, such as *.jpg*, *.bmp*, and *.tif*.

Block E-mail Files
    Performs active screening of email files, such as *.ost*, *.pst*, and *.mbox*.

Monitor Executable and System Files
    Performs passive screening (reporting only) of both executable files and system files, such as *.ocx* and *.dll* files.

Similar to disk quota templates, when you modify a file-screen template, you'll be given the choice to apply the template changes to all file screens that are based on this template, to only those file screens that haven't been modified since the file-screen template was created, or to apply the updated template only to any new file screens.

See Also

Recipe 9.13 for more on managing file screens and Recipe 9.14 on managing file-screen exceptions

9.13   Managing File Screens

Problem

You want to create a file screen to control what types of files users can save to a file server.

Solution

Using a graphical user interface

1. Open the File Server Management MMC snap-in. Navigate to File Server Management → File Server Resource Manager → File Screening Management.

2. Right-click on File Screens and select "Create file screen." Under File Screen path, specify the directory that this file screen should apply to or click Browse to navigate to it using Windows Explorer.

3. To base the file screen on a file-screen template, select "Derive properties from this file-screen template (recommended)," and select the template from the drop-down box. To manually specify a file screen, select the "Define custom file screen" properties radio button. Click on Custom Properties to define the properties for this file screen; this process is similiar to the steps used in defining a file-screen template in Recipe 9.12.

4. Click Create.

Using a command-line interface

The following command will create a passive file screen based on the Prevent Saving of Music Files template:

```
> filescrn screen add /Path:d:\users\* /type:Passive
/Add-Filegroup."Music Files"
```

Discussion

When you create a new file screen, you can either define its properties manually or base it on a file-screen template that you've already created. The advantage to using a template is that any future changes you make to the template can automatically apply to any file screens, whereas you'll need to update any manually created file screens one at a time.

 Keep in mind that the file-screen capability in R2 is only capable of restricting files on the basis of their three-letter file extensions. If a user were to rename a restricted file with an innocuous extension such as *.txt*, the file-screen mechanism would not restrict their ability to save that file.

See Also

Recipe 9.11 for more on creating file groups, Recipe 9.12 on creating file-screen templates, and Recipe 9.14 on file-screen exceptions

9.14   Managing File-Screen Exceptions

Problem

You want to create an exception to a file screen.

Solution

Using a graphical user interface

1. Open the File Server Management MMC snap-in. Navigate to File Server Management → File Server Resource Manager → File Screening Management.

2. Right-click on File Screens and select "Create file screen exception."

3. Under Exception path specify the directory that this exception should apply to or click Browse to navigate to it using Windows Explorer.

4. Under File Groups, select one or more file groups to be excluded from file screening. Place checkmarks next to a pre-existing group, or click Create or Edit to create or modify existing file groups.

5. Click OK.

 Editing an existing file group here will affect every file screen, file-screen template, file-screen exception, and storage report that uses this file group. Be sure to understand the implications of this before you modify an existing file group during this process.

Using a command-line interface

The following command will create a file-screen exception that will allow file types defined in the Image Files file group to be saved:

```
> filescrn exception add /Path:D:\shared\marketing
  /add-filegroup:"Image Files"
```

Discussion

File-screen exceptions, as their name suggests, are used in situations in which you need to allow one or more file types to be stored in a particular subdirectory of a parent directory that's been configured with a file screen. For example, you may have configured a file screen to prevent users from saving image files to your file server, but your marketing department may have a legitimate need to save this type of information for use in brochures, mailers, etc. When configured on a subfolder, a file-screen exception will override any file-screen rules that have been derived from a parent folder. You can configure a file-screen exception only on a folder that doesn't already have a file screen configured; you need to assign the exception to a subfolder of the parent folder that's been configured with the file screen.

See Also

Recipe 9.12 for more on file-screen templates and Recipe 9.13 for more on configuring file screens

9.15 Configuring File Server Reporting

Problem

You want to create reports for the File Server Resource Manager.

Solution

Using a graphical user interface

1. Open the File Server Management MMC snap-in. Navigate to File Server Resource Manager, right-click on Storage Report Management, and select "Schedule a new report task."

2. On the Settings tab, click Add under the Scope option to specify the files and folders to include in the report. Under Report data, select one or more reports to generate. Click Edit Parameters to modify any reports that contain configurable parameters. Under Report Formats, select one or more of the following:
   - DHTML
   - HTML
   - XML

- CSV
- Text

3. On the Delivery tab, place a checkmark next to "Send reports to the following administrators." Enter one or more email addresses, separated by semicolons.

4. On the Schedule tab, click Create Schedule. Click New to specify the date and time that the task should run.

5. Click OK.

 To generate reports immediately, right-click on Storage Report Management and select "Generate reports now."

Using a command-line interface

The following command will add a scheduled task to create a disk quota report:

```
> storrept reports add /report:QuotaUse /Task:createdailyreports /Scope:D:\shared
    /Name:"Quota Usage Report" /MinUse:75
```

Discussion

One of the improvements with Windows Server 2003 R2 is the built-in reporting functionality within the file-server role. You can generate any of the following reports on a scheduled basis or on the fly:

- Duplicate Files
- File Screening Audit
- Files by File Group
- Files by Owner
- Large Files
- Least Recently Accessed Files
- Most Recently Accessed Files
- Quota Usage

To run a report or a set of reports, you need to specify the folder that the reports should pertain to, and what format the reports should be produced in. The report will be stored on the file server's local hard drive, and you can also email the reports to one or more users. By default, any reports that you produce will be stored in the following locations:

Incident Reports
    %systemdrive%\StorageReports\Incident. These are the reports that are generated when a user exceeds a disk quota threshold or violates a file-screen restriction.

Scheduled Reports
    %systemdrive%\StorageReports\Scheduled

On-demand Reports
    %systemdrive%\StorageReports\Interactive

You can modify these default locations in the File Server Resource Manager options screen.

See Also

Recipe 9.16 for more on configuring file-server options

9.16   Managing File Server Options

Problem

You want to enable optional settings for a Windows file server, such as file screen auditing and email notifications.

Solution

Using a graphical user interface

1. Open the File Server Management MMC snap-in. Navigate to File Server Management.
2. Right-click on File Server Resource Manager and select Configure options.
3. On the Email notifications tab, configure the following options:
   - SMTP Server name or IP address
   - Default administrator recipients
   - Default "From" email address
4. To modify File Server Management reports, click on the Storage Reports tab. Select the report that you wish to modify and click Edit Parameters.
5. To modify the location in which reports are stored, click on the Report Locations tab. You can manually specify or browse to specify the following three storage locations:
   - Incident reports folder
   - Scheduled reports folder
   - On-demand reports folder
6. On the File Screen Audit tab, place a checkmark next to "Record file screening activity in auditing database."
7. Click OK when you've made your changes.

Using a command-line interface

The following command will modify the default recipients of File Server Manager reports:

```
> storrept admin options /from:admin@rallencorp.com
    /adminemails:"admin@rallencorp.com;itsupport@rallencorp.com"
```

Discussion

The File Server Resource Manager Options screen allows you to set a number of configuration items for your file server using a series of configuration tabs. The E-Mail Notifications tab is critical if you wish to receive any email notifications of users who violate disk quota or file-screen settings, or if you wish to distribute storage reports via email. Individual reports can be configured on the Storage Reports tab, where you can modify parameters for a number of reports.

By using File Server Resource Manager, you can record file screening activity in an auditing database. The information saved in this database is used to generate the File Screen Audit Report. When the file server role is installed, the following reports have configurable parameters that can be managed from this tab:

File Screening Audit
> You can modify the minimum number of days since the file screening event occurred (0 by default) for an item to be included in this report. You can also configure the report so that it reports activity for All Users (default) or only for selected users.

Files by File Group
> You can report on all file groups or on just one or more individual file groups that you specify.

Files by Owner
> You can report on all file owners or only specific users. You can also restrict the report to report only on particular filenames using the ? and * wildcards. For example, *.mp3 will report on all users who own MP3 files on your file server.

Large Files
> You can specify the minimum file size that will be included in the report; the default is 5,000 MB. You can also restrict the report to report only on particular filenames using the ? and * wildcards.

Least Recently Accessed Files
> You can specify the minimum number of days since the last time the file was accessed, as well as restrict filenames using ? and *. By default, this report will show information for files that have not been accessed within the last 90 days.

Most Recently Accessed Files

Here you'll specify the maximum number of days since the last time the file was accessed, as well as restrict filenames using ? and *. By default, this report will show information for all files that have been accessed at least once within the last seven days.

Quota Usage

You can restrict the report to show only users who have used up at least a certain percentage of their quota. This value defaults to 0, which means that it will report on the quota usage for all users. Setting this value to 50, for example, will display results for only those users who have used up at least 50 percent of their disk quota.

See Also

Recipe 9.15 for more on configuring file-server reporting

CHAPTER 10

Group Policy Objects

10.0 Introduction

Active Directory Group Policy Objects (GPOs) can customize virtually any aspect of a computer or user's desktop. They can also be used to install applications, secure a computer, run logon/logoff or startup/shutdown scripts, and much more. You can assign a GPO to a local computer, site, domain, or Organizational Unit. This is called scope of management (SOM), because only the users or computers that fall under the scope of the computer, OU, site, or domain will process the GPO. Assigning a GPO to a SOM is referred to as *linking* the GPO. You can further restrict the application of GPOs by using security groups to filter which users or groups they will apply to.

With Windows Server 2003 servers and Windows XP workstations, you can also use a WMI filter to restrict the application of a GPO. A WMI filter is simply a WMI query that can search against any information on a client's computer. If the WMI filter returns a true value (i.e., the client computer matches the conditions that are specified in the filter), the GPO will be processed; otherwise, it will not. So not only do you have all of the SOM options for applying GPOs, you can now use any WMI information available on the client's computer to determine whether GPOs should be applied. For more on the capabilities of GPOs, we recommend Chapter 7 of *Active Directory,* Third Edition, by Joe Richards et al. (O'Reilly).

Group policies are defined by a set of files that are replicated to each domain controller in a domain and a groupPolicyContainer (GPC) object that is stored in the cn=Policies,cn=System,*<DomainDN>* container. GPC objects contain information related to software deployment, wireless deployments, IPSec assignments, and metadata about the version of the GPO. GPC objects are used for linking to OUs, sites, and domains. The guts of GPOs are stored on the filesystem of each domain controller in group policy template (GPT) files. These can be found in the *%SystemRoot%\SYSVOL\sysvol\<DomainDNSName>\Policies* directory.

So why are there two storage points for GPOs? The need for the Active Directory object is obvious: to be able to link GPOs to other types of objects, the GPOs need to be represented in Active Directory. Group Policy Templates are stored in the filesystem to reduce the amount of data that needs to be replicated within Active Directory.

Managing GPOs

While the new capabilities of GPOs were significant in Windows 2000 Active Directory, the one obvious thing that was lacking were good tools for managing them. The dual storage nature of GPOs creates a lot of problems. First, Microsoft did not provide a scriptable interface for accessing and manipulating GPO settings. Second, there were no tools for copying or migrating GPOs from a test environment to production. In Windows 2000, the primary tool for managing GPOs was the Group Policy Editor (GPE), now known as the Group Policy Object Editor (GPOE). The main function of GPOE is to modify GPO settings; it does not provide any other management capabilities.

Microsoft realized these were major issues for group policy adoption, so they developed the Group Policy Management Console (GPMC). The GPMC is a MMC snap-in that provides the kitchen sink of GPO management capabilities: you can create, delete, import, copy, back up, restore, and model GPO processing from a single interface. Perhaps what is even better is the scriptable API that comes with the GPMC. Pretty much every function you can accomplish with the GPMC tool, you can do via a script.

The only major feature that is still lacking is the ability to directly modify the settings of a GPO via command line or script. That can be done with only the GPOE. However, the GPMC provides numerous options for migrating GPOs, which addresses the majority of the problems people face today.

You can download the GPMC from the following site: *http://www.microsoft.com/ windowsserver2003/gpmc/default.mspx*. It requires at least version 1.1 of the .NET Framework on Windows Server 2003 or Windows XP SP1 or SP2. (Windows XP SP 1 requires hotfix Q326469 as well.) The GPMC cannot be run on Windows 2000. You can, however, manage Windows 2000–based Active Directory GPOs with the GPMC as long as you run it from one of the previously mentioned platforms.

Another tool that you can download from the Microsoft web site is GPInventory. This is an incredibly useful tool that will allow you to perform a software inventory for users and computers in a domain or OU, and to track information about the roll-out of GPOs in AD, such as computers that have not applied new GPO information.

The majority of solutions presented in this chapter use GPMC. In fact, most of these recipes would not have had workable solutions were it not for the GPMC. It is for this reason that we highly recommend downloading it and becoming familiar with it. Most of the command-line solutions we provide will use one of the scripts provided in the GPMC install. A whole host of precanned scripts have already been written, in a mix of VBScript and JavaScript, which serve as great command-line tools and good examples to start scripting GPOs. These scripts are available by default in the *%ProgramFiles%\GPMC\scripts* directory. You can execute them one of two ways, either by using *cscript*:

```
> cscript listallgpos.wsf
```

or, if you make *cscript* your default WSH interpreter, by executing the file directly. To make *cscript* your default interpreter, run this command:

```
> cscript //H:cscript
```

The complete documentation for the GPM API is available in the *gpmc.chm* file in the *%ProgramFiles%\GPMC\scripts* directory or from MSDN (*http://msdn.microsoft.com*).

10.1 Finding the GPOs in a Domain

Problem

You want to find all of the GPOs that have been created in a domain.

Solution

Using a graphical user interface

1. Open the GPMC snap-in.
2. In the left pane, expand the Forest container.
3. Expand the Domains container.
4. Browse to the domain of the target GPO.
5. Expand the Group Policy Objects container. All of the GPOs in the domain will be listed under that container.

Using a command-line interface

You can generate a list of all GPOs in a domain using the *liastallgpos.wsf* script, as well as DSQuery and AdFind:

```
> listallgpos.wsf [/domain:<DomainDNSName>] [/v]

> dsquery * domainroot -filter (objectcategory=grouppolicycontainer) -att
r displayname

> adfind -default -f (objectclass=grouppolicycontainer) displayname
```

You can also use the *gpotool* utility from the Windows Server 2003 Resource Kit to display the GPOs:

```
> gpotool [/domain:<DomainDNSName>] [/verbose]
```

Using VBScript

```
' This code displays all of the GPOs for a domain.
' ------ SCRIPT CONFIGURATION ------
strDomain   = "<DomainDNSName>"    ' e.g. rallencorp.com
' ------ END CONFIGURATION ---------

set objGPM = CreateObject("GPMgmt.GPM")
set objGPMConstants = objGPM.GetConstants( )

' Initialize the Domain object
set objGPMDomain = objGPM.GetDomain(strDomain, "", objGPMConstants.UseAnyDC)

' Create an empty search criteria
set objGPMSearchCriteria = objGPM.CreateSearchCriteria
set objGPOList = objGPMDomain.SearchGPOs(objGPMSearchCriteria)

' Print the GPOs
WScript.Echo "Found " & objGPOList.Count & " GPOs in " & strDomain & ":"
for each objGPO in objGPOList
    WScript.Echo "   " & objGPO.DisplayName
next
```

Discussion

See the "Introduction" to this chapter for more on how GPOs are stored in Active Directory.

Using VBScript

You can find the GPOs in a domain by using the GPMDomain.SearchGPOs method. The only parameter you need to pass to SearchGPOs is a GPMSearchCriteria object, which can be used to define criteria for your search. In this case, we created a GPMSearchCriteria object without additional criteria so that all GPOs are returned. The SearchGPOs method returns a GPMGPOCollection object, which is a collection of GPMGPO objects.

See Also

MS KB 216359 (How to Identify Group Policy Objects in the Active Directory and SYSVOL) and MSDN: GPMDomain.SearchGPOs

10.2 Creating a GPO

Problem

You want to create a Group Policy Object within Active Directory.

Solution

Using a graphical user interface

1. Open the GPMC snap-in.
2. In the left pane, expand the Forest container, expand the Domains container, and browse to the domain of the target GPO.
3. Right-click on the Group Policy Objects container and select New.
4. Enter the name of the GPO and click OK.

Using a command-line interface

```
> creategpo.wsf <GPOName> [/domain:<DomainDNSName>]
```

Using VBScript

```
' This code creates an empty GPO.
' ------ SCRIPT CONFIGURATION ------
strGPO      = "<GPOName>"          ' e.g. "Sales GPO"
strDomain   = "<DomainDNSName>"    ' e.g. "rallencorp.com"
' ------ END CONFIGURATION ---------

set objGPM = CreateObject("GPMgmt.GPM")
set objGPMConstants = objGPM.GetConstants( )

' Initialize the Domain object
set objGPMDomain = objGPM.GetDomain(strDomain, "", objGPMConstants.UseAnyDC)

' Create the GPO and print the results
set objGPO = objGPMDomain.CreateGPO( )
WScript.Echo "Successfully created GPO"
objGPO.DisplayName = strGPO
WScript.Echo "Set GPO name to " & strGPO
```

Discussion

When you create a GPO through the GPMC, it is initially empty with no settings or links configured. See Recipe 10.6 for more on modifying GPO settings, and Recipe 10.14 for creating a link.

Using VBScript

To create a GPO, first instantiate a GPMDomain object for the domain to add the GPO to. This is accomplished with the GPM.GetDomain method. Then it is just a matter of calling the `GPMDomain.CreateGPO` method (with no parameters) to create an empty GPO. A `GPM.GPO` object is returned from this method, which you then use to set the display name of the GPO.

See Also

MS KB 216359 (How to Identify Group Policy Objects in the Active Directory and SYSVOL) and MSDN: GPMDomain.CreateGPO

10.3 Copying a GPO

Problem

You want to copy the properties and settings of a GPO into another GPO.

Solution

Using a graphical user interface

1. Open the GPMC snap-in.
2. In the left pane, expand the Forest container, expand the Domains container, browse to the domain of the source GPO, and expand the Group Policy Objects container.
3. Right-click on the source GPO and select Copy.
4. Right-click on the Group Policy Objects container and select Paste.
5. Select whether you want to use the default permissions or to preserve the existing permissions from the GPO being copied, and click OK.
6. A status window will pop up that will indicate whether the copy was successful. Click OK to close.
7. Rename the new GPO by right-clicking it in the left pane and selecting Rename.

Using a command-line interface

```
> copygpo.wsf <SourceGPOName> <TargetGPOName>
```

Using VBScript

```
' This code copies a source GPO to a new GPO.
' ------ SCRIPT CONFIGURATION ------
strSourceGPO = "<SourceGPOName>"  ' e.g. SalesGPO
strNewGPO    = "<NewGPOName>"     ' e.g. Marketing GPO
strDomain    = "<DomainDNSName>"  ' e.g. rallencorp.com
' ------ END CONFIGURATION ------

set objGPM = CreateObject("GPMgmt.GPM")
set objGPMConstants = objGPM.GetConstants( )
```

```
' Initialize the Domain object
set objGPMDomain = objGPM.GetDomain(strDomain, "", objGPMConstants.UseAnyDC)

' Find the source GPO
set objGPMSearchCriteria = objGPM.CreateSearchCriteria
objGPMSearchCriteria.Add objGPMConstants.SearchPropertyGPODisplayName, _
                         objGPMConstants.SearchOpEquals, cstr(strSourceGPO)
set objGPOList = objGPMDomain.SearchGPOs(objGPMSearchCriteria)
if objGPOList.Count = 0 then
   WScript.Echo "Did not find GPO: " & strGPO
   WScript.Echo "Exiting."
   WScript.Quit
elseif objGPOList.Count > 1 then
   WScript.Echo "Found more than one matching GPO. Count: " & _
               objGPOList.Count
   WScript.Echo "Exiting."
   WScript.Quit
else
   WScript.Echo "Found GPO: " & objGPOList.Item(1).DisplayName
End if

' Copy from source GPO to target GPO
set objGPMResult = objGPOList.Item(1).CopyTo(0, objGPMDomain, strNewGPO)

' This will throw an exception if there were any errors
' during the actual operation.
on error resume next
objGPMResult.OverallStatus( )
if objGPMResult.Status.Count > 0 then
   WScript.Echo "Status message(s): " & objGPMResult.Status.Count
   for i = 1 to objGPMResult.Status.Count
      WScript.Echo objGPMResult.Status.Item(i).Message
   next
   WScript.Echo vbCrLf
end if

' Display the results
if Err.Number <> 0 then
   WScript.Echo "Error copying GPO."
   WScript.Echo "Error: " & Err.Description
else
   WScript.Echo "Copy successful to " & strNewGPO & "."
end if
```

Discussion

Prior to the GPMC tool, two of the big problems with managing GPOs in large environments were migrating them from one forest to another and copying them from one domain to another within the same forest. It is common to have a test forest where GPOs are initially created, configured, and tested before moving them into production. The problem before GPMC was that once you had the GPO the way you wanted it in the test forest, there was no easy or well-publicized way to move it to the production forest.

With the GPMC, you can simply copy GPOs between domains and even forests. Copying GPOs between forests requires a trust to be in place between the two target domains (or a cross-forest trust in place between the two forests). If this is not possible, you can import GPOs, which is similar to a copy operation except that a trust is not needed. A GPO import uses a backup of the source GPO in order to create the new GPO. See Recipe 10.7 for more information on importing a GPO.

Some properties of GPOs, such as security group filters, UNC paths, and Restricted Groups may vary slightly from domain to domain; for example, a logon script that runs from \\SERVERA\share in the source domain may need to run on \\SERVERB\share in the target domain. In that case, you can use a GPMC migration table to help facilitate the transfer of those types of references to the target domain. For more information on migration tables, see the GPMC help file and Recipe 10.8.

Using VBScript

To copy a GPO, you have to first find the source GPO. To do this, use a GPMSearchCriteria object to find the GPO that is equal to the display name of the GPO specified in the configuration section. Use an if else conditional statement to ensure that only one GPO is returned. If zero is returned or more than one are returned, you have to abort the script.

Now that you have a GPMGPO object, you're ready to copy the GPO using the GPMGPO.CopyTo method. The first parameter to CopyTo is a flag that indicates how permissions in the source GPO should be handled when copying them to the new GPO. Specify 0 to use the default setting (see the GPMC help file for the other values). The second parameter is the GPMDomain object of the domain the GPO should be copied to. The last parameter is the display name of the new GPO.

See Also

Recipe 10.7 for importing a GPO, Recipe 10.8, and MSDN: GPMGPO.CopyTo

10.4   Deleting a GPO

Problem

You want to delete a GPO.

Solution

Using a graphical user interface

1. Open the GPMC snap-in.
2. In the left pane, expand the Forest container, expand the Domains container, browse to the domain of the target GPO, and expand the Group Policy Objects container.
3. Right-click on the target GPO and select Delete.
4. Click OK to confirm.

Using a command-line interface

```
> deletegpo.wsf <GPOName> [/domain:<DomainDNSName>]
```

 To retain the links to the deleted GPO, (in case you will be re-creating it with the same name), use the /keeplinks switch. Otherwise, all links will be deleted along with the GPO.

Using VBScript

```
' This code deletes the specified GPO.
' ------ SCRIPT CONFIGURATION ------
strGPO      = "<GPOName>"         ' e.g. "My New GPO"
strDomain   = "<DomainDNSName>"   ' e.g. "rallencorp.com"
' ------ END CONFIGURATION ---------

set objGPM = CreateObject("GPMgmt.GPM")
set objGPMConstants = objGPM.GetConstants( )

' Initialize the Domain object
set objGPMDomain = objGPM.GetDomain(strDomain, "", objGPMConstants.UseAnyDC)

' Find the GPO
set objGPMSearchCriteria = objGPM.CreateSearchCriteria
objGPMSearchCriteria.Add objGPMConstants.SearchPropertyGPODisplayName, _
                    objGPMConstants.SearchOpEquals, cstr(strGPO)
set objGPOList = objGPMDomain.SearchGPOs(objGPMSearchCriteria)
if objGPOList.Count = 0 then
   WScript.Echo "Did not find GPO: " & strGPO
   WScript.Echo "Exiting."
   WScript.Quit
elseif objGPOList.Count > 1 then
   WScript.Echo "Found more than one matching GPO. Count: " & _
             objGPOList.Count
   WScript.Echo "Exiting."
   WScript.Quit
else
   WScript.Echo "Found GPO: " & objGPOList.Item(1).DisplayName
end if
```

```
' Delete the GPO
objGPOList.Item(1).Delete
WScript.Echo "Successfully deleted GPO: " & strGPO
```

Discussion

When you delete a GPO through the GPMC, it attempts to find all links to the GPO in the domain and will delete them if the user has permissions to delete the links. If the user does not have the necessary permissions to remove the links, the GPO will still get deleted, but the links will remain intact. Any links external to the domain the GPO is in are not automatically deleted. For this reason, it is a good practice to view the links to the GPO before you delete it. Links to deleted GPOs show up as "Not Found" in GPMC.

Using VBScript

Use a GPMSearchCriteria object to find the GPO that is equal to the display name of the GPO specified in the configuration section. Use an if else conditional statement to ensure that only one GPO is returned. If zero or more than one are returned, abort the script. If only one is returned, use the GPMGPO.Delete method to delete the GPO.

See Also

Recipe 10.13 for viewing the links for a GPO and MSDN: GPMGPO.Delete

10.5   Viewing the Settings of a GPO

Problem

You want to view the settings that have been defined on a GPO.

Solution

Using a graphical user interface

1. Open the GPMC snap-in.
2. In the left pane, expand the Forest container, expand the Domains container, browse to the domain of the target GPO, and expand the Group Policy Objects container.
3. Click on the target GPO.
4. In the right pane, click on the Settings tab.
5. Click the Show All link to display all configured settings.

Using a command-line interface

```
> getreportsforgpo.wsf "<GPOName>" <ReportLocation> [/domain:<DomainDNSName>]
```

Using VBScript

```vbscript
' This code generates a HTML report of all the properties
' and settings for a GPO.
' ------ SCRIPT CONFIGURATION ------
strGPO         = "<GPOName>"         ' e.g. Sales GPO
strDomain      = "<DomainDNSName>"   ' e.g. rallencorp.com
strReportFile  = "<FileNameAndPath>" ' e.g. c:\gpo_report.html
' ------ END CONFIGURATION ---------

set objGPM = CreateObject("GPMgmt.GPM")
set objGPMConstants = objGPM.GetConstants( )

' Initialize the Domain object
set objGPMDomain = objGPM.GetDomain(strDomain, "", objGPMConstants.UseAnyDC)

set objGPMSearchCriteria = objGPM.CreateSearchCriteria
objGPMSearchCriteria.Add objGPMConstants.SearchPropertyGPODisplayName, _
                        objGPMConstants.SearchOpEquals, cstr(strGPO)
set objGPOList = objGPMDomain.SearchGPOs(objGPMSearchCriteria)

if objGPOList.Count = 0 then
   WScript.Echo "Did not find GPO: " & strGPO
   WScript.Echo "Exiting."
   WScript.Quit
elseif objGPOList.Count > 1 then
   WScript.Echo "Found more than one matching GPO. Count: " & _
              objGPOList.Count
   WScript.Echo "Exiting."
   WScript.Quit
else
   WScript.Echo "Found GPO: " & objGPOList.Item(1).DisplayName
end if

set objGPMResult = objGPOList.Item(1).GenerateReportToFile( _
                       objGPMConstants.ReportHTML, _
                                     strReportFile)

' This will throw an exception if there were any errors
' during the actual operation.
on error resume next
objGPMResult.OverallStatus( )

if objGPMResult.Status.Count > 0 then
   WScript.Echo "Status message(s): " & objGPMResult.Status.Count
   for i = 1 to objGPMResult.Status.Count
     WScript.Echo objGPMResult.Status.Item(i).Message
   next
   WScript.Echo vbCrLf
end if
```

```
' Display the result
if Err.Number <> 0 then
   WScript.Echo "Error generating report."
   WScript.Echo "Error: " & Err.Description
else
   WScript.Echo "Reported saved to " & strReportFile
end if
```

Discussion

The GPMC can generate an XML or HTML report that contains all of the settings in
a GPO. See Recipe 10.6 for more on how to modify GPO settings.

Using VBScript

Use a GPMSearchCriteria object to find the GPO that is equal to the display name of
the GPO specified in the configuration section. Use an if else conditional statement
to ensure that only one GPO is returned. If zero or more than one are returned, abort
the script. If only one is returned, you can use the GPMGPO.GenerateReportToFile
method to generate a report of all the settings in the GPO. The first parameter for
GenerateReportToFile is a constant that determines the type of report to generate (i.e.,
HTML or XML). The second parameter is the path of the file to store the report.

See Also

MSDN: GPMGPO.GenerateReportToFile

10.6   Modifying the Settings of a GPO

Problem

You want to modify the settings associated with a GPO.

Solution

Using a graphical user interface

1. Open the GPMC snap-in.
2. In the left pane, expand the Forest container, expand the Domains container,
   browse to the domain of the target GPO, and expand the GPO container.
3. Right-click on the target GPO and select Edit. This will bring up the GPOE.
4. Browse through the Computer Configuration or User Configuration settings and
   modify them as necessary.

Using a command-line interface or VBScript

You cannot modify the settings of a GPO with any of the command-line tools or APIs, but you can copy and import settings as described in Recipe 10.3 and Recipe 10.7.

Discussion

The one function that the GPMC tool and API cannot do is modify GPO settings. This still must be done from within the GPOE. You can, however, launch GPOE from within GPMC as described in the GUI solution. Not having a scriptable way to modify GPO settings has been a big roadblock with managing GPOs, especially across multiple forests. Copying or importing GPOs can help with migrating settings across forests.

gpedit can be launched from the command line with the following syntax:

```
gpedit.msc /gpobject:"LDAP://CN={GUID of the GPO},CN=Policies,CN=System,<DomainDN>
```

See Also

Recipe 10.3 for copying a GPO, Recipe 10.5 for viewing the settings of a GPO, and Recipe 10.7 for importing settings into a GPO

10.7 Importing Settings into a GPO

Problem

You want to import settings from one GPO to another.

Solution

Using a graphical user interface

1. Open the GPMC snap-in.
2. In the left pane, expand the Forest container, expand the Domains container, browse to the domain of the target GPO, and expand the Group Policy Objects container.
3. Right-click on the target GPO and select Import Settings.
4. Click Next.
5. Click the Backup button if you want to take backup of the GPO you are importing into.
6. Click Next.
7. Select the backup folder location and click Next.
8. Select the backup instance you want to import from and click Next.

9. It then will scan to see if there are any security principals or UNC paths in the GPO being imported from. If there are, it will give you an option to modify those settings.

10. Click Next.

11. Click Finish.

Using a command-line interface

```
> importgpo.wsf "<GPOBackupLocation>" "<OrigGPOName>" "<NewGPOName>"
```

Using VBScript

```
' This code imports the settings from a GPO that has been backed up into
' an existing GPO.
' ------ SCRIPT CONFIGURATION ------
strGPOImportTo    = "<GPOName>"         ' e.g. "Sales GPO"
strDomain         = "<DomainDNSName>"   ' e.g. "rallencorp.com"
strBackupLocation = "<BackupLocation>"  ' e.g. "c:\GPMC Backups"

' GUID representing the specific backup
' e.g.{3E53B39B-C29B-44FF-857B-8A84528804FF}
strBackupID       = "<BackupGUID>"
' ------ END CONFIGURATION ---------

set objGPM = CreateObject("GPMgmt.GPM")
set objGPMConstants = objGPM.GetConstants( )

' Initialize the Domain object
set objGPMDomain = objGPM.GetDomain(strDomain, "", objGPMConstants.UseAnyDC)

' Locate GPO backup
set objGPMBackupDir = objGPM.GetBackupDir(strBackupLocation)
set objGPMBackup = objGPMBackupDir.GetBackup(strBackupID)
WScript.Echo "Backup found:"
WScript.Echo "  ID: " & objGPMBackup.ID
WScript.Echo "  Timestamp: " & objGPMBackup.TimeStamp
WScript.Echo "  GPO ID: " & objGPMBackup.GPOID
WScript.Echo "  GPO Name: " & objGPMBackup.GPODisplayName
WScript.Echo "  Comment: " & objGPMBackup.Comment
WScript.Echo

' Find GPO to import into
set objGPMSearchCriteria = objGPM.CreateSearchCriteria
objGPMSearchCriteria.Add objGPMConstants.SearchPropertyGPODisplayName, _
                         objGPMConstants.SearchOpEquals, cstr(strGPOImportTo)
set objGPOList = objGPMDomain.SearchGPOs(objGPMSearchCriteria)
if objGPOList.Count = 0 then
    WScript.Echo "Did not find GPO: " & strGPO
    WScript.Echo "Exiting."
    WScript.Quit
elseif objGPOList.Count > 1 then
    WScript.Echo "Found more than one matching GPO. Count: " & _
```

```
                        objGPOList.Count
         WScript.Echo "Exiting."
         WScript.Quit
      else
         WScript.Echo "Found GPO: " & objGPOList.Item(1).DisplayName
      end if

      ' Perform the import
      set objGPMResult = objGPOList.Item(1).Import(0,objGPMBackup)

      ' This will throw an exception if there were any errors
      ' during the actual operation.
      on error resume next
      objGPMResult.OverallStatus( )

      if objGPMResult.Status.Count > 0 then
         WScript.Echo "Status message(s): " & objGPMResult.Status.Count
         for i = 1 to objGPMResult.Status.Count
            WScript.Echo objGPMResult.Status.Item(i).Message
         next
         WScript.Echo vbCrLf
      end if

      ' Print results
      if Err.Number <> 0 then
         WScript.Echo "Error importing GPO " & objGPMBackup.GPODisplayName
         WScript.Echo "Error: " & Err.Description
      else
         WScript.Echo "Import successful."
         WScript.Echo "GPO '" & objGPMBackup.GPODisplayName & _
                   "' has been imported into GPO '" & _
                   objGPOList.Item(1).DisplayName & "'"
      end if
```

Discussion

The GPMC import function uses a backup of the source GPO to create the new
"imported" GPO. This means you must first back up the source GPO using GPMC.
You can then import the settings from that GPO into a new GPO, which may be in
the same domain or a completely different forest. Importing a GPO is a great way to
help facilitate transferring GPO settings from a test environment to production.

Some properties of GPOs, such as security group filters or UNC paths, may vary
slightly from domain to domain; a logon script that runs from \\SERVERA\share in
the source domain may need to run on \\SERVERB\share in the target domain, for
example. In this case, you can use a GPMC migration table to help facilitate the
transfer of those kinds of references to the target domain. For more information on
migration tables, see the GPMC help file and Recipe 10.8.

Using VBScript

To import the settings of a backup, you have to first instantiate a GPMBackup object of the source backup by specifying the backup ID (a GUID) with the GPMBackupDir. GetBackup method. If you need to programmatically search for the backup ID, you can use the GPMBackup.SearchBackups method to find the most recent backup or a backup with a particular display name.

Next, instantiate a GPMGPO object of the GPO you're importing into. To do this, use a GPMSearchCriteria object to find the GPO that is equal to the display name of the GPO specified in the configuration section. Use an if else conditional statement to ensure that only one GPO is returned. If zero or more than one are returned, abort the script. If only one is returned, use the GPMGPO.Import method to import the settings. The first parameter to the Import method is a flag that determines how security principals and UNC path mapping is done; 0 is the default to not copy security settings. You can also use a migration table to do mappings if necessary. The second parameter is the GPMBackup object instantiated earlier. The rest of the script performs some error handling and prints the results.

See Also

Recipe 10.3 for copying a GPO, Recipe 10.8, Recipe 10.23 for backing up a GPO, and MSDN: GPMGPO.Import

10.8   Creating a Migration Table

Problem

You want to create a migration table to assist in copying or migrating a GPO from one domain or forest to another.

Solution

Using a graphical user interface

1. Open the Group Policy Management Console. Navigate to the forest and domain containing the GPOs you wish to migrate or copy.
2. Right-click on the Group Policy Objects node and select Open Migration Table Editor.
3. You will begin with a blank migration table. To populate the source fields from existing data, click on Tools → Populate from GPO or Tools → Populate from Backup. Select the GPO or the backup that you wish to import. Optionally, place a checkmark next to "During scan, include security principals from the DACL on the GPO." Click OK.

4. Modify the Destination Name column of any entries to match their format in the destination forest or domain.

5. To add a new entry, enter the name of the item in the Source Name column. In the Source Type column, select one of the following:

   - User
   - Computer
   - Domain Local Group
   - Domain Global Group
   - Universal Group
   - UNC Path
   - Free Text or SID

6. To delete an entry, right-click on the entry and select Delete.

7. To configure an entry to use the same information as configured in the source GPO, right-click on the entry and select Set Destination → Same As Source.

8. To configure an entry to use the relative name of the destination, right-click on the entry and select Set Destination → Map by Relative Name. For example, if you have an entry for the salesuser@rallencorp.com user in a GPO that you wish to copy to the *mycompany.com* forest, selecting Map by Relative Name will populate the entry in the destination GPO as salesuser@mycompany.com.

9. To ensure that you have properly formatted all entries in the table, click Tools → Validate Table, then click File → Save or File → Save As to save the migration table.

Using a command-line interface

```
> createmigrationtable.wsf <DestinationFileName> /GPO:<DestinationGPO> /MapByName
```

Discussion

One of the convenient new features of the GPMC is the ability to copy a GPO's settings from one GPO to another, or to migrate GPOs between domains or forests. In some cases, certain entries in the GPO may need to be modified to suit the needs of the destination domain or forest. For example, a UNC for user home directories will likely need to be modified to correspond to a server or DFS share in the destination, as well as individual user or group names. To address this need, you can create and populate a migration table to automatically transform the necessary entries on one or more GPOs.

Using a command-line interface

To create a migration table from the command line, use the *createmigrationtable.wsf* script that is included in the *~\Scripts* folder of the GPMC. The script will require two arguments: the destination file name and the GPO that it should be populated from.

As an alternative to the /GPO: switch, you can use /BackupLocation: to populate the migration table from a GPO backup. By default, a migration table that you create using this script will use Same As Source mapping, or you can specify the /MapByName parameter to use relative name mapping.

See Also

Recipe 10.3 for more on copying a GPO and Recipe 10.7 for information on importing settings into a GPO

10.9   Creating Custom Group Policy Settings

Problem

You want to deploy settings via Group Policy that are not covered by the default set of GPO templates that come with Active Directory.

Solution

The GPE comes preloaded with a number of default *templates* (also called *ADM files*) that define a number of settings that can be controlled via GPO. To control and deploy settings for additional or third-party applications, you'll need to create your own custom ADM files to manage the settings you require. You'll create this file in Notepad or another simple text editor, and save it as *<FileName>.adm*. For example, the following ADM file will allow you to disable dynamic DNS registration for Windows 2000 clients:

```
Class Machine

Category !!AdministrativeServices

Category !!DNSClient


Policy !!DisableDynamicUpdate
Keyname "System\CurrentControlSet\Services\Tcpip\Parameters"
Explain !!DisableDynamicUpdate_Help
Valuename "DisableDynamicUpdate"
End Policy


End Category ;;DNS Client

End Category ;;AdministrativeServices

[strings]
AdministrativeServices="System"
DNSClient="DNS Client"
```

```
DisableDynamicUpdate="Disable Dynamic Update"
DisableDynamicUpdate_Help="Stops the client from dynamically registering all adapters
with DNS.\n\nWhen this setting is enabled it changes the DisableDynamicUpdate value
to 1 in HKEY_LOCAL_MACHINE\SYSTEM\CurrentControlSet\Services\Tcpip\Parameters\n\nWhen
this setting is disabled, the value is set back to its default of zero. Note that
when the policy is disabled, the registry value may be deleted from the registry.\n\
nSee Q246804 for more details."

;End of Strings
```

To import this template into the GPE, follow these steps:

1. Open the GPMC snap-in.

2. In the left pane, expand the Forest container, expand the Domains container, browse to the domain of the target GPO, and expand the Group Policy Objects container.

3. Drill down to User Configuration or Computer Configuration, as appropriate. Right-click on Administrative Templates and select Add/Remove Template.

4. Click Add and browse to the location of the ADM file you created, and then click Open.

5. Click Close, and then browse to the new node you've just added to the Administrative Templates folder.

6. If you don't see the new settings you've created, right-click on the righthand pane, select View → Filtering, and remove the checkmark next to "Only show policy settings that can be fully managed." Then click OK to return to the GPO Editor. (This happens because the GPO Editor displays only *policy* settings by default, while the settings contained in a custom ADM file are considered *preferences*.

Discussion

When you create a custom ADM file for a Group Policy Object, the new template is automatically uploaded to the *%SystemRoot%\SYSVOL\sysvol\domain name\Policies\ {GPO GUID}\Adm* folder on the DC that is performing the updates to the GPO, typically the PDC Emulator. Because the *SYSVOL* folder is included in the Active Directory replication process, the new ADM file will be automatically replicated to all other instances of the GPO.

See Also

MS KB 323639 (How to Create Custom Administrative Templates in Windows 2000), MS KB 259576 (Group policy application rules for domain controllers), MS KB 316977 (Group Policy Template Behavior in Windows Server 2003), MS KB 816662 (Recommendations for managing Group Policy administrative template (.adm) files)

10.10 Assigning Logon/Logoff and Startup/Shutdown Scripts in a GPO

Problem

You want to assign either user logon/logoff scripts or computer startup/shutdown scripts in a GPO.

Solution

Using a graphical user interface

1. Open the GPMC snap-in.
2. In the left pane, expand the Forest container, expand the Domains container, browse to the domain of the target GPO, and expand the Group Policy Objects container.
3. Right-click on the target GPO and select Edit. This will bring up the GPOE.
4. If you want to assign a computer startup or shutdown script, browse to Computer Configuration → Windows Settings → Scripts. If you want to assign a user logon or logoff script, browse to User Computer → Windows Settings → Scripts.
5. In the right pane, double-click on the type of script you want to add.
6. Click the Add button.
7. Select the script by typing the name of it in or browsing to its location.
8. Optionally, type any script parameters in the Script Parameters field.
9. Click OK twice.

Discussion

When you assign a script in a GPO, you can either reference a script that is stored locally on the domain controller somewhere under the *SYSVOL* share, or in a UNC path to a remote file server. The default storage location is in the *SYSVOL* share in the *<DomainName>\scripts* folder—e.g., *\\rallencorp.com\sysvol\rallencorp.com\scripts*. The logon script can also be set as an attribute of the user object (scriptPath). This is provided as legacy support for users migrated from NT 4.0 domains and requires the script to be stored in the *Netlogon* share. You should choose one method of specifying the logon script or the other—but not both, as this will cause the logon script to run twice.

10.11 Installing Applications with a GPO

Problem

You want to install an application on a group of computers using a GPO.

Solution

Using a graphical user interface

1. Open the GPMC snap-in.

2. In the left pane, expand the Forest container, expand the Domains container, browse to the domain of the target GPO, and expand the Group Policy Objects container.

3. Right-click on the target GPO and select Edit. This will bring up the GPOE.

4. Expand Software Settings under Computer Configuration or User Configuration (depending on which you want to target the installation for).

5. Right-click on Software Installation and select New → Package.

6. Browse to the network share that has the MSI package for the application and click OK. Be sure to specify a UNC path such as *\\servername\share\installer.msi*. If you enter a local file path on the DC such as *c:\packages\pro.msi*, the client will not be able to access the installer.

7. Select whether you want to assign the application or publish it, and click OK. You can also click Advanced to further define how you want to deploy the software installation package.

Discussion

Installing applications with a GPO is a powerful feature, but you must be careful about the impact it can have on your network throughput and clients. If the MSI package you are installing is several megabytes in size, it will take a while for it to download to the client computer. This can result in sluggish performance on the client, especially over a heavily utilized connection. (Software installation does not occur over slow links, by default.) You'll also want to make sure you've thoroughly tested the application before deployment. After you've configured the GPO to install an application, it will be only a short period of time before it has been installed on all targeted clients. If there is a bug in the application or the installer program is faulty, the impact could be severe to your user base and support staff alike.

Your two options for deploying an application are to assign it or publish it. If you assign an application using the "deploy at logon" option, it will get automatically installed on the targeted clients when users log on to those machines. If you publish an application or assign it without choosing this option, it will be installed the first time a user double-clicks on a shortcut to the application or attempts to open a file that requires the application. A published application can also be installed manually from the Add/Remove Programs applet in the Control Panel on the target computers. You can assign an application to both user and computer objects, but you can publish applications only to users.

 If you need to exert more granular control over your software installations than is enabled by Group Policy, you should investigate leveraging the additional capabilities of dedicated deployment software such as Microsoft's Systems Management Server.

10.12 Disabling the User or Computer Settings in a GPO

Problem

You want to disable either the user or computer settings of a GPO.

Solution

Using a graphical user interface

1. Open the GPMC snap-in.
2. In the left pane, expand the Forest container, expand the Domains container, browse to the domain of the target GPO, and expand the Group Policy Objects container.
3. Right-click on the target GPO and select GPO Status.
4. You can either select User Configuration Settings Disabled to disable the user settings or Computer Configuration Settings Disabled to disable the computer settings.

Using VBScript

```
' This code can enable or disable the user or computer settings of a GPO.
' ------ SCRIPT CONFIGURATION ------
strGPO      = "<GPOName>"        ' e.g. "Sales GPO"
strDomain   = "<DomainDNSName>"  ' e.g. "rallencorp.com"
boolUserEnable = False
boolCompEnable = True
' ------ END CONFIGURATION ---------

set objGPM = CreateObject("GPMgmt.GPM")
set objGPMConstants = objGPM.GetConstants( )

' Initialize the Domain object
set objGPMDomain = objGPM.GetDomain(strDomain, "", objGPMConstants.UseAnyDC)

' Find the specified GPO
set objGPMSearchCriteria = objGPM.CreateSearchCriteria
objGPMSearchCriteria.Add objGPMConstants.SearchPropertyGPODisplayName, _
```

```
                    objGPMConstants.SearchOpEquals, cstr(strGPO)
set objGPOList = objGPMDomain.SearchGPOs(objGPMSearchCriteria)
if objGPOList.Count = 0 then
    WScript.Echo "Did not find GPO: " & strGPO
    WScript.Echo "Exiting."
    WScript.Quit
elseif objGPOList.Count > 1 then
    WScript.Echo "Found more than one matching GPO. Count: " & _
                  objGPOList.Count
    WScript.Echo "Exiting."
    WScript.Quit
else
    WScript.Echo "Found GPO: " & objGPOList.Item(1).DisplayName
end if

' You can comment out either of these if you don't want to set one:

objGPOList.Item(1).SetUserEnabled boolUserEnable
WScript.Echo "User settings: " & boolUserEnable

objGPOList.Item(1).SetComputerEnabled boolCompEnable
WScript.Echo "Computer settings: " & boolCompEnable
```

Discussion

GPOs consist of two parts, a user and a computer section. The user section contains settings that are specific to a user that logs in to a computer, while the computer section defines settings that apply to the computer regardless of which user logs in. You can enable or disable either the user configuration or computer configuration sections of a GPO, or both. By disabling both, you effectively disable the GPO. This can be useful if you want to stop a GPO from applying settings to clients, but you do not want to delete it, remove the links, or clear the settings.

Disabling the user configuration or the computer configuration is useful in environments that have separate OUs for computers and users. Typically, you would disable the computer configuration for GPOs linked to the users' OU and vice versa. Disabling half of the GPO in this way makes GPO processing more efficient and can improve performance both during logon and when Group Policy Objects perform a background refresh (every 5 minutes by default on domain controllers, every 90 minutes by default on clients and member servers).

Using VBScript

First, we have to find the target GPO. To do this, we use a GPMSearchCriteria object to find the GPO that is equal to the display name of the GPO specified in the configuration section. We use an if else conditional statement to ensure that only one GPO is returned. If zero or more than one are returned, we abort the script. If only one is returned, we call the SetUserEnabled and SetComputerEnable methods to either enable or disable the settings per the configuration.

See Also

MSDN: GPMGPO.SetUserEnabled and MSDN: GPMGPO.SetComputerEnabled

10.13 Listing the Links for a GPO

Problem

You want to list all of the links for a particular GPO.

Solution

Using a graphical user interface

1. Open the GPMC snap-in.
2. In the left pane, expand the Forest container, expand the Domains container, browse to the domain of the target GPO, and expand the Group Policy Objects container.
3. Click on the GPO you want to view the links for.
4. In the right pane, the defined links for the GPO will be listed under Links.

Using a command-line interface

```
> dumpgpoinfo.wsf "<GPOName>"
```

Using VBScript

```
' This code lists all the sites, OUs, and domains a GPO is linked to.
' ------ SCRIPT CONFIGURATION ------
strGPO      = "<GPOName>"        ' e.g. "SalesGPO"
strForest   = "<ForestName>"     ' e.g. "rallencorp.com"
strDomain   = "<DomainDNSName>"  ' e.g. "rallencorp.com"
' ------ END CONFIGURATION ---------

set objGPM = CreateObject("GPMgmt.GPM")
set objGPMConstants = objGPM.GetConstants( )

' Initialize the Domain object
set objGPMDomain = objGPM.GetDomain(strDomain, "", objGPMConstants.UseAnyDC)
' Initialize the Sites Container object
set objGPMSitesContainer = objGPM.GetSitesContainer(strForest, _
                        strDomain, "", objGPMConstants.UseAnyDC)
' Find the specified GPO
set objGPMSearchCriteria = objGPM.CreateSearchCriteria
objGPMSearchCriteria.Add objGPMConstants.SearchPropertyGPODisplayName, _
                        objGPMConstants.SearchOpEquals, cstr(strGPO)
set objGPOList = objGPMDomain.SearchGPOs(objGPMSearchCriteria)
if objGPOList.Count = 0 then
   WScript.Echo "Did not find GPO: " & strGPO
   WScript.Echo "Exiting."
```

```
      WScript.Quit
   elseif objGPOList.Count > 1 then
      WScript.Echo "Found more than one matching GPO. Count: " & _
                  objGPOList.Count
      WScript.Echo "Exiting."
      WScript.Quit
   else
      WScript.Echo "Found GPO: " & objGPOList.Item(1).DisplayName
   end if

   ' Search for all SOM links for this GPO
   set objGPMSearchCriteria = objGPM.CreateSearchCriteria
   objGPMSearchCriteria.Add objGPMConstants.SearchPropertySOMLinks, _
                       objGPMConstants.SearchOpContains, objGPOList.Item(1)
   set objSOMList = objGPMDomain.SearchSOMs(objGPMSearchCriteria)
   set objSiteLinkList = objGPMSitesContainer.SearchSites(objGPMSearchCriteria)

   if objSOMList.Count = 0 and objSiteLinkList.Count = 0 Then
      WScript.Echo "No Site, Domain, or OU links found for this GPO"
   else
      WScript.Echo "Links:"
      for each objSOM in objSOMList
         select case objSOM.Type
            case objGPMConstants.SOMDomain
               strSOMType = "Domain"
            case objGPMConstants.SOMOU
               strSOMType = "OU"
         end select
         ' Print GPO Domain and OU links
         WScript.Echo "  " & objSOM.Name & " (" & strSOMType & ")"
      next

      ' Print GPO Site Links
      for each objSiteLink in objSiteLinkList
         WScript.Echo "  " & objSiteLink.Name & " (Site)"
      next
   end if
```

Discussion

See the "Introduction" for this chapter for more information on GPO linking and SOMs.

Using VBScript

First, we have to find the target GPO. To do this, we use a GPMSearchCriteria object to find the GPO that is equal to the display name of the GPO specified in the configuration section. We use an if else conditional statement to ensure that only one GPO is returned. If none or more than one are returned, we abort the script. If only one is returned, we search for all SOMs (domain, OUs, and sites) that have the GPO linked using the GPMSitesContainer.SearchSites and GPMDomain.SearchSOMs methods.

See Also

The introduction to this chapter, Recipe 10.14 for creating a GPO link to an OU, MSDN: GPMDomain.SearchSOMs, and MSDN: GPMSitesContainer.SearchSites

10.14 Creating a GPO Link to an OU

Problem

You want to apply the GPO settings to the users and/or computers in an OU. This is called *linking* a GPO to an OU.

Solution

Using a graphical user interface

1. Open the GPMC snap-in.
2. In the left pane, expand the Forest container, expand the Domains container, and browse to the target domain.
3. Right-click on the OU you want to link and select Link an Existing GPO.
4. Select from the list of available GPOs and click OK.

Using VBScript

```
' This code links a GPO to an OU
' ------ SCRIPT CONFIGURATION ------
strGPO     = "<GPOName>"        ' e.g. "Sales GPO"
strDomain  = "<DomainDNSName>"  ' e.g. "rallencorp.com"
strOU      = "<OrgUnitDN>"      ' e.g. "ou=Sales,dc=rallencorp,dc=com"
intLinkPos = -1 ' set this to the position the GPO evaluated at
                ' a value of -1 signifies appending it to the end of the list
' ------ END CONFIGURATION ---------

set objGPM = CreateObject("GPMgmt.GPM")
set objGPMConstants = objGPM.GetConstants( )

' Initialize the Domain object
set objGPMDomain = objGPM.GetDomain(strDomain, "", objGPMConstants.UseAnyDC)

' Find the specified GPO
set objGPMSearchCriteria = objGPM.CreateSearchCriteria
objGPMSearchCriteria.Add objGPMConstants.SearchPropertyGPODisplayName, _
objGPMConstants.SearchOpEquals, cstr(strGPO)
set objGPOList = objGPMDomain.SearchGPOs(objGPMSearchCriteria)
if objGPOList.Count = 0 then
    WScript.Echo "Did not find GPO: " & strGPO
    WScript.Echo "Exiting."
    WScript.Quit
elseif objGPOList.Count > 1 then
```

```
        WScript.Echo "Found more than one matching GPO. Count: " & _
                     objGPOList.Count
        WScript.Echo "Exiting."
        WScript.Quit
else
        WScript.Echo "Found GPO: " & objGPOList.Item(1).DisplayName
end if

' Find the specified OU
set objSOM = objGPMDomain.GetSOM(strOU)
if IsNull(objSOM) then
        WScript.Echo "Did not find OU: " & strOU
        WScript.Echo "Exiting."
        WScript.Quit
else
        WScript.Echo "Found OU: " & objSOM.Name
end if

on error resume next

set objGPMLink = objSOM.CreateGPOLink( intLinkPos, objGPOList.Item(1) )

if Err.Number <> 0 then
        WScript.Echo "There was an error creating the GPO link."
        WScript.Echo "Error: " & Err.Description
else
        WScript.Echo "Sucessfully linked GPO to OU"
end if
```

Discussion

Linking a GPO is the process whereby you assign a scope of management (SOM), which can be an OU, site, or domain. The solutions show how to link a GPO to an OU, but they could be easily modified to link to a site or domain.

See Recipe 5.15 for details on how to link an OU by modifying the gpLink attribute, instead of using the GPMC interface.

Using VBScript

To link a GPO, we first have to find the target GPO. We use a GPMSearchCriteria object to find the GPO that is equal to the display name of the GPO specified in the configuration section. We use an if else conditional statement to ensure that only one GPO is returned. If zero or more than are are returned, we abort the script. If only one GPO is returned, we instantiate a GPMSOM object by passing the name of the OU to be linked to the GPMDomain.GetSOM method. Once we instantiate this object, we can call GPMSOM.CreateGPOLink to create a GPO link to the OU.

If the OU in question already has GPOs linked to it, the VBScript solution will, by default, insert the new link at the end of the list of linked GPOs.

See Also

MS KB 248392 (Scripting the Addition of Group Policy Links) and MSDN: GPM-SOM.CreateGPOLink

10.15 Blocking Inheritance of GPOs on an OU

Problem

You want to block inheritance of GPOs on an OU.

Solution

Using a graphical user interface

1. Open the GPMC snap-in.
2. In the left pane, expand the Forest container, expand the Domains container, and browse to the target domain.
3. Right-click on the OU you want to block inheritance for and select Block Inheritance.

Using VBScript

```
' This code blocks inheritance of GPOs on the specified OU
' ------ SCRIPT CONFIGURATION ------
strDomain   = "<DomainDNSName>" ' e.g. "rallencorp.com"
strOU       = "<OrgUnitDN>"      ' e.g. "ou=Sales,dc=rallencorp,dc=com"
boolBlock   = TRUE              ' e.g. set to FALSE to not block inheritance
' ------ END CONFIGURATION ---------

set objGPM = CreateObject("GPMgmt.GPM")
set objGPMConstants = objGPM.GetConstants( )

' Initialize the Domain object
set objGPMDomain = objGPM.GetDomain(strDomain, "", objGPMConstants.UseAnyDC)

' Find the specified OU
set objSOM = objGPMDomain.GetSOM(strOU)
if IsNull(objSOM) then
   WScript.Echo "Did not find OU: " & strOU
   WScript.Echo "Exiting."
   WScript.Quit
else
   WScript.Echo "Found OU: " & objSOM.Name
```

```
    end if

    ' on error resume next

    objSOM.GPOInheritanceBlocked = boolBlock

    if Err.Number <> 0 then
        WScript.Echo "There was an error blocking inheritance."
        WScript.Echo "Error: " & Err.Description
    else
        WScript.Echo "Successfully set inheritance blocking on OU to " & boolBlock
    end if
```

Discussion

By default, GPOs are inherited down through the directory tree. If you link a GPO to a top-level OU, that GPO will apply to any objects within the child OUs. Sometimes that may not be what you want, so you can disable inheritance as described in the solutions.

Try to avoid blocking inheritance when possible because it can make determining what settings should be applied to a user or computer difficult. If someone sees that a GPO is applied at a top-level OU, they may think it applies to any object under it. Using the Resultant Set of Policies (RSoP) snap-in can help identify what settings are applied to a user or computer (see Recipe 10.25).

Using VBScript

To block inheritance, we first have to get a GPMSOM object for the OU by calling the GPMDomain.GetSOM method. The only parameter to this method is the DN of the OU (or leave blank to reference the domain itself). Next, we call the GPMSOM.GPOInheritanceBlocked method, which should be set to either TRUE or FALSE depending if you want inheritance blocked or not.

See Also

Recipe 10.25 and MSDN: GPMDomain.GetSOM and MSDN: GPMSOM.GPOInheritanceBlocked

10.16 Enforcing the Settings of a GPO Link

Problem

You want to ensure that a GPO's settings are enforced regardless of any "Block Inheritance" settings that have been enforced further down the scope of management (SOM).

Solution

Using a graphical user interface

1. Open the GPMC snap-in.

2. In the left pane, expand the Forest container, expand the Domains container, browse to the domain of the target GPO, and expand the container containing the link you want to enforce.

3. Right-click on the link you want to configure and place a checkmark next to Enforced. To remove the Enforced setting, right-click on the link and remove the checkmark.

Using VBScript

```
' This code enforces a link to a GPO.
' ------ SCRIPT CONFIGURATION ------
strGPO      = "<GPOName>"      ' e.g. SalesGPO
strForest   = "<ForestName>"   ' e.g. rallencorp.com
strDomain   = "<DomainName>"   ' e.g. rallencorp.com
strLinkName = "<LinkName>"     ' e.g. "Finance" for an OU link,
                               ' "rallencorp.com" for a domain,
                               ' "Default-First-Site-Link" for a site
boolEnforced = TRUE            ' FALSE to disable the enforced setting
' ------ END CONFIGURATION ---------

set objGPM = CreateObject("GPMgmt.GPM")
set objGPMConstants = objGPM.GetConstants( )

' Initialize the Domain object
set objGPMDomain = objGPM.GetDomain(strDomain, "", objGPMConstants.UseAnyDC)
' Initialize the Sites Container object
set objGPMSitesContainer = objGPM.GetSitesContainer(strForest, _
                          strDomain, "", objGPMConstants.UseAnyDC)
' Find the specified GPO
set objGPMSearchCriteria = objGPM.CreateSearchCriteria
objGPMSearchCriteria.Add objGPMConstants.SearchPropertyGPODisplayName, _
                    objGPMConstants.SearchOpEquals, cstr(strGPO)
set objGPOList = objGPMDomain.SearchGPOs(objGPMSearchCriteria)
if objGPOList.Count = 0 then
   WScript.Echo "Did not find GPO: " & strGPO
   WScript.Echo "Exiting."
   WScript.Quit
elseif objGPOList.Count > 1 then
   WScript.Echo "Found more than one matching GPO. Count: " & _
             objGPOList.Count
   WScript.Echo "Exiting."
   WScript.Quit
else
   WScript.Echo "Found GPO: " & objGPOList.Item(1).DisplayName
   strGUID = objGPOList.Item(1).ID
end if
```

```
' Search for all SOM links for this GPO
set objGPMSearchCriteria = objGPM.CreateSearchCriteria
objGPMSearchCriteria.Add objGPMConstants.SearchPropertySOMLinks, _
                         objGPMConstants.SearchOpContains, objGPOList.Item(1)
set objSOMList = objGPMDomain.SearchSOMs(objGPMSearchCriteria)
set objSiteLinkList = objGPMSitesContainer.SearchSites(objGPMSearchCriteria)

if objSOMList.Count = 0 and objSiteLinkList.Count = 0 Then
    WScript.Echo "No Site, Domain, or OU links found for this GPO"
else
    for each objSOM in objSOMList
        if strcomp(objSOM.Name, strLinkName, vbTextCompare) = 0 then
            set colGPOLinks = objSOM.getGPOLinks()
            for each objGPOLink in colGPOLinks
                if strcomp(objGPOLink.GPOID,strGUID,vbTextCompare) = 0 then
                    objGPOLink.Enforced = boolEnforced
                    WScript.Echo("Enforced GPO " & strGPO & _
                                 " link to " & strLinkName)
                end if
            next
        end if
    next

    ' Print GPO Site Links
    for each objSiteLink in objSiteLinkList
        if strcomp(objSiteLink.Name, strLinkName, vbTextCompare) = 0 then
            set colGPOLinks = objSiteLink.getGPOLinks()
            for each objGPOLink in colGPOLinks
                if strcomp(objGPOLink.GPOID,strGUID,vbTextCompare) = 0 then
                    objGPOLink.Enforced = boolEnforced
                        WScript.Echo("Enforced GPO " & strGPO & _
                                     " link to " & strLinkName)
                end if
            next
        end if
    next
end if
```

Discussion

As a counterpoint to the ability to block inheritance of a GPO for a particular site, domain, or OU, an administrator can configure a particular GPO link as Enforced, meaning that the settings contained in that GPO will be configured for that SOM regardless of the presence of any Block Inheritance configuration. This is useful in a decentralized environment, for example, where a central IT department has configured a certain Group Policy baseline that it wishes to enforce regardless of what individual departments may have configured on their own. Just like security filtering and Block Inheritance, though, we recommend that you use this function sparingly, as it can create complex troubleshooting issues when trying to determine where and how Group Policy application is failing.

Remember that the Enforced setting is configured against a particular *link* to a GPO, not against the GPO itself. This means that one GPO can be linked to several locations, but not all of those links need to be enforced.

Using VBScript

It is unfortunately not possible to zero in on an individual Group Policy link through VBScript, since the IGPMSearchCriteria interface does not allow you to search for a particular link by any sort of display name or GUID. As such, the script in this recipe will set the Enforced flag for every link associated with a particular GPO, which may or may not be what you intended to achieve.

See Also

Recipe 10.15 and MSDN:IGPMSearchCriteria, MSDN:GPMC Object Model

10.17 Applying a Security Filter to a GPO

Problem

You want to configure a GPO so that it applies only to members of a particular security group.

Solution

Using a graphical user interface

1. Open the GPMC snap-in.
2. In the left pane, expand the Forest container, expand the Domains container, browse to the target domain, and expand the Group Policy Objects container.
3. Click on the GPO you want to modify.
4. In the right pane under Security Filtering, click the Add button.
5. Use the Object Picker to select a group and click OK.
6. Highlight Authenticated Users and click the Remove button.
7. Click OK to confirm.

Using a command-line interface

```
> setgpopermissions.wsf "<GPOName>" "<GroupName>" /permission:Apply
> setgpopermissions.wsf "<GPOName>" "Authenticated Users" /permission:None
```

Using VBScript

```
' This code adds a security group filter permission to a GPO
' and removes the Authenticated Users filter permission.
' ------ SCRIPT CONFIGURATION ------
strGPO        = "<GPOName>"         ' e.g. "Sales GPO"
strDomain     = "<DomainDNSName>"   ' e.g. "rallencorp.com"
strGroupAdd   = "<GroupName>"       ' e.g. "SalesUsers"
strGroupRemove =  "Authenticated Users"
' ------ END CONFIGURATION ---------

set objGPM = CreateObject("GPMgmt.GPM")
set objGPMConstants = objGPM.GetConstants( )

' Initialize the Domain object
set objGPMDomain = objGPM.GetDomain(strDomain, "", objGPMConstants.UseAnyDC)

' Find the specified GPO
set objGPMSearchCriteria = objGPM.CreateSearchCriteria
objGPMSearchCriteria.Add objGPMConstants.SearchPropertyGPODisplayName, _
                         objGPMConstants.SearchOpEquals, cstr(strGPO)
set objGPOList = objGPMDomain.SearchGPOs(objGPMSearchCriteria)
if objGPOList.Count = 0 then
   WScript.Echo "Did not find GPO: " & strGPO
   WScript.Echo "Exiting."
   WScript.Quit
elseif objGPOList.Count > 1 then
   WScript.Echo "Found more than one matching GPO. Count: " & _
               objGPOList.Count
   WScript.Echo "Exiting."
   WScript.Quit
else
   WScript.Echo "Found GPO: " & objGPOList.Item(1).DisplayName
end if

' Get permission objects to Apply GPO
set objGPMPerm1 = objGPM.CreatePermission(strGroupAdd, _
                         objGPMConstants.PermGPOApply, False)
set objGPMPerm2 = objGPM.CreatePermission(strGroupRemove, _
                         objGPMConstants.PermGPOApply, False)

' Get the existing set of permissions on the GPO
set objSecurityInfo = objGPOList.Item(1).GetSecurityInfo( )

' Add the new permission
objSecurityInfo.Add objGPMPerm1
' Remove Authenticate users
objSecurityInfo.Remove objGPMPerm2

on error resume next

' Apply the permission to the GPO
objGPOList.Item(1).SetSecurityInfo objSecurityInfo
if Err.Number <> 0 then
```

```
        WScript.Echo "There was an error setting the security filter."
        WScript.Echo "Error: " & Err.Description
    else
        WScript.Echo "Added Apply permission for group " & strGroupAdd
        WScript.Echo "Removed Apply permission for group " & strGroupRemove
    end if
```

Discussion

You can use security filtering to restrict the users, groups, or computers that a GPO applies to by granting or denying the `Apply Group Policy` permission on the ACL of the GPO. By default, `Authenticated Users` are granted the `Apply Group Policy` right on all new GPOs, so you will also need to remove this right if you want to restrict the GPO to be applied only to members of one specific group.

As a rule, you should avoid using Deny permissions as part of any custom security filter, because this can lead to confusion with accounts that are members of groups with conflicting filter settings. For example, if a user is a member of a group that has Deny set in the filter and is also a member of a group that is allowed to apply the policy, the Deny setting will always win. This can be difficult to troubleshoot, particularly if nested group memberships are involved.

Be very careful when changing permissions on GPOs. If you create a very restricted GPO and apply a security filter to it, be sure to also put tight controls on who can modify the GPO and how. If for some reason that security filter were removed (resulting in no security filters), the restrictive GPO could be applied to every user or computer in the domain.

Using VBScript

First, we have to find the target GPO. We use a `GPMSearchCriteria` object to find the GPO that is equal to the display name of the GPO specified in the configuration section. We use an `if else` conditional statement to ensure that only one GPO is returned. If none or more than one were returned, we abort the script. If only one GPO is returned, we create two `GPM.CreatePermission` objects for the group we want to add as a security filter and for the `Authenticated Users` group. Next, we use the `GPMGPO.GetSecurityInfo` to retrieve the current ACL on the GPO. Finally, we add the permission to the ACL for the group we want as the new security filter, and we remove the permission for `Authenticated Users`.

See Also

MSDN: GPM.CreatePermission and MSDN: GPMGPO.GetSecurityInfo

10.18 Delegating Administration of GPOs

Problem

You want to delegate permissions on GPOs and related tasks within Active Directory.

Solution

Using a graphical user interface

To delegate the ability to create GPOs, do the following:

1. Open the Group Policy Management Console.
2. Navigate to the Group Policy Objects node and click on the Delegation tab.
3. To add permissions for a new user or group to create GPOs, click Add. Use the object picker to select the object you want and click OK.

To delegate permissions on a particular GPO, follow these steps:

1. Open the Group Policy Management Console.
2. Navigate to the GPO that you want to delegate permissions for and click on the Delegation tab.
3. To add permissions for a new user or group, click Add. Use the object picker to select the object you want and click OK.
4. In the Permissions drop-down box, select "Read, Edit Settings" or "Edit Settings, Delete, and Modify Security," then click OK.

To delegate Group Policy–related tasks on a particular site, domain, or OU, do the following:

1. Open the Group Policy Management Console.
2. Navigate to the site, domain, or OU that you want to delegate permissions for and click on the Delegation tab.
3. In the Permission drop-down, select Link GPOs, Perform Group Policy Modeling Analyses, or Read Group Policy Results Data.
4. To add permissions for a new user or group, click Add. Use the object picker to select the object you want and click OK.
5. In the Permissions drop-down box, select "This container only" or "This container and all child containers," then click OK.

Discussion

In addition to using Active Directory users and groups to control how GPOs are applied within a site, domain, or OU, you can also use ACLs to delegate permissions over GPOs to allow you to decentralize the administration of them in your organization.

You can delegate the ability to do the following:

- Create GPOs
- Manage the settings of an individual GPO
- Link GPOs to a site, domain, or OU
- Create WMI filters
- Manage an individual WMI filter

While the ability to delegate administration in this manner is quite simple to implement, it's critical that you fully understand the security implications that it carries with it. For example, the ability to link GPOs to an entire site or domain should be granted only to highly trusted administrators since it can have far-reaching implications for the performance and behavior of your network.

See Also

MS KB 250842 (Troubleshooting Group Policy application problems) and Recipe 10.17 for more on using security filtering to control GPO behavior

10.19 Importing a Security Template

Problem

You want to import a security template into a GPO.

Solution

Using a graphical user interface

1. Open the GPMC snap-in.
2. In the left pane, expand the Forest container, expand the Domains container, browse to the domain of the GPO you want to target, and expand the Group Policy Objects container.
3. Right-click on the target GPO and select Edit.
4. Navigate to Computer Configuration → Windows Settings.
5. Right-click on Security Settings and select Import Policy.
6. Browse to the template you want to import and click Open.

Discussion

Rather than manually configuring the plethora of security settings available in Windows 2000 and Windows Server 2003, you can use a template.

Some common security templates include the following:

compatws.inf
Used for workstations that need backward compatibility with legacy applications or networks.

hisec*.inf
Used for a high-security configuration. *hisecdc.inf* corresponds to a domain controller. *hisecws.inf* is for a secure workstation or member server.

secure*.inf
Used for situations in which you want a secure configuration, but the settings in the *hisec*.inf* templates are a bit over-the-top. Sufficient for most environments.

It's important to test the settings created by these templates before deploying them in a production network, since it may be necessary to modify one or more to meet the needs of your unique environment.

> To configure security settings for a local computer or for computers not configured in an Active Directory domain, you can use the secedit command-line utility with the /configure switch.

See Also

Windows Server 2003 Security Guide (*http://www.microsoft.com/technet/security/prodtech/windowsserver2003/w2003hg/sgch00.mspx*), MS KB 216735 (Methods Used to Apply Security Settings Throughout an Enterprise), MS KB 816297 (How to Define Security Templates by Using the Security Templates Snap-in in Windows Server 2003), and MS KB 816585 (How to Apply Predefined Security Templates in Windows Server 2003)

10.20 Creating a WMI Filter

> WMI filters can be configured only on a Windows Server 2003 domain controller, and they will apply only to Windows Server 2003– and Windows XP–based clients.

Problem

You want to create a WMI filter.

Solution

Using a graphical user interface

1. Open the GPMC snap-in.
2. In the left pane, expand the Forest container, expand the Domains container, browse to the target domain, and click the WMI Filters container.
3. Right-click on the WMI Filters container and select New.
4. Enter a name and description for the filter.
5. Click the Add button.
6. Select the appropriate namespace, enter a WQL query, and click OK.
7. Repeat steps 5 and 6 for as many queries as you need to add.
8. Click the Save button.

Using VBScript

At the time of publication of this book, there were no GPM methods available for creating WMI filters.

Discussion

WMI filters are new in Windows Server 2003 and provide another way to filter how GPOs are applied to clients. WMI filters live in Active Directory as objects under the WMIPolicy container within the System container for a domain. A WMI filter consists of a WMI Query Language (WQL) query that when linked to a GPO will be run against all clients that the GPO applies to. If the WQL returns a true value (that is, it returns nonempty results from the WQL query), the GPO will continue to process. If the WQL query returns false (nothing is returned from the query), the GPO will not be processed.

The great thing about WMI filters is that the vast amount of information that is available in WMI on a client becomes available to filter GPOs. You can query against CPU, memory, disk space, hotfixes installed, service packs installed, applications installed, running processes, and the list goes on and on.

For example, if you want to create a GPO that applies only to computers that are running Windows XP Professional, it would have been really difficult to accomplish under Windows 2000 Active Directory. You would have either needed to create a security group that contained all of those computers as members (and apply a security filter) or to move all of those workstations to a particular OU. With a WMI filter, this becomes trivial to create. (Bear in mind, however, that there is client performance overhead associated with WMI queries, as each computer will need to process the WMI query to determine whether a particular GPO should or should not be applied.) Here is a sample WQL query that would return true when run on a Windows XP Professional workstation:

```
select * from Win32_OperatingSystem
  where Caption = "Microsoft Windows XP Professional"
```

See Also

Recipe 10.21 for applying a WMI filter to a GPO and MSDN: Querying with WQL

10.21 Applying a WMI Filter to a GPO

 WMI filters can be configured only on a Windows Server 2003 domain controller, and they will apply only to Windows Server 2003– and Windows XP–based clients.

Problem

You want to apply a WMI filter to a GPO.

Solution

Using a graphical user interface

1. Open the GPMC snap-in.
2. In the left pane, expand the Forest container, expand the Domains container, browse to the domain of the GPO you want to target, and expand the Group Policy Objects container.
3. Single-click on the target GPO.
4. At the bottom of the righthand pane, you can select from the list of WMI filters.
5. After you've selected the WMI filter, click Yes to confirm.

Using VBScript

```
' This code links an existing WMI filter with a GPO.
' ------ SCRIPT CONFIGURATION ------
strGPO        = "<GPOName>"        ' e.g. "Sales GPO"
strDomain     = "<DomainDNSName>"  ' e.g. "rallencorp.com"

' e.g. {D715559A-7965-45A6-864D-AEBDD9934415}
strWMIFilterID = "<WMIFilterID>"
' ------ END CONFIGURATION ---------

set objGPM = CreateObject("GPMgmt.GPM")
set objGPMConstants = objGPM.GetConstants( )

' Initialize the Domain object
set objGPMDomain = objGPM.GetDomain(strDomain, "", objGPMConstants.UseAnyDC)
```

```
' Find the GPO
set objGPMSearchCriteria = objGPM.CreateSearchCriteria
objGPMSearchCriteria.Add objGPMConstants.SearchPropertyGPODisplayName, _
                         objGPMConstants.SearchOpEquals, _
                         cstr(strGPO)
set objGPOList = objGPMDomain.SearchGPOs(objGPMSearchCriteria)
if objGPOList.Count = 0 then
   WScript.Echo "Did not find GPO: " & strGPO
   WScript.Echo "Exiting."
   WScript.Quit
elseif objGPOList.Count > 1 then
   WScript.Echo "Found more than one matching GPO. Count: " & _
                objGPOList.Count
   WScript.Echo "Exiting."
   WScript.Quit
else
   WScript.Echo "Found GPO: " & objGPOList.Item(1).DisplayName
end if

on error resume next

' Retrieve the WMI filter
strWMIFilter = "MSFT_SomFilter.Domain=""" & _
               strDomain & """,ID=""" & _
               strWMIFilterID & """"
set objWMIFilter = objGPMDomain.GetWMIFilter(strWMIFilter)
if Err.Number <> 0 then
   WScript.Echo "Did not find WMI Filter: " & strWMIFilterID
   WScript.Echo "Exiting."
   WScript.Quit
else
   WScript.Echo "Found WMI Filter: " & objWMIFilter.Name
end if

' Link the filter and print the result
objGPOList.Item(1).SetWMIFilter(objWMIFilter)
if Err.Number <> 0 then
   WScript.Echo "Failed to set WMI filter."
   WScript.Echo "Error: " & err.description
else
   WScript.Echo "Set WMI filter successfully."
end if
```

Discussion

You can link only one WMI filter to a GPO at any time. This is not an overly restrictive limitation, though, because you can still link more than one GPO to a site, domain, or OU. If you need multiple WMI filters to apply to a GPO, copy the GPO and apply a different WMI filter to it. See Recipe 10.20 for more information on WMI filters.

Keep in mind that requiring your clients to process multiple WMI filters will have an impact on their performance at logon time and during the GPO background refresh process.

Using VBScript

We use a `GPMSearchCriteria` object to find the GPO that is equal to the display name of the GPO specified in the configuration section. We use an `if else` conditional statement to ensure that only one GPO is returned. If no GPOs are returned or if more than one is returned, we abort the script. If only one GPO is returned, we call `GPMDomain.GetWMIFilter` to instantiate a `GPMWMIFilter` object based on the WMI filter GUID specified in the configuration section. (If you need to programmatically search for the WMI filter ID, you can use the `GPMDomain.SearchWMIFilters` method.) After we retrieve the `GPMWMIFilter` object, we call the `GPMGPO.SetWMIFilter` method to set the filter for the GPO.

See Also

MSDN: GPMDomain.GetWMIFilter and MSDN: GPMGPO.SetWMIFilter

10.22 Configuring Loopback Processing for a GPO

Problem

You want to configure a GPO to use loopback processing that will enforce consistent computer settings regardless of which user logs on to a computer.

Solution

Using a graphical user interface

1. Open the GPMC snap-in.
2. Navigate to the GPO that you want to configure. Right-click on the GPO and select Edit Settings.
3. Navigate to Computer Configuration → System → Group Policy. Double-click on "User Group Policy loopback processing mode." Select the radio button next to Enabled.
4. In the Mode drop-down box, select either Merge or Replace. (See the "Discussion" for more information on these two options.)
5. Click OK.

Discussion

GPOs are applied to user/computer combinations on an Active Directory network based on the site, domain, and OU that the user and computer objects belong to. If the user and computer are located in two separate locations, the user will receive the GPOs that apply to the user's container combined with those that apply to the computer's container. However, there may be cases where you want a user to receive Group Policy based solely on the location of the computer objects. In this case, you will enable loopback processing in one of two modes:

Merge Mode
> In this mode, any GPOs that are associated with the user will be applied first. The GPOs associated with the computer object will be applied after the GPOs associated with the user object, thereby giving them a higher precedence than the user GPOs. In this case, the user will still receive any GPO settings associated with his user object, but settings configured for the computer will override in the case of any conflicts.

Replace Mode
> In this mode, only the list of GPOs that apply to the computer object will be applied.

See Also

MS KB 231287 (Loopback Processing of Group Policy)

10.23 Backing Up a GPO

Problem

You want to back up a GPO.

Solution

Using a graphical user interface

1. Open the GPMC snap-in.
2. In the left pane, expand the Forest container, expand the Domains container, browse to the domain of the GPO you want to back up, and expand the Group Policy Objects container.
3. Right-click on the GPO you want to back up and select Back Up.
4. For Location, enter the folder path to store the backup files.
5. For Description, enter a descriptive name for the backup.
6. Click the Back Up button.

7. You will see a progress bar and status message that indicates if the backup was successful.

8. Click OK to exit.

Using a command-line interface

```
> backupgpo.wsf "<GPOName>" "<BackupFolder>" /comment:"<BackupComment>"
```

Using VBScript

```
' This code backs up a GPO to the specified backup location.
' ------ SCRIPT CONFIGURATION ------
strGPO      = "<GPOName>"        ' e.g. "Default Domain Policy"
strDomain   = "<DomainDNSName>"  ' e.g. "rallencorp.com"
strLocation = "<BackupFolder>"   ' e.g. "c:\GPMC Backups"
strComment  = "<BackupComment>"  ' e.g. "Default Domain Policy Weekly"
' ------ END CONFIGURATION ---------

set objGPM = CreateObject("GPMgmt.GPM")
set objGPMConstants = objGPM.GetConstants( )

' Initialize the Domain object
set objGPMDomain = objGPM.GetDomain(strDomain, "", objGPMConstants.UseAnyDC)

' Find the GPO you want to back up
set objGPMSearchCriteria = objGPM.CreateSearchCriteria
objGPMSearchCriteria.Add objGPMConstants.SearchPropertyGPODisplayName, _
                         objGPMConstants.SearchOpEquals, cstr(strGPO)
set objGPOList = objGPMDomain.SearchGPOs(objGPMSearchCriteria)
if objGPOList.Count = 0 then
   WScript.Echo "Did not find GPO: " & strGPO
   WScript.Echo "Exiting."
   WScript.Quit
elseif objGPOList.Count > 1 then
   WScript.Echo "Found more than one matching GPO. Count: " & _
                objGPOList.Count
   WScript.Echo "Exiting."
   WScript.Quit
else
   WScript.Echo "Found GPO: " & objGPOList.Item(1).DisplayName
End if

' Kick off the backup
On Error Resume Next
set objGPMResult = objGPOList.Item(1).Backup(strLocation, strComment)
' Call the OverallStatus method on the GPMResult.
' This will throw an exception if there were any
' errors during the actual operation.
objGPMResult.OverallStatus( )
if objGPMResult.Status.Count > 0 then
   WScript.Echo "Status messages:" & objGPMResult.Status.Count
   for i = 1 to objGPMResult.Status.Count
   WScript.Echo objGPMResult.Status.Item(i).Message
```

```
      next
      WScript.Echo strXML
   end if

   ' Print the results
   if Err.Number <> 0 then
      WScript.Echo "The backup failed."
      WScript.Echo "Attempted to backup GPO '" & strGPO & "' to location " & strLocation
      WScript.Echo "Error: " & err.description
   else
      set objGPMBackup = objGPMResult.Result
      WScript.Echo "Backup completed successfully."
      WScript.Echo "GPO ID: "  & objGPMBackup.GPOID
      WScript.Echo "Timestamp: " & objGPMBackup.TimeStamp
      WScript.Echo "Backup ID: " & objGPMBackup.ID
   end if
```

Discussion

The GPMC provides a way to back up individual (or all) GPOs. A GPO backup consists of a set of folders and files that catalog the GPO settings, filters and links, and is created in the backup location you specify. You can back up a GPO to a local drive or over the network to a file server. Restoring a GPO is just as easy and is described in Recipe 10.24.

Prior to GPMC, the only way to back up GPOs was by backing up the System State on a domain controller. The System State includes Active Directory and the *SYSVOL* share (both components are needed to completely back up a GPO). To restore a GPO using this method, you'd have to boot into DS Restore mode and perform an authoritative restore of the GPO(s) you were interested in. Needless to say, the GPMC method is significantly easier.

A good practice is to back up your GPO backups. Since all the backup information is captured in a series of files, you can back up that information to media, which provides two levels of restore capability. You could restore the last backup taken, which could be stored on a domain controller or file server, or you could go to tape and restore a previous version.

In the folder you specify to store the GPO backups is a list of folders that have GUIDs for names. This does not make it very easy to distinguish which backups are for which GPOs. A quick way to find that out is to use the *querybackuplocation.wsf* script. This will list each of the folder GUID names and the corresponding GPO it is for:

```
> querybackuplocation.wsf "c:\gpmc backups"
```

Using VBScript

We use a GPMSearchCriteria object to find the GPO that is equal to the display name of the GPO specified in the configuration section. We use an if else conditional statement to ensure that only one GPO is returned. If none or more than one is returned, we abort the script. If only one is returned, we call the GPMGPO.Backup method to back up the GPO. The first parameter is the directory to store the GPO backup files, and the second parameter is a comment that can be stored with the backup. This comment may come in handy later for doing searches against the backups on a server, so you may want to think about what to put for it.

See Also

Recipe 10.24 for restoring a GPO and MSDN: GPMGPO.Backup

10.24 Restoring a GPO

Problem

You want to restore a GPO.

Solution

Using a graphical user interface

1. Open the GPMC snap-in.
2. In the left pane, expand the Forest container, expand the Domains container, browse to the domain of the GPO you want to back up, and expand the Group Policy Objects container.
3. Right-click on the GPO you want to restore, and select "Restore from Backup."
4. Click Next.
5. Select the backup folder location and click Next.
6. Select the backup you want to restore and click Next.
7. Click Finish.
8. You will see the restore status window. After it completes, click OK to close the window.

Using a command-line interface

```
> restoregpo.wsf "<BackupFolder>" "<GPOName>"
```

Using VBScript

```
' This code restores a GPO from a backup.
' ------ SCRIPT CONFIGURATION ------
strGPO      = "<GPOName>"        ' e.g. "Sales Users GPO"
strDomain   = "<DomainDNSName>"  ' e.g. "rallencorp.com"
strLocation = "<BackupFolder>"   ' e.g. "c:\GPMC Backups"
strBackupID = "<BackupGUID>"     ' e.g. "{85CA37AC-0DB3-442B-98E8-537291D26ED3}"
' ------ END CONFIGURATION ---------
```

```
set objGPM = CreateObject("GPMgmt.GPM")
set objGPMConstants = objGPM.GetConstants( )

' Initialize the Domain object
set objGPMDomain = objGPM.GetDomain(strDomain, "", objGPMConstants.UseAnyDC)

' Make sure backup location and ID are valid
set objGPMBackupDir = objGPM.GetBackupDir(strLocation)
set objGPMBackup = objGPMBackupDir.GetBackup(strBackupID)
WScript.Echo "Backup found:"
WScript.Echo "   ID: " & objGPMBackup.ID
WScript.Echo "   Timestamp: " & objGPMBackup.TimeStamp
WScript.Echo "   GPO ID: " & objGPMBackup.GPOID
WScript.Echo "   GPO Name: " & objGPMBackup.GPODisplayName
WScript.Echo "   Comment: " & objGPMBackup.Comment
WScript.Echo

' Perform restore
set objGPMResult = objGPMDomain.RestoreGPO(objGPMBackup, _
                                        objGPMConstants.DoNotValidateDC)
' This will throw an exception if there were any errors
' during the actual operation.
on error resume next
objGPMResult.OverallStatus( )
if objGPMResult.Status.Count > 0 then
    WScript.Echo "Status message(s): " & objGPMResult.Status.Count
    for i = 1 to objGPMResult.Status.Count
        WScript.Echo objGPMResult.Status.Item(i).Message
    next
    WScript.Echo vbCrLf
end if

' Print result
if Err.Number <> 0 then
    WScript.Echo "Error restoring GPO " & objGPMBackup.GPODisplayName
    WScript.Echo "Error: " & Err.Description
else
    WScript.Echo "Restore successful."
    WScript.Echo "GPO '" & objGPMBackup.GPODisplayName & _
                "' has been restored."
end if
```

Discussion

To restore a GPO using GPMC, you first need a valid backup of the GPO. The procedure for backing up a GPO is described in Recipe 10.23. You can then restore the GPO, even if the GPO has been deleted. To restore a deleted GPO, use the following steps:

1. Right-click on the Group Policy Objects container in the target domain and select Manage Backups.

2. Highlight the GPO you want to restore and click the Restore button

3. Click Yes to confirm.

4. Click OK after the restore completes.

If you don't have a valid backup of the GPO, but you do have another GPO that is identical or similar to the one you want to restore (perhaps in another forest), you can copy that GPO to replace the one you want to restore.

Keep in mind that restoring a GPO does not restore the links that were associated with that GPO, since the gpLink attribute is configured on the container that the GPO was linked to and not the container itself. See Recipe 10.3 for more on copying GPOs.

Using VBScript

To restore a GPO, ypu have to first get a handle to the backup you are going to restore from. This is done by instantiating an object to the backup location with GPM.GetBackupDir and then calling GPMBackupDir.GetBackup with the GUID of the backup to be restored. To programmatically search for the backup ID, use the GPMBackup.SearchBackups method to find the most recent backup or a backup with a particular display name.

After obtaining a GPMBackup object, call the GPMDomain.RestoreGPO method. The first parameter is the GPMBackup object that represents the backup to restore. The second parameter is a validation flag—use the constant that causes the restore to not be validated against a domain controller.

See Also

Recipe 10.3 for copying a GPO, Recipe 10.23 for backing up a GPO, and MSDN: GPMDomain.RestoreGPO

10.25 Simulating the RSoP

Problem

You want to simulate the Resultant Set of Policies (RSoP) based on OU, site, and security group membership. This is also referred to as Group Policy Modeling.

Solution

This must be run against a Windows Server 2003 domain controller.

Using a graphical user interface

1. Open the GPMC snap-in.

2. In the left pane, right-click Group Policy Modeling and select Group Policy Modeling Wizard.

3. Select a domain controller to process the query and click Next.

4. Under User Information and/or Computer Information, either seclect the container you want to simulate to contain the user or computer, or select a specific user or computer account, and click Next.

5. Select a site if necessary, and specify whether you wish to simulate a slow link or loopback processing, and then click Next.

6. If you selected a target user container or user account in step 4, you will be presented with an option to simulate different group membership. Click Next when you are done.

7. If you selected a target computer container or computer account in step 4, you will be presented with an option to simulate different group membership. Click Next when you are done.

8. If you selected a target user container or user account in step 4, you will be presented with an option to simulate any additional WMI filters. Click Next when you are done.

9. If you selected a target computer container or computer account in step 4, you will be presented with an option to simulate any additional WMI filters. Click Next when you are done.

10. Click Next to start the simulation.

11. Click Finish.

12. In the right pane of the GPMC window, the results of the simulation will be displayed.

Discussion

With GPMC, you can simulate the RSoP based on user-defined OU, site, group, and domain membership. This is very powerful because it allows you to create one or more GPOs, simulate them being applied to a user and computer, and determine whether any changes are necessary before deployment.

See Also

Recipe 10.26 for viewing the RSoP

10.26 Viewing the RSoP

Problem

You want to view the actual RSoP for a user and computer. This is a great tool for determining if policies are being applied correctly on a client.

Solution

Using a graphical user interface

The RSoP snap-in is available only on Windows Server 2003 and Windows XP.

Open the RSoP snap-in by running *rsop.msc* from the command line. This will cause the RSoP snap-in to evaluate the group policies for the target computer and pop open a MMC console so that you can browse the applied settings.

You can target a different computer by right-clicking the top of the tree in the left pane and selecting Change Query. You will then be prompted for the name of the computer to query.

You can also gather this information by using the Group Policy Results Wizard in the GPMC.

Using a command-line interface

```
> gpresult
```

With the Windows Server 2003 version of *gpresult*, you can specify a /S option and the name of a computer to target, which allows you to run the command remotely. With Windows 2000, there is a /S option, but it enables super-verbose mode. There is no way to target another computer with the Windows 2000 version. For a complete list of options with either version, run gpresult /? from a command line.

Discussion

If you implement more than a few GPOs, it can get confusing as to what settings will apply to users. To address this problem, you can query the resultant set of policy on a client to determine what settings have been applied.

The registry on the target computer is another source of information. You can view the list of policies that were applied to the computer by viewing the subkeys under this key:

```
HKEY_CURRENT_USER\Software\Microsoft\Windows\CurrentVersion\Group Policy\History
```

The settings that were applied are not stored in the registry, but you can obtain the GPO name, distinguished name, SYSVOL location, version, and where the GPO is linked.

See Also

Recipe 10.25 for simulating the RSoP

10.27 Refreshing GPO Settings on a Computer

Problem

You've made some changes to a GPO and want to apply them to a computer by refreshing the group policies for the computer.

Solution

Using a command-line interface

On Windows Server 2003 or Windows XP, use this command:

```
> gpupdate [/target:{Computer | User}]
```

On Windows 2000, use this command:

```
> secedit /refreshpolicy [machine_policy | user_policy]
```

Discussion

By default, Group Policy settings will refresh automatically every 5 minutes on a domain controller and every 90 minutes on clients and member servers. To force GPO settings to refresh sooner than that, you will need to run the *gpupdate* utility on the client computer. The new *gpupdate* command is a much-needed improvement over the older *secedit* utility that was used to refresh Group Policy in Windows 2000. With *gpupdate*, you can force all settings to be applied with the /force option (the default is only changed settings). You can apply the computer or user settings of GPOs using the /target option, and you can force a logoff or reboot after the settings have been applied using the /logoff and /boot options.

See Also

MS KB 298444 (A Description of the Group Policy Update Utility)

10.28 Restoring a Default GPO

Problem

You've made changes to the Default Domain Security Policy, Default Domain Controller Security Policy, or both, and now want to reset them to their original configuration.

Solution

Using a command-line interface

The following command would replace both the Default Domain Security Policy and Default Domain Controller Security Policy on a Windows Server 2003 domain controller. You can specify Domain or DC instead of Both, to only restore one or the other:

```
> dcgpofix /target:Both
```

Note that this must be run from a domain controller in the target domain where you want to reset the GPO.

To recreate the default GPOs in a Windows 2000 domain, download the Windows 2000 Default Group Policy Restore Tool (*recreatedefpol.exe*) from *http://www. microsoft.com/downloads/details.aspx?FamilyID=b5b685ae-b7dd-4bb5-ab2a-976d6873129d&DisplayLang=en*.

Discussion

If you've made changes to the default GPOs in Windows Server 2003 and would like to revert back to the original settings, the *dcgpofix* utility is your solution. *dcgpofix* works with a particular version of the schema. If the version it expects to be current is different from what is in Active Directory, it will not restore the GPOs. You can work around this by using the /ignoreschema switch, which will restore the GPO according to the version *dcgpofix* thinks is current. The only time you might experience this issue is if you install a service pack on a domain controller (*dc1*) that extends the schema but these changes have not yet replicated to a second domain controller (*dc2*). If you try to run *dcgpofix* from *dc2*, you will receive the error since a new version of the schema and the *dcgpofix* utility was installed on *dc1*.

In Windows 2000, the *recreatedefpols.exe* utility will instruct you to log out after running the utility, and then log back on to complete the process using the administrative account that should be added as an EFS Recovery Agent.

## CHAPTER 11

Schema

11.0 Introduction

The Active Directory schema contains the blueprint for how objects are structured and secured, what data they can contain, and even how they can be viewed. Having a good understanding of the schema is paramount for any Active Directory administrator. Understanding key concepts, such as class inheritance, class types, attribute syntax, and attribute indexing options is critical to being able to adequately design an Active Directory infrastructure and should be considered mandatory for any developer that is writing applications or automation scripts that utilize Active Directory.

If you are one of the lucky few who is designated as a schema administrator (i.e., a member of the *Schema Admins* group), then the importance of the schema is already well known to you. This chapter serves as a guide to accomplishing many of the day-to-day tasks of schema administrators. For a more in-depth discussion of the schema, we suggest reading Chapter 4 of *Active Directory*, Third Edition, by Joe Richards et al. (O'Reilly).

The Anatomy of Schema Objects

An interesting feature of Active Directory not common among other LDAP implementations is that the schema is stored within Active Directory itself as a set of objects. This means that you can use similar interfaces and programs to manage the schema as you would any other type of object.

All schema objects are stored in the Schema container (for example, cn=schema,cn=configuration,<ForestRootDN>). The schema is comprised of two classes of objects, classSchema and attributeSchema. Unsurprisingly, the classSchema objects define classes and attributeSchema objects define attributes. The Schema container contains a third type of object called subSchema, also known as the abstract schema, which is defined in the LDAP version 3 specification (RFC 2251). There is only a single subSchema object in the Schema container, named cn=Aggregate, and it contains a summary of the entire schema.

Tables 11-1 and 11-2 contain useful attributes of classSchema objects and attributeSchema objects, respectively.

Table 11-1. Attributes of classSchema objects

Attribute	Description
adminDescription	Description of the class.
auxiliaryClass	Multivalued attribute containing any auxiliary classes defined for the class.
cn	Relative distinguished name of the class.
defaultHidingValue	Boolean that determines whether objects of this class are hidden by default in administrative GUIs.
defaultSecurityDescriptor	Default security descriptor applied to objects of this class.
governsID	OID for the class.
isDefunct	Boolean that indicates whether the class is defunct (i.e., deactivated).
lDAPDisplayName	Name used when referencing the class in searches or when instantiating or modifying objects of this class.
mayContain	Multivalued attribute that contains a list of attributes that can be optionally set on the class.
mustContain	Multivalued attribute that contains a list of attributes that must be set on the class.
objectClassCategory	Integer representing the class's type. Can be one of 1 (structural), 2 (abstract), 3 (auxiliary), or 0 (88).
possibleInferiors	Multivalued list of other object classes this object can contain.
possSuperiors	Multivalued list of object classes this object can be subordinate to.
rDNAttID	Naming attribute (i.e., RDN) of instances of the class.
schemaIDGUID	GUID of the class.
showInAdvancedViewOnly	Boolean that indicates whether instances of this class should be shown only in Advanced mode in the administrative GUIs.
subClassOf	Parent class.
systemAuxiliaryClass	Multivalued attribute containing any auxiliary classes defined for the class. This can be modified only internally by Active Directory.
systemFlags	Integer representing additional properties of the class.
systemMayContain	Multivalued attribute that contains a list of attributes that can be optionally set on the class. This can be modified only internally by Active Directory.
systemMustContain	Multivalued attribute that contains a list of attributes that must be set on the class. This can be modified only internally by Active Directory.
systemPossSuperiors	Multivalued list of object classes this object can be subordinate to. This can be modified only internally by Active Directory.

Table 11-2. Attributes of attributeSchema objects

Attribute	Description
adminDescription	Description of the attribute.
attributeID	OID for the attribute.
attributeSecurityGUID	GUID of the property set (if any) that an attribute is a member of.
attributeSyntax	OID representing the syntax of the attribute. This is used in conjunction with oMSyntax to define a unique syntax.
cn	Relative distinguished name of the attribute.
isDefunct	Boolean that indicates if the attribute is defunct (i.e., deactivated).
isMemberOfPartialAttributeSet	Boolean that indicates if the attribute is a member of the partial attribute set (i.e., the global catalog).
isSingleValued	Boolean that indicates whether the attribute is single-valued or multivalued.
linkID	If this is populated, it will contain an integer that represents a link (either forward or backward) to another attribute.
lDAPDisplayName	Name used when referencing the attribute in searches or when populating it on objects. Note that this value may not be the same as cn.
oMSyntax	An integer representing the OSI Abstract Data Manipulation (OM) type of the attribute. This is used in conjunction with attributeSyntax to determine a unique syntax for the attribute.
schemaIDGUID	GUID of the attribute.
searchFlags	Integer representing special properties related to searching with the attribute. This includes how the attribute is indexed and if it is used in ANR searches.
systemFlags	Integer representing additional properties of the attribute.

11.1 Registering the Active Directory Schema MMC Snap-in

Problem

You want to use the Active Directory Schema MMC snap-in for the first time on an administrative computer.

Solution

Before you can use the Active Directory Schema MMC snap-in, you have to register the DLL associated with it. This can be done with the *regsvr32* utility using the following command:

```
> regsvr32 schmmgmt.dll
```

If the command is successful, you'll see the following message:

```
DllRegisterServer in schmmgmt.dll succeeded.
```

Discussion

Most of the Active Directory MMC snap-ins do not require that you manually register the associated DLL. Microsoft requires this with the Active Directory Schema snap-in, however, due to the sensitive nature of modifying the schema. This doesn't actually do much to prevent users from using it, but at least it isn't available by default. And regardless, only members of the *Schema Admins* group have permission to modify the schema anyway, so making this snap-in available should not pose much of a risk.

The *schmmgmt.dll* file is installed as part of the *adminpak.msi* Administrative Tools installer, or else it is installed by default on a domain controller when it is first promoted. If you want to use the Schema snap-in on a nondomain controller machine and you have not installed the *adminpak.msi* package, you'll need to specify the full path to *schmmgmt.dll* when using *regsvr32*. This can be found in the \i386 directory of a Windows Server CD.

See Also

MS KB 320337 (How to Manage the Active Directory Schema in Windows 2000) and MS KB 326310 (How to Manage the Active Directory Schema in Windows Server 2003 Enterprise Edition)

11.2   Enabling Schema Updates

 This is necessary only when the Schema FSMO role owner is running Windows 2000.

Problem

You want to enable schema modifications on the Schema FSMO. This is a necessary first step before you can extend the schema.

Solution

Using a graphical user interface

1. Open the Active Directory Schema snap-in.
2. Click on Active Directory Schema in the left pane.
3. Right-click on Active Directory Schema and select Operations Master.
4. Check the box beside "Allow schema modifications."
5. Click OK.

Using a command-line interface

To enable modifications to the schema, use the following command:

```
> reg add HKEY_LOCAL_MACHINE\System\CurrentControlSet\Services\NTDS\Parameters /t
REG_DWORD /v "Schema Update Allowed" /d 1
```

To disable modifications to the schema, use the following command:

```
> reg delete HKEY_LOCAL_MACHINE\System\CurrentControlSet\Services\NTDS\Parameters /v
"Schema Update Allowed" /f
```

Using VBScript

```
' This code enables or disables schema mods on Schema FSMO.
' ------ SCRIPT CONFIGURATION -----.
' TRUE to enable schema mods and FALSE to disable
boolSetReg  = TRUE

' Name of the Schema FSMO or "." to run locally
strDC = "<SchemaFSMOName>"
' ------ END CONFIGURATION ---------

const HKEY_LOCAL_MACHINE = &H80000002
set objReg = GetObject("winmgmts:\\" & strDC & "\root\default:StdRegProv")
strKeyPath  = "System\CurrentControlSet\Services\NTDS\Parameters"
strValueName = "Schema Update Allowed"

if boolSetReg = TRUE then
   strValue = 1
   intRC = objReg.SetDWORDValue(HKEY_LOCAL_MACHINE,strKeyPath, _
                               strValueName,strValue)
   if intRC > 0 then
      WScript.Echo "Error occurred: " & intRC
   else
      WScript.Echo strValueName & " value set to " & strValue
   end if
else
   intRC = objReg.DeleteValue(HKEY_LOCAL_MACHINE,strKeyPath,strValueName)
   if intRC > 0 then
      WScript.Echo "Error occurred: " & intRC
   else
      WScript.Echo strValueName & " value deleted"
   end if
end if
```

Discussion

When the Schema FSMO role owner is running Windows 2000, you must explicitly enable schema modifications on the server before extending the schema. To enable this, you need to create a key value called Schema Update Allowed with a value of 1 under the following key:

```
HKEY_LOCAL_MACHINE\System\CurrentControlSet\Services\NTDS\Parameters
```

To disable schema modifications, set the value to 0 or delete it from the registry.

 This is no longer necessary when the Schema FSMO owner is running Windows Server 2003. Microsoft removed this registry hack as a requirement for extending the schema.

See Also

MS KB 285172 (Schema Updates Require Write Access to Schema in Active Directory)

11.3   Generating an OID to Use for a New Class or Attribute

Problem

You want to generate an OID to use with a new class or attribute that you intend to add to the schema.

Solution

To implement schema extensions for production use, you should use an OID from your company or organization's OID branch. To determine if your company already has an assigned OID, see these sites:

- *http://www.iana.org/assignments/enterprise-numbers*
- *http://www.alvestrand.no/objectid/*

If your organization does not have an assigned OID, go to your country's national registry to request one. The list of registries can be found at the following site: *http://www.iso.ch/iso/en/aboutiso/isomembers/index.html*.

Once you have a base OID, you can create branches from that OID however you want. For example, if you had a base OID of 1.2.3.4, you could start new class OIDs under 1.2.3.4.1 and new attributes under 1.2.3.4.2. In that case, the first class OID you would create would be 1.2.3.4.1.1 and the first attribute OID would be 1.2.3.4.2.1.

Discussion

An OID is nothing more than a string of numbers separated by periods (.). OIDs were initially defined by the ITU-T in X.208 and have been used to uniquely identify a variety of things including SNMP MIB objects and LDAP schema classes and attributes. OIDs are hierarchical, and the national registries are responsible for managing and assigning OID branches.

See Also

Recipe 11.2 for more on enabling schema updates and Recipe 11.4 for more on generating a GUID to use for a new class or attribute

11.4 Generating a GUID to Use for a New Class or Attribute

Problem

You want to generate a GUID to use for the schemaIDGUID attribute of a new class or attribute you intend to add to the schema.

Solution

There are several ways to go about generating a GUID. If you do not specify the schemaIDGUID when initially creating a class or attribute, one will automatically be generated for you. So you could add the class or attribute to the schema of a test forest and then use the schemaIDGUID that was generated in that forest.

You can also programmatically generate a GUID using Perl, VB, C++, or C#, but you cannot do so natively within VBScript. The Windows API supports a CoCreateGUID method that can be used to generate a GUID. If you are stuck with VBScript, you can wrap the CoCreateGUID method in an ActiveX DLL using VB and then use that DLL from within VBScript.

Finally, you can use a tool such as *uuidgen.exe*, which is available in the Microsoft Platform SDK, to generate GUIDs. *uuidgen* doesn't require any parameters (although there are a few options that can be seen by running uuidgen -h), and it can generate as many GUIDs as you need.

If you intend to use LDIF files for extending the schema (highly recommended), then you need to encode any GUIDs in base64 notation. This is necessary because GUIDs are stored as octet strings (binary data) in Active Directory. The LDIF specification requires any binary data to be encoded in base64. Again, VBScript does not support base64 encoding natively, but other languages like Perl have modules available that do. Here is a sample Perl script that uses the *uuidgen* utility to generate a GUID, the Win32::Lanman module to convert the GUID to binary, and the MIME::Base64 module to encode it:

```
#!perl
use MIME::Base64;
use Win32::Lanman;

# Get the string GUID
my $str_guid = `uuidgen.exe`;
chomp $str_guid;
```

```
# Convert to a binary GUID
my $bin_guid = Win32::Lanman::StringToGuid($str_guid);

# Base64 encode binary GUID
my $b64_guid = encode_base64($bin_guid);

print "$b64_guid\n";
```

 You can avoid using *uuidgen.exe* altogether by using the Win32::
Guidgen module or Data::UUID (for Unix), both of which can generate
text-based GUIDs.

Discussion

The schemaIDGUID attribute defines the GUID or unique identifier for classes and
attributes in the schema. It is a good practice to define this attribute in your schema
extensions when creating new classes or attributes. This is especially true if the new
class or attribute will be associated with any extended rights or property sets, which
reference schema objects by GUID. If you do not explicitly set this value, the method
you use for creating or modifying extended rights to use that class will have to
dynamically determine the schemaIDGUID for each forest it is implemented in, which is
not very clean.

11.5   Extending the Schema

Problem

You want to extend the schema to support new classes and attributes in Active
Directory.

Solution

Extending the schema is a straightforward process that consists of adding new
classes or attributes, or modifying existing ones in the schema. While extending the
schema is not hard, due to the sensitive nature of the schema, you should implement
a schema extension process that thoroughly tests any extensions before you put them
in your production forest. Here is a suggested summary of what your schema extension process should be:

1. Meet with clients and determine if there is a business justification for integrating
    their application with Active Directory. Determine if there are any existing
    attributes that would fulfill the desired requirements.

2. Examine the extensions and determine what impact, if any, they will have on your
    Active Directory environment (e.g., adding an attribute to the global catalog).

3. Try out the extensions in a test environment. Observe any peculiarities.

4. Document the extensions.

5. Extend the schema in your production Active Directory.

For more information on defining a schema extension process, see Chapter 12 of *Active Directory*, Third Edition, by Joe Richards et al. (O'Reilly).

Discussion

One thing to be cautious of when developing a schema extension process is not to make it an overly bureaucratic process that can require several weeks to complete. At the same time, you want to ensure that any schema changes that you make are well thought out, tested, and documented thoroughly to avoid encountering trouble-shooting issues later. While some organizations may want to strictly limit schema extensions, there is nothing inherently bad about properly extending the schema; it is one of the core features and advantages over Active Directory's predecessor, Windows NT 4.0.

See Also

Recipe 11.8 for adding a new attribute, Recipe 11.10 for adding a new class, and MS KB 283791 (How to Modify Schema Information Using the Ldifde Utility)

11.6   Preparing the Schema for Upgrade

Problem

You want to prepare the Active Directory schema for an application installation, such as an Active Directory upgrade to Windows Server 2003.

Solution

From a graphical user interface

To prepare your Active Directory forest for a Windows upgrade, do the following:

1. Log on to the Schema Master FSMO of your AD forest.

2. Click Start → Run or open a command prompt.

3. Run the command `adprep /forestprep`. Read the warning message that appears and press C, followed by Enter.

To verify that `adprep /forestprep` has completed successfully, do the following:

1. Open the ADSI Edit MMC snap-in and open a connection to the Configuration NC.

2. Verify that the following object exists:

```
CN=Windows2003Update,CN=ForestUpdates,CN=Configuration,<ForestRootDN>
```

To extend the Active Directory schema to prepare for a Windows Server 2003 upgrade, follow these steps:

1. Log on to the Infrastructure Master FSMO for the domain.
2. Click Start → Run or open a command prompt.
3. Run the command `adprep /domainprep`. Read the warning message that appears and press C, followed by Enter.

Discussion

Just like some third-party applications, major upgrades to the Windows operating system itself will usually require that the Active Directory schema be extended with new classes and attributes. To automate this process, Active Directory includes the *adprep* utility to perform these modifications. *adprep* needs to be run once for the entire forest using the `/forestprep` switch and once for each domain that will be upgraded using the `/domainprep` switch. In the case of a Windows Server 2003 upgrade, you can view the schema extensions that will be performed by this utility by looking at the *.ldf* files in the \i386 directory on the Windows Server 2003 CD. These files contain LDIF entries for adding and modifying new and existing classes and attributes. Since the `/forestprep` process extends and modifies the schema, you must perform this task using credentials that belong to both the *Schema Admins* and *Enterprise Admins* groups.

After `/forestprep` has completed, `/domainprep` will create new containers and objects within each Domain NC, as well as modify ACLs on some objects and the behavior of the Everyone security principal. Before you can run `/domainprep`, you need to ensure that the updates from `/forestprep` have replicated to all domain controllers in the forest using the method described in this recipe. `/domainprep` needs to be run on the Infrastructure Master of the domain, using Domain Admin credentials.

See Also

Recipe 3.3 for more on verifying the promotion of a domain controller, MS KB 325379 (How to Upgrade Windows 2000 Domain Controllers to Windows Server 2003), MS KB 331161 (Hotfixes to Install on Windows 2000 Domain Controllers Before Running adprep /forestprep), and MS KB 314649 (Windows Server 2003 adprep /forestprep Command Causes Mangled Attributes in Windows 2000 Forests that Contain Exchange 2000 Servers)

11.7   Documenting Schema Extensions

Problem

You want to document your schema extensions.

Solution

There are several different ways you can document schema extensions. If you require LDIF files of the schema extensions before you extend the schema, you can use the files themselves as a simple self-documenting system. You can put comments in LDIF files by putting # at the beginning of a line, or else use the new schema analyzer functionality available with the Active Directory Application Partition (ADAM). We recommend a combination of these options, and recommend that any company that needs to extend the schema of their customer's Active Directory should include LDIF files, regardless of whether you use that method to actually extend the schema.

The AD Schema Analyzer is a useful new tool that can document your existing schema, as well as create a file to help you modify the schema. To use the Schema Analyzer, do the following:

1. Click Start → All Programs → ADAM → ADAM Tools Command Prompt. Run the program *adschemaanalyzer* from the command prompt.
2. Click File → Load target schema. To load the current Active Directory schema, enter your username, password, and domain name, and then click OK.
3. Click File → Load base schema. Enter your username, password, and domain name, and then click OK.
4. Place a checkmark next to each class, attribute, and property set that you wish to export.
5. Click File → Create LDIF file. Enter a path and name of the file to export, and click Save.

Discussion

There are no hard and fast rules for documenting schema extensions. Documenting schema extensions in some fashion, even a rudimentary one, should be a requirement of any schema extension process you adopt. If you have the resources and time, you can even develop a much more elaborate documentation system using the Web or even an object-modeling system.

See Also

RFC 2849 (The LDAP Data Interchange Format (LDIF)—Technical Specification)

11.8 Adding a New Attribute

Problem

You want to add a new attribute to the schema.

Solution

 For Windows 2000 Active Directory, you need to enable schema modifications before proceeding. See Recipe 11.2 for more information.

Using a graphical user interface

1. Open the Active Directory Schema snap-in.
2. In the left pane, right-click on the Attributes folder and select Create Attribute.
3. Click the Continue button to confirm that you want to extend the schema.
4. Enter the information for the new attribute.
5. Click OK.

Using a command-line interface

You can create new attributes by using *ldifde* and an LDIF file that contains the properties to be set on the attribute. The following text shows a sample LDIF file called *create_attr.ldf* that creates an attribute called rallencorp-LanguagesSpoken:

```
dn: cn=rallencorp-LanguagesSpoken,cn=schema,cn=configuration,<ForestRootDN>
changetype: add
objectclass: attributeSchema
lDAPDisplayName: rallencorpLanguagesSpoken
attributeId: 1.3.6.1.4.1.999.1.1.28.3
oMSyntax: 20
attributeSyntax: 2.5.5.4
isSingleValued: FALSE
searchFlags: 1
description: "Languages a user speaks"
```

Then run the following command:

```
> ldifde -v -i -f create_attr.ldf
```

You can also use AdMod to add a schema attribute as follows:

```
> admod –b cn=rallencorpLanguagesSpoken,cn=schema,cn=configuration,
    <ForestRootDN> objectClass::attributeSchema
    lDAPDisplayName::rallencorpLanguagesSpoken
    attributeId::1.3.6.1.4.1.999.1.1.28.3
    omSyntax::20
    attributeSyntax::2.5.5.4
    isSingleValued::FALSE
    searchFlags::1
    description::"Languages a user speaks"
    -add
```

Using VBScript

```
' This code illustrates how to create an attribute
' called rallencorp-LanguagesSpoken.

set objRootDSE = GetObject("LDAP://RootDSE")
set objSchemaCont = GetObject("LDAP://" & _
                        objRootDSE.Get("schemaNamingContext") )
set objAttr = objSchemaCont.Create("attributeSchema", _
                        "cn=rallencorp-LanguagesSpoken")
objAttr.Put "lDAPDisplayName", "rallencorp-LanguagesSpoken"
objAttr.Put "attributeId", "1.3.6.1.4.1.999.1.1.28.3"
objAttr.Put "oMSyntax", 20
objAttr.Put "attributeSyntax", "2.5.5.4"
objAttr.Put "isSingleValued", FALSE
objAttr.Put "description", "Languages a user speaks"
objAttr.Put "searchFlags", 1  ' index the attribute
objAttr.SetInfo
WScript.Echo "Attribute created"
```

Discussion

To create an attribute, you need to add an attributeSchema object to the Schema container. Typically, when you extend the schema, you perform several additions or modifications at once. The order of your extensions is very important. You can't create a class, assign an attribute, and then create the attribute; you obviously need to create the attribute before it can be assigned to the class. Even if you create the attribute before you assign it to a class, you must reload the schema before doing the class assignment. Reloading the schema is described in more detail in Recipe 11.25.

Most of the attributes that can be set on attributeSchema objects are pretty straightforward, but a couple of them require a little explanation. The attributeSyntax and oMSyntax attributes together define the syntax, or the type of data that can be contained in the attribute. Table 11-3 shows the possible combinations of these two attributes and the resulting syntax.

Table 11-3. attributeSyntax and oMSyntax combinations

Name	attributeSyntax	oMSyntax	Description
AccessPointDN	2.5.5.14	127	Type of distinguished name taken from X.500.
Boolean	2.5.5.8	1	TRUE or FALSE value.
CaseExactString	2.5.5.3	27	Case-sensitive string.
CaseIgnoreString	2.5.5.4	20	Case-insensitive string.
DirectoryString	2.5.5.12	64	Case-insensitive Unicode string.
DN	2.5.5.1	127	String representing a distinguished name.

Table 11-3. attributeSyntax and oMSyntax combinations (continued)

Name	attributeSyntax	oMSyntax	Description
DNWithBinary	2.5.5.7	127	Octet string that has the following format: `B:CharCount:BinaryValue:ObjectDN` where *CharCount* is the number of hexadecimal digits in *BinaryValue*, *BinaryValue* is the hexadecimal representation of the binary value, and *ObjectDN* is a distinguished name.
DNWithString	2.5.5.14	127	Octet string that contains a string value and a DN. A value with this syntax has the following format: `S:CharCount:StringValue:ObjectDN` where *CharCount* is the number of characters in the *StringValue* string and *ObjectDN* is a distinguished name of an object in Active Directory.
Enumeration	2.5.5.9	10	Defined in X.500 and treated as an integer.
GeneralizedTime	2.5.5.11	24	Time-string format defined by ASN.1 standards. See ISO 8601 and X.680.
IA5String	2.5.5.5	22	Case-sensitive string containing characters from the IA5 character set.
Integer	2.5.5.9	2	32-bit integer.
Integer8	2.5.5.16	65	64-bit integer, also known as a large integer.
NTSecurityDescriptor	2.5.5.15	66	Octet string that contains a security descriptor.
NumericString	2.5.5.6	18	String that contains digits.
OctetString	2.5.5.10	4	Array of bytes used to store binary data.
OID	2.5.5.2	6	String that contains digits (0–9) and decimal points (.).
ORName	2.5.5.7	127	Taken from X.400; used for X.400 to RFC 822 mapping.
PresentationAddress	2.5.5.13	127	String that contains OSI presentation addresses.
PrintableString	2.5.5.5	19	Case-sensitive string that contains characters from the printable character set.
ReplicaLink	2.5.5.10	127	Used by Active Directory internally.
Sid	2.5.5.17	4	Octet string that contains a security identifier (SID).
UTCTime	2.5.5.11	23	Time-string format defined by ASN.1 standards.

The searchFlags attribute is a bit flag that defines special properties related to searching with the attribute. Table 11-4 contains the values that can be set for this attribute. The values are cumulative, so to index an attribute and include it in ANR searches, you would set a value of 5 (1 + 4).

Table 11-4. searchFlags bit values

Value	Description
1	Index over attribute. See Recipe 11.12 for more information.
2	Index over container and attribute.
4	Include as part of Ambiguous Name Resolution (ANR). Should be used in addition to 1. See Recipe 11.15 for more information.
8	Preserve attribute in tombstone objects. This will ensure that the value of a particular attribute will be retained when the object is tombstoned, so that it will be repopulated automatically if you need to reanimate the object.
16	Copy attribute when duplicating an object. See Recipe 11.13 for more information.
32	Create a tuple index for this attribute. This improves the response time for searches that put a wildcard in front of the search string for the attribute (e.g., `givenname=*on`).
128	Set the confidential bit on this attribute, which requires normal users to be assigned additional permissions to be able to read its contents. (This is new with Windows Server 2003 Service Pack 1.)

See Also

Recipe 4.15 for setting a bit flag, Recipe 11.10 for adding a new class, and Recipe 11.25 for reloading the schema

11.9   Viewing an Attribute

Problem

You want to view the properties of an attribute.

Solution

Using a graphical user interface

1. Open the Active Directory Schema snap-in.
2. In the left pane, click on the Attributes folder.
3. In the right pane, double-click the attribute you want to view.
4. Click on each tab to view the available properties.

Using a command-line interface

In the following command, replace *<AttrCommonName>* with the common name (not LDAP display dame) of the attribute you want to view:

```
> dsquery * cn=schema,cn=configuration,<ForestRootDN> -scope onelevel -attr *\
-filter "(&(objectcategory=attributeSchema)(cn=<AttrCommonName>))"
```

You can also use AdFind to view the properties of an attribute as follows:

```
> adfind -schema -f (ldapdisplayname=<AttributeName>)
```

You can also use a shortcut syntax for this command, as follows:

```
> adfind -sc s:<AttributeName>
```

Using VBScript

```
' This code displays the attributes for the specified attributeSchema object
' Refer to Recipe 4.2 for the DisplayAttributes( ) function code.
' ------ SCRIPT CONFIGURATION ------
' Set to the common name (not LDAP display dame) of the attribute
strAttrName = "<AttrCommonName>"    ' e.g. surname
' ------ END CONFIGURATION ---------

set objRootDSE = GetObject("LDAP://RootDSE")
set objAttr = GetObject("LDAP://cn=" & strAttrName & "," & _
                        objRootDSE.Get("schemaNamingContext"))
objAttr.GetInfo
WScript.Echo "Properties for " & strAttrName & ":"
DisplayAttributes(objAttr.ADsPath)
```

Discussion

In the CLI and VBScript solutions, we mention that you need to specify the common name (or cn) of the attribute you want to view. The common name is a source of confusion for many people. For example, the surname attribute has the following distinguished name in the *rallencorp.com* forest:

```
cn=surname,cn=schema,cn=configuration,dc=rallencorp,dc=com
```

The problem is that most applications refer to attributes by their LDAP display name as defined in the lDAPDisplayName attribute for the attributeSchema object, which is typically different from the cn attribute. As an example, the surname attribute uses surname for its common name (cn), but sn for its LDAP display name (lDAPDisplayName).

In the CLI solution, to use the LDAP display name instead of cn when using DSQuery, simply change (cn=<AttrCommonName>) to (lDAPDisplayName=<AttrLDAPName>).

For AdMod, change −rb cn=<AttrCommonName> to −f (lDAPDisplayName=<AttrLDAPName>. In the VBScript solution, it is not that simple. When using cn, we can call GetObject since we know the DN of the attributeSchema object. If you want to use the lDAPDisplayName attribute instead, you'll need to do an ADO query and use search criteria similar to those in the CLI solution.

One attribute of note that is defined on attributeSchema objects is the systemFlags bit flag, which is used to define a few miscellaneous properties about an attribute. Table 11-5 contains the bits associated with systemFlags. The values are cumulative, so a value of 17 (1 + 16) would indicate that the attribute is part of the base Active Directory installation and is not replicated.

Table 11-5. systemFlags bit values

Value	Description
1	Not replicated among domain controllers.
4	Dynamically constructed by Active Directory.
16	Part of the base Active Directory installation. This value cannot be set.

See Also

Recipe 4.2 for viewing the attributes of an object and Recipe 4.12 for searching with a bitwise filter

11.10 Adding a New Class

Problem

You want to add a new class to the schema.

Solution

 For Windows 2000 Active Directory, you need to enable schema modifications before proceeding. See Recipe 11.2 for more information.

Using a graphical user interface

1. Open the Active Directory Schema snap-in.
2. In the left pane, right-click on the Classes folder and select "Create Class...."
3. Click the Continue button to confirm that you want to extend the schema.
4. Enter the information for the new class and click Next.
5. Enter any mandatory and optional attributes and click Finish.

Using a command-line interface

You can create new classes by using *ldifde* and an LDIF file that contains the properties to be set on the class. The following text shows a sample LDIF file called *create_ class.ldf* that creates a class called `rallencorp-SalesUser`:

```
dn: cn=rallencorp-SalesUser,cn=schema,cn=configuration,<ForestRootDN>
changetype: add
objectclass: classSchema
lDAPDisplayName: rallencorp-SalesUser
governsId: 1.3.6.1.4.1.999.1.1.28.4
objectClassCategory: 3
subClassOf: top
description: Auxiliary class for Sales user attributes
```

```
adminDescription: Auxiliary class for Sales user attributes
mayContain: rallencorp-Building
mayContain: rallencorp-Theatre
```

Then run the following command:

```
> ldifde -v -i -f create_class.ldf
```

You can also add a new class using AdMod, as follows:

```
> admod -b cn=rallencorp-SalesUser,cn=schema,cn=configuration,<ForestRootDN>
    objectclass::classSchema lDAPDisplayName::rallencorp-SalesUser
    governsId::1.3.6.1.4.1.999.1.1.28.4 objectClassCategory::3
    subClassOf::top description::"Auxiliary class for Sales user"
    adminDescription::"Auxiliary class for Sales user"
    mayContain::rallencorp-Building;rallencorp-Theatre
    -add
```

Using VBScript

```
' This code creates a class in the schema called rallencorp-SalesUser.
' It is assumed that the script is being run by a member of Schema Admins

set objRootDSE = GetObject("LDAP://RootDSE")
set objSchemaCont = GetObject("LDAP://" & _
                               objRootDSE.Get("schemaNamingContext") )
set objClass = objSchemaCont.Create("classSchema", _
                               "cn=rallencorp-SalesUser")
objClass.Put "lDAPDisplayName", "rallencorp-SalesUser"
objClass.Put "governsId", "1.3.6.1.4.1.999.1.1.28.4"
objClass.Put "objectClassCategory", 3
objClass.Put "subClassOf", "top"
objClass.Put "adminDescription", "Auxilliary class for Sales user attributes"
objClass.Put "mayContain", Array("rallencorp-Building","rallencorp-Theatre")
objClass.SetInfo
WScript.Echo "Class created"
```

Discussion

To create a new class, you need to create a classSchema object in the Schema container. The important attributes to set include:

governsId
: Defines the OID for the class

objectClassCategory
: Defines the class type

subClassOf
: Defines the parent class

mayContain *and* mustContain
: Defines any optional and mandatory attributes for instantiated objects of the class

The lDAPDisplayName also needs to be set and should be equal to the common name (cn) as a general rule. Even though many of the default classes do not use the same name for the common name and LDAP display name, using the same name is highly recommended to avoid confusion when referencing the class. Another best practice is to set the schemaIDGUID of the class, which is especially important if you are doing anything with extended rights.

See Also

The "Introduction" of this chapter for attributes of classSchema objects, Recipe 11.3 for generating an OID, Recipe 11.4 for generating a GUID, Recipe 11.19 for more on object class type, Recipe 11.21 for setting the default security for a class, and Recipe 11.25 for reloading the schema cache

11.11 Viewing a Class

Problem

You want to view the attributes of a class.

Solution

Using a graphical user interface

1. Open the Active Directory Schema snap-in.
2. In the left pane, click on the Classes folder.
3. In the right pane, double-click the class you want to view.
4. Click on each tab to view the available properties.

Using a command-line interface

In the following command, replace <ClassCommonName> with the common name (not LDAP display name) of the class you want to view:

```
> dsquery * cn=<ClassCommonName>,cn=schema,cn=configuration,<ForestRootDN> -scope\
base -attr *
```

You can also use adfind to view the properties of a class as follows:

```
> adfind –schema –rb cn=<ClassCommonName>
```

Using VBScript

```
' This code prints out the attributes for the specified class.
' Recipe 4.2 for the code for the DisplayAttributes( ) function.
' ------ SCRIPT CONFIGURATION ------
' Set to the common name (not LDAP display dame)
' of the class you want to view.
strClassName = "<ClassCommonName>"    ' e.g. user
```

```
' ------ END CONFIGURATION ---------
set objRootDSE = GetObject("LDAP://RootDSE")
set objClass = GetObject("LDAP://cn=" & strClassName & "," & _
                         objRootDSE.Get("schemaNamingContext"))
objClass.GetInfo
WScript.Echo "Properties for " & strClassName
DisplayAttributes(objClass.ADsPath)
```

Discussion

See Table 11-1, at the beginning of this chapter, for a list of the important classSchema attributes and their descriptions.

See Also

Recipe 4.2 for viewing the attributes of an object

11.12 Indexing an Attribute

Problem

You want to index an attribute so that searches using that attribute are faster.

Solution

 For Windows 2000 Active Directory you need to enable schema modifications before proceeding. See Recipe 11.2 for more information.

Using a graphical user interface

1. Open the Active Directory Schema snap-in.
2. In the left pane, click on the Attributes folder.
3. In the right pane, double-click the attribute you want to index.
4. Check the box beside "Index this attribute in the Active Directory."
5. Click OK.

Using a command-line interface

You can index an attribute by using the *ldifde* utility and an LDIF file that contains the following:

```
dn: cn=<AttrCommonName>,cn=schema,cn=configuration,<ForestRootDN>
changetype: modify
replace: searchFlags
searchFlags: 1
-
```

If the LDIF file were named *index_attribute.ldf*, you would run the following command:

```
> ldifde -v -i -f index_attribute.ldf
```

You can also enable the appropriate searchFlags value using admod, as follows:

```
> admod -b cn=<AttrCommonName>,cn=schema,cn=configuration,<ForestRootDN> searchFlags:
:1
```

Using VBScript

```
' This code indexes an attribute.
' ------ SCRIPT CONFIGURATION ------
' Set to the common name (not LDAP display name) of the attribute
strAttrName = "<AttrCommonName>"    ' e.g. rallencorp-LanguagesSpoken
' ------ END CONFIGURATION ---------

set objRootDSE = GetObject("LDAP://RootDSE")
set objAttr = GetObject("LDAP://cn=" & strAttrName & "," &
                        objRootDSE.Get("schemaNamingContext"))
objAttr.Put "searchFlags", 1
objAttr.SetInfo
WScript.Echo "Indexed attribute: " & strAttrName
```

> The CLI and VBScript solutions assume that searchFlags wasn't pre-
> viously set; if a value is present, they just blindly overwrite it. See
> Recipe 4.15 for a better solution that will enable the bit you want
> without overwriting any previous settings.

Discussion

To index an attribute, you need to enable the 1 bit (0001) in the searchFlags attribute for the attributeSchema object.

searchFlags is a bit flag attribute that is used to set various properties related to searching with the attribute. Table 11-5, earlier in this chapter, contains the various bit flags that can be set with searchFlags. When setting searchFlags, you may often need to set a couple bits together. For example, all Ambiguous Name Resolution (ANR) attributes must also be indexed, which means searchFlags should be set to 5 (1 + 4).

You can find the attributes that are indexed in the schema by using the following search criteria:

Base
    cn=Schema,cn=Configuration,<ForestRootDN>

Filter
    (&(objectcategory=attributeSchema)(searchFlags:1.2.840.113556.1.4.803:=1))

Scope
    onelevel

Alternatively, to find attributes that aren't indexed, change the previous search filter to the following:

```
(&(objectcategory=attributeSchema)(!(searchFlags:1.2.840.113556.1.4.803:=1)))
```

See Also

Recipe 4.15 for modifying a bit flag attribute, Recipe 11.8 for adding a new attribute, and MS KB 243311 (Setting an Attribute's searchFlags Property to Be Indexed for ANR)

11.13 Modifying the Attributes That Are Copied When Duplicating a User

Problem

You want to add an attribute to the list of attributes that are copied when duplicating a user with the ADUC snap-in.

Solution

 For Windows 2000 Active Directory you need to enable schema modifications before proceeding. See Recipe 11.2 for more information.

Using a graphical user interface

1. Open the Active Directory Schema snap-in.
2. In the left pane, click on the Attributes folder.
3. In the right pane, double-click the attribute you want to edit.
4. Check the box beside "Attribute is copied when duplicating a user."
5. Click OK.

Using a command-line interface

You can cause an attribute to get copied when duplicating a user by using the *ldifde* utility and an LDIF file that contains the following:

```
dn: cn=rallencorp-LanguagesSpoken,cn=schema,cn=configuration,<ForestRootDN>
changetype: modify
replace: searchFlags
searchFlags: 16
-
```

If the LDIF file were named *add_dup_user_attr.ldf*, you would run the following command:

```
> ldifde -v -i -f add_dup_user_attr.ldf
```

You can also modify the searchFlags attribute using AdMod, as follows:

```
> admod -b <AttributeDN> searchFlags::16
```

Using VBScript

```
' This code adds an attribute to the list of attributes that get
' copied when duplicating a user.
' ------ SCRIPT CONFIGURATION ------
' Set to the common name (not LDAP display dame) of the attribute
strAttrName = "<AttrCommonName>"    ' e.g. rallencorp-LanguagesSpoken
' ------ END CONFIGURATION ---------

set objRootDSE = GetObject("LDAP://RootDSE")
set objAttr = GetObject("LDAP://cn=" & strAttrName & "," & objRootDSE.
Get("schemaNamingContext"))
objAttr.Put "searchFlags", 16
objAttr.SetInfo
WScript.Echo "New copied attribute: " & strAttrName
```

> The CLI and VBScript solutions assume that searchFlags wasn't previously set; if a value is present, they just blindly overwrite it. See Recipe 4.15 for a better solution that will enable the bit you want without overwriting any previous settings.

Discussion

The Active Directory Users and Computers snap-in queries the schema for the list of attributes that should be copied whenever you right-click on a user and select Copy. This flag is purely informational and does not impose any restrictions or result in any impact on the DIT, unlike indexing an attribute.

To find out which attributes are copied when duplicating a user, use the following search criteria:

Base
    cn=Schema,cn=Configuration,<ForestRootDN>
Filter
    (&(objectcategory=attributeSchema)(searchFlags:1.2.840.113556.1.4.803:=16))
Scope
    onelevel

Alternatively, to find attributes that aren't copied, change the previous search filter to the following:

```
(&(objectcategory=attributeSchema)(!(searchFlags:1.2.840.113556.1.4.803:=16)))
```

See Also

Recipe 4.15 for modifying a bit flag attribute and Recipe 11.8 for adding a new attribute

11.14 Adding Custom Information to ADUC

Problem

You want schema information that you've created to be visible in the ADUC snap-in.

Solution

Using VBScript

```
Set oFileSystem = WScript.CreateObject("Scripting.FileSystemObject")
sSystemFolder =  oFileSystem.GetSpecialFolder(1)
set oRootDSE = Getobject("LDAP://RootDSE")

' The display specifier for US English is 409; modify this
' for another locale if necessary.
set oCont = GetObject("LDAP://" & "CN=409, CN=DisplaySpecifiers," &
oRootDSE.get("configurationNamingContext"))
Set oDisplay = oCont.GetObject("displaySpecifier","cn=user-Display")

'Add Attribute Display Names
oDisp.PutEx 3,"attributeDisplayNames" , Array("BudgetCode,BudgetCode")
oDisp.SetInfo

'Add this field to the Right-Click Context Menu
iCount = 0
If Not IsEmpty(oDisp.shellContextMenu) Then
   aMenu = oDisp.GetEx("shellContextMenu")
   iCount = iCount + 1
End If
sNewMenu = CStr(iCount) & ",&Budget code...,budgetshell.vbs"
oDisp.PutEx 3,"shellContextMenu" , Array(sNewMenu)
oDisp.SetInfo
Set sOutFile = oFileSystem.CreateTextFile(sSystemFolder & "\budgetshell.vbs",True)
sOutFile.WriteLine "Set Args = Wscript.Arguments"
sOutFile.WriteLine "Set oUser = GetObject(Args(0))"
sOutFile.WriteLine "MsgBox " & Chr(34) & "Budget Code" & Chr(34) & " & vbCRLF & " &
Chr(34) & "Budget Code: " & Chr(34) & " & oUser.BudgetCode & vbCRLF & " & Chr(34)
sOutFile.WriteLine "Set oUser = Nothing"
sOutFile.WriteLine "WScript.Quit"
sOutFile.Close
'Allow for updates
iCount = 0
If Not IsEmpty(oDisp.adminContextMenu) Then
   aMenu = oDisp.GetEx("adminContextMenu")
   iCount = iCount + 1
End If
sNewMenu = CStr(iCount) & ",&Budget Code...,budgetadmin.vbs"
oDisp.PutEx 3,"adminContextMenu" , Array(sNewMenu)
oDisp.SetInfo
MsgBox "Adding Admin Context Menu Program"
Set sOutFile = oFileSystem.CreateTextFile(sSystemFolder & "\budgetadmin.vbs",True)
sOutFile.WriteLine "Set Args = Wscript.Arguments"
```

```
sOutFile.WriteLine "Set oUser = GetObject(Args(0))"
sOutFile.WriteLine "temp = InputBox(" & Chr(34) & "Current Budget Code: " & Chr(34) &
" & oUser.BudgetCode & vbCRLF & " & Chr(34) & "New Budget Code" & Chr(34) & ")"
sOutFile.WriteLine "if temp <> " & Chr(34) & Chr(34) & " then oUser.Put " & Chr(34) &
"BudgetCode" & Chr(34) & ",temp"
sOutFile.WriteLine "oUser.SetInfo"
sOutFile.WriteLine "Set oUser = Nothing"
sOutFile.WriteLine "WScript.Quit"
sOutFile.Close
Set oDisp = Nothing
Set oCont = Nothing
Set oRoot = Nothing
Set oFileSystem = Nothing
WScript.Quit
```

 It's important that you run the script listed in this recipe only one time; otherwise you may wind up with duplicate entries in the ADUC context menu.

Discussion

Modifying the default MMC snap-ins is a nontrivial task, but it can be accomplished using VBScript to add information to the display specifiers in the Configuration NC. Let's say that you've extended the user class in your forest with an auxiliary class that stores the user's budget code for their expense reports, and you want to be able to view and edit this information using ADUC. You can create a VBScript that will display and modify this information from the right-click context menu, as shown in this recipe.

Another option would be to create a VBScript file that simply displays the necessary message boxes to display and/or update the user attribute in question, after which you could use ADSI Edit or AdMod to configure your display specifiers to call that script whenever appropriate.

If you saved such a script to the \\dc1\share\updatebudget.vbs path, for example, you could then add the following information to the adminContextMenu attribute of cn=user-Display,cn=409,cn=DisplaySpecifiers,cn=Configuration,<ForestRootDN>:

```
4, &Update Budget Information,\\dc1\share\updatebudget.vbs
```

See Also

MSDN: Display Specifiers and MS KB 299646 (How to Add Custom Attributes to the DSFind Pick list)

11.15 Modifying the Attributes Included with ANR

Problem

You want to modify the attributes that are included as part of ANR.

Solution

 For Windows 2000 Active Directory, you need to enable schema modifications before proceeding. See Recipe 11.2 for more information.

Using a graphical user interface

1. To proceed, you must have first indexed the attribute.
2. Open the Active Directory Schema snap-in.
3. In the left pane, click on the Attributes folder.
4. In the right pane, double-click the attribute you want to edit.
5. Check the box beside ANR.
6. Click OK.

Using a command-line interface

You can include an attribute as part of ANR by using the *ldifde* utility and an LDIF file that contains the following:

```
dn: cn=rallencorp-LanguagesSpoken,cn=schema,cn=configuration,<ForestRootDN>
changetype: modify
replace: searchFlags
searchFlags: 5
-
```

If the LDIF file were named *add_anr_attr.ldf*, you'd run the following command:

```
> ldifde -v -i -f add_anr_attr.ldf
```

You can also modify the searchFlags attribute using AdMod, as follows:

```
> admod –b <AttributeDN> searchFlags::5
```

Using VBScript

```
' This code will make an attribute part of the ANR set.
' ------ SCRIPT CONFIGURATION ------
' Set to the common name (not LDAP display dame) of the attribute
strAttrName = "<AttrCommonName>"    ' e.g. rallencorp-LanguagesSpoken
' ------ END CONFIGURATION ---------

set objRootDSE = GetObject("LDAP://RootDSE")
set objAttr = GetObject("LDAP://cn=" & strAttrName & "," & _
```

```
                    objRootDSE.Get("schemaNamingContext"))
objAttr.Put "searchFlags", 5
objAttr.SetInfo
WScript.Echo "New ANR attribute: " & strAttrName
```

 The CLI and VBScript solutions assume that searchFlags wasn't previously set; if a value is present, they just blindly overwrite it. Check out
Recipe 4.15 for a better solution that will enable the bit you want
without overwriting any previous settings.

Discussion

ANR is an efficient search algorithm that allows for a complex search filter to be
written using a single comparison. For example, a search for (anr=Jim Smith) would
translate into the following query:

- An OR filter with every attribute in the ANR set against Jim Smith*
- A filter for givenName = Jim* and sn = Smith*
- A filter for givenName = Smith* and sn = Jim*

These filters are ORed together and then processed by Active Directory. Since all
default ANR attributes are also indexed, the query return should come back quickly.

Here is a list of the default attributes that are included as part of ANR searches. The
LDAP display name of the attribute is shown first, with the common name in
parenthesis:

- displayName (Display-Name)
- givenName (Given-Name)
- legacyExchangeDN (Legacy-Exchange-DN)
- msDS-AdditionalSamAccountName (ms-DS-Additional-Sam-Account-Name)
- physicalDeliveryOfficeName (Physical-Delivery-Office-Name)
- name (RDN)
- sAMAccountName (SAM-Account-Name)
- sn (Surname)

 msDS-AdditionalSamAccountName was added as an ANR attribute in
Windows Server 2003.

One requirement of any new ANR attribute is that the attribute must be also
indexed. ANR searches are intended to be very fast, so if a nonindexed attribute were
added to the set, it could dramatically impact the performance of the searches.
Therefore, Active Directory requires that each added attribute be indexed.

You can use adfind with the –stats+only switch to verify what the ANR expansion actually looks like. You can find out which attributes are included in the ANR set by using the following search criteria:

Base
>   cn=Schema,cn=Configuration,*<ForestRootDN>*

Filter
>   (&(objectcategory=attributeSchema)(searchFlags:1.2.840.113556.1.4.803:=4))

Scope
>   onelevel

Alternatively, to find attributes that aren't included in ANR, change the previous search filter to the following:

>   (&(objectcategory=attributeSchema)(!(searchFlags:1.2.840.113556.1.4.803:=4)))

See Also

Recipe 4.15 for modifying a bit flag attribute, Recipe 11.8 for adding a new attribute, MS KB 243299 (Ambiguous Name Resolution for LDAP in Windows 2000), and MS KB 243311 (Setting an Attribute's searchFlags Property to Be Indexed for ANR)

11.16 Modifying the Set of Attributes Stored on a Global Catalog

Problem

You want to add or remove an attribute in the global catalog.

Solution

 For Windows 2000 Active Directory, you need to enable schema modifications before proceeding. See Recipe 11.2 for more information.

Using a graphical user interface

1. Open the Active Directory Schema snap-in.
2. In the left pane, click on the Attributes folder.
3. In the right pane, double-click the attribute you want to edit.
4. Check the box beside "Replicate this attribute to the Global Catalog" to add to the global catalog, or uncheck to remove the global catalog.
5. Click OK.

Using a command-line interface

You can add an attribute to the global catalog by using the *ldifde* utility and an LDIF file that contains the following:

```
dn: cn=<AttrCommonName>,cn=schema,cn=configuration,<ForestRootDN>
changetype: modify
replace: isMemberOfPartialAttributeSet
isMemberOfPartialAttributeSet: TRUE
-
```

If the LDIF file were named *add_gc_attr.ldf*, you would run the following command:

```
> ldifde -v -i -f add_gc_attr.ldf
```

You can also modify this property using AdMod, as follows:

```
> admod -b cn=<AttrCommonName>,cn=schema,cn=configuration,<ForestRootDN>
isMemberOfPartialAttributeSet::TRUE
```

Using VBScript

```
' This code adds an attribute to the global catalog.
' ------ SCRIPT CONFIGURATION ------
' Set to the common name (not LDAP display name) of the attribute.
strAttrName = "<AttrCommonName>"  ' e.g. surname
' Set to TRUE to add to GC, set to FALSE to remove from GC
boolAddtoGC = TRUE
' ------ END CONFIGURATION ---------

set objRootDSE = GetObject("LDAP://RootDSE")
set objAttr = GetObject("LDAP://cn=" & strAttrName & "," & _
                        objRootDSE.Get("schemaNamingContext"))
objAttr.Put "isMemberOfPartialAttributeSet", boolAddtoGC
objAttr.SetInfo
WScript.Echo "Added attribute to GC: " & strAttrName
```

Discussion

Each domain controller in a forest replicates a copy of the Domain naming context for its own domain, as well as copies of the forest-wide Configuration and Schema partitions. However, domain controllers do not replicate Domain naming contexts for other domains in the forest. When enabled as a global catalog server, a domain controller will make partial, read-only replicas of all the objects in other domains in the forest.

Searching against the global catalog is useful when you need to perform a single search across several naming contexts at once. The global catalog stores only a subset of each object's attributes, which is why it is considered a partial replica. Attributes stored in the global catalog are considered part of the PAS. Any attributes that you add to the PAS should be ones you'd want to use as part of global catalog searches that are not present already.

You can add to the attributes that are stored in the global catalog by setting the isMemberOfPartitalAttributeSet attribute of an attributeSchema object to TRUE. Likewise, to remove an attribute from the PAS, set isMemberOfPartitalAttributeSet to FALSE for the target attribute.

 With Windows 2000, anytime you added an attribute to the PAS a full sync of all of the global catalog contents was done for every global catalog server. This could have a major impact on replication in some multidomain environments, as the amount of data that needed to replicate across your forest could be significant. Fortunately, this limitation was removed in Windows Server 2003 so that a full sync is no longer performed. Removing an attribute from the partial attribute list does not force a global catalog sync, even under Windows 2000.

You can find which attributes are included in the global catalog by using a query with the following criteria:

Base
> cn=Schema,cn=Configuration,<*ForestRootDN*>

Filter
> (&(objectcategory=attributeSchema)(isMemberOfPartitalAttributeSet=TRUE))

Scope
> onelevel

Alternatively, to find attributes that aren't in the global catalog, you only need to change part of the previous filter to the following:

> (isMemberOfPartialAttributeSet=FALSE)

See Also

MS KB 229662 (How to Control What Data Is Stored in the Global Catalog), MS KB 230663 (How to Enumerate Attributes Replicated to the Global Catalog), MS KB 232517 (Global Catalog Attributes and Replication Properties), MS KB 248717 (How to Modify Attributes That Replicate to the Global Catalog), MS KB 257203 (Common Default Attributes Set for Active Directory and Global Catalog), and MS KB 313992 (How to Add an Attribute to the Global Catalog in Windows 2000)

11.17 Finding the Nonreplicated and Constructed Attributes

Problem

You want to find the attributes that are not replicated or are constructed by Active Directory.

Solution

Using a graphical user interface

1. Open LDP.
2. From the menu, select Connection → Connect.
3. For Server, enter the name of a domain controller (or leave blank to do a server-less bind).
4. For Port, enter 389.
5. Click OK.
6. From the menu, select Connection → Bind.
7. Enter credentials of a domain user.
8. Click OK.
9. From the menu, select Browse → Search.
10. For BaseDN, type the Schema Container DN (for example, cn=schema, cn=configuration,dc=rallencorp,dc=com).
11. For Scope, select One Level.
12. To find nonreplicated attributes, use the following for Filter:

    (&(objectcategory=attributeSchema)(systemFlags:1.2.840.113556.1.4.803:=1))
13. To find constructed attributes, use the following for Filter:

    (&(objectcategory=attributeSchema)(systemFlags:1.2.840.113556.1.4.803:=4))
14. Click Run.

Using a command-line interface

To find the nonreplicated attributes using DSQuery, use the following command:

```
> dsquery * cn=schema,cn=configuration,<ForestRootDN> -attr "cn" -filter
"(&(objectcategory=attributeSchema)(systemFlags:1.2.840.113556.1.4.803:=1))"
```

To find the nonreplicated attributes using AdFind, use the following:

```
> adfind -schema -bit -f "(&(objectcategory=attributeSchema)(systemFlags:AND:=1))"
```

To find the constructed attributes using DSQuery, use the following command:

```
> dsquery * cn=schema,cn=configuration,<ForestRootDN> -attr "cn" -filter
"(&(objectcategory=attributeSchema)(systemFlags:1.2.840.113556.1.4.803:=4))"
```

To find the constructed attributes using AdFind, use the following:

```
> adfind -schema-bit -f "(&(objectcategory=attributeSchema)(systemFlags:AND:=4))"
```

Using VBScript

```
' This script will print out the nonreplicated and constructed attributes.

set objRootDSE = GetObject("LDAP://RootDSE")
strBase    = "<LDAP://" & objRootDSE.Get("SchemaNamingContext") & ">;"
strFilter  = "(&(objectcategory=attributeSchema)" _
             & "(systemFlags:1.2.840.113556.1.4.803:=1));"
strAttrs   = "cn;"
strScope   = "onelevel"

set objConn = CreateObject("ADODB.Connection")
objConn.Provider = "ADsDSOObject"
objConn.Open "Active Directory Provider"
set objRS = objConn.Execute(strBase & strFilter & strAttrs & strScope)
objRS.MoveFirst
WScript.Echo "Nonreplicated attributes: "
while Not objRS.EOF
    Wscript.Echo "  " & objRS.Fields(0).Value
    objRS.MoveNext
wend

strFilter = "(&(objectcategory=attributeSchema) " _
            & "(systemFlags:1.2.840.113556.1.4.803:=4));"
set objRS = objConn.Execute(strBase & strFilter & strAttrs & strScope)
objRS.MoveFirst
WScript.Echo ""
WScript.Echo "Constructed attributes: "
while Not objRS.EOF
    Wscript.Echo "  " & objRS.Fields(0).Value
    objRS.MoveNext
wend
```

Discussion

The systemFlags attribute of attributeSchema objects defines a few special attribute properties, including whether an attribute is not replicated between domain controllers and whether it is dynamically constructed by Active Directory.

Most attributes are replicated after they are updated on an object, but some never replicate between domain controllers. These attributes are considered nonreplicated. An example of a nonreplicated attribute you may be familiar with is the lastLogon attribute that stores the last logon time for user and computer objects. Whenever a user or computer logs in to Active Directory, the authenticating domain controller updates the user or computer's lastLogon attribute, but the update does not get replicated out to other domain controllers.

Constructed attributes are automatically maintained by Active Directory and cannot be set manually. A good example of a constructed attribute is the new msDS-Approx-Immed-Subordinates available in Windows Server 2003. That attribute contains the approximate number of child objects within a container. Obviously this attribute wouldn't be of much value if you had to maintain it, so Active Directory does it automatically.

One of the downsides to constructed attributes is that you cannot search against them. For example, we cannot perform a search to find all containers that have more than 10 objects in them (i.e., msDS-Approx-Immed-Subordinates>10). This would return an operations error. Constructed attributes can be returned only as part of the attribute set for a query and cannot be used as part of the query itself.

To find the nonreplicated or constructed attributes, you have to use a bitwise LDAP filter against attributeSchema objects. A bit value of 1 indicates the attribute is non-replicated and a value of 4 indicates the attribute is constructed.

See Also

Recipe 4.12 for searching with a bitwise filter

11.18 Finding the Linked Attributes

Problem

You want to find attributes that are linked.

Solution

Using a graphical user interface

1. Open LDP.
2. From the menu, select Connection → Connect.
3. For Server, enter the name of a domain controller (or leave blank to do a server-less bind).
4. For Port, enter 389.
5. Click OK.
6. From the menu, select Connection → Bind.
7. Enter credentials of a domain user.
8. Click OK.
9. From the menu, select Browse → Search.
10. For BaseDN, type the Schema container DN (e.g., cn=schema, cn=configuration,dc=rallencorp,dc=com).
11. For Scope, select One Level.
12. To find linked attributes, use the following for Filter:

        (&(objectcategory=attributeSchema)(linkid=*))
13. Click Run.

Using a command-line interface

You can return a list of linked attributes using either the built-in DSQuery tool or AdMod. To use DSQuery, use the following syntax:

```
> dsquery * cn=schema,cn=configuration,<ForestRootDN> -scope onelevel -filter
"(&(objectcategory=attributeSchema)(linkid=*))" -attr cn linkID
```

To return a list of linked attributes with AdMod, use the following:

```
> adfind -schema -f "(&(objectcategory=attributeSchema)(linkid=*))" cn linkID))"
```

Using VBScript

```
' This code prints out all of the attributes that are linked
' and their corresponding linkID values.
set objRootDSE = GetObject("LDAP://RootDSE")
strBase    = "<LDAP://" & objRootDSE.Get("SchemaNamingContext") & ">;"
strFilter  = "(&(objectcategory=attributeSchema)(linkid=*));"
strAttrs   = "cn,linkid;"
strScope   = "onelevel"

set objConn = CreateObject("ADODB.Connection")
objConn.Provider = "ADsDSOObject"
objConn.Open "Active Directory Provider"
set objRS = objConn.Execute(strBase & strFilter & strAttrs & strScope)
objRS.MoveFirst
while Not objRS.EOF
    Wscript.Echo objRS.Fields(1).Value & " : " & objRS.Fields(0).Value
    objRS.MoveNext
wend
```

Discussion

The values of some attributes in Active Directory are linked. For example, if you set the manager attribute on one user object to be the DN of a second user object, the reports attribute on the second user object will automatically contain the first user object's DN. In this example, the manager attribute, or the attribute that gets set, is considered the *forward* link, and the reports attribute, or the attribute that automatically gets calculated, is called the *back link*. Another common example is group membership. The member attribute of the group object represents the forward link, while the memberOf attribute of the corresponding object (e.g., *user*) represents the back link.

You can identify which attributes are linked in the schema by searching for attributeSchema objects that have a linkID attribute that contains some value. The linkID value for a forward-link attribute will be an even, positive number. The corresponding back-link attribute will be the forward linkID plus 1. For example, the manager attribute linkID is 42, and the back-link reports attribute has a linkID of 43.

11.19 Finding the Structural, Auxiliary, Abstract, and 88 Classes

Problem

You want to list the structural, auxiliary, abstract, and 88 classes.

Solution

Using a graphical user interface

1. Open the Active Directory Schema snap-in.
2. In the left pane, click on the Classes folder.
3. In the right pane, the list of all the classes will be displayed. The Type column contains the type of class. Even though you can click on the column header, it currently does not sort the classes by type.

Using a command-line interface

You can return the list of Active Directory classes using either DSQuery or AdFind. DSQuery takes the following syntax:

```
> dsquery * cn=schema,cn=configuration,<ForestRootDN> -limit 0 -scope onelevel
-filter "(objectcategory=classSchema)" -attr lDAPDisplayName objectclasscategory
```

AdFind requires the following syntax:

```
> adfind -schema -f "(objectcategory=classSchema)" lDAPDisplayName
objectClassCategory
```

Using VBScript

```
' This code prints out classes of a particular type
' ------ SCRIPT CONFIGURATION ------
' Set the following to TRUE or FALSE depending if you want to
' view or not view classes of the type defined by the variable
boolShowStructural = TRUE
boolShowAuxiliary  = TRUE
boolShowAbstract   = TRUE
boolShow88         = TRUE
' ------ END CONFIGURATION ---------

set objRootDSE = GetObject("LDAP://RootDSE")
set objSchemaCont = GetObject("LDAP://cn=schema," & _
                         objRootDSE.Get("configurationNamingContext"))
objSchemaCont.Filter = Array("classSchema")
WScript.Echo "Loading classes, this will take a few seconds."
for each objClass in objSchemaCont
   WScript.StdOut.Write(".")
```

```
        if objClass.Get("objectClassCategory") = 0 then
            str88 = str88 & vbTab & objClass.Get("lDAPDisplayName") & vbCrlf
        elseif objClass.Get("objectClassCategory") = 1 then
            strStruct = strStruct & vbTab & _
                        objClass.Get("lDAPDisplayName") & vbCrlf
        elseif objClass.Get("objectClassCategory") = 2 then
            strAbst = strAbst & vbTab & objClass.Get("lDAPDisplayName") & vbCrlf
        elseif objClass.Get("objectClassCategory") = 3 then
            strAux = strAux & vbTab & objClass.Get("lDAPDisplayName") & vbCrlf
        else
            WScript.Echo "Unknown class type: " & _
                        objClass.Get("lDAPDisplayName") & vbCrlf
        end if
next
WScript.Echo vbCrlf

if boolShowStructural = TRUE then
    WScript.Echo "Structural Classes: "
    WScript.Echo strStruct
    WScript.Echo
end if

if boolShowAbstract = TRUE then
    WScript.Echo "Abstract Classes: "
    WScript.Echo strAbst
    WScript.Echo
end if

if boolShowAuxiliary = TRUE then
    WScript.Echo "Auxiliary Classes: "
    WScript.Echo strAux
    WScript.Echo
end if

if boolShow88 = TRUE then
    WScript.Echo "88 Classes: "
    WScript.Echo str88
    WScript.Echo
end if
```

Discussion

There are four supported class types in the Active Directory schema. The class type is defined by the objectClassCategory attribute on classSchema objects. Each class type is used for a different purpose relating to organizing and inheriting classes. Table 11-6 describes each type.

Table 11-6. Object class category values

Name	Value	Description
88	0	Legacy class type defined by the original X.500 standards. It should not be used for new classes.
Structural	1	Used for instantiating objects. Can be comprised of abstract, auxiliary, and other structural classes.
Abstract	2	Used to define a high-level grouping of attributes that can be used as part of other abstract or structural class definitions. Objects cannot be instantiated using an abstract class.
Auxiliary	3	Used as a collection of attributes that can be applied to other abstract, auxiliary, or structural classes.

11.20 Finding the Mandatory and Optional Attributes of a Class

Problem

You want to view the mandatory and optional attributes of a class.

Solution

Using a graphical user interface

1. Open the Active Directory Schema snap-in.

2. In the left pane, click on the Classes folder.

3. In the right pane, double-click the class you want to view.

4. Click on the Attributes tab.

Using a command-line interface

You can enumerate the mandatory and optional attributes of a class using either DSQuery or AdFind. DSQuery takes the following syntax:

```
> dsquery * cn=<ClassCommonName>,cn=schema,cn=configuration,<ForestRootDN> -l
-attr mayContain mustContain systemMayContain systemMustContain
```

To list these attributes using AdFind, use the following syntax:

```
> adfind -schema -rb cn=<ClassCommonName> mayContain mustContain systemMayContain
systemMustContain
```

Using VBScript

```
' This code displays the mandatory and optional attributes for a class.
' ------ SCRIPT CONFIGURATION ------
```

```
' Set to common name of class to view
strClassName = "<ClassCommonName>"    ' e.g. Surname
' ------ END CONFIGURATION ---------

set objRootDSE = GetObject("LDAP://RootDSE")
set objClass = GetObject("LDAP://cn=" & strClassName & "," & _
                         objRootDSE.Get("schemaNamingContext"))

WScript.Echo "Class: " & strClassName & vbCrlf

' Need to enable this so that if an attribute is not set, it won't die
on error resume next

WScript.Echo "mayContain:"
for each strVal in objClass.Get("mayContain")
   WScript.Echo vbTab & strVal
next

WScript.Echo vbCrlf & "systemMayContain:"
for each strVal in objClass.Get("systemMayContain")
   WScript.Echo vbTab & strVal
next

WScript.Echo vbCrlf & "mustContain:"
for each strVal in objClass.Get("mustContain")
   WScript.Echo vbTab & strVal
next

WScript.Echo vbCrlf & "systemMustContain:"
for each strVal in objClass.Get("systemMustContain")
   WScript.Echo vbTab & strVal
next
```

Discussion

The mayContain and systemMayContain attributes define the optional attributes for a class, while the mustContain and systemMustContain attributes contain the mandatory attributes. The systemMayContain and systemMustContain attributes are set by Active Directory itself and cannot be modified. You can only populate the mustContain attribute when a class is first created; you cannot add attributes to it after the fact. This is so that you are not inadvertently able to modify a class such that existing instances of that class become invalid.

It is also worth noting that each of the solutions displays only the attributes defined directly on the class. It will not show any inherited attributes that are defined by inherited classes.

11.21 Modifying the Default Security of a Class

Problem

You want to modify the default security that is applied to objects instantiated from a particular structural class.

Solution

 For Windows 2000 Active Directory, you need to enable schema modifications before proceeding. See Recipe 11.2 for more information.

Using a graphical user interface

1. Open the Active Directory Schema snap-in.
2. In the left pane, click on the Classes folder.
3. In the right pane, double-click the class you want to modify the security for.
4. Click the Default Security tab.
5. Modify the security as necessary.
6. Click OK.

Using a command line interface

```
> admod -b cn=<ClassShortName>,cn=schema,cn=Configuration,<ForestRootDN>
defaultSecurityDescriptor::"O:AOG:DAD:(A;;RPWPCCDCLCSWRCWDWOGA;;;S-1-0-0)"
```

Using VBScript

```
' This code modifies the defaultSecurityDescriptor of a class
' Refer to Recipe 4.2 for the DisplayAttributes( ) function code.
' ------ SCRIPT CONFIGURATION ------
' Set to the common name (not LDAP display dame) of the class
strClassName = "<ClassCommonName>"    ' e.g. User
' ------ END CONFIGURATION ---------

set objRootDSE = GetObject("LDAP://RootDSE")
set objClass = GetObject("LDAP://cn=" & strAttrName & "," & _
                    objRootDSE.Get("schemaNamingContext"))
objClass.Put "defaultSecurityDescriptor", _
   "O:AOG:DAD:(A;;RPWPCCDCLCSWRCWDWOGA;;;S-1-0-0)"
objClass.SetInfo
WScript.Echo "Default Security Descriptor modified"
```

Discussion

Whenever a new object is created in Active Directory, a default security descriptor (SD) is applied to it along with any inherited security from its parent container. The default security descriptor is stored in the `defaultSecurityDescriptor` attribute of the `classSchema` object. If you modify the default SD, every new object will get that SD, but it does not affect any existing objects.

Using a command-line interface

The `defaultSecurityDescriptor` attribute is stored in Active Directory using the Security Descriptor Definition Language (SDDL) format, and will return data formatted similar to the following:

```
"O:AOG:DAD:(A;;RPWPCCDCLCSWRCWDWOGA;;;S-1-0-0)"
```

For more information on formulating SDDL strings, see the Platform Software Development Kit (SDK) or MSDN.

 When creating your own Active Directory classes, we recommend against setting a default security descriptor, as this feature can create issues when working with delegated permissions.

See Also

MS KB 265399 (How to Change Default Permissions for Objects That Are Created in the Active Directory) and MSDN: Security Descriptor String Format

11.22 Managing the Confidentiality Bit

Problem

You want to manage the confidentiality of a schema attribute.

Solution

Using VBScript

```
' This code safely modifies the confidentiality bit of an attribute.
' ------ SCRIPT CONFIGURATION ------
strAttribute = "<schemaAttributeDN>"
 ' e.g. "cn=SalesUser-Description,cn=Schema,
 ' cn=Configuration,dc=rallencorp,dc=com"
strAttr = "searchFlags"          ' e.g. rallencorp-UserProperties
boolEnableBit = <TRUEorFALSE> ' e.g. TRUE
intBit = 128
' ------ END CONFIGURATION ---------

set objAttribute = GetObject("LDAP://" & strAttribute)
```

```
intBitsOrig = objAttribute.Get(strAttr)
intBitsCalc = CalcBit(intBitsOrig, intBit, boolEnableBit)

if intBitsOrig <> intBitsCalc then
    objObject.Put strAttr, intBitsCalc
    objObject.SetInfo
    WScript.Echo "Changed " & strAttr & " from " & intBitsOrig & " to " & intBitsCalc
else
    WScript.Echo "Did not need to change " & strAttr & " (" & intBitsOrig & ")"
end if


Function CalcBit(intValue, intBit, boolEnable)

    CalcBit = intValue

    if boolEnable = TRUE then
        CalcBit = intValue Or intBit
    else
        if intValue And intBit then
            CalcBit = intValue Xor intBit
        end if
    end if

End Function
```

Discussion

The confidentiality bit is a new addition to Windows Server 2003 Service Pack 1 that allows you to restrict access to attributes that should not be accessible to all users. For example, you may have created an attribute to store user Social Security Number information. Even though this attribute may be populated for every user object in the directory, you will likely wish to restrict access to that specific attribute to only a subset of your personnel. The confidentiality bit is set in the searchFlags attribute by setting bit 8 (128) to a value of 1. Once you've done this, the Read permission on that attribute will not be sufficient to access the information stored in it; you'll need to grant the Control_Access permission to allow a user or group to view the contents of the attribute using LDP. (Unfortunately, the current version of *dsacls* does not allow you to set the Control_Access permission via the command line.)

While the confidentiality bit is a great improvement in Active Directory security, it does have two significant limitations. The first is that there is not a supported mechanism to set the confidentiality bit on any attributes that are a part of the base schema; you can, however, obtain a list of these attributes by searching for attributes that have bit 4 (16 in decimal) set to 1.

There is an unsupported mechanism for setting the confidentiality bit on a base attribute, by modifying the appropriate searchFlags value on a domain controller, that has not yet been upgraded to Windows Server 2003 SP1. Be aware that this is unsupported, however, and that Microsoft will likely not offer you any technical support for any issues that arise as a result. This solution is more fully documented in Chapter 11 of *Active Directory*, Third Edition, by Joe Richards et al. (O'Reilly).

Second, there are certain default permissions included with Active Directory that will still allow certain security principals to access the information stored in confidential attributes; these groups include the Administrators group, Account Operators, and any user or group who has the Full Control permission on an object containing a confidential attribute.

See Also

Recipe 4.15 for more on modifying a bitwise attribute and How the Active Directory Schema Works: *http://www.microsoft.com/technet/prodtechnol/windowsserver2003/library/TechRef/e3525d00-a746-4466-bb87-140acb44a603.mspx*

11.23 Deactivating Classes and Attributes

Problem

You want to deactivate a class or attribute in the schema because you no longer need it.

Solution

Using a graphical user interface

1. Open the Active Directory Schema snap-in.
2. In the left pane, click on the Classes folder.
3. In the right pane, double-click the class you want to deactivate.
4. Uncheck the box beside "Class is active."
5. Click OK.

Using a command-line interface

You can deactivate a class using the *ldifde* utility and an LDIF file that contains the following lines:

```
dn: cn=<SchemaObjectCommonName>,cn=schema,cn=configuration,<ForestRootDN>
changetype: modify
replace: isDefunct
isDefunct: TRUE
-
```

If the LDIF file were named *deactivate_class.ldf*, you would run the following command:

```
> ldifde -v -i -f deactivate_class.ldf
```

You can also deactivate a class using AdMod, as follows:

```
> admod –b cn=<SchemaObjectCommonName>,cn=schema,cn=configuration,<ForestRootDN>
isDefunct::TRUE
```

Using VBScript

```
' This code deactivates a class or attribute.
' ------ SCRIPT CONFIGURATION ------
strName = "<SchemaObjectCommonName>"   ' e.g. rallencorp-LanguagesSpoken
' ------ END CONFIGURATION ---------
set objRootDSE = GetObject("LDAP://RootDSE")
set objSchemaObject = GetObject("LDAP://cn=" & strName & "," & _
                                objRootDSE.Get("schemaNamingContext"))
objSchemaObject.Put "isDefunct", TRUE
objSchemaObject.SetInfo
WScript.Echo "Schema object deactivated: " & strName
```

Discussion

There is no supported way to delete classes or attributes defined in the schema. You can, however, deactivate them, also known as making them defunct. Before you deactivate a class you should make sure that no instantiated objects of that class exist. If you want to deactivate an attribute, you should make sure no object classes define the attribute as mandatory. After you've verified the class or attribute is no longer being used, you can deactivate by setting the isDefunct attribute to TRUE. You can always reactivate it at a later time by simply setting isDefunct to FALSE. With Windows Server 2003 Active Directory, you can even redefine the class or attribute while it is defunct. This gives you much more flexibility over reusing classes or attributes you may have added before, but no longer want.

See Also

Recipe 11.24 for redefining classes and attributes

11.24 Redefining Classes and Attributes

 This recipe requires the Windows Server 2003 forest functional level.

Problem

You want to redefine a class or attribute that was previously created.

Solution

To redefine a class or attribute, you must first deactivate it by setting the `isDefunct` attribute to TRUE (see Recipe 11.23 for more details). If you are deactivating a class, make sure no objects are instantiated that use the class. If you are deactivating an attribute, make sure it isn't populated on any objects and remove it from any classes that have it defined as part of `mayContain` and `mustContain`. After the class or attribute has been deactivated, you can modify (i.e., redefine) the LDAP display name (`lDAPDisplayName`), the OID (`governsID` or `attributeID`), the syntax (`attributeSyntax` and `oMSyntax`), and the `schemaIDGUID`. The one attribute that you cannot modify is the common name.

Discussion

Redefining schema objects is a new feature of Windows Server 2003. Although you still cannot delete schema objects in Windows Server 2003, you can work around many of the reasons that would cause you to want to delete a schema object by redefining it instead. Redefining schema objects comes in handy if you accidentally mistype an OID (`governsID/attributeID`) or `lDAPDisplayName`, or no longer need an attribute you previously created. You can reuse it by renaming the attribute and giving it a different syntax.

 You could delete schema objects in W2K pre-SP3 but we won't get into that since it was unsupported then as well. See *http://www.winnetmag.com/Articles/Index.cfm?ArticleID=27096* for more information.

See Also

Recipe 11.23 for deactivating classes and attributes

11.25 Reloading the Schema Cache

Problem

You want to reload the schema cache so schema extensions take effect immediately.

Solution

Using a graphical user interface

1. Open the Active Directory Schema snap-in.
2. In the left pane, click on Active Directory Schema.
3. Right-click on the label and select "Reload the Schema."

Using a command-line interface

You can reload the schema by using the *ldifde* utility and an LDIF file that contains the following:

```
dn:
changetype: modify
add: schemaUpdateNow
schemaUpdateNow: 1
-
```

If the LDIF file were named *reload.ldf*, you would run the following command:

```
> ldifde -v -i -f reload.ldf
```

You can also reload the schema cache using AdMod, as follows:

```
> admod -b "" schemaupdatenow::1
```

Using VBScript

```
set objRootDSE = GetObject("LDAP://dc1/RootDSE")
objRootDSE.Put "schemaUpdateNow", 1
objRootDSE.SetInfo
WScript.Echo "Schema reloaded"
```

Discussion

Each domain controller maintains a complete copy of the schema in memory to make access to the schema very fast. This is called the *schema cache*. When you extend the schema on the Schema FSMO role owner, the change is written to the schema cache, and not committed to disk yet. The schema automatically commits any changes to the schema every five minutes if a change has taken place, but you can also do it manually/programmatically by writing to the schemaUpdateNow operational attribute of the RootDSE on the Schema FSMO role owner. Once that is done, any changes to the schema cache are written to disk.

It is necessary to force a schema cache update if your schema extensions reference newly created attributes or classes. For example, let's say that you want to create one new auxiliary class that contains one new attribute. To do that, you would first need to create the attribute and then create the auxiliary class. As part of the auxiliary class's definition, you would need to reference the new attribute, but unless you reload the schema cache, an error would be returned stating that the attribute does not exist. For this reason, you need to add an additional step. First you create the attribute, then reload the schema cache, and finally create the auxiliary class. Here is what an LDIF representation would look like:

```
dn: cn=rallencorp-TestAttr,cn=schema,cn=configuration,dc=rallencorp,dc=com
changetype: add
objectclass: attributeSchema
lDAPDisplayName: rallencorp-TestAttr
attributeId: 1.3.6.1.4.1.999.1.1.28.312
```

```
oMSyntax: 20
attributeSyntax: 2.5.5.4
isSingleValued: FALSE
searchFlags: 1

dn:
changetype: modify
add: schemaUpdateNow
schemaUpdateNow: 1
-

dn: cn=rallencorp-TestClass,cn=schema,cn=configuration,dc=rallencorp,dc=com
changetype: add
objectclass: classSchema
lDAPDisplayName: rallencorp-TestClass
governsId: 1.3.6.1.4.1.999.1.1.28.311
subClassOf: top
objectClassCategory: 3
mayContain: rallencorp-TestAttr
```

See Also

Recipe 11.8 for adding a new attribute to the schema and Recipe 11.10 for adding a new class to the schema

11.26 Managing the Schema Master FSMO

Problem

You want to view, transfer, or seize the Schema Master FSMO for your Active Directory Forest.

Solution

Using a graphical user interface

To view the current Schema Master FSMO role holder, do the following:

1. Open the Active Directory Schema snap-in.
2. Right-click on Active Directory Schema in the left pane and select Operations Master.

To transfer the Schema Master to another server, follow these steps:

1. Open the Active Directory Schema snap-in. Right-click on Active Directory Schema and select "Connect to Domain Controller." Select the DC that you wish to transfer the FSMO role to.
2. Right-click on Active Directory Schema in the left pane and select Operations Master.
3. Click the Change button.

4. Click OK twice.

5. You should then see a message stating whether the transfer was successful.

Using a command-line interface

To query the owner of the Schema Master FSMO role, you can use the `dsquery` server command shown here:

```
> dsquery server -hasfsmo schema
```

To transfer the Schema Master to another server, follow these steps:

```
> ntdsutil roles conn "co t s <NewRoleOwner>" q "transfer Schema Master" q q
```

To forcibly seize the Schema Master to another DC, do the following:

```
> ntdsutil roles conn "co t s <NewRoleOwner>" q "seize Schema Master" q q
```

Using VBScript

```
' This code prints the Schema Master role owner for the specified forest.

strSchemaDN = objRootDSE.Get("schemaNamingContext")

' Schema Master
set objSchemaFsmo = GetObject("LDAP://" & strSchemaDN)
Wscript.Echo "Schema Master: " & objSchemaFsmo.fsmoroleowner

' This code transfers the Schema Master role to another server
Set dse = GetObject("LDAP://localhost/RootDSE")
set myDomain = GetObject("LDAP://" & dse.get("defaultNamingContext"))
dse.Put "becomeSchemaMaster",1
dse.SetInfo

' This code seizes the Schema Master role to another server
set myDomain = GetObject("LDAP://" & dse.get("defaultNamingContext"))
dse.Put "becomeSchemaMaster",1
dse.SetInfo
```

Discussion

Several Active Directory operations, such as updating the schema, are sensitive and therefore need to be restricted to a single domain controller to prevent corruption of the AD database. This is because Active Directory cannot guarantee the proper evaluation of these functions in a situation where they may be invoked from more than one DC. The FSMO mechanism is used to limit these functions to a single DC.

The first domain controller in a new forest is assigned the two forest-wide FSMO roles, the schema master and domain naming master. The first domain controller in a new domain gets the other three domain-wide roles. If you need to decommission the domain controller that is currently the Schema Master role owner (either permanently or for a significant period of time), you'll want to transfer the role beforehand.

If the Schema Master becomes unavailable before you can transfer it, you'll need to seize the role (see Recipe 3.32).

 If you seize the Schema Master FSMO to another server, you should reformat and reinstall the original role holder before returning it to your production environment.

See Also

Recipe 3.30, Recipe 3.31, and Recipe 3.32 for more on viewing, transferring, and seizing FSMO roles; and MS KB 324801 (How to view and transfer FSMO roles in Windows Server 2003)

## CHAPTER 12

Site Topology

12.0 Introduction

Active Directory needs information about the underlying network to determine how domain controllers should replicate and what domain controller(s) are optimal for a given client to authenticate with. This network information is often referred to as the site or replication *topology*, and consists of numerous object types that represent various aspects of the network.

At a high level, a site is a logical collection of high-speed LAN segments. One or more subnets can be associated with a site, and this mapping is used to determine which site a client belongs to, based on its IP address. Sites are connected via site links, which are analogous to WAN connections. Finally, each domain controller in a site has one or more connection objects, which define a replication connection to another domain controller.

These site topology objects are contained under the Sites container within the Configuration naming context. Figure 12-1 shows an example of the site topology hierarchy using the Active Directory Sites and Services snap-in.

Directly under the Sites container are the individual site containers, plus containers that store the site link objects (cn=Inter-site Transports) and subnets (cn=Subnets). There are three objects included within a site:

- An NTDS Site Settings (nTDSSiteSettings) object that contains attributes that can customize replication behavior for the whole site
- A License Site Settings (licensingSiteSettings) object that can be used to direct hosts within the site to the appropriate licensing server
- A Servers container

The Servers container contains a server object for each of the domain controllers that are members of the site, along with any other servers that need to be represented in the site topology (e.g., DFS servers).

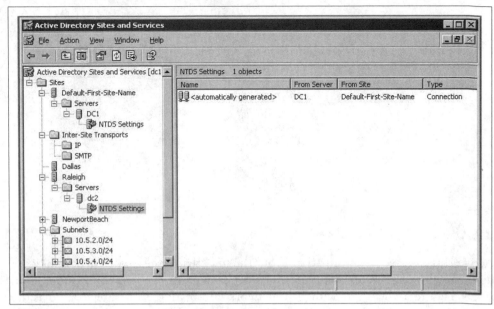

Figure 12-1. Site topology hierarchy

A server object can contain a NTDS Settings (nTDSDSA) object, which distinguishes domain-controller server objects from other server objects. The NTDS Settings object stores several attributes that are used to customize replication behavior for a specific domain controller. The NTDS Settings object can contain one or more nTDSConnection objects, which define the replication connections between domain controllers.

The Anatomy of Site Topology Objects

Tables 12-1 through 12-7 contain some of the important attributes of the various site topology objects.

Table 12-1. Attributes of site objects

Attribute	Description
cn	RDN of the object. This is the name of the site (e.g., Raleigh).
gpLink	Contains a prioritized list of GPOs that are linked to the site.
siteObjectBL	Multivalued attribute that contains a list of distinguished names for each subnet that is associated with the site.

Table 12-2. Attributes of nTDSSiteSettings objects

Attribute	Description
cn	RDN of the object, which is always equal to NTDS Site Settings.
interSiteTopologyGenerator	Distinguished name of the NTDS Settings object of the current ISTG.

Table 12-2. Attributes of nTDSSiteSettings objects (continued)

Attribute	Description
msDS-Preferred-GC-Site	If universal group caching is enabled, this contains the distinguished name of the site that domain controllers should refresh their cache from. This attribute is new to Windows Server 2003. See Recipe 7.13 for more information.
options	Bit flag that determines if universal group caching is enabled, whether site link transitivity is disabled, and if replication schedules should be ignored. For more information see Recipe 12.6.
schedule	Octet string that represents the default replication schedule for the site.

Table 12-3. Attributes of subnet objects

Attribute	Description
cn	RDN of the object. Contains the network number and bit mask for the subnet (e.g., 10.1.3.0/24).
siteObject	Distinguished name of the site object the subnet is associated with.

Table 12-4. Attributes of siteLink objects

Attribute	Description
cn	RDN of the object. Contains the name of the link.
cost	Number that represents the site link cost. See Recipe 12.15 for more information.
replInterval	Interval in minutes that replication occurs over the site link.
schedule	Octet string that represents the replication schedule for the site link.
siteList	Multimultivalued list of distinguished names of each site that is associated with the site link. See Recipe 12.13 for more information.

Table 12-5. Attributes of server objects

Attribute	Description
bridgeheadTransportList	Multivalued attribute that contains the list of transports (e.g., IP or SMTP) for which the server is a preferred bridgehead server.
cn	RDN of the object. This is set to the hostname of the associated server.
dNSHostName	Fully qualified domain name of the server. This attribute is automatically maintained for domain controllers.
serverReference	Distinguished name of the corresponding computer object contained within one of the domain-naming contexts.

Table 12-6. Attributes of nTDSDSA (NTDS Settings) objects

Attribute	Description
cn	RDN of the object, which is always equal to NTDS Settings.
invocationID	GUID that represents the DIT (*ntds.dit*) on the domain controller.
hasMasterNCs	Multivalued attribute containing the list of writable naming contexts (does not include application partitions) stored on the domain controller.

Table 12-6. Attributes of nTDSDSA (NTDS Settings) objects (continued)

Attribute	Description
hasPartialReplicaNCs	Multivalued attribute containing the list of read-only naming contexts stored on the domain controller. This will be populated only if the domain controller is a global catalog server.
msDS-Behavior-Version	Number that represents the functional level (i.e., operating system) of the domain controller. This attribute is new to Windows Server 2003.
msDS-HasDomainNCs	Contains the distinguished name of the writable domain naming context stored on the domain controller. This attribute is new to Windows Server 2003.
msDs-HasInstantiatedNCs	A combination of all available read-only and writable naming contexts stored on the domain controller. This attribute is new to Windows Server 2003.
msDS-hasPartialReplicaNCs	Multivalued attribute that contains distinguished names of each read-only naming context stored on the domain controller. This will be populated only if the domain controller is a global catalog server. This attribute is new to Windows Server 2003.
msDS-hasMasterNCs	Multivalued attribute that contains distinguished names of each writeable naming context and application partition stored on the domain controller. This attribute is new to Windows Server 2003.
options	Bit flag that determines if domain controller is a global catalog server.
queryPolicyObject	If set, the distinguished name of the LDAP query policy object to be used by the domain controller.

Table 12-7. Attributes of nTDSConnection objects

Attribute	Description
cn	RDN of the object. For KCC-generated connections, this is a GUID.
enabledConnection	Boolean that indicates if the connection is available to be used.
fromServer	Distinguished name of the NTDS Settings object of the domain controller this connection replicates with.
ms-DS-ReplicatesNCReason	Multivalued attribute that stores reason codes for why the connection exists. There will be one entry per naming context the connection is used for.
options	Bit flag where a value of 1 indicates the connection was created by the KCC and a value of 0 means the connection was manually created. See Recipe 12.29 for more information.
schedule	Octet string that represents the replication schedule for the site link.
transportType	Distinguished name of the transport type (e.g., IP or SMTP) that is used for the connection.

12.1   Creating a Site

Problem

You want to create a site.

Solution

Using a graphical user interface

1. Open the Active Directory Sites and Services snap-in.
2. Right-click on the Sites container and select New Site.
3. Beside Name, enter the name of the new site.
4. Under Link Name, select a site link for the site.
5. Click OK twice.

Using a command-line interface

Create an LDIF file called *create_site.ldf* with the following contents:

```
dn: cn=<SiteName>,cn=sites,cn=configuration,<ForestRootDN>
changetype: add
objectclass: site

dn: cn=Licensing Site Settings,cn=<SiteName>,cn=sites,cn=configuration,
<ForestRootDN>
changetype: add
objectclass: licensingSiteSettings

dn: cn=NTDS Site Settings,cn=<SiteName>,cn=sites,cn=configuration,<ForestRootDN>
changetype: add
objectclass: nTDSSiteSettings

dn: cn=Servers,cn=<SiteName>,cn=sites,cn=configuration,<ForestRootDN>
changetype: add
objectclass: serversContainer
```

Then run the following command:

```
> ldifde -v -i -f create_site.ldf
```

You can also create a site by issuing the following four AdMod commands:

```
> admod -b "cn=Licensing Site Settings,cn=<SiteName,
cn=sites,cn=configuration,<ForestRootDN>" objectclass::licensingSiteSettings -add
> admod -b "cn=NTDS Site Settings,cn=<SiteName,
cn=sites,cn=configuration,<ForestRootDN>" objectclass::nTDSSiteSettings -add
> admod -b "cn=NTDS Site Settings,cn=<SiteName,
cn=sites,cn=configuration,<ForestRootDN>" objectclass::nTDSSiteSettings -add
> admod -b cn=Servers,cn=<SiteName>,cn=sites,cn=configuration,<ForestRootDN>"
objectclass::serversContainer -add
```

Using VBScript

```
' This code creates the objects that make up a site.
' ------ SCRIPT CONFIGURATION ------
strSiteName = "<SiteName>"   ' e.g. Dallas
' ------ END CONFIGURATION ---------

set objRootDSE = GetObject("LDAP://RootDSE")
```

```
set objSitesCont = GetObject("LDAP://cn=sites," & _
                            objRootDSE.Get("configurationNamingContext") )
' Create the site
set objSite = objSitesCont.Create("site","cn=" & strSiteName)
objSite.SetInfo

' Create the Licensing Site Settings object
set objLicensing = objSite.Create("licensingSiteSettings", _
                            "cn=Licensing Site Settings")
objLicensing.SetInfo

' Create the NTDS Site Settings object
set objNTDS = objSite.Create("nTDSSiteSettings","cn=NTDS Site Settings")
objNTDS.SetInfo

' Create the Servers container
set objServersCont = objSite.Create("serversContainer","cn=Servers")
objServersCont.SetInfo

WScript.Echo "Successfully created site " & strSiteName
```

Discussion

To create a site in Active Directory, you have to create a number of objects. The first is a site object, which is the root of all the other objects. The site object contains the following:

licensingSiteSettings

> This object isn't mandatory but is created automatically when creating a site with AD Sites and Services. It is intended to point clients to a license server for the site.

nTDSSiteSettings

> This object stores replication-related properties about a site, such as the replication schedule, current ISTG role holder, and whether universal group caching is enabled.

serversContainer

> This container is the parent of the server objects that are part of the site. All the domain controllers that are members of the site will be represented in this container.

After these objects are created, you've essentially created an empty site. If you didn't do anything else, the site would not be of much value. To make it usable, you need to assign subnet objects to it (see Recipe 12.11), and add the site to a siteLink object to link the site to other sites (see Recipe 12.14). At that point, you can promote or move domain controllers into the site, and it should be fully functional.

See Also

Recipe 12.11, Recipe 12.14, and MS KB 318480 (How to Create and Configure an Active Directory Site in Windows 2000)

12.2   Listing the Sites

Problem

You want to obtain the list of sites in a forest.

Solution

Using a graphical user interface

1. Open the Active Directory Sites and Services snap-in.
2. Click on the Sites container.
3. The list of sites will be displayed in the right pane.
4. Double-click on a site to view its properties.

Using a command-line interface

Run one of the following commands to list the sites in a forest:

```
> dsquery site
```

or:

```
> adfind -config -rb cn=sites -f (objectcategory=site)
```

Run one of the following commands to view the properties for a particular site:

```
> dsget site "<SiteName>"
```

or:

```
> adfind -config -rb "cn=<SiteName>",cn=sites
```

Using VBScript

```
' This code lists all of the site objects.

set objRootDSE = GetObject("LDAP://RootDSE")
set objSitesCont = GetObject("LDAP://cn=sites," & _
                             objRootDSE.Get("configurationNamingContext") )
objSitesCont.Filter = Array("site")
for each objSite in objSitesCont
   Wscript.Echo "  " & objSite.Get("cn")
next
```

Discussion

Site objects are stored in the Sites container (for example, cn=sites, cn=configuration,dc=rallencorp,dc=com) in the Configuration Naming Context (CNC). For more information on creating sites, see Recipe 12.1.

12.3 Renaming a Site

Problem

You want to rename a site.

Solution

Using a graphical user interface

1. Open the Active Directory Sites and Services snap-in.
2. Click on the Sites container.
3. In the right pane, right-click the site you want to rename and select Rename.
4. Enter the new name of the site and press Enter.

Using a command-line interface

The following command will change the RDN of a site:

```
> dsmove "<SiteDN>" -newname "<NewSiteName>"
```

You can also rename a site using AdMod, using the following syntax:

```
> admod -b "<SiteDN>" -rename "<NewSiteName>"
```

Using VBScript

```
' This code renames a site object.
' ------ SCRIPT CONFIGURATION ------
strSiteOldName = "<OldSiteName>" ' e.g. Raleigh
strSiteNewName = "<NewSiteName>" ' e.g. Raleigh-Durham
' ------ END CONFIGURATION ---------

Set objRootDSE = GetObject("LDAP://RootDSE")
strConfigurationNC = objRootDSE.Get("configurationNamingContext")

strSitesContainer = "LDAP://cn=Sites," & strConfigurationNC
strOldSiteDN = "LDAP://cn=" & strSiteOldName & ",cn=Sites," & strConfigurationNC

Set objSitesContainer = GetObject(strSitesContainer)
objSitesContainer.MoveHere strOldSiteDN, strSiteNewName
```

Discussion

Renaming a site in Active Directory involves changing the cn of the site object. The largest concern with renaming a site, as with any other AD object, is to ensure that no applications reference the site by name. A best practice to avoid this pitfall is to reference AD objects by their GUIDs, which will not change even when the object is renamed.

See Also

MSDN: Object Names and Identities and MSDN: Using objectGUID to Bind to an Object

12.4 Deleting a Site

Problem

You want to delete a site.

Solution

Using a graphical user interface

1. Open the Active Directory Sites and Services snap-in.
2. Click on the Sites container.
3. In the right pane, right-click the site you want to delete and select Delete.
4. Click Yes twice.

Using a command-line interface

```
> dsrm <SiteDN> -subtree -noprompt
```

Alternately, you can remove a site and its associated objects by issuing the following AdMod command:

```
> admod -b "cn=<SiteName>,cn=sites,cn=configuration,<ForestRootDN>" -del -treedelete
```

Using VBScript

```
' This code deletes a site and all child containers.
' ------ SCRIPT CONFIGURATION ------
strSiteName = "<SiteName>"    ' e.g. Dallas
' ------ END CONFIGURATION ---------

set objRootDSE = GetObject("LDAP://RootDSE")
set objSite = GetObject("LDAP://cn=" & strSiteName & ",cn=sites," & _
                         objRootDSE.Get("configurationNamingContext") )
objSite.DeleteObject(0)
WScript.Echo "Successfully deleted site " & strSiteName
```

Discussion

When deleting a site, be very careful to ensure that no active server objects exist within it. If you delete a site that contains domain controllers, it will disrupt replication for all domain controllers in that site. A more robust VBScript solution would be to first perform an ADO query for all server objects using the distinguished name of the site as the base DN. If no servers were returned, then you could safely delete the site. If server objects were found, you should move them before deleting the site.

It is also worth noting that deleting a site does not delete any of the subnets or site links that are associated with the site. This would be another good thing to add to the VBScript solution. That is, before you delete the site, delete any subnets and site links that are associated with the site or, more likely, associate them with a different site.

See Also

Recipe 12.1 for more on creating a site and Recipe 12.7 for creating a subnet

12.5 Delegating Control of a Site

Problem

You want to delegate permission of an AD site to allow it to be administered by another user or group.

Solution

Using a graphical user interface

The following example will delegate administration of the managedBy attribute of a site:

1. Open the Active Directory Sites and Services snap-in.
2. Click on the Sites container.
3. In the right pane, right-click the site you want to delegate and select Delegate Control.
4. Click Next to bypass the initial Welcome screen of the Delegation of Control wizard.
5. Click Add to select the users or groups that you want to delegate control to. Click Next to continue.
6. Select "Create a custom task to delegate" and click Next.
7. Click "Only the following objects in the folder." Place a checkmark next to site objects and click Next.
8. Place a checkmark next to "Write managedBy." Click Next to continue.
9. Click Finish.

Using a command-line interface

The following code will allow a group called *SiteAdmins* to manage the managedBy attribute of sites within *rallencorp.com*:

```
> dsacls cn=Sites,cn=Configuration,dc=rallencorp,dc=com /I:S /G
rallencorp.com\SiteAdmins:WP;;managedBy
```

Using VBScript

```
' This VBScript code grants write access to the managedBy attribute of a site.

' ------ SCRIPT CONFIGURATION ------
strSiteDN = "<SiteDN>"   ' e.g. cn=SalesGroup,ou=Sales,dc=rallencorp,dc=com"
strUserOrGroup = "<UserOrGroup>"   ' e.g. joe@rallencorp.com or RALLENCORP\joe
' ------ END CONFIGURATION ---------

set objSite = GetObject("LDAP://" & strSiteDN)

'############################
' Constants
'############################
' ADS_ACETYPE_ENUM
Const ADS_ACETYPE_ACCESS_ALLOWED_OBJECT = &h5
Const ADS_FLAG_OBJECT_TYPE_PRESENT = &h1
Const ADS_RIGHT_DS_WRITE_PROP = &h20

' From schemaIDGUID of description attribute
Const MANAGEDBY_ATTRIBUTE = "{0296c120-40da-11d1-a9c0-0000f80367c1}"

'############################
' Create ACL
'############################
set objSD = objSite.Get("nTSecurityDescriptor")
set objDACL = objSD.DiscretionaryAcl

' Set WP for member attribute
set objACE = CreateObject("AccessControlEntry")
objACE.Trustee     = strUserOrGroup
objACE.AccessMask  = ADS_RIGHT_DS_WRITE_PROP
objACE.AceFlags    = 0
objACE.Flags       = ADS_FLAG_OBJECT_TYPE_PRESENT
objACE.AceType     = ADS_ACETYPE_ACCESS_ALLOWED_OBJECT
objACE.ObjectType  = MANAGEDBY_ATTRIBUTE

objDACL.AddAce objACE

'############################
' Set ACL
'############################
objSD.DiscretionaryAcl = objDACL
objSite.Put "nTSecurityDescriptor", objSD
objSite.SetInfo
WScript.Echo "Delegated control of description attribute for " & strSiteDN & " to "
& strUser
```

Discussion

Using a graphical user interface

Delegating control over a site can be done via the Delegation of Control wizard, or by using *dsacls* at the command line or a VBScript. The Delegation of Control wizard allows you to delegate one preconfigured task—managing Group Policy links—or create a custom task to delegate. When delegating a custom task, you must first determine whether you are delegating permission over the entire site and all objects contained therein or whether you are only going to delegate control over specific child objects. (For example, you can delegate control over all computer objects within a site.) Once you've made this determination, you'll then specify the specific permissions that you're delegating; you can delegate anything from Full Control of the entire object down to granting read permissions on a single attribute.

See Also

MS KB 310997 (Active Directory Services and Windows 2000 or Windows Server 2003 domains) and MS KB 315676 (How to Delegate Administrative Authority in Windows 2000)

12.6 Configuring Universal Group Caching for a Site

 This recipe requires the Windows Server 2003 forest functional level.

Problem

You want to configure a site so that it does not require access to a global catalog server during most user logins.

Solution

Using a graphical user interface

1. Open the Active Directory Sites and Services snap-in.
2. In the left pane, browse to the site you want to enable group caching for and click on it.
3. In the right pane, double-click on the NTDS Site Settings object.
4. Under Universal Group Membership Caching, check the box beside Enable Universal Group Caching.
5. If you want to force the cache refresh from a particular site, select a site; otherwise, leave the default set to <Default>.
6. Click OK.

Using a command-line interface

You can use *ldifde* to enable universal group caching. Create a file called *enable_univ_cache.ldf* with the following contents, but change *<SiteName>* to the name of the site you want to enable, and *<ForestRootDN>* to the distinguished name of the forest root domain:

```
dn: cn=NTDS Site Settings,cn=<SiteName>,cn=sites,cn=configuration,<ForestRootDN>
changetype: modify
replace: options
options: 32
-
```

Then use the following command to import the change:

```
> ldifde -i -f enable_univ_cache.ldf
```

You can also perform this change using AdMod, using the following syntax:

```
> admod -b "cn=NTDS Site Settings,cn=<SiteName>,cn=sites,cn=
configuration,<ForestRootDN>" options::32
```

 To explicitly set the site that domain controllers in this site should use to refresh universal group membership, configure the msDS-Preferred-GC-Site attribute on the NTDS Site Settings object with the DN of the desired site.

Using VBScript

```
' This code safely enables universal group caching for the specified site.
' ------ SCRIPT CONFIGURATION ------
strSiteDN = "<SiteDN>"       ' e.g. cn=Raleigh,cn=Sites,cn=Configuration,
                             ' dc=rallencorp,dc=com
strAttr = "options"
boolEnableCaching = TRUE  ' Set to false to disable UG caching
intBit = 32
' ------ END CONFIGURATION ---------

set objSite = GetObject("LDAP://" & strSiteDN)
intBitsOrig = objObject.Get(strAttr)
intBitsCalc = CalcBit(intBitsOrig, intBit, boolEnableBit)

if intBitsOrig <> intBitsCalc then
   objSite.Put strAttr, intBitsCalc
   objSite.SetInfo
   WScript.Echo "Changed " & strAttr & " to " & boolEnableCaching
else
   WScript.Echo "Did not need to change " & strAttr & " value."
end if

Function CalcBit(intValue, intBit, boolEnable)

   CalcBit = intValue

   if boolEnableCaching = TRUE then
      CalcBit = intValue Or intBit
   else
      if intValue And intBit then
```

```
        CalcBit = intValue Xor intBit
    end if
  end if

  End Function
```

Discussion

In Windows 2000 Active Directory, an authenticating domain controller is required to contact a global catalog server (if it is not one itself) in order to process any client authentication requests. This is necessary because of the need to verify universal group memberships for any clients attempting to access the domain. *Universal group caching* was introduced in Windows Server 2003 to reduce the impact of this requirement. Universal group caching can be enabled on a site-by-site basis and allows domain controllers to cache universal group information locally. This largely removes the need to query the global catalog during client logon, though a global catalog will still need to be contacted the first time a new user logs on because no membership information will be cached in that case. The local DC will also need to contact a GC at regular intervals to update its cached information.

You can enable universal group caching manually by enabling the 100,000 bit (32 in decimal) on the options attribute of the NTDS Site Settings object. The CLI solutions blindly write a value of 32 to that attribute, which is not ideal since it will overwrite any existing values that may already be in place. The VBScript solution provides a safer and more elegant solution for setting a bit flag attribute such as options.

See Also

Recipe 4.12 for more on viewing bitwise attributes, Recipe 4.15 for information on configuring bitwise values, and MS KB 269181 (How to Query Active Directory by Using a Bitwise Filter)

12.7 Creating a Subnet

Problem

You want to create a subnet.

Solution

Using a graphical user interface

1. Open the Active Directory Sites and Services snap-in.
2. Right-click on the Subnets container and select New Subnet.
3. Enter the Address and Mask and then select which site the subnet is part of.
4. Click OK.

Using a command-line interface

Create an LDIF file called *create_subnet.ldf* with the following contents:

```
dn: cn=<Subnet>,cn=subnets,cn=sites,cn=configuration,<ForestRootDN>
changetype: add
objectclass: subnet
siteObject: cn=<SiteName>,cn=sites,cn=configuration,<ForestRootDN>
```

Then run the following command:

```
> ldifde -v -i -f create_subnet.ldf
```

You can also create a subnet using AdMod, as follows:

```
> admod -b "cn=<Subnet>,cn=subnets,cn=sites,cn=configuration,<ForestRootDN>"
objectClass::subnet siteObject::"cn=<SiteName,
cn=sites,cn=configuration,<ForestRootDN>" -add
```

Using VBScript

```
' This code creates a subnet object and associates it with a site.
' ------ SCRIPT CONFIGURATION ------
strSubnet = "<Subnet>"      ' e.g. 10.5.3.0/24
strSite   = "<SiteName>"    ' e.g. Dallas
' ------ END CONFIGURATION ---------

set objRootDSE = GetObject("LDAP://RootDSE")
set objSubnetsCont = GetObject("LDAP://cn=subnets,cn=sites," & _
                               objRootDSE.Get("configurationNamingContext") )
set objSubnet = objSubnetsCont.Create("subnet", "cn=" & strSubnet)
objSubnet.Put "siteObject", "cn=" & strSite & ",cn=sites," & _
                            objRootDSE.Get("configurationNamingContext")
objSubnet.SetInfo

WScript.Echo "Successfully created subnet " & strSubnet
```

Discussion

Subnet objects reside in the Subnets container in the Configuration NC (e.g., cn=subnets,cn=sites,cn=configuration,dc=rallencorp,dc=com). The RDN of the subnet should be the subnet address and bit-mask combination (e.g., 10.5.3.0/24). The other important attribute to set is siteObject, which should contain the DN of the site that the subnet is associated with.

See Also

MS KB 323349 (How to Configure Subnets in Windows Server 2003 Active Directory)

12.8   Listing the Subnets

Problem

You want to list the subnet objects in Active Directory.

Solution

Using a graphical user interface

1. Open the Active Directory Sites and Services snap-in.
2. Click on the Subnets container.
3. The list of subnets will be displayed in the right pane.
4. To view the properties of a specific subnet, double-click on the one you want to view.

Using a command-line interface

The following command will list all subnets:

```
> dsquery subnet
```

The following command will display the properties for a particular subnet. Replace *<Subnet>* with the subnet address and mask (e.g., 10.5.3.0/24):

```
> dsget subnet "<Subnet>"
```

You can also list all configured subnets with AdFind, as follows:

```
> adfind -config -f (objectCategory=subnet)
```

To display the properties of a particular subnet with AdFind, use this syntax:

```
> adfind -config -rb "cn=<Subnet>,cn=subnets,cn=sites"
```

Using VBScript

```
' This code lists all the subnets stored in Active Directory.
set objRootDSE = GetObject("LDAP://RootDSE")
set objSubnetsCont = GetObject("LDAP://cn=subnets,cn=sites," & _
                             objRootDSE.Get("configurationNamingContext") )
objSubnetsCont.Filter = Array("subnet")
for each objSubnet in objSubnetsCont
   Wscript.Echo "  " & objSubnet.Get("cn")
next
```

Discussion

To display the site that subnets are associated with, include the siteObject attribute as one of the attributes to return from the query. For example, the second-to-last line of the VBScript solution could be modified to return the site by using this code:

```
Wscript.Echo "  " & objSubnet.Get("cn") & " : " & objSubnet.Get("siteObject")
```

See Also

MS KB 323349 (How to Configure Subnets in Windows Server 2003 Active Directory)

12.9 Finding Missing Subnets

Problem

You want to find the subnets that are missing from your site topology. Missing subnets can result in clients not authenticating against the most optimal domain controller, which can degrade performance.

Solution

Having all of your subnets in Active Directory is important because a client that attempts to log on from a subnet that is not associated with any site may authenticate with any domain controller in the domain. This can result in the logon process taking longer to complete. Unfortunately, Microsoft has not provided an easy way to rectify this problem.

Under Windows 2000, the only source of missing subnet information is the System event 5778. Here is an example:

```
Event Type:         Information
Event Source:       NETLOGON
Event Category:        None
Event ID:       5778
Date:               1/27/2003
Time:               12:07:04 AM
User:               N/A
Computer:       DC2
Description:
'JSMITH-W2K' tried to determine its site by looking up its IP address ('10.21.85.34')
in the Configuration\Sites\Subnets container in the DS.  No subnet matched the IP
address.  Consider adding a subnet object for this IP address.
```

The only way to dynamically determine missing subnets is to query each domain controller for 5778 events and map the IP addresses specified within the events to a subnet you add to the site topology.

With Windows Server 2003, things are not that much better. One of the issues with the 5778 events under Windows 2000 is that they can easily fill up your System event log if you have many missing subnets. In Windows 2003, Microsoft decided to instead display a summary event 5807 that states that some number of connection attempts have been made by clients that did not map to a subnet in the site topology. Here is an example:

```
Event Type:      Warning
Event Source:       NETLOGON
Event Category:        None
```

```
Event ID:         5807
Date:             1/10/2003
Time:             10:59:53 AM
User:             N/A
Computer:         DC1
Description:
During the past 4.18 hours there have been 21 connections to this Domain Controller
from client machines whose IP addresses don't map to any of the existing sites in the
enterprise. Those clients, therefore, have undefined sites and may connect to any
Domain Controller including those that are in far distant locations from the clients.
A client's site is determined by the mapping of its subnet to one of the existing
sites. To move the above clients to one of the sites, please consider creating subnet
object(s) covering the above IP addresses with mapping to one of the existing sites.
The names and IP addresses of the clients in question have been logged on this
computer in the following log file '%SystemRoot%\debug\netlogon.log' and,
potentially, in the log file '%SystemRoot%\debug\netlogon.bak' created if the former
log becomes full. The log(s) may contain additional unrelated debugging information.
To filter out the needed information, please search for lines which contain text
'NO_CLIENT_SITE:'. The first word after this string is the client name and the second
word is the client IP address. The maximum size of the log(s) is controlled by the
following registry DWORD value 'HKEY_LOCAL_MACHINE\SYSTEM\CurrentControlSet\Services\
Netlogon\Parameters\LogFileMaxSize'; the default is 20000000 bytes. The current
maximum size is 20000000 bytes.  To set a different maximum size, create the above
registry value and set the desired maximum size in bytes.

For more information, see Help and Support Center at http://go.microsoft.com/fwlink/
events.asp.
```

Instead of scraping the event logs on every domain controller, you can look at the *%SystemRoot%\debug\netlogon.log* file on each domain controller and parse out all of the NO_CLIENT_SITE entries. This is still far from an easy process, but at least the event logs are no longer cluttered with 5778 events.

Here is an example of some of the NO_CLIENT_SITE entries from the *netlogon.log* file:

```
01/16 15:50:07 RALLENCORP: NO_CLIENT_SITE: RALLEN-TEST4 164.2.45.157
01/16 15:50:29 RALLENCORP: NO_CLIENT_SITE: SJC-BACKUP 44.25.26.142
01/16 16:19:58 RALLENCORP: NO_CLIENT_SITE: RALLEN-TEST4 164.2.45.157
01/16 16:20:07 RALLENCORP: NO_CLIENT_SITE: RALLEN-TEST4 164.2.45.157
01/16 16:50:07 RALLENCORP: NO_CLIENT_SITE: RALLEN-TEST4 164.2.45.157
01/16 16:57:00 RALLENCORP: NO_CLIENT_SITE: JSMITH-W2K1 10.61.80.19
01/16 17:20:08 RALLENCORP: NO_CLIENT_SITE: RALLEN-TEST4 164.2.45.157
01/16 17:50:08 RALLENCORP: NO_CLIENT_SITE: RALLEN-TEST4 164.2.45.157
```

If you wanted to get creative and automate a solution to do this, you could write a script that goes out to each domain controller, opens the *netlogon.log* file and retrieves NO_CLIENT_SITE entries. You could then examine all of the IP addresses and create subnets in Active Directory that would contain them. You could associate all of those subnets with a default site or even use the Default-First-Site-Name site. Then once a week (or whenever), you could look at the sites that were created or that were associated with the default site and determine what site they should actually be associated with.

Another potential solution would be to create a subnet object that is a supernet of all of the physical subnets on your network, and then associate this logical subnet with a site that would not otherwise be authenticating users. Any users that authenticate against this site will do so only because their specific subnet is not defined elsewhere in Active Directory.

See Also

MS KB 909423 (TechNet Support WebCast: Configuring Subnets for Active Directory Sites in Windows Server 2003)

12.10 Deleting a Subnet

Problem

You want to delete a subnet object.

Solution

Using a graphical user interface

1. Open the Active Directory Sites and Services snap-in.
2. Click on the Subnets container.
3. The list of subnets will be displayed in the right pane.
4. Right-click on the subnet you wish to remove and select Delete.
5. Click Yes to confirm.

Using a command-line interface

You can delete a subnet object using the built-in *dsrm* utility or AdMod. The *dsrm* utility takes the following syntax:

```
> dsrm cn=<SubnetName>,cn=subnets,cn=sites,cn=configuration,<ForestRootDN>
```

To remove a subnet using AdMod, use this syntax:

```
> admod -b cn=<SubnetName>,cn=subnets,cn=sites,cn=configuration,<ForestRootDN> -del
```

Using VBScript

```
strSubnetName = "cn=<SubnetName>" ' e.g. "cn=10.0.0.0/8"
strParentDN = cn=subnets,cn=sites,cn=configuration," _
            & strForestDN
strForestDN = "<ForestRootDN>" ' e.g. "dc=rallencorp,dc=com"

set objContainer = GetObject("LDAP://" & strParentDN)
objContainer.Delete "subnet", strSubnetName
```

Discussion

Using VBScript

This script example uses the `IADsContainer::Delete` method to delete the subnet object. To use this method, you must first bind to the parent container of the object. You then call `Delete` by passing the object class along with the RDN of the object that you want to delete.

The `Delete` method is a safer alternative to the `DeleteObject` method because you need to be more explicit about what you are deleting. With `DeleteObject`, you only have to specify the distinguished name of an object and it will summarily delete it. For example, the following code will delete a subnet object using `DeleteObject`:

```
strSubnetDN = "<SubnetDN>"
set objSubnet = GetObject("LDAP://" & strObjectDN)
objSubnet.DeleteObject(0)
```

As you can see, if a user accidentally or maliciously mistypes an inappropriate DN, the result could be disastrous. Using the `DeleteObject` method puts more constraints on the delete operation.

See Also

Recipe 4.25 for deleting a container object, MS KB 258310 (Viewing Deleted Objects in Active Directory), MSDN: IADsContainer::Delete, and MSDN: IADsDeleteOps:: DeleteObject

12.11 Changing a Subnet's Site Assignment

Problem

You want to change the site object that a particular subnet is associated with.

Solution

Using a graphical user interface

1. Open the Active Directory Sites and Services MMC snap-in (*dssite.msc*).
2. Browse to Sites → Subnets; then right-click on the subnet that you wish to modify and select Properties.
3. In the Site drop-down box, select the name of the site that this subnet should be associated with and click OK.

Using a command-line interface

```
> admod cn=<SubnetName>,cn=Subnets,cn=Sites,cn=Configuration,<ForestRootDN>
siteObject::<NewSiteDN>
```

For <*SubnetName*>, use the format "192.168.1.0/24", for example.

Using VBScript

```
' This code updates the site assignment of a subnet object.
' ------ SCRIPT CONFIGURATION ------
strNewSiteName = "<SiteName>" ' e.g. "Raleigh"
strSubnetName = "<SubnetName>" ' e.g. "192.168.1.0/24"
' ------ END CONFIGURATION ---------

set objRootDSE = GetObject("LDAP://RootDSE")
set objSiteSettings = GetObject("LDAP://cn=" & _strSubnetName & _
                                "cn=subnets,cn=sites," & _
                                objRootDSE.Get("ConfigurationNamingContext"))

objSiteSettings.Put "siteObject", _
                    "cn=" & strNewSiteName & ",cn=sites," & _
                    objRootDSE.Get("ConfigurationNamingContext")
objSiteSettings.SetInfo
WScript.Echo("Site membership updated successfully!")
```

Discussion

Since the site topology that you create in Active Directory is meant to map to your physical network topology, an Active Directory subnet object can be associated with only a single AD site at any one time. If you modify your site configuration or need to delete a site object for any reason, you should configure any subnets associated with that site that are still active on your network so that they are associated with another Active Directory site. This will ensure that any clients that reside on those subnets will be able to locate resources such as domain controllers appropriately, without sending authentication requests across site links unnecessarily.

See Also

Recipe 12.9 to find missing subnets on your network and Recipe 12.10 for more on deleting subnet objects

12.12 Creating a Site Link

Problem

You want to create a site link to connect two or more sites together.

Solution

Using a graphical user interface

1. Open the Active Directory Sites and Services snap-in.
2. Expand the Sites container.
3. Expand the Inter-Site Transports container.
4. Right-click on IP (or SMTP) and select New Site Link.
5. For Name, enter the name for the site link.
6. Under "Sites not in this site link," select at least two sites and click the Add button.
7. Click OK.

Using a command-line interface

The following LDIF would create a site link connecting the SJC and Dallas sites:

```
dn: cn=Dallas-SJC,cn=IP,cn=inter-site
transports,cn=sites,cn=configuration,<ForestRootDN>
changetype: add
objectclass: siteLink
siteList: cn=SJC,cn=sites,cn=configuration,<ForestRootDN>
siteList: cn=Dallas,cn=sites,cn=configuration,<ForestRootDN>
```

If the LDIF file were named *create_site_link.ldf*, you'd then run the following command:

```
> ldifde -v -i -f create_site_link.ldf
```

You can also create a site link using AdMod, as follows:

```
> admod -b "cn=<SiteLinkName>,cn=IP,cn=inter-site
    transports,cn=sites,cn=configuration,<ForestRootDN>"
    objectclass::sitelink
    "sitelist:++:cn=<FirstSite>,cn=sites,cn=configuration,
    <ForestRootDN>;
    cn=<SecondSite>,cn=sites,cn=configuration,<ForestRootDN>"
    cost::50 replInterval::180
    -add
```

Using VBScript

```
' This code creates a site link.
' ------ SCRIPT CONFIGURATION ------
intCost  = 100            ' site link cost
intReplInterval = 180     ' replication interval in minutes
strSite1 = "<Site1>"      ' e.g. SJC
strSite2 = "<Site2>"      ' e.g. Dallas
strLinkName = strSite1 & " - " & strSite2
' ------ END CONFIGURATION ---------

' Taken from ADS_PROPERTY_OPERATION_ENUM
const ADS_PROPERTY_UPDATE = 2
```

```
set objRootDSE = GetObject("LDAP://RootDSE")
set objLinkCont = GetObject( _
                "LDAP://cn=IP,cn=Inter-site Transports,cn=sites," & _
                objRootDSE.Get("configurationNamingContext") )
set objLink = objLinkCont.Create("siteLink", "cn=" & strLinkName)
strSite1DN = "cn=" & strSite1 & ",cn=sites," & _
                objRootDSE.Get("configurationNamingContext")
strSite2DN = "cn=" & strSite2 & ",cn=sites," & _
                objRootDSE.Get("configurationNamingContext")
objLink.PutEx ADS_PROPERTY_UPDATE, "siteList", Array(strSite1DN,strSite2DN)
objLink.Put "cost", intCost
objLink.Put "replInterval", intReplInterval
objLink.SetInfo

WScript.Echo "Successfully created link: " & strLinkName
```

Discussion

Without site links, domain controllers would not be able to determine the optimal partners to replicate with. The cost that is associated with a site defines how expensive the link is. A lower cost is less expensive (or faster) than a higher cost. Link costs are inversely proportional to bandwidth, so a faster link should be configured with a lower cost than a low-speed one. Site link costs are manually configured items, which means that the administrator can control how inter-site replication should take place on the network.

See Also

Chapter 13 for more information on replication and MS KB 316812 (How to Create and Configure a Site Link in Active Directory in Windows 2000)

12.13 Finding the Site Links for a Site

Problem

You want to list the site links that are associated with a site.

Solution

Using a graphical user interface

1. Open LDP and from the menu, select Connection → Connect.
2. For Server, enter the name of a domain controller (or leave blank to do a server-less bind).
3. For Port, enter 389.
4. Click OK.
5. From the menu, select Connection → Bind.

6. Enter the credentials of the domain user.

7. Click OK.

8. From the menu, select Browse → Search.

9. For BaseDN, type the Inter-Site Transports container DN (e.g., cn=Inter-siteTransports,cn=sites,cn=configuration,dc=rallencorp,dc=com).

10. For Scope, select Subtree.

11. For Filter, enter the following:

```
(&(objectcategory=siteLink)(siteList=cn=<SiteName>,
cn=sites,cn=configuration,<ForestRootDN>))
```

12. Click Run.

Using a command-line interface

You can list the site links associated with a particular site using DSQuery or AdFind. DSQuery requires the following syntax:

```
> dsquery * "cn=inter-site transports,cn=sites,cn=configuration,<ForestRootDN>"
-filter "(&(objectcategory=siteLink)(siteList=cn=<SiteName>,
cn=sites,cn=configuration,<ForestRootDN>))" -scope subtree -attr name
```

To obtain this information using AdFind, use the following:

```
> adfind -config -f "(&(objectcategory=siteLink)(siteList=cn=<SiteName>
,cn=sites,cn=configuration,<ForestRootDN>))" name
```

Using VBScript

```
' This code displays the site links associated with the specified site.
' ------ SCRIPT CONFIGURATION ------
strSiteName = "<SiteName>"  ' e.g. Raleigh
' ------ END CONFIGURATION ---------

set objRootDSE = GetObject("LDAP://RootDSE")
strSiteDN = "cn=" & strSiteName & ",cn=sites," & _
            objRootDSE.Get("ConfigurationNamingContext")

strBase     = "<LDAP://cn=Inter-site Transports,cn=sites," _
              & objRootDSE.Get("ConfigurationNamingContext") & ">;"
strFilter   = "(&(objectcategory=siteLink)" & _
              "(siteList=" & strSiteDN & "));"
strAttrs    = "name;"
strScope    = "subtree"

set objConn = CreateObject("ADODB.Connection")
objConn.Provider = "ADsDSOObject"
objConn.Open "Active Directory Provider"
set objRS = objConn.Execute(strBase & strFilter & strAttrs & strScope)

WScript.Echo "Total site links for " & strSiteName & ": " & objRS.RecordCount
if objRS.RecordCount > 0 then
```

```
    objRS.MoveFirst
    while Not objRS.EOF
        Wscript.Echo vbTab & objRS.Fields(0).Value
        objRS.MoveNext
    wend
end if
```

Discussion

A site can be included as a part of zero or more site links. A site with no site links would be considered orphaned from the site topology, since there is no way to determine how and where it connects into the topology. Branch office sites may have only a single site link back to a hub, while a hub site may have numerous links that connect it to the rest of the world.

Finding the site links associated with a site consists of performing a query for all siteLink objects that have the DN of the site included in the siteList attribute for a link. The siteList attribute is a multivalued attribute that contains all the sites that are connected via the site link.

12.14 Modifying the Sites That Are Part of a Site Link

Problem

You want to modify the sites associated with a site link.

Solution

Using a graphical user interface

1. Open the Active Directory Sites and Services snap-in.
2. In the left pane, expand Sites → Inter-Site Transports.
3. Click either the IP or SMTP folder, depending where the site link is stored.
4. In the right pane, double-click on the link you want to modify.
5. Under the General tab, you can add and remove sites that are associated with the site link.
6. Click OK.

Using a command-line interface

Create an LDIF file called *modify_site_link.ldf* with the following contents. Replace *<LinkName>* with the name of the link and *<SiteName>* with the site to add to the link:

```
dn: cn=<LinkName>,cn=IP,cn=inter-site
transports,cn=sites,cn=configuration,<ForestRootDN>
changetype: modify
add: siteList
```

```
siteList: cn=<SiteName>,cn=sites,cn=configuration,<ForestRootDN>
-
```

Then run the following command:

```
> ldifde -v -i -f modify_site_link.ldf
```

You can also add sites to a site link using AdMod, as follows:

```
> admod -b "cn=<LinkName>,cn=IP,cn=inter-site
transports,cn=sites,cn=configuration,<ForestRootDN>" siteList:++:"cn=<SiteName>
,cn=sites,cn=configuration,<ForestRootDN>"
```

Using VBScript

```
' This code adds a site to an existing site link.
' ------ SCRIPT CONFIGURATION ------
strSite = "<SiteName>" ' e.g. Burlington
strLink = "<LinkName>" ' e.g. DEFAULTIPSITELINK
' ------ END CONFIGURATION ---------

' Taken from ADS_PROPERTY_OPERATION_ENUM
const ADS_PROPERTY_APPEND = 3

set objRootDSE = GetObject("LDAP://RootDSE")
set objLink = GetObject("LDAP://cn=" & strLink & _
                    ",cn=IP,cn=Inter-site Transports,cn=sites," & _
                    objRootDSE.Get("configurationNamingContext") )
strSiteDN = "cn=" & strSite & ",cn=sites," & _
            objRootDSE.Get("configurationNamingContext")
objLink.PutEx ADS_PROPERTY_APPEND, "siteList", Array(strSiteDN)
objLink.SetInfo

WScript.Echo "Successfully modified link: " & strLink
```

Discussion

To associate a site with a site link, add the DN of the site to the siteList attribute of the siteLink object that represents the link. To remove a site from a link, remove the DN associated with the site from the siteList attribute. For example, to remove a site from a site link using AdMod, replace siteList:++: with siteList:--:.

See Also

Recipe 12.13 for finding the links associated with a site

12.15 Modifying the Cost for a Site Link

Problem

You want to modify the cost for a site link.

Solution

Using a graphical user interface

1. Open the Active Directory Sites and Services snap-in.
2. In the left pane, expand Sites → Inter-Site Transports.
3. Click either the IP or SMTP folder, depending where the site link is stored.
4. In the right pane, double-click on the link you want to modify.
5. Under the General tab, you can change the cost for the site link.
6. Click OK.

Using a command-line interface

Create an LDIF file called *modify_site_link_cost.ldf* with the following contents. Replace *<LinkName>* with the name of the link you want to modify and *<LinkCost>* with the cost.

```
dn: cn=<LinkName>,cn=IP,cn=inter-site
transports,cn=sites,cn=configuration,<ForestRootDN>
changetype: modify
replace: cost
cost: <LinkCost>
-
```

Then run the following command:

```
> ldifde -v -i -f modify_site_link_cost.ldf
```

You can also modify the cost of a site link using AdMod, as follows:

```
> admod -b "cn=<LinkName>,cn=IP,cn=inter-site
transports,cn=sites,cn=configuration,<ForestRootDN>" cost::<LinkCost>
```

Using VBScript

```
' This code modifies the cost attribute of a site link.
' ------ SCRIPT CONFIGURATION ------
strLink = "<SiteLink>"    ' e.g. DEFAULTIPSITELINK
intCost = <LinkCost>      ' e.g. 200
' ------ END CONFIGURATION ---------

set objRootDSE = GetObject("LDAP://RootDSE")
set objLink = GetObject("LDAP://cn=" & strLink & _
                    ",cn=IP,cn=Inter-site Transports,cn=sites," & _
                    objRootDSE.Get("configurationNamingContext") )
objLink.Put "cost", intCost
objLink.SetInfo

WScript.Echo "Successfully modified link: " & strLink
```

Discussion

The cost attribute is one of the most important attributes of siteLink objects. cost is used by the KCC to determine what connection objects should be created to allow domain controllers to replicate data.

cost is inversely proportional to bandwidth; the lower the cost, the greater the bandwidth. The number you use for the cost is also arbitrary; the default is 100. You could use 100–1,000 as the range for your site link costs, or you could use 1–10. The actual number isn't important, so long as you configure the values to be relative based on the other site links you've configured. The costs that you assign to your site links should be configured according to the physical topology of your network, where you assign the lowest costs to the highest-speed links, and higher costs to lower-speed links such as a backup ISDN link between two sites.

12.16 Enabling Change Notification for a Site Link

Problem

You want to enable change notification between sites so that replication will occur as changes occur rather than according to a set schedule.

Solution

Using a graphical user interface

1. Open ADSI Edit from the Windows Support Tools. Create or open a connection to the Configuration Container, then browse to CN=Configuration,<*ForestRootDN*> → CN=Sites → CN=Inter-Site Transports → CN=IP.

2. Right-click on the site link object that you want to modify and select Properties.

3. Scroll to the options attribute. If the attribute has not been set, click Edit and enter a value of 1. Click OK.

4. If there is an existing value in place, perform a bitwise OR with 1 and the existing value, click Edit, and enter the new value. Click OK.

Using a command-line interface

```
> admod cn=<SiteLinkName>,cn=IP,cn=Inter-site
Transports,cn=Sites,cn=Configuration,cn=<ForestRootDN> options::1
```

Since options is a bitwise operator, your best option will be to make this modification using ADSI Edit or the VBScript solution that follows.

Using VBScript

```
' This code safely modifies a bit flag attribute.
' ------ SCRIPT CONFIGURATION ------
strSiteLink = "<SiteLinkDN>"         ' e.g. cn=jsmith,cn=users,dc=rallencorp,dc=com
strAttr = "options"
boolEnableBit = <TRUEorFALSE>  ' e.g. TRUE to enable
intBit = 1
' ------ END CONFIGURATION ---------

set objSiteLink = GetObject("LDAP://" & strSiteLink)
intBitsOrig = objSiteLink.Get(strAttr)
intBitsCalc = CalcBit(intBitsOrig, intBit, boolEnableBit)

if intBitsOrig <> intBitsCalc then
   objSiteLink.Put strAttr, intBitsCalc
   objSiteLink.SetInfo
   WScript.Echo "Changed " & strAttr & " from " & intBitsOrig & " to " & intBitsCalc
else
   WScript.Echo "Did not need to change " & strAttr & " (" & intBitsOrig & ")"
end if


Function CalcBit(intValue, intBit, boolEnable)

   CalcBit = intValue

   if boolEnable = TRUE then
      CalcBit = intValue Or intBit
   else
      if intValue And intBit then
         CalcBit = intValue Xor intBit
      end if
   end if

End Function
```

Discussion

By default, intra-site replication occurs on the basis of change notifications where replication occurs almost immediately after a change occurs, while domain controllers in different sites will only replicate with each other on a set schedule. To configure a particular site link to use the change-notification mechanism for replication, you can set bit 1 of its options attribute. Keep in mind that this will create more frequent replication traffic on the site link in question, but it will ensure that changes made in one site can be replicated to the other site much more quickly than by using the default inter-site replication schedules.

See Also

Recipe 4.15 for more on modifying bitwise attributes and Recipe 12.17 for more on modifying replication schedules

12.17 Modifying Replication Schedules

Problem

You want to change the times of day or week that a particular site link (IP or SMTP) is available for replication.

Solution

1. Open the Active Directory Sites and Services snap-in.
2. In the left pane, expand Sites → Inter-Site Transports.
3. Click either the IP or SMTP folder, depending where the site link is stored.
4. In the right pane, double-click on the link you want to modify.
5. On the General tab, click Change Schedule.
6. Click OK.
7. Select the times and days of the week that you wish to allow or disallow, and select the Replication Available or Replication Not Available radio button, as appropriate.
8. Click OK twice to save your changes.

Using a command-line interface

To configure a site link to be available 24 hours a day, 7 days a week, use the following syntax:

```
> admod -b cn=<SiteLinkName>,cn=<TransportName>,cn=Inter-site
Transports,cn=sites,cn=configuration,<ForestRootDN> schedule::0
```

Using VBScript

```
' The following script will display the availability schedule
' for a particular site link.

Days = Array _
    ("Sunday", "Monday", "Tuesday", "Wednesday", "Thursday", "Friday", "Saturday")

Set objSiteLink = GetObject _
    ("LDAP://<SiteLinkDN>")
arrHours = objSiteLink.Get("schedule")

For i = 1 To LenB(arrHours)
    arrHoursBytes(i-1) = AscB(MidB(arrHours, i, 1))
    WScript.Echo "MidB returns: " & MidB(arrHours, i, 1)
    WScript.Echo "arrHoursBytes: " & arrHoursBytes(i-1)
    wscript.echo vbcrlf
Next

intCounter = 0
```

```
    intLoopCounter = 0
    WScript.echo "Day  Byte 1   Byte 2   Byte 3"
    For Each HourByte In arrHoursBytes
        arrHourBits = DisplayLogonHourBits(HourByte)

        If intCounter = 0 Then
            WScript.STDOUT.Write Days(intLoopCounter) & Space(2)
            intLoopCounter = intLoopCounter + 1
        End If

        For Each HourBit In arrHourBits
            WScript.STDOUT.Write HourBit
            intCounter = 1 + intCounter

            If intCounter = 8 or intCounter = 16 Then
                Wscript.STDOUT.Write Space(1)
            End If

            If intCounter = 24 Then
                WScript.echo vbCr
                intCounter = 0
            End If
        Next
    Next

    Function DisplayLogonHourBits(x)
        Dim arrBits(7)
        For i = 7 to 0 Step -1
            If x And 2^i Then
                arrBits(i) = 1
            Else
                arrBits(i) = 0
            End If
        Next
        DisplayLogonHourBits = arrBits
    End Function
```

Discussion

When you configure an inter-site replication link, you can specify a particular schedule during which the link will be available for replication. By default, inter-site links
can pass replication traffic 24 hours a day, 7 days a week, but you can restrict this so
that it is only available for specific hours of the day and/or days of the week. This
might be useful for a heavily utilized link that you do not want to have overloaded
with replication traffic. For example, a bank headquarters may wish to stop replication traffic during a two-hour time period at the end of every day while its branch
offices are transmitting daily report information.

Using VBScript

The schedule attribute of a siteLink object is a binary object, rather than a simple string like most of the other attributes we've discussed. Because of this, manipulating it directly is a bit trickier than simply inserting a new string in place of an old one. In the VBScript example shown in this recipe, we use a VBScript function that manipulates the various bits of the attribute to display the correct values.

See Also

Recipe 13.4 to force replication from one DC to another, MS KB 232263 (Replication Schedule for Intrasite Replication Partners), and MSDN: schedule attribute [AD Schema]

12.18 Disabling Site Link Transitivity or Site Link Schedules

Problem

You want to disable site link transitivity to control replication manually.

Solution

Using a graphical user interface

1. Open the Active Directory Sites and Services snap-in.
2. In the left pane, expand Sites → Inter-Site Transports.
3. Right-click either the IP or SMTP folder, depending on which protocol you want to disable transitivity or ignore schedules for.
4. Select Properties.
5. To disable site link transitivity, uncheck "Bridge all site links."
6. To ignore site link schedules, check "Ignore schedules."
7. Click OK.

Using a command-line interface

You can modify the options attribute of a site link object using an LDIF file and *ldifde*, but since the attribute is a bit flag, you are better off using the GUI or VBScript solutions that look at the current value of options and modify it accordingly. *ldifde* doesn't handle this type of logic.

Using VBScript

```
' This code can disable site link transitivity and site
' schedules for all links of the IP transport.
' The code for the CalcBit function can be found in Recipe 4.15
 ------ SCRIPT CONFIGURATION ------
boolDisableTrans = <TrueOrFalse>   ' e.g. TRUE
boolIgnoreSchedules = <TrueOrFalse> ' e.g. FALSE
' ------ END CONFIGURATION ---------

set objRootDSE = GetObject("LDAP://RootDSE")
set objLink = GetObject( _
                "LDAP://cn=IP,cn=Inter-site Transports,cn=sites," & _
                objRootDSE.Get("configurationNamingContext") )

intBitsOrg = objLink.Get("options")
intBits = CalcBit(intBitsOrg, 2, boolDisableTrans)
intBits = CalcBit(intBitsOrg, 1, boolIgnoreSchedules)

if objLink.Get("options") <> intBits then
    objLink.Put "options", intBits
    objLink.SetInfo
    WScript.Echo "Successfully modified link transitivity for " & strLink
else
    WScript.Echo "Did not need to modify link transitivity for " & strLink
end if
```

Discussion

Active Directory site links are transitive, which means that if site A is linked to site B, and site B is linked to site C, then site A is also linked (through site B) to site C. The KCC uses transitivity by default when making decisions about creating connection objects. You can, however, disable this behavior if you so choose. Typically, this is not something you'll want to do without a very good reason. Disabling transitivity may be necessary, for example, in some Windows 2000 deployments that have a lot of sites and find that the KCC is having a hard time keeping up. With Windows Server 2003, the KCC has been greatly improved and site link transitivity should not cause these problems.

The other reason you might want to disable transitivity is if you need to make replication more deterministic—that is, you want to exert more manual control over the process. Disabling transitivity makes it much easier to determine where the KCC will attempt to establish connection objects, because the KCC on a domain controller will not be able to replicate with domain controllers that are not in sites that are directly linked.

We mention site link schedules here primarily because the same attribute (i.e., options) that determines site link transitivity also determines if link schedules are enforced. If you enable the ignore schedules option for a particular transport (i.e., IP or SMTP), the KCC ignores any preconfigured link schedules. If you later disable this setting, link schedules will go back into effect.

See Also

Recipe 4.15 for more on setting a bit flag attribute

12.19 Creating a Site Link Bridge

Problem

You want to create a site link bridge because you've disabled site link transitivity.

Solution

Using a graphical user interface

1. Open the Active Directory Sites and Services snap-in.
2. In the left pane, expand Sites → Inter-Site Transports.
3. Right-click either the IP or SMTP folder, depending which protocol you want to create a site link bridge for.
4. Select New Site Link Bridge.
5. Highlight two or more site links in the left box.
6. Click the Add button.
7. Click OK.

Using a command-line interface

Create an LDIF file called *create_site_link_bridge.ldf* with the following contents, where `<Link1>` and `<Link2>` refer to the site links to be bridged:

```
dn: cn=<BridgeName>,cn=IP,cn=inter-site
transports,cn=sites,cn=configuration,<ForestRootDN>
changetype: add
objectclass: siteLinkBridge
siteLinkList: cn=<Link1>,cn=IP,cn=Inter-site Transports,cn=sites,cn=configuration,
<ForestRootDN>
siteLinkList: cn=<Link2>,cn=IP,cn=Inter-site Transports,cn=sites,cn=configuration,
<ForestRootDN>
```

Then run the following command:

```
> ldifde -v -i -f create_site_link_bridge.ldf
```

You can also create a site link bridge using AdMod, as follows:

```
> admod -b "cn=<BridgeName>,cn=IP,cn=inter-site
   transports,cn=sites,cn=configuration,<ForestRootDN>"
   objectclass::sitelinkBridge
   "sitelist:++:cn=<FirstSiteLink>,cn=IP,cn=inter-site
   transports,cn=sites,cn=configuration,<ForestRootDN>;
   cn=<SecondSiteLink>,cn=IP,cn=inter-site
   transports,cn=sites,cn=configuration,<ForestRootDN>"
   -add
```

Using VBScript

```
' This code creates a site link bridge between two site links.
' ------ SCRIPT CONFIGURATION ------
strLink1 = "<Link1>"        ' e.g. AMS-LON
strLink2 = "<Link2>"        ' e.g. SJC-RTP
strBridge = "<BridgeName>"  ' e.g. AMER-EUR
' ------ END CONFIGURATION ---------

set objRootDSE = GetObject("LDAP://RootDSE")
set objLinkCont = GetObject( _
                "LDAP://cn=IP,cn=Inter-site Transports,cn=sites," & _
                objRootDSE.Get("configurationNamingContext") )
set objBridge = objLinkCont.Create("siteLinkBridge", "cn=" & strBridge)
strLink1DN = "cn=" & strLink1 & _
            ",cn=IP,cn=Inter-site Transports,cn=sites," & _
            objRootDSE.Get("configurationNamingContext")
strLink2DN = "cn=" & strLink2 & _
            ",cn=IP,cn=Inter-site Transports,cn=sites," & _
            objRootDSE.Get("configurationNamingContext")
objBridge.Put "siteLinkList", Array(strLink1DN,strLink2DN)
objBridge.SetInfo

WScript.Echo "Successfully created bridge: " & strBridge
```

Discussion

If you've disabled site link transitivity or have networks that lack direct routes between sites, you will need to create *site link bridges*. Creating a site link bridge to link several links is analogous to creating a site link to link several sites. Let's take an example where site link transitivity is disabled and we have four sites, among which site A has a link to site B and site C has a link to site D. If we want domain controllers in sites A and B to replicate with sites C and D, we need to create a site link bridge to bridge the A–B link with the C–D link.

See Also

Recipe 12.18 for disabling site link transitivity

12.20 Finding the Bridgehead Servers for a Site

Problem

You want to find the bridgehead servers for a site.

Solution

Using a graphical user interface

1. Open the Replication Monitor from the Support Tools (*replmon.exe*).
2. From the menu, select View → Options.

3. In the left pane, right-click on Monitored Servers and select Add Monitored Server.

4. Use the Add Monitored Server Wizard to add a server in the site you want to find the bridgehead server(s) for.

5. In the left pane, right-click on the server and select Show BridgeHead Servers → In This Server's Site.

Using a command-line interface

```
> repadmin /bridgeheads [<ServerName>] [/verbose]
```

The /bridgeheads option is valid only with the Windows Server 2003 version of *repadmin*. There is no such option in the Windows 2000 version.

Using VBScript

```
' This code finds the bridgehead servers for the specified site.
' ------ SCRIPT CONFIGURATION ------
strServer = "<ServerName>" ' server to target query against, e.g. dc01
strSite = "<SiteName>"      ' name of site to query
                            ' e.g. Default-First-Site-Name
' ------ END CONFIGURATION ---------

set objIadsTools = CreateObject("IADsTools.DCFunctions")
intRes = objIadsTools.GetBridgeHeadsInSite(Cstr(strServer),Cstr(strSite),0)

if intRes = -1 then
    Wscript.Echo "Bridge heads: " & objIadsTools.LastErrorText
    WScript.Quit
end if

for count = 1 to intRes
    WScript.Echo vbTab & objIadsTools.BridgeHeadName(count)
next
```

Discussion

Bridgehead servers are responsible for replicating data between sites. Instead of all domain controllers replicating the same naming contexts outside of the site, the bridgehead servers act as a funnel for replication into and out of a site. Any domain controller in a site can become a bridgehead server, and bridgeheads are designated by the KCC for each writable partition in the site. You can control which servers are designated as bridgehead servers by defining preferred bridgehead servers (see Recipe 12.21 for more on how to do this).

See Also

MS KB 271997 (Description of Bridgehead Servers in Windows 2000)

12.21 Setting a Preferred Bridgehead Server for a Site

Problem

You want to set a preferred bridgehead server for a site.

Solution

Using a graphical user interface

1. Open the Active Directory Sites and Services snap-in.
2. In the left pane, expand Sites, expand the site where the server you want to set as a bridgehead is contained, and expand the Servers container.
3. Right-click on the server you want to set as the bridgehead and select Properties.
4. Highlight IP, SMTP, or both, depending on the protocol(s) for which you want the server to be a bridgehead.
5. Click the Add button.
6. Click OK.

Using a command-line interface

Create an LDIF file called *set_bridgehead_server.ldf* with the following contents:

```
dn: cn=<DCName>,cn=servers,cn=<SiteName>,cn=sites,cn=configuration,<ForestRootDN>
changetype: modify
add: bridgeheadTransportList
bridgeheadTransportList: cn=IP,cn=Inter-site
Transports,cn=sites,cn=configuration,<ForestRootDN>
-
```

Then run the following command:

```
> ldifde -v -i -f set_bridgehead_server.ldf
```

You can also set the preferred bridgehead server with AdMod, using the following syntax:

```
Admod -b cn=<DCName>,cn=servers,cn=<SiteName,
cn=sites,cn=configuration,<ForestRootDN> bridgeheadTransportList:++:"cn=IP,
cn=Inter-site transports,cn=sites,cn=configuration,<ForestRootDN>"
```

Using VBScript

```
' This code sets a preferred bridgehead server for a particular transport.
' ------ SCRIPT CONFIGURATION ------
strServer     = "<DomainControllerName>"  ' e.g. dc1
strServerSite = "<SiteName>"              ' e.g. Default-First-Site-Name
strTransport  = "<TransportName>"         ' e.g. either IP or SMTP
' ------ END CONFIGURATION ---------

set objRootDSE = GetObject("LDAP://RootDSE")
```

```
set objServer = GetObject("LDAP://cn=" & strServer & ",cn=Servers,cn=" & _
                          strServerSite & ",cn=sites," & _
                          objRootDSE.Get("configurationNamingContext") )
objServer.Put "bridgeHeadTransportList", _
              "cn=" & strTransport & ",cn=Inter-site Transports,cn=sites," _
                 & objRootDSE.Get("configurationNamingContext")
objServer.SetInfo

WScript.Echo "Successfully set bridgehead server: " & strServer
```

Discussion

Setting a preferred bridgehead server can give you more control over which domain controllers participate in inter-site replication, but it is also limiting. The KCC typically selects bridgehead servers dynamically, but if you set preferred bridgehead servers, the KCC will not select new ones if the preferred servers become unavailable. Therefore, you should ensure that if you do select preferred bridgehead servers, you select at least two for a given partition in a site.

 As a general rule, you shouldn't set preferred bridgehead servers if at all possible.

See Also

MS KB 271997 (Description of Bridgehead Servers in Windows 2000)

12.22 Listing the Servers

Problem

You want to list the server objects in the site topology.

Solution

Using a graphical user interface

1. Open LDP.
2. From the menu, select Connection → Connect.
3. For Server, enter the name of a domain controller (or leave blank to do a server-less bind).
4. For Port, enter 389.
5. Click OK.
6. From the menu, select Connection → Bind.
7. Enter the credentials of a domain user.

8. Click OK.

9. From the menu, select Browse → Search.

10. For BaseDN, type the Sites container's DN (for example, `cn=sites,cn=configuration,dc=rallencorp,dc=com`).

11. For Scope, select Subtree.

12. For Filter, enter (objectcategory=server).

13. Click Run.

You can also view the servers in your site topology by using the Active Directory Sites and Services MMC snap-in (*dssite.msc*) and manually browsing the site topology.

Using a command-line interface

```
> dsquery server [-site <SiteName>]
```

To list all servers in the site topology using AdFind, use the following syntax:

```
> adfind -config -f (objectcategory=server)
```

To restrict the results to a specific site, do the following:

```
> adfind -config -rb cn=<SiteName>,cn=sites -f (objectcategory=server)
```

Using VBScript

```
' This code lists the server objects in the site topology.

set objRootDSE = GetObject("LDAP://RootDSE")
strBase    = "<LDAP://cn=sites," & _
                objRootDSE.Get("ConfigurationNamingContext") & ">;"
strFilter = "(objectcategory=server);"
strAttrs  = "distinguishedName;"
strScope  = "subtree"

set objConn = CreateObject("ADODB.Connection")
objConn.Provider = "ADsDSOObject"
objConn.Open "Active Directory Provider"
set objRS = objConn.Execute(strBase & strFilter & strAttrs & strScope)
objRS.MoveFirst
while Not objRS.EOF
    Wscript.Echo objRS.Fields(0).Value
    objRS.MoveNext
wend
```

Discussion

Each Active Directory domain controller is represented in the site topology by a server object that is associated with a specific site. Replication decisions are made based on links from this site to other sites that contain domain controllers.

Other types of services can also add server objects to the site topology. The way you can distinguish which ones are domain controllers is the presence of a NTDS Settings (nTDSDSA) object that is a child of the server object. Only domain controllers will have that object.

12.23 Moving a Domain Controller to a Different Site

Problem

You want to move a domain controller to a different site. This may be necessary if you promoted the domain controller without first adding its subnet to Active Directory. In that case, the domain controller will be added to the Default-First-Site-Name site.

Solution

Using a graphical user interface

1. Open the Active Directory Sites and Services snap-in.
2. In the left pane, expand Sites, expand the site where the server you want to move is contained, and expand the Servers container.
3. Right-click on the server you want to move and select Move.
4. Select the site to move the server to.
5. Click OK.

Using a command-line interface

You can move a domain controller to a new site using either the built-in DSMove utility or AdMod. DSMove takes the following syntax:

```
> dsmove "cn=<ServerName>,cn=servers,cn=<CurrentSite>,
cn=sites,cn=configuration,<ForestRootDN>" -newparent "cn=servers,cn=<NewSite>,
cn=sites,cn=configuration,<ForestRootDN>"
```

To move a DC using AdMod, use the following:

```
> admod -b "cn=<ServerName>,cn=servers,cn=<CurrrentSite,
cn=sites,cn=configuration,<ForestRootDN> -move "cn=servers,cn=<NewSite,>
cn=sites,cn=configuration,<ForestRootDN>
```

Using VBScript

```
' This code moves a server to a different site.
' ------ SCRIPT CONFIGURATION ------
' Should contain the common name of the server object
strDC = "<DomainControllerName>" ' e.g. dc02
' Name of servers current site
strCurrentSite = "<CurrentSite>" ' e.g. Default-First-Site-Name
' Name of site you want to move server to
```

```
strNewSite = "<NewSite>"          ' e.g. Raleigh
' ------ END CONFIGURATION ---------

strConfigDN = GetObject("LDAP://RootDSE").Get("configurationNamingContext")
strServerDN = "LDAP://cn=" & strDC & ",cn=servers,cn=" & _
                     strCurrentSite & ",cn=sites," & strConfigDN
strNewParentDN = "LDAP://cn=servers,cn=" & strNewSite & ",cn=sites," & strConfigDN

Set objCont = GetObject(strNewParentDN)
objCont.MoveHere strServerDN, "cn=" & strDC
```

Discussion

After you move a server to a new site, you might want to monitor replication to and from that server to make sure that any new connections that are needed get created and start replicating. See Recipe 13.2 for more on viewing the replication status of a server.

See Also

MS KB 214677 (Automatic Detection of Site Membership for Domain Controllers)

12.24 Configuring a Domain Controller to Cover Multiple Sites

Problem

You want to configure a domain controller to cover multiple sites, which will cause clients in all of those sites to use that domain controller for authentication and directory lookups.

Solution

Using a graphical user interface

1. Run *regedit.exe* from the command line or click Start → Run.
2. In the left pane, expand *HKEY_LOCAL_MACHINE\SYSTEM\CurrentControlSet\Services\Netlogon\Parameters*.
3. If the SiteCoverage value does not exist, right-click on Parameters in the left pane and select New → Multi-String Value. For the name, enter SiteCoverage.
4. In the right pane, double-click on the value and enter each site the server should cover on a separate line.
5. Click OK.

Using a command-line interface

```
> reg add HKLM\System\CurrentControlSet\Services\Netlogon\Parameters /v
"SiteCoverage" /t REG_MULTI_SZ /d <Site1>\0<Site2>
```

Using VBScript

```
' This code configures a domain controller to cover multiple sites.
' ------ SCRIPT CONFIGURATION ------
strDC     = "<DomainControllerName>"       ' e.g. dc01
arrSites  = Array("<Site1>","<Site2>") ' Array of sites to cover
' ------ END CONFIGURATION ---------

strNTDSReg = "SYSTEM\CurrentControlSet\Services\Netlogon\Parameters"
const HKLM = &H80000002
set objReg = GetObject("winmgmts:\\" & strDC & "\root\default:StdRegProv")
objReg.SetMultiStringValue HKLM, strNTDSReg, _
                  "SiteCoverage", _
                  arrSites
WScript.Echo "Site coverage set for " & strDC
```

Discussion

In an Active Directory environment, it is perfectly valid to have a site that does not contain its own domain controller. In fact, if you model the site topology after your real network, some sites will lack their own domain controllers unless you've deployed a branch office architecture or have very few sites. If you create sites without any domain controllers, the site links between the sites will determine which domain controllers will *cover* or advertise their services to the site. When a domain controller covers for a remote site, it needs to publish site-specific DNS resource records that clients in the remote site can use to find the domain controller. Active Directory will select DCs to cover DC-less sites automatically, but you can hardcode the list of sites a specific domain controller should cover by modifying the Registry as described in the Solution section.

See Also

MS KB 200498 (Configure a Domain Controller for Membership in Multiple Sites)

12.25 Viewing the Site Coverage for a Domain Controller

Problem

You want to view the sites that a domain controller covers.

Solution

Using a command-line interface

In the following command, replace *<DomainControllerName>* with the name of the domain controller you want to view site coverage for:

```
> nltest /server:<DomainControllerName> /DsGetSiteCov
```

Using VBScript

Although you cannot use it directly from a scripting language like VBScript, Microsoft provides a DsGetDcSiteCoverage method that can be used by languages such as Visual Basic and C++ to retrieve site coverage information. In fact, the nltest command shown in the CLI solution is a wrapper around this method.

Discussion

Recipe 12.24 describes how to configure a domain controller to cover multiple sites. Recipe 12.26 describes how you can prevent a domain controller from covering for any sites other than its own.

See Also

MSDN: DsGetDcSiteCoverage

12.26 Disabling Automatic Site Coverage for a Domain Controller

Problem

You want to prevent a domain controller from covering sites outside of the one it resides in.

Solution

Using a graphical user interface

1. Run *regedit.exe* from the command line or Start → Run.
2. Expand *HKEY_LOCAL_MACHINE\SYSTEM\CurrentControlSet\Services\Netlogon\Parameters*.
3. Right-click on Parameters and select New → DWORD Value.
4. For the name, enter AutoSiteCoverage.
5. Double-click on the new value, enter 0 under Value data, and click OK.

Using a command-line interface

```
> reg add HKLM\System\CurrentControlSet\Services\Netlogon\Parameters /v\
AutoSiteCoverage /t REG_DWORD /d 0
```

Using VBScript

```
' This code disables auto site coverage.
strNetlogonReg = "SYSTEM\CurrentControlSet\Services\Netlogon\Parameters"
const HKLM = &H80000002
Set objReg = GetObject("winmgmts:root\default:StdRegProv")
```

```
objReg.SetDWORDValue HKLM, strNetlogonReg, "AutoSiteCoverage", 0
WScript.Echo "Site coverage disabled"
```

Discussion

If you want to reduce the load on a domain controller, one way is to prevent it from covering for other sites. Automatic site coverage happens when a site does not contain any member domain controllers.

See Also

Recipe 12.25 for viewing the site coverage for a domain controller

12.27 Finding the Site for a Client

Problem

You want to find which site a client computer is located in.

Solution

Using a command-line interface

In the following command, replace *<HostName>* with the name of the host you want to find the site for:

```
> nltest /server:<HostName> /DsGetSite
```

 You'll use the /server:*<HostName>* parameter even if you are specifying a client computer.

Using VBScript

Although you cannot use it directly from a scripting language like VBScript, Microsoft provides a DsGetSiteName method that can be used by languages such as Visual Basic and C++ to retrieve site coverage information. In fact, the nltest command shown in the CLI solution is a wrapper around this method.

The IADsTool interface provides a wrapper around this method:

```
set objIadsTools = CreateObject("IADsTools.DCFunctions")
strSite = objIadsTools.DsGetSiteName("<HostName>")
Wscript.Echo "Site: " & strSite
```

Discussion

Each domain controller has a server object that is contained within a site. Clients are different—they are associated with a site based on their IP address and the corresponding subnet that it matches is in the Subnets container. The client site information is important because it determines the domain controller the client authenticates with. If the client's IP address does not match the subnet range of any of the subnets stored in Active Directory, it will randomly pick a site to use, which means it could authenticate against any domain controller in the domain. See Recipe 12.28 for a way to hardcode the site association for a client.

See Also

Recipe 12.28 for forcing a host into a particular site, MS KB 247811 (How Domain Controllers Are Located in Windows), and MSDN: DsGetSiteName

12.28 Forcing a Host into a Particular Site

Problem

You want to force a host to be in a particular site.

Solution

Using a graphical user interface

1. Run *regedit.exe* from the command line or Start → Run.
2. Expand *HKEY_LOCAL_MACHINE\SYSTEM\CurrentControlSet\Services\Net-logon\Parameters*.
3. Right-click on Parameters and select New → String Value.
4. Enter SiteName for the name.
5. Double-click on the new value, enter the name of the site under Value data, and click OK.

Using a command-line interface

```
> reg add HKLM\System\CurrentControlSet\Services\Netlogon\Parameters /v SiteName /t\
REG_SZ /d <SiteName>
```

Using VBScript

```
' This code forces the host the script is run on to use a particular host.
' ------ SCRIPT CONFIGURATION ------
strSite = "<SiteName>"   ' e.g. Raleigh
' ------ END CONFIGURATION ---------

strNetlogonReg = "SYSTEM\CurrentControlSet\Services\Netlogon\Parameters"
const HKLM = &H80000002
set objReg = GetObject("winmgmts:root\default:StdRegProv")
objReg.SetStringValue HKLM, strNetlogonReg, "SiteName", strSite
WScript.Echo "Set SiteName to " & strSite
```

Discussion

You can bypass the part of the DC Locator process that determines a client's site by hardcoding it in the Registry. This is generally not recommended and should primarily be used as a troubleshooting tool. If a client is experiencing authentication delays due to a misconfigured site or subnet object, you can hardcode its site so that it temporarily points to a more optimal location (and domain controller) to see if this alleviates the problem. However, in a situation like this, your ultimate goal should be to properly configure your sites and subnets so that the DC Locator process can function without this kind of manual intervention.

See Also

Recipe 12.27 for finding the site for a client and MS KB 247811 (How Domain Controllers Are Located in Windows)

12.29 Creating a Connection Object

Problem

You want to create a connection object to manually set up replication between two servers.

Solution

Using a graphical user interface

1. Open the Active Directory Sites and Services snap-in.
2. In the left pane, expand Sites, expand the site that contains the connection object you want to check, expand the Servers container, and expand the server for which you want to create the connection object.
3. Right-click on the NTDS Settings object and select Create New Active Directory Connection.
4. Select the replication partner and click OK.
5. Enter the name for the connection and click OK.

Using a command-line interface

```
> repadmin /add <PartitionDN> <DC1DNSName> <DC2DNSName>
```

Discussion

Hopefully you will not need to create connection objects manually, since creating and maintaining connection objects is the job of the KCC. It can be a lot of work to keep your connection objects up-to-date by yourself, especially if you have a large topology. The KCC uses complex algorithms to determine the best partners for a domain controller to replicate with. The Windows 2000 KCC had problems generating very large topologies, but the Windows Server 2003 version is significantly better.

It is sometimes necessary to create connections manually if you find a replication problem and need to get replication going again between one or more sites. By creating a connection and forcing replication to occur over that connection, you can get servers back in sync quickly.

See Also

Recipe 12.30 for listing the connection objects for a server

12.30 Listing the Connection Objects for a Server

Problem

You want to view the connection objects associated with a domain controller.

Solution

Using a graphical user interface

1. Open the Active Directory Sites and Services snap-in.
2. In the left pane, expand Sites, expand the site that contains the connection object you want to check, expand the Servers container, expand the server that contains the connection object, and click on the NTDS Settings object.
3. In the right pane, under the name column, it will display which connection objects were automatically generated by the KCC and which ones were manually generated.

Using a command-line interface

```
> repadmin /showconn [<DomainControllerName>]
```

Using VBScript

```
' This code lists the connection objects for a server.
' ------ SCRIPT CONFIGURATION ------
strServer = "<ServerName>"  ' e.g. dc01
strSite   = "<SiteName>"    ' e.g. MySite1
' ------ END CONFIGURATION ---------

set objRootDSE = GetObject("LDAP://RootDSE")
set objNTDSCont = GetObject("LDAP://cn=NTDS Settings,cn=" & strServer & _
                     ",cn=servers,cn=" & strSite & ",cn=sites," & _
                     objRootDSE.Get("configurationNamingContext") )
```

```
objNTDSCont.Filter = Array("ntdsConnection")
WScript.Echo "Connection objects for " & strSite & "\" & strServer
for each objConn in objNTDSCont
    if objConn.Get("options") = 0 then
        Wscript.Echo "  " & objConn.Get("cn") & " (MANUAL)"
    else
        Wscript.Echo "  " & objConn.Get("cn") & " (AUTO)"
    end if
next
```

Another option for programmatically getting the connection objects for a server is to use the GetDSAConnections method from the IADsTool interface.

Discussion

Connection objects are used to replicate inbound changes to a domain controller. By viewing the connection objects for a server, you can see what domain controllers it receives updates from. Connection objects are created automatically by the KCC, but can be created manually if necessary.

See Also

Recipe 12.29 for creating a connection object

12.31 Load-Balancing Connection Objects

Problem

You want to evenly distribute connection objects between bridgehead servers in a site.

Solution

Using a command-line interface

To see what changes the Active Directory Load Balancing (ADLB) utility would make, run the following command without the /commit option. To actually make the changes in Active Directory, use the /commit option:

```
> adlb /server:<DomainControllerName> -site:<SiteName> [/commit] [/verbose]
```

This utility is available in the Windows Server 2003 Resource Kit.

Discussion

Bridgeheads can become overloaded or end up with too many connection objects in relation to other bridgeheads in the domain. The Active Directory Load Balancing (ADLB) tool allows you to balance the load of connection objects among bridgehead servers within a site. The Windows Server 2003 algorithms are much better than Windows 2000 at load-balancing connection objects across servers, but that process happens only when new connection objects are added. You can use the *adlb* tool to load-balance existing connection objects more efficiently at any time.

We recommend first viewing the changes *adlb* would make before using the /commit option. Though the tool has matured to the point that it will typically make good decisions for your topology, it is still always good to do a sanity check to ensure *adlb* doesn't mess up your replication topology.

12.32 Finding the ISTG for a Site

Problem

You want to find the Inter-Site Topology Generator (ISTG) for a site.

Solution

Using a graphical user interface

1. Open the Active Directory Sites and Services snap-in.
2. Click on the site you are interested in.
3. In the right pane, double-click on the NTDS Site Settings object.

    The ISTG will be displayed under ISTG if one is present.

Using a command-line interface

In Windows Server 2003, you can query for this information using *repadmin* or DSQuery:

```
> repadmin /istg <DomainControllerName>

> dsquery * "cn=NTDS Site Settings,cn=<SiteName>,cn=sites,<ForestRootDN>" -attr
intersitetopologygenerator
```

> You can leave off the <DomainControllerName> switch to query the local DC for this information.

These commands are available only with Windows Server 2003. You can also use AdFind for both Windows 2000 and Windows Server 2003, as follows:

```
> adfind -config -rb "cn=ntds site settings,cn=<SiteName>,cn=sites"
intersitetopologygenerator
```

Using VBScript

```
' This code finds the ISTG for the specified site.
' ------ SCRIPT CONFIGURATION ------
strSiteName = <SiteName>  ' e.g. Raleigh
' ------ END CONFIGURATION ---------

set objRootDSE = GetObject("LDAP://RootDSE")
set objSiteSettings = GetObject("LDAP://cn=NTDS Site Settings,cn=" & _
                                strSiteName & ",cn=sites," & _
                                objRootDSE.Get("ConfigurationNamingContext"))
on error resume next
strISTGDN = objSiteSettings.Get("interSiteTopologyGenerator")
if (strISTGDN <> "") then
    set objNTDSSettings = GetObject("LDAP://" & strISTGDN)
    set objServer = GetObject( objNTDSSettings.Parent )
    WScript.Echo "ISTG for site " & strSiteName & " is " & _
                 objServer.Get("dnsHostName")
else
    WScript.Echo "No ISTG found for site " & strSiteName
end if
```

Discussion

One domain controller in every site is picked as the ISTG for that site. While each domain controller is responsible for creating its own intra-site connection objects, the ISTG for a site is responsible for creating the inter-site connection objects for the bridgehead servers in the site.

The current ISTG for a site is stored in the interSiteTopologyGenerator attribute of the site's NTDS Site Settings object. The distinguished name of ISTG's NTDS Settings object is stored in the interSiteTopologyGenerator attribute.

Disabling inter-site topology generation is synonymous with disabling the KCC for a site. See Recipe 12.36 for more information on disabling the KCC.

See Also

Recipe 12.33 for moving the ISTG, Recipe 12.36, MS KB 224815 (The Role of the Inter-Site Topology Generator in Active Directory Replication), and MS KB 224599 (Determining the Inter-Site Topology Generator (ISTG) of a Site in the Active Directory)

12.33 Transferring the ISTG to Another Server

Problem

You want to move the ISTG for a site to another domain controller. This happens automatically if you take the current ISTG offline, but you may want to transfer the role to a server that is more optimal in your environment.

Solution

Using a graphical user interface

1. Open ADSI Edit.
2. Connect to the Configuration NC if it is not already displayed in the left pane.
3. In the left pane, browse to Configuration NC → Sites.
4. Click on the site you want to transfer the ISTG for.
5. In the right pane, double-click CN=NTDS Site Settings.
6. Modify the interSiteTopologyGenerator attribute to include the NTDS Settings object of the domain controller you want to transfer the ISTG role to.
7. Click OK.

Using a command-line interface

```
> admod -b "cn=NTDS Site Settings,cn=<SiteName>,
cn=sites,cn=configuration,<ForestRootDN>" interSiteTopologyGenerator::"cn=NTDS Site
Settings,cn=<NewISTGName>,cn=servers,cn=<SiteName>,
cn=sites,cn=configuration,<ForestRootDN>
```

Using VBScript

```
' This code forces a new ISTG in a site.
' ------ SCRIPT CONFIGURATION ------
' Name of site to transfer ISTG in
strSiteName = "<SiteName>"          ' e.g. Raleigh
' Site the new ISTG server is in
strNewISTGSite = "<ISTGSiteName>" ' e.g. Raleigh
' Common name of server object for new ISTG
strNewISTGName = "<DomainControllerName>"  ' e.g. dc01
' ------ END CONFIGURATION ---------

set objRootDSE = GetObject("LDAP://RootDSE")
set objSiteSettings = GetObject("LDAP://cn=NTDS Site Settings,cn=" & _
                           strSiteName & ",cn=sites," & _
                           objRootDSE.Get("ConfigurationNamingContext"))
strCurrentISTG = objSiteSettings.Get("interSiteTopologyGenerator")

objSiteSettings.Put "interSiteTopologyGenerator", _
```

```
                    "cn=NTDS Settings,cn=" & strNewISTGName & _
                    ",cn=servers,cn=" & strNewISTGSite & ",cn=sites," & _
                    objRootDSE.Get("ConfigurationNamingContext")
    objSiteSettings.SetInfo
    WScript.Echo "ISTG for " & strSiteName & " changed from:"
    WScript.Echo "   " & strCurrentISTG
    WScript.Echo "To"
    WScript.Echo "   " & objSiteSettings.Get("interSiteTopologyGenerator")
```

Discussion

The current ISTG for a site is stored in the interSiteTopologyGenerator attribute of the site's NTDS Site Settings object. The distinguished name of the ISTG's NTDS Settings object is stored in that attribute as well.

Domain controllers communicate their presence as the ISTG by writing to the interSiteTopologyGenerator attribute at a set interval. If you want another domain controller to assume the role of the ISTG, you need to write the distinguished name of that domain controller's NTDS Settings object to the interSiteTopologyGenerator attribute of the NTDS Site Settings object for the site.

Two registry settings govern the ISTG registration process, both of which are stored under the *HKEY_LOCAL_MACHINE\System\CurrentControlSet\Services\NTDS\Parameters* key. The interval (in minutes) in which the current ISTG should write to the interSiteTopologyGenerator attribute to inform the other DCs in the site that it is still the ISTG is stored in the KCC site generator renewal interval (minutes) value. The default is 30 minutes. The other value is named KCC site generator failover (minutes) and contains the time in minutes that each domain controller in the site should wait for the interSiteTopologyGenerator attribute to be written to before attempting to register itself as the ISTG. The default is 60 minutes.

See Also

MS KB 224815 (The Role of the Inter-Site Topology Generator in Active Directory Replication)

12.34 Triggering the KCC

Problem

You want to trigger the KCC.

Solution

Using a graphical user interface

1. Open the Active Directory Sites and Services snap-in.
2. In the left pane, browse to the NTDS Settings object for the server you want to trigger the KCC for.

3. Right-click on NTDS Settings, select All Tasks, and check Replication Topology.

4. Click OK.

Using a command-line interface

```
> repadmin /kcc <DomainControllerName>
```

Using VBScript

```
' This code triggers the KCC on a DC.
' ------ SCRIPT CONFIGURATION ------
strDC = "<DomainControllerName>"  ' e.g. dc01
' ------ END CONFIGURATION ---------

set objIadsTools = CreateObject("IADsTools.DCFunctions")
intRes = objIadsTools.TriggerKCC(Cstr(strDC),0)

if intRes = -1 then
    Wscript.Echo objIadsTools.LastErrorText
else
    Wscript.Echo "KCC successfully triggered"
end if
```

Discussion

The KCC runs every 15 minutes by default on all domain controllers to generate the intra-site topology connections. The KCC that runs on the server that is selected as the ISTG generates inter-site topology connections to other sites from the bridge-head servers in its site. In some situations—such as when you create new site, siteLink, or subnet objects—you may want to run the KCC immediately so that any new connections between domain controllers are created right away.

See Also

Recipe 12.35 for determining if the KCC is completing successfully, the *iadstools.doc* file that is installed with the Support Tools for more information on IADsTools, and MS KB 224815 (The Role of the Inter-Site Topology Generator in Active Directory Replication)

12.35 Determining Whether the KCC Is Completing Successfully

Problem

You want to determine whether the KCC is completing successfully.

Solution

Using a graphical user interface

1. Open the Event Viewer of the target domain controller.
2. Click on the Directory Service log.
3. In the right pane, click on the Source heading to sort by that column.
4. Scroll down to view any events with Source: NTDS KCC.

Using a command-line interface

The following command will display any KCC errors found in the Directory Service log:

```
> dcdiag /v /test:kccevent /s:<DomainControllerName>
```

Discussion

The only way to debug issues with the KCC is by looking for NTDS KCC events in the Directory Service event log. If you suspect a problem or perhaps are seeing errors, you can increase the amount of logging in the event log by enabling diagnostics logging for the KCC. When KCC diagnostics logging is enabled, each KCC exception logs a significant amount of information to the event log that may help you pinpoint the problem. See Recipe 16.2 for more information on enabling diagnostics logging.

12.36 Disabling the KCC for a Site

Problem

You want to disable the KCC for a site and generate your own replication connections between domain controllers.

Solution

Using a graphical user interface

1. Open ADSI Edit.
2. Connect to the Configuration Naming Context if it is not already displayed.
3. In the left pane, browse to the *cn=Sites* folder.
4. Click on the site you want to disable the KCC for.
5. In the right pane, double-click CN=NTDS Site Settings.

6. Modify the options attribute. To disable only intra-site topology generation, enable the 00001 bit (decimal 1). To disable inter-site topology generation, enable the 10000 bit (decimal 16). To disable both, enable the 10001 bits (decimal 17).

7. Click OK.

Using a command-line interface

You can disable the KCC for *<SiteName>* by using the *ldifde* utility and an LDIF file that contains the following:

```
dn: cn=NTDS Site Settings,<SiteName>,cn=sites,cn=configuration,<ForestRootDN>
changetype: modify
replace: options
options: <OptionsValue>
-
```

If the LDIF file were named *disable_kcc.ldf*, you would run the following command:

```
> ldifde -v -i -f disable_kcc.ldf
```

You can also perform this change using AdMod, as follows:

```
> admod -b "cn=NTDS Site Settings,cn=<SiteName>,
cn=sites,cn=configuration,<ForestRootDN> options::<OptionsValue>
```

 Both of these solutions simply overwrite the value of the options attribute without checking to see if any current value may be in place. See Recipe 4.15 for a safer method to modify bitwise values.

Using VBScript

```
' This code disables the KCC for a site.
' ------ SCRIPT CONFIGURATION ------
strSiteName = "<SiteName>" ' e.g. Default-First-Site-Name
boolDisableIntra = TRUE    ' set to TRUE/FALSE to disable/enable intra-site
boolDisableInter = TRUE    ' set to TRUE/FALSE to disable/enable inter-site
' ------ END CONFIGURATION ---------

strAttr = "options"
set objRootDSE = GetObject("LDAP://RootDSE")
set objObject = GetObject("LDAP://cn=NTDS Site Settings,cn=" _
                          & strSiteName & ",cn=sites," & _
                          objRootDSE.Get("configurationNamingContext") )

intBitsOrig = objObject.Get(strAttr)
intBitsCalc = CalcBit(intBitsOrig, 1, boolDisableIntra)
WScript.Echo "Checking the KCC Intra-site generation flag:"
if intBitsOrig <> intBitsCalc then
    objObject.Put strAttr, intBitsCalc
    objObject.SetInfo
    WScript.Echo "  Changed " & strAttr & " from " & _
                 intBitsOrig & " to " & intBitsCalc
```

```
else
   WScript.Echo "  Did not need to change " & strAttr & _
            " (" & intBitsOrig & ")"
end if

intBitsOrig = objObject.Get(strAttr)
intBitsCalc = CalcBit(intBitsOrig, 16, boolDisableInter)
WScript.Echo "Checking the KCC Inter-site generation flag:"
if intBitsOrig <> intBitsCalc then
   objObject.Put strAttr, intBitsCalc
   objObject.SetInfo
   WScript.Echo "  Changed " & strAttr & " from " & intBitsOrig & _
            " to " & intBitsCalc
else
   WScript.Echo "  Did not need to change " & strAttr & " (" & _
            intBitsOrig & ")"
end if
```

Discussion

In some cases, you may want to disable the KCC from generating the intra-site topology connections, inter-site topology connections, or both. The connection objects that the KCC dynamically creates determine how domain controllers replicate with each other. Disabling the KCC was sometimes necessary with Windows 2000 due to scalability issues with the KCC and very large topologies. In Windows Server 2003, the KCC has been greatly improved, and, hopefully, you will not need to disable the KCC. We recommend against disabling the KCC unless you have really good reasons, because you will have to pay close attention to any domain controller or site topology changes and manually adjust the connection objects accordingly.

Disabling the KCC can be done only at the site level. You have to modify the NTDS Site Settings object of the site for which you want to disable the KCC. The options attribute (a bit flag) on this object determines whether the KCC runs. If the 00001 bit is enabled, intra-site topology generation is disabled; if the 10000 bit is enabled (16 in decimal), inter-site topology generation is disabled. See Recipe 4.15 for more on the proper way to set bit flags.

See Also

Recipe 4.15 for more on setting bit flags, Recipe 12.29 for creating a connection object manually, MS KB 242780 (How to Disable the Knowledge Consistency Checker from Automatically Creating Replication Topology), and MS KB 245610 (How to Disable the Knowledge Consistency Checker Inter-Site Topology Generation for All Sites)

12.37 Changing the Interval at Which the KCC Runs

Problem

You want to change the interval at which the KCC runs.

Solution

Using a graphical user interface

1. Run *regedit.exe* from the command line or Start → Run.
2. Expand *HKEY_LOCAL_MACHINE\SYSTEM\CurrentControlSet\Services\NTDS\ Parameters*.
3. Right-click on Parameters and select New → DWORD Value.
4. Enter the following for the name: `Repl topology update period (secs)`.
5. Double-click on the new value, and under Value data enter the KCC interval in number of seconds (900 is the default).
6. Click OK.

Using a command-line interface

```
> reg add HKLM\System\CurrentControlSet\Services\NTDS\Parameters /v "Repl topology\
update period (secs)" /t REG_DWORD /d <NumSecs>
```

Using VBScript

```
' This code changes the interval in which the KCC runs.
' ------ SCRIPT CONFIGURATION ------
intNumSecs = <NumSecs>   ' Number of seconds between intervals
                         ' 900 is default
' ------ END CONFIGURATION ---------

strNetlogonReg = "SYSTEM\CurrentControlSet\Services\NTDS\Parameters"
const HKLM = &H80000002
Set objReg = GetObject("winmgmts:root\default:StdRegProv")
objReg.SetDWORDValue HKLM, strNetlogonReg, _
                "Repl topology update period (secs)", _
                intNumSecs
WScript.Echo "KCC interval set to " & intNumSecs
```

Discussion

By default, the KCC checks its connections every 15 minutes and makes changes as necessary. You can modify this interval by simply modifying the registry. This was necessary with many Windows 2000 implementations that had large topologies. In that case, the KCC might have taken longer than 15 minutes to run or else it would have monopolized the CPU. Changing the KCC to run every hour instead of 15 minutes would help ensure that it would have enough time to complete. With Windows Server 2003, Microsoft made significant improvements to the scalability of the KCC, and we recommend running the KCC at the default interval.

There is another related registry setting you should also be aware of. By default, the KCC waits five minutes after Active Directory starts up before it runs. You can change this delay by creating a REG_DWORD value called Repl topology update delay (secs) under the *HKLM\System\CurrentControlSet\Services\NTDS\Parameters* key. The data for the value should be the number of seconds to wait after startup before the KCC starts. The default is 300, which is 5 minutes.

See Also

MS KB 271988 (Replication Topology Updates)

Replication

13.0   Introduction

Replication is one of the most important and perhaps complex components of Active Directory. The infrastructure behind Active Directory replication, including the site topology, connection objects, and the KCC, was covered in Chapter 12. This chapter focuses strictly on some of the tasks and processes associated with replicating data and checking replication health. For an in-depth overview of how replication works in Active Directory, we suggest reading Chapter 5 in *Active Directory*, Third Edition, by Joe Richards et al. (O'Reilly).

13.1   Determining Whether Two Domain Controllers Are in Sync

Problem

You want to determine whether two domain controllers are in sync and have no objects to replicate to each other.

Solution

Using a command-line interface

By running the following command you can compare the up-to-dateness vector on the two DCs:

```
> repadmin /showchanges <DestinationDC's FQDN> <SourceDCGUID> <NamingContext>
```

For example, the following illustrates the syntax needed to compare the up-to-dateness vectors using *dc2.rallencorp.com* as the destination DC and the GUID of *dc1.rallencorp* as the source, checking replication on the Domain NC:

```
> repadmin /showchanges dc1.rallencorp.com 5f09d979-1795-4ca1-9fc3-04efd
2bb721 dc-rallencorp,dc=com
```

```
Building starting position from destination server dc1.rallencorp.com

Source Neighbor:
dc=rallencorp,dc=com
==== INBOUND NEIGHBORS ========================================

dc=rallencorp,dc=com
    Default-First-Site-Name\DC2 via RPC
        DC object GUID: 5f09d979-1795-4ca1-9fc3-04efd22bb721
        Address: 5f09d979-1795-4ca1-9fc3-04efd22bb721._msdcs.rallencorp.com
        DC invocationID: accbf436-4577-4191-9a42-16f49e01db5d
        SYNC_ON_STARTUP DO_SCHEDULED_SYNCS WRITEABLE
        USNs: 12384/OU, 12384/PU
        Last attempt @ 2006-02-26 10:04:08 was successful.

Destination's up-to-date vector:
accbf436-4577-4191-9a42-16f49e01db5d @ USN 12393
e197616c-7465-43f2-a502-bac90df20b09 @ USN 14059

==== SOURCE DC: 5f09d979-1795-4ca1-9fc3-04efd22bb721._msdcs.rallencorp.com ====

No Changes
```

The Windows 2000 version of *repadmin* requires you to use a different syntax, running a command against both DCs to allow you to manually compare the information that's automatically displayed by the /showchanges switch in Windows Server 2003. Here is the equivalent syntax:

```
> repadmin /showvector <NamingContextDN> <DC1Name>
> repadmin /showvector <NamingContextDN> <DC2Name>
```

Using VBScript

```
' This code prints the up-to-dateness vector for the DCs defined in
' the array arrDCList for the naming context defined by strNCDN.
' ------ SCRIPT CONFIGURATION ------
' Set to the DN of the naming context you want to check the DCs against
strNCDN = "<NamingContextDN>"    ' e.g. dc=amer,dc=rallencorp,dc=com
' Enter 2 or more DCs to compare
arrDCList = Array("<DC1Name>","<DC2Name>")
' ------ END CONFIGURATION ---------

set objIadsTools = CreateObject("IADsTools.DCFunctions")

for each strDC in arrDCList
   WScript.Echo "Replication partner USNs for " & strDC & ":"
   intUSN = objIadsTools.GetHighestCommittedUSN(Cstr(strDC),0)
   if intUSN = -1 then
      Wscript.Echo "Error retrieving USN: " & objIadsTools.LastErrorText
      WScript.Quit
   end if
   WScript.Echo vbTab & strDC & " = " & intUSN
```

```
    intRes = objIadsTools.GetReplicationUSNState(Cstr(strDC), _
                                    Cstr(strNCDN),0,0)
    if intRes = -1 then
        Wscript.Echo "Error retrieving USNs: " & objIadsTools.LastErrorText
        WScript.Quit
    end if
    for count = 1 to intRes
        WScript.Echo vbTab & objIadsTools.ReplPartnerName(count) &
                " = " & objIadsTools.ReplPartnerUSN(count)
    next
    WScript.Echo
next
```

Discussion

To determine if two or more DCs are in sync from a replication standpoint, you need to compare their up-to-dateness vectors. Each domain controller stores what it thinks is the highest update sequence number (USN) for every DC that replicates a naming context. This is called the *up-to-dateness vector*. If you want to compare DC1 and DC2, you'd first want to get the up-to-dateness vector for DC1 and compare DC1's highest USN against what DC2 thinks DC1's highest USN is. If they are different, then you can deduce that DC2 has not yet replicated all the changes from DC1. Next, compare the reverse to see if DC1 is in sync with DC2.

See Also

IadsTools.doc in the Support Tools for more information on the IADsTools' interface

13.2   Viewing the Replication Status of Several Domain Controllers

Problem

You want to take a quick snapshot of replication activity for one or more domain controllers.

Solution

Using a command-line interface

The following command will show the replication status of all the domain controllers in the forest, as shown in the output that follows:

```
> repadmin /replsum

Replication Summary Start Time: 2006-02-26 11:01:34

Beginning data collection for replication summary, this may take awhile:
  .....
```

```
Source DC          largest delta  fails/total  %%  error
DC1                     15m:22s     0 /   3      0
DC2                        :12s     0 /   3      0


Destination DC     largest delta  fails/total  %%  error
DC1                        :05s     0 /   3      0
DC2                     15m:22s     0 /   3      0
```

You can also use * as a wildcard character to view the status of a subset of domain controllers. The following command will display the replication status of only the servers that begin with the name dc-rtp:

```
> repadmin /replsum dc-rtp*
```

 This command is available only with the Windows Server 2003 version of *repadmin*.

Discussion

The new /replsum option in *repadmin* is a great way to quickly determine if there are any replication issues. This command should be your starting point if you suspect any replication problems. If you are running /replsum against a lot of domain controllers, you can use the /sort option to sort the returned table output by any of the table columns. You can also use the /errorsonly option to display only the replication partners who are encountering errors.

13.3 Viewing Unreplicated Changes Between Two Domain Controllers

Problem

You want to find the unreplicated changes between two domain controllers.

Solution

Using a graphical user interface

1. Open the Replication Monitor from the Support Tools (*replmon.exe*).
2. From the menu, select View → Options.
3. On the General tab, check the boxes beside Show Transitive Replication Partners and Extended Data.
4. Click OK.
5. In the left pane, right-click on Monitored Servers and select Add Monitored Server.

6. Use the Add Monitored Server Wizard to add one of the domain controllers you want to compare (we'll call it *dc1*).

7. In the left pane, under the server you just added, expand the naming context that you want to check for unreplicated changes.

8. Right-click on the other domain controller you want to compare (we'll call it *dc2*) and select "Check Current USN and Un-replicated Objects."

9. Enter credentials if necessary and click OK.

10. If some changes have not yet replicated from *dc2* to *dc1*, a box will pop up that lists the unreplicated objects.

11. To find out what changes have yet to replicate from *dc1* to *dc2*, repeat the same steps, except add *dc2* as a monitored server and check for unreplicated changes against *dc1*.

Using a command-line interface

Run the following command to find the differences between two domain controllers. Use the /statistics option to view a summary of the changes:

```
> repadmin /showchanges <DC1Name> <DC2GUID> <NamingContextDN>
> repadmin /showchanges <DC2Name> <DC1GUID> <NamingContextDN>
```

The Windows 2000 version of *repadmin* has a different syntax to accomplish the same thing. Here is the equivalent syntax:

```
> repadmin /getchanges <NamingContextDN> <DC1Name> <DC2GUID>
> repadmin /getchanges <NamingContextDN> <DC2Name> <DC1GUID>
```

Using VBScript

```
' This code uses the IADsTools interface to print the unreplicated
' changes for the naming context defined by strNCDN for the DCs
' defined by strDC1Name and strDC2Name.
' ------ SCRIPT CONFIGURATION ------
strNCDN    = "<NamingContextDN>"  ' e.g. dc=rallencorp,dc=com
strDC1Name = "<DC1Name>"          ' e.g. dc1.rallencorp.com
strDC2Name = "<DC2Name>"          ' e.g. dc2.rallencorp.com
' ------ END CONFIGURATION ---------

set objIadsTools = CreateObject("IADsTools.DCFunctions")

' ----------------------------------
' Have to get the GUIDs of both servers in order to identify
' the correct partner in the GetReplicationUSNState call
' ==============================
strDC1GUID = objIadsTools.GetGuidForServer(Cstr(strDC1Name), _
                                 Cstr(strDC1Name),0)
strDC2GUID = objIadsTools.GetGuidForServer(Cstr(strDC2Name), _
                                 Cstr(strDC2Name),0)
```

```
' ----------------------------------
' Need to get what each DC thinks is the highest USN for the other
' The USN is needed in the call to GetMetaDataDifferences to return
' the unreplicated changes
' ----------------------------------
intRes = objIadsTools.GetReplicationUSNState(Cstr(strDC1Name), _
                                             Cstr(strNCDN),0,0)
if intRes = -1 then
   Wscript.Echo objIadsTools.LastErrorText
   WScript.Quit
end if
for count = 1 to intRes
   if strDC2GUID = objIadsTools.ReplPartnerGuid(count) then
      intDC2USN = objIadsTools.ReplPartnerUSN(count)
   end if
next
if intDC2USN = "" then
   WScript.Echo strDC2Name & " is not a replication partner with " & _
                strDC1Name
end if
intRes = objIadsTools.GetReplicationUSNState(Cstr(strDC2Name), _
                                             Cstr(strNCDN),0,0)
if intRes = -1 then
   Wscript.Echo objIadsTools.LastErrorText
   WScript.Quit
end if
for count = 1 to intRes
   if strDC1GUID = objIadsTools.ReplPartnerGuid(count) then
      intDC1USN = objIadsTools.ReplPartnerUSN(count)
   end if
next
if intDC2USN = "" then
   WScript.Echo strDC1Name & " is not a replication partner with " & _
                strDC2Name
end if

' ----------------------------------
' Now that we have retrieved the highest USN for both partners,
' the GetMetaDataDifferences method will return what needs to be
' replicated
' ----------------------------------
intRes = objIadsTools.GetMetaDataDifferences(Cstr(strDC1Name), _
                                             Cstr(intDC1USN), _
                                             Cstr(strNCDN),0)
if intRes = -1 then
   Wscript.Echo objIadsTools.LastErrorText
   WScript.Quit
end if
WScript.Echo "Data on " & strDC1Name & " but not " & strDC2Name & ":"
for count = 1 to intRes
   WScript.Echo count & ". " & _
                   objIadsTools.MetaDataDifferencesObjectDN(count)
   WScript.Echo vbTab & " Attribute:    " & _
                   objIadsTools.MetaDataDifferencesAttribute(count)
```

```
        WScript.Echo vbTab & " Write time:   " & _
                        objIadsTools.MetaDataDifferencesLastWriteTime(count)
        WScript.Echo vbTab & " Orig Server: " & _
                        objIadsTools.MetaDataDifferencesOrigServer(count)
        WScript.Echo vbTab & " Orig USN:     " & _
                        objIadsTools.MetaDataDifferencesOrigUSN(count)
    next
    WScript.Echo

    intRes = objIadsTools.GetMetaDataDifferences(Cstr(strDC2Name), _
                                        Cstr(intDC2USN), _
                                        Cstr(strNCDN), 0)

    if intRes = -1 then
        Wscript.Echo objIadsTools.LastErrorText
        WScript.Quit
    end if
    WScript.Echo "Data on " & strDC2Name & " but not " & strDC1Name & ":"
    for count = 1 to intRes
        WScript.Echo count & ". " & _
                        objIadsTools.MetaDataDifferencesObjectDN(count)
        WScript.Echo vbTab & " Attribute:    " & _
                        objIadsTools.MetaDataDifferencesAttribute(count)
        WScript.Echo vbTab & " Write time:   " & _
                        objIadsTools.MetaDataDifferencesLastWriteTime(count)
        WScript.Echo vbTab & " Orig Server: " & _
                        objIadsTools.MetaDataDifferencesOrigServer(count)
        WScript.Echo vbTab & " Orig USN:     " & _
                        objIadsTools.MetaDataDifferencesOrigUSN(count)
    next
```

Discussion

All three solutions show how to display the current unreplicated changes between two domain controllers. This can be useful in troubleshooting replication on your network, particularly if you are finding inconsistent information between one or more domain controllers. The repadmin /showchanges command has several additional options you can use to display the changes, including saving the output to a file for later comparison. Also, with the /statistics option, you can view a summary of the changes.

See Also

IadsTools.doc in the Support Tools for more information on the IADsTools interface

13.4 Forcing Replication from One Domain Controller to Another

Problem

You want to force replication between two partners.

Solution

Using a graphical user interface

1. Open the Active Directory Sites and Services snap-in.
2. Browse to the NTDS Setting object for the domain controller you want to replicate to.
3. In the right pane, right-click on the connection object corresponding to the domain controller you want to replicate from and select Replicate Now.

Using a command-line interface

The following command will perform a replication sync from *<DC2Name>* to *<DC1Name>* of the naming context specified by *<NamingContextDN>*:

```
> repadmin /replicate <DC1Name> <DC2Name> <NamingContextDN>
```

The Windows 2000 version of *repadmin* has a different syntax to accomplish the same thing. Here is the equivalent syntax:

```
> repadmin /sync <NamingContextDN> <DC1Name> <DC2GUID>
```

Using VBScript

```
' This code initiates a replication event between two DCs
' for a naming context
' ------ SCRIPT CONFIGURATION ------
strDC1Name = "<DC1Name>"    ' e.g. dc1
strDC2Name = "<DC2Name>"    ' e.g. dc2
strNamingContextDN = "<NamingContextDN>"    ' e.g. dc=rallencorp,dc=com
' ------ END CONFIGURATION ---------

set objIadsTools = CreateObject("IADsTools.DCFunctions")
intRes = objIadsTools.ReplicaSync(Cstr(strDC1Name),_
                                  Cstr(strNamingContextDN),_
                                  Cstr(strDC2Name), 0, 0)
if intRes = -1 then
   Wscript.Echo "Error: " & objIadsTools.LastErrorText
else
   WScript.Echo "Replication intitiated from " & strDC2Name & _
                " to " & strDC1Name
end if
```

Discussion

Each solution shows how to replicate all unreplicated changes from a source domain controller to a destination domain controller. This sync is a one-way operation. If you want to ensure that both domain controllers are in sync, you'll need to follow the same procedure in the opposite direction, replicating both from DC1 to DC2 and from DC2 to DC1. It's important to remember that all replication takes place as a pull operation. For example, DC2 notifies DC1 that it has changes available, after which DC1 pulls the changes it needs from DC2. For replication to occur in the opposite direction, DC1 will notify DC2 that it has changes available, and DC2 will pull those changes from DC1.

 With *repadmin*, you can replicate a single object instead of any unreplicated object in a naming context by using the /replsingleobj option. This option is available only with the Windows Server 2003 version of *repadmin*.

See Also

Recipe 13.3 for viewing unreplicated changes between two domain controllers, MS KB 232072 (Initiating Replication Between Active Directory Direct Replication Partners), and *IadsTools.doc* in the Support Tools for more information on the IADsTools interface

13.5 Enabling and Disabling Replication

Problem

You want to enable or disable inbound or outbound replication on a domain controller.

Solution

Using a command-line interface

To disable outbound replication on a domain controller, use the following syntax:

    > repadmin /options +DISABLE_OUTBOUND_REPL

To re-enable outbound replication, enter the following:

    > repamin /options -DISABLE_OUTBOUND_REPL

To disable inbound replication, use the following syntax:

    > repadmin /options +DISABLE_INBOUND_REPL

To re-enable inbound replication, use the following:

    > repadmin /options -DISABLE_INBOUND_REPL

Discussion

When you are making major changes to Active Directory, particularly in cases where you are extending the schema, it is recommended that you disable outbound replication on the DC that you're modifying. This will allow you to test any changes that you've made on a single DC without propagating those changes to the remainder of your directory. If you make a mistake or find that the changes you've made are otherwise unacceptable, you can restore a single DC rather than being faced with the prospect of performing a disaster recovery operation on your entire domain.

It's important to note that disabling outbound replication on a domain controller will not have any effect on inbound replication; the DC in question will still receive updates from its other replication partners unless you disable inbound replication on them as well.

In a worst-case scenario, you can disable replication for an entire forest by issuing the following command:

```
> repadmin /options * +DISABLE_INBOUND_REPL
```

See Also

MS KB 321153 (How to Disable or Enable Active Directory Replication in Windows 2000)

13.6   Changing the Intra-Site Replication Interval

Problem

You want to change the number of seconds that a domain controller in a site waits before replicating within the site.

Solution

Using a graphical user interface

1. Run *regedit.exe* from the command line or Start → Run.
2. Expand *HKEY_LOCAL_MACHINE\SYSTEM\CurrentControlSet\Services\NTDS\ Parameters*.
3. If a value entry for "Replicator notify pause after modify (secs)" does not exist, right-click on Parameters and select New → DWORD Value. For the name, enter Replicator notify pause after modify (secs).
4. Double-click on the value and enter the number of seconds to wait before notifying intra-site replication partners.
5. Click OK.

Using a command-line interface

With the following command, change *<NumSeconds>* to the number of seconds you want to set the intra-site replication delay to:

```
> reg add HKLM\System\CurrentControlSet\Services\NTDS\Parameters /v "Replicator
notify pause after modify (secs)" /t REG_DWORD /d <NumSeconds>
```

Using VBScript

```
' This code sets the intra-site delay interval.
' ------ SCRIPT CONFIGURATION ------
strDC      = "<DomainControllerName>" ' DC you want to configure
intNumSeconds = <NumSeconds>  ' Time in seconds to delay
' ------ END CONFIGURATION ---------

const HKLM = &H80000002
strNTDSReg = "SYSTEM\CurrentControlSet\Services\NTDS\Parameters"
set objReg = GetObject("winmgmts:\\" & strDC & _
                       "\root\default:StdRegProv")
objReg.SetDWORDValue HKLM, strNTDSReg, _
                     "Replicator notify pause after modify (secs)", _
                     intNumSeconds
WScript.Echo "Intra-site replication delay set to " & intNumSeconds
```

Discussion

After a change has been made to a domain controller's local copy of Active Directory, it waits for a period of time before sending change-notification requests to its intra-site replication partners. The default delay on Windows 2000 domain controllers is five minutes; for Windows Server 2003, the default delay has been changed to 15 seconds. You can customize this notification delay by changing the registry value "Replicator notify pause after modify (secs)" on the domain controllers, as described in the Solution section.

 If you are upgrading a Windows 2000 domain controller to Windows Server 2003, Microsoft recommends removing the 5-minute value after upgrading to Windows Server 2003 in order to utilize the new default of 15 seconds.

See Also

MS KB 214678 (How to Modify the Default Intra-Site Domain Controller Replication Interval)

13.7   Changing the Intra-Site Notification Delay

Problem

You want to change how long a domain controller waits before notifying domain controllers within a site that updates are available.

Solution

Using a graphical user interface

1. Open ADSI Edit.

2. If an entry for the Configuration naming context you want to browse is not already displayed, do the following:

    a. Right-click on ADSI Edit in the right pane and click "Connect to…."

    b. Fill in the information for the Configuration NC. Click on the Advanced button if you need to enter alternate credentials.

3. In the left pane, browse to CN=Configuration,<*ForestRootDN*> → CN=Partitions. Right-click on the domain partition designated by the short name of the domain (CN=RALLENCORP for *rallencorp.com*) and select Properties.

4. Double-click on the following attributes and modify their values as appropriate:

    • msDS-Replication-Notify-First-DSA-Delay

    • msDS-Replication-Notify-Subsequent-DSA-Delay

Using a command-line interface

Create a file called *modify_replication_interval.ldf* with the following contents:

```
dn: <DomainPartitionCrossRefDN>
changetype: modify
replace: msDS-Replication-Notify-First-DSA-Delay
msDS-Replication-Notify-First-DSA-Delay: <FirstDelayInSeconds>
-
replace: msDS-Replication-Notify-Subsequent-DSA-Delay
msDS-Replication-Notify-Subsequent-DSA-Delay: <NextDelayInSeconds>
```

Then import the changes into Active Directory using the following syntax:

```
ldifde -i -v modify_replication_interval.ldf
```

You can also make the changes using AdMod, as follows:

```
admod -b cn=<DomainPartition>,cn=Partitions,cn=Configuration,<ForestRootDN> msDS-
Replication-Notification-First-DSA-Delay::<FirstDelayInSeconds> msDS-Replication-
Notify-Subsequent-DSA-Delay::<NextDelayInSeconds>
```

Using VBScript

```
' This code sets the replication delay for an application partition.
' ------ SCRIPT CONFIGURATION ------
strDomainPartDN = "<DomainPartitionDN>"  ' e.g. cn=rallencorp,dc=rallencorp,dc=com
intFirstDelay = <FirstDelayInSeconds>
intNextDelay  = <NextDelayInSeconds>
' ------ END CONFIGURATION ---------

set objRootDSE = GetObject("LDAP://RootDSE")
strBase     = "<LDAP://cn=Partitions," & _
                 objRootDSE.Get("ConfigurationNamingContext") & ">;"
strFilter   = "(&(objectcategory=crossRef)(nCName=" & strDomainPartDN & "));"
strAttrs    = "cn,distinguishedName;"
strScope    = "onelevel"
set objConn = CreateObject("ADODB.Connection")
objConn.Provider = "ADsDSOObject"
objConn.Open "Active Directory Provider"
set objRS = objConn.Execute(strBase & strFilter & strAttrs & strScope)

if objRS.RecordCount <> 1 then
   WScript.Echo "Did not find a match for " & strDomainPartDN
else
   objRS.MoveLast
   set objAppPart = GetObject("LDAP://" & _
                    objRS.Fields("distinguishedName").Value )
   objAppPart.Put "msDS-Replication-Notify-First-DSA-Delay", intFirstDelay
   objAppPart.Put "msDS-Replication-Notify-Subsequent-DSA-Delay", intNextDelay
   objAppPart.SetInfo
   Wscript.Echo "Modified " & objRS.Fields("distinguishedName").Value
end if
```

Discussion

Because Active Directory assumes that DCs within a site are connected by high-speed links, intra-site replication occurs as changes are made rather than adhering to a specific schedule. In Windows 2000, anytime you made a change on a domain controller, that DC would wait five minutes before beginning to notify its replication partners that it had changes available, as we discussed in the previous recipe. The 2000 DC would then notify all of its configured partners one at a time in 30-second intervals. To change these values in Windows 2000, you need to modify the following Reg_DWORD values in the Windows 2000 Registry:

```
HKEY_LOCAL_MACHINE\SYSTEM\CurrentControlSet
\Services\NTDS\Parameters\Replicator notify pause after modify (secs)

HKEY_LOCAL_MACHINE\SYSTEM\CurrentControlSet
\Services\NTDS\Parameters\Replicator notify pause between DSAs(secs)
```

In Windows Server 2003, the intra-site replication intervals have been reduced so that the initial delay is 15 seconds, after which a 2003 DC will notify its replication partners in 3-second intervals. This greatly reduces the *convergence time* within a site—that is, the amount of time it takes for domain controllers within a site to synchronize with one another.

 There are some updates that are deemed of sufficient importance that the initial 15-second delay does not apply. This is known as *urgent replication*, and applies to critical directory updates such as locking out an account, changing the account lockout or password policy of a domain, and changing the password of a domain-controller computer account.

See Also

MS KB 214678 (How to Modify the Default Intra-Site Domain Controller Replication Interval), and MS KB 305476 (Initial synchronization requirements for Windows 2000 Server and Windows Server 2003 operations master role holders)

13.8   Changing the Inter-Site Replication Interval

Problem

You want to set the replication schedule for a site link.

Solution

Using a graphical user interface

1. Open the Active Directory Sites and Services snap-in.
2. Expand the Inter-Site Transport container.
3. Click on the IP container.
4. In the right pane, double-click on the site link you want to modify the replication interval for.
5. Enter the new interval beside "Replicate every."
6. Click OK.

Using a command-line interface

To change the replication interval, create an LDIF file named *set_link_rep_interval. ldf* with the following contents:

```
dn: cn=<LinkName>,cn=ip,cn=Inter-Site Transports,cn=sites,
cn=configuration,<ForestRootDN>
changetype: modify
replace: replInterval
replInterval: <NewInterval>
-
```

Then run the following command:

```
> ldifde -v -i -f set_link_rep_interval.ldf
```

You can also make this change using AdMod, as follows:

```
> admod -b cn=<LinkName>,cn=ip,cn=Inter-Site
Transports,cn=sites,cn=configuration,<ForestRootDN> replInterval::<NewInterval>
```

Using VBScript

```
' This code sets the replication interval for a site link.
' ------ SCRIPT CONFIGURATION ------
strLinkName   = "<LinkName>"  ' cn of the link you want to configure
intNewInterval = <NewInterval> ' replication interval in minutes
' ------ END CONFIGURATION ---------

set objRootDSE = GetObject("LDAP://RootDSE")
set objLink = GetObject("LDAP://cn=" & strLinkName & _
                    ",cn=IP,cn=Inter-site Transports,cn=sites," & _
                    objRootDSE.Get("configurationNamingContext") )
objLink.Put "replInterval", intNewInterval
objLink.SetInfo
WScript.Echo "Set interval for link " & objLink.Get("cn") & _
            " to " & intNewInterval
```

Discussion

To configure the inter-site replication interval between two sites, you need to set the replInterval attribute on the site-link object that connects the two sites. The value of the attribute should be the replication interval in minutes. The default value is 180 minutes (3 hours), and the minimum is 15 minutes.

These solutions assume the use of IP transport, but SMTP transport can be used as well. However, keep in mind that you cannot use an SMTP link to replicate the Domain naming context, only the Schema and Configuration NCs as well as Global Catalog information.

See Also

MS KB 224815 (The role of the Inter-site Topology Generator in Active Directory Replication), and "Administering Intersite Replication" in the Windows Server 2003 Operations Guide

13.9 Disabling Inter-Site Compression of Replication Traffic

Problem

You want to disable inter-site compression of replication traffic.

Solution

You need to modify the options attribute of the site-link object that connects the sites you want to disable compression for. Site-link objects are stored in the following location:

```
cn=IP,cn=Inter-site Transports,cn=Sites,cn=Configuration,<ForestRootDN>
```

The options attribute is a bit flag. In order to disable compression, you must set bit 4, or 0100 in binary. If the attribute is currently unset, you can simply set it to 4. If it contains a value, you should see Recipe 4.15 for more information on properly setting bit flags.

Discussion

By default, data replicated inter-site is compressed. By contrast, intra-site replication traffic is not compressed. It is useful to compress inter-site traffic if the traffic is going over a WAN on the assumption that the less traffic the better. The trade-off to reducing WAN traffic is increased CPU utilization on the bridgehead servers replicating the data. If CPU utilization is an issue on your bridgehead servers and you aren't as concerned about the amount of traffic being replicated, you should consider disabling inter-site compression.

See Also

Recipe 4.15 for setting bit-flag attributes

13.10 Checking for Potential Replication Problems

Problem

You want to determine whether replication is succeeding.

Solution

The following two commands will help identify problems with replication on a source domain controller:

```
> dcdiag /test:replications
> repadmin /showrepl /errorsonly
```

Discussion

For a more detailed report, you can use the Replication Monitor (*replmon.exe*). The Generate Status Report option will produce a lengthy report of site topology and replication information, and will provide details on any errors encountered. The Directory Service event log can also be an invaluable source of replication and KCC problems.

See Also

Recipe 13.2 for viewing the replication status of several domain controllers

13.11 Enabling Enhanced Logging of Replication Events

Problem

You want to enable enhanced logging of replication events.

Solution

Enable diagnostics logging for five Replication Events. See Recipe 16.2 for more information.

See Also

MS KB 220940 (How to Enable Diagnostic Event Logging for Active Directory Services)

13.12 Enabling Strict or Loose Replication Consistency

Problem

You want to enable strict or loose replication consistency.

Solution

Using a graphical user interface

1. Run *regedit.exe* from the command line or Start → Run.
2. Expand *HKEY_LOCAL_MACHINE\SYSTEM\CurrentControlSet\Services\NTDS\ Parameters*.
3. If the Strict Replication Consistency value does not exist, right-click on Parameters and select New → DWORD Value. For the name, enter Strict Replication Consistency.
4. In the right pane, double-click on the value and enter 1 to enable strict consistency or 0 to enable loose consistency.
5. Click OK.

Using a command-line interface

To enable strict consistency, run the following command:

```
> reg add HKLM\System\CurrentControlSet\Services\NTDS\Parameters /v "Strict
Replication Consistency" /t REG_DWORD /d 1
```

To enable loose consistency, run the following command:

```
> reg add HKLM\System\CurrentControlSet\Services\NTDS\Parameters /v "Strict\
Replication Consistency" /t REG_DWORD /d 0
```

Using VBScript

```
' This code enables strict or loose consistency on the specified DC.
' ------ SCRIPT CONFIGURATION ------
intEnableStrict = 1   ' 1 = strict consistency, 0 = loose consistency
strDC = "<DomainControllerName>"
' ------ END CONFIGURATION ---------

const HKLM = &H80000002
strNTDSReg = "SYSTEM\CurrentControlSet\Services\NTDS\Parameters"
set objReg = GetObject("winmgmts:\\" & strDC & _
                        "\root\default:StdRegProv")
objReg.SetDWORDValue HKLM, strNTDSReg, "Strict Replication Consistency", _
                intEnableStrict
WScript.Echo "Strict Replication Consistency value set to " & _
            intEnableStrict
```

Discussion

Up until Windows 2000 Service Pack 3, domain controllers followed a *loose replication consistency* model whereby lingering objects could get reinjected into Active Directory and replicate among all the domain controllers. A *lingering object* is one that was previously deleted, but got reintroduced because a domain controller did not successfully replicate for the duration of the time defined by the tombStoneLifetime attribute, or because the object was restored using a backup that was older than the tombStoneLifetime. See the "Introduction" of Chapter 17 for more on the tombStoneLifetime attribute. Windows 2000 SP2 and earlier domain controllers would replicate the lingering object throughout the naming context. Loose consistency thus has the potential to cause some security risks since an object you thought was deleted is now back in the forest again.

Some post-SP2 hotfixes and SP3 introduced *strict replication consistency*. Under strict replication, a domain controller will stop replicating with a destination domain controller when it determines that the source is attempting to replicate a lingering object. Event ID 1084 will get logged in the Directory Service event log indicating that it couldn't replicate the lingering object. Although strict replication can halt replication, it is the preferable method and is a good check to ensure lingering objects do not infiltrate your forest. For this reason, you must monitor your domain controllers to ensure they are replicating on a regular basis and that they do not have any 1084 events.

See Also

The "Introduction" of Chapter 17 for more on the `tombStoneLifetime` attribute, MS KB 317097 (Lingering Objects Prevent Active Directory Replication from Occurring), and MS KB 314282 (Lingering Objects May Remain After You Bring an Out-of-Date Global Catalog Server Back Online)

13.13 Finding Conflict Objects

Problem

You want to find conflict objects that are a result of replication collisions.

Solution

Using a graphical user interface

1. Open LDP from the Windows Support Tools.
2. From the menu, select Connection → Connect.
3. For Server, enter the name of a domain controller (or leave blank to do a serverless bind).
4. For Port, enter 389 or 3268 for the global catalog.
5. Click OK.
6. From the menu, select Connection → Bind.
7. Enter credentials (if necessary) of a user that can view the object.
8. Click OK.
9. From the menu, select Browse → Search.
10. For BaseDN, type the base DN from where you want to start the search.
11. For Scope, select the appropriate scope.
12. For Filter, enter (name=*\0ACNF:*).
13. Click Run.

Using a command-line interface

The following command finds all conflict objects within the whole forest:

```
> dsquery * forestroot -gc -attr distinguishedName -scope subtree -filter
"(name=*\0ACNF:*)"
```

You can also perform this query with AdFind as follows:

```
> adfind -b -gc -t "(name=*\0ACNF:*)" -dn
```

Using VBScript

```
' This code finds any conflict objects in a forest.
' If the search times out, you may need to change strBase to
' a specific OU or container
' ------ SCRIPT CONFIGURATION ------
strBase   = "<GC://" & "<ForestRootDN>" & ">;"
' ------ END CONFIGURATION ---------

strFilter = "(name=*\0ACNF:*);"
strAttrs  = "distinguishedName;"
strScope  = "Subtree"

set objConn = CreateObject("ADODB.Connection")
objConn.Provider = "ADsDSOObject"
objConn.Open
Set objRS = objConn.Execute(strBase & strFilter & strAttrs & strScope)

WScript.Echo objRS.RecordCount & " conflict objects found"
while not objRS.EOF
   Wscript.Echo objRS.Fields.Item("distinguishedName").Value
   objRS.MoveNext
wend
```

Discussion

Any distributed multimaster system has to deal with replication collisions, and Active Directory is no different. A collision can occur if an object is created on one domain controller and before that object has time to replicate out, an object with at least the same name is created on a different domain controller. So which object wins? With Active Directory, the following steps are used to determine which object is retained as is and which one is considered a conflict object:

1. AD will compare the version number of the objects. In Active Directory, version numbers are incremented every time you make a change to an object; the higher the version number, the more changes have been made to the object.

2. If the version numbers are the same, AD then compares the timestamps of when each object was created. The object that was created more recently will be retained and the older one will be renamed.

3. If the statistically improbable happens and two objects or attributes possess identical timestamps and version numbers, AD will take one final step to resolve the conflict by maintaining the object that originated from the DC with the higher GUID, and renaming the object that originated from the DC with the lower GUID.

When the losing object is renamed, the format of the renamed object is:

    <ObjectName>\0CNF:<ObjectGUID>

where <ObjectName> is the original name of the object, followed by a null termination character, followed by CNF:, followed by the object's GUID.

It is good to periodically scan your Active Directory tree to ensure you do not have a lot of conflict objects hanging around and to remove any that exist. It is a bit problematic to find conflict objects in a single query because the filter to find them is not optimized. In all three solutions, you have to perform a leading- and trailing-match pattern search (with *), and this can easily time out if you have a lot of objects. You may want to restrict your initial search to a few containers so that the search is quicker. Most notably, you'll want to search against your containers that house computer objects because these can frequently generate conflict objects. This can occur when a computer account is created, joined to a domain, and then the computer reboots. After the computer starts up, if it authenticates against a domain controller that has not replicated the new computer object, the domain controller will add a new object, which eventually results in a conflict.

See MS KB 297083 for more information on how to handle conflict objects after you've identified them.

See Also

MS KB 218614 (Replication Collisions in Windows 2000), and MS KB 297083 (How to Rename an Object After a Replication Collision Has Occurred)

13.14 Finding Orphaned Objects

Problem

You want to find orphaned objects within Active Directory

Solution

Using a graphical user interface

1. Open the ADUC snap-in.
2. If you need to change domains, right-click on "Active Directory Users and Computers" in the left pane, select "Connect to Domain," enter the domain name, and click OK.
3. If the LostAndFound container is not visible in the lefthand pane, click on View and place a check mark next to Advanced Features.

   You will see a list of any orphaned objects in the righthand pane.

Using a command-line interface

You can query for orphaned objects using either the built-in DSQuery utility or AdFind. DSQuery takes the following syntax:

```
> dsquery * cn=LostAndFound,<DomainDN> -scope onelevel -attr *
```

To use AdFind, enter the following:

```
> adfind -default -rb cn=LostAndFound -s onelevel
```

Using VBScript

```
' Using "" for the second parameter means that the there will be no
' indentation for the first level of objects displayed.
DisplayLostAndFound "LDAP://cn=LostAndFound,<DomainDN>", ""

' DisplayLostAndFound takes the ADsPath of the LostAndFound container
' and recursively displays all objects contained within it
Function DisplayLostAndFound( strADsPath, strSpace)
   set objObject = GetObject(strADsPath)
   Wscript.Echo strSpace & strADsPath
   for each objChildObject in objObject
      DisplayLostAndFound objChildObject.ADsPath, strSpace & " "
   next
End Function
```

Discussion

Because of the distributed nature of Active Directory, there exists the possibility that an administrator working on one DC can attempt to create or move a user into a container object such as an OU at the same time that another administrator *deletes* that OU from another DC. When this occurs, the leaf object becomes orphaned and is moved into the LostAndFound container within the Domain NC. You can view the lastKnownParent attribute of an object in this container to determine the OU or container that was deleted, and then delete the object or move it to a different container as appropriate.

From a procedural standpoint, objects being moved to the LostAndFound container should be a rare event. If it is happening frequently or if there are a large number of objects in the container, you should review the change-control procedures that are in place on your network to ensure that object moves and deletions are more tightly coordinated.

See Also

MS KB 271946 (Replication Does Not Work When There Is a Name Conflict on a Global Catalog) and MSDN: Lost-And-Found Class [AD Schema]

13.15 Listing the Replication Partners for a DC

Problem

You want to find the replication partners for a particular DC.

Solution

Using a graphical user interface

1. Open Active Directory Sites and Services.

2. Browse to Sites → *<SiteName>* → Servers → *<DCName>* → NTDS Settings.

3. The replication partners that have been configured for the DC in question will appear in the righthand pane. Double-click on any connection object to view its properties.

Using a command-line interface

You can query for replication connections using either the built-in DSQuery utility or AdFind. DSQuery takes the following syntax:

```
> dsquery * "cn=NTDS Settings,cn=<DCName,cn=Servers,cn=<SiteName,
cn=Sites,cn=Configuration,<ForestRootDN> -filter (objectcategory=NTDSConnection)
-attr *
```

To use AdFind, enter the following:

```
> adfind –config –rb "cn=NTDS Settings,cn=<DCName>,cn=Servers,cn=<SiteName>,cn=Sites"
–f (objectcategory=NTDSConnection)
```

Using VBScript

```
' This code searches for ntdsConnection Objects within the Sites container.
' ------ SCRIPT CONFIGURATION ------
strSite = "<SiteName>" ' e.g. "cn=Raleigh"
strForestDN = "<ForestRootDN>" ' e.g. "dc=rallencorp,dc=com"
strBaseDN    = "<LDAP://" & strSite & _
               ",cn=Sites,cn=Configuration," & strForestDN & ">;"
               ' BaseDN should be the search base
strFilter  = "(objectclass=NTDSConnection);"
strAttrs   = "fromServer;"
strScope   = "Subtree"
' ------ END CONFIGURATION ---------

set objConn = CreateObject("ADODB.Connection")
objConn.Provider = "ADsDSOObject"
objConn.Open "Active Directory Provider"
set objRS = objConn.Execute(strBaseDN & strFilter & strAttrs & strScope)
objRS.MoveFirst
While Not objRS.EOF
    Wscript.Echo objRS.Fields(0).Value
    objRS.MoveNext
Wend
WScript.Echo("Search complete!")
```

Discussion

By default, Active Directory's replication topology is created by the KCC, which runs on every DC to dynamically create and maintain *connection objects*. (The KCC will run every 15 minutes by default to determine if there have been any changes to the site topology that require modifications to the connection objects KCC has created.) Each connection object corresponds to an inbound replication connection—that is, a remote DC that will contact the local DC whenever it has changes available. Any connection object that is listed as <automatically generated> in Active Directory Sites and Services was created by the KCC. You can create additional connection objects manually, but these objects will not be kept up-to-date by the KCC in the event that a remote DC is relocated or taken offline.

See Also

MS KB 251250 (NTFRS Event ID 13557 Is Recorded When Duplicate NTDS Connection Objects Exist) and MS KB 232538 (Unsuccessful Replication Without Partner Listed)

13.16 Viewing Object Metadata

Problem

You want to view metadata for an object. The object's replPropertyMetaData attribute stores metadata information about the most recent updates to every attribute that has been set on the object.

Solution

Using a graphical user interface

1. Open LDP.
2. From the menu, select Connection → Connect.
3. For Server, enter the name of a domain controller or domain that contains the object.
4. For Port, enter 389.
5. Click OK.
6. From the menu, select Connection → Bind.
7. Enter credentials (if necessary) of a user that can view the object.
8. Click OK.
9. From the menu, select Browse → Replication → View Metadata.
10. For Object DN, type the distinguished name of the object you want to view.
11. Click OK.

Using a command-line interface

In the following command, replace *<ObjectDN>* with the distinguished name of the object for which you want to view metadata:

```
> repadmin /showobjmeta <DomainControllerName> <ObjectDN>
```

This command was called /showmeta in the Windows 2000 version of *repadmin*. Also, the parameters were switched in that version; *<ObjectDN>* came before *<DomainControllerName>*.

Using VBScript

```
' This code displays the metadata for the specified object.
' ------ SCRIPT CONFIGURATION ------
strObjectDN = "<ObjectDN>"        ' e.g. dc=rallencorp,dc=com
strDC    = "<DomainControllerName>"  ' e.g. dc1
' ------ END CONFIGURATION ---------

set objIadsTools = CreateObject("IADsTools.DCFunctions")
intRes = objIadsTools.GetMetaData(Cstr(strDC),Cstr(strObjectDN),0)

if intRes = -1 then
   Wscript.Echo objIadsTools.LastErrorText
   WScript.Quit
end if

for count = 1 to intRes
   WScript.Echo count & ". " & objIadsTools.MetaDataName(count)
   WScript.Echo vbTab & " Version:    " & _
                     objIadsTools.MetaDataVersionNumber(count)
   WScript.Echo vbTab & " Last Write: " & _
                     objIadsTools.MetaDataLastWriteTime(count)
   WScript.Echo vbTab & " Local USN:  " & _
                     objIadsTools.MetaDataLocalUSN(count)
   WScript.Echo vbTab & " Source USN: " & _
                     objIadsTools.MetaDataSourceUSN(count)
   WScript.Echo vbTab & " Server:     " & _
                     objIadsTools.MetaDataServerName(count)
next
```

Discussion

Object metadata can be an invaluable source of information when you need to troubleshoot replication problems or find out the last time an attribute was set for a particular object. In fact, a quick way to determine if two domain controllers have the same copy of an object is to look at the metadata for the object on both servers. If they both have the same metadata, then they have the same version of the object.

Unfortunately, the replPropertyMetaData attribute is stored as an octet string, so in Windows 2000, you could not simply read the attribute to view all of the metadata information. In the VBScript solution, the IADsTools GetMetaData method is a wrapper around the `DsReplicaGetInfo` method call. This method understands the format of the `replPropertyMetaData` attribute and can return it into a readable format. The following data is stored for each attribute that has been set on the object:

Attribute ID
Attribute that was updated.

Attribute version
Number of originating writes to the property.

Local USN
USN of the property on the local DC. This will be the same as the originating DC if the originating DC and local DC are the same.

Originating USN
USN stored with the property when the update was made on the originating DC.

Originating DC
DC that the originating write was made on.

Time/Date
Time and date that the property was changed in UTC.

In Windows Server 2003 and ADAM, you also have access to the `msDS-ReplAttributeMetaData` and `msDS-ReplValueMetaData` attributes, which provide much object metadata in XML-formatted output, as shown through this AdFind query:

```
> adfind -default -rb cn=administrator,cn=users msds-replattributemetadata

Using server: dc2.rallencorp.com:389
Directory: Windows Server 2003
Base DN: cn=administrator,cn=users,DC=rallencorp,DC=com

dn:CN=Administrator,CN=Users,DC=rallencorp,DC=com
>msDS-ReplAttributeMetaData: <DS_REPL_ATTR_META_DATA>
    <pszAttributeName>isCriticalSystemObject</pszAttributeName>
    <dwVersion>1</dwVersion>
    <ftimeLastOriginatingChange>2006-02-26T14:24:08Z</ftimeLastOriginatingChange>
    <uuidLastOriginatingDsaInvocationID>e197616c-7465-43f2-a502-
bac90df20b09</uuidLastOriginatingDsaInvocationID>
    <usnOriginatingChange>8194</usnOriginatingChange>
    <usnLocalChange>7298</usnLocalChange>
    <pszLastOriginatingDsaDN>CN=NTDS Settings,CN=DC1,CN=Servers,CN=Default-First-
Site-Name,CN=Sites,CN=Configuration,DC=rallencorp,DC=com</pszLastOriginatingDsaDN>
    </DS_REPL_ATTR_META_DATA>
```

```
>msDS-ReplAttributeMetaData: <DS_REPL_ATTR_META_DATA>
    <pszAttributeName>objectCategory</pszAttributeName>
    <dwVersion>1</dwVersion>
    <ftimeLastOriginatingChange>2006-02-26T14:24:08Z</ftimeLastOriginatingChange>
    <uuidLastOriginatingDsaInvocationID>e197616c-7465-43f2-a502-
bac90df20b09</uuidLastOriginatingDsaInvocationID>
    <usnOriginatingChange>8194</usnOriginatingChange>
    <usnLocalChange>7298</usnLocalChange>
    <pszLastOriginatingDsaDN>CN=NTDS Settings,CN=DC1,CN=Servers,CN=Default-First-
Site-Name,CN=Sites,CN=Configuration,DC=rallencorp,DC=com</pszLastOriginatingDsaDN>
</DS_REPL_ATTR_META_DATA>
```

See Also

IadsTools.doc in the Support Tools for more information on the IADsTools interface

CHAPTER 14
DNS and DHCP

14.0 Introduction

Active Directory is tightly coupled with the Domain Name System (DNS) name resolution service. Windows clients (running Windows 2000 or later) and domain controllers alike use DNS to locate domain controllers that are housed in a particular site
or that serve a particular function (like a Global Catalog server). Each domain controller requires numerous resource records (RRs) to be present in DNS so that it can
advertise its services as a domain controller, global catalog server, PDC Emulator, etc.

One of the innovative uses of Active Directory is as a store for DNS data. Instead of
using the primary and secondary zone transfer method, or even the more recent
NOTIFY method (RFC 1996) to replicate zone data between non-AD-integrated
DNS servers, AD-integrated zones store the zone data in Active Directory and use the
same replication process used to replicate other data between domain controllers.
The one catch with AD-integrated zones is that the DNS server must also be a
domain controller, and overloading DNS server responsibilities on your domain controllers may not be something you want to do if you plan on supporting a large volume of DNS requests. You can integrate forward and reverse lookup zones into
Active Directory, as well as *stub zones*, a new feature of Windows Server 2003 that is
used to maintain information about remote DNS zones and to reduce zone transfer
traffic across WAN links. For a detailed description of resource records, zone types,
and much more on DNS, see Chapter 6 in *Active Directory*, Third Edition, by Joe
Richards et al. (O'Reilly).

The Anatomy of a DNS Object

The only time DNS data is stored in Active Directory is if you have a zone that is AD-
integrated. When using standard primary and secondary zones that are not AD-integrated, the DNS data is stored locally in the filesystem of each DNS server in *zone files*.
If you have an AD-integrated zone under Windows 2000, a container is created in the
following location: `cn=<ZoneName>,cn=MicrosoftDNS,cn=System,<DomainDN>`, where
<ZoneName> is the name of the zone.

For Windows Server 2003, you can use application partitions to store DNS data in an alternate location. By default, there are three options:

- Store DNS data on all domain controllers in a domain (this is the only option available for Windows 2000).
- Store DNS data on all domain controllers that are DNS servers in the domain.
- Store DNS data on all domain controllers that are DNS servers in the forest.

The default location for the second option is dc=DomainDNSZones,<DomainDN>; for the third option, it is dc=ForestDNSZones,<ForestDN>. These two locations are actually application partitions that are replicated only to the domain controllers that are DNS servers in the domain or forest, respectively.

Inside the MicrosoftDNS container is a dnsZone object for each AD-integrated zone. Inside the dnsZone container are dnsNode objects that store all resource records associated with a particular node. In the following textual representation of an A record, the *dc1.rallencorp.com* name is considered a node (generally the left side of the resource record):

```
dc1.rallencorp.com. 600 IN A 6.10.57.21
```

There could be multiple resource records associated with the *dc1.rallencorp.com* name, so Microsoft decided to implement each distinct name as a dnsNode object. The dnsNode object has a dnsRecord attribute, which is multivalued and contains all of the resource records associated with that node. Unfortunately, the contents of that attribute are stored in a binary format and are not directly readable.

Tables 14-1 and 14-2 contain some of the interesting attributes that are available on dnsZone and dnsNode objects.

Table 14-1. Attributes of dnsZone objects

Attribute	Description
dc	Relative distinguished name of the zone. For example, the dc=domaindnszones,dc=rallencorp,dc=com dnsZone object has a dc attribute value of rallencorp.com
dnsProperty	Binary-formatted string that stores configuration information about the zone.
msDS-Approx-Immed-Subordinates	Approximate number of nodes contained within the zone. This is new to Windows Server 2003.

Table 14-2. Attributes of dnsNode objects

Attribute	Description
dc	Relative distinguished name of the node.
dnsRecord	Binary-formatted multivalued attribute that stores the resource records associated with the node.
dnsTombstoned	Boolean that indicates whether the node is marked for deletion. FALSE means it is not and TRUE means that it is

14.1   Creating a Forward Lookup Zone

Problem

You want to create a forward lookup zone. A forward lookup zone maps FQDNs to IP addresses or other names.

Solution

Using a graphical user interface

1. Open the DNS Management snap-in.

2. If an entry for the DNS server you want to connect to does not exist, right-click on DNS in the left pane and select "Connect to DNS Server." Select "This computer" or "The following computer," enter the server you want to connect to (if applicable), and click OK.

3. Expand the server in the left pane and click on Forward Lookup Zones.

4. Right-click on Forward Lookup Zones and select New Zone.

5. Click Next.

6. Select the zone type and click Next.

7. If you selected to store the zone data in Active Directory, next you will be asked which servers you want to replicate the DNS data to. Click Next after you make your selection.

 Step 7 applies only to DNS servers that are installed on Windows Server 2003 domain controllers. If you still have Windows 2000 DNS servers in your environment, choose the option to replicate the zone to all domain controllers in your domain.

8. Enter the zone name and click Next.

9. Fill out the information for the remaining screens. They will vary depending on whether you are creating a primary, secondary, or stub zone.

Using a command-line interface

The following command creates an AD-integrated zone:

```
> dnscmd <DNSServerName> /zoneadd <ZoneName> /DsPrimary
```

Using VBScript

```
' This code creates an AD-integrated forward zone.
' ------ SCRIPT CONFIGURATION ------
strServer = "<DNSServerName>"  ' e.g. dc1.rallencorp.com
strNewZone = "<ZoneName>"       ' e.g. othercorp.com
' ------ END CONFIGURATION ---------
```

```
set objDNS = GetObject("winMgmtr:\\" & strServer & "\root\MicrosoftDNS")
set objDNSZone = objDNS.Get("MicrosoftDNS_Zone")
strNull = objDNSZone.CreateZone(strNewZone, 0 , True)
WScript.Echo "Created zone " & strNewZone
```

Discussion

Using a command-line interface

When you create an AD-integrated zone with the /DsPrimary switch, you can additionally include a /dp switch and specify an application partition to add the zone to. Here is an example:

```
> dnscmd /zoneadd <ZoneName> /DsPrimary /dp domaindnszones.rallencorp.com
```

Using VBScript

The DNS WMI Provider is Microsoft's first comprehensive DNS API. You can create and modify zones, query and manage resource records, and manipulate DNS server configuration. In the VBScript solution, the CreateZone method of the MicrosoftDNS_Zone class was used to create the forward zone. The DNS WMI Provider is available only for Windows Server 2003 DNS; it cannot be used on Windows 2000 DNS servers.

See Also

Recipe 14.2 for creating a reverse lookup zone, MS KB 323445 (How to Create a New Zone on a DNS Server in Windows Server 2003), MSDN: DNS WMI Provider, and MSDN: CreateZone Method of the MicrosoftDNS_Zone Class

14.2   Creating a Reverse Lookup Zone

Problem

You want to create a reverse lookup zone. A reverse lookup zone maps IP addresses to names.

Solution

Using a graphical user interface

1. Open the DNS Management snap-in.
2. If an entry for the DNS server you want to connect to does not exist, right-click on DNS in the left pane and select "Connect to DNS Server." Select "This computer" or "The following computer," then enter the server you want to connect to (if applicable) and click OK.
3. Expand the server in the left pane and click on Reverse Lookup Zones.
4. Right-click on Reverse Lookup Zones and select New Zone.

5. Click Next.

6. Select the zone type (Primary, Secondary, or Stub zone). To AD-integrate the zone, place a check mark next to "Store the zone in Active Directory (available only if DNS server is a domain controller)" and click Next.

7. If you selected to store the zone data in Active Directory, next you will be asked which servers you want to replicate the DNS data to: all DNS servers in the forest, all DNS servers in the domain, all domain controllers in the domain, or all DCs that are hosting a particular application partition. Click Next after you make your selection.

 Step 7 applies only to DNS servers that are installed on Windows Server 2003 domain controllers. If you still have Windows 2000 DNS servers in your environment, choose the option of replicate the zone to all domain controllers in your domain.

8. Type the Network ID for the reverse zone or enter a reverse zone name to use.

9. Fill out the information for the remaining screens. They will vary depending on if you are creating a primary, secondary, or stub zone.

Using a command-line interface

The following command creates an AD-integrated reverse zone:

```
> dnscmd <DNSServerName> /zoneadd <ZoneName> /DsPrimary
```

Using VBScript

```
' This code creates an AD-integrated reverse zone.
' ------ SCRIPT CONFIGURATION ------
strServer  = "<DNSServerName>"  ' e.g. dc1.rallencorp.com
strNewZone = "<ZoneName>"        ' e.g. 8.10.192.in-addr.arpa.
' ------ END CONFIGURATION ---------

set objDNS = GetObject("winMgmts:\\" & strServer & "\root\MicrosoftDNS")
set objDNSZone = objDNS.Get("MicrosoftDNS_Zone")
strNull = objDNSZone.CreateZone(strNewZone, 0 , True)
WScript.Echo "Created zone " & strNewZone
```

Discussion

Creating a reverse zone is very similar to creating a forward zone. See Recipe 14.1 for more information.

See Also

MS KB 323445 (How to Create a New Zone on a DNS Server in Windows Server 2003) and MSDN: CreateZone Method of the MicrosoftDNS_Zone Class

14.3 Viewing a Server's Zones

Problem

You want to view the zones on a server.

Solution

Using a graphical user interface

1. Open the DNS Management snap-in.
2. Right-click on DNS in the left pane and select "Connect to DNS Server."
3. Enter the server you want to connect to and click Enter.
4. In the left pane, expand the server and click Forward Lookup Zones and Reverse Lookup Zones to view the hosted zones.

Using a command-line interface

```
> dnscmd <DNSServerName> /enumzones
```

Using VBScript

```
' This code lists the zones that are hosted by the specified server.
' ------ SCRIPT CONFIGURATION ------
strServer = "<DNSServerName>"   ' e.g. dc1.rallencorp.com
' ------ END CONFIGURATION ---------

set objDNS = GetObject("winMgmts:\\" & strServer & "\root\MicrosoftDNS")
set objDNSServer = objDNS.Get("MicrosoftDNS_Server.Name="".""")
set objZones = objDNS.ExecQuery("Select * from MicrosoftDNS_Zone " & _
                                "Where DnsServerName = '" & _
                                objDNSServer.Name & "'")
WScript.Echo "Zones on " & objDNSServer.Name
for each objZone in objZones
    WScript.Echo " " & objZOne.Name
next
```

Discussion

Using a graphical user interface

When you click on either the Forward Lookup Zones or Reverse Lookup Zones in the lefthand pane of the DMS MMC, the right pane contains a Type column that displays the zone type for each zone.

Using a command-line interface

When using the /enumzones switch without any more parameters, it displays all zones on the server. You can specify additional filters that limit the types of zones returned.

With the Windows 2000 version of *dnscmd*, you can specify up to two filters (for example, using the /enumzones /primary /forward switch combination will display all primary forward zones on the server):

```
Filter1:
    /Primary
    /Secondary
    /Cache
    /Auto-Created
Filter2:
    /Forward
    /Reverse
```

With the Windows Server 2003 version of *dnscmd*, the filter behavior has changed. Instead of having two levels of criteria, you can specify one or more of the following:

/Primary
> Lists both standard and Active Directory–integrated primary zones

/Secondary
> Lists all standard secondary zones

/Forwarder
> Lists all zones that forward unresolvable queries to another DNS server

/Stub
> Lists all stub zones hosted on a server

/Cache
> Lists zones that are loaded into cache on the server

/Auto-Created
> Lists zones that were created automatically during the DNS server installation

/Forward
> Lists all forward lookup zones

/Reverse
> Lists all reverse lookup zones

/Ds
> Lists all Active Directory–integrated zones

/File
> Lists zones that are stored in text files

/DomainDirectoryPartition
> Lists zones that are stored in the DomainDNSZones partition

/ForestDirectoryPartition
> Lists zones that are stored in the ForestDNSZones partition

/CustomDirectoryPartition
> Lists zones that are stored in a user-created directory partition

```
/LegacyDirectoryPartition
```
Lists zones that are stored in the domain NC
```
/DirectoryPartition <PartitionName>
```
Lists zones that are stored in a particular application partition

Using VBScript

A WQL query was used to find all MicrosoftDNS_Zone objects. You can add additional criteria to the WQL Select statement to return a subset of zones supported on the server.

See Also

MSDN: MicrosoftDNS_Zone

14.4   Converting a Zone to an AD-Integrated Zone

Problem

You want to convert a standard primary zone to an AD-integrated zone. This causes the contents of the zone to be stored and replicated in Active Directory instead of in a text file on the local server.

Solution

Using a graphical user interface

1. Open the DNS Management snap-in.
2. Right-click on DNS in the left pane and select "Connect to DNS Server."
3. Enter the server you want to connect to and click Enter.
4. If you want to convert a forward zone, expand the Forward Lookup Zone folder. If you want to convert a reverse zone, expand the Reverse Lookup Zone folder.
5. Right-click on the zone you want to convert and select Properties.
6. Beside Type, click the Change button.
7. Check the box beside "Store the zone in Active Directory."
8. Click OK twice.

Using a command-line interface

```
> dnscmd <ServerName> /zoneresettype <ZoneName> /DsPrimary
```

Using VBScript

```
' This code converts a zone to AD-integrated.
' ------ SCRIPT CONFIGURATION ------
strZone  = "<ZoneName>"    ' e.g. rallencorp.com
```

```
strServer = "<ServerName>"  ' e.g. dc1.rallencorp.com
' ------ END CONFIGURATION ---------

set objDNS = GetObject("winMgmts:\\" & strServer & "\root\MicrosoftDNS")
set objDNSServer = objDNS.Get("MicrosoftDNS_Server.Name=""."""")
set objDNSZone = objDNS.Get("MicrosoftDNS_Zone.ContainerName=""" & _
                            strZone & """",DnsServerName=""" & _
                            objDNSServer.Name & """",Name=""" & strZone & """""")
strNull = objDNSZone.ChangeZoneType(0, True)
objDNSZone.Put_
WScript.Echo "Converted " & strZone & " to AD-Integrated"
```

Discussion

See the "Introduction" to this chapter, "Moving AD-Integrated Zones into an Application Partition," and Chapter 6 of *Active Directory*, Third Edition, by Joe Richards et al. (O'Reilly) for more on AD-integrated zones.

See Also

MS KB 198437 (How to Convert DNS Primary Server to Active Directory Integrated), MS KB 227844 (Primary and Active Directory Integrated Zones Differences), and MSDN: ChangeZoneType Method of the MicrosoftDNS_Zone Class

14.5 Moving AD-Integrated Zones into an Application Partition

 This recipe requires the Windows Server 2003 domain functional level.

Problem

You want to move AD-integrated zones into an application partition.

Solution

Using a graphical user interface

1. Open the DNS Management snap-in.

2. If an entry for the DNS server you want to connect to does not exist, right-click on DNS in the left pane and select Connect to DNS Server. Select "This computer" or "The following computer," enter the server you want to connect to (if applicable), and click OK.

3. Expand the server in the left pane and expand either Forward Lookup Zones or Reverse Lookup Zones, depending on the type of zone.

4. Right-click on the name of the zone and select Properties.

5. Click on the Change button beside Replication.

6. Select the application partition you want to move the zone into.

7. Click OK twice.

Using a command-line interface

The following command will move a zone to the default application partition that replicates across all domain controllers in the domain that are configured as DNS servers:

```
> dnscmd <DNSServerName> /zonechangedirectorypartition <ZoneName> /domain
```

Using VBScript

At the time of publication of this book, the DNS WMI Provider did not support programmatically moving a zone into an application partition.

Discussion

With Windows 2000 Active Directory, if you had AD-integrated zones, those zones were replicated to every domain controller in the domain where they were stored. In many cases, not every domain controller also served as a DNS server, which resulted in increased and unnecessary traffic to replicate zone changes to DCs that did not require the data.

Windows Server 2003 provides an elegant solution to this issue by using application partitions. Application partitions are user-defined partitions that can be configured to replicate with any domain controller in a forest. This provides a lot more flexibility for how you store and replicate your AD-integrated zones. You could, in fact, have a few domain controllers from each domain act as DNS servers for all of your AD domains.

See Also

Chapter 18 for more information on application partitions

14.6   Configuring Zone Transfers

Problem

You want to enable zone transfers to specific secondary nameservers.

Solution

Using a graphical user interface

1. Open the DNS snap-in.
2. In the left pane, expand the server node and expand either Forward Lookup Zone or Reverse Lookup Zone depending on the type of zone you want to manage.
3. Right-click on the zone and select Properties.
4. Select the Zone Transfers tab.
5. Select either the option to restrict zone transfers to those servers listed on the Name Servers tab or the option to restrict zone transfers to specific IP addresses. See the "Discussion" section for more on these two options.

Using a command-line interface

The following command enables zone transfers for the *test.local* zone and specifies they can only occur with servers that have NS records in the zone (i.e., servers listed within the Name Servers tab of the DNS snap-in):

```
> dnscmd <ServerName> /ZoneResetSecondaries test.local /SecureNs
```

The next command enables zone transfers for same zone, but specifies they can only occur with hosts whose IP addresses are 172.16.11.33 and 172.16.11.34:

```
> dnscmd <ServerName> /ZoneResetSecondaries test.local /SecureList 172.16.11.33
  172.16.11.34
```

Using VBScript

```
' This code creates a nameserver (NS) record on a DNS server.

strDNSServer = "<servername>"
strContainer = "<containername>"
strOwner = "<ownername>"
intRecordClass = 1
intTTL = 600
strNSHost = "<nameservername>"
strComputer = "."

set objWMIService = GetObject _
    ("winmgmts:\\" & strComputer & "\root\MicrosoftDNS")
set objItem = objWMIService.Get("MicrosoftDNS_NSType")
errResult = objItem.CreateInstanceFromPropertyData _
    (strDNSServer, strContainer, strOwner, intRecordClass, intTTL, strNSHost)

' This code configures the allowed secondaries for zone transfer and notify

' XFR constants
const ZONE_SECSECURE_NO_SECURITY = 0
const ZONE_SECSECURE_NS_ONLY     = 1
const ZONE_SECSECURE_LIST_ONLY   = 2
```

```
const ZONE_SECSECURE_NO_XFR       = 3

' NOTIFY constants
const ZONE_NOTIFY_OFF             = 0
const ZONE_NOTIFY_ALL_SECONDARIES = 1
const ZONE_NOTIFY_LIST_ONLY       = 2

' ------ SCRIPT CONFIGURATION ------
strZone   = "<ZoneName>"    ' e.g. rallencorp.com
strServer = "<ServerName>"  ' e.g. dc1.rallencorp.com

' use one of the above XFR constants
intSecureSecondaries = ZONE_SECSECURE_LIST_ONLY
arrSecondaries = Array("1.1.1.2","1.1.1.3")

' use one of the above NOTIFY constants
intNotify = ZONE_NOTIFY_LIST_ONLY
arrNotify = Array("<IP1>","<IP2>")
' ------ END CONFIGURATION --------

set objDNS = GetObject("winMgmts:\\" & strServer & "\root\MicrosoftDNS")
set objDNSServer = objDNS.Get("MicrosoftDNS_Server.Name=""."""")
set objDNSZone = objDNS.Get("MicrosoftDNS_Zone.ContainerName=""" & _
                    strZone & """,DnsServerName=""" & _
                    objDNSServer.Name & """,Name=""" & strZone & """")
strNull = objDNSZone.ResetSecondaries(arrSecondaries,intSecureSecondaries, _
                                arrNotify,intNotify)
objDNSZone.Put_
WScript.Echo "Updated secondaries for zone transfer and notify"
```

Discussion

Depending on your environment, your DNS implementation may require that you create secondary zones to allow for load balancing for busy DNS servers or remote sites connected by slow links. In this situation, you want to allow zone transfers to occur between your AD-integrated DNS servers and your secondary servers, but you want to restrict which hosts can initiate zone transfers with your AD-integrated nameservers. Allowing anyone to initiate a zone transfer with your domain controllers could provide an attacker with information for mapping out your network; it is therefore critical that you limit which hosts can pull zone transfers from your servers.

If you are using only Active Directory–integrated zones, the Name Servers tab will be automatically populated with a list of all nameservers that are authoritative for the selected zone, and this is the recommended choice when you have a large network with many nameservers deployed. If any of your nameservers are using standard zone files, however, you will need to populate this tab manually for any secondary nameservers you deploy.

Specifying a list of IP addresses for hosts that can initiate zone transfers may be more secure since it is more specific, but this approach has the trade-off of adding the additional management overhead of keeping track of the IP addresses of all nameservers on your network, so you should follow this approach only if your network is small and you have relatively few nameservers deployed. Another disadvantage of this approach is that if you forget to add some IP addresses of nameservers to your list, zone information stored on those servers could become stale, causing name resolution to fail for some of your clients. This could result in some of your users experiencing difficulties in accessing network resources.

Note that on Windows 2000 nameservers, the default setting is to allow zone transfers with any host that requests them. This setting is inherently insecure as it allows attackers to use *nslookup* to display all resource records on your servers, so be sure to use the steps outlined in this recipe to change the setting on your servers to one of the two settings described here. Windows Server 2003 DNS is more secure by default because in the case of file-based zones, it is configured to allow zone transfers only with servers listed on the Name Servers tab of a zone. In the case of Active Directory–integrated zones, it is configured to disallow zone transfers entirely since they generally aren't needed in an Active Directory environment.

See Also

MS KB 164017 (Explanation of a DNS Zone Transfer)

14.7 Configuring Forwarding

Problem

You want to configure forwarding to allow for name resolution outside of your corporate network.

Solution

Using a graphical user interface

1. Open the DNS Management snap-in.
2. Connect to the DNS Server you want to modify. In the left pane, right-click on DNS and select "Connect to DNS Server." Select "The following computer" and enter the target server name. Click OK.
3. Right-click on the server and select Properties.
4. Click the Forwarders tab.
5. To configure a global forwarder, make sure "All other DNS domains" is selected under DNS domain, type an IP under "Selected domain's forwarder IP address list," click Add, and then click Apply.
6. To configure a conditional forwarder for a specific domain, click the New button.
7. Enter the domain name and click OK.

8. Add IPs as described for global forwarders in Step 5.

9. From the Forwarders tab, you can also set the number of seconds that the server waits before forward queries time out. You can also disable the use of recursion for certain domains. Both of these can be set on a per-domain basis.

Using a command-line interface

The following command sets the default forwarders. Replace *<IPsOfForwarders>* with a space-separated list of IP addresses for the nameservers to forward requests to.

```
> dnscmd <ServerName> /resetforwarders <IPsOfForwaders>
```

For example:

```
> dnscmd dns01 /resetforwarders 10.22.3.4 10.22.3.5
```

The following command creates a domain-based forwarder:

```
> dnscmd <ServerName> /zoneadd <DomainName> /forwarder <IPsOfForwarders>
```

The following command configures the default forwarder timeout:

```
> dnscmd <ServerName> /config /forwardingtimeout <NumSeconds>
```

The following command configures the forwarder timeout for a specific domain:

```
> dnscmd <ServerName> /config <DomainName> /forwardertimeout <NumSeconds>
```

Using VBScript

```
' This code enumerates the default forwarders.
' ------ SCRIPT CONFIGURATION ------
strServer = "<ServerName> "  ' e.g. dns1.rallencorp.com
' ------ END CONFIGURATION ---------

set objDNS = GetObject("winMgmts:\\" & strServer & "\root\MicrosoftDNS")
set objDNSServer = objDNS.Get("MicrosoftDNS_Server.Name="".""")
for each strForwarder in objDNSServer.Forwarders
   Wscript.Echo strForwarder
Next


' This code sets the default forwarders.
' ------ SCRIPT CONFIGURATION ------
strServer = "<ServerName>"  ' e.g. dns1.rallencorp.com
arrForwarders = Array("<IP1>","<IP2>")
' ------ END CONFTGURATION ---------

set objDNS = GetObject("winMgmts:\\" & strServer & "\root\MicrosoftDNS")
set objDNSServer = objDNS.Get("MicrosoftDNS_Server.Name="".""")
objDNSServer.Forwarders = arrForwarders
objDNSServer.Put_
Wscript.Echo "Successfully set default forwarders"
```

```
' This code sets the forwarders for a specific domain.
' ------ SCRIPT CONFIGURATION ------
strServer = "<ServerName>"    ' e.g. dns01
strNewZone = "<ZoneName>"     ' e.g. othercorp.com
arrMasterIPs = Array("<IP1>","<IP2>") ' replace <IPx> with IPs of master server
' ------ END CONFIGURATION ---------
on error resume next
set objDNS = GetObject("winMgmts:\\" & strServer & "\root\MicrosoftDNS")
set objDNSZone = objDNS.Get("MicrosoftDNS_Zone")
strNull = objDNSZone.CreateZone(strNewZone,3,false,"",arrMasterIPs)
if Err then
   WScript.Echo "Error occurred creating zone: " & Err.Description
else
   WScript.Echo "Domain forwarder created."
end if
```

Discussion

Nameservers have long supported the notion of *forwarders*. Rather than sending all unresolved queries to the root Internet nameservers, you can use forwarders to send queries to a specific server or set of servers, perhaps hosted by your ISP or by a partner corporation. This allows you to better control the name resolution process on your network.

Microsoft has extended this capability in Windows Server 2003 to support *conditional forwarding*. With conditional forwarding, you can forward unresolved queries for specific domains to different nameservers. The most common use of conditional forwarding is when you have two or more noncontiguous namespaces. Consider, for example, a merger between the *rallencorp.com* and *othercorp.com* corporations. Normally, for the nameservers of *rallencorp.com* to resolve queries for *othercorp.com*, the queries would have to first be forwarded to the root Internet nameservers. With conditional forwarding, you can configure the *rallencorp.com* DNS servers so that all requests for *othercorp.com* should be sent directly to the *othercorp.com* nameservers and all other unresolved queries should be sent to the Internet, and vice versa. The trade-off for this feature is the additional CPU processing that's necessary to examine each query and forward it to the appropriate server, rather than just funneling all unresolved queries to a single external server.

See Also

MS KB 304491 (Conditional Forwarding in Windows Server 2003) and MS KB 811118 (Support WebCast: Microsoft Windows Server 2003 DNS: Stub Zones and Conditional Forwarding)

14.8 Delegating Control of a Zone

Problem

You want to delegate control of managing the resource records in a zone.

Solution

Using a graphical user interface

1. Open the DNS Management snap-in.

2. If an entry for the DNS server you want to connect to does not exist, right-click on DNS in the left pane and select "Connect to DNS Server." Select "This computer" or "The following computer," then enter the server you want to connect to (if applicable) and click OK.

3. Expand the server in the left pane and expand either Forward Lookup Zones or Reverse Lookup Zones, depending on the type of zone.

4. Right-click on the name of the zone and select Properties.

5. Click on the Security tab.

6. Click the Add button.

7. Use the Object Picker to locate the user or group to which you want to delegate control.

8. Under Permissions, check the Full Control box.

9. Click OK.

Using a command-line interface

The following command grants full control over managing the resource records in an AD-Integrated zone:

```
> dsacls dc=<ZoneName>,cn=MicrosoftDNS,<DomainOrAppPartitionDN> /G
<UserOrGroup>:GA;;
```

Using VBScript

```
' This code grants full control for the specified user or group over
' an AD-Integrated zone.
' ------ SCRIPT CONFIGURATION ------
strZoneDN = "dc=<ZoneName>,cn=MicrosoftDNS,<DomainOrAppPartitionDN>"
strUserOrGroup = "<UserOrGroup>"  ' e.g. joe@rallencorp.com or RALLENCORP\joe
' ------ END CONFIGURATION ---------

set objZone = GetObject("LDAP://" & strZoneDN)
'###########################
' Constants
'###########################
```

```
' ADS_ACETYPE_ENUM
Const ADS_ACETYPE_ACCESS_ALLOWED_OBJECT = &h5

' ADS_FLAGTYPE_ENUM
Const ADS_FLAG_OBJECT_TYPE_PRESENT = &h1

' ADS_RIGHTS_ENUM
Const ADS_RIGHT_GENERIC_ALL = &h10000000

'###########################
' Create ACL
'###########################

set objSD = objZone.Get("nTSecurityDescriptor")
set objDACL = objSD.DiscretionaryAcl

' Full Control
set objACE1 = CreateObject("AccessControlEntry")
objACE1.Trustee    = strUserOrGroup
objACE1.AccessMask = ADS_RIGHT_GENERIC_ALL
objACE1.AceFlags   = 0
objACE1.Flags      = ADS_FLAG_OBJECT_TYPE_PRESENT
objACE1.AceType    = ADS_ACETYPE_ACCESS_ALLOWED_OBJECT

objDACL.AddAce objACE1

'###########################
' Set ACL
'###########################
objSD.DiscretionaryAcl = objDACL
objZone.Put "nTSecurityDescriptor", objSD
objZone.SetInfo
WScript.Echo "Delegated control of " & strZoneDN & " to " & strUserOrGroup
```

Discussion

By default, members of the *DNSAdmins* group have control over DNS server and
zone configuration. You can delegate control of individual AD-integrated zones by
modifying permissions on the zone object in AD. The solutions show examples for
how to grant Full Control to an additional user or group over a particular zone.

See Also

MS KB 256643 (Unable to Prevent DNS Zone Administrator from Creating New
Zones)

14.9 Creating and Deleting Resource Records

Problem

You want to create and delete resource records in a zone.

Solution

Using a graphical user interface

1. Open the DNS Management snap-in.

2. If an entry for the DNS server you want to connect to does not exist, right-click on DNS in the left pane and select "Connect to DNS Server." Select "This computer" or "The following computer," then enter the server you want to connect to (if applicable) and click OK.

3. If you want to add or delete a record in a forward zone, expand the Forward Lookup Zone folder. If you want to add or delete a record for a reverse zone, expand the Reverse Lookup Zone folder.

To create a resource record, do the following:

1. In the left pane, right-click the zone and select the option that corresponds to the record type you want to create—e.g., New Host (A).

2. Fill in all required fields.

3. Click OK.

To delete a resource record, do the following:

1. In the left pane, click on the zone the record is in.

2. In the right pane, right-click on the record you want to delete and select Delete.

3. Click Yes to confirm.

Using a command-line interface

To add a resource record, use the following command:

```
> dnscmd <DNSServerName> /recordadd <ZoneName> <NodeName> <RecordType> <RRData>
```

The following command adds an A record in the *rallencorp.com* zone:

```
> dnscmd dc1 /recordadd rallencorp.com wins01 A 19.25.52.2.25
```

To delete a resource record, use the following command:

```
> dnscmd <DNSServerName> /recorddelete <ZoneName> <NodeName> <RecordType> <RRData>
```

The following command deletes an A record in the *rallencorp.com* zone:

```
> dnscmd dc1 /recorddelete rallencorp.com wins01 A 19.25.52.2.25
```

Using VBScript

```
' This code shows how to add an A record and PTR record using
' the DNS WMI Provider.
' ------ SCRIPT CONFIGURATION ------
strForwardRRAdd = "test-xp.rallencorp.com. IN A 192.32.64.13"
strReverseRRAdd = "13.64.32.192.in-addr.arpa IN PTR test-xp.rallencorp.com"
strForwardDomain = "rallencorp.com"
```

```
strReverseDomain = "192.in-addr.arpa."
' ------ END CONFIGURATION ---------

set objDNS = GetObject("winMgmts:root\MicrosoftDNS")
set objRR = objDNS.Get("MicrosoftDNS_ResourceRecord")
set objDNSServer = objDNS.Get("MicrosoftDNS_Server.Name="".""")

' Create the A record
strNull = objRR.CreateInstanceFromTextRepresentation( _
                objDNSServer.Name, _
                strForwardDomain, _
                strForwardRRAdd, _
                objOutParam)
set objRR2 = objDNS.Get(objOutParam)
WScript.Echo "Created Record: " & objRR2.TextRepresentation

' Create the PTR record
strNull = objRR.CreateInstanceFromTextRepresentation( _
                objDNSServer.Name, _
                strReverseDomain, _
                strReverseRRAdd, _
                objOutParam)
set objRR2 = objDNS.Get(objOutParam)
WScript.Echo "Created Record: " & objRR2.TextRepresentation


' This code shows how to delete an A and PTR record for the record
' we created in the previous example.

strHostName  = "test-xp.rallencorp.com."

set objDNS = GetObject("winMgmts:root\MicrosoftDNS")
set objDNSServer = objDNS.Get("MicrosoftDNS_Server.Name="".""")

set objRRs = objDNS.ExecQuery(" select * " & _
                        " from MicrosoftDNS_ResourceRecord " & _
                        " where OwnerName = """ & strHostName & """" & _
                        " Or RecordData = """ & strHostName & """")
if objRRs.Count < 1 then
   WScript.Echo "No matches found for " & strHostName
else
   for each objRR in objRRs
      objRR.Delete_
      WScript.Echo "Deleted " & objRR.TextRepresentation
   next
end if
```

Discussion

Using a graphical user interface

The DNS Management snap-in is good for creating a small number of records, but if you need to add or delete more than a couple of dozen, then we'd recommend writing a batch file around *dnscmd* or using the DNS WMI Provider to automate the process.

Using a command-line interface

Adding A, CNAME, and PTR resource records is pretty straightforward as far as the data you must enter, but other record types, such as SRV, require quite a bit more data. The help pages for /recordadd and /recorddelete display the required information for each record type. For example, to add an SRV record using *dnscmd*, you need to specify the priority, weight, port, and hostname of the record as in the following example:

```
> dnscmd /recordadd dc1.rallencorp.com SRV 50 100 88 _kerberos
```

Using VBScript

The first example creates A and PTR records using the `CreateInstanceFrom TextRepresentation` method, which is a `MicrosoftDNS_ResourceRecord` method that allows you to create resource records by passing in the textual version of the record. This is the textual representation of the A record used in the example:

```
test-xp.rallencorp.com IN A 192.32.64.13
```

The first parameter to this method is the DNS server name, the second is the name of the domain to add the record to, the third is the resource record, and the last is an out parameter that returns a reference to the new resource record.

The second example finds all resource records that match a certain hostname and deletes them. This is done by first using a WQL query to find all resource records where the `OwnerName` equals the target hostname (this will match any A records) and where `RecordData` equals the target hostname (this will match any PTR records). The `Delete_` method is called on each matching record, removing them from the DNS server.

See Also

MSDN: MicrosoftDNS_ResourceRecord

14.10 Querying Resource Records

Problem

You want to query resource records.

Solution

Using a graphical user interface

The DNS Management snap-in does not provide an interface for searching resource records.

Using a command-line interface

In the following command, replace *<RecordType>* with the type of resource record you want to find (e.g., A, CNAME, SRV) and *<RecordName>* with the name or IP address of the record to match:

```
> nslookup -type=<RecordType> <RecordName>
```

Using VBScript

```
' This code prints the resource records that match
' the specified name.
' ------ SCRIPT CONFIGURATION ------
strQuery = "<RecordName>"
' ------ END CONFIGURATION ---------

set objDNS = GetObject("winMgmts:root\MicrosoftDNS")
set objDNSServer = objDNS.Get("MicrosoftDNS_Server.Name="".""")
set objRRs = objDNS.ExecQuery(" select * " & _
                        " from MicrosoftDNS_ResourceRecord" & _
                        " where  OwnerName = """ & strQuery & """" & _
                        " Or  DomainName = """ & strQuery & """" & _
                        " Or RecordData = """ & strQuery & """")
if objRRs.Count < 1 then
    WScript.Echo "No matches found for " & strHostName & " of " _
                & strRecordType & " type"
else
    for each objRR in objRRs
        WScript.Echo objRR.TextRepresentation
    next
end if
```

Discussion

Using a command-line interface

You can leave off the -type switch, and the command will find any A, PTR, and CNAME records that match *<RecordName>*.

You can also run *nslookup* from interactive mode, which can be entered by typing nslookup at a command prompt with no additional parameters, or switch back and forth between query types by using the q=ANY command to reset *nslookup*.

Using VBScript

In the VBScript solution, a WQL query was used to find all matching resource records. This is a good example of how powerful the DNS WMI Provider can be. The query attempts to find any object of the MicrosoftDNS_ResourceRecord class that has an OwnerName, DomainName, or RecordData field equal to the *<RecordName>*. This is not the most efficient query if the server supports multiple large zones, so you may want to restrict it to search for specific types of records by adding criteria to match RecordType = *<Type>*.

See Also

MSDN: MicrosoftDNS_ResourceRecord, RFC 1035 (Domain Names – Implementation and Specification), and RFC 1700 (DNS Parameters)

14.11 Modifying the DNS Server Configuration

Problem

You want to modify the DNS Server settings.

Solution

Using a graphical user interface

1. Open the DNS Management snap-in.
2. If an entry for the DNS server you want to connect to does not exist, right-click on DNS in the left pane and select "Connect to DNS Server." Select "This computer" or "The following computer," then enter the server you want to connect to (if applicable) and click OK.
3. Right-click on the server and select Properties.
4. There will be several tabs you can choose from to edit the server settings.
5. Click OK to commit the changes after you've completed your modifications.

Using a command-line interface

With the following command, replace *<Setting>* with the name of the setting to modify and *<Value>* with the value to set:

```
> dnscmd <DNSServerName> /config  /<Setting> <Value>
```

The following command enables the EnableDnsSec setting on *dns01*:

```
> dnscmd dns01 /config /EnableDnsSec 1
```

The following command disables the NoTcp setting on the local host:

```
> dnscmd /config /NoTcp 0
```

The following command sets the DsPollingInterval setting to 60 on *dns02*:

```
> dnscmd dns02 /config /DsPollingInterval 60
```

For the complete list of settings, run dnscmd /config from the command-line.

Using VBScript

```
set objDNS = GetObject("winMgmts:root\MicrosoftDNS")
set objDNSServer = objDNS.Get("MicrosoftDNS_Server.Name=""."""")
objDNSServer.<Setting> = <Value>  ' e.g. objDNSServer.AllowUpdate = TRUE
objDNSServer.Put
```

Discussion

The Microsoft DNS server supports a variety of settings to configure everything from scavenging and forwarders to logging. With the DNS Management snap-in, the settings are spread over several tabs in the Properties property page. You can get a list of these settings by simply running `dnscmd /config` from a command line. For the CLI and VBScript solutions, the setting names are nearly identical. In the VBScript solution, be sure to call the `Put_` method after you are done configuring settings in order for the changes to take effect.

See Also

MSDN: MicrosoftDNS_Server

14.12 Scavenging Old Resource Records

Problem

You want to scavenge old resource records. DNS scavenging is the process whereby resource records are automatically removed if they are not updated after a period of time. Typically, this applies only to resource records that were added via DDNS, but you can also scavenge manually created static records as well. DNS scavenging is a recommended practice so that your DNS zones are automatically kept clean of stale resource records.

Solution

The following solutions will show how to enable automatic scavenging on all AD-integrated zones.

Using a graphical user interface

1. Open the DNS Management snap-in.

2. If an entry for the DNS server you want to connect to does not exist, right-click on DNS in the left pane and select "Connect to DNS Server." Select "This computer" or "The following computer," enter the server you want to connect to (if applicable), and click OK.

3. Click on the server, right-click on it, and select "Set Aging/Scavenging for all zones."

4. Check the box beside "Scavenge stale resource records."

5. Configure the No-Refresh and Refresh intervals as necessary, and click OK.

6. Check the box beside "Apply these settings to the existing Active Directory–integrated zones" and click OK.

7. Right-click on the server again and select Properties.

8. Select the Advanced tab.

9. Check the box beside "Enable automatic scavenging of stale resource records."

10. Configure the scavenging period as necessary.

11. Click OK.

Using a command-line interface

```
> dnscmd <DNSServerName> /config /ScavengingInterval <ScavengingMinutes>
> dnscmd <DNSServerName> /config /DefaultAgingState 1
> dnscmd <DNSServerName> /config /DefaultNoRefreshInterval <NoRefreshMinutes>
> dnscmd <DNSServerName> /config /DefaultRefreshInterval <RefreshMinutes>
> dnscmd <DNSServerName> /config ..AllZones /aging 1
```

Using VBScript

```
' This code enables scavenging for all AD-integrated zones.
' ------ SCRIPT CONFIGURATION ------
strServer = "<DNSServerName>"
intScavengingInterval = <ScavengingMinutes>
intNoRefreshInterval  = <NoRefreshMinutes>
intRefreshInterval    = <RefreshMinutes>
' ------ END CONFIGURATION ---------

set objDNS = GetObject("winMgmts:\\" & strServer & "\root\MicrosoftDNS")
set objDNSServer = objDNS.Get("MicrosoftDNS_Server.Name=""."""")

objDNSServer.ScavengingInterval         = intScavengingInterval
objDNSServer.DefaultNoRefreshInterval   = intNoRefreshInterval
objDNSServer.DefaultRefreshInterval     = intRefreshInterval
objDNSServer.DefaultAgingState          = TRUE
objDNSServer.Put_
WScript.Echo "Configured server scavenging settings"

set objZones = objDNS.ExecQuery("Sclect * from MicrosoftDNS_Zone " & _
                        "Where DnsServerName = '" & _
                                objDNSServer.Name & "'" & _
                        " And DsIntegrated = TRUE")
WScript.Echo "Configuring AD-integrated zones: "
for each objZone in objZones
    WScript.Echo " " & objZone.Name & " HERE: " & objZone.Aging
    objZone.Aging = 1
    objZone.Put_
next
```

Discussion

There are four settings that you need to be aware of before enabling scavenging. You must use caution when enabling scavenging, because an incorrect configuration could lead to resource records getting deleted by mistake.

The first setting you have to configure is the *scavenging interval*. This is the interval in which the DNS server will kick off the scavenging process. It is disabled by default so that scavenging does not take place unless you enable this setting. The default value is 168 hours, which is equivalent to 7 days.

The second setting is the *default aging configuration setting* for new zones. If you want all new zones to be configured for scavenging, set this to 1.

The next two settings control how records get scavenged. The *no-refresh interval* determines how long before a dynamically updated record can be updated again. This setting is necessary to reduce how often a DNS server has to update its timestamp of the resource record. The default value is 168 hours (7 days). This means that after a resource record has been dynamically updated, the server will not accept another dynamic update for the same record for another 7 days. However, if the IP address or some other data for the record changes, the server will still accept the new information.

The *refresh interval* setting is the amount of time after the no-refresh interval during which a client can update its record before it is considered old or stale. The default value for this setting is also 168 hours (7 days). If you use the default values, the combination of the no-refresh interval and refresh interval would mean that a dynamically updated record would not be considered stale for up to 14 days after its most recent update. Combine this with the default scavenging interval, and it could be up to 21 days before a record is deleted if the record became stale immediately after the last scavenge process completed: 7 days (no refresh) + 7 days (refresh) + up to 7 days (scavenge process).

The solutions in this recipe show you how to configure these settings for all zones that are hosted on a server; however, you can configure these settings for individual zones as well. In the GUI solution, you would do this by accessing the Properties sheet of an individual zone rather than the server node; in *dnscmd*, simply specify the zone name after the /aging, /scavenginginterval, /defaultagingstate, /defaultnorefreshinterval, or /defaultrefreshinterval.

14.13 Clearing the DNS Cache

Problem

You want to clear the DNS cache. The DNS cache contains resource records that are cached by the server or workstation for a period of time in memory so that repeated requests for the same record can be returned immediately. There are two types of DNS cache. One pertains to the cache on the Windows DNS *client* resolver (this can refer to both server and workstation operating systems when they are requesting DNS information from a server), and the other refers to the cache used by the Microsoft DNS *server* software.

Solution

To flush the client resolver cache, use the following command:

```
> ipconfig /flushdns
```

To flush the DNS server cache, use any of the following solutions.

Using a graphical user interface

1. Open the DNS Management snap-in.
2. Right-click on DNS in the left pane and select "Connect to DNS Server."
3. Enter the server you want to connect to and click Enter.
4. Right-click on the server and select Clear Cache.

Using a command-line interface

The following command will clear the cache on *<DNSServerName>*. You can leave out the *<DNSServerName>* parameter to simply run the command against the local server:

```
> dnscmd <DNSServerName> /clearcache
```

Using VBScript

```
' This code clears the DNS server cache on the specified server.
' ------ SCRIPT CONFIGURATION ------
strServer = "<DNSServerName>"    ' e.g. dc1.rallencorp.com
' ------ END CONFIGURATION ---------

set objDNS = GetObject("winmgmts:\\" & strServer & "\root\MicrosoftDNS")
set objDNSServer = objDNS.Get("MicrosoftDNS_Server.Name=""."""")
set objDNSCache  = objDNS.Get("MicrosoftDNS_Cache.ContainerName=""..Cache""" & _
                             ",DnsServerName=""" & objDNSServer.Name & _
                             """,Name=""..Cache""")
objDNSCache.ClearCache
WScript.Echo "Cleared server cache"
```

Discussion

The client resolver cache is populated whenever a DNS lookup is performed on a workstation or server (e.g., with *nslookup*). It's important to remember that this cache will store both positive DNS responses as well as negative ones. For example, if lost network connectivity causes DNS queries for an external resource like a mail server to fail, those queries will continue to fail until the cache refreshes: the queries have been *negatively cached*.

The second type of cache is in place only on Microsoft DNS servers. It is a cache of all DNS requests that the server has made while processing queries from various clients. You can view this cache by browsing the Cached Lookups folder for a server in the DNS Management snap-in. This folder is not shown by default, so you'll need to select Advanced from the View menu.

With both the client and server cache, records are removed from the cache after the record's TTL value expires. The TTL is used to age records so that clients and servers will request an updated copy of the record at a later point in order to receive any changes that may have occurred.

14.14 Verifying That a Domain Controller Can Register Its Resource Records

Problem

You want to verify DNS is configured correctly so that a domain controller can register its resource records, which are needed for clients to be able to locate various AD services.

Solution

Using a command-line interface

 This test is available only with the Windows Server 2003 version of *dcdiag*.

With the following *dcdiag* command, replace *dc1* with the DNS name of the domain that the domain controller is in. This command has to be run from the domain controller you want to test, not from an administrative workstation.

```
> dcdiag /test:RegisterInDNS /DnsDomain:dc1

   Starting test: RegisterInDNS
      DNS configuration is sufficient to allow this domain controller to
      dynamically register the domain controller Locator records in DNS.

      The DNS configuration is sufficient to allow this computer to dynamically
      register the A record corresponding to its DNS name.

      ........................ dc1 passed test RegisterInDNS
```

Discussion

With the default setup, domain controllers attempt to dynamically register the resource records necessary for them to be located by Active Directory clients and other domain controllers. Domain controllers must have their resource records populated in DNS in order to function, but it can be very tedious and error-prone to register all of the records manually. This is why allowing the domain controllers to use dynamic DNS (DDNS) to automatically register and update their records can be much easier from a support standpoint.

The Windows Server 2003 version of *dcdiag* provides a new RegisterInDNS switch that allows you to test whether or not the DC can register its records. In the solution above, we showed the output if the domain controller passes the test.

Here is the output if an error occurs:

```
Starting test: RegisterInDNS
    This domain controller cannot register domain controller Locator DNS
    records. This is because either the DNS server with IP address
    6.10.45.14 does not support dynamic updates or the zone rallencorp.com is
    configured to prevent dynamic updates.

    In order for this domain controller to be located by other domain members
    and domain controllers, the domain controller Locator DNS records must be
    added to DNS. You have the following options:

    1. Configure the rallencorp.com zone and the DNS server with IP address
    6.10.45.14 to allow dynamic updates. If the DNS server does not
    support dynamic updates, you might need to upgrade it.

    2. Migrate the rallencorp.com zone to a DNS server that supports dynamic
    updates (for example, a Windows 2000 DNS server).

    3. Delegate the zones _msdcs.rallencorp.com, _sites.rallencorp.com,
    _tcp.rallencorp.com, and _udp.rallencorp.com to a DNS server that supports
    dynamic updates (for example, a Windows 2000 DNS server); or

    4. Manually add to the DNS records specified in the
    systemroot\system32\config\netlogon.dns file.

    DcDiag cannot reach a conclusive result because it cannot interpret the
    following message that was returned: 9501.

    ........................ dc1 failed test RegisterInDNS
```

As you can see, the output of *dcdiag* offers several options for resolving the problem. The information provided will also vary depending on the error encountered.

See Also

Recipe 14.16 for registering a domain controller's resource records

14.15 Enabling DNS Server Debug Logging

Problem

You want to enable DNS debug logging to troubleshoot issues related to DNS queries or updates.

Solution

Using a graphical user interface

1. From the Administrative Tools, open the DNS Management snap-in.
2. Connect to the DNS Server you want to modify. In the left pane, right-click on DNS and select "Connect to DNS Server." Select "The following computer" and enter the target server name. Click OK.
3. Right-click on the server and select Properties.
4. Click on the Debug Logging tab (or the Logging tab in Windows 2000).
5. Select what you want to log and the location of the logfile (in Windows 2000, the logfile location is hardcoded to *%systemroot%\system32\dns\dns.log*).
6. Click OK.

Using a command-line interface

Use the following four commands to enable debug logging. For the log level, you have to add together the event codes you want logged and specify the result in hex. The available event codes can be found in Table 14-3.

```
> dnscmd <ServerName> /Config /LogLevel <EventFlagSumInHex>
```

Use the following command to specify the location of the logfile:

```
> dnscmd <ServerName> /Config /LogFilePath <DirectoryAndFilePath>
```

Use the following command to log only entries that pertain to certain IP addresses:

```
> dnscmd <ServerName> /Config /LogIPFilterList <IPAddress1>[,<IPAddress2>...]
```

Use the following command to specify the maximum logfile size:

```
> dnscmd <ServerName> /Config /LogFileMaxSize <NumberOfBytesInHex>
```

Use the following command to disable debug logging:

```
> dnscmd <ServerName> /Config /LogLevel 0
```

Using VBScript

```vbscript
' This code enables DNS debug logging.
' ------ SCRIPT CONFIGURATION ------
strServer     = "<ServerName>"             ' e.g. dc1
' The log level must be in decimal, not hex like dnscmd
intLogLevel   = <EventFlagSumInDecimal>    ' e.g. 65535
arrFilterList = Array("<IPAddress1>")      ' e.g. 192.168.1.12
strFilePath   = <DirectoryAndFilePath>     ' e.g. c:\dnslog.txt
intFileSize   = <NumberOfBytesInDecimal>   ' e.g. 50000000
' ------ END CONFIGURATION ---------

set objDNS = GetObject("winMgmts:\\" & strServer & "\root\MicrosoftDNS")
set objDNSServer = objDNS.Get("MicrosoftDNS_Server.Name="".""")
objDNSServer.LogLevel = intLogLevel
objDNSServer.LogIPFilterList = arrFilterList
```

```
objDNSServer.LogFilePath = strFilePath
objDNSServer.LogFileMaxSize = intFileSize
objDNSServer.Put_
WScript.Echo "Enabled DNS Debug Logging on " & strServer

' To disable debug logging, set the intLogLevel variable to 0
```

Discussion

With the DNS Server debug log, you can record all DNS operations received and initiated by the server, including queries, updates, zone transfers, etc. If you need to troubleshoot a particular host, you can use the LogIPFilterList setting in *dnscmd* or the WMI DNS Provider to restrict the log to operations performed only for or by that host.

The most important debug log setting is the log level. With the DNS snap-in, you can select from a list of available options. With Windows Server 2003, the DNS snap-in provides an intuitive interface for selecting the required options. On Windows 2000, you are presented with a list of checkboxes and you have to figure out which ones need to be used in conjunction with one another. You have a similar issue with CLI and VBScript solutions, where you need to determine what log level you want to set.

Table 14-3 contains all of the event codes with their hexadecimal and decimal values.

Table 14-3. DNS debug logging event codes

Hexadecimal value	Decimal value	Descriptions
0x0	0	No logging. This is the default.
0x1	1	Query transactions.
0x10	16	Notifications transactions.
0x20	32	Update transactions.
0xFE	254	Nonquery transactions.
0x100	256	Question packets.
0x200	512	Answer packets.
0x1000	4096	Send packets.
0x2000	8192	Receive packets.
0x4000	16384	UDP packets.
0x8000	32768	TCP packets.
0xFFFF	65535	All packets.
0x10000	65536	AD write transactions.
0x20000	131072	AD update transactions.
0x1000000	16777216	Full packets.
0x80000000	2147483648	Write-through transactions.

DNS debug logging can come in handy if you want to look at the dynamic update requests a particular DNS Server is processing. For example, if a client or DHCP server is attempting to dynamically register records, you can enable the Update Transactions log category on the DNS Server you think should be processing the updates. If you don't see any update transactions, this can indicate that another server is processing the dynamic update requests.

 Transactions are not immediately written to the debug logfile as they occur. They are buffered and written to the file after a certain number of requests are processed.

See Also

MSDN: MicrosoftDNS_Server

14.16 Registering a Domain Controller's Resource Records

Problem

You want to manually force registration of a domain controller's resource records. This may be necessary if you've made some configuration changes on your DNS servers to allow your domain controllers to start dynamically registering resource records.

Solution

Using a command-line interface

```
> nltest /dsregdns /server:<DomainControllerName>
```

Discussion

The Windows Server 2003 version of *nltest* provides a /dsregdns switch that allows you to force registration of the domain-controller-specific resource records. You can also force reregistration of its resource records by restarting the NetLogon service on the domain controller. The NetLogon service automatically attempts to reregister a domain controller's resource records every hour, so if you can wait that long, you do not need to use *nltest*.

See Also

Recipe 14.14 for verifying if a domain controller is registering its resource records

14.17 Deregistering a Domain Controller's Resource Records

Problem

You want to manually deregister a domain controller's resource records.

Solution

Using a command-line interface

With the following *nltest* command, replace *<DomainControllerName>* with the FQDN of the domain controller you want to deregister and *<DomainDNSName>* with the FQDN of the domain of which the domain controller is a member:

```
> nltest /dsderegdns:<DomainControllerName> /dom:<DomainDNSName>
```

Discussion

When a domain controller is demoted from a domain, it dynamically deregisters its resource records. This is a nice feature of the demotion process because it means you do not have to manually remove all of the resource records or wait for scavenging to remove them. If, however, you have a domain controller that crashes and you do not plan on bringing it back online, you'll need to remove the records manually or wait for the scavenging process to take place.

You can use the DNS Mgmt MMC snap-in and even the *dnscmd.exe* utility to manually remove them one by one, or you can use *nltest*, as shown in the solution.

The /dsderegdns switch also has /DomGUID and /DsaGUID options if you want to delete the records that are based on the domain GUID and DSA GUID, respectively. You need to know the actual GUIDs of the domain and domain controller to use those switches, so if you don't have them handy, it would be easier to delete them using the DNS Management MMC snap-in.

14.18 Preventing a Domain Controller from Dynamically Registering All Resource Records

Problem

You want to prevent a domain controller from dynamically registering its resource records using DDNS. If you manually register a domain controller's resource records, you'll want to prevent those domain controllers from attempting to dynamically register them. If you do not disable them from sending dynamic update requests, you may see annoying error messages on your DNS servers that certain DDNS updates are failing.

Solution

Using a command-line interface

```
> reg add HKLM\System\CurrentControlSet\Services\Netlogon\Parameters /v
UseDynamicDNS /t REG_DWORD /d 0
The operation completed successfully.

> net stop netlogon
The Net Logon service is stopping.
The Net Logon service was stopped successfully.

> del %SystemRoot%\system32\config\netlogon.dnb

> net start netlogon
The Net Logon service is starting.......
The Net Logon service was started successfully.
```

Using VBScript

```
' This code prevents a DC from registering resource records dynamically.
' It must be run directly on the server.

' Create Registry Value
const HKLM = &H80000002
set oReg=GetObject("winmgmts:root\default:StdRegProv")
strKeyPath = "System\CurrentControlSet\Services\Netlogon\Parameters"
if oReg.SetDWORDValue(HKLM,strKeyPath,"UseDynamicDNS",1) <> 0 then
   WScript.Echo "Error creating registry value"
else
   WScript.Echo "Created registry value successfully"
end if

' Stop Netlogon service
strService = "Netlogon"
set objService = GetObject("WinMgmts:root/cimv2:Win32_Service.Name='" & _
                           strService & "'")
if objService.StopService <> 0 then
   WScript.Echo "Error stopping " & strService & " service"
else
   WScript.Echo "Stopped " & strService & " service successfully"
end if

' Delete netlogon.dnb file
set WshShell = CreateObject("WScript.Shell")
set objFSO = CreateObject("Scripting.FileSystemObject")
set objFile = objFSO.GetFile( _
                     WshShell.ExpandEnvironmentStrings("%SystemRoot%") _
                & "\system32\config\netlogon.dnb" )
```

```
   objFile.Delete
   WScript.Echo "Deleted netlogon.dnb successfully"

   ' Start Netlogon service
   if objService.StartService <> 0 then
      WScript.Echo "Error starting " & strService & " service"
   else
      WScript.Echo "Started " & strService & " service successfully"
   end if

   WScript.Echo
   WScript.Echo "Done"
```

Discussion

By default, domain controllers attempt to dynamically register their Active Directory–related resource records every hour via the NetLogon service. You can prevent a domain controller from doing this by setting the UseDynamicDNS value to 0 under *HKEY_LOCAL_MACHINE\System\CurrentControlSet\Services\Netlogon\Parameters*. After you set that value, you should stop the NetLogon service, remove the *%SystemRoot%\system32\config\netlogon.dnb* file, and then restart NetLogon. It is necessary to remove the *netlogon.dnb* file because it maintains a cache of the resource records that are dynamically updated. This file will get re-created when the NetLogon service restarts.

See Also

Recipe 14.19 for preventing certain resource records from being dynamically registered, MS KB 198767 (How to Prevent Domain Controllers from Dynamically Registering DNS Names), and MS KB 246804 (How to Enable/Disable Windows 2000 Dynamic DNS Registrations)

14.19 Preventing a Domain Controller from Dynamically Registering Certain Resource Records

Problem

You want to prevent a domain controller from dynamically registering certain resource records. It is sometimes advantageous to prevent certain resource records from being dynamically registered. For example, if you want to reduce the load on the PDC Emulator for a domain, you can prevent some of its SRV records from being published, which would reduce the amount of client traffic the server receives.

Solution

Using a command-line interface

This command will disable the Ldap, Gc, and GcIpAddress resource records from being dynamically registered:

```
> reg add HKLM\System\CurrentControlSet\Services\Netlogon\Parameters /v
 DnsAvoidRegisterRecords /t REG_MULTI_SZ /d Ldap\0Gc\0GcIpAddress
The operation completed successfully.

> net stop netlogon
The Net Logon service is stopping.
The Net Logon service was stopped successfully.

> del %SystemRoot%\system32\config\netlogon.dnb

> net start netlogon
The Net Logon service is starting.......
The Net Logon service was started successfully.
```

Using VBScript

```
' This code prevents a DC from registering the resource records
' associated with the Ldap, Gc, and GcIpAddress mnemonics and must be run
' directly on the server.

' Create Registry Value
const HKLM = &H80000002
set objReg = GetObject("winmgmts:root\default:StdRegProv")
strKeyPath = "System\CurrentControlSet\Services\Netlogon\Parameters"
' prevent Ldap, Gc, and GCIpAddress records from being registered
arrValues  = Array("Ldap","Gc","GcIpAddress")
if objReg.SetMultiStringValue(HKLM,strKeyPath,"DnsAvoidRegisterRecords", _
                              arrValues) <> 0 then
   WScript.Echo "Error creating registry value"
else
   WScript.Echo "Created registry value successfully"
end if

' Stop Netlogon service
strService = "Netlogon"
set objService = GetObject("WinMgmts:root/cimv2:Win32_Service.Name='" & _
                           strService & "'")
if objService.StopService <> 0 then
   WScript.Echo "Error stopping " & strService & " service"
else
   WScript.Echo "Stopped " & strService & " service successfully"
end if

' Delete netlogon.dnb file
On Error Resume Next
set WshShell = CreateObject("WScript.Shell")
set objFSO = CreateObject("Scripting.FileSystemObject")
```

```
set objFile = objFSO.GetFile( _
                    WshShell.ExpandEnvironmentStrings("%systemroot%") _
                    & "\system32\config\netlogon.dnb")
objFile.Delete
if (Err.Number <> 0) then
   WScript.Echo "Error deleting netlogon.dnb: " & Err.Description
else
   WScript.Echo "Deleted netlogon.dnb successfully"
end if

' Start Netlogon service
if objService.StartService <> 0 then
   WScript.Echo "Error starting " & strService & " service"
else
   WScript.Echo "Started " & strService & " service successfully"
end if

WScript.Echo
WScript.Echo "Done"
```

Discussion

The procedure to disable registration of certain resource records is very similar to
that described in Recipe 14.18 for preventing all resource records from being dynamically registered, except in this case you need to create a value called
DnsAvoidRegisterRecords under the *HKEY_LOCAL_MACHINE\System\CurrentCon-
trolSet\Services\Netlogon\Parameters* key. The type for DnsAvoidRegisterRecords should
be REG_MULTI_SZ, and the data should be a whitespace-separated list of mnemonics.
Mnemonics are used to represent various resource records that domain controllers
register. The complete list of mnemonics is included in Table 14-4.

You can also control these values using Group Policy, in *Computer
Configuration\Administrative Templates\System\Netlogon.*

Table 14-4. Registry mnemonics for resource records

Registry mnemonic	Resource record type	Resource record name
LdapIpAddress	A	*<DnsDomainName>*
Ldap	SRV	_ldap._tcp.*<DnsDomainName>*
LdapAtSite	SRV	_ldap._tcp.*<SiteName>*._sites.*<DnsDomainName>*
Pdc	SRV	_ldap._tcp.pdc._msdcs.*<DnsDomainName>*
Gc	SRV	_ldap._tcp.gc._msdcs.*<DnsForestName>*
GcAtSite	SRV	_ldap._tcp.*<SiteName>*._sites.gc._msdcs.*<DnsForestName>*
DcByGuid	SRV	_ldap._tcp.*<DomainGuid>*.domains._msdcs.*<DnsForestName>*

Table 14-4. Registry mnemonics for resource records (continued)

Registry mnemonic	Resource record type	Resource record name
GcIpAddress	A	_gc._msdcs.<*DnsForestName*>
DsaCname	CNAME	<*DsaGuid*>._msdcs.<*DnsForestName*>
Kdc	SRV	_kerberos._tcp.dc._msdcs.<*DnsDomainName*>
KdcAtSite	SRV	_kerberos._tcp.dc._msdcs.<*SiteName*>._sites. <*DnsDomainName*>
Dc	SRV	_ldap._tcp.dc._msdcs.<*DnsDomainName*>
DcAtSite	SRV	_ldap._tcp.<*SiteName*>._sites.dc._msdcs. <*DnsDomainName*>
Rfc1510Kdc	SRV	_kerberos._tcp.<*DnsDomainName*>
Rfc1510KdcAtSite	SRV	_kerberos._tcp.<*SiteName*>._sites. <*DnsDomainName*>
GenericGc	SRV	_gc._tcp.<*DnsForestName*>
GenericGcAtSite	SRV	_gc._tcp.<*SiteName*>._sites.<*DnsForestName*>
Rfc1510UdpKdc	SRV	_kerberos._udp.<*DnsDomainName*>
Rfc1510Kpwd	SRV	_kpasswd._tcp.<*DnsDomainName*>
Rfc1510UdpKpwd	SRV	_kpasswd._udp.<*DnsDomainName*>

See Also

Recipe 14.18 for preventing all resource records from being dynamically registered, MS KB 246804 (How to Enable/Disable Windows 2000 Dynamic DNS Registrations), MS KB 267855 (Problems with Many Domain Controllers with Active Directory Integrated DNS Zones), and the Windows Server 2003 Branch Office Planning and Deployment Guide (*http://go.microsoft.com/fwlink/?LinkId=28523*)

14.20 Allowing Computers to Use a Different Domain Suffix from Their AD Domain

Problem

You want to allow computers to use a different domain suffix than their AD domain.

Solution

The following solutions work only for Windows Server 2003 domains. Read the "Discussion" for a workaround for Windows 2000.

Using a graphical user interface

1. Open ADSI Edit.
2. Connect to the domain you want to edit.
3. Right-click on the domainDNS object and select Properties.
4. Edit the msDS-AllowedDNSSuffixes attribute and enter the DNS suffix you want to add.
5. Click OK.

Using a command-line interface

Create an LDIF file called *add_dns_suffix.ldf* with the following contents:

```
dn: <DomainDN>
changetype: modify
add: msDS-AllowedDNSSuffixes
msDS-AllowedDNSSuffixes: <DNSSuffix>
-
```

Then run the following command:

```
> ldifde -v -i -f add_dns_suffix.ldf.ldf
```

You can also make this change using AdMod, as follows:

```
> admod –b <DomainDN> msDS-AllowedDNSSuffixes:+:<DNSSuffix>
```

Using VBScript

```
' This code adds a domain suffix that can be used by clients in the domain.
' ------ SCRIPT CONFIGURATION ------
strDNSSuffix = "<DNSSuffix>"        ' e.g. othercorp.com
strDomain    = "<DomainDNSName>"    ' e.g. amer.rallencorp.com
' ------ END CONFIGURATION ---------

set objRootDSE = GetObject("LDAP://" & strDomain & "/RootDSE")
set objDomain = GetObject("LDAP://" & objRootDSE.Get("defaultNamingContext") )
objDomain.Put "msDS-AllowedDNSSuffixes", strDNSSuffix
objDomain.SetInfo

WScript.Echo "Added " & strDNSSuffix & " to suffix list."
```

Discussion

Windows 2000, Windows XP, and Windows Server 2003 member computers dynamically maintain the dNSHostName and servicePrincipalName attributes of their corresponding computer object in Active Directory with their current hostname. By default, those attributes can only contain hostnames that have a DNS suffix equal to the Active Directory domain the computer is a member of.

If the computer's DNS suffix is not equal to the Active Directory domain, as may be the case during a domain migration or a corporate merger or consolidation, 5788 and 5789 events will be generated in the System event log on the domain controllers the clients attempt to update. These events report that the dnsHostName and servicePrincipalName attributes could not be updated due to an incorrect domain suffix. For Windows Server 2003 domains, you can avoid this by adding the computer's DNS suffix to the msDS-AllowedDNSSuffixes attribute on the domain object (e.g., dc=rallencorp,dc=com).

With Windows 2000, the only workaround for this issue is to grant the Self principal the ability to write the dNSHostName and servicePrincipalName attribute for computer objects. Here are the steps:

1. Open ADSI Edit.
2. Right-click on the domain object and select Properties.
3. Click the Security tab.
4. Click the Add button.
5. Enter Self in the object picker and click OK.
6. Click the Advanced button.
7. Under the Name column, double-click on SELF.
8. Click the Properties tab.
9. Beside "Apply onto," select Computer objects.
10. Under Permissions, check the Allow box for Write dNSHostName and Write servicePrincipalName.
11. Click OK until you close all the windows.

 It is worth noting that if you implement this method, it is possible for someone to cause a computer to write any name into those attributes and, therefore, advertise itself as another computer.

See Also

MS KB 258503 (DNS Registration Errors 5788 and 5789 When DNS Domain and Active Directory Domain Name Differ)

14.21 Authorizing a DHCP Server

Problem

You want to permit (i.e., authorize) a DHCP server to process DHCP requests from clients. This is necessary only if the DHCP server is a member of an Active Directory domain.

Solution

Using a graphical user interface

Windows 2000 DHCP servers cannot be authorized with the Windows Server 2003 version of the DHCP snap-in unless the DHCP server has Service Pack 2 or higher installed.

1. Open the DHCP snap-in.
2. In the left pane, right-click on DHCP and select Add Server.
3. Type in the name of the DHCP server you want to target and click OK.
4. Click on the server entry in the left pane.
5. Right-click on the server and select Authorize.

If the DHCP server is not a member of an Active Directory domain, you will not see the Authorize option.

Using a command-line interface

The following command authorizes a DHCP server in Active Directory:

```
> netsh dhcp add server <DHCPServerName> <DHCPServerIP>
```

This example shows how to authorize the DHCP server named *dhcp01.rallencorp.com* with IP 192.168.191.15:

```
> netsh dhcp add server dhcp01.rallencorp.com 192.168.191.15
```

Using VBScript

```
' The following script prints out the list of
' authorized DHCP Servers in Active Directory.
' ------ SCRIPT CONFIGURATION ------
strForestRootDN = "<ForestRootDN>"  ' e.g. dc=rallencorp,dc=com
' ------ END CONFIGURATION ---------
set objCont = GetObject("LDAP://CN=DhcpRoot,CN=NetServices,CN=Services," & _
                        "CN=Configuration," & strForestRootDN)
colDHCPServers = objCont.GetEx("dhcpServers")
for each strDHCPServer in colDHCPServers
   Wscript.Echo strDHCPServer
next
```

Discussion

Windows 2000 and Windows Server 2003–based DHCP servers that belong to an Active Directory domain must be authorized before they can give leases to clients. This feature helps reduce the danger of a rogue Windows 2000 or Windows Server 2003 DHCP server that an end user sets up, perhaps even unintentionally.

However, this still doesn't prevent someone from plugging in a non-Windows DHCP server (e.g., a Linksys router with the DHCP server enabled) and causing clients to receive bad leases. A rogue DHCP server can provide incorrect lease information or deny lease requests altogether, ultimately causing a denial of service for clients on your network.

If the DHCP server service is enabled on a domain controller, it is automatically authorized. A DHCP server that is a member server of an Active Directory domain performs a query in Active Directory to determine whether it is authorized. If it is, it will respond to DHCP requests; if not, it will not respond to requests.

A standalone Windows DHCP server that is not a member of an Active Directory domain sends out a DHCPINFORM message when it first initializes. If an authorized DHCP server responds to the message, the standalone server will not respond to any further DHCP requests. If it does not receive a response from a DHCP server, it will respond to client requests and distribute leases.

DHCP servers are represented in Active Directory as objects of the dhcpClass class, in the cn=NetServices,cn=Services,cn=Configuratation,<ForestRootDN> container. The relative distinguished name of these objects is the IP address of the DHCP server. There is also an object in the same container named cn=dhcpRoot, which is created after the first DHCP server is authorized. It has an attribute named dhcpServers that contains all authorized servers. We enumerated this attribute in the VBScript solution to display all authorized servers.

By default, only members of the *Enterprise Admins* group can authorize DHCP servers. However, you can delegate the rights to authorize a DHCP server. Do the following to delegate the necessary permissions to a group called *DHCP Admins*:

1. Open ADSI Edit from the Support Tools while logged on as a member of the *Enterprise Admins* group.
2. In the left pane, expand the Configuration Container → CN=Configuration → CN=Services → CN=NetServices.
3. Right-click on CN=NetServices and select Properties.
4. Select the Security tab.
5. Click the Advanced button.
6. Click the Add button.
7. Use the object picker to select the *DHCP Admins* group.
8. Check the boxes under "Allow for Create dHCPClass objects" and "Delete dHCPClass objects."
9. Click OK until all dialog boxes are closed.
10. Back in ADSI Edit, right-click on CN=dhcpRoot (if you've previously authorized DHCP Servers) and select Properties.

11. Select the Security tab.

12. Click the Advanced button.

13. Click the Add button.

14. Use the object picker to select the *DHCP Admins* group.

15. Check the boxes under Allow for "Write for all properties."

16. Click OK until all dialog boxes are closed.

Using a graphical user interface

You can quickly determine whether a DHCP server has been authorized by looking at its server node in the left pane of the DHCP snap-in. If the icon has a little red flag, it isn't authorized; if the flag is green, it is authorized.

Using a command-line interface

To see the list of authorized servers using the command line, run the following command:

```
> netsh dhcp show server
```

See Also

MS KB 279908 (Unexpected Results in the DHCP Service Snap-In After Using NETSH to Authorize DHCP), MS KB 300429 (How to Install and Configure a DHCP Server in an Active Directory Domain in Windows 2000), MS KB 303351 (How to Use Netsh.exe to Authorize, Unauthorize and List DHCP Servers in Active Directory), and MS KB 306925 (After a new DHCP server is authorized, the original DHCP server becomes unauthorized and cannot be authorized again in Windows 2000 Server)

14.22 Locating Unauthorized DHCP Servers

Problem

You want to locate any unauthorized or rogue DHCP servers on your network.

Solution

Using a command-line interface

Here's how to search for rogue DHCP servers from a workstation with an IP address of 10.0.0.101 while disregarding a known, valid DHCP server residing on 10.0.0.200:

```
> dhcploc 10.0.0.101 10.0.0.200
```

Discussion

The DHCP authorization process in Active Directory will prevent any Windows 2000 or Windows Server 2003 DHCP servers from offering up IP addresses without first being authorized by a member of the *Enterprise Admins* group. However, this mechanism does not extend to Windows NT 4.0 DHCP servers or non-Windows devices, such as a Linksys router that also functions as a DHCP server. The *dhcploc* utility in the Windows Support Tools will display an output of all DHCP traffic that it receives, with a *** displayed next to traffic that it receives from unauthorized servers, as follows:

```
14:24:28 (IP)0.0.0.0     NACK     (S)10.0.0.40     ***

14:24:28 (IP)10.0.0.103 OFFER     (S)10.0.0.60     ***

14:24:28 (IP)10.0.0.201 ACK       (S)10.0.0.30

14:24:23 (IP)10.0.0.203 ACK       (S)10.0.0.30

14:24:25 (IP)10.0.0.4 OFFER       (S)10.0.0.30

14:24:35 (IP)10.0.0.2 OFFER       (S)10.0.0.40

14:24:36 (IP)10.0.0.3 OFFER       (S)10.0.0.26     ***
```

See Also

Recipe 14.21 for more on authorizing DHCP servers in Active Directory

14.23 Restricting DHCP Administrators

Problem

You want to restrict who can administer your DHCP servers in your domain.

Solution

Using a graphical user interface

1. Open the Active Directory Users and Computers MMC snap-in.
2. In the console tree, click Active Directory Users and Computers → Domain-Name → Users.
3. In the details pane, click DHCP Administrators.
4. Click Action → Properties → Members.
5. Remove all users and groups you do not want to have administering your DHCP server by clicking their names and then clicking Remove.

6. To add new DHCP administrators, click Add, provide the user or group name, and then click OK.

7. Click OK.

Using a command-line interface

Add a member to a group with DSMod by passing the -addmbr option:

```
> dsmod group "<GroupDN>" -addmbr "<MemberDN>"
```

To add a group member with AdMod, use the following syntax:

```
> admod -b "<GroupDN>" member:+:"<MemberDN>"
```

Remove a member from a group with DSMod by passing the -rmmbr option:

```
> dsmod group "<GroupDN>" -rmmbr "<MemberDN>"
```

To remove a group member with AdMod, use the following syntax:

```
> admod -b "<GroupDN>" member:-:"<MemberDN>"
```

Replace the complete membership list with DSMod by passing the -chmbr option:

```
> dsmod group "<GroupDN>" -chmbr "<Member1DN Member2DN  . . . >"
```

To replace the membership of a group with AdMod, use the following two commands:

```
> admod -b "<GroupDN>" :-
> admod -b "<GroupDN>" member++::"<Member1DN>;<Member2DN>;<Member3DN>"
```

Using VBScript

```
' This code adds a member to the DHCP Administrators group.
' ------ SCRIPT CONFIGURATION ------
strGroupDN = "<GroupDN>"   ' e.g. "cn=DHCP Administrators,cn=Users,<DomainDN>
strMemberDN = "<MemberDN>" ' e.g. cn=jsmith,cn=users,dc=rallencorp,dc=com
' ------ END CONFIGURATION --------

set objGroup = GetObject("LDAP://" & strGroupDN)
' Add a member
objGroup.Add("LDAP://" & strMemberDN)

' This code removes a member from the DHCP Administrators group.

set objGroup = GetObject("LDAP://" & strGroupDN)
objGroup.Remove("LDAP://" & strMemberDN)
```

Discussion

Windows Server 2003 is better than its predecessors about supporting role separation. Most roles can be assigned independently of one another rather than just making a user a Domain Admin or an Enterprise Admin. This is great for security administrators who want to ensure that users have only enough rights to perform their assigned tasks. For example, a user Fred might need to modify an enterprise-wide object. You could just add Fred to the *Enterprise Admin* groups to solve the problem. However, Fred now has access to virtually any object in the entire forest and could cause irreparable harm to your network, not to mention compromise all security in place. Instead, you can grant Fred access to just that object.

This can be done in separate ways. One method is the "Delegation of Control" wizard. Another way is that Windows has several built-in groups that are created and populated when specific services are installed. One such group is *DHCP Administrators*, which is created when the first DHCP server is brought up in a domain. You can control administrative access to the DHCP function of these servers through this group membership.

 Nondomain joined computers also have a *DHCP Administrators* group. This is a local group on each computer and must be managed separately on each sever.

See Also

"To add a user or group as a DHCP administrator" in the Windows Server 2003 documentation, and "Delegate ability to authorize DHCP server to a nonenterprise administrator" in the Windows Server 2003 documentation

## CHAPTER 15

Security and Authentication

15.0 Introduction

The default Windows 2000 Active Directory installation was not as secure as it could have been. It allowed anonymous queries to be executed, which could take up valuable processing resources, and it did not place any requirements on encrypting or signing traffic between clients and domain controllers. As a result, usernames, passwords, and search results could be sent over the network in clear text. Fortunately, with Windows Server 2003, things have been tightened up significantly. LDAP traffic is signed by default, and anonymous queries are disabled by default. Additionally, Transport Layer Security (TLS), the more flexible cousin of Secure Sockets Layer (SSL), is supported in Windows Server 2003, which allows for end-to-end encryption of traffic between domain controllers and clients.

Active Directory's ACL model provides ultimate flexibility for securing objects throughout a forest; you can restrict access down to the attribute level if you need to. With this flexibility comes increased complexity. An object's ACL is initially generated from the default ACL for the object's class, inherited permissions, and permissions directly applied on the object.

An ACL is a collection of ACEs, which defines the permission and properties that a security principal can use on the object to which the ACL is applied. Defining these entries and populating the ACL is the foundation of Active Directory security and delegation.

In this chapter, we will explore some of the common tasks of managing permissions in Active Directory. If you are looking for a detailed guide to Active Directory permissions, we suggest reading Chapter 11 in *Active Directory*, Third Edition, by Joe Richards et al. (O'Reilly).

In order for ACLs to be of use, a user must first authenticate to Active Directory. *Kerberos* is the primary network authentication system used by Active Directory. Kerberos is a standards-based system originally developed at MIT that has been widely implemented at universities. We will also be covering some Kerberos-related tasks in this chapter that you will be likely to encounter in an Active Directory environment. For a complete review of Kerberos, we recommend *Kerberos: The Definitive Guide* by Jason Garman (O'Reilly).

15.1 Enabling SSL/TLS

Problem

You want to enable SSL/TLS access to your domain controllers so clients can encrypt LDAP traffic to the servers.

Solution

Using a graphical user interface

1. Open the Control Panel on a domain controller.
2. Open the "Add or Remove Programs" applet.
3. Click on Add/Remove Windows Components.
4. Check the box beside Certificate Services and click Yes to verify.
5. Click Next.
6. Select the type of authority you want the domain controller to be (select "Enterprise root CA" if you are unsure) and click Next.
7. Type the common name for the CA, select a validity period, and click Next.
8. Enter the location for certificate database and logs, and click Next.
9. After the installation completes, click Finish.
10. Now open the Domain Controller Security Policy GPO.
11. Navigate to Computer Configuration → Windows Settings → Security Settings → Public Key Policies.
12. Right-click on Automatic Certificate Request Settings and select New → Automatic Certificate Request.
13. Click Next.
14. Under Certificate Templates, click on Domain Controller and click Next.
15. Click Finish.
16. Right-click on Automatic Certificate Request Settings and select New → Automatic Certificate Request.
17. Click Next.
18. Under Certificate Templates, click on Computer and click Next.
19. Click Finish.

Discussion

After Windows 2000 domain controllers obtain certificates, they open up ports 636 and 3289. Port 636 is for LDAP over SSL/TLS and port 3269 is used for global catalog queries performed over SSL/TLS. See Recipe 15.2 for more information on how to query a domain controller using SSL/TLS.

Installing and configuring a Public Key Infrastructure (PKI) to support the certificate templates and certificate requests described here is outside the scope of this book; for more information please refer to *Windows Server 2003 Security Cookbook* by Mike Danseglio and Robbie Allen (O'Reilly).

See Also

MS KB 247078 (How to Enable Secure Socket Layer (SSL) Communication Over LDAP For Windows 2000 Domain Controllers), MS KB 281271 (Windows 2000 Certification Authority Configuration to Publish Certificates in Active Directory of Trusted Domain), and MS KB 321051 (How to Enable LDAP over SSL with a Third-Party Certification Authority)

15.2   Encrypting LDAP Traffic with SSL, TLS, or Signing

Problem

You want to encrypt LDAP traffic using SSL, TLS, or signing.

Solution

Using a graphical user interface

Most of the GUI-based tools on a Windows Server 2003, Windows XP, or Windows 2000 SP3 machine automatically sign and encrypt traffic between the server and client. This includes the following tools:

- Active Directory Domains and Trusts
- Active Directory Sites and Services
- Active Directory Schema
- Active Directory Users and Computers
- ADSI Edit
- Group Policy Management Console
- Object Picker

With ADSI Edit, you can also specify the port number to use when browsing a partition. View the settings for a connection by right-clicking on the partition and selecting Settings. Click the Advanced button and enter 636 for LDAP over SSL or 3269 for the global catalog over SSL.

The Windows Server 2003 version of LDP supports encryption using the StartTLS and StopTLS operations, which are available from the Options → TLS menu. With the Windows 2000 version, you can use SSL by going to Connection → Connect and entering 636 or 3269 for the port.

Using a command-line interface

The DS command-line tools support LDAP signing and encryption when run from Windows Server 2003 or Windows XP against a Windows 2000 SP3 or Windows Server 2003 domain controller. This includes DSAdd, DSMod, DSrm, DSMove, DSGet, and DSQuery.

Using VBScript

```
' This code shows how to enable SSL and secure authentication using ADSI.

ADS_SECURE_AUTHENTICATION = 1
ADS_USE_SSL = 2

set objLDAP = GetObject("LDAP:")
set objOU = objLDAP.OpenDSObject("LDAP://ou=Sales,dc=rallencorp,dc=com", _
                                "administrator@rallencorp.com", _
                                "MyAdminPassword", _
                                ADS_SECURE_AUTHENTICATION + ADS_USE_SSL)
WScript.Echo objOU.Get("ou")
' This code shows how to enable SSL and secure authentication using ADO.

' Constants taken from ADS_AUTHENTICATION_ENUM
ADS_SECURE_AUTHENTICATION = 1
ADS_USE_SSL = 2

set objConn = CreateObject("ADODB.Connection")
objConn.Provider = "ADsDSOObject"
objConn.Properties("User ID") = "administrator@rallencorp.com"
objConn.Properties("Password") = "MyAdminPassword"
objConn.Properties("Encrypt Password") = True
objConn.Properties("ADSI Flag") = ADS_SECURE_AUTHENTICATION + ADS_USE_SSL
objConn.Open "Active Directory Provider"
set objRS = objConn.Execute("<LDAP://cn=users,dc=rallencorp,dc=com>;" & _
                            "(cn=*);" & "cn;" & "onelevel")
objRS.MoveFirst
while Not objRS.EOF
    Wscript.Echo objRS.Fields(0).Value
    objRS.MoveNext
wend
```

Discussion

An out-of-the-box installation of Windows 2000 Active Directory did not provide any default data encryption over the network between clients and domain controllers when using most of the standard tools. If you run Network Monitor (*netmon. exe*) while using tools that perform simple LDAP binds, you'll see LDAP requests, usernames, and passwords going over the network in plain text. Obviously this is not the most secure configuration, so with Windows Server 2003 most of the AD tools sign and encrypt traffic from the clients to the domain controllers by default.

To use the more secure Windows Server 2003 tools against Windows 2000 domain controllers, you need to install at least Service Pack 3 on the Windows 2000 domain controllers. The new versions of the tools cannot be run directly on Windows 2000, so you must use a Windows XP or Windows Server 2003 machine to host them.

See Also

Recipe 15.1 for enabling SSL/TLS, Recipe 15.3 for disabling LDAP encryption, MS KB 325465 (Windows 2000 Domain Controllers Require SP3 or Later When Using Windows Server 2003 Administration Tools), MS KB 304718 (Administering Windows Server-Based Computers Using Windows XP Professional-Based Clients), and MSDN: ADS_AUTHENTICATION_ENUM

15.3 Disabling LDAP Signing or Encryption

Problem

You want to disable LDAP signing and/or encryption.

Solution

Using the Registry

If you need to temporarily disable LDAP encryption or signing for troubleshooting purposes, browse to the *HKLM\Software\Microsoft\Windows\CurrentVersion\Admin-Debug\ADsOpenObjectFlags* key on the client that is running the administrative tool. Create a DWORD entry called `ADsOpenObjectFlags` and set it to one of the following values:

    1 To disable LDAP signing

    2 To disable LDAP encryption

    3 To disable both LDAP signing and LDAP encryption

Discussion

If you want to take advantage of some of the new features of the Active Directory administration tools, but have not installed SP3 on your Windows 2000 domain controllers yet, you can disable signing on the Windows XP or Windows Server 2003 machine. It is worth stating the obvious that this is insecure and defeats one of the major benefits of the new tools, but you may have no other choice.

See Also

Recipe 15.2 to enable LDAP signing and encryption

15.4 Enabling Anonymous LDAP Access

Problem

You want to enable anonymous LDAP access for clients. In Windows 2000 Active Directory, anonymous queries were enabled by default, although they were restricted. With Windows Server 2003 Active Directory, anonymous queries are disabled by default except for querying the RootDSE.

Solution

Using a graphical user interface

1. Open ADSI Edit.
2. In the Configuration partition, browse to cn=Services → cn=Windows NT → cn=Directory Service.
3. In the left pane, right-click on the Directory Service object and select Properties.
4. Double-click on the dSHeuristics attribute.
5. If the attribute is empty, set it with the value 0000002.
6. If the attribute has an existing value, make sure the seventh digit is set to 2.
7. Click OK twice.

Using VBScript

```
' This code enables or disables anonymous query mode for a forest.
' ------ SCRIPT CONFIGURATION ------
boolEnableAnonQuery = 2  ' e.g. 2 to enable, 0 to disable
' ------ END CONFIGURATION ---------

set objRootDSE = GetObject("LDAP://RootDSE")
set objDS = GetObject( _
            "LDAP://cn=Directory Service,cn=Windows NT,cn=Services," _
            & objRootDSE.Get("configurationNamingContext") )
strDSH = objDS.Get("dSHeuristics")

for i = len(strDSH) to 6
   strDSH = strDSH & "0"
next

strNewDSH = Left(strDSH,6) & boolEnableAnonQuery
strNewDSH = strNewDSH & Right(strDSH, len(strDSH) - 7 )

WScript.Echo "Old value: " & strDSH
WScript.Echo "New value: " & strNewDSH
```

```
if strDSH <> strNewDSH then
    objDS.Put "dSHeuristics", strNewDSH
    objDS.SetInfo
    WScript.Echo "Successfully set anon query mode to " & boolEnableAnonQuery
else
    WScript.Echo "Anon query mode already set to " & boolEnableAnonQuery
end if
```

Discussion

To enable anonymous access, you have to modify the dSHeuristics attribute of the cn=Directory Service,cn=Windows NT,cn=Services,ConfigurationDN object. The dSHeuristics attribute is an interesting attribute used to control certain behavior in Active Directory. For example, you can enable "List Object Mode" (see Recipe 15.20) by setting the dSHeuristics flag.

The dSHeuristics attribute consists of a series of digits that, when set, enable certain functionality. To enable anonymous access, the seventh digit must be set to 2. By default, dSHeuristics does not have a value. If you set it to enable anonymous access, the value would be 0000002.

After enabling anonymous access, the assumption is you'll want to grant access for anonymous users to retrieve certain data from Active Directory. To do that, grant the ANONYMOUS LOGON user access to the parts of the directory you want anonymous users to search. You must grant the access from the root of the directory down to the object of interest. See MS KB 320528 for an example of how to enable the anonymous user to query the email addresses of user objects.

See Also

Recipe 15.20, MS KB 320528 (How to Configure Active Directory to Allow Anonymous Queries), and MS KB 326690 (Anonymous LDAP Operations to Active Directory Are Disabled on Windows Server 2003 Domain Controllers)

15.5 Restricting Hosts from Performing LDAP Queries

Problem

You want domain controllers to reject LDAP queries from certain IP addresses. This can be useful if you want to prohibit domain controllers from responding to LDAP queries for certain applications or hosts.

Solution

Using a command-line interface

The following adds network 10.0.0.0 with mask 255.255.255.0 to the IP deny list:

```
> ntdsutil "ipdeny list" conn "co t s <DomainControllerName>" q
```

```
IP Deny List: Add 10.0.0.0 255.255.255.0
*[1] 10.0.0.0 GROUP MASK      255.255.255.0

NOTE: * | D - uncommitted addition | deletion
IP Deny List: Commit
 [1] 10.10.10.0 GROUP MASK      255.255.255.0

NOTE: * | D - uncommitted addition | deletion
```

Discussion

The IP deny list is stored as an octet string in the `lDAPIPDenyList` attribute of a query policy. See Recipe 4.27 for more information on the LDAP query policy.

When the IP deny list is set, domain controllers that are using the default query policy will not respond to LDAP queries from any IP address specified in the deny list address range. To test whether a certain IP address would be denied, run Test $x.x.x.x$ (where $x.x.x.x$ is an IP address) from the IP Deny List subcommand in *ntdsutil*.

By setting the IP deny list on the default query policy, you would effectively restrict the IP address range from querying any domain controller in the forest. If you need to restrict queries only for a specific domain controller, you'll need to create a new LDAP query policy and apply it to only the domain controller in question.

See Also

Recipe 4.27 for more information on the LDAP query policy and MS KB 314976 (How to Use the Ntdsutil Utility to Deny Access to IP Addresses in Windows 2000)

15.6 Restricting Anonymous Access to Active Directory

Problem

You want to enable or disable anonymous access to the information stored in the Active Directory database.

Solution

Using a graphical user interface

1. Open the Active Directory Users and Computers (ADUC) snap-in.

2. If you need to change domains, right-click on Active Directory Users and Computers in the left pane, select "Connect to Domain," enter the domain name, and click OK.

3. Navigate to the Builtin container. Double-click on the Pre-Windows 2000 Compatible Access group.

4. Click the Members tab.

5. Select the Everyone group and click the Remove button. Click Yes and then OK to confirm.

6. Select the Anonymous Logon user and click the Remove button. Click Yes and then OK to confirm.

7. If the Authenticated Users group is not present in the group membership list, click Add to include it and then click OK.

Using a command-line interface

You have three command-line choices to modify the Pre-Windows 2000 Access security group: net localgroup, DSMod, or AdMod. net localgroup takes the following syntax:

```
> net localgroup "Pre-Windows 2000 Compatible Access" Everyone /delete
> net localgroup "Pre-Windows 2000 Compatible Access" "Anonymous Logon" /delete
> net localgroup "Pre-Windows 2000 Compatible Access" "Authenticated Users" /add
```

To update the group membership using DSMod so that it only includes Authenticated Users, enter the following:

```
> dsmod group "cn=Pre-Windows 2000 Compatible Access,cn=Builtin,
<DomainDN>" -chmbr "cn=S-1-5-11,cn=ForeignSecurityPrincipals,<DomainDN>"
```

To use AdMod, use the following syntax:

```
> admod -b "cn=Pre-Windows 2000 Compatible Access,cn=Builtin,
<DomainDN>" member::"cn=S-1-5-11,cn=ForeignSecurityPrincipals,<DomainDN>"
```

Using VBScript

```
' This code adds a member to a group.
' ------ SCRIPT CONFIGURATION ------
StrAnonAccessDN = "cn=Pre-Windows 2000 Compatible Access," & _
   cn=Builtin,<DomainDN>"
strAuthUsersDN = "cn=S-1-5-11,cn=ForeignSecurityPrincipals,<DomainDN>"
Const ADS_PROPERTY_CLEAR = 1    ' Used to clear the existing membership
' ------ END CONFIGURATION ---------

set objAnonAccessDN = GetObject("LDAP://" & strGroupDN)

' Remove any existing groups with anonymous access
objAnonAccessDN.PutEx ADS_PROPERTY_CLEAR, "member", 0
objAnonAccessDN.SetInfo

' Now add auth users only
objGroup.Add("LDAP://" & strAuthUsersDN)
```

Discussion

Anonymous access to Active Directory is controlled by membership in the *Pre-Windows 2000 Compatible Access* security group, located in the cn=Builtin container. This group is named like that because some legacy applications and operating systems, most notably Windows NT 4.0 RAS servers, required anonymous access to the information stored in AD in order to function properly. The default membership of this group depends on whether you selected "Permissions compatible with pre-Windows 2000 operating systems" or "Permissions compatible with only Windows 2000 and Windows 2003" when you ran *dcpromo*. If you selected the former, the *Everyone* group and the *Anonymous Logon* SID were added to Pre-Windows 2000 Compatible Access; if the latter, only *Authenticated Users* was added.

In the DSMod, AdMod, and VBScript solutions, the *Authenticated Users* group was specified using an SID and it resides in the `ForeignSecurityPrincipals` container. This is because *Well-Known SIDs* such as *Everyone* (S-1-1-0) and *Authenticated Users* (S-1-5-11) are not maintained within Active Directory itself and are therefore stored in the FSP container.

See Also

MS KB 303973 (How to Add Users to the Pre-Windows 2000 Compatible Access Group) and MS KB 243330 (Well-Known Security Identifiers in Windows Operating Systems)

15.7   Using the Delegation of Control Wizard

Problem

You want to delegate control over objects in Active Directory to a user or group.

Solution

Using a graphical user interface

1. Open the Active Directory Users and Computers (ADUC) or Active Directory Sites and Services snap-in, depending on the type of object you want to delegate.

2. In the left pane, browse to the object you want to delegate control on.

3. Right-click on the object and select Delegate Control. Only certain objects support the "Delegation of Control Wizard," so this option will not show up for every type of object.

4. Click Next.

5. Click the Add button and use the Object Picker to select the users or groups you want to delegate control to.

6. Click Next.

7. If the task you want to delegate is an option under "Delegate the following common tasks," place a check mark next to it and click Next. If the task is not present, select "Create a custom task to delegate" and click Next. If you selected the latter option, you will need to go perform two additional steps:

a. Select the object type you want to delegate.

b. Click Next.

c. Select the permissions you want to delegate.

d. Click Next.

8. Click Finish.

Using a command-line Interface

To grant permissions from the command line, use the following syntax:

```
> dsacls <ObjectDN> /g<Permissions>
```

For example, the following syntax will delegate the permission to read and write information to the description property:

```
> dsacls <ObjectDN> RPWP;description;
```

Discussion

The Delegation of Control Wizard is Microsoft's attempt to ease the pain of trying to set permissions for common tasks. Because Active Directory permissions are so granular, they can also be cumbersome to configure. The Delegation of Control Wizard helps in this regard, but it is still limited in functionality. The default tasks that can be delegated are fairly minimal, although you can add more tasks as described in Recipe 15.8. Another limitation is that you can only add new permissions; you cannot undo or remove permissions that you previously set with the wizard. To do that, you have to use the ACL Editor directly as described in Recipe 15.10 or use *dsrevoke*.

See Also

Recipe 15.9 for more on using *dsrevoke* and Recipe 15.8 for customizing the Delegation of Control wizard.

15.8 Customizing the Delegation of Control Wizard

Problem

You want to add or remove new delegation options in the Delegation of Control Wizard.

Solution

Open the Delegation of Control Wizard INF file (*%SystemRoot%\Inf\Delegwiz.inf*) on the computer you want to modify the wizard for.

Under the [DelegationTemplates] section, you'll see a line like the following:

```
Templates = template1, template2, template3, template4, template5, template6,
template7, template8, template9,template10, template11, template12, template13
```

You need to append a new template name. In this case, we'll follow the same naming convention and create a template named `template14`. The line now looks like this:

```
Templates = template1, template2, template3, template4, template5, template6,
template7, template8, template9,template10, template11, template12, template13,
template14
```

Scroll to the end of the file and append a new template section. You can use the other template sections as examples. Here is the generic format:

```
[<TemplateName>]
AppliesToClasses = <CommaSeparatedOfObjectClassesInvokedFrom>

Description = "<DescriptionShownInWizard>"

ObjectTypes = <CommaSeparatedListOfObjectClassesThatAreSet>

[<TemplateName>.SCOPE]
<Permission entries for Scope>

[<TemplateName>.<ObjectClass1>]
<Permission entries for ObjectClass1>

[<TemplateName>.<ObjectClass2>]
<Permission entries for ObjectClass2>


    . . .
```

`<TemplateName>` is the same as what we used in the [DelegationTemplates] section—i.e., `template14`.

In the `AppliesToClasses` line, replace `<CommaSeparatedObjectClassesInvokedFrom>` with a comma-separated list of LDAP display names of the classes that can be delegated. This delegation action will show up on the classes listed here only when you select Delegate Control from a snap-in. To make our new template entry apply to domain objects, OUs, and containers, we would use this line:

```
AppliesToClasses = domainDNS,organizationalUnit,container
```

In the `Description` line, replace `<DescriptionShownInWizard>` with the text you want shown in the wizard that describes the permissions being delegated. Here is a sample description for delegating full control over `inetOrgPerson` objects:

```
Description = "Create, delete, and manage user and inetOrgPerson accounts"
```

In the `ObjectTypes` line, replace `<CommaSeparatedListOfObjectClassesThatAreSet>` with a comma-separated list of object classes to be delegated. In this example, permissions will be modified for user and `inetOrgPerson` objects:

```
ObjectTypes = user,inetOrgPerson
```

Next, define the actual permissions to set when this action is selected. You can define two different types of permissions. You can use a [<*TemplateName*>.SCOPE] section to define permissions that are set on the object that is used to start the wizard. This will be one of the object classes defined in the AppliesToClass line. This is commonly used in the context of containers and organizational units to specify create, modify, or delete child objects of a particular type. For example, to grant the ability to create (CC) or delete (DC) user and inetOrgPerson objects, you would use the following:

```
[template14.SCOPE]
user=CC,DC
inetOrgPerson=CC,DC
```

As you can see, each permission (e.g., create child) is abbreviated to a two-letter code (e.g., CC). Table 15-1 lists the valid codes.

Table 15-1. Permissions and abbreviated codes

Abbreviated code	Permission
RP	Read Property
WP	Write Property
CC	Create Child
DC	Delete Child
GA	Full Control

It is perfectly valid to leave out a SCOPE section if it is not needed. The rest of the lines are used to specify permissions that should be set on the object classes defined by the ObjectTypes line.

To grant full control over all existing user and inetOrgPerson objects, we'll use these entries:

```
[template14.user]
@=GA

[template14.inetOrgPerson]
@=GA
```

This is very similar to the previous example, except that here SCOPE is replaced with the names of the object classes the permissions apply to. The @ symbol is used to indicate that the permission applies to all attributes on the object. You can get more granular by replacing @ with the name of the attribute the permission applies to. For example, this would grant read and write permissions on the department attribute for inetOrgPerson objects:

```
[template14.inetOrgPerson]
department=RP,WP
```

You can also enable control access rights using the `CONTROLRIGHT` designator instead of @ or an attribute name; you just need to specify the LDAP display name of the control access right you want to enable. The following section enables the `Reset Password` right on `inetOrgPerson` objects and enables read and write access to the `pwdLastSet` attribute:

```
[template14.inetOrgPerson]
CONTROLRIGHT="Reset Password"
pwdLastSet=RP,WP
```

Discussion

You can completely customize the tasks that can be delegated with the Delegation of Control Wizard, but you still have the problem of getting the *Delegwiz.inf* file on all the clients that need to use the new settings. You can manually copy it to the computers that need it, or you can use Group Policy to automate the distribution of it.

See Also

Recipe 15.7 for more on using the Delegation of Control wizard

15.9   Revoking Delegated Permissions

Problem

You want to remove permissions that you've delegated to a domain or an OU.

Solution

Using a graphical user interface

1. Open the Active Directory Users and Computers MMC snap-in (*dsa.msc*). Right-click on the object that you wish to modify and select Properties.
2. From the Security tab, highlight the permissions entry that you wish to revoke and click Remove, then OK.

Using a command-line interface

The following command will remove any permissions that have been delegated directly to the `RALLENCORP\jsmith` user over the `Finance` Organizational Unit:

```
> dsrevoke /remove "/root:ou=Finance,dc=rallencorp,dc=com" RALLENCORP\jsmith
```

Discussion

While the Delegation of Control wizard makes it trivial to grant permissions to objects within Active Directory, one thing that it lacks is an Undo button. To help address this, Microsoft has made the *dsrevoke* command-line utility a free download

---

from its site (*http://www.microsoft.com/downloads/details.aspx?FamilyID=77744807-c403-4bda-b0e4-c2093b8d6383&DisplayLang=en*). The *dsrevoke* utility will remove any permissions that have been delegated to a security principal on a domain or an OU, with the following limitations:

- You can use *dsrevoke* only on a domain or an OU; if you've delegated permissions over individual objects, you'll need to remove these manually.
- *dsrevoke* removes only object permissions; if you've assigned any user rights through Group Policy they'll need to be removed separately.
- You can't use *dsrevoke* to remove any permissions that have been delegated to the Schema or Configuration NCs.

See Also

Best Practices for Delegating Active Directory Administration:

> *http://www.microsoft.com/downloads/details.aspx?FamilyID=631747a3-79e1-48fa-9730-dae7c0a1d6d3&DisplayLang=en*

15.10 Viewing the ACL for an Object

Problem

You want to view the ACL for an object.

Solution

Using a graphical user interface

1. Open the ACL Editor. You can do this by viewing the properties of an object (right-click on the object and select Properties) with a tool such as ADUC or ADSI Edit. Select the Security tab. To see the Security tab with ADUC, you must select View → Advanced Features from the menu.
2. Click the Advanced button to view a list of the individual ACEs.

Using a command-line interface

```
> dsacls <ObjectDN>
```

Using VBScript

Unfortunately, the code to view the ACEs in an ACL is quite messy and long. This will be included as part of the code on the web site for the book (*http://www.oreilly.com/catalog/activedckbk*).

Discussion

Viewing an object's ACL is a common task and should already be familiar to most administrators. The ACL Editor is useful for checking the permissions that have been set on objects, especially after running the Delegation of Control Wizard. In addition to viewing permissions, the options available in the GUI include viewing auditing settings and the owner of the object. Knowing the owner of an object is important because ownership confers certain inherent rights.

Because the ACL Editor is the same for NTFS permissions and properties as it is for Active Directory objects, you should feel comfortable with the look and feel of the interface; it is exactly the same as file and folder permissions. We also highly recommend getting familiar with the Advanced View of the ACL Editor, as this is truly the view in which you can determine what is going on with permissions. The Basic view presents a list of security principals that have permissions configured, but it will not always show every configured ACE entry. The Advanced view will show the complete picture, including the scope of permissions for ACEs down to the object and even the attribute level.

See Also

Recipe 15.14 for changing an ACL and Recipe 16.15 for auditing of object access

15.11 Customizing the ACL Editor

Problem

You want to set permissions on attributes that do not show up in the default Active Directory Users and Computers ACL Editor.

Solution

The ACL Editor in ADUC shows only a subset of the object's attributes on which permissions can be set. These can be seen in the ACL Editor by clicking the Advanced button, adding or editing a permission entry, and selecting the Properties tab.

An attribute can have a read permission, write permission, or both, either of which can be set to Allow or Deny. If the attribute you want to secure is not in the list, you will need to modify the *%SystemRoot%\system32\dssec.dat* file on the computer that you're running the ACL Editor from.

There are sections for each object class represented in square brackets—e.g., [user]. Underneath that heading is a list of attributes that you can configure to display or not display in the ACL Editor.

These are the first few lines for the [user] section:

```
[user]
aCSPolicyName=7
adminCount=7
allowedAttributes=7
```

The value to the right of the attribute determines whether it is shown in the ACL Editor. The valid values include the following:

0   Both Read Property and Write Property are displayed for the attribute.

1   Write property is displayed for the attribute.

2   Read property is displayed for the attribute.

7   No entries are displayed for the attribute.

If the attribute is not defined, then the default value (specified by @, if present) is used.

Discussion

Much like the Delegation of Control Wizard, you can customize the attributes that are shown in the ACL Editor, but you still need to distribute the *dssec.dat* file to all computers that need to see the change.

A good example of when this recipe is needed is for delegating the ability to unlock accounts. This is common in larger organizations when you want to assign this task to the help desk without giving them additional rights on user objects. In this case, you need to set the lockoutTime to 0 in the [user] section of the *dssec.dat* file.

See Also

MS KB 296490 (How to Modify the Filtered Properties of an Object) and MS KB 294952 (How To Delegate the Unlock Account Right)

15.12 Viewing the Effective Permissions on an Object

Problem

You want to view the effective permissions that a user or group has for a particular object.

Solution

Using a graphical user interface

1. Open the ACL Editor. You can do this by viewing the properties of an object (right-click on the object and select Properties) with a tool such as ADUC or ADSI Edit. Select the Security tab. To see the Security tab with ADUC, you must select View → Advanced Features from the menu.

2. Click the Advanced button.

3. Select the Effective Permissions tab.

4. Click the Select button to bring up the Object Editor.

5. Find the user or group you for which want to see the effective permissions.

6. The results will be shown under Effective Permissions.

 The Effective Permissions tab is available only in the Windows Server 2003 version of the ACL Editor. For Windows 2000, you'll need to use the *acldiag* command-line solution.

Using a command-line interface

```
> acldiag <ObjectDN> /geteffective:<UserOrGroup>
```

Discussion

Viewing the permissions on an object does not tell the whole story as to what the actual translated permissions are for a user or group on that object. The *effective permissions* of an object take into account all group membership and any inherited permissions that might have been applied further up the tree. While this is a useful new tool in Windows Server 2003 to analyze permissions, it is still unfortunately only a best guess. Even with the improvements in 2003, there are still some situations in which certain permissions will not be reflected.

See Also

MS KB 323309 (Effective Permissions Are Displayed Incorrectly)

15.13 Configuring Permission Inheritance

Problem

You want to configure permission inheritance on an Active Directory container to determine whether a child object should automatically receive any permissions that you've granted to its parent object.

Solution

1. Open the ACL Editor. You can do this by viewing the properties of an object (right-click on the object and select Properties) with a tool such as Active Directory Users and Computers (ADUC) or ADSI Edit. Select the Security tab. If the Security tab is not visible within ADUC, you must select View → Advanced Features from the menu.

2. Click the Advanced button to view a list of the individual ACEs.

3. To turn off inheritance, remove the check mark next to "Allow inheritable permissions from the parent to propagate to this object and all child objects. Include these with entries defined explicitly here."

4. You will be given the option to "Copy the existing permissions onto the object as explicitly assigned permissions," to "Remove all inherited permissions (all explicitly-assigned permissions will remain in place)," or to "Cancel the operation."

5. To re-enable permission inheritance from objects further up the directory structure, reinsert the check mark listed in Step 3.

Using a VBScript

To disable permission inheritance (i.e., to configure an object such that only explicitly assigned permissions apply), use the following syntax:

```
> dsacls <ObjectDN> /P:N
```

To enable permission inheritance, do the following:

```
> dsacls <ObjectDN> /P:Y
```

Using VBScript

```
' This code enables or disables the "Allow inheritable permissions..."
' setting on an AD object.
' ------ SCRIPT CONFIGURATION ------
Const SE_DACL_PROTECTED = &H1000    ' set to 0 to enable inheritance
strObject = "<ObjectDN>" ' e.g. ou=Finance,dc=rallencorp,dc=com
' ------ END CONFIGURATION ---------

Set objObject = GetObject("LDAP://" & strObject
Set objntSD = objObject.Get("nTSecurityDescriptor")
intNTSDControl = objNtSD.Control

' Disable the bit for "allow inheritable permissions".
intNTSDControl = intNTSDControl And SE_DACL_PROTECTED
objntSD.Control = intNTSDControl
objObject.Put "nTSecurityDescriptor", objntSD
objObject.SetInfo

Wscript.Echo "Inheritable permissionss disabled!"
```

Discussion

Similar to NTFS permissions on the filesystem, Active Directory permissions on container objects can be set to inherit or trickle down to objects further down the directory structure. This process can greatly simplify assigning permissions, as you can assign a common set of permissions high up in the directory structure and have those permissions filter down to all of the OUs and objects below. In some cases, though, you might want to turn off permissions inheritance to configure a different set of permissions entirely for a child object or container.

One thing to keep in mind when enabling or disabling inheritance is that there are a number of AD security principals protected by the AdminSDHolder process that will receive a specific set of permissions regardless of the inheritance settings you configure. These groups include *Enterprise Admins*, *Schema Admins*, *Domain Admins*, and *Administrators* in Windows 2000, with the addition of *Account Operators*, *Server Operators*, *Print Operators*, *Backup Operators*, and *Cert Publishers* in Windows Server 2003 or with certain hotfixes in Windows 2000. In addition, some Active Directory–aware applications depend on inheritance being in place in order to function efficiently.

See Also

"AdminSDHolder, or where did my permissions go?": *http://msmvps.com/blogs/ulfbsimonweidner/archive/2005/05/29/49659.aspx* and MS KB 232199 (Description and Update of the Active Directory AdminSDHolder Object)

15.14 Changing the ACL of an Object

Problem

You want to change the ACL on an object to grant or restrict access to it for a user or group.

Solution

Using a graphical user interface

1. Open the ACL Editor. You can do this by viewing the properties of an object (right-click on the object and select Properties) with a tool such as ADUC or ADSI Edit. Select the Security tab. To see the Security tab with ADUC, you must select View → Advanced Features from the menu.

2. Click the Advanced button to view a list of the individual ACEs.

3. Click Add to specify a new user or group, then place check marks next to the permissions that you want to assign and click OK.

4. To remove an ACE, highlight the entry and click Remove. If the Permissions entry is inherited from further up the directory tree, the option to remove the permission will not be available unless you remove the check mark next to "Allow inheritable permissions from the parent to propagate to this object and all child objects...." With this check mark in place, you will only have the option to remove any permissions that have <not inherited> listed in the "Inherited From" column.

Using a command-line interface

To grant permissions from the command line, use the following syntax:

```
> dsacls <ObjectDN> /g<Permissions>
```

To deny permissions, replace /g with /d.

Using VBScript

See Recipes 7.11, 8.2, 14.8, and 18.9 for several examples of modifying an ACL with VBScript.

Discussion

Changing the ACL of an object is a common task for administrators in any but the most basic AD implementations because, as shown in Recipes 15.7 and 15.8, the Delegation of Control Wizard is limited and cumbersome to extend and deploy. The GUI and command-line methods are useful for one-off changes to permissions, but for making global changes to a number of objects, you should consider using a script to automate the process.

See Also

Recipes 7.11, 8.2, 14.8, 15.7, 15.8, 18.9, and MS KB 281146 (How to Use Dsacls.exe in Windows 2000)

15.15 Changing the Default ACL for an Object Class in the Schema

Problem

You want to change the default ACL for an object class in the schema.

Solution

Using a graphical user interface

1. Open the Active Directory Schema snap-in.
2. In the left pane, browse to the class you want to modify.
3. Right-click on it and select Properties.
4. Select the Default Security tab.
5. Use the ACL Editor to change the ACL.
6. Click OK.

The Default Security tab is available only in the Windows Server 2003 version of the Active Directory Schema snap-in. See MS KB 265399 for the manual approach that is needed with Windows 2000.

Discussion

Each instantiated object in Active Directory has an associated structural class that defines a default security descriptor (the `defaultSecurityDescriptor` attribute). When an object is created, the default security descriptor is applied to it. This, along with inheritable permissions from the parent container, determines how an object's security descriptor is initially defined. If you find that you are modifying the default security descriptor on a particular type of object every time it is created, you may want to modify its default security descriptor. (Another option would be to use a script that would modify the ACL at the same time that the object was created.)

See Also

Recipe 15.16 for comparing the ACL of an object to the default defined in the schema, Recipe 15.17 for resetting the ACL of an object to the default defined in the schema, Recipe 11.1 for more on registering the Active Directory Schema snap-in, and MS KB 265399 (How to Change Default Permissions for Objects That Are Created in the Active Directory)

15.16 Comparing the ACL of an Object to the Default Defined in the Schema

Problem

You want to determine if an object has the permissions defined in the schema for its object class as part of its ACL.

Solution

Using a command-line interface

```
> acldiag <ObjectDN> /schema
```

Discussion

For more on the default security descriptor (SD), see Recipe 15.15. *acldiag* will determine if the object possesses the security descriptor that's defined in the schema—if you've modified the security descriptor, *acldiag* will compare the object's SD against the currently defined SD, not the Active Directory default.

See Also

Recipe 15.17 for resetting an object's ACL to the default defined in the schema

15.17 Resetting an Object's ACL to the Default Defined in the Schema

Problem

You want to reset an object's ACL to the one defined in the schema for the object's object class.

Solution

Using a graphical user interface

 This is available only in the Windows Server 2003 version of the ACL Editor.

1. Open the ACL Editor. You can do this by viewing the properties of an object (right-click on the object and select Properties) with a tool such as ADUC or ADSI Edit. Select the Security tab. To see the Security tab with ADUC, you must select View → Advanced Features from the menu.

2. Click the Advanced button.

3. Click the Default button.

4. Click OK twice.

Using a command-line interface

```
> dsacls <ObjectDN> /s
```

Discussion

For more on the default security descriptor, see Recipe 15.15.

15.18 Preventing the LM Hash of a Password from Being Stored

Problem

You want to prevent the LM hash for new passwords from being stored in Active Directory. The LM hash is primarily used for backward compatibility with Windows 95 and 98 clients; it is susceptible to brute force attacks.

Solution

For Windows 2000, you need to create the following Registry key on all domain controllers: `HKLM\SYSTEM\CurrentControlSet\Control\Lsa\NoLMHash`. Note that this is a key and not a value entry. Also, this is supported only on W2K SP2 and later domain controllers.

For Windows Server 2003, the `NoLMHash` key has turned into a DWORD value entry under the `HKLM\SYSTEM\CurrentControlSet\Control\Lsa` key. This value should be set to 1. You can accomplish this by modifying the Default Domain Controller Security Policy as described next.

Using a graphical user interface

1. Open the Default Domain Controller Security Policy snap-in.
2. In the left pane, expand Local Policies → Security Options.
3. In the right pane, double-click on "Network security: Do not store LAN Manager hash value on next password change."
4. Check the box beside "Define this policy setting."
5. Click the Enabled radio button.

Discussion

If you do not have Windows 98 or older clients in your domain, you should consider disabling the storage of the LM password hash for users. The LM hash uses an old algorithm (pre-Windows NT 4.0) and is considered to be relatively weak compared to the NT hash that is also stored.

 The LM hash is generated only for passwords that are shorter than 15 characters. So if you are one of the few people who have a password longer than this, the LM hash is not stored for you.

In addition to making this change on the server side, you should configure your network clients as described in Recipe 15.19. Finally, to clear any existing LM hashes that have already been stored in AD, you will need to force a password change for the users in question.

See Also

MS KB 299656 (How to Prevent Windows from Storing a LAN Manager Hash of Your Password in Active Directory and Local SAM Databases)

15.19 Enabling Strong Domain Authentication

Problem

You want to ensure that users can only authenticate to Active Directory using strong authentication protocols.

Solution

Using a graphical user interface

1. Open the Group Policy Management Console snap-in.

2. In the left pane, expand the Forest container, expand the Domains container, browse to the domain you want to administer, and expand the Group Policy Objects container.

3. Right-click on the GPO that controls the configuration of your domain controllers and select Edit. (By default, this is the Default Domain Controller Policy, but it may be a different GPO in your environment.) This will bring up the Group Policy Object Editor.

4. Browse to Computer Configuration → Windows Settings → Security Settings → Local Policies → Security Options.

5. Double-click on "Network security: LAN Manager Authentication Level." Place a check mark next to "Define this policy setting."

6. Select "Send NTLMv2 responses only/refuse LM & NTLM." Click OK.

7. Wait for Group Policy to refresh, or type gpupdate /force from the command prompt of a Windows Server 2003 domain controller. On a Windows 2000 DC, use the secedit command with the /refreshpolicy switch.

Discussion

Microsoft operating systems have supported different flavors of LAN Manager (LM) and NT LAN Manager (NTLM) authentication since the earliest days of Windows. LM authentication is an extremely old and weak authentication protocol that should no longer be used in production environments unless absolutely necessary. By default, Windows 2000 Active Directory supported client authentication attempts using LM, NTLM, or NTLMv2; Windows Server 2003 supports only NTLM and NTLMv2 out of the box.

The strongest NTLM authentication scheme you can select is to refuse LM and NTLM authentication from any client, and to only respond to clients using NTLMv2. Depending on your client configuration, though, enabling this option may require changes on the client side as well. You can apply the same setting to a GPO linked to your Active Directory domain to ensure that all of your clients will use NTLMv2 instead of older, weaker protocols.

See Also

MS KB 239869 (How to Enable NTLM 2 Authentication) and MS KB 299656 (How to Prevent Windows from Storing a LAN Manager Hash of Your Password in Active Directory and Local SAM databases)

15.20 Enabling List Object Access Mode

Problem

You want to prevent any authenticated user from being able to browse the contents of Active Directory by default. Enabling List Object Access mode means that users will need explicit permissions to see directory listings of containers.

Solution

Using a graphical user interface

1. Open ADSI Edit.
2. In the Configuration partition, browse to cn=Services → cn=Windows NT → cn=Directory Service.
3. In the left pane, right-click on the Directory Service object and select Properties.
4. Double-click on the dSHeuristics attribute.
5. If the attribute is empty, set it with the value 001. If the attribute has an existing value, make sure the third digit (from the left) is set to 1.
6. Click OK twice.

Using VBScript

```
On Error Resume Next ' necessary if dsHeuristics is not
                     ' already set

' This code enables or disables list object mode for a forest.
' ------ SCRIPT CONFIGURATION ------
boolEnableListObject = 1  ' e.g. 1 to enable, 0 to disable
' ------ END CONFIGURATION ---------

set objRootDSE = GetObject("LDAP://RootDSE")
set objDS = GetObject( _
              "LDAP://cn=Directory Service,cn=Windows NT,cn=Services," _
              & objRootDSE.Get("configurationNamingContext") )
strDSH = objDS.Get("dSHeuristics")
if len(strDSH) = 1 then
   strDSH = strDSH & "0"
end if
```

```
strNewDSH = Left(strDSH,2) & boolEnableListObject
if len(strDSH) > 3 then
    strNewDSH = strNewDSH & Right(strDSH, len(strDSH) - 3)
end if

WScript.Echo "Old value: " & strDSH
WScript.Echo "New value: " & strNewDSH

if strDSH <> strNewDSH then
    objDS.Put "dSHeuristics", strNewDSH
    objDS.SetInfo
    WScript.Echo "Successfully set list object mode to " & _
                boolEnableListObject
else
    WScript.Echo "List object mode already set to " & boolEnableListObject
end if
```

Discussion

List Object Access mode is useful if you want your users to view only a subset of objects when doing a directory listing of a particular container, or you do not want them to be able to list the objects in a container at all. By default, the Authenticated Users group is granted the List Contents access control right over objects in a domain. If you remove or deny this right on a container by modifying the ACL, users will not be able to get a listing of the objects in that container using tools such as ADUC or ADSI Edit.

To limit the objects that users can see when they pull up an object listing, you first need to enable List Object Access mode as described in the solution. You should then remove the List Contents access control right on the target container. Lastly, you'll need to grant the List Object right to the objects that the users or groups should be able to list.

Enabling List Object Access mode can significantly increase the administration overhead for configuring ACLs in Active Directory. It can also impact performance on a domain controller since it will take considerably more time to verify ACLs before returning information to a client.

Using VBScript

While we discussed error handling in Chapter 1, this script actually requires the On Error Resume Next command in order to function. This is because, without this line in place, the script will throw an error if the dsHeuristics attribute is not set.

See Also

MSDN: Controlling Object Visibility and Microsoft's High-Volume Hosting Site at *http://www.microsoft.com/serviceproviders/deployment/hvh_ad_deploy.asp*

15.21 Modifying the ACL on Administrator Accounts

Problem

You want to modify the ACL for user accounts that are members of one of the administrative groups.

Solution

Using one of the methods described in Recipe 15.14, modify the ACL on the `cn=AdminSDHolder,cn=Systems,<DomainDN>` object in the domain that the administrator accounts reside in. The ACL on this object gets applied every hour to all user accounts that are members of the administrative groups.

Discussion

If you've ever tried to directly modify the ACL on a user account that was a member of one of the administrative groups in Active Directory, or you modified the ACL on the OU containing an administrative account, and then wondered why the account's ACL was overwritten later, you've come to the right place. The Admin SD Holder feature of Active Directory is one that many administrators stumble upon after much grinding of teeth. However, after you realize the purpose for it, you'll understand it is a necessary feature.

Once an hour, a process on the PDC Emulator that we'll refer to as the Admin SD Holder process (but is actually known as the *sdprop* (SD Propagator) thread) compares the ACL on the `AdminSDHolder` object to the ACL on the accounts that are in administrative groups in the domain as well as the groups themselves. If it detects a difference, it will overwrite the account or Group ACL and disable inheritance.

 If you later remove a user from an administrative group, you will need to reapply any inherited permissions and enable inheritance if necessary. The Admin SD Holder process will not take care of this for you.

The Admin SD Holder process is intended to subvert any malicious activity by a user that has been delegated rights over an OU or container that contains an account that is in one of the administrative groups. An OU administrator could, for example, modify permissions inheritance on an OU to attempt to lock out the *Domain Admins* group; this permission change would be reverted the next time that the SD Propagator thread runs.

These are the groups included as part of the Admin SD Holder processing:

- *Administrators*
- *Account Operators*
- *Cert Publishers*

- *Backup Operators*
- *Domain Admins*
- *Enterprise Admins*
- *Print Operators*
- *Schema Admins*
- *Server Operators*

The *administrator* and *krbtgt* user accounts are also specifically checked during the Admin SD Holder process.

See Also

MS KB 232199 (Description and Update of the Active Directory AdminSDHolder Object), MS KB 306398 (AdminSDHolder Object Affects Delegation of Control for Past Administrator Accounts), and MS KB 817433 (Delegated Permissions Are Not Available and Inheritance Is Automatically Disabled)

15.22 Viewing and Purging Your Kerberos Tickets

Problem

You want to view and possibly purge your Kerberos tickets.

Solution

Both the *kerbtray* and *klist* utilities can be found in the Resource Kit.

Using a graphical user interface

1. Run *kerbtray.exe* from the command line or Start → Run.
2. A new icon (green) should show up in the system tray. Double-click on that icon. This will allow you to view your current tickets.
3. To purge your tickets, right-click on the *kerbtray* icon in the system tray and select Purge Tickets.
4. Close the *kerbtray* window and reopen it by right-clicking on the *kerbtray* icon and selecting List Tickets.

Using a command-line interface

Run the following command to list your current tickets:

```
> klist tickets
```

Run the following command to purge your tickets:

```
> klist purge
```

Discussion

Active Directory uses Kerberos as its preferred network authentication system. When you authenticate to a Kerberos Key Distribution Center (KDC), which in Active Directory terms is a domain controller, you are issued one or more tickets. These tickets identify you as a certain principal in Active Directory and can be used to authenticate you to other Kerberized services. This type of ticket is known as a *ticket-granting-ticket*, or TGT. Once you've obtained a TGT, the client can use the TGT to gain access to a Kerberized service by querying the Ticket Granting Service on the KDC; if the KDC verifies that the user is authorized to access the service in question, it will issue a *service ticket* that allows the client to use the particular service.

Kerberos is a fairly complicated system that cannot be done justice in a single paragraph. If you want more information on tickets and how the Kerberos authentication system works, see *Kerberos: The Definitive Guide* by Jason Garman (O'Reilly).

See Also

RFC 1510 (The Kerberos Network Authentication Service V5) and MS KB 232179 (Kerberos Administration in Windows 2000)

15.23 Forcing Kerberos to Use TCP

Problem

Clients are experiencing authentication problems, and you've determined it is due to UDP fragmentation of Kerberos traffic. You want to force Kerberos traffic to use the TCP protocol instead.

Solution

Using a graphical user interface

1. Run *regedit.exe* from the command line or from Start → Run.
2. In the left pane, expand HKEY_LOCAL_MACHINE → System → Current-ControlSet → Control → Lsa → Kerberos → Parameters.
3. Right-click on Parameters and select New → DWORD value. Enter MaxPacketSize for the value name.
4. In the right pane, double-click on MaxPacketSize and enter 1.
5. Click OK.

Using a command-line interface

```
> reg add "HKLM\SYSTEM\CurrentControlSet\Control\Lsa\Kerberos\Parameters" /v\
"MaxPacketSize" /t REG_DWORD /d 1
```

Using VBScript

```
' This code forces Kerberos to use TCP.
' ------ SCRIPT CONFIGURATION ------
strComputer = "<ComputerName>"  ' e.g. rallen-w2k3
' ------ END CONFIGURATION ---------

const HKLM = &H80000002
strRegKey = "SYSTEM\CurrentControlSet\Control\Lsa\Kerberos\Parameters"
set objReg = GetObject("winmgmts:\\" & strComputer & _
                       "\root\default:StdRegProv")
objReg.SetDwordValue HKLM, strRegKey, "MaxPacketSize", 1
WScript.Echo "Kerberos forced to use TCP for " & strComputer
```

Discussion

If you have users that are experiencing extremely slow logon times (especially over VPN) or they are seeing the infamous "There are currently no logon servers available to service the logon request," then they may be experiencing UDP fragmentation of Kerberos traffic. This occurs because UDP is a *connectionless protocol*, so UDP packets that arrive out of order will be dropped by the destination router. One way to help identify if there is a problem with Kerberos is to have the users run the following command:

```
> netdiag /test:kerberos
```

Another source of information is the System event log on the clients. Various Kerberos-related events are logged there if problems with authentication occur.

For more information about Kerberos and UDP, see MS KB 244474 (How to Force Kerberos to Use TCP Instead of UDP).

See Also

MS KB 244474 (How to Force Kerberos to Use TCP Instead of UDP in Windows Server 2003, in Windows XP, and in Windows 2000)

15.24 Modifying Kerberos Settings

Problem

You want to modify the default Kerberos settings that define things, such as maximum ticket lifetime.

Solution

Using a graphical user interface

1. Open the Domain Security Policy snap-in.
2. In the left pane, expand Account Policies → Kerberos Policy.

3. In the right pane, double-click on the setting you want to modify.

4. Enter the new value and click OK.

Discussion

There are several Kerberos-related settings you can customize, most of which revolve around either increasing or decreasing the maximum lifetime for Kerberos user and service tickets. In most environments, the default settings are sufficient, but the ones you can modify are listed in Table 15-2.

 Change the default settings with caution, as doing so could cause operational problems and compromise security if done incorrectly.

Table 15-2. Kerberos policy settings

Setting	Default value
Enforce user logon restrictions	Enabled
Maximum lifetime for service ticket	600 minutes
Maximum lifetime for user ticket	10 hours
Maximum lifetime for user ticket renewal	7 days
Maximum tolerance for computer clock synchronization	5 minutes

See Also

MS KB 231849 (Description of Kerberos Policies in Windows 2000) and MS KB 232179 (Kerberos Administration in Windows 2000)

15.25 Viewing Access Tokens

Problem

You want to view the access tokens that are created for a user account that has authenticated to Active Directory.

Using a command-line interface

```
> tokensz /compute_tokensize /package:negotiate /target_server:host/<DCName>
/user:<Username> /domain:<DomainName> /password:<Password> /dumpgroups
```

Discussion

When an Active Directory security principal receives a TGT from the Kerberos Key Distribution Center, the TGT contains a Privilege Attribute Certificate (PAC). This PAC contains several pieces of authentication data, such as the groups that a user belongs to (including all nested group memberships). In the majority of AD environments, this PAC is created without issue, but some larger environments can run into instances of token bloat. This occurs when a user belongs to a large number of groups (estimates start around 70 to 120), and the size of the PAC becomes too large for the TGT to handle. This issue can manifest itself through authentication issues or through Group Policy Objects not applying properly. You can use the *tokensz.exe* utility, downloadable from *http://go.microsoft.com/fwlink/?LinkId=25830*, to compute the token size for a user relative to the maximum allowable size, as well as to list the groups that a user belongs to.

You can resolve this issue by streamlining the number of groups that the user or users belong to, which would have the added benefit of simplifying the process of assigning permissions and applying Group Policy Objects. If this isn't possible, you can apply the hotfix referenced in MS KB 327825 or modify the `HKLM\System\CurrentControlSet\Control\Lsa\Kerberos\Parameters\MaxTokenSize` DWORD value on your domain computers. This issue is more relevant on Windows 2000 domain controllers, since Windows Server 2003 has made a number of improvements to alleviate the need to modify this value.

If you determine that you need to modify the `MaxTokenSize` value, use the following formula as a guideline:

    1200 + 40d + 80s

In this equation, `1200` denotes a suggested amount of overhead that's used by the PAC; you can use the *tokensz* utility to determine the size for the domain in question. d refers to the number of domain local security groups that a representative user is a member of, plus any universal security groups in other domains that the user belongs to, plus any groups represented in the user's `sIDHistory` attribute. s refers to the number of global security groups a representative user belongs to, plus any universal security groups within the user's own domain.

See Also

MS KB 327825 (New Resolution for Problems That Occur When Users Belong to Many Groups), MS KB 263693 (Group Policy May Not Be Applied to Users Belonging to Many Groups), MS KB 280830 (Kerberos Suthentication May Not Work if User Is a Member of Many Groups), and Troubleshooting Kerberos Errors: *http://www.microsoft.com/technet/prodtechnol/windowsserver2003/technologies/security/tkerberr.mspx*

## CHAPTER 16

Logging, Monitoring, and Quotas

16.0 Introduction

This chapter deals with tracking the activity and usage of various Active Directory components. When you need to troubleshoot a problem, often the first place you look is logfiles. With Active Directory, there are several different logfiles, and each has different ways to increase or decrease the verbosity of information that is logged. Viewing log messages can be a useful troubleshooting step, but you should also look at *performance metrics* to determine if system hardware or a particular service is being overutilized. In this chapter, we'll review a couple of ways you can view performance metrics, as well as monitor Active Directory performance. For more extensive monitoring, we suggest looking at NetPro's Active Directory monitoring tools (*http://www.netpro.com/*), Microsoft Operations Manager (*http://microsoft.com/mom/*), or similar products from other vendors such as NetIQ. In addition to the typical items that you would monitor on a Windows Server (e.g., disk space usage, physical and virtual memory errors, processor utilization), you should also monitor AD-specific performance metrics. This extends to monitoring replication activity, Event Log information, and the status of services like the File Replication Service (FRS).

We'll also cover a somewhat-related topic called *quotas*, which allow you to monitor and limit the number of objects that a security principal (user, group, or computer) can create within a partition. This feature, introduced in Windows Server 2003, attempts to close a hole that existed in Windows 2000 where users that had access to create objects in Active Directory could create as many of those objects as they wanted. These users could even cause a denial-of-service attack by creating objects until the disk drive on the domain controllers filled to capacity. This kind of attack is not likely to happen in most environments, but the possibility should still be considered and protected against.

The Anatomy of a Quota Object Container

Quota objects are stored in the NTDS Quotas container in all Windows Server 2003–based naming contexts and application partitions except for the schema naming context (quotas cannot be associated with the schema NC). By default, this container is hidden from view within tools such as Active Directory Users and Computers, but can be seen by selecting View → Advanced Features from the menu. The quota object container has an objectClass of msDS-QuotaContainer and contains several attributes that define default quota behavior. Table 16-1 lists some of the important attributes of msDS-QuotaContainer objects.

Table 16-1. Attributes of msDS-QuotaContainer objects

Attribute	Description
cn	RDN of quota container objects. By default, this is equal to NTDS Quotas.
msDS-DefaultQuota	The default quota applied to all security principals that do not have another quota specification applied. See Recipe 16.20 for more details.
msDS-QuotaEffective	A constructed attribute that contains the effective quota of the security principal that is viewing the attribute. See Recipe 16.21 for more details.
msDS-QuotaUsed	A constructed attribute that contains the quota usage of the security principal that is viewing the attribute. See Recipe 16.21 for more details.
msDS-TombstoneQuotaFactor	Percentage that tombstone objects count against a quota. The default is 100, which means a tombstone object has equal weighting to a normal object. See Recipe 16.19 for more details.
msDS-TopQuotaUsage	Multivalued attribute that contains information about the security principals with the top quota usage. See Recipe 16.21 for more details.

The Anatomy of a Quota Object

Quota objects have an objectClass of msDS-QuotaControl, which defines three attributes that relate to quotas. Table 16-2 contains these attributes and provides a description for each.

Table 16-2. Attributes of msDS-QuotaControl objects

Attribute	Description
cn	RDN of the quota object.
msDS-QuotaAmount	Number of objects that can be created by the security principals that the quota applies to. See Recipe 16.17 for more information.
msDS-QuotaTrustee	SID of the security principal that the quota applies to. This can be a user, group, or computer SID. See Recipe 16.17 for more information.

16.1 Enabling Extended dcpromo Logging

Problem

You want to enable extended *dcpromo* logging. This can be useful if you are experiencing problems during the Domain Controller promotion or demotion process and the *dcpromo* logfiles are not providing enough information to indicate the problem.

Solution

These solutions are slightly different on Windows 2000. See the "Discussion" section for more information. To enable the maximum amount of logging, use 16711683 (FF0003 in hexadecimal) as the flag value. For a complete description of the possible bit values, see MS KB 221254.

Using a graphical user interface

1. Run *regedit.exe* from the command line or Start → Run.
2. In the left pane, expand *HKEY_LOCAL_MACHINE\Software\Microsoft\Windows\CurrentVersion\AdminDebug\dcpromoui*.
3. If the LogFlags value does not exist, right-click on *dcpromoui* in the left pane and select New → DWORD Value. For the name, enter LogFlags.
4. In the right pane, double-click on the LogFlags value and enter the flag value you want to set.
5. Click OK.

Using a command-line interface

With the following command, `<FlagValue>` needs to be the decimal version (not hexadecimal) of the flag value:

```
> reg add HKLM\Software\Microsoft\Windows\CurrentVersion\AdminDebug\dcpromoui /v
"LogFlags" /t REG_DWORD /d <FlagValue>
```

Using VBScript

```
' This code sets the dcpromoui logging flag (for Windows Server 2003 only).
' ------ SCRIPT CONFIGURATION ------
strDC   = "<DomainControllerName>"  ' e.g. dc01
intFlag = <FlagValue>                ' Flag value in decimal, e.g. 16711683
' ------ END CONFIGURATION ---------

const HKLM = &H80000002
strDcpromoReg = "Software\Microsoft\Windows\CurrentVersion\AdminDebug\dcpromoui"
set objReg = GetObject("winmgmts:\\" & strDC & "\root\default:StdRegProv")
objReg.SetDwordValue HKLM, strDcpromoReg, "LogFlags", intFlag
WScript.Echo "Dcpromoui flag set to " & intFlag
```

Discussion

As described in Recipe 3.6, the *dcpromo* wizard creates a couple of logfiles in *%SystemRoot%\debug* when it is executed, which can be useful in troubleshooting promotion or demotion problems. Typically, the default amount of logging that is done in the *dcpromoui.log* file is sufficient to identify most problems, but you can increase it as described in the Solution section.

The location of the log flags registry value changed from Windows 2000 to Windows Server 2003. In Windows 2000, the value is located here:

```
HKLM\Software\Microsoft\Windows\CurrentVersion\AdminDebug\dcpromoui
```

In Windows Server 2003, the value is located here (this is the value that was used in the Solutions section):

```
HKLM\Software\Microsoft\Windows\CurrentVersion\AdminDebug\dcpromoui\LogFlags
```

See Also

Recipe 3.6 for more on troubleshooting *dcpromo* problems and MS KB 221254 (Registry Settings for Event Detail in the Dcpromoui.log File)

16.2   Enabling Diagnostics Logging

Problem

You want to enable diagnostics event logging because the current level of logging is not providing enough information to help pinpoint the problem you are troubleshooting.

Solution

Using a graphical user interface

1. Run *regedit.exe* from the command line or Start → Run.

2. In the left pane, expand the following Registry key: *HKEY_LOCAL_MACHINE\System\CurrentControlSet\Services\NTDS\Diagnostics*.

3. In the right pane, double-click on the diagnostics logging entry you want to increase, and enter a number (0–5) based on how much you want logged.

4. Click OK.

Using a command-line interface

```
> reg add HKLM\SYSTEM\CurrentControlSet\Services\NTDS\Diagnostics /v
"<LoggingSetting>" /t REG_DWORD /d <0-5>
```

Using VBScript

```
' This code sets the specified diagnostics logging level.
' ------ SCRIPT CONFIGURATION ------
strDC    = "<DomainControllerName>"  ' e.g. dc01
strLogSetting = "<LoggingSetting>"   ' e.g. 1 Knowledge Consistency Checker
intFlag = <FlagValue>                ' Flag value in decimal, e.g. 5
' ------ END CONFIGURATION ---------

const HKLM = &H80000002
strRegKey = "SYSTEM\CurrentControlSet\Services\NTDS\Diagnostics"
set objReg = GetObject("winmgmts:\\" & strDC & "\root\default:StdRegProv")
objReg.SetDwordValue HKLM, strRegKey, "LogFlags", intFlag
WScript.Echo "Diagnostics logging for " & strLogSetting _
             & " set to " & intFlag
```

Discussion

A useful way to troubleshoot specific problems you are encountering with Active Directory is to increase the diagnostics logging level. Diagnostics logging can be enabled for individual components of AD. For example, if you determine the KCC is not completing every 15 minutes, you can enable diagnostics logging for the "1 Knowledge Consistency Checker" setting.

These settings are stored under *HKLM\SYSTEM\CurrentControlSet\Services\NTDS\ Diagnostics*. By default, all settings are set to 0, which disables diagnostic logging, but you can increase it by setting it to a number from 1 through 5. As a general rule, a value of 1 is used for minimum logging, 3 for medium logging, and 5 for maximum logging. It is a good practice to ease your way up to 5 because some diagnostics logging settings can generate a bunch of events in the event log, which may make it difficult to read, along with increasing resource utilization on the domain controller.

Here is the complete list of diagnostics logging settings for Windows Server 2003. Note that settings 20–24 are not available on Windows 2000–based domain controllers:

```
1 Knowledge Consistency Checker
2 Security Events
3 ExDS Interface Events
4 MAPI Interface Events
5 Replication Events
6 Garbage Collection
7 Internal Configuration
8 Directory Access
9 Internal Processing
10 Performance Counters
11 Initialization/Termination
12 Service Control
13 Name Resolution
14 Backup
15 Field Engineering
16 LDAP Interface Events
17 Setup
```

```
18 Global Catalog
19 Inter-site Messaging
20 Group Caching
21 Linked-Value Replication
22 DS RPC Client
23 DS RPC Server
24 DS Schema
```

See Also

MS KB 220940 (How to Enable Diagnostic Event Logging for Active Directory Services)

16.3   Enabling NetLogon Logging

Problem

You want to enable NetLogon logging to help with troubleshooting client account logon, lockout, or domain-controller location issues.

Solution

Using a command-line interface

To enable NetLogon logging, use the following command:

```
> nltest /dbflag:0x2080ffff
```

To disable NetLogon logging, use the following command:

```
> nltest /dbflag:0x0
```

Discussion

The *netlogon.log* file located in *%SystemRoot%\Debug* can be invaluable for trouble-shooting client logon and related issues. When enabled at the highest setting (0x2080ffff), it logs useful information such as the site the client is in, the domain controller the client authenticated against, additional information related to the DC Locator process, account password expiration information, account lockout information, and even Kerberos failures.

The NetLogon logging level is stored in the following registry value:

```
HKLM\System\CurrentControlSet\Services\Netlogon Parameters\DBFlag
```

 If you set that registry value manually instead of using *nltest*, you'll need to restart the NetLogon service for it to take effect.

One of the issues with the *netlogon.log* file is that it can quickly grow to several megabytes, which makes it difficult to peruse. A new tool available for Windows XP and Windows Server 2003 called *nlparse* can filter the contents of the *netlogon.log* file so that you'll see only certain types of log entries. The *nlparse* tool is part of the Account Lockout and Management Tools that Microsoft made available from the following web page (assuming the tools haven't moved):

> *http://www.microsoft.com/downloads/details.aspx?FamilyID=7af2e69c-91f3-4e63-8629-b999adde0b9e&DisplayLang=en*

See Also

MS KB 109626 (Enabling Debug Logging for the Netlogon Service), MS KB 247811 (How Domain Controllers Are Located in Windows), and MS KB 273499 (Description of Security Event 681)

16.4 Enabling GPO Client Logging

Problem

You want to troubleshoot GPO processing issues on a client or server by enabling additional logging in the Application event log.

Solution

Using a graphical user interface

1. Run *regedit.exe* from the command line or Start → Run.
2. In the left pane, expand *HKEY_LOCAL_MACHINE\Software\Microsoft\Windows NT\CurrentVersion*.
3. If the Diagnostics key doesn't exist, right-click on CurrentVersion and select New → Key. Enter Diagnostics for the name and hit Enter.
4. Right-click on Diagnostics and select New → DWORD value. Enter RunDiagnosticLoggingGroupPolicy for the value name.
5. In the right pane, double-click on RunDiagnosticLoggingGroupPolicy and enter 1.
6. Click OK.

Using a command-line interface

```
> reg add "HKLM\SOFTWARE\Microsoft\Windows NT\CurrentVersion\Diagnostics" /v
"RunDiagnosticLoggingGroupPolicy" /t REG_DWORD /d 1
```

Using VBScript

```
' This code enables GPO logging on a target computer.
' ------ SCRIPT CONFIGURATION ------
strComputer = "<ComputerName>"  ' e.g. rallen-w2k3
```

```
' ------ END CONFIGURATION ---------

const HKLM = &H80000002
strRegKey = "SOFTWARE\Microsoft\Windows NT\CurrentVersion\Diagnostics"
set objReg = GetObject("winmgmts:\\" & strComputer _
                       & "\root\default:StdRegProv")
objReg.SetDwordValue HKLM, strRegKey, "RunDiagnosticLoggingGroupPolicy", 1
WScript.Echo "Enabled GPO logging for " & strComputer
```

Discussion

If you experience problems with client GPO processing, such as a GPO not getting applied even though you think it should, there are a few different tools that can help you troubleshoot the problem. One way to get detailed information about what GPOs are applied on a client is by enabling additional GPO event logging. If you set the RunDiagnosticLoggingGroupPolicy Registry value to 1, extensive logging will be written to the Application event log. Events detailing the beginning of the GPO processing cycle, what GPOs are applied, and any errors encountered will all be logged. The following is an example of a log message that shows which GPOs will be applied on the host *DC1*. To disable this logging, either delete the RunDiagnosticLoggingGroupPolicy key or set the value to 0.

Here is a sample event log message:

```
Event Type:        Error
Event Source:      Userenv
Event Category:      None
Event ID:       1031
Date:             5/26/2003
Time:             5:52:13 PM
User:             NT AUTHORITY\SYSTEM
Computer:       DC1
Description:
Group Policy objects to be applied: "Default Domain Policy" "Default Domain
Controllers Policy" .
```

You can also use the new Group Policy Management Console (GPMC) to troubleshoot Group Policy Processing, particularly the Resultant Set of Policy (RSoP) wizard.

See Also

MS KB 186454 (How to Enable User Environment Event Logging in Windows 2000)

16.5   Enabling Kerberos Logging

Problem

You want to enable Kerberos logging on a domain controller to troubleshoot authentication problems.

Solution

Using a graphical user interface

1. Run *regedit.exe* from the command line or Start → Run.

2. In the left pane, expand *HKEY_LOCAL_MACHINE\System\CurrentControlSet\Control\Lsa\Kerberos\Parameters*.

3. If the LogLevel value doesn't already exist, right-click on Parameters and select New → DWORD value. Enter LogLevel for the value name and click OK.

4. In the right pane, double-click on LogLevel and enter 1.

5. Click OK.

Using a command-line interface

```
> reg add HKLM\SYSTEM\CurrentControlSet\Control\Lsa\Kerberos\Parameters /v
"LogLevel" /t REG_DWORD /d 1
```

Using VBScript

```
' This code enables Kerberos logging for the specified domain controller.
' ------ SCRIPT CONFIGURATION ------
strDC = "<DomainControllerName>"  ' e.g. dc01
' ------ END CONFIGURATION ---------

const HKLM = &H80000002
strRegKey = "SYSTEM\CurrentControlSet\Control\Lsa\Kerberos\Parameters"
set objReg = GetObject("winmgmts:\\" & strDC & "\root\default:StdRegProv")
objReg.SetDwordValue HKLM, strRegKey, "LogLevel", 1
WScript.Echo "Enable Kerberos logging for " & strDC
```

Discussion

If you are experiencing authentication problems or would like to determine whether you are experiencing any Kerberos-related issues, enabling Kerberos logging will cause Kerberos errors to be logged in the System event log. The Kerberos events can point out if the problem is related to clock skew, an expired ticket, an expired password, etc. For a good overview of some of the Kerberos error messages, see MS KB 230476.

Here is a sample event:

```
Event Type:        Error
Event Source:        Kerberos
Event Category:        None
Event ID:       3
Date:               5/26/2003
Time:               5:53:43 PM
User:               N/A
Computer:       DC01
Description:
```

```
 A Kerberos Error Message was received:
         on logon session
  Client Time:
  Server Time: 0:53:43.0000 5/27/2003 Z
  Error Code: 0xd KDC_ERR_BADOPTION
  Extended Error: 0xc00000bb KLIN(0)
  Client Realm:
  Client Name:
  Server Realm: RALLENCORP.COM
  Server Name: host/ dc01.rallencorp.com
  Target Name: host/dc01.rallencorp.com@RALLENCORP.COM
  Error Text:
  File: 9
  Line: ab8
  Error Data is in record data.
```

See Also

MS KB 230476 (Description of Common Kerberos-Related Errors in Windows 2000)
and MS KB 262177 (How to Enable Kerberos Event Logging)

16.6   Viewing DNS Server Performance Statistics

Problem

You want to view DNS Server performance statistics.

Solution

Using a graphical user interface

1. Open the Performance Monitor.
2. Click on System Monitor in the left pane.
3. In the right pane, click the + button. This will bring up the page to add counters.
4. Under "Select counters from computer," enter the DNS server you want to target.
5. Select the DNS performance object.
6. Select the counters you want to add and click the Add button.
7. Click Close.

Using a command-line interface

```
> dnscmd <DNSServerName> /statistics
```

Using VBScript

```
' This code displays all statistics for the specified DNS server.
' ----- SCRIPT CONFIGURATION ------
strServer = "<DNSServerName>"    ' e.g. dc1.rallencorp.com
```

```
' ------ END CONFIGURATION ---------
set objDNS = GetObject("winmgmts:\\" & strServer & "\root\MicrosoftDNS")
set objDNSServer = objDNS.Get("MicrosoftDNS_Server.Name=""."""")
set objStats = objDNS.ExecQuery("Select * from MicrosoftDNS_Statistic ")
for each objStat in objStats
   WScript.Echo " " & objStat.Name & " : " & objStat.Value
next
```

Discussion

The Microsoft DNS Server keeps track of dozens of performance metrics. These metrics include the number of queries, updates, transfers, directory reads, and directory writes processed by the server. If you can pump these metrics into an enterprise management system, you can track DNS usage and growth over time.

These statistics can also be useful to troubleshoot load-related issues. If you suspect a DNS Server is being overwhelmed with DNS update requests, you can look at the Dynamic Update Received/sec counter and see if it is processing an unusually high number of updates.

Using a command-line interface

You can obtain a subset of the statistics by providing a *statid* after the /statistics option. Each statistics category has an associated number (i.e., statid). For a complete list of categories and their statids, run the following command:

```
> dnscmd /statistics /?
```

Here is an example of viewing the Query (statid = 2) and Query2 (statid = 4) statistics:

```
> dnscmd /statistics 6
DNS Server . statistics:

Queries and Responses:
----------------------
Total:
    Queries Received =      14902
    Responses Sent   =      12900
UDP:
    Queries Recvd    =      14718
    Responses Sent   =      12716
    Queries Sent     =      23762
    Responses Recvd  =          0
TCP:
    Client Connects  =        184
    Queries Recvd    =        184
    Responses Sent   =        184
    Queries Sent     =          0
    Responses Recvd  =          0

Queries:
--------
```

```
Total        =     14902
    Notify   =         0
    Update   =      2207
    TKeyNego =       184
    Standard =     12511
        A    =      1286
        NS   =        29
        SOA  =      2263
        MX   =         0
        PTR  =         1
        SRV  =      8909
        ALL  =         0
        IXFR =         0
        AXFR =         0
        OTHER=        23

Command completed successfully.
```

Using VBScript

You can obtain a subset of statistics by adding a where clause to the WQL query. The following query would match only counters that start with "Records":

```
select * from MicrosoftDNS_Statistic where Name like 'Records%'
```

See Also

MSDN: MicrosoftDNS_Statistic

16.7   Monitoring the File Replication Service

Problem

You want to monitor the performance of the File Replication Service (FRS).

Solution

Using a graphical user interface

1. Double-click on *frsdiag.exe* in the Windows Resource Kit
2. Under Target Server(s), select Local Machine, or click Browse to select a remote machine to diagnose.
3. Click GO.

Using a command-line interface

The following will display the polling interval for *dc1.rallencorp.com*:

```
> ntfrsutl poll dc1.rallencorp.com
```

The sets parameter will display all active replication sets on *dc1.rallencorp.com*, as follows:

```
> ntfrsutl sets dc1.rallencorp.com
```

Discussion

The FRS used by Windows 2000 and Windows Server 2003 to replicate the contents of the *SYSVOL* shared folder, as well as any Distributed File System (DFS) folders you've configured. Anytime that FRS detects a change that's been made to a file or folder within one of these shared folders, it will replicate the updated object to other servers within the replica set. Because FRS allows for multimaster file replication (similar to the database replication performed by AD itself), any server in the replica set is able to make changes to *SYSVOL* or DFS folders, and the File Replication Service will distribute those changes accordingly.

You can monitor the File Replication Service using either *frsdiag* from the Resource Kit, or the Ultrasound utility, which is a free download from the Microsoft web site. Ultrasound requires access to a database to store its information: either a SQL server instance or the free MSDE database that can also be downloaded from the Microsoft site.

See Also

MS KB 221111 (Description of FRS Entries in the Registry), MS KB 319553 (How to restrict FRS Replication Traffic to a Specific Static Port), and MS KB 272279 (How to Troubleshoot the File Replication Service and the Distributed File System)

16.8   Monitoring the Windows Time Service

Problem

You want to verify the correct functioning of the Windows Time Service.

Solution

Using a command-line interface

The following syntax will verify that the Windows Time Service is functioning on *dc1.rallencorp.com* and *dc2.rallencorp.com*:

```
> w32tm /monitor /computers:dc1.rallencorp.com,dc2.rallencorp.com
```

Discussion

Because Active Directory relies on Kerberos for authentication, it's critical that all of your domain controllers, member servers and clients maintain a consistent time across the network; if any computer's clock is off by more than five minutes by default, it will not be able to authenticate to Active Directory. You can use the *w32tm* utility to verify time synchronization on one or more computers using the `/monitor` switch, as well as using the `/resync` switch to prompt a computer to immediately resynchronize its clock with its authoritative time source.

See Also

Recipe 3.17 to configure a DC to use an external time source, MS KB 257187 (RPC Error Messages Returned for Active Directory Replication When Time Is Out of Synchronization), and MS KB 816042 (How to Configure an Authoritative Time Server in Windows Server 2003)

16.9 Enabling Inefficient and Expensive LDAP Query Logging

Problem

You want to log inefficient and expensive LDAP queries to the Directory Services event log.

Solution

To log a summary report about the total number of searches, total expensive searches, and total inefficient searches to the Directory Services event log, set the 15 Field Engineering diagnostics logging setting to 4. This summary is generated every 12 hours during the garbage collection cycle.

To log an event to the Directory Services event log every time an expensive or inefficient search occurs, set the 15 Field Engineering diagnostics logging setting to 5.

See Recipe 16.2 for more on enabling diagnostics logging.

Discussion

A search is considered *expensive* if it has to visit a large number of objects in Active Directory. The default threshold for an expensive query is 10,000. That means any search that visits 10,000 or more objects would be considered expensive. A search is considered *inefficient* if it returns less than 10 percent of the total objects it visits. If a query visited 10,000 objects and only returned 999 of them (less than 10 percent), it would be considered inefficient. The default bottom limit for an inefficient query is 1,000. If it returned 1,000 instead, it would not be considered inefficient. To summarize, with 1,000 being the default bottom threshold, no search that visits less than 1,000 entries (even if it visited 999 and returned 0) would be considered inefficient.

Here is a sample summary report event that is logged when 15 Field Engineering is set to 4:

```
Event Type:        Information
Event Source:        NTDS General
Event Category:        Field Engineering
Event ID:        1643
Date:                5/24/2003
Time:                7:24:24 PM
User:                NT AUTHORITY\ANONYMOUS LOGON
Computer:        DC1
Description:
Internal event: Active Directory performed the following number of search operations
within this time interval.

Time interval (hours): 9
Number of search operations: 24679

During this time interval, the following number of search operations were
characterized as either expensive or inefficient.

Expensive search operations: 7
Inefficient search operations: 22
```

If you set 15 Field Engineering to 5, the summary event is logged during the garbage collection cycle, and event 1644 is generated every time an expensive or inefficient search occurs. Setting this value can provide useful information if you are running applications that regularly generate expensive or inefficient queries. Notice that this event provides details on all aspects of the search, including the client IP, authenticating user, search base DN, search filter, attributes, controls, number of entries visited, and number of entries returned. This was taken from a Windows Server 2003 domain controller. Windows 2000 does not provide quite as much detail:

```
Event Type:        Information
Event Source:        NTDS General
Event Category:        Field Engineering
Event ID:        1644
Date:                5/24/2003
Time:                7:50:40 PM
User:                RALLENCORP\rallen
Computer:        DC1
Description:
Internal event: A client issued a search operation with the following options.

Client: 192.168.4.14
Starting node: DC=rallencorp,DC=com
Filter: (description=*)
Search scope: subtree
Attribute selection: cn
Server controls:

Visited entries: 10340
Returned entries: 1000
```

With the default settings, the query shown in the above event is considered both expensive and inefficient. It is expensive because it visited more than 10,000 entries. It is inefficient because it returned less than 10 percent of those entries.

You can customize what a domain controller considers *expensive* and *inefficient* by creating a couple of registry values under the HKLM\SYSTEM\CurrentControlSet\ Services\NTDS\Parameters key. You can create a value named Expensive Search Results Threshold of type DWORD and specify the number of entries a search would need to visit to be considered expensive. Similarly, you can create a value named Inefficient Search Results Threshold of type DWORD and specify the minimum number of entries visited where a match returning less than 10 percent would be considered inefficient.

 If you want to see all the LDAP queries that are being sent to a domain controller, a quick way to do that would be to set the 15 Field Engineering setting to 5 and Expensive Search Results Threshold to 0. This would cause the domain controller to consider every search as expensive and log all the LDAP searches. While this can be very useful, you should use it with care as it could quickly fill your event log. Be sure to allow sufficient disk space for your Event Logs to avoid any issues with low disk space on your domain controllers.

See Also

Recipe 16.2 for enabling diagnostics logging

16.10 Using the STATS Control to View LDAP Query Statistics

Problem

You want to use the STATS LDAP control to test the efficiency of a query.

Solution

Using a graphical user interface

1. Open LDP from the Windows Support Tools.
2. From the menu, select Connection → Connect.
3. For Server, enter the name of a domain controller (or leave blank to do a server-less bind).
4. For Port, enter 389.
5. Click OK.
6. From the menu, select Connection → Bind.

7. Enter the credentials of a user to perform the search.

8. Click OK.

9. From the menu, select Options → Control.

10. For the Windows Server 2003 version of LDP, you can select Search Stats from the Load Predefined selection. For Windows 2000, add a control with the OID 1.2.840.113556.1.4.970.

11. Click OK.

12. From the menu, select Browse → Search.

13. Enter your search criteria and then click the Options button.

14. Under Search Call Type, be sure that Extended is selected.

15. Click OK and then click Run.

Using a command-line interface

The AdFind command-line utility has four switches that will display efficiency statistics for any query:

-stats

> Enables the STATS control to return statistics about the query, along with the actual results of the query.

-statsonly

> Returns *only* the statistics about the query, and suppresses the actual query results.

-stats+

> Similar to -stats, but also displays additional advanced analysis about the query.

-stats+only

> Just like -stats+, but will suppress the actual results of the query and only display the query statistics.

Discussion

The STATS control is a useful way to obtain statistics about the performance of an LDAP query. With the STATS control, you can find out information such as the amount of time it took the server to process the query, how many entries were visited versus returned, what the search filter expanded to, and if any indexes were used. Here is an example of what the STATS control returns for a search for all group objects in the cn=Users container:

```
***Searching . . .
ldap_search_ext_s(ld, "cn=users,DC=rallencorp,DC=com", 2, "(objectcategory=group)",
attrList, 0, svrCtrls, ClntCtrls, 20, 1000 ,&msg)
Result <0>:
Matched DNs:
```

```
Stats:
        Call Time:          10 (ms)
        Entries Returned:        17
        Entries Visited:         17
        Used Filter:
(objectCategory=CN=Group,CN=Schema,CN=Configuration,DC=rallencorp,DC=com) \
        Used Indexes:       INTERSECT_INDEX:17:I;
```

A couple things are worth noting here. First, the search visited only 17 entries and ended up returning all 17. In terms of the definitions defined in Recipe 16.9, this query is both *inexpensive* and *efficient*. You can also see that the filter used, (objectcategory=group), was expanded to (objectCategory=CN=Group,CN=Schema, CN=Configuration,DC=rallencorp,DC=com). The syntax of the objectCategory attribute is a distinguished name, but Active Directory provides a shortcut so that you need to use only the LDAP display name of the class instead. Internally, Active Directory converts the display name to the distinguished name, as shown here. Finally, we can see that our search used an index, INTERSECT_INDEX:17:I.

Let's look at another example, except this time we'll perform an ANR search for Jim Smith:

```
***Searching . . .
ldap_search_ext_s(ld, "ou=Sales,DC=rallencorp,DC=com", 2, "(anr=Jim Smith)",
attrList,  0, svrCtrls, ClntCtrls, 20, 1000 ,&msg)
Result <0>:
Matched DNs:
Stats:
        Call Time:          20 (ms)
        Entries Returned:         1
        Entries Visited:          2
        Used Filter:          ( |  (displayName=Jim Smith*) (givenName=Jim Smith*)
(legacyExchangeDN=Jim Smith)  (msDS-AdditionalSamAccountName=Jim Smith*)
(physicalDeliveryOfficeName=Jim Smith*)  (proxyAddresses=Jim Smith*) (name=Jim
Smith*)  (sAMAccountName=Jim Smith*)
(sn=Jim Smith*)  ( &  (givenName=Jim*)  (sn=Smith*) )  ( & (givenName=Smith*)
(sn=Jim*) ) )
        Used Indexes:       idx_givenName:10:N;idx_givenName:10:N;idx_sn:9:N;idx_
sAMAccountName:8:N;idx_name:7:N;idx_proxyAddresses:6:N;idx_
physicalDeliveryOfficeName:5:N;idx_msDS-AdditionalSamAccountName:4:N;idx_
legacyExchangeDN:3:N;idx_givenName:2:N;idx_displayName:1:N;
```

You can see from the second line that we used a very simple filter (anr=Jim Smith). If you look down a little farther at Used Filter:, you can see a better example of search-filter expansion. Like the objectCategory example earlier, ANR is a shorthand way to do something complex. A simple one-term search filter expands into a multiterm filter that searches across numerous attributes. (For more on the behavior of ANR, see Recipe 11.15.) The point of showing this is that the STATS control is very powerful and can be an invaluable tool when trying to troubleshoot or optimize LDAP queries.

See Also

Recipe 4.4 for using LDAP controls, Recipe 4.8 for searching for objects, Recipe 11.15 for more on ANR, and Recipe 16.9 for more on expensive and inefficient searches

16.11 Using Perfmon to Monitor AD

Problem

You want to use the Performance Monitor to examine the performance of Active Directory.

Solution

Using a graphical user interface

1. Open the Performance Monitor.
2. Click on System Monitor in the left pane.
3. Press Ctrl-I. This will bring up the page to add counters.
4. Under "Select counters from computer," enter the name of the domain controller you want to target.
5. Select the NTDS performance object.
6. Select the counters you want to monitor.
7. After you're done with your selections, click Close.

Discussion

There are several Performance Monitor counters that can be very valuable for monitoring and troubleshooting Active Directory. The NTDS performance object has counters for address book lookups; inbound and outbound replication; LDAP reads, writes, and searches; Kerberos authentication; and the Security Account Manager (SAM).

Here is a list of some of the most useful NTDS counters. We've also included their Performance Monitor explanation, which you can view by clicking on the Explain button in the Add Counters dialog box.

DRA Inbound Bytes Total/sec
    Shows the total number of bytes replicated in. It is the sum of the number of uncompressed bytes (never compressed) and the number of compressed bytes (after compression).

DRA Inbound Objects/sec

Shows the number of objects received from neighbors through inbound replication. A *neighbor* is a domain controller from which the local domain controller replicates locally.

DRA Inbound Values Total/sec

Shows the total number of object property values received from inbound replication partners. Each inbound object has one or more properties, and each property has zero or more values. A zero value indicates property removal.

DRA Outbound Bytes Total/sec

Shows the total number of bytes replicated out. It is the sum of the number of uncompressed bytes (never compressed) and the number of compressed bytes (after compression).

DRA Outbound Objects/sec

Shows the number of objects replicated out.

DRA Outbound Values Total/sec

Shows the number of object property values sent to outbound replication partners.

DRA Pending Replication Synchronizations

Shows the number of directory synchronizations that are queued for this server but not yet processed.

DS Client Binds/sec

Shows the number of *ntdsapi.dll* binds per second serviced by this DC.

DS Directory Reads/sec

Shows the number of directory reads per second.

DS Directory Searches/sec

Shows the number of directory searches per second.

DS Directory Writes/sec

Shows the number of directory writes per second.

KDC AS Requests

Shows the number of Authentication Server (AS) requests serviced by the Kerberos Key Distribution Center (KDC) per second. AS requests are used by client to obtain a ticket-granting ticket.

KDC TGS Requests

Shows the number of Ticket Granting Server (TGS) requests serviced by the KDC per second. TGS requests are used by the client to obtain a ticket to a resource.

Kerberos Authentications

Shows the number of times per second that clients use a ticket for this DC to authenticate to this DC.

LDAP Bind Time
> Shows the time, in milliseconds, taken for the last successful LDAP bind.

LDAP Client Sessions
> Shows the number of currently connected LDAP client sessions.

LDAP Searches
> Shows the percentage of directory searches coming from LDAP.

LDAP Searches/sec
> Shows the rate at which LDAP clients perform search operations.

LDAP Successful Binds
> Shows the percentage of LDAP bind attempts that are successful.

LDAP Successful Binds/sec
> Shows the number of LDAP binds per second.

LDAP Writes
> Shows the percentage of directory writes coming from LDAP.

LDAP Writes/sec
> Shows the rate at which LDAP clients perform write operations.

16.12 Using Perfmon Trace Logs to Monitor AD

Problem

You want to enable Perfmon Trace Logs to view system-level calls related to Active Directory.

Solution

1. Open the Performance Monitor.
2. In the left pane, expand Performance Logs and Alerts.
3. Right-click on Trace Logs and select New Log Settings.
4. Enter a name for the log and click OK.
5. Click the Add button.
6. Highlight one or more of the Active Directory providers and click OK.
7. Use the tabs to configure additional settings about the log.
8. When you are done, click OK.
9. Unless you've scheduled it to run at a different time, the trace log you created should show up in the right pane next to a green icon, which indicates that it is running.
10. To stop the Trace Log, right-click on it in the right pane and select Stop.
11. Now open up a command prompt (*cmd.exe*).

12. Use cd to change into the directory where the trace logfiles are stored (*c:\perflogs* by default).

13. Run the following command:

```
> tracerpt <LogFileName>
```

This command is available by default with Windows Server 2003. On Windows 2000, you'll need to use the Resource Kit utility called *tracedmp.exe* with the same syntax.

The *tracerpt/tracedmp* commands generate a *summary.txt* file that summarizes all of the events by total. A second file called *dumpfile.csv* is created that can be imported into Excel or viewed with a text viewer to show the details of each event.

Discussion

Trace Logs capture detailed system and application level events. Applications support Trace Log capability by developing a Trace Log Provider. Active Directory supports several providers that log low-level system calls related to Kerberos, LDAP, and DNS, to name a few. This can be an extremely valuable tool for debugging or just exploring the inner workings of Active Directory. Trace Logs can be resource intensive, so you should enable them with care.

Here is an example of what the *summary.txt* file looks like on a domain controller that had all of the Active Directory–related Trace Log Providers enabled:

```
Files Processed:
        AD_000001.etl
Total Buffers Processed 5
Total Events  Processed 193
Total Events  Lost      0
Start Time              Friday, May 23, 2003
End Time                Friday, May 23, 2003
Elapsed Time            24 sec
+---------------------------------------------------------------------------+
|Event Count Event Name          Event Type  Guid                          |
+---------------------------------------------------------------------------+
|   1        EventTrace          Header      {68fdd900-4a3e-11d1-84f4-0000f80464e3}|
|  69        SamNameById         Start       {25059476-899f-11d2-819e-0000f875a064}|
|  69        SamNameById         End         {25059476-899f-11d2-819e-0000f875a064}|
|   2        KerbInitSecurityContext End     {52e82f1a-7cd4-47ed-b5e5-fde7bf64cea6}|
|   2        KerbInitSecurityContext Start   {52e82f1a-7cd4-47ed-b5e5-fdc7bf64cea6}|
|   1        KerbAcceptSecurityContext Start {94acefe3-9e56-49e3-9895-7240a231c371}|
|   1        KerbAcceptSecurityContext End   {94acefe3-9e56-49e3-9895-7240a231c371}|
|   1        SamGetAliasMem      Start       {1cf5fd19-1ac1-4324-84f7-970a634a91ee}|
|   1        SamGetAliasMem      End         {1cf5fd19-1ac1-4324-84f7-970a634a91ee}|
|  14        LdapRequest         End         {b9d4702a-6a98-11d2-b710-00c04fb998a2}|
|  14        LdapRequest         Start       {b9d4702a-6a98-11d2-b710-00c04fb998a2}|
|   1        DsLdapBind          Start       {05acd009-daeb-11d1-be80-00c04fadfff5}|
|   1        DsLdapBind          End         {05acd009-daeb-11d1-be80-00c04fadfff5}|
|   8        DsDirSearch         End         {05acd000-daeb-11d1-be80-00c04fadfff5}|
|   8        DsDirSearch         Start       {05acd000-daeb-11d1-be80-00c04fadfff5}|
+---------------------------------------------------------------------------+
```

Here you can see that over a 24-second period, there was 1 LDAP bind request (DsLdapBind), 8 directory searches (DsDirSearch), and 14 total LDAP requests (LdapRequest).

The *dumpfile.csv* contains entries for every event that was generated during the time period. Here is an example of an entry for one of the DsDirSearch requests (note that the lines will wrap due to their length so we've added a blank line in between for separation):

```
DsDirSearch, Start, 0x000003F4, 126982224636242128, 61350, 440530, "DS", 3, 3,
1141178432, 2694848000, "192.168.5.26", "deep", "OU=Sales,DC=rallencorp,DC=com", "0,
0

DsDirSearch, End, 0x000003F4, 126982224636342271, 61350, 440540, "DS", 3, 5,
1157955648, 2694848000, "0", "
(&(objectCategory=CN=Person,CN=Schema,CN=Configuration,DC=rallencorp,DC=com)
(objectClass=user)) 0, 0
```

Based on just those two lines (disregarding most of the numeric values), we can deduce that a user on the host with IP address 192.168.5.26 performed an LDAP query for user objects in the Sales OU. Pretty neat, huh?

See Also

MS KB 302552 (How to Create and Configure Performance Monitor Trace Logs in Windows 2000)

16.13 Creating an Administrative Alert

Problem

You want to define a threshold for a performance counter that should cause an alert to be generated.

Solution

1. Open the Performance Monitor.
2. In the left pane, expand "Performance Logs and Alerts."
3. Right-click on Alerts and select New Alert Settings.
4. Enter a name for the alert and click OK.
5. On the General tab, enter a description for the alert in the Comment field.
6. Click the Add button.
7. Highlight one or more of the Active Directory providers and click OK.
8. For each counter, for "Alert when the value is...," specify Under or Over. For Limit, specify the threshold value that should trigger the alert.

9. For "Sample data every," specify how often the performance counter should be updated.

10. On the Schedule tab, specify the time that the scan should begin and end.

11. On the Action tab, specify the action that the OS should take when the alert is generated. You can choose from one or more of the following:

    - Log an entry in the application event log.
    - Send a network message.
    - Start a performance data log.
    - Run an external program.

12. Click OK.

Discussion

There are any number of options for monitoring the ongoing performance of the Windows operating system, whether the machine in question is a domain controller, member server, or workstation. For larger environments, you can look into add-on tools like the Microsoft Operations Manager (MOM) or third-party utilities from NetPro, NetIQ, and others. For a built-in solution, however, the Performance MMC snap-in can monitor performance metrics and send various administrative alerts.

See Also

Recipe 16.14 for configuring an alert to email an operator or administrator, MS KB 243625 (How to Configure Administrative Alerts in Windows 2000), and MS KB 248345 (How to Create a Log Using System Monitor in Windows)

16.14 Emailing an Administrator on a Performance Alert

Problem

You want to create an alert that will notify an administrator via email if a performance alert is generated.

Solution

Using VBScript

```
' This code will send a simple email message
' from a computer that is running its own SMTP server

'------------Script Configuration--------------------
strSubject = "Low hard disk space on server dc1."
strFromLine = "admin@rallencorp.com"
```

```
strToLine = "oncall@rallencorp.com"
strText = "Available disk space on the C:\ drive of dc1." & _
   "rallencorp.com has gone below 100MB."
'-------------------------------------------------------

Set objMessage = CreateObject("CDO.Message")
objMessage.Subject = strSubject
objMessage.From = strFromLine
objMessage.To = strToLine
objMessage.TextBody = strText
objMessage.Send
```

Discussion

A common request among Windows system administrators is to have the ability to
email an on-call administrator when a critical performance alert is generated—for
example, when a domain controller is experiencing a critical hardware failure. It is a
relatively simple matter to send email through VBScript using Collaborative Data
Objects (CDO), which are built into Windows XP and Windows Server 2003. You
can either hardcode the appropriate alert messages into the VBScript code and maintain multiple scripts for the various alerts that you create, or you can generate command-line arguments within the Performance Alert and use those alerts to customize
the output of a single, more generic script. Using the Performance MMC, you can
submit one or more of the following as command-line arguments to a script that's
been fired in response to an alert:

- Date/time
- The value that was measured by the alert
- The name of the alert
- The name of the counter being measured
- The value of the limit that was exceeded
- A manually defined text string

You can also use a number of third-party tools to implement this solution, such as
the open source Blat (*http://www.blat.net*) SourceForge project, which allows you to
send SMTP or NNTP messages from a command line.

Using VBScript

The script example in this recipe assumes that the computer that's running the
script is itself running the SMTP service. To send a message using a remote SMTP
server, you'll need to specify the following additional information before sending
the message:

```
objMessage.Configuration.Fields.Item _
("http://schemas.microsoft.com/cdo/configuration/sendusing") = 2

'Name or IP of the remote SMTP Server
```

```
objMessage.Configuration.Fields.Item _
("http://schemas.microsoft.com/cdo/configuration/smtpserver") = "smtp.myserver.com"

'Port being used by the SMTP server (port 25 by default)
objMessage.Configuration.Fields.Item _
("http://schemas.microsoft.com/cdo/configuration/smtpserverport") = 25

objMessage.Configuration.Fields.Update
```

See Also

MS KB 280391 (How to Send Digitally Signed Messages by Using CDOSYS/ CDOEX) and MS KB 248698 (How to Send Mail from an Active Server Page by Using CDOEX with Exchange 2000 Server or Exchange Server 2003)

16.15 Enabling Auditing of Directory Access

Problem

You want to enable auditing of directory access and modifications. Audit events are logged to the Security event log.

Solution

Using a graphical user interface

1. Open the Domain Controller Security Policy snap-in.
2. In the left pane, expand Local Policies and click on Audit Policy.
3. In the right pane, double-click "Audit directory service access."
4. Make sure the box is checked beside "Define these policy settings."
5. Check the box beside Success and/or Failure.
6. Click OK.

Using a command-line interface

```
> auditpol \\<DomainControlerName> /enable /directory:all
```

Discussion

You can log events to the Security event log for every successful and/or failed attempt to access or modify the directory, which is referred to as *auditing*. Auditing is enabled via the Security Settings section of a GPO that's linked to the Domain Controllers OU, using the "Audit directory service access" setting. Once this is enabled, you need to use the ACL Editor to define auditing in the SACL of the objects and containers you want to monitor.

By default, the domain object has an inherited audit entry for the *Everyone* security principal for all object access and modifications. That means once you enable auditing in the Domain Controller Security Policy and this configuration change replicates out, domain controllers will log events for any directory access or modification to any part of the directory. As you can imagine, auditing every access to Active Directory can generate a lot of events, so you'll either want to disable auditing of the *Everyone* group and apply more specific auditing instead, or else keep a close eye on your domain controllers to ensure that they are not adversely affected while auditing is enabled.

Here is a sample event that was logged after the *Administrator* account created a contact object called foobar in the Sales OU:

```
Event Type:        Success Audit
Event Source:      Security
Event Category:      Directory Service Access
Event ID:     566
Date:              5/26/2003
Time:              7:24:10 PM
User:              RALLENCORP\administrator
Computer:     DC1
Description:
Object Operation:
        Object Server:      DS
        Operation Type:     Object Access
        Object Type:        organizationalUnit
        Object Name:        OU=Sales,DC=rallencorp,DC=com
        Handle ID:          -
        Primary User Name:      DC1$
        Primary Domain:      RALLENCORP
        Primary Logon ID:      (0x0,0x3E7)
        Client User Name:       administrator
        Client Domain:      RALLENCORP
        Client Logon ID:       (0x0,0x3B4BE)
        Accesses:       Create Child

        Properties:
        Create Child
        contact

        Additional Info:      CN=foobar,OU=Sales,DC=rallencorp,DC=com
        Additional Info2:      CN=foobar,OU=Sales,DC=rallencorp,DC=com
        Access Mask:       0x1
```

 It can also be useful to enable Audit Account Management in the GPO that's linked to the Domain Controllers OU. This provides additional information about account-management operations—for example, finding what account deleted a certain object.

See Also

MS KB 232714 (How to Enable Auditing of Directory Service Access), MS KB 314955 (How to Audit Active Directory Objects in Windows 2000), MS KB 314977 (How to Enable Active Directory Access Auditing in Windows 2000), and MS KB 814595 (How to Audit Active Directory Objects in Windows Server 2003)

16.16 Enabling Auditing of Registry Keys

Problem

You want to enable auditing of any changes to one or more Registry keys.

Using a graphical user interface

To enable auditing of a Registry key on an individual domain controller, do the following:

1. Create a Group Policy Object (or enable an existing GPO) that enables the following settings under Computer Configuration → Window Settings → Security Settings → Local Policies → Audit Policy:

   - Audit object access: Success

   - Audit object access: Failure

2. Link the GPO to the container containing the DC you wish to audit.

3. On the DC you want to audit, open *regedit.exe* from the command line or from Start → Run.

4. Navigate to the Registry key that you want to enable auditing on.

5. Right-click on the key and select Permissions. Click Advanced and select the Auditing tab.

6. Click Add to select a user or group to audit, then click OK. For Apply Onto, select "This key only," "This key and subkeys," or "Subkeys only."

7. Under Access, select the actions that should be audited, and click OK.

If you need to enable auditing of the same Registry keys on multiple computers, a much more efficient solution would be to use a GPO as follows:

1. Create a Group Policy Object (or modifying an existing GPO) that enables the following settings under Computer Configuration → Window Settings → Security Settings → Local Policies → Audit Policy:

   - Audit object access: Success

   - Audit object access: Failure

2. Navigate to Computer Configuration → Windows Settings → Security Settings → Registry.

3. Right-click on Registry and select "Add key." On the "Select Registry key" screen, navigate to the key that you want to audit and click OK.

4. Right-click on the key and select Permissions. Click Advanced and select the Auditing tab.

5. Click Add to select a user or group to audit, then click OK. For Apply Onto, select "This key only," "This key and subkeys," or "Subkeys only."

6. Under Access, select the actions that should be audited, and click OK.

7. Link the GPO to the container containing the DC you wish to audit.

Discussion

Before you can enable auditing on specific Registry keys, you must create an audit policy that enables auditing of object access events, both Success and Failure events. You can enable auditing by modifying an existing Group Policy Object or by creating a brand-new GPO that you've created expressly for this purpose. Maintaining a number of single-purpose GPOs can make for easier Group Policy troubleshooting, but can lead to performance implications if clients need to process too many GPOs at logon and during the background refresh of Group Policy. As is usually the case, the definition of "too many" will vary from one environment to the next; it's important to monitor the performance of your clients to determine which approach is appropriate for your network. Once you've enabled auditing of a specific key or keys, information about the activity that you've chosen to audit will appear in the Security event log of the computer where the event took place.

See Also

Recipe 10.6 for more on modifying the settings of a Group Policy Object, MS KB 810088 (CPU Usage May Be High After You Turn On Auditing for HKEY_LOCAL_MACHINE\System), and MS KB 841001 (Event IDs 560 and 562 appear many times in the security event log)

16.17 Creating a Quota

 This recipe requires a Windows Server 2003 domain controller.

Problem

You want to limit the number of objects a security principal can create in a partition by creating a quota.

Solution

Using a command-line interface

```
> dsadd quota -part <PartitionDN> -qlimit <QuotaLimit> -acct <PrincipalName>
  [-rdn <QuotaName>]
```

The following command creates a quota specification that allows the *RALLEN-CORP\rallen* user to create only five objects in the dc-rallencorp,dc=com partition:

```
> dsadd quota -part dc=rallencorp,dc=com -qlimit 5 -acct RALLENCORP\rallen
```

Discussion

Quotas are a new feature in Windows Server 2003 that allows an administrator to limit the number of objects that a user (or group of users) can create. This is similar in nature to the quota for creating computer objects found in Windows 2000 (see Recipe 8.12 for more details), except that the quotas in Windows Server 2003 apply to the creation of all object types.

There are three things that need to be set when creating a quota specification, including:

Partition
> Currently, quotas can apply only to an entire partition. You cannot create a quota that pertains only to a subtree in a partition. You can create quotas for any partition, including application partitions, except for the schema naming context. The reasoning behind this restriction is that the schema is a highly protected area of the directory, and you shouldn't need to restrict how many objects get created there.

Target security principal
> A quota can be defined for any type of security principal. The msDS-QuotaTrustee attribute on the quota object stores the target principal in the form of an SID.

Limit
> This determines how many objects the target security principal can create.

The quota limit is a combination of the new objects that a user creates plus any tombstone objects that are created by that user. If a user creates an object and then deletes another object, that would count as two objects toward any quotas that apply to the user. This is because when an object is deleted, a tombstone object is created in its place, which counts as another object creation. If a user creates an object and later deletes the same object, this would count as only one object against their quota. Once the tombstone object is removed from Active Directory, which happens after 60 days by default (or 180 in an AD forest created from scratch on a 2003 Service Pack 1 server), the user's quota will be decremented accordingly. By default, a tombstone object counts as one object, but that is configurable. See Recipe 16.19 for more on changing the tombstone quota factor.

Since quotas can be assigned to both users and groups, it is conceivable that multiple quotas may apply to a user. In this case, the quota with the highest limit will be in force for the user. You can also create a default quota for a partition that applies to all security principals. See Recipe 16.20 for more information on configuring the default quota.

 Quotas do not apply to members of the *Enterprise Admins* and *Domain Admins* groups. Even if you've configured a default quota for all users, members of those administrative groups will not have any restrictions.

See Also

Recipe 8.12 for more on the computer object quota, the "Introduction" to this chapter for more on the attributes of quota objects, Recipe 16.18 for finding the quotas assigned to a security principal, Recipe 16.19 for changing the tombstone quota factor, and Recipe 16.20 for setting a default quota

16.18 Finding the Quotas Assigned to a Security Principal

 This recipe requires a Windows Server 2003 domain controller.

Problem

You want to find the quotas that have been configured for a security principal (i.e., user, group, or computer).

Solution

Using a command-line interface

```
> dsquery quota <PartitionDN> -acct <PrincipalName>
```

The following command searches for quotas that have been assigned to the *RALLEN-CORP\rallen* user in the dc=rallencorp,dc=com partition:

```
> dsquery quota dc=rallencorp,dc=com -acct RALLENCORP\rallen
```

Discussion

The DSQuery solution will find only quotas that have been directly assigned to a security principal; it will not list quotas that have been assigned to any group objects that the principal may be a member of. The msDS-QuotaTrustee attribute on quota objects defines a SID that the quota applies to. The dsquery quota command will look up the SID for the specified account and match that against quota objects that reference that SID. Unfortunately, this doesn't quite show the whole picture. A user could have a quota assigned directly, which the DSQuery command would show, but the user could also be part of one or more groups that have quotas assigned. These won't show up using DSQuery.

A more robust solution would entail retrieving the tokenGroups attribute of the user, which contains a list of SIDs for all expanded group memberships, and then querying each of those groups to determine whether any of them have quotas assigned. This is actually the type of algorithm that is used to determine a user's effective quota, as shown in Recipe 16.21.

See Also

Recipe 16.17 for creating a quota and Recipe 16.21

16.19 Changing How Tombstone Objects Count Against Quota Usage

 This recipe requires a Windows Server 2003 domain controller.

Problem

You want to change the relative weight of tombstone objects in quota calculations.

Solution

Using a graphical user interface

1. Open ADSI Edit.
2. Connect to the partition on which you want to modify this setting (this setting must be changed for each partition that you want to configure).
3. In the left pane, expand the root of the partition.
4. Right-click on cn=NTDS Quotas and select Properties.
5. Set the msDS-TombstoneQuotaFactor attribute to a value between 0 and 100.
6. Click OK.

Using a command-line interface

Create an LDIF file called *change_tombstone_quota.ldf* with the following contents:

```
dn: cn=NTDS Quotas,<PartitionDN>
changetype: modify
replace: msDs-TombstoneQuotaFactor
msDs-TombstoneQuotaFactor: <0-100>
-
```

Then run the following command:

```
> ldifde -v -i -f change_tombstone_quota.ldf
```

You can also make the change using DSMod or AdMod. DSMod takes the following syntax:

```
> dsmod partition <PartitionDN> -qtmbstawt <0-100>
```

You can make the change with AdMod, as follows:

```
> admod -b <PartitionDN> msDs-TombstoneQuotaFactor::<0-100>
```

Using VBScript

```
' This code modifies the tombstone quota factor for the specified partition.
' ------ SCRIPT CONFIGURATION ------
strPartitionDN = "<PartitionDN>"   ' e.g. dc=rallencorp,dc=com
intTombstoneFactor = <0-100>       ' e.g. 50
' ------ END CONFIGURATION ---------

set objPart = GetObject("LDAP://cn=NTDS Quotas," & strPartitionDN )
objPart.Put "msDs-TombstoneQuotaFactor", intTombstoneLifetime
objPart.SetInfo
WScript.Echo "Set the tombstone quota factor for " & _
             strPartitionDN & " to " & intTombstoneFactor
```

Discussion

The tombstone quota factor is a percentage that determines how much each tombstone object counts against a security principal's quota usage. By default, tombstone objects count as one object. This means if a user's quota is set to 10 and the user deletes 10 objects, that user will not be able to create or delete any other objects until those tombstone objects have been purged from Active Directory.

The msDs-TombstoneQuotaFactor attribute on the NTDS Quota container for each partition defines the tombstone quota factor. As mentioned previously, the default is that tombstone objects count 100 percent of a normal object; thus, the msDs-TombstoneQuotaFactor attribute contains 100 by default. If you modify this attribute to contain a value of 50 and a user has a quota limit of 10, then that user could delete a maximum of 20 objects (i.e., create 20 tombstone objects) because 20×50 percent = 10. As another example, you may not care about how many objects your users delete; in this case, you'd want to set the tombstone quota factor to 0 so that tombstoned objects would not count against a user's NTDS Quota at all.

See Also

MSDN: ms-DS-Tombstone-Quota-Factor attribute [AD Schema] and MSDN: ms-DS-Quota-Container class [AD Schema]

16.20 Setting the Default Quota for All Security Principals in a Partition

 This recipe requires a Windows Server 2003 domain controller.

Problem

You want to set a default quota for all security principals.

Solution

Using a graphical user interface

1. Open ADSI Edit.
2. Connect to the partition you want to modify (this setting must be changed for each partition that you want to configure).
3. In the left pane, expand the root of the partition.
4. Right-click on cn=NTDS Quotas and select Properties.
5. Set the msDS-DefaultQuota attribute to the number of objects that security principals should be allowed to create if they are not assigned another quota.
6. Click OK.

Using a command-line interface

Create an LDIF file called *set_default_quota.ldf* with the following contents:

```
dn: cn=NTDS Quotas,<NTDS Quotas DN>
changetype: modify
replace: msDs-DefaultQuota
msDs-DefaultQuota: <NumberOfObjects>
-
```

Then run the following command:

```
> ldifde -v -i -f set_default_quota.ldf
```

You can also make the change using DSMod or AdMod. DSMod takes the following syntax:

```
> dsmod partition <NTDS Quotas DN> -qdefault <DefaultQuota>
```

You can make the change with AdMod, as follows:

```
> admod -b <NTDS Quotas DN> msDs-DefaultQuota::<DefaultQuota>
```

Using VBScript

```
' This code sets the default quota for the specified partition.
' ------ SCRIPT CONFIGURATION ------
strPartitionDN = "<PartitionDN>"        ' e.g. dc=rallencorp,dc=com
intDefaultQuota = <NumberOfObjects>     ' e.g. 10
' ------ END CONFIGURATION ---------

set objPart = GetObject("LDAP://cn=NTDS Quotas," & strPartitionDN )
objPart.Put "msDs-DefaultQuota", intDefaultQuota
objPart.SetInfo
WScript.Echo "Set the default quota for " & _
             strPartitionDN & " to " & intDefaultQuota
```

Discussion

The easiest way to apply a default quota to all of your users is to modify the msDS-DefaultQuota attribute on the NTDS Quotas container for the target partition. This attribute contains the default quota limit that is used if no other quotas have been assigned to a security principal. A value of -1 means that no quota exists; security principals can create and/or tombstone as many objects as they wish.

You should be careful when setting the default quota because it applies to every non-administrator security principal. If you set the default to 0, for example, computers would not be able to dynamically update their DNS records in an AD-integrated zone because that creates an object. This may not be applicable in your environment, but the point is that you need to consider the impact of the default quota and test it thoroughly before implementing it.

16.21 Finding the Quota Usage for a Security Principal

 This recipe requires a Windows Server 2003 domain controller.

Problem

You want to find the quota usage for a certain security principal.

Solution

The quota usage of a security principal can be determined a few different ways. First, you can use DSGet. Here is an example:

```
> dsget user "<UserDN>" -part <PartitionDN> -qlimit -qused
```

This displays the effective quota limit and how much of the quota has been used for a particular user. You can use similar parameters with dsget computer and dsget group to find the quota usage for those types of objects.

Users can find their own quota usage by querying the msDs-QuotaUsed and msDs-QuotaEffective attributes on the cn=NTDS Quotas container for a partition. These two attributes are constructed, which means they are dynamically calculated based on the user that is accessing them (see Recipe 11.17 for more on constructed attributes). The msDs-QuotaUsed attribute returns how much of the quota has been used by the user, and the msDs-QuotaEffective attribute contains the quota limit.

Alternatively, view the msDs-TopQuotaUsage attribute on a partition's cn=NTDS Quotas container, which contains the users with the top quota usage. This attribute is multivalued, with each value being XML-like text that contains the SID and how much of the quota the principal has used. See the "Discussion" section for an example.

Discussion

If you implement quotas, you'll certainly need to tell users what their quotas are (or provide instructions on how they can find out for themselves). Currently, there are a few ways to determine quota usage, as outlined in the Solution section.

Perhaps the most interesting is obtaining the top-quota usage. Each value of the msDs-TopQuotaUsage attribute contains an entry that details the top quota users in the database, listed in decreasing order of quota usage. Each value of the msDs-TopQuotaUsage attribute contains blocks of data formatted in an XML-like language. Each block has the SID of the security principal (<ownerSID>), quota used (<quotaUsed>), number of tombstone objects created (<tombstonedCount>), and the number of objects that are still active (<liveCount>) (i.e., not tombstoned). Here is an example of what the attribute can contain:

```
>> Dn: CN=NTDS Quotas,DC=rallencorp,DC=com
        3> msDS-TopQuotaUsage:
<MS_DS_TOP_QUOTA_USAGE>
        <partitionDN> DC=rallencorp,DC=com </partitionDN>
        <ownerSID> S-1-5-21-1422208173-2062366415-1864960452-512 </ownerSID>
        <quotaUsed> 152 </quotaUsed>
        <tombstonedCount> 2 </tombstonedCount>
        <liveCount> 150 </liveCount>
</MS_DS_TOP_QUOTA_USAGE>
;
<MS_DS_TOP_QUOTA_USAGE>
        <partitionDN> DC=rallencorp,DC=com </partitionDN>
        <ownerSID> S-1-5-18 </ownerSID>
        <quotaUsed> 43 </quotaUsed>
        <tombstonedCount> 32 </tombstonedCount>
        <liveCount> 11 </liveCount>
</MS_DS_TOP_QUOTA_USAGE>
;
```

```
<MS_DS_TOP_QUOTA_USAGE>
        <partitionDN> DC=rallencorp,DC=com </partitionDN>
        <ownerSID> S-1-5-32-544 </ownerSID>
        <quotaUsed> 14 </quotaUsed>
        <tombstonedCount> O </tombstonedCount>
        <liveCount> 14 </liveCount>
</MS_DS_TOP_QUOTA_USAGE>
```

See Also

Recipe 16.18 for more on finding the quotas that are assigned to a security principal

## CHAPTER 17

Backup, Recovery, DIT Maintenance, and Deleted Objects

17.0 Introduction

The AD Directory Information Tree (DIT) is implemented as a transactional database using the Extensible Storage Engine (ESE). The primary database file is named *ntds.dit* and is stored in the *%SystemRoot%\NTDS* folder by default, but can be relocated during the initial promotion process or manually via *ntdsutil* (see Recipe 17.8 for more details).

Each database write transaction is initially stored in a logfile called *edb.log*, which is stored in the same directory as *ntds.dit* by default, though you can modify this either during or after the initial dcpromo process. That logfile can grow to 10 MB in size, after which additional logfiles are created (e.g., *edb00001.log*), each of which can also grow to up to 10 MB in size. After the transactions in the logfiles are committed to the database, the logfiles are purged, beginning with the log containing the oldest transactions. (This process is referred to as *circular logging*.) These logfiles are useful when a domain controller is shut down unexpectedly because when the DC comes back online, Active Directory can replay the logfiles and apply any transactions that might not have been written to disk before the DC shut down. The *edb.chk* file stores information about the last transaction that was actually committed to the database; AD uses this information to determine which transactions in the logfiles still need to be committed. Finally, two 10 MB files called *res1.log* and *res2.log* are used as placeholders in case the disk runs out of space; if this happens, these files are deleted to free up enough space to allow Active Directory to commit any final changes before the DC is shut down.

In order to recover portions of Active Directory, or the entire directory itself, you need to have a solid backup strategy in place. You can back up Active Directory while it is online, which means you do not need to worry about scheduling regular downtime simply to perform backups. Restoring Active Directory is also a relatively simple process. To do any type of restore, you have to boot into offline mode, more commonly referred to as Directory Services (DS) Restore Mode, in which the Active

Directory database is not active. You can then restore a single object, an entire subtree, or the entire database if necessary. For a detailed discussion on backing up and restoring Active Directory, see Chapter 13 in *Active Directory*, Third Edition, by Joe Richards et al. (O'Reilly).

You also need to be familiar with how deleted objects are treated in Active Directory, which can affect your backup procedures. When an object is deleted, a copy of the object is stored in the Deleted Object container. This *tombstone object* has most of the original object's attribute values removed to save space in the *NTDS.DIT* file. These objects are stored in the `cn=Deleted Objects` container in the naming context that the original object was located in. The deleted object is named using the following format: `<OrigName>\0ADEL:<ObjectGUID>`, where `<OrigName>` is the original RDN of the object, `<ObjectGUID>` is the GUID of the original object, and `\0A` is a null-terminated character. For example, if you deleted the `jsmith` user object, its tombstone object would have a distinguished name similar to the following:

```
CN=jsmith\0ADEL:fce1ca8e-a5ec-4a29-96e1-c8013e533d2c,CN=Deleted
Objects,DC=rallencorp,DC=com
```

After a period of time known as the *tombstone lifetime* (60 days is the default for pre-SP1 Windows Server 2003 forests), the tombstone object is finally removed from Active Directory. At that point, no remnants of the former object exist in Active Directory.

 The default tombstone lifetime changed with Windows Server 2003 Service Pack 1. A 2003 forest that has been upgraded to SP1 will retain the original 60-day tombstone lifetime; however, a forest created from scratch with SP1 integrated will have a tombstone lifetime of 180 days.

Tombstone objects are important to understand with regard to your backup strategy because you should not keep backups longer than the tombstone lifetime. If you attempt to restore a backup that is older than the tombstone lifetime, it may introduce objects that were deleted, but for which a tombstone object no longer exists. Under normal conditions, if you do a nonauthoritative restore from backup, objects that were valid when the backup was taken but that were subsequently deleted will not be readded as a part of the restore process. A check is done before injecting new objects via the nonauthoritative restore to determine if a tombstone object exists for it. If a tombstone object exists for it, Active Directory knows that the object was deleted after the backup and will not restore it. If the tombstone object has already expired (e.g., the backup is older than 60 days), Active Directory has no way to determine if the object was previously deleted and will happily readd it. Reinjected deleted objects are referred to as *lingering* or *zombie objects*.

The tombstone lifetime value is stored in the `tombStoneLifetime` attribute on the following object: `cn=Directory Service,cn=Windows NT,cn=Services,cn=Configuration,` `<ForestRootDN>`.

The Anatomy of a Deleted Object

Deleted objects are stored in the `Deleted Objects` container of a naming context. You cannot browse that container by default. You need to enable an LDAP control, as explained in Recipe 17.18, to view deleted objects. Table 17-1 contains some of the attributes that are stored with deleted objects.

 The attributes that are preserved in tombstone objects are determined by `attributeSchema` objects that have bit 3 enabled (8 in decimal) in the `searchFlags` attribute.

Table 17-1. Useful attributes of deleted objects

Attribute	Description
isDeleted	The value for this attribute is TRUE for deleted objects.
lastKnownParent	Distinguished name of container the object was contained in. This is new in Windows Server 2003.
Name	RDN of the object's current location.
userAccountControl	This attribute is retained when the original object is deleted. This applies only to user and computer objects.
objectSID	This attribute is copied from the original object after it is deleted. This applies only to user and computer objects.
sAMAccountName	This attribute is copied from the original object after it is deleted. This applies only to user and computer objects.
sidHistory	Beginning with Windows Server 2003 Service Pack 1, the sidHistory attribute is now included in this list of attributes that are retained with tombstoned objects.

17.1   Backing Up Active Directory

Problem

You want to back up Active Directory to tape or disk.

Solution

Back up the System State, which includes, among other things, the Active Directory–related files on the domain controller. Here are the directions for backing up the System State using the NtBackup utility that comes installed on Windows 2000 and Windows Server 2003 computers.

Using a graphical user interface

1. Go to Start → All Programs (or Programs for Windows 2000) → Accessories → System Tools → Backup.
2. Click the Advanced Mode link.

3. Click the Backup tab.

4. Check the box beside System State.

5. Check the box beside any other files, directories, or drives you would also like to back up.

6. For "Backup destination," select either File or Tape, depending on where you want to back up the data to.

7. For "Backup media or file name," type either the name of a file or select the tape to save the backup to.

8. Click the Start Backup button twice.

Using a command-line interface

The NtBackup utility supports several command-line parameters that you can use to initiate backups without ever bringing up the GUI.

For the complete list of supported commands on Windows 2000, see MS KB 300439 (How to Use Command Line Parameters With the "Ntbackup" Command).

For the complete list of supported commands on Windows Server 2003, see MS KB 814583 (How to Use Command Line Parameters with the Ntbackup Command in Windows Server 2003).

Discussion

Fortunately, domain controllers can be backed up while online. Having the ability to perform online backups makes the process very easy. And since Active Directory is included as part of the System State on domain controllers, you are required to back up only the System State, although you can back up other folders and drives as necessary. (As a best practice, it is also a good idea to back up the system drive as well.) On a domain controller, the System State includes the following:

- Boot files
- Registry
- COM+ class registration database
- Active Directory files
- System Volume (SYSVOL)
- Certificates database (if running Certificate Server)

See Also

Recipe 17.21 for modifying the tombstone lifetime, MS KB 216993 (Backup of the Active Directory Has 60-Day Useful Life), MS KB 240363 (How to Use the Backup Program to Back Up and Restore the System State in Windows 2000), MS KB 300439 (How to Use Command Line Parameters With the "Ntbackup" Command),

MS KB 326216 (How to Use the Backup Feature to Back Up and Restore Data in Windows Server 2003), and MS KB 814583 (How to Use Command Line Parameters with the Ntbackup Command in Windows Server 2003)

17.2   Restarting a Domain Controller in Directory Services Restore Mode

Problem

You want to restart a domain controller in DS Restore Mode.

Solution

To enter DS Restore Mode, you must reboot the server at the console. Press F8 after the power-on self test (POST), which will bring up a menu, as shown in Figure 17-1. From the menu, select Directory Services Restore Mode.

```
Windows Advanced Options Menu
Please select an option:

    Safe Mode
    Safe Mode with Networking
    Safe Mode with Command Prompt

    Enable Boot Logging
    Enable VGA Mode
    Last Known Good Configuration (your most recent settings that worked)
    Directory Services Restore Mode (Windows domain controllers only)
    Debugging Mode

    Start Windows Normally
    Reboot
    Return to OS Choices Menu

Use the up and down arrow keys to move the highlight to your choice.
```

Figure 17-1. Boot options

Discussion

The Active Directory database is live and locked by the system whenever a domain controller is booted into normal mode. If you want to perform integrity checks, restore part of the database or otherwise manipulate the Active Directory database in some way, you have to reboot into DS Restore Mode. In this mode, Active Directory does not start up and the database files (e.g., *ntds.dit*) are not locked.

It is not always practical to be logged into the console of the server when you need to reboot it into DS Restore Mode. You can work around this by modifying the *boot.ini* file for the server to automatically boot into DS Restore Mode after reboot. You can then use Terminal Services to log on to the machine remotely while it is in that mode. See MS KB 256588 for more information on how to enable this capability. Be careful if you try to access DS Restore Mode via Terminal Services. Unless you have configured everything properly, you may end up with the domain controller booted into DS Restore Mode and not be able to access it via Terminal Services.

See Also

MS KB 256588 (Using Terminal Services for Remote Administration of Windows 2000 DCs in Directory Service Restore Mode)

17.3 Resetting the Directory Service Restore Mode Administrator Password

Problem

You want to reset the DS Restore Mode administrator password. This password is set individually (i.e., not replicated) on each domain controller and is initially configured when you promote the domain controller into a domain.

Solution

Using a graphical user interface

For this to work you must be booted into DS Restore Mode (see Recipe 17.2 for more information).

1. Go to Start → Run.
2. Type compmgmt.msc and press Enter.
3. In the left pane, expand System Tools → Local Users and Computers.
4. Click on the Users folder.
5. In the right pane, right-click on the Administrator user and select Set Password.
6. Enter the new password and confirm, then click OK.

Using a command-line interface

With the Windows Server 2003 version of *ntdsutil*, you can change the DS Restore Mode administrator password of a domain controller while it is live (i.e., not in DS Restore Mode). Another benefit of this new option is that you can run it against a remote domain controller. Here is the sample output when run against domain controller DC1:

```
> ntdsutil "set dsrm password" "reset password on server DC1"
ntdsutil: set dsrm password
Reset DSRM Administrator Password: reset password on server DC1
Please type password for DS Restore Mode Administrator Account: **********
Please confirm new password: **********
Password has been set successfully.
```

Microsoft added a new utility called *setpwd* in Windows 2000 Service Pack 2 and later. It works similarly to the Windows Server 2003 version of *ntdsutil* by allowing you to reset the DS Restore Mode password while a domain controller is live. It can also be used remotely.

Discussion

You may be thinking that having a separate DS Restore Mode administrator password can be quite a pain. Yet another thing you have to maintain and update on a regular basis, right? But if you think about it, you'll see that it is quite necessary.

Generally, you boot a domain controller into DS Restore Mode when you need to perform some type of maintenance on the Active Directory database. To do this, the database needs to be offline. But if the database is offline, then there is no way to authenticate against it. Because of this, the system has to use another user repository, so it reverts back to the legacy SAM database. The DS Restore Mode administrator account and password are stored in the SAM database, just as with standalone Windows servers.

The one disadvantage to the solutions presented in this recipe is that you have to reset the DSRM password on one machine at a time. To help automate this process, Directory Services MVP Dean Wells of MSE Technology (*http://www.msetechnology.com*) has created a batch script that will change the password on every DC in a forest. The script requires the Windows 2000 *setpwd* utility to be present in the system path on each DC that it's being run on, and can be found here: *http://www.mail-archive.com/activedir@mail.activedir.org/msg29990.html*.

See Also

Recipe 17.2 for booting into Directory Services Restore Mode, MS KB 239803 (How to Change the Recovery Console Administrator Password on a Domain Controller), and MS KB 322672 (How to Reset the Directory Services Restore Mode Administrator Account Password in Windows Server 2003)

17.4 Performing a Nonauthoritative Restore

Problem

You want to perform a nonauthoritative restore of a domain controller. This can be useful if you want to quickly restore a domain controller that failed due to a hardware problem.

Solution

Using a graphical user interface

1. You must first reboot into Directory Services Restore Mode (see Recipe 17.2 for more information).

2. Open the NT Backup utility; go to Start → All Programs (or "Programs for Windows 2000") → Accessories → System Tools → Backup.

3. Click the Advanced Mode link.

4. Under the Welcome tab, click the Restore Wizard button and click Next.

5. Check the box beside System State and any other drives you want to restore and click Next.

6. Click the Advanced button.

7. Select "Original location" for "Restore files to."

8. For the "How to Restore" option, select "Replace existing files" and click Next.

9. For the Advanced Restore Options, be sure that the following are checked: "Restore Security Settings," "Restore junction points," and "Preserve existing mount volume points." Then click Next.

10. Click Finish.

11. Restart the computer.

Discussion

If you encounter a failed domain controller that you cannot bring back up (e.g., multiple hard disks fail), you have two options for restoring it. One option is to remove the domain controller completely from Active Directory (as outlined in Recipe 3.7) and then repromote it back in. This is known as the *restore from replication* method, because you are essentially bringing up a brand-new domain controller and letting replication restore all the data on the server. On Windows Server 2003 domain controllers, you can also use the Install From Media option described in Recipe 3.2 to expedite this process.

The other option is described in the Solution section. You can restore the domain controller from a good backup. This method involves getting into DS Restore Mode, restoring the System State and any necessary system drive(s), and then rebooting. As long as the domain controller comes up clean, it should start participating in Active Directory replication once again and replicate any changes that have occurred since the backup was taken. This method is generally the fastest for restoring a domain controller, particularly if the server is the only DC located in a remote site.

For a detailed discussion of the advantages and disadvantages of each option, see Chapter 13 in *Active Directory*, Third Edition, by Joe Richards et al. (O'Reilly).

See Also

Recipe 17.2 for getting into Directory Services Restore Mode, MS KB 240363 (How to Use the Backup Program to Back Up and Restore the System State in Windows 2000), and MS KB 811944 (Computer Does Not Start After You Use Windows Backup to Restore the System State)

17.5 Performing an Authoritative Restore of an Object or Subtree

Problem

You want to perform an authoritative restore of one or more objects, but not the entire Active Directory database.

Solution

Follow the same steps as Recipe 17.4, except that once the restore has completed, do not restart the computer.

To restore a single object, run the following:

```
> ntdsutil "auth restore" "restore object cn=jsmith,ou=Sales,dc=rallencorp,dc=com" q
```

To restore an entire subtree, run the following:

```
> ntdsutil "auth restore" "restore subtree ou=Sales,dc=rallencorp,dc=com" q
```

Restart the computer.

There are some issues related to restoring user, group, computer, and trust objects that you should be aware of. See MS KB 216243 and MS KB 280079 for more information.

Discussion

If an administrator or user accidentally deletes an important object or entire subtree from Active Directory, you can restore it. Fortunately, the process isn't very painful. The key is having a good backup that contains the objects you want to restore. If you don't have a backup with the objects in it, you are, for the most part, out of luck. (See Recipe 17.19 for another option to restore deleted objects in Windows Server 2003.)

To restore one or more objects, you need to follow the same steps as performing a nonauthoritative restore. The only difference is that after you do the restore, you need to use *ntdsutil* to mark the objects in question as authoritative on the restored domain controller. After you reboot the domain controller, it will then receive information from its replication partners and process updates for any objects that have been changed since the backup that was restored on the machine, except for the objects or subtree that were marked as authoritative. For those objects, Active Directory modifies the restored objects in such a way that they will become authoritative and replicate out to the other domain controllers.

 Performing an authoritative restore of user or group objects will require additional considerations, as detailed in MS KB 280079. (Authoritative restore of groups can result in inconsistent membership information across domain controllers.)

You can also use *ntdsutil* without first doing a restore in situations where an object has accidentally been deleted, but the change has not yet replicated to all domain controllers. The trick here is that you need to find a domain controller that has not had the deletion replicated yet, and either stop it from replicating or make the object authoritative before it sends its replication updates. Take a look at Recipe 13.5 for more information on controlling inbound and outbound replication on a domain controller.

See Also

Recipe 17.2 for booting into Directory Services Restore Mode, Recipe 17.19 for restoring a deleted object, MS KB 216243 (Authoritative Restore of Active Directory and Impact on Trusts and Computer Accounts), and MS KB 280079 (Authoritative Restore of Groups Can Result in Inconsistent Membership Information Across Domain Controllers)

17.6 Performing a Complete Authoritative Restore

Problem

You want to perform a complete authoritative restore of the Active Directory database because a significant failure has occurred.

Solution

Follow the same steps as Recipe 17.4, except that after the restore has completed, do not restart the computer.

Run the following command to restore the entire database:

```
> ntdsutil "auth restore" "restore database" q
```

Restart the computer.

Discussion

In a production environment, you should never have to perform an authoritative restore of the entire Active Directory database unless you have encountered a drastic situation such as a forest recovery scenario. It is a drastic measure, and you will almost inevitably lose data as a result. Before you even attempt such a restore, you may want to contact Microsoft Support to make sure that all options have been exhausted. However, you should still test the authoritative restore process in a lab environment and make sure that you have the steps properly documented in case you ever do need to use it.

See Also

Recipe 17.2 for getting into Directory Services Restore Mode, MB KB 216243 (Authoritative Restore of Active Directory and Impact on Trusts and Computer Accounts), MS KB 241594 (How to Perform an Authoritative Restore to a Domain Controller in Windows 2000), and MS KB 280079 (Authoritative Restore of Groups Can Result in Inconsistent Membership Information Across Domain Controllers)

17.7   Checking the DIT File's Integrity

Problem

You want to check the integrity and semantics of the DIT file to verify that there is no corruption or bad entries.

Solution

Using a command-line interface

First, reboot into Directory Services Restore Mode. Then run the following commands:

```
> ntdsutil files integrity q q
> ntdsutil "semantic database analysis" "verbose on" go
```

Discussion

The Active Directory DIT file (*ntds.dit*) is implemented as a transactional database. Microsoft uses the ESE database (also called Jet Blue) for Active Directory, which has been used for years in other products such as Microsoft Exchange.

Since the Active Directory DIT is ultimately a database, it can suffer from many of the same issues that traditional databases do. The ntdsutil integrity command checks for any low-level database corruption and ensures that the database headers are correct and the tables are in a consistent state. It reads every byte of the database and can take quite a while to complete, depending on how large your DIT file is. The time it takes is also greatly dependent on your hardware, but some early estimates from Microsoft for Windows 2000 put the rate at 2 GB an hour.

Whereas the ntdsutil integrity command verifies the overall structure and health of the database files, the ntdsutil semantics command looks at the contents of the database. It will verify, among other things, reference counts, replication metadata, and security descriptors. If any errors are reported back, you can run go fixup to attempt to correct them. You should have a recent backup handy before doing this and perform this step only as a troubleshooting option, preferably under the direction of a Microsoft PSS engineer, since in the worst case the corruption cannot be fixed or the state of your AD database may even become worse after the go fixup command completes.

See Also

Recipe 17.2 for booting into Directory Services Restore Mode and MS KB 315136 (How to Complete a Semantic Database Analysis for the Active Directory Database by Using Ntdsutil.exe)

17.8   Moving the DIT Files

Problem

You want to move the Active Directory DIT files to a new drive to improve performance or capacity.

Solution

Using a command-line interface

First, reboot into DS Restore Mode. Then, run the following commands, in which *<DriveAndFolder>* is the new location where you want to move the files (e.g., *d:\ NTDS*):

```
> ntdsutil files "move db to <DriveAndFolder>" q q
> ntdsutil files "move logs to <DriveAndFolder>" q q
```

Discussion

You can move the Active Directory database file (*ntds.dit*) independently of the logfiles. The first command in the solution moves the database, and the second moves the logs. You may also want to consider running an integrity check against the database after you've moved it to ensure that nothing went wrong during the move. See Recipe 17.7 for more details.

See Also

Recipe 17.2 for booting into Directory Services Restore Mode, Recipe 17.7 for checking DIT file integrity, MS KB 257420 (How to Move the Ntds.dit File or Log Files), MS KB 315131 (How to Use Ntdsutil to Manage Active Directory Files from the Command Line in Windows 2000), and MS KB 816120 (How to Use Ntdsutil to Manage Active Directory Files from the Command Line in Windows Server 2003)

17.9   Repairing or Recovering the DIT

Problem

You need to repair or perform a soft recovery of the Active Directory DIT because a power failure or some other failure caused the domain controller to enter an unstable state.

Solution

Using a command-line interface

First, reboot into DS Restore Mode.

Run the following command to perform a soft recovery of the transaction logfiles:

```
> ntdsutil files recover q q
```

If you continue to experience errors, you may need to run a repair, which does a low-level repair of the database but can result in loss of data:

```
> ntdsutil files repair q q
```

If either the recover or repair operations are successful, you should then check the integrity of the AD database (see Recipe 17.7).

Discussion

You should (hopefully) never need to recover or repair your Active Directory database. A recovery may be needed after a domain controller unexpectedly shuts down, perhaps due to a power loss, and certain changes were never committed to the database. When it boots back up, a soft recovery is automatically done in an attempt to reapply any changes that were contained in the transaction logfiles. Since Active Directory does this automatically, it is unlikely that running the ntdsutil recover command will be of much help. ntdsutil repair, on the other hand, can fix low-level problems, but it can also result in a loss of data which cannot be predicted. *Use at your own peril!*

I recommend that you use extreme caution when performing a repair, and you may want to engage Microsoft Support first in case something goes wrong. If you try the repair and it makes things worse, you should consider rebuilding the domain controller from scratch. See Recipe 3.7 for forcibly removing a failed domain controller from your domain.

See Also

Recipe 17.2 for booting into Directory Services Restore Mode, Recipe 17.7 for checking the integrity of the DIT, MS KB 315131 (How to Use Ntdsutil to Manage Active Directory Files from the Command Line in Windows 2000), and MS KB 816120 (How to Use Ntdsutil to Manage Active Directory Files from the Command Line in Windows Server 2003)

17.10 Performing an Online Defrag Manually

 This recipe must be run against a Windows Server 2003 domain controller.

Problem

You want to initiate an online defragmentation to optimize the disk space that's being used by the *ntds.dit* file.

Solution

Using a graphical user interface

1. Open LDP from the Windows Support Tools.
2. From the menu, select Connection → Connect.
3. For Server, enter the name of the target domain controller.
4. For Port, enter 389.
5. Click OK.
6. From the menu, select Connection → Bind.
7. Enter the credentials of a user from one of the administrator groups.
8. Click OK.
9. From the menu, select Browse → Modify.
10. Leave the Dn blank.
11. For Attribute, enter "DoOnlineDefrag".
12. For Values, enter 180.
13. For Operation, select Add.
14. Click Enter.
15. Click Run.

Using a command-line interface

Create an LDIF file called *online_defrag.ldf* with the following contents:

```
dn:
changetype: modify
replace: DoOnlineDefrag
DoOnlineDefrag: 180
-
```

Then run the following command:

```
> ldifde -v -i -f online_defrag.ldf
```

You can also perform an online defrag using AdMod:

```
> admod -b "" doOnlineDefrag::180
```

Using VBScript

```
' This code kicks off an online defrag to run for up to 180 seconds.
' ------ SCRIPT CONFIGURATION ------
strDC = "<DomainControllerName>"  ' e.g. dc01
' ------ END CONFIGURATION ---------

set objRootDSE = GetObject("LDAP://" & strDC & "/RootDSE")
objRootDSE.Put "DoOnlineDefrag", 180
objRootDSE.SetInfo
WScript.Echo "Successfully initiated an online defrag"
```

Discussion

New to Windows Server 2003 is the ability to initiate an online defragmentation. By default, the online defrag process runs every 12 hours on each domain controller. This process defrags the Active Directory database (*ntds.dit*) by combining whitespace generated from deleted objects, but does not reduce the size of the database file.

To start an online defrag, simply write the DoOnlineDefrag attribute to the RootDSE with a value equal to the maximum time the defrag process should run (in seconds). You must be a member of one of the administrator groups in the domain controller's domain in order to write to this attribute.

See Also

Recipe 17.14 for performing an offline defrag and MS KB 198793 (The Active Directory Database Garbage Collection Process)

17.11 Performing a Database Recovery

Problem

You want to perform a recovery of the Active Directory database when other methods have failed.

Solution

Using a command-line interface

Reboot the DC into Directory Services Restore Mode.

To perform an integrity check of the Active Directory database, enter the following:

```
> esentutl /g "<PathToNTDS.DIT>"/!10240 /8 /o
```

To perform a recovery of the AD database, enter the following:

```
> esentutl /r "<PathToNTDS.DIT>" /!10240 /8 /o
```

To perform a repair of the database, use the following syntax:

```
> esentutl /p "<PathToNTDS.DIT>" /!10240 /8 /o
```

Discussion

When attempting to recover the *ntds.dit* database, you may occasionally encounter a situation where *ntdsutil* is unable to repair whatever damage has occurred. You may run into error messages similar to the following:

```
Operation failed because the database was inconsistent.

Initialize jet database failed; cannot access file.

Error while performing soft recovery.
```

Because the AD database is based on the ESE, you also have access to the *esentutl* database utility that can perform a number of operations against the *ntds.dit* file, including defragmentation, database recovery or repair, and integrity checks. (For a complete description of each operation, type esentutl /? at the command line.)

If the *ntdsutil* recovery options listed elsewhere in this chapter fail, you can attempt to repair AD using this ESE utility. Many of the operations that you can perform with *esentutl* have the potential to exacerbate data loss, so be certain that you have a viable backup in place before attempting any of them. In fact, in some cases it may actually be simpler and quicker to simply restore from a known good backup to get your domain or forest back online again.

See Also

MS KB 305500 (Cannot Repair the Active Directory Database by Using the Ntdsutil Tool) and MS KB 280364 (How to Recover from Event ID 1168 and Event ID 1003 Error Messages)

17.12 Creating a Reserve File

Problem

You want to create another reserve file on the disk containing the *ntds.dit* file to guard against AD failures caused by disk space shortages.

Solution

Using a command-line interface

The following command will create an empty reserve file, 250 MB in size, in the same directory as the *ntds.dit* file:

```
> fsutil file createnew <PathToNTDS.DIT>\reservefile 256000000
```

For example, the following will create the reserve file in *c:\windows\ntds*:

```
> fsutil file createnew c:\windows\ntds\reservefile 256000000
```

Discussion

By default, Active Directory creates two files called *res1.log* and *res2.log* in the same directory as the *ntds.dit* database. Each of these files is 10 MB in size and is used to hold in reserve the last 20 MB of space on the drive hosting the AD database files. If a domain controller runs out of space on that drive, Active Directory will use the space being held by *res1.log* and *res2.log* to commit any uncommitted transactions before shutting down so that no information is lost. If you wish to set aside more space than this, you can create a reserve file to set aside additional space; this reserve file can then be manually deleted to free up disk space. This can provide an additional safeguard against a user or administrator inadvertently filling up the drive that's hosting the *ntds.dit* file, or to guard against a virus or a malicious user performing a denial-of-service attack by intentionally filling up the drive.

 To prevent accidental or malicious bloating of the *ntds.dit* itself, you can also establish quotas to restrict the number of objects that can be created by a user.

See Also

Recipe 16.17 for more on creating Active Directory quotas and Recipe 16.19 for configuring how tombstoned objects affect quotas

17.13 Determining How Much Whitespace Is in the DIT

Problem

You want to find the amount of whitespace in your DIT. A lot of whitespace in the DIT may mean that you could regain enough space on the disk to warrant performing an offline defrag.

Solution

Using a graphical user interface

1. Run *regedit.exe* from the command line or Start → Run.

2. Expand *HKEY_LOCAL_MACHINE\SYSTEM\CurrentControlSet\Services\NTDS\Diagnostics*.

3. In the right pane, double-click on 6 Garbage Collection.

4. For Value data, enter 1.

5. Click OK.

Using a command-line interface

```
> reg add HKLM\System\CurrentControlSet\Services\NTDS\Diagnostics /v "6 Garbage
Collection" /t REG_DWORD /d 1
```

Using VBScript

```
' This code enables logging of DIT whitespace information in the event log.
' ------ SCRIPT CONFIGURATION ------
strDCName = "<DomainControllerName>"   ' e.g. dc1
' ------ END CONFIGURATION ---------

const HKLM = &H80000002
strNTDSReg = "SYSTEM\CurrentControlSet\Services\NTDS\Diagnostics"
set objReg = GetObject("winmgmts:\\" & strDCName & "\root\default:StdRegProv")
objReg.SetDWORDValue HKLM, strNTDSReg, "6 Garbage Collection", 1
WScript.Echo "Garbage Collection logging set to 1"
```

Discussion

By setting the 6 Garbage Collection diagnostics logging option, event 1646 will get generated after the garbage collection process runs. Here is a sample 1646 event:

```
Event Type:        Information
Event Source:        NTDS Database
Event Category:        Garbage Collection
Event ID:        1646
Date:                5/25/2003
Time:                9:52:46 AM
User:                NT AUTHORITY\ANONYMOUS LOGON
Computer:        DC1
Description:
Internal event: The Active Directory database has the following amount of free hard
disk space remaining.

Free hard disk space (megabytes): 100
Total allocated hard disk space (megabytes): 1024
```

This shows that domain controller *dc1* has a 1 GB DIT file with 100 MB that is free (i.e., whitespace).

See Also

Recipe 17.14 for performing an offline defrag

17.14 Performing an Offline Defrag to Reclaim Space

Problem

You want to perform an offline defrag of the Active Directory DIT to reclaim whitespace in the DIT file.

Solution

Using a command-line interface

1. First, reboot into Directory Services Restore Mode.

2. Next, check the integrity of the DIT, as outlined in Recipe 17.7.

3. Now, you are ready to perform the defrag operation. Run the following command to create a compacted copy of the DIT file. You should check to make sure the drive on which you create the copy has plenty of space. A rule of thumb is that it should have at least 115 percent of the size of the current DIT available:

   ```
   > ntdsutil files "compact to <TempDriveAndFolder>" q q
   ```

4. Next, you need to delete the transaction logfiles in the current NTDS directory:

   ```
   > del <CurrentDriveAndFolder>\*.log
   ```

5. You may want to keep a copy of the original DIT file for a short period of time to ensure that nothing catastrophic happens to the compacted DIT. This does not replace the need for a System State backup and a backup of the domain controller's system drive; it is simply a temporary measure to provide a fallback if the move process itself goes wrong. If you are going to copy or move the original version, be sure you have enough space in its new location:

   ```
   > move <CurrentDriveAndFolder>\ntds.dit <TempDriveAndFolder>\ntds_orig.dit
   > move <TempDriveAndFolder>\ntds.dit <CurrentDriveAndFolder>\ntds.dit
   ```

   > Due to the size and the sensitive nature of the NTDS files, you cannot move them through normal Windows Explorer or command prompt commands; these files can only be moved using the *ntdsutil* options outlined here.

6. Repeat the steps in Recipe 17.7 to ensure the new DIT is not corrupted. If it is clean, reboot into normal mode and monitor the event log. If no errors are reported in the event log, make sure the domain controller is backed up as soon as possible.

Discussion

Performing an offline defragmentation of your domain controllers can reclaim disk space if you've deleted a large number of objects from Active Directory. You should perform an offline defrag when (and if) this occurs only if you actively require the disk space back—e.g., when following a spin-off in which you've migrated a large number of objects into a separate domain. The database will reuse whitespace and grow organically as required. Typically, the database grows year over year as more objects are added, so an offline defrag should seldom be required. An offline defrag always carries a small element of risk, so it should not be done unnecessarily.

You might want to consider doing an offline defrag after the upgrade to Windows Server 2003. A new feature called *single instance storage for security descriptors* can greatly reduce the amount of space your DIT requires. With this new feature, unique security descriptors are stored once regardless of how many times they are used, whereas in Windows 2000 the same security descriptor would be stored individually on each object that used it.

The key thing to plan ahead of time is your disk space requirements. If you plan on creating the compacted copy of the DIT on the same drive as the current DIT, you need to make sure that drive has 115 percent of the size of the DIT available. If you plan on storing the original DIT on the same drive, you'll need to make sure you have at least that much space available.

See Also

Recipe 17.2 for booting into Directory Services Restore Mode, Recipe 17.7 for checking the integrity of the DIT, MS KB 198793 (The Active Directory Database Garbage Collection Process), MS KB 229602 (Defragmentation of the Active Directory Database), and MS KB 232122 (Performing Offline Defragmentation of the Active Directory Database)

17.15 Changing the Garbage Collection Interval

Problem

You want to change the default garbage-collection interval.

Solution

Using a graphical user interface

1. Open ADSI Edit.
2. In the left pane, expand cn=Configuration → cn=Services → cn=Windows NT.
3. Right-click on cn=Directory Service and select Properties.

---

4. Edit the garbageColPeriod attribute and set it to the interval in hours that the garbage collection process should run (the default is 12 hours).

5. Click OK.

Using a command-line interface

Create an LDIF file called *change_garbage_period.ldf* with the following contents:

```
dn: cn=Directory Service,cn=Windows NT,cn=Services,cn=Configuration,<ForestRootDN>
changetype: modify
replace: garbageCollPeriod
garbageCollPeriod: <IntervalInHours>
-
```

Then run the following command:

```
> ldifde -v -i -f change_garbage_period.ldf
```

You can also modify the garbage collection period using AdMod:

```
> adfind -config -rb "cn=Directory Servce,cn=Windows NT,cn=Services" -s base -dsq |
admod  garbageCollPeriod::<IntervalInHours>
```

Using VBScript

```
' This code changes the default garbage-collection interval.
' ------ SCRIPT CONFIGURATION ------
intGarbageColl = <IntervalInHours>
' ------ END CONFIGURATION ---------

set objRootDSE = GetObject("LDAP://RootDSE")
set objDSCont = GetObject("LDAP://cn=Directory Service,cn=Windows NT," & _
          "cn=Services," & objRootDSE.Get("configurationNamingContext") )
objDSCont.Put "garbageCollPeriod", intGarbageColl
objDSCont.SetInfo
WScript.Echo "Successfully set the garbage collection interval to " & _
          intGarbageColl
```

Discussion

When an object is deleted from the Configuration naming context, a Domain naming context, or an application partition, the object is *tombstoned* by renaming the object, moving it to the Deleted Object container, and clearing the value of most of its attributes to save space in the *ntds.dit* file. This tombstone object remains in Active Directory for the duration of the tombstone lifetime (60 days for Windows Server 2003, 180 days for fresh installations of 2003 Service Pack 1) before it gets completely removed. See Recipe 17.21 for more information on the tombstone lifetime.

A garbage-collection process runs on each domain controller that automatically removes expired tombstone objects. This process runs every 12 hours by default, but you can change it to run more or less frequently by setting the garbageCollPeriod attribute on the `cn=DirectoryService,cn=WindowsNT,cn=Services,cn=Configuration,` *<RootDomainDN>* object to the frequency in hours.

See Also

Recipe 17.21 for modifying the tombstone lifetime, Recipe 17.16 for logging the number of tombstones that get garbage-collected, and MS KB 198793 (The Active Directory Database Garbage Collection Process)

17.16 Logging the Number of Expired Tombstone Objects

Problem

You want to log the number of expired tombstone objects that are removed from Active Directory during each garbage-collection cycle.

Solution

Using a graphical user interface

1. Run *regedit.exe* from the command line or Start → Run.
2. Expand *HKEY_LOCAL_MACHINE\SYSTEM\CurrentControlSet\Services\NTDS\ Diagnostics*.
3. In the right pane, double-click on 6 Garbage Collection.
4. For Value data, enter 3.
5. Click OK.

Using a command-line interface

```
> reg add HKLM\System\CurrentControlSet\Services\NTDS\Diagnostics /v "6 Garbage
Collection" /t REG_DWORD /d 3
```

Using VBScript

```
' This code enables garbage-collection logging.
' ------ SCRIPT CONFIGURATION ------
strDCName = "<DomainControllerName>"
intValue = 3
' ------ END CONFIGURATION ---------

const HKLM = &H80000002
strNTDSReg = "SYSTEM\CurrentControlSet\Services\NTDS\Diagnostics"
set objReg = GetObject("winmgmts:\\" & strDCName & "\root\default:StdRegProv")
objReg.SetDWORDValue HKLM, strNTDSReg, "6 Garbage Collection," intValue
WScript.Echo "Garbage Collection logging enabled"
```

Discussion

Here is a sample event that is logged when the 6 Garbage Collection diagnostics logging level is set to 3 or higher:

```
Event Type:        Information
Event Source:      NTDS General
Event Category:       Garbage Collection
Event ID:        1006
Date:            6/24/2003
Time:            11:29:31 AM
User:            NT AUTHORITY\ANONYMOUS LOGON
Computer:        DC1
Description:
Internal event: Finished removing deleted objects that have expired (garbage
collection). Number of expired deleted objects that have been removed: 229.
```

See Also

Recipe 16.2 for more on diagnostics logging and Recipe 17.15 for more on the garbage-collection process

17.17 Determining the Size of the Active Directory Database

Problem

You want to determine the size of the Active Directory database.

Solution

Using a command-line interface

If you are in DS Restore Mode, you can use *ntdsutil* to report the size of the Active Directory database:

```
> ntdsutil files info
```

If you are not in DS Restore Mode and run this command, you will receive the following error message:

```
*** Error: Operation only allowed when booted in DS restore mode
       "set SAFEBOOT_OPTION=DSREPAIR" to override - NOT RECOMMENDED!
```

As you can see, it is possible to override this failure by setting the SAFEBOOT_OPTION environment variable to DSREPAIR, but we do not recommend this unless you know what you are doing. By setting this environment variable, the *ntdsutil* command will not stop you from performing other commands that should not be done while the database is online. This can obviously be quite dangerous.

Another method, which is safer and easier, is to bring up a command shell by going to Start → Run, typing cmd.exe, and pressing Enter. Then type cd <NTDSDir>, where <NTDSDir> is the full path to the *ntds.dit* file. Finally, run the *dir* command; the output will show the size of the files.

Discussion

The size of the Active Directory database on a domain controller is the size of the *ntds.dit* file. This file can vary slightly in size between domain controllers, even within the same domain, due to unreplicated changes or differences with nonreplicated data.

You should monitor the size of this file on one or more domain controllers in each of your domains to ensure that you have adequate disk space. Also, by knowing the average size of your DIT, you can quickly recognize if it spikes dramatically, perhaps due to a new application that is writing data to the directory.

If you find that you are running out of disk space, you have a couple of options. You could move the Active Directory files to a new drive with more capacity. Alternatively, you can perform an offline defragmentation if the DIT file contains a lot of whitespace.

See Also

Recipe 17.8 for moving the DIT files, Recipe 17.13 for determining how much whitespace is in the DIT, and Recipe 17.14 for performing an offline defragmentation of the Active Directory database

17.18 Searching for Deleted Objects

Problem

You want to search for deleted objects.

Solution

Using a graphical user interface

1. Open LDP from the Windows Support Tools.
2. From the menu, select Connection → Connect.
3. For Server, enter the name of a domain controller you want to target (or leave blank to do a serverless bind).
4. For Port, enter 389.
5. Click OK.
6. From the menu, select Connection → Connect.

7. Enter credentials of a user that is an administrator for the domain.

8. Click OK.

9. From the menu, select Options → Controls.

10. For Windows Server 2003, select the Return Deleted Objects control under Load Predefined. For Windows 2000, type `1.2.840.113556.1.4.417` for the Object Identifier and click the Check In button.

11. Click OK.

12. From the menu, select Browse → Search.

13. For BaseDN, enter: `cn=Deleted Objects,<DomainDN>`.

14. For Scope, select One Level.

15. For Filter, enter: `(isDeleted=TRUE)`.

16. Click the Options button.

17. Under Search Call Type, select Extended.

18. Click OK.

19. Click Run.

Using a command-line interface

To view all of the deleted objects in the current domain, use the following syntax:

```
> adfind -default -rb "cn=Deleted Objects" -showdel
```

Using VBScript

It is currently not possible to search for deleted objects with ADSI or ADO.

Discussion

When an object is deleted in Active Directory, it is not completely deleted. The original object is renamed, most of its attributes are cleared, and it is moved to the `Deleted Objects` container within the naming context that it was deleted from. See the "Introduction" in this chapter for more on tombstone objects.

Both the `Deleted Objects` container and tombstone objects themselves are hidden by default in tools such as ADUC and ADSI Edit. To query tombstone objects, you need to enable the Return Deleted Objects LDAP control, which has an OID of `1.2.840.113556.1.4.417`. When that control is enabled, you can perform searches for tombstone objects by specifying a search filter that contains `(isDeleted=TRUE)` in it. Only members of the administrator groups can perform searches for tombstone objects.

See Also

MSDN: Retrieving Deleted Objects

17.19 Undeleting a Single Object

Problem

You want to undelete or *reanimate* an object that has been deleted from your Windows Server 2003 Active Directory domain.

 This recipe requires Windows Server 2003 Active Directory.

Solution

Using a graphical user interface

1. Open LDP from the Windows Support Tools.
2. From the menu, select Connection → Connect.
3. For Server, enter the name of a domain controller or domain that contains the object.
4. For Port, enter 389.
5. Click OK.
6. From the menu, select Connection → Bind.
7. Enter the credentials of a user that can view deleted objects.
8. Click OK.
9. Click on Options → Controls. In the Load Pre-defined drop-down box, select "Return deleted objects." Click OK.
10. From the menu, select View → Tree.
11. For BaseDN, type <CN=Deleted Objects,<DomainDN>>.
12. Click OK.
13. Click the + sign next to the Deleted Objects container in the right-hand pane to browse the deleted objects in your domain.
14. Double-click on the object that you want to undelete.
15. Right-click on the object and select Modify.
16. In the Edit Entry Attribute box, enter isDeleted. Leave the Value box blank. Select Delete from the Operation radio buttons, and then click Enter.
17. Enter distinguishedName in the Edit Entry Attribute box, and enter the DN that the restored object should have. Select Replace from the Operation radio buttons, and then click Enter.
18. Once you've entered both changes, click Run.

Using a command line interface

```
> adfind -default -f "name=<ObjectRDN>*" -showdel -dsq |
admod -undel
```

Discussion

When an Active Directory object is deleted, it is placed in the cn=Deleted Objects container within the domain naming context. To save space in the *ntds.dit* file, most of the object's attribute values are cleared; only a small subset are actually retained, including:

- SID
- ObjectGUID
- LastKnownParent
- sAMAccountName
- SIDHistory (Windows Server 2003 SP1 only)

Once you've manually reanimated an object, you'll need to manually restore any additional attributes that were not saved when the object was tombstoned; e.g., for a user object, you'll want to reconfigure their home directory, logon script information, and the like. You'll also need to re-enter the user into any necessary security and distribution groups so that he can receive the necessary access to resources that he possessed before his account was deleted.

Another option when restoring a single object is to perform a System State restore on a domain controller, and then use *ntdsutil* to mark the individual object or subtree as *authoritative*. This has the downside of causing downtime on a domain controller, since you'll need to reboot it into Directory Services Restore mode to perform the restore. However, it saves you the manual effort of re-establishing most user account attributes since these will be automatically repopulated as part of the restore process.

See Also

MS KB 840001 (How to restore deleted user accounts and their group membership in Active Directory), MSDN: Considerations for Active Directory Services Backup, and the other recipes in this chapter for more on AD backups, restores, and disaster recovery

17.20 Undeleting a Container Object

Problem

You want to undelete a container object such as an OU that contained other objects when it was deleted.

This recipe requires Windows Server 2003.

Solution

Using a graphical user interface

Use the steps in Recipe 17.19 to first undelete the container object. Then undelete each individual child object that was contained within the container, specifying the container's DN in the restored object's DN. Alternately, perform a System State restore and use *ntdsutil* to mark the restored OU as authoritative, as described in Recipe 17.5.

Performing an authoritative restore of user or group objects will require additional considerations, as detailed in MS KB 280079 (Authoritative restore of groups can result in inconsistent membership information across domain controllers).

Using a command line interface

```
> adfind -default -rb "cn=Deleted Objects" -f "(name=<ContainerRDN>*)"
  -showdel -dsq | admod –undel
> adfind -default -rb "cn=Deleted Objects" -f
  ("lastKnownParent=<ParentContainerDN>") –showdel –dsq | admod -undel
```

Discussion

When you delete an Active Directory container object, it also deletes any child objects that are housed within that container. Restoring an entire OU, for example, therefore requires you to restore both the container itself as well as all of the child objects contained within it. This is relatively simple to perform from the command line since you can restrict your query to those objects that have the appropriate value listed in the lastKnownParent attribute. However, just as when you reanimate an individual object, each of these child objects will need to have its individual attributes re-established. Therefore, when restoring a container object, your most efficient method will be to perform a System State restore and to use *ntdsutil* to mark the restored OU as authoritative.

See Also

MSDN:Restoring Deleted Object[Active Directory]

17.21 Modifying the Tombstone Lifetime for a Domain

Problem

You want to change the default tombstone lifetime for a domain.

Solution

Using a graphical user interface

1. Open ADSI Edit.
2. In the left pane, expand cn=Configuration → cn=Services → cn=Windows NT.
3. Right-click on cn=Directory Service and select Properties.
4. Set the tombstoneLifetime attribute to the number of days that tombstone objects should remain in Active Directory before getting removed completely (the default is 60 days in Windows Server 2003, 180 days for AD environments installed from scratch on a Service Pack 1 server).
5. Click OK.

Using a command-line interface

Create an LDIF file called *change_tombstone_lifetime.ldf* with the following contents:

```
dn: cn=Directory Service,cn=Windows NT,cn=Services,cn=Configuration,<ForestRootDN>
changetype: modify
replace: tombstoneLifetime
tombstoneLifetime: <NumberOfDays>
-
```

Then run the following command:

```
> ldifde -v -i -f change_tombstone_lifetime.ldf
```

You can also make this change using AdMod, as follows:

```
> admod -b "cn=Directory Service,cn=Windows
NT,cn=Services,cn=Configuration,<ForestRootDN> tombstoneLifetime::<NumberOfDays>
```

Using VBScript

```
' This code modifies the default tombstone lifetime.
' ------ SCRIPT CONFIGURATION ------
intTombstoneLifetime = <NumberOfDays>
' ------ END CONFIGURATION ---------

set objRootDSE = GetObject("LDAP://RootDSE")
set objDSCont = GetObject("LDAP://cn=Directory Service,cn=Windows NT," & _
                "cn=Services," & objRootDSE.Get("configurationNamingContext") )
objDSCont.Put "tombstoneLifetime", intTombstoneLifetime
objDSCont.SetInfo
WScript.Echo "Successfully set the tombstone lifetime to " & _
             intTombstoneLifetime
```

Discussion

In Windows Server 2003, the default tombstone lifetime for Active Directory is 60 days. This was increased to 180 days in Service Pack 1 due to numerous customers (particularly those in higher education) needing to extend this value from its original default, but you will see this value populated automatically only in a forest that was created from scratch on a server that already has Service Pack 1 installed. If you upgrade an existing 2003 domain controller to SP1, the tombstone lifetime will stay at 60 days unless you manually increase it using one of the solutions in this recipe.

It is not recommended that you lower the tombstone lifetime unless you have a very good reason for doing so, since lowering this value below the 60-day default, also lowers the length of time a backup of Active Directory is good for. See the "Introduction" to this chapter and Recipe 17.18 for more information on tombstone (deleted) objects and the tombstone lifetime.

See Also

Recipe 17.15 for more on the garbage collection process, MS KB 198793 (The Active Directory Database Garbage Collection Process), MS KB 216993 (Backup of the Active Directory Has 60-Day Useful Life), and MS KB 314282 (Lingering Objects May Remain After You Bring an Out-of-Date Global Catalog Server Back Online)

## CHAPTER 18

Application Partitions

18.0 Introduction

Active Directory domain controllers, when first installed, host exactly three pre-defined partitions. The *Configuration naming context* is replicated to all domain controllers in the forest, and contains information that is needed forest-wide such as the site topology and LDAP query policies. The *Schema naming context* is also replicated forest-wide and contains all of the schema objects that define how data is stored and structured in Active Directory. The third partition is the *Domain naming context*, which is replicated to all of the domain controllers that host a particular domain.

Windows Server 2003 introduces a new type of partition called an *application partition*, which is very similar to the other naming contexts except that you can configure which domain controllers in the forest will replicate the data that's contained within it. Examples include the *DomainDnsZones* partition, which is replicated across all AD-Integrated DNS servers in the same domain, and *ForestDnsZones*, which is replicated across all AD-integrated DNS servers in the forest. This capability gives administrators much more flexibility over how they can store and replicate the data that is contained in Active Directory. If you need to replicate a certain set of data to only two different sites, for example, you can create an application partition that will only replicate the data to the domain controllers in those two sites rather than replicating the data to additional DCs that have no need of it.

See Chapter 14 for more on DNS-related management tasks, as well as Chapter 3 in *Active Directory*, Third Edition, by Joe Richards et al. (O'Reilly) for more details on application partitions.

Application Partitions are new to Windows Server 2003, so this entire chapter applies only to Windows Server 2003 domain controllers. Windows 2000 domain controllers cannot host application partitions.

The Anatomy of an Application Partition

Application partitions are stored in Active Directory in a similar fashion as a Domain NC. In fact, application partitions and Domain NCs consist of the same two types of objects: a domainDNS object and a crossRef object that resides under the Partitions container in the Configuration Naming Context (CNC). Application partitions have a similar naming convention as domains and can be named virtually anything you want. You can create an application partition that uses the current namespace within the forest. For example, in the *rallencorp.com* (dc=rallencorp,dc=com) forest, you could create an *apps.rallencorp.com* (dc=apps,dc=rallencorp,dc=com) application partition. Alternatively, a name that is part of a new tree can also be used, for example, *apps.local* (dc=apps,dc=local). Application partitions can also be subordinate to other application partitions.

Tables 18-1 and 18-2 contain some of the interesting attributes of domainDNS and crossRef objects as they apply to application partitions.

Table 18-1. Attributes of domainDNS objects

Attribute	Description
dc	Relative distinguished name of the application partition.
instanceType	This attribute must be set to 5 when creating an application partition. See Recipe 18.1 for more information.
msDs-masteredBy	List of nTDSDSA object DNs of the domain controllers that replicate the application partition. See Recipe 18.4 for more information.

Table 18-2. Attributes of crossRef objects

Attribute	Description
cn	Relative distinguished name of the crossRef object. This value is generally a GUID for application partitions.
dnsRoot	Fully qualified DNS name of the application partition.
msDS-NC-Replica-Locations	List of nTDSDSA object DNs of the domain controllers that replicate the application partition. See Recipe 18.4 for more information.
msDS-SDReferenceDomain	Domain used for security descriptor translation. See Recipe 18.8 for more information.
nCName	Distinguished name of the application partition's corresponding domainDNS object.
systemFlags	Bit flag that identifies if the crossRef represents an application. See Recipe 18.2 for more information.

18.1   Creating and Deleting an Application Partition

Problem

You want to create or delete an application partition. Application partitions are useful if you need to replicate data to a subset of locations where you have domain controllers. Instead of replicating the application data to all domain controllers in a domain, you can use an application partition to replicate the data to only the domain controllers of your choosing.

Solution

Using a command-line interface

Use the following command to create an application partition on a domain controller:

```
> ntdsutil "dom man" conn "co to se <DomainControllerName>" q "create nc
<AppPartitionDN> NULL" q q
```

Use the following command to delete an application partition:

```
> ntdsutil "dom man" conn "co to se <DomainControllerName>" q "delete nc
<AppPartitionFQDN>" q q
```

Discussion

To create an application partition, you'll use the *ntdsutil* utility to create a domainDNS object that serves as the root container for the partition. A crossRef object is automatically created in the Partitions container in the Configuration NC. Conversely, when removing an application partition, you only need to remove the crossRef object and the domainDNS is automatically deleted. When you delete an application partition, all objects within the partition also get deleted. Tombstone objects are not created for any of the objects within the application partition or for the application partition itself.

See Also

MS KB 322669 (How to Manage the Application Directory Partition and Replicas in Windows Server 2003), MSDN: Creating an Application Directory Partition, and MSDN: Deleting an Application Directory Partition

18.2   Finding the Application Partitions in a Forest

Problem

You want to find the application partitions that have been created in a forest.

Solution

Using a graphical user interface

1. Open LDP from the Windows Support Tools.
2. From the menu, select Connection → Connect.
3. For Server, enter the name of a DC.
4. For Port, enter 389.
5. Click OK.
6. From the menu, select Connection → Bind.
7. Enter a user and password with the necessary credentials.
8. Click OK.
9. From the menu, select Browse → Search.
10. For BaseDN, type the DN of the Partitions container (for example, cn=partitions,cn=configuration,dc=rallencorp,dc=com).
11. For Filter, enter:

    ```
    (&(objectcategory=crossRef)(systemFlags:1.2.840.113556.1.4.803:=5))
    ```

12. For Scope, select One Level.
13. Click the Options button.
14. For Attributes, type **dnsRoot**.
15. Click OK.
16. Click Run.

Using a command-line interface

Use the following command to find all of the application partitions in a forest:

```
> dsquery * cn=partitions,cn=configuration,<ForestDN> -filter
"(&(objectcategory=crossRef)(systemFlags:1.2.840.113556.1.4.803:=5))"
-scope onelevel -attr dnsRoot
```

You can also find application partitions in a forest using AdFind:

```
> adfind -bit -config -rb cn=partitions -f
"(&(objectcategory=crossref)(systemFlags:AND:=5))" dnsroot
```

Using VBScript

```
' This code displays the application partitions contained in the
' default forest

set objRootDSE = GetObject("LDAP://RootDSE")
strBase    = "<LDAP://cn=Partitions," & _
              objRootDSE.Get("ConfigurationNamingContext") & ">;"
strFilter  = "(&(objectcategory=crossRef)" & _
              "(systemFlags:1.2.840.113556.1.4.803:=5));"
```

```
strAttrs    = "cn,ncName;"
strScope    = "onelevel"

set objConn = CreateObject("ADODB.Connection")
objConn.Provider = "ADsDSOObject"
objConn.Open "Active Directory Provider"
set objRS = objConn.Execute(strBase & strFilter & strAttrs & strScope)

objRS.MoveFirst
while not objRS.EOF
   Wscript.Echo objRS.Fields("nCName").Value
   objRS.MoveNext
wend
```

Discussion

To get the list of application partitions in the Solution, we queried all crossRef objects in the Partitions container that have the systemFlags attribute with the 0101 bits set (5 in decimal). To do this, a logical AND bit-wise filter was used. See Recipe 4.12 for more on searching with a bitwise filter.

You can take a shortcut by not including the bitwise OID in the search filter, and changing it to systemFlags=5. This currently produces the same results in the test forest as with the bitwise filter, but there are no guarantees since it is a bit flag attribute. You may encounter circumstances in which an application partition would have another bit set in systemFlags that would yield a different value.

In each solution, the dnsRoot attribute was printed for each application partition, which contains the DNS name of the application partition. You can also retrieve the nCName attribute, which contains the distinguished name of the application partition.

See Also

Recipe 4.12

18.3 Adding or Removing a Replica Server for an Application Partition

Problem

You want to add or remove a replica server for an application partition. After you've created an application partition, you should make at least one other server a replica server in case the first server fails.

Solution

Using a command-line interface

Use the following command to add a replica server for an application partition:

```
> ntdsutil "dom man" conn "co to se <DomainControllerName>" q "add nc replica
<AppPartitionDN> <DomainControllerName>" q q
```

Use the following command to remove a replica server for an application partition:

```
> ntdsutil "dom man" conn "co to se <DomainControllerName>" q "remove nc replica
<AppPartitionDN> <DomainControllerName>" q q
```

You can also add a replica using AdMod:

```
> adfind –config –rb cn=partitions –f "(dnsRoot=<PartitionDNSName>)" -dsq | admod
msDS-NC-Replica-Locations:+:"cn=ntds settings,
cn=<DCName,cn=servers,cn=<SiteName,cn=sites,cn=configuration,<ForestRootDN>"
```

Using VBScript

```
' This code adds or removes a replica server for the
' specified application partition
' ------ SCRIPT CONFIGURATION ------
strAppPart = "<AppPartitionFQDN>" ' DNS name of the application partition

' Hostname of server to add as replica for app partition.
' This needs to match the common name for the DC's server object.
strServer = "<DomainControllerName>" ' e.g. dc01

' Set to True to add server as new replica or False to remove
boolAdd    = True
' ------ END CONFIGURATION ---------

' Constants taken from ADS_PROPERTY_OPERATION_ENUM
const ADS_PROPERTY_APPEND = 3
const ADS_PROPERTY_DELETE = 4

set objRootDSE = GetObject("LDAP://RootDSE")

' -----------------------------------------------------------
' First find the NTDS Settings object for the server
' -----------------------------------------------------------
strBase    = "<LDAP://cn=Sites," & _
             objRootDSE.Get("ConfigurationNamingContext") & ">;"
strFilter  = "(&(objectcategory=server)(cn=" & strServer & "));"
strAttrs   = "cn,distinguishedName;"
strScope   = "subtree"
set objConn = CreateObject("ADODB.Connection")
objConn.Provider = "ADsDSOObject"
objConn.Open "Active Directory Provider"
set objRS = objConn.Execute(strBase & strFilter & strAttrs & strScope)
if objRS.RecordCount <> 1 then
   WScript.Echo "Did not find a match for server " & strServer
   WScript.Quit
```

```
else
   objRS.MoveLast
   strServerDN = "cn=NTDS Settings," & _
                objRS.Fields("distinguishedName").Value
   ' Make sure the NTDS Settings object actually exists
   set objNTDSDSA = GetObject("LDAP://" & strServerDN)
   Wscript.Echo "Found server: "
   WScript.Echo strServerDN
   Wscript.Echo
end if


' --------------------------------------------------------------------
' Now need to find the crossRef object for the application partition
' --------------------------------------------------------------------
strBase   = "<LDAP://cn=Partitions," & _
             objRootDSE.Get("ConfigurationNamingContext") & ">;"
strFilter = "(&(objectcategory=crossRef)" & _
             "(dnsRoot=" & strAppPart & "));"
strAttrs  = "cn,distinguishedName;"
strScope  = "onelevel"
set objRS = objConn.Execute(strBase & strFilter & strAttrs & strScope)
if objRS.RecordCount <> 1 then
   WScript.Echo "Did not find a match for application partition " & _
               strAppPart
   WScript.Quit
else
   objRS.MoveLast
   set objAppPart = GetObject("LDAP://" & _
                   objRS.Fields("distinguishedName").Value )
   Wscript.Echo "Found app partition: "
   WScript.Echo objRS.Fields("distinguishedName").Value
   WScript.Echo
end if


' ----------------------------------------------------
' Lastly, either add or remove the replica server
' ----------------------------------------------------
if boolAdd = TRUE then
   objAppPart.PutEx ADS_PROPERTY_APPEND, "msDS-NC-Replica-Locations", _
                   Array(strServerDN)
   objAppPart.SetInfo
   WScript.Echo "Added server to replica set"
else
   objAppPart.PutEx ADS_PROPERTY_DELETE, "msDS-NC-Replica-Locations", _
                   Array(strServerDN)
   objAppPart.SetInfo
   WScript.Echo "Removed server from replica set"
end if
```

Discussion

When you initially create an application partition, there is only one domain controller that hosts the application partition, namely the one you created the application

partition on. You can add any other domain controllers in the forest as replica servers assuming the domain controllers are running Windows Server 2003. The list of replica servers is stored in the msDS-NC-Replica-Locations attribute on the crossRef object for the application partition in the Partitions container. That attribute contains the distinguished name of each replica server's nTDSDSA object. To add a replica server, simply add the DN of the new replica server. To remove a replica server, remove the DN corresponding to the server you want to remove. Behind the scene, the KCC gets triggered anytime there is a change to that attribute, at which point it will either cause the application partition to get replicated to the target domain controller or it will remove the replica from the target DC. When a domain controller is demoted, it should automatically remove itself as a replica server for any application partitions that it replicated.

See Also

Recipe 18.4 for finding the replica servers for an application partition and MS KB 322669 (How to Manage the Application Directory Partition and Replicas in Windows Server 2003)

18.4   Finding the Replica Servers for an Application Partition

Problem

You want to find the replica servers for an application partition.

Solution

Using a graphical user interface

1. Open ADSI Edit.
2. Connect to the configuration naming context of the forest the application partition is in, if it is not already present in the left pane.
3. Expand the configuration naming context and click on the Partitions container.
4. In the right pane, right-click on the crossRef object that represents the application partition and select Properties.
5. Under Attributes, select the msDS-NC-Replica-Locations attribute.

Using a command-line interface

```
> ntdsutil "dom man" conn "co to se <DomainControllerName>" q "list nc replicas
<AppPartitionDN>" q q
```

You can also list replica servers using AdFind:

```
> adfind -config -rb cn=partitions -f "(dnsRoot=<PartitionDNSName>)" dnsRoot msDS-NC-
Replica-Locations
```

Using VBScript

```
' This code displays the DN of each domain controller's
' NTDSDSA object that is a replica server for the
' specified app partition
' ------ SCRIPT CONFIGURATION ------
' Fully qualified DNS name of app partition
strAppPart = "<AppPartitionFQDN>"    ' e.g. apps.rallencorp.com
' ------ END CONFIGURATION ---------

set objRootDSE = GetObject("LDAP://RootDSE")
strBase    = "<LDAP://cn=Partitions," & _
               objRootDSE.Get("ConfigurationNamingContext") & ">;"
strFilter  = "(&(objectcategory=crossRef)(dnsRoot=" & strAppPart & "));"
strAttrs   = "msDS-NC-Replica-Locations;"
strScope   = "onelevel"
set objConn = CreateObject("ADODB.Connection")
objConn.Provider = "ADsDSOObject"
objConn.Open "Active Directory Provider"
set objRS = objConn.Execute(strBase & strFilter & strAttrs & strScope)
if objRS.RecordCount <> 1 then
   WScript.Echo "Did not find a match for application partition " & _
               strAppPart
   WScript.Quit
else
   objRS.MoveLast
   if objRS.Fields("msDS-NC-Replica-Locations").Properties.Count > 0 then
      Wscript.Echo "There are no replica servers for app partition " & _
               strAppPart
   else
      Wscript.Echo "Replica servers for app partition " & strAppPart & ":"
      for each strNTDS in objRS.Fields("msDS-NC-Replica-Locations").Value
         WScript.Echo " " & strNTDS
      next
   end if
end if
```

Discussion

The list of replica servers for an application partition is stored in the multivalued
msDS-NC-Replica-Locations attribute on the crossRef object for the application partition. This object is located in the Partitions container in the Configuration naming
context.

See Also

Recipe 18.3 for adding and removing replica servers

18.5 Finding the Application Partitions Hosted by a Server

Problem

You want to find the application partitions that a particular server is hosting. Before you decommission a server, it is good to check to see if it hosts any application partitions and if so, to add another replica server to replace it.

Solution

Using a graphical user interface

1. Open LDP from the Windows Support tools.
2. From the menu, select Connection → Connect.
3. For Server, enter the name of a DC.
4. For Port, enter 389.
5. Click OK.
6. From the menu, select Connection → Bind.
7. Enter a user and password with the necessary credentials.
8. Click OK.
9. From the menu, select Browse → Search.
10. For BaseDN, type the DN of the Partitions container (for example, cn=partitions,cn=configuration,dc=rallencorp,dc=com).
11. For Filter, enter:

    ```
    (&(objectcategory=crossRef)(systemFlags:1.2.840.113556.1.4.803:=5)
    (msDS-NC-Replica-Locations=cn=NTDS Settings,cn=<DomainControllerName>,
    cn=servers,cn=<SiteName>,cn=sites, cn=configuration,<ForestDN>))
    ```

12. For Scope, select One Level.
13. Click the Options button.
14. For Attributes, type **dnsRoot**.
15. Click OK.
16. Click Run.

Using a command-line interface

Use the following command to find all of the application partitions hosted by a domain controller. To run this command, you need the distinguished name of the forest root domain (*<ForestDN>*), the common name of the DC's server object (*<DomainControllerName>*), and the common name of the site object the server is in (*<SiteName>*).

```
> dsquery * "cn=partitions,cn=configuration,<ForestDN>" -scope onelevel -attr
dnsRoot -filter "(&(objectcategory=crossRef)(systemFlags:1.2.840.113556.1.4.803:=5)
(msDS-NC-Replica-Locations=cn=NTDS Settings,cn=<DomainControllerName>,
cn=servers,cn=<SiteName>,cn=sites,cn=configuration,<ForestDN>))"
```

You can also display the application partitions hosted by a particular DC using
AdFind:

```
> adfind -config -rb cn=partitions -s onelevel -bit -f
"(&(objectcategory=crossRef)(systemFlags:AND:=5)(msDS-NC-Replica-Locations=cn=NTDS
Settings,cn=<DomainControllerName>,cn=servers,cn=<SiteName,
cn=sites,cn=configuration,<ForestRootDN>))"
```

Using VBScript

```
' This code finds the application partitions hosted by the specified server.
' ------ SCRIPT CONFIGURATION ------
' Hostname of server to add as replica for app partition.
' This needs to match the common name for the DC's server object.
strServer = "<DomainControllerName>"   ' e.g. dc01
' ------ END CONFIGURATION ---------


' -----------------------------------------------------------
' First need to find the NTDS Settings object for the server
' -----------------------------------------------------------
set objRootDSE = GetObject("LDAP://RootDSE")
strBase    = "<LDAP://cn=Sites," & _
               objRootDSE.Get("ConfigurationNamingContext") & ">;"
strFilter  = "(&(objectcategory=server)(cn=" & strServer & "));"
strAttrs   = "cn,distinguishedName;"
strScope   = "subtree"
set objConn = CreateObject("ADODB.Connection")
objConn.Provider = "ADsDSOObject"
objConn.Open "Active Directory Provider"
set objRS = objConn.Execute(strBase & strFilter & strAttrs & strScope)
if objRS.RecordCount <> 1 then
   WScript.Echo "Did not find a match for server " & strServer
   WScript.Quit
else
   objRS.MoveLast
   strServerDN = "cn=NTDS Settings," & _
                 objRS.Fields("distinguishedName").Value
   Wscript.Echo "Found server object: "
   WScript.Echo strServerDN
   Wscript.Echo
end if


' -----------------------------------------------------------
' Find the crossRef objects that are hosted by the server
' -----------------------------------------------------------
strBase = "<LDAP://cn=Partitions," & _
          objRootDSE.Get("ConfigurationNamingContext") & ">;"
strFilter  = "(&(objectcategory=crossRef)" & _
             "(msDS-NC-Replica-Locations=" & strServerDN & "));"
```

```
strAttrs  = "nCName;"
strScope  = "onelevel"
set objRS = objConn.Execute(strBase & strFilter & strAttrs & strScope)
if objRS.RecordCount = 0 then
   WScript.Echo "Server " & strServer & _
                 " does not host any application partitions"
   WScript.Quit
else
   Wscript.Echo "App partitions hosted by server " & strServer & ": "
   objRS.MoveFirst
   while not objRS.EOF
      WScript.Echo " " & objRS.Fields("nCName").Value
      objRS.MoveNext
   wend
end if
```

Discussion

As described in Recipe 18.3 and Recipe 18.4, the msDS-NC-Replica-Locations
attribute on crossRef objects contains the list of replica servers for a given application partition. Each of the solutions illustrates how to perform a query using this
attribute to locate all of the application partitions a particular domain controller is a
replica server for. For the GUI and CLI solutions, you need to know the distinguished name of the nTDSDSA object for the target domain controller. The VBScript
solution tries to dynamically determine the distinguished name given a server name.

See Also

Recipes 18.3 and 18.4 for finding the replica servers for an application partition

18.6 Verifying Application Partitions Are Instantiated on a Server Correctly

Problem

You want to verify that an application partition is instantiated on a replica server.
After you add a domain controller as a replica server for an application partition, the
data in the application partition needs to fully replicate to that domain controller
before it can be used on that domain controller.

Solution

Using a command-line interface

Use the following command to determine if there are any problems with application
partitions on a domain controller:

```
> dcdiag /test:checksdrefdom /test:verifyreplicas /test:crossrefvalidation /s:
<DomainControllerName>
```

These tests are valid only with the Windows Server 2003 version of *dcdiag*.

You can also verify the state of a particular application partition by using *ntdsutil* as follows:

1. Type ntdsutil.
2. Type domain management (or just do ma) to go to the Domain Management menu.
3. Type connections (or just co) to go to the Connections menu.
4. Type connect to server *<ServerName>*.
5. Type q to return to the Domain Management menu.
6. Type list nc replicas *<AppPartitionDN>*. (You can shorten list nc replicas to just l nc rep.)

Discussion

The *dcdiag* CheckSDRefDom, VerifyReplicas, and CrossRefValidation tests can help determine if an application partition has been instantiated on a server and if there are any problems with it. Here is the *dcdiag* help information for those three tests:

CrossRefValidation
> This test looks for cross-references that are in some way invalid.

CheckSDRefDom
> This test checks that all application directory partitions have appropriate security descriptor reference domains.

VerifyReplicas
> This test verifies that all application directory partitions are fully instantiated on all replica servers.

Another way you can check to see if a certain application partition has been instantiated on a domain controller yet is to look at the msDS-HasInstantiatedNCs attribute for the server's nTDSDSA object. That attribute has DN with Binary syntax and contains a list of all the application partitions that have been successfully instantiated on the server. Unfortunately, tools such as ADSI Edit and DSQuery do not interpret DN with Binary attributes correctly, but it can be viewed with LDP. In addition, you can use AdFind as follows:

```
adfind -config -rb cn=dc1,cn=servers,cn=default-first-site-name,cn=site
s -f "msds-HasInstantiatedNCs=B:8:00000005:dc=apps,dc=local" -dn
```

This will return results similar to the following:

```
AdFind V01.27.00cpp Joe Richards (joe@joeware.net) November 2005

Using server: dc1.rallencorp.com:389
Directory: Windows Server 2003
Base DN: cn=dc1,cn=servers,cn=default-first-site-name,cn=sites,CN=Configuration,
DC=rallencorp,DC=com

dn:CN=NTDS Settings,CN=DC1,CN=Servers,CN=Default-First-Site-Name,CN=Sites,CN=Con
figuration,DC=rallencorp,DC=com

1 Objects returned
```

See Also

MSDN: ms-DS-Has-Instantiated-NCs attribute [AD Schema]

18.7 Setting the Replication Notification Delay for an Application Partition

Problem

Two replication-related settings that you can customize for application partitions (or any naming context for which change notification is enabled) include the first and subsequent replication delay after a change to the partition has been detected. The first replication delay is the time that a domain controller waits before it notifies its first replication partner that there has been a change. The subsequent replication delay is the time that the domain controller waits after it has notified its first replication partner before it will notify its next partner. You may need to customize these settings so that replication happens as quickly as you need it to for data in the application partition.

Solution

Using a graphical user interface

1. Open ADSI Edit.
2. Connect to the configuration naming context of the forest that the application partition is in if a connection is not already present in the left pane.
3. Expand the configuration naming context and click on the Partitions container.
4. In the right pane, right-click on the crossRef object that represents the application partition and select Properties.
5. Set the msDS-Replication-Notify-First-DSA-Delay and msDS-Replication-Notify-Subsequent-DSA-Delay attributes to the number of seconds you want for each delay (see the "Discussion" section for more details).
6. Click OK.

Using a command-line interface

The Windows Server 2003 version of *repadmin* supports setting the notification delays. (This option is not supported by the Windows 2000 version of *repadmin*.)

```
> repadmin /notifyopt <AppPartitionDN> /first:<FirstDelayInSeconds> /subs:
<NextDelayInSeconds>
```

You can also change both of these parameters using AdMod, as follows:

```
> admod -b <AppPartitionCrossRefDN> msDS-Replication-Notify-First-DSA-Delay::
<FirstDelayInSeconds>
> admod -b <AppPartitionCrossRefDN> msDS-Replication-Notify-Subsequent-DSA-Delay::
<NextDelayInSeconds>
```

Using VBScript

```
' This code sets the replication delay for an application partition
' ------ SCRIPT CONFIGURATION ------
strAppPartDN = "<AppPartitionDN>"   ' e.g. dc=apps,dc=rallencorp,dc=com
intFirstDelay = <FirstDelayInSeconds>
intNextDelay  = <NextDelayInSeconds>
' ------ END CONFIGURATION ---------

set objRootDSE = GetObject("LDAP://RootDSE")
strBase      = "<LDAP://cn=Partitions," & _
                objRootDSE.Get("ConfigurationNamingContext") & ">;"
strFilter    = "(&(objectcategory=crossRef)(nCName=" & strAppPartDN & "));"
strAttrs     = "cn,distinguishedName;"
strScope     = "onelevel"
set objConn = CreateObject("ADODB.Connection")
objConn.Provider = "ADsDSOObject"
objConn.Open "Active Directory Provider"
set objRS = objConn.Execute(strBase & strFilter & strAttrs & strScope)

if objRS.RecordCount <> 1 then
   WScript.Echo "Did not find a match for " & strAppPartDN
else
   objRS.MoveLast
   set objAppPart = GetObject("LDAP://" & _
                   objRS.Fields("distinguishedName").Value )
   objAppPart.Put "msDS-Replication-Notify-First-DSA-Delay", intFirstDelay
   objAppPart.Put "msDS-Replication-Notify-Subsequent-DSA-Delay", intNextDelay
   objAppPart.SetInfo
   Wscript.Echo "Modified " & objRS.Fields("distinguishedName").Value
end if
```

Discussion

The settings that control the notification delay are stored in the msDS-Replication-Notify-First-DSA-Delay and msDS-Replication-Notify-Subsequent-DSA-Delay attributes on the application partition's crossRef object in the Partitions container. The time values are stored as seconds. The default for application partitions is 15 seconds for the first delay and 5 seconds for each subsequent delay.

See Also

MSDN: Application Directory Partition Replication [Active Directory], MSDN: Modifying Application Directory Partition Configuration [Active Directory], MSDN: ms-DS-Replication-Notify-First-DSA-Delay, and MSDN: ms-DS-Replication-Notify-Subsequent-DSA-Delay

18.8 Setting the Reference Domain for an Application Partition

Problem

Whenever you create an object in Active Directory, the default security descriptor that's defined in the schema for the object's class is applied to the object. This default security descriptor may reference specific groups, such as *Domain Admins*, but it is not specific to a domain. This makes a lot of sense for domain naming contexts, where the *Domain Admins* group in question would be the one that's defined in the domain in question. But for application partitions that don't contain a *Domain Admins* group, it is not so straightforward. Which domain's *Domain Admins* group do you use? To work around this issue, you can set a default security descriptor reference domain for an application partition by setting the msDS-SDReferenceDomain attribute of the partition's crossRef object.

Solution

Using a graphical user interface

1. Open ADSI Edit.
2. Connect to the Configuration naming context of the forest the application partition is in if it is not already present in the left pane.
3. Expand the Configuration naming context and click on the Partitions container.
4. In the right pane, right-click on the crossRef object that represents the application partition and select Properties.
5. Under Attributes, select the msDS-SDReferenceDomain attribute.
6. Enter the Distinguished Name for the appropriate domain and click OK.

Using a command-line interface

```
> ntdsutil "dom man" conn "co to se <DomainControllerName>" q "set nc ref domain
<AppPartitionDN> <DomainDN>" q q
```

You can also set the reference domain using AdMod:

```
> adfind –config –rb cn=partitions –f "(dnsRoot=<PartitionDNSName>)" -dsq | admod
msDS-SDReferenceDomain::"<DomainDN>"
```

Using VBScript

```
' This code sets the SD reference domain for the specified app partition
' ------ SCRIPT CONFIGURATION ------
' DN of reference domain
strRefDomainDN = "<DomainDN>"          ' e.g. dc=emea,dc=rallencorp,dc=com
' Fully qualified DNS name of app partition
strAppPart = "<AppPartitionFQDN>"      ' e.g. app.rallencorp.com
' ------ END CONFIGURATION ---------

set objRootDSE = GetObject("LDAP://RootDSE")
strBase = "<LDAP://cn=Partitions," & _
            objRootDSE.Get("ConfigurationNamingContext") & ">;"
strFilter  = "(&(objectcategory=crossRef)(dnsRoot=" & _
               strAppPart & "));"
strAttrs   = "nCName,msDS-SDReferenceDomain,distinguishedName;"
strScope   = "onelevel"
set objConn = CreateObject("ADODB.Connection")
objConn.Provider = "ADsDSOObject"
objConn.Open "Active Directory Provider"
set objRS = objConn.Execute(strBase & strFilter & strAttrs & strScope)
if objRS.RecordCount <> 1 then
   WScript.Echo "Did not find a match for application partition " & _
                strAppPart
   WScript.Quit
else
   objRS.MoveLast
   WScript.Echo "Current Reference Domain: " & _
                objRS.Fields("msDS-SDReferenceDomain").Value
   set objCrossRef = GetObject("LDAP://" & _
                     objRS.Fields("distinguishedName").Value )
   objCrossRef.Put "msDS-SDReferenceDomain", strRefDomainDN
   objCrossRef.SetInfo
   WScript.Echo "New Reference Domain: " & _
                objCrossRef.Get("msDS-SDReferenceDomain")
end if
```

Discussion

If you don't set the msDS-SDReferenceDomain attribute for an application partition, then a specific hierarchy will be followed to determine the default security descriptor domain. These are the guidelines:

- If the application partition is created as part of a new tree, the forest root domain is used as the default domain.
- If the application partition is a child of a domain, the parent domain is used as the default domain.
- If the application partition is a child of another application partition, the parent application partition's default domain is used.

See Also

Recipe 11.21 for more on setting the default security descriptor for a class and Recipe 18.1 for creating an application partition

18.9 Delegating Control of Managing an Application Partition

Problem

You want to delegate control over the management of an application partition.

Solution

Using a graphical user interface

1. Open ADSI Edit.

2. Connect to the Configuration naming context of the forest the application partition is in if it is not already present in the left pane.

3. Expand the Configuration naming context and click on the Partitions container.

4. In the right pane, right-click on the crossRef object that represents the application partition and select Properties.

5. Click the Security tab.

6. Click the Advanced button.

7. Click the Add button.

8. Use the object picker to find the user or group you want to delegate control to and click OK.

9. Click the Properties tab.

10. Under Allow, check the boxes beside Write msDS-NC-Replica-Locations, Write msDS-SDReferenceDomain, Write msDS-Replication-Notify-First-DSA-Delay, and Write msDS-Replication-Notify-Subsequent-DSA-Delay.

11. Click OK.

Using a command-line interface

```
> dsacls <AppPartitionCrossRefDN> /G <UserOrGroup>:RPWP;msDS-NC-Replica-Locations
> dsacls <AppPartitionCrossRefDN> /G <UserOrGroup>:RPWP;msDS-SDReferenceDomain
> dsacls <AppPartitionCrossRefDN> /G <UserOrGroup>:RPWP;msDS-Replication-Notify-
First-DSA-Delay
> dsacls <AppPartitionCrossRefDN> /G <UserOrGroup>:RPWP;msDS-Replication-Notify-
Subsequent-DSA-Delay
```

As is the case with most permissions, you should exercise care when delegating the ability to create or modify application partitions. Because application partitions reside within Active Directory, allowing them to be placed indiscriminately or setting the initial and subsequent replication delays too low can bring your network to a grinding halt.

Using VBScript

```
' This script delegates control over the four key attributes
' of an app partition to the specified user or group.
' ------ SCRIPT CONFIGURATION ------
' Fully qualified DNS name of app partition
strAppPart = "<AppPartitionFQDN>"  ' e.g. apps.rallencorp.com
' User or group to delegate control to
strUser = "<UserOrGroup>"  ' e.g. joe@rallencorp.com or RALLENCORP\joe
' ------ END CONFIGURATION ---------

'###########################
' Constants
'###########################

' ADS_ACETYPE_ENUM
Const ADS_ACETYPE_ACCESS_ALLOWED        = &h0
Const ADS_ACETYPE_ACCESS_ALLOWED_OBJECT = &h5

' ADS_FLAGTYPE_ENUM
Const ADS_FLAG_OBJECT_TYPE_PRESENT = &h1

' ADS_RIGHTS_ENUM
Const ADS_RIGHT_DS_WRITE_PROP = &h20
Const ADS_RIGHT_DS_READ_PROP  = &h10

' schemaIDGUID values
Const REPLICA_LOCATIONS          = "{97de9615-b537-46bc-ac0f-10720f3909f3}"
Const SDREFERENCEDOMAIN          = "{4c51e316-f628-43a5-b06b-ffb695fcb4f3}"
Const NOTIFY_FIRST_DSA_DELAY     = "{85abd4f4-0a89-4e49-bdcc-6f35bb2562ba}"
Const NOTIFY_SUBSEQUENT_DSA_DELAY = "{d63db385-dd92-4b52-b1d8-0d3ecc0e86b6}"

'###########################
' Find App Partition
'###########################

set objRootDSE = GetObject("LDAP://RootDSE")
strBase = "<LDAP://cn=Partitions," & _
          objRootDSE.Get("ConfigurationNamingContext") & ">;"
strFilter  = "(&(objectcategory=crossRef)(dnsRoot=" & _
             strAppPart & "));"
strAttrs   = "cn,distinguishedName;"
strScope   = "onelevel"
set objConn = CreateObject("ADODB.Connection")
objConn.Provider = "ADsDSOObject"
objConn.Open "Active Directory Provider"
```

```
Set objRS = objConn.Execute(strBase & strFilter & strAttrs & strScope)
if objRS.RecordCount <> 1 then
   WScript.Echo "Did not find a match for " & strAppPart
else
   objRS.MoveLast
   set objAppPart = GetObject("LDAP://" & _
                    objRS.Fields("distinguishedName").Value )
end if

'############################
' Create ACL
'############################

set objSD = objAppPart.Get("ntSecurityDescriptor")
set objDACL = objSD.DiscretionaryAcl

' Read/Write Property: msDS-NC-Replica-Locations
set objACE1 = CreateObject("AccessControlEntry")
objACE1.Trustee    = strUser
objACE1.AccessMask = ADS_RIGHT_DS_WRITE_PROP Or ADS_RIGHT_DS_READ_PROP
objACE1.AceFlags   = 0
objACE1.Flags      = ADS_FLAG_OBJECT_TYPE_PRESENT
objACE1.AceType    = ADS_ACETYPE_ACCESS_ALLOWED_OBJECT
objACE1.ObjectType = REPLICA_LOCATIONS   '

' Read/Write Property: msDS-SDReferenceDomain
set objACE2 = CreateObject("AccessControlEntry")
objACE2.Trustee    = strUser
objACE2.AccessMask = ADS_RIGHT_DS_WRITE_PROP Or ADS_RIGHT_DS_READ_PROP
objACE2.AceFlags   = 0
objACE2.Flags      = ADS_FLAG_OBJECT_TYPE_PRESENT
objACE2.AceType    = ADS_ACETYPE_ACCESS_ALLOWED_OBJECT
objACE2.ObjectType = SDREFERENCEDOMAIN

' Read/Write Property: msDS-Replication-Notify-First-DSA-Delay
set objACE3 = CreateObject("AccessControlEntry")
objACE3.Trustee    = strUser
objACE3.AccessMask = ADS_RIGHT_DS_WRITE_PROP Or ADS_RIGHT_DS_READ_PROP
objACE3.AceFlags   = 0
objACE3.Flags      = ADS_FLAG_OBJECT_TYPE_PRESENT
objACE3.AceType    = ADS_ACETYPE_ACCESS_ALLOWED_OBJECT
objACE3.ObjectType = NOTIFY_FIRST_DSA_DELAY

' Read/Write Property: msDS-Replication-Notify-Subsequent-DSA-Delay
set objACE4 = CreateObject("AccessControlEntry")
objACE4.Trustee    = strUser
objACE4.AccessMask = ADS_RIGHT_DS_WRITE_PROP Or ADS_RIGHT_DS_READ_PROP
objACE4.AceFlags   = 0
objACE4.Flags      = ADS_FLAG_OBJECT_TYPE_PRESENT
objACE4.AceType    = ADS_ACETYPE_ACCESS_ALLOWED_OBJECT
objACE4.ObjectType = NOTIFY_SUBSEQUENT_DSA_DELAY

objDACL.AddAce objACE1
objDACL.AddAce objACE2
```

```
objDACL.AddAce objACE3
objDACL.AddAce objACE4

'###########################
' Set ACL
'###########################
objSD.DiscretionaryAcl = objDACL
objAppPart.Put "ntSecurityDescriptor", objSD
objAppPart.SetInfo
WScript.Echo "Delegated control of " & strAppPart & " to " & strUser
```

Discussion

If you want to delegate control of management of application partitions, you must grant control over four key attributes. Here is a description of each attribute and what can be accomplished by having control over it:

msDS-NC-Replica-Locations
> By having write access to this attribute, a user can add replica servers for the application partition. See Recipe 18.3 for more information.

msDS-SDReferenceDomain
> By having write access to this attribute, a user can define the default security descriptor domain for the application partition. See Recipe 18.8 for more information.

msDS-Replication-Notify-First-DSA-Delay
> See Recipe 18.7 for more information.

msDS-Replication-Notify-Subsequent-DSA-Delay
> See Recipe 18.7 for more information.

If you want to delegate control over managing objects within the application partition, you need to follow the same procedures you would when delegating control over objects in a domain naming context. See Recipe 14.8 for more information on delegating control.

See Also

Recipe 14.8, Recipe 15.7 for delegating control, Recipe 18.3 for more on adding and removing replica servers, Recipe 18.7 for more on the replication delay attributes, and Recipe 18.8 for more on the default security descriptor domain

CHAPTER 19

Active Directory Application Mode

19.0 Introduction

Active Directory Application Mode (ADAM) was released in November 2003 on the Microsoft web site. ADAM is a lightweight LDAP platform that allows developers and administrators to work with AD objects such as users, groups, and organizational units, without worrying about the overhead of running a full-blown copy of the Active Directory directory service. ADAM can run on Windows XP or Windows 2003 computers, and you can run multiple instances of ADAM on a single Windows 2003 machine. Because ADAM runs as a standalone service, you can start, stop, install or remove ADAM instances without affecting or interfering with any underlying AD infrastructure. ADAM can leverage domain authentication, local machine users and groups, or it can authenticate users based on security principals that you've created within ADAM itself. (It's important to note that these are separate from Active Directory security principals, which cannot be created within an ADAM instance.) ADAM can also be used to replicate data between non-AD computers such as ISA configuration between a farm of ISA 2004 servers configured as a workgroup.

 You cannot run multiple ADAM instances on a Windows XP computer, only on Windows Server 2003 and R2 servers.

The newest version of ADAM, ADAM Service Pack 1, has been packaged with Windows Server 2003 R2; it has a number of improvements over the initial release of ADAM, including:

Creating user objects in the Configuration partition
> By default, any ADAM user object you create is scoped to only the partition it was created in. By creating user objects in the Configuration partition, you can grant them permissions to resources in any partition within an ADAM instance.

This also allows you to configure an ADAM user to administer ADAM, rather than requiring a Windows user to do so.

Password resets chained to Windows

Any password changes made within ADAM to a proxy object such as a userProxy can be forwarded through to the appropriate Windows authentication store.

VLV searching

The new version of ADAM can leverage the VLV function of Windows Server 2003, which allows you to display a subset of the results of a query without needing to return every single entry.

For more detailed information on ADAM, refer to Chapter 18 of *Active Directory*, Third Edition, by Joe Richards et al. (O'Reilly).

19.1   Installing ADAM

Problem

You want to install a new instance of ADAM.

Solution

Using a graphical user interface

To install ADAM on a Windows Server 2003 R2 server, do the following:

1. Click Start → Control Panel → Add/Remove Programs.
2. Click Add/Remove Windows Components.
3. Select Active Directory Services, and click Details.
4. Place a checkmark next to Active Directory Application Mode (ADAM). Click OK and then Next to continue.
5. If prompted, provide the path to the Windows Server 2003 R2 Disc 2 media.
6. Click Finish when all files have copied.

To install ADAM on Windows XP or Windows Server 2003, do the following:

1. Double-click on the ADAM installer. Click Next to begin.
2. After reading the License Agreement, select the radio button next to "I agree" and click Next.
3. Click Finish when all files have copied.

Using a command-line interface

To perform a silent install of ADAM, use the following syntax:

```
> <ADAM Installer File> /q
```

The /q switch is not supported by the ADAM installer that is included with R2; to perform an unattended install of an ADAM instance on R2, see Recipe 19.2 and Recipe 19.3.

Discussion

At its most basic level, an ADAM installation will simply copy the necessary program files and DLLs to the machine in question without creating an ADAM instance or performing any other configuration steps. This can be useful if you want to include ADAM as part of a base image that you deploy to your application developers, while allowing them to create their own ADAM instances and configuration sets as they see fit. By using the /q switch on the ADAM installation file, you can deploy it during Windows setup or through an automated batch file.

If the ADAM installation encounters any errors, these will be logged in the *%windir%\Debug\adamsetup.log* file.

See Also

Recipe 19.2, Recipe 19.3, MS KB 840991 (Active Directory Application Mode Does Not Function Correctly in Windows Server 2003 or Windows XP), MSDN: About Active Directory Application Mode [ADAM], and Chapter 18 of *Active Directory*, Third Edition, by Joe Richards et al. (O'Reilly)

19.2   Creating a New ADAM Instance

Problem

You want to create a new ADAM instance.

Solution

Using a graphical user interface

1. Click on Start → All Programs → ADAM → Create an ADAM instance. Click Next to begin.
2. Select the radio button next to "A unique instance" and click Next.
3. Enter the name of the ADAM instance and click Next.
4. Enter the LDAP and SSL port numbers that will be used to access this instance; these default to 50000 and 50001 on a domain controller or any computer that is already listening on the default LDAP port. Otherwise, the LDAP and SSL ports that ADAM chooses during the installation will be 389 and 636.

If you've already installed an ADAM instance on ports 50000 and 50001, the ADAM installer will choose the next two ports available; the second ADAM instance would choose ports 50002 and 50003, then 50004 and 50005, and so on.

5. Click Next to continue.

6. Specify whether you want to create an Application Directory Partition for this instance. You can use any partition name isn't already being used, such as cn=IntranetApplication,dc=rallencorp,dc=com. Click Next to continue.

7. Specify the directory that will house the ADAM instance data as well as its data recovery files. These will both default to *c:\Program Files\Microsoft ADAM\ <instance name>\data*. Click Next.

8. On the Service Account Selection screen, configure the account under whose security context this instance will run. By default, the Network service account is selected, or you can click the radio button next to "This account" and specify a different account.

9. On the ADAM administrator's screen, specify the user or group account that will have administrative rights to this ADAM instance. This defaults to the currently logged-on user, or you can click the radio button next to "This account" and specify a different user or group. Click Next.

10. Specify whether you want to import additional LDIF files into this ADAM instance. See Recipe 19.7 for more information.

11. Click Next twice and then Finish to create the new ADAM instance.

Using a command-line interface

Create an answer file similar to the one listed here. Save it as *adam_install.txt*.

```
[ADAMInstall]

; Install a unique ADAM instance
InstallType=Unique

; Specify the name of the new instance
InstanceName=IntranetApplication

; Specify the ports to be used by LDAP.
LocalLDAPPortToListenOn=50000
LocalSSLPortToListenOn=50001

; Create a new application partition
NewApplicationPartitionToCreate="cn=IntranetApplication,dc=rallencorp,dc=com"

; The following line specifies the directory to use for ADAM data files.
DataFilesPath=C:\Program Files\Microsoft ADAM\IntranetApplication\data
```

```
; The following line specifies the directory to use for ADAM log files.
LogFilesPath=D:\ADAM Log Files\IntranetApplication\logs

; The following line specifies the .ldf files to import into the ADAM schema.
ImportLDIFFiles="ms-inetorgperson.ldf" "ms-user.ldf"
```

Then enter the following command at the Run line or from the Windows command prompt:

```
> adaminstall.exe /answer:<driveletter>:\<pathname>\<answerfile.txt>
```

Discussion

An ADAM *instance* refers to a single installation of ADAM on a particular server or workstation. A single Windows 2003 computer can host multiple instances of ADAM simultaneously; they are all independently managed and use different LDAP and LDAPS ports to communicate. Just as you can have multiple web servers operating on the same computer, with one using TCP port 80 and one using TCP port 8081, you can likewise have multiple ADAM instances running simultaneously on different ports.

When you create an ADAM instance, you also have the option to create an application directory partition to associate with the instance. An ADAM instance can have zero, one, or multiple application partitions associated with it that will be used to store ADAM application data such as security principals as well as user and group information.

See Also

Recipe 19.7, MSDN: Binding to an Instance [ADAM], and Chapter 18 of *Active Directory*, Third Edition, by Joe Richards et al. (O'Reilly)

19.3   Creating a New Replica of an ADAM Configuration Set

Problem

You want to create a new replica of an existing ADAM configuration set.

Solution

Using a graphical user interface

1. Click on Start → All Programs → ADAM → Create an ADAM instance. Click Next to begin.
2. Select the radio button next to "A replica of an existing instance" and click Next.
3. Enter the name of the instance that you want to connect to and click Next.

4. Enter the LDAP and SSL port numbers that will be used to access this instance; these default to 50000 and 50001 on a domain controller or any computer that is already listening on the default LDAP port. Otherwise, the LDAP and SSL ports that ADAM chooses during the installation will be 389 and 636.

 If you've already installed an ADAM instance on ports 50000 and 50001, the ADAM installer will choose the next two ports available; the second ADAM instance would choose ports 50002 and 50003, then 50004 and 50005, and so on.

5. On the Join a Configuration Set screen, enter the name of a server hosting an existing replica of this instance, and the port number used to connect to it. Click Next to continue.

6. On the Administrative Credentials for the Configuration Set screen, specify a user or group account that has administrative rights to this ADAM instance. This defaults to the currently logged-on user, or you can click the radio button next to "This account" and specify a different user or group. Click Next.

7. On the Copy Application Partitions screen, select the application directory partitions that you would like to replicate to the local server. Use the Add, Remove, Select All, and Remove All buttons to select the appropriate partitions. Click Next to continue.

8. Specify the directory that will house the ADAM instance data as well as its data recovery files. These will both default to *c:\Program Files\Microsoft ADAM\ <instance name>\data*. Click Next.

9. On the Service Account Selection screen, configure the account under whose security context this instance will run. By default, the Network service account is selected, or you can click the radio button next to "This account" and specify a different account.

10. On the ADAM Administrators screen, specify the user or group account that will have administrative rights to this ADAM instance. This defaults to the currently logged-on user, or you can click the radio button next to "This account" and specify a different user or group. Click Next.

11. Click Next and then Finish to create the new ADAM replica.

Using a command-line interface

Create an answer file similar to the one listed here. Save it as *new_replica_install.txt*.

```
[ADAMInstall]

[ADAMInstall]
; Install a replica of an existing ADAM instance.
InstallType=Replica
; Specify the name of the new replica.
```

```
InstanceName=IntranetApplication
; Specify the ports used for LDAP and SSL.
LocalLDAPPortToListenOn=50000
LocalSSLPortToListenOn=50001
; The following line specifies the directory to use for ADAM data files.
DataFilesPath=C:\Program Files\Microsoft ADAM\IntranetApplication\data
; The following line specifies the directory to use for ADAM log files.
LogFilesPath=D:\ADAM Log Files\IntranetApplication\logs
; Specify the name of the a computer hosting an existing replica
SourceServer=servername
SourceLDAPPort=389
```

Then enter the following command at the Run line or from the Windows command prompt:

```
> adaminstall.exe /answer:<driveletter>:\<pathname>\<answerfile.txt>
```

Discussion

Similar to Active Directory itself, ADAM uses *multimaster replication* that allows multiple computers to host, read, and make updates to one or more *configuration sets*. An ADAM *replica* is a computer that is hosting one instance of a particular configuration set. Unlike Active Directory, you can host replica instances on computers that are running any Windows XP or Windows Server 2003 computer; you are not restricted to replicating data only to your domain controllers. Conversely, you are also no longer forced to replicate data to *all* of your domain controllers unnecessarily; this can be quite useful in the case of data that is locally interesting, but that perhaps doesn't need to be replicated throughout your entire AD environment.

See Also

Recipe 19.2 for creating a new ADAM instance, MSDN: Using Application Directory Partitions [ADAM], and Chapter 18 of *Active Directory*, Third Edition, by Joe Richards et al. (O'Reilly)

19.4   Stopping and Starting an ADAM Instance

Problem

You want to start or stop an ADAM instance.

Solution

Using a graphical user interface

1. Open the Services MMC snap-in.
2. Select the name of the ADAM instance that you want to manage.
3. Right-click on the instance name and select Start, Stop, Pause, Resume, or Restart, as needed.

Using a command-line interface

To stop an ADAM instance, enter the following:

```
> net stop <instance_name>
```

To start an ADAM instance, enter the following:

```
> net start <instance_name>
```

Using VBScript

```
' The following code will stop or start an ADAM instance
'--------------- SCRIPT CONFIGURATION -----------------
strComputer = "."
strInstanceName - "<IntranetApplication>" ' ie "ADAM_IntranetApplication"
'------------------------------------------------------
Set objWMIService = GetObject("winmgmts:" _
    & "{impersonationLevel=impersonate}!\\" & strComputer & "\root\cimv2")

Set colServiceList - objWMIService.ExecQuery _
    ("Select * from Win32_Service where Name='" & strInstanceName & "'")

For Each objService in colServiceList
    errReturn = objService.StartService() ' change this method name to
                                          ' .StopService() to stop the
                                          ' ADAM instance.
Next
```

Discussion

When you install an ADAM instance on a computer (regardless of whether it is a new or replica instance), the instance will advertise itself as a typical Windows Service with the naming convention of ADAM_<InstanceName>, where <InstanceName> is the name you specified when you installed the instance. If you need to modify the display name of the service after you've installed the ADAM instance, you can use the built-in sc utility as follows:

```
> sc \\<servername> config <servicename> displayname = "<display name>"
```

See Also

Recipe 19.6 for listing the ADAM instances installed on a computer, MSDN: Service-ControllerStatusEnumeration, MSDN: Service Control Utilities [SDK Tools], and Chapter 18 of *Active Directory*, Third Edition, by Joe Richards et al. (O'Reilly)

19.5 Changing the Ports Used by an ADAM Instance

Problem

You want to change the LDAP or SSL ports that are being used by a particular ADAM instance.

Solution

```
> dsdbutil
>    activate instance <instancename>
>    LDAP port <port>
>    SSL port <port>
> quit
```

Discussion

If you need to change the LDAP and/or SSL port that an instance is using to communicate, you must first stop the instance using one of the methods specified in Recipe 19.4. Once the instance has stopped, use *dsdbutil* as shown in the Solution.

See Also

Recipe 19.4 for more on starting and stopping ADAM instances and Chapter 18 of *Active Directory*, Third Edition, by Joe Richards et al. (O'Reilly)

19.6 Listing the ADAM Instances Installed on a Computer

Problem

You want to list all of the ADAM instances installed on a computer.

Solution

Using a command-line interface

To list all ADAM instances installed on a computer, enter the following:

```
> dsdbutil
```

From the dsbutil: prompt, enter the following:

```
> list instances
```

Using VBScript

```
' The following code will list all ADAM instances on the local computer
'---------------- SCRIPT CONFIGURATION -----------------
strComputer = "."
'-------------------------------------------------------
```

```
Set objWMIService = GetObject("winmgmts:" _
    & "{impersonationLevel=impersonate}!\\" & strComputer & "\root\cimv2")

Set services = objWMIService.ExecQuery _
    ("Select * from Win32_Service where Name Like '%ADAM_%'")

If services.Count = 0 Then
    Wscript.Echo "No ADAM instances found."
Else
    For Each service in services
        Wscript.Echo service.Name & " -- " & service.State
    Next
End If
```

Discussion

As we discussed in Recipe 19.4, a single computer can host multiple ADAM instances running on different ports, each of which will advertise itself as a typical Windows Service. These services will have a naming convention of ADAM_ *<InstanceName>*, where *<InstanceName>* is the name that you specified when you installed the instance. (The name of the service will remain the same even if you change the display name or description of the service at a later time, which can make the *services.msc* snap-in a less-than-desirable option for stopping and starting ADAM instances if you make a habit of renaming them.) By querying for service names that include the string "ADAM" using something like '%ADAM_%' in the WQL query, you can return the ADAM instances that are installed on a local or remote computer.

The method discussed in this recipe will not help you, however, if someone has modified the Registry key containing the name of the ADAM instance. Locating ADAM services can be a difficult task if someone in your organization is trying to hide his ADAM instances. One possible solution if you are having difficulty with this type of information gathering would be to perform a port scan on one or more target computers; once you've obtained a list of listening ports, you can connect to each one in turn and look for an LDAP response.

See Also

Recipe 19.4, MSDN: Querying with WQL [WMI], MSDN: WQL Operators [WMI], and Chapter 18 of *Active Directory*, Third Edition, by Joe Richards et al. (O'Reilly)

19.7 Extending the ADAM Schema

Problem

You want to extend the ADAM Schema with new classes or attributes.

Solution

Using a command-line interface

To extend the ADAM Schema from the command-line, you'll need to create an LDIF file containing the necessary schema extensions, and then import it using the LDIFDE command, or use a tool like AdMod to perform the changes. ADAM comes with a number of such LDIF files pre-installed that you can import during the ADAM installation process. If you did not import these files during installation, you can do so after the fact using the following syntax:

```
> ldifde -i -f <driveletter>:\<pathname>\contact.ldf –s<servername>:<portnumber>-k
-j . -c "CN=Schema,CN=Configuration" #schemaNamingContext
```

Discussion

The schema that you receive when you install ADAM contains a subset of the classes and attributes that exist in the Active Directory Schema. You have the same ability to extend the schema in ADAM as you do in AD, which means that you can expand and modify the schema to be the same as the AD Schema, or to match any changes made by your third-party or home-grown applications. Because of this, ADAM is a great place to test potential schema modifications that you want to make in Active Directory. Because the schema extension process works the same in both AD and ADAM, and because you can easily install, uninstall, and reinstall ADAM instances, you can use ADAM to quickly test new extensions, tweaking the definitions until you get exactly what you want.

Every instance of ADAM will have at least two partitions: the Configuration partition and the Schema partition; you can create additional application partitions during or after installation as described in Chapter 18. Similar to the Active Directory Schema NC, the ADAM Schema partition contains definitions of classes and attributes that can be used to create objects within a particular ADAM instance. An ADAM Schema is unique to an individual ADAM instance; changes to the schema in one instance will not affect the schema in other, separate instances. ADAM comes with a number of pre-configured LDIF files that you can import to create common object types such as user, contact, and inetorgperson objects. You can import these LDIF files during the initial creation of an ADAM instance as well as after the instance has been created.

Using a command-line interface

When updating the ADAM Schema, be sure to use the version of *ldifde* that came with ADAM rather than any earlier versions of the utility.

See Also

Recipe 19.2, MSDN: Adding User Classes [ADAM], MSDN: Adding Contact Classes [ADAM], MSDN: Extending the Active Directory Application Mode Schema [ADAM], and Chapter 18 of *Active Directory*, Third Edition, by Joe Richards et al. (O'Reilly)

19.8   Managing ADAM Application Partitions

Problem

You want to add or remove an application partition to house ADAM data.

Solution

Using a graphical user interface

To add an application partition, do the following:

1. Open *ldp.exe* from the Windows Support Tools. Click Connection → Connect to bind to an ADAM instance, and Connection → Bind to provide credentials to bind to the instance.
2. Click on Browse → Add child.
3. For DN, enter a distinguished name for the application partition.
4. Under Edit entry, enter ObjectClass in the Attribute box and container in the Values box and then click Enter.
5. Under Edit entry, enter instanceType for the Attribute and 5 in the Values box, and then click Enter.
6. Click Run.

To remove an application partition, do the following:

1. Open ADAM ADSI Edit. If necessary, create and bind to a connection of your ADAM instance.
2. Browse to the Partitions container (CN=Partitions). Right-click on the application directory partition that you want to delete, and then click Delete.
3. Click Yes to confirm.

Using a command-line interface

Use the following sequence of commands to create an ADAM application partition:

```
> dsmgmt
>    create nc <ApplicationPartitionDN> container <ComputerName>:<PortNumber>
>      quit
> quit
```

Use the following command to delete an application partition:

```
> dsmgmt
>    delete nc <ApplicationPartitionDN>
>      quit
> quit
```

Using VBScript

```
' This code creates an application partition off of the
' root of the default forest.
' ------ SCRIPT CONFIGURATION ------
strAppPart = "<AppPartitionName>" ' DN of the app partition to delete
strServer  = "<DomainControllerName>" ' DNS name of DC to host app partition
strDescr   = "<Description>"  ' Descriptive text about the app partition
' ------ END CONFIGURATION ---------

set objRootDSE = GetObject("LDAP://" & strServer & "/RootDSE")
set objLDAP = GetObject("LDAP://" & strServer & "/" & _
                        objRootDSE.Get("rootDomainNamingContext") )
set objAppPart = objLDAP.Create("domainDNS", "dc=" & strAppPart)
objAppPart.Put "instancetype", 5
objAppPart.Put "description", strDescr
objAppPart.SetInfo
WScript.Echo "Created application partition: " & strAppPart

' This code deletes the specified application partition
' ------ SCRIPT CONFIGURATION ------
strAppPart = "<AppPartitionDN>"  ' DN of the app partition to delete
' ------ END CONFIGURATION ---------

set objRootDSE = GetObject("LDAP://RootDSE")
strBase = "<LDAP://cn=Partitions," & _
          objRootDSE.Get("ConfigurationNamingContext") & ">;"
strFilter   = "(&(objectcategory=crossRef)(nCName=" & _
              strAppPart & "));"
strAttrs   = "cn,distinguishedName;"
strScope   = "onelevel"

set objConn = CreateObject("ADODB.Connection")
objConn.Provider = "ADsDSOObject"
objConn.Open "Active Directory Provider"
set objRS = objConn.Execute(strBase & strFilter & strAttrs & strScope)

if objRS.RecordCount <> 1 then
   WScript.Echo "Did not find a match for " & strAppPart
else
   objRS.MoveLast
   set objAppPart = GetObject("LDAP://" & _
                             objRS.Fields("distinguishedName").Value )
   objAppPart.DeleteObject(0)
   Wscript.Echo "Deleted " & objRS.Fields("distinguishedName").Value
end if
```

Discussion

An ADAM installation creates up to three partitions by default: Configuration, Schema, and an application. The Configuration and Schema partitions get created automatically during the creation of a new ADAM instance; you can create application partitions during the initial installation or after the instance has been created. If you're installing a replica of an existing ADAM configuration set, the existing Schema and Configuration partitions are automatically replicated to the new instance. The Configuration partition stores information about ADAM replication and partitions, while the Schema partition contains definitions for the types of objects that you can create within the ADAM instance. (These partitions correspond quite closely to the Configuration and Schema naming contexts within Active Directory.)

When you create a new application directory partition, you need to specify a *distinguished name* for the partition; this name needs to be unique within your environment.

See Also

MSDN: Using Application Directory Partitions [ADAM], MSDN: Creating an Application Directory Partition [ADAM], MSDN: Deleting an Application Directory Partition [ADAM], and Chapter 18 of *Active Directory*, Third Edition, by Joe Richards et al. (O'Reilly)

19.9   Managing ADAM Organizational Units

Problem

You want to create or delete OUs within an ADAM instance.

Solution

Using a graphical user interface

1. Open ADAM ADSI Edit. If necessary, create and bind to a connection of your ADAM instance.
2. Right-click on the instance and select New → Object.
3. Under "Select a class," click on organizationalUnit and click Next.
4. For the value of the ou attribute, type AdamUsers and click Next.
5. Click Finish.
6. To delete an OU, right-click on the object in question and select Delete.

Using a command-line interface

To create an ADAM OU from the command-line, use the following syntax:

```
> admod -h <ComputerName>:<PortNumber> -b <OU DN>
  objectClass::organizationalUnit -add
```

To delete an OU, replace the –add switch with –del in the previous statement.

Using VBScript

```
' The following code will add a new OU to an ADAM instance
'--------------- SCRIPT CONFIGURATION -----------------
strComputerName = "<ComputerName>" ' Use "localhost" for the local computer
strPort = "<PortNumber>"            ' the LDAP port number to connect to
strAppPart = "<Application Partition DN>"
'------------------------------------------------------

Set objDomain = GetObject("LDAP://" & strComputerName & _
                          ":" & strPort & "/" & strAppPart)
Set objOU = objDomain.Create("organizationalUnit", "ou=Finance")
objOU.SetInfo

' The following code will delete the OU you just created
objOU.Delete "organizationalUnit", "ou=Finance"
```

Discussion

Creating OUs in ADAM is identical to creating them within Active Directory. Just like in AD, ADAM OUs are containers that can contain other objects such as users, groups, contacts, or other OUs. You can also delegate permissions to an OU, allowing a user or group to have rights to the OU itself and to objects within that OU.

Using a command-line interface

A useful feature of AdFind and AdMod is that, if you are working on ADAM or AD on the local machine, you can use a period (.) for the hostname and it will expand that into *localhost* for you.

See Also

Recipe 19.19 for more on managing ADAM permissions, Chapter 5 for more on managing Active Directory OUs, and Chapter 18 of *Active Directory*, Third Edition, by Joe Richards et al. (O'Reilly)

19.10 Managing ADAM Users

Problem

You want to create or delete user objects within an ADAM instance.

Solution

Using a graphical user interface

1. Open ADAM ADSI Edit. If necessary, create a connection and bind to the necessary ADAM instance.
2. Right-click on the container that should house the user and select New → Object.
3. Under "Select a class," click on "user" and click Next.
4. For the value of the cn attribute, type Joe Smith and click Next.
5. Click Finish.

Using a command-line interface

```
> admod -h <ComputerName>:<PortNumber> -b <OU DN>
  objectClass::user -add
```

Using VBScript

```
' The following code will add a new OU to an ADAM instance
'---------------- SCRIPT CONFIGURATION -----------------
strComputerName = "<ComputerName>" ' Use "localhost" for the local computer
strPort = "<PortNumber>"            ' the LDAP port number to connect to
strAppPart = "<Application Partition DN>" ' ie "o=rallencorp,c=us"
strUserDN = "<UserDN>"              ' ie "Joe Smith"
strUPN - "<UserPrincipalName>"      ' ie "joe@rallencorp.com"
'------------------------------------------------------

Set objOU = GetObject("LDAP://" & strComputerName & _ ":" & strPort & _
                  "/" & strAppPart))
Set objUser = objOU.Create("user", strUserDN)
objUser.Put "displayName", strUserDN
objUser.Put "userPrincipalName", strUPN
objUser.SetInfo
```

Discussion

Creating users in ADAM is quite similar to creating users in Active Directory. The most significant difference is that ADAM users do not have the sAMAccountName attribute. You could conceivably define such an attribute within ADAM and associate it with the user class, but it will not have the same properties that it does in Active Directory, particularly the AD constraint in which sAMAccountName uniqueness is enforced across a domain. ADAM also would not be able to use a manually-created attribute like that for user logons the way that sAMAccountName is used in AD.

If you create an ADAM user on a Windows Server 2003 or R2 computer without creating a password for it, the object will be disabled until you enable it using LDP or an ADSI script.

See Also

Recipe 19.11 to configure the password for an ADAM user, MSDN: Managing Users [ADAM], MSDN: Set or Modify the Password of an ADAM User [ADAM], and Chapter 18 of *Active Directory*, Third Edition, by Joe Richards et al. (O'Reilly)

19.11 Changing the Password for an ADAM User

Problem

You want to change the password for an ADAM user.

Solution

Using a graphical user interface

1. Open LDP from the Windows Support Tools.
2. Click Connection → Connect, and then enter the server name and port number used by your ADAM instance.
3. Click Options → Connection Options.
4. In the Option Name drop-down, select LDAP_OPT_SIGN, type 1 in Value, and then click Set.
5. Select LDAP_OPT_ENCRYPT, type 1 in Value, click Set and then Close.
6. Click Connection → Bind, and then enter a username and password to bind to the ADAM instance.
7. Click on View → Tree. Leave the BaseDN value blank and click OK.
8. Navigate to the DN of the container within the application partition containing the ADAM user in question.
9. Right-click the CN=<UserName> user object, and then click Modify.
10. Enter userpassword as the attribute to be modified, and then enter the new password under Values.
11. Click Enter, and then click Run.

Using VBScript

```
' The following code will set the password for an ADAM user
'--------------- SCRIPT CONFIGURATION ----------------
Const ADS_SECURE_AUTHENTICATION =   1
Const ADS_USE_SSL               =   2
```

```
Const ADS_USE_SIGNING          =  64
Const ADS_USE_SEALING          = 128

Const ADS_OPTION_PASSWORD_PORTNUMBER = 6
Const ADS_OPTION_PASSWORD_METHOD     = 7

Const ADS_PASSWORD_ENCODE_REQUIRE_SSL = 0
Const ADS_PASSWORD_ENCODE_CLEAR       = 1

strComputerName = "<ComputerName>" ' Use "localhost" for the local computer
strPort = "<PortNumber>"           ' the LDAP port number to connect to
intPort = CInt(strPort)
strUserDN = "<UserDN>"             ' ie "Joe Smith"

lngAuth = ADS_USE_SIGNING Or ADS_USE_SEALING Or _
          ADS_SECURE_AUTHENTICATION
'--------------------------------------------------------

' Bind to the user whose password you want to change
Set objUser = GetObject _
    ("LDAP://" & strComputerName & ":"  & strPort & "/" & strUserDN, _
      vbNullString, vbNullString, lngAuth)

' Set the password for the user.
objUser.SetOption ADS_OPTION_PASSWORD_PORTNUMBER, intPort
objUser.SetOption ADS_OPTION_PASSWORD_METHOD, _
                  ADS_PASSWORD_ENCODE_CLEAR

' In a production script, this should be read in as a script argument
' rather than being embedded in clear-text within the script itself
objUser.SetPassword "ADAMComplexPassword1234"

If Err.Number <>0 Then
    WScript.Echo "Error:    Set password failed with error " _
                            & Hex(Err.Number)
Else
    WScript.Echo "Success:  Password set for user"
    WScript.Echo "          " & objUser.ADsPath
End If
```

Discussion

To create user objects within an ADAM instance, you first need to import the optional LDIF that are provided with ADAM installer into the ADAM schema, including *ms-User.ldf*, *ms-InetOrgPerson.ldf*, and *ms-UserProxy.ldf*. The *ms-user.ldf* file allows you to create Person, organizational-Person, and User objects. Any ADAM user objects that you create on a Windows Server 2003 computer will adhere to whatever local or domain password and account lockout policies are in place on the server that's hosting the ADAM instance. You can use the procedures listed here to change the password for an ADAM user, or to set a password for an ADAM user that was created without specifying an initial password.

Using a command-line interface

You can also use *ldifde* to set or change an ADAM user's password, but it requires a 128-bit SSL connection with a certificate installed on the computer that's running the ADAM instance.

You can also perform this using the –kerbenc switch in `admod`, as follows:

```
> admod -h . -b cn=jsmith,o=test userpassword::mypasswordQ1 -kerbenc
```

See Also

MS KB 263991 (How to Set a User's Password with LDIFDE), MSDN: Setting User Passwords [ADAM], and Chapter 18 of *Active Directory*, Third Edition, by Joe Richards et al. (O'Reilly)

19.12 Enabling and Disabling an ADAM User

Problem

You want to enable or disable an ADAM user object.

Solution

Using a graphical user interface

1. Open ADAM ADSI Edit. If necessary, create and bind to a connection of your ADAM instance.
2. Navigate to the user in question, right-click and select Properties.
3. Scroll to the msDS-UserAccountDisabled attribute and click Edit.
4. Click True, and then click OK.
5. To re-enable the ADAM user account, modify the msDS-UserAccountDisabled attribute to have a value of `False`.

Using a command-line interface

To disable an ADAM user from the command-line, enter the following syntax:

```
> admod -h <ComputerName>:<PortNumber> -b <User DN>
  msDS-UserAccountDisabled::TRUE
```

To enable or re-enable a user account, change `TRUE` to `FALSE` in the previous command.

When configuring this attribute, `TRUE` and `FALSE` are case-sensitive and must be specified using all uppercase letters.

Using VBScript

```
' The following code will enable or disable an ADAM user
'--------------- SCRIPT CONFIGURATION -----------------
strComputerName = "<ComputerName>" ' Use "localhost" for the local computer
strPort = "<PortNumber>"           ' the LDAP port number to connect to
strUserDN = "<UserDN>"             ' ie "Joe Smith"
'------------------------------------------------------

Set objUser = GetObject _
    ("LDAP://" & strComputerName & ":"  & strPort & "/" & strUserDN)

objUser.Put "msDS-UserAccountDisabled", "FALSE"    ' set this to TRUE to disable
objUser.SetInfo
```

Discussion

ADAM users can be enabled or disabled by modifying the `msDS-UserAccountDisabled` property. A new ADAM user will be enabled by default when you first create it, unless the password you've assigned for it doesn't meet the requirements of the password policy, which is in effect on the machine. This restriction doesn't apply to ADAM instances that are being housed on Windows XP Professional computers, since ADAM support on XP is primarily intended for standalone development tasks rather than hosting enterprise-caliber applications.

See Also

Recipe 19.11 for more on setting the password of an ADAM user, MSDN: ms-DS-User-Account-Disabled Attribute [AD Schema], and Chapter 18 of *Active Directory*, Third Edition, by Joe Richards et al. (O'Reilly)

19.13 Managing ADAM Groups

Problem

You want to create or delete a group object within ADAM.

Solution

Using a graphical user interface

1. Open ADAM ADSI Edit. If necessary, create and bind to a connection of your ADAM instance.
2. Right-click on the instance and select New → Object.
3. Under "Select a class," click on group and click Next.
4. For the value of the cn attribute, type AdamGroup and click Next.
5. Leave the value of the groupType attribute blank to create a security-enabled global group and click Next.

6. Click Finish.

7. To delete a group object, right-click on the object in question and select Delete.

Using a command-line interface

To disable an ADAM user from the command line, enter the following syntax:

```
> admod -h <ComputerName>:<PortNumber> -b <Group DN>
  objectClass::group -add
```

 To delete a group object, change –add to –del in the previous command.

Using VBScript

```
' The following code will create a group object
'---------------- SCRIPT CONFIGURATION -----------------
strComputerName = "<ComputerName>" ' Use "localhost" for the local computer
strPort = "<PortNumber>"            ' the LDAP port number to connect to
strOUDN = "<OUDN>"                  ' ie "ou=AdamUsers,o=rallencorp,c=us"
strGroupName = "<GroupName>"        ' ie "cn=FinanceGroup"
'-----------------------------------------------------

Set objOU = GetObject("LDAP://" & strComputerName _
                       & ":" & strPort & "/" & strOUDN)
Set objGroup = objOU.Create("group", strGroupName)
objGroup.SetInfo

' The following code snippet will delete the group you just created
objOU.delete "group", strGroupName
```

Discussion

Group objects in ADAM are greatly simplified compared to their Active Directory counterparts, since the notion of security and distribution groups as two separate entities does not exist. In addition, all ADAM groups have the same scope: an ADAM group that has been created within an application partition can only be used within that partition; a security principal that's been created in the Configuration NC can be used in all naming contexts in that ADAM instance. This means that a group or user that was created in Instance1 cannot be used to assign permissions on objects in Instance2 or be added to a group in Instance2. Windows security principals can be assigned permissions in any application partition. And just like ADAM user objects, ADAM group objects do not contain the sAMAccountName attribute.

When you first install an ADAM instance, you have four default groups that are installed in the CN=Roles container: *Administrators*, *Instances*, *Readers*, and *Users*.

See Also

MSDN: Enumerating Users and Groups [ADAM], MSDN: Creating Groups [ADAM], MSDN: Deleting Groups [MSDN], and Chapter 18 of *Active Directory*, Third Edition, by Joe Richards et al. (O'Reilly)

19.14 Managing ADAM Group Memberships

Problem

You want to manage the groups that an ADAM user is a member of.

Solution

Using a graphical user interface

1. Open ADAM ADSI Edit. Connect and bind to the ADAM instance you want to manage.

2. Navigate to the group in question, right-click and select Properties.

3. Scroll to the member attribute and click Edit.

4. To add a Windows user to the group, click Add Windows Account and enter the name of the Windows account. To add an ADAM user, click Add ADAM Account and enter the DN of the user you wish to add. Repeat this to add additional users.

5. To remove members, click on the CN of the object you wish to remove, and then click Remove. Repeat this to remove additional users from the group.

6. To enumerate a user's group memberships, scroll to the user in question, right-click and select Properties. Double-click on the memberOf attribute to view all group memberships for this user.

Using a command-line interface

To add an ADAM user to a group from the command-line, enter the following syntax:

```
> admod -h <ComputerName>:<PortNumber> -b <Group DN>
  member:+:"SID=<UserSID>"
```

To add multiple users at one time, change + to ++ in the previous command and separate the User DNs with a semicolon.

To remove a single user, change + to - in the previous command.

To remove multiple users, change + to -- in the previous command and separate the User DNs with a semicolon.

Using VBScript

```
' The following code will modify an ADAM group membership
'---------------- SCRIPT CONFIGURATION -----------------
Const ADS_PROPERTY_DELETE = 4
strComputerName = "<ComputerName>" ' Use "localhost" for the local computer
strPort = "<PortNumber>"           ' the LDAP port number to connect to
strGroupName = "<GroupName>"       ' ie "cn=FinanceGroup"
strUserName = "<UserName>"         ' ie "cn=Joe Smith,
                                         ou=AdamUsers,o=rallencorp,c=us"
'-------------------------------------------------------

Set objGroup = GetObject _
        ("LDAP://" & strComputerName & ":" & strPort & "/" & strGroupDN)
Set objUser = GetObject _
        ("LDAP://" & strComputerName & ":" & strPort & "/" & strUserDN)

' the following code will add a user object to a group
objGroup.Add objUser.AdsPath

' the following code will remove a user object from a group
objGroup.PutEx ADS_PROPERTY_DELETE, "member", _ Array(strUserName)
objGroup.SetInfo

' the following code will enumerate all members of a group
For Each objUser in objGroup.Members
    Wscript.Echo objUser.Name
Next

' the following code will enumerate all the groups that a user belongs to
arrMembersOf = objUser.GetEx("memberOf")

For Each strMemberOf in arrMembersOf
  WScript.Echo strMemberOf
Next
```

Discussion

ADAM group objects can contain both ADAM users and Windows security principals, which allows you to assign permissions to data stored in ADAM instances using a consistent method. In the case of groups that were created within a specific application partition, they can only be assigned permissions within that partition; groups that were created within the Configuration partition can be assigned permissions to objects in any partition within the ADAM instance.

Using a command-line interface

To insert a Windows principal into an ADAM group, you need to either know the `ForeignSecurityPrincipal` or the `userProxy` object that the Windows user is tied to within the ADAM instance; otherwise, you need to add the user by its SID as done here.

See Also

Recipe 19.13 for more on managing groups, MSDN: Adding a User to a Group [ADAM], MSDN: Removing Members from Groups [ADAM], and Chapter 18 of *Active Directory*, Third Edition, by Joe Richards et al. (O'Reilly)

19.15 Viewing and Modifying ADAM Object Attributes

Problem

You want to view the attributes of an object within an ADAM instance.

Solution

Using a graphical user interface

1. Open ADAM ADSI Edit. If necessary, create and bind to a connection of your ADAM instance.

2. Navigate to the object in question, right-click and select Properties. To view only the mandatory attributes for an object, remove the checkmark next to "Show optional attributes." To view only the optional attributes for an object, place a checkmark next to "Show optional attributes" and remove the checkmark next to "Show mandatory attributes."

3. Scroll through object's properties. To modify a particular property, select the property and select Edit.

4. To insert a value into a single-valued attribute, enter the value and click OK. To remove a value from a single-valued attribute, click Clear.

5. To insert one or more values into a multivalued attribute, enter each value and click Add. To remove one or more values from a multivalued attribute, select the value and click Remove.

Using a command-line interface

To view the attributes of an object, enter the following

```
> adfind -h <ComputerName>:<PortNumber> -b <Object DN> -s base
```

To restrict the AdFind output to only a few attributes, specify the name of each attribute you want to view after the ObjectDN; to view multiple attributes, separate each one with spaces in-between. You can also use the –excl switch to display all but one or two attributes.

To insert a value into a single-valued attribute, enter the following syntax:

```
> admod -h <ComputerName>:<PortNumber> -b <Object DN>
  <AttributeName>::<Value>
```

To insert multiple values into a multivalued attribute, change + to ++ in the previous command and separate the values with a semicolon.

To clear an attribute's value (whether a single- or a multivalued attribute), enter the following:

```
> admod -h <ComputerName>:<PortNumber> -b <Object DN>
  <AttributeName>:-
```

To remove a single value from a multivalued attribute, change - to -- in the previous command.

Using VBScript

```
' The following code will list all attributes of an object
'--------------- SCRIPT CONFIGURATION ----------------
strComputerName = "<ComputerName>" ' Use "localhost" for the local computer
strPort = "<PortNumber>"           ' the LDAP port number to connect to
strObjectDN = "<ObjectDN>"         ' ie "ou=AdamUsers,o=rallencorp,c=us"
strObjectType = "<ObjectType>"     ' ie "organizationalunit", "group", "user"
strAttributeName = "<AttributeName>" ' ie "description
strAttributeValue = "<AttributeValue>" ' ie "Description of this object"
'-----------------------------------------------------

Set objObject = GetObject _
        ("LDAP://" & strComputerName & ":" & strPort & "/" & strGroupDN)
Set objObjectProperties = GetObject("LDAP://" & strComputerName & _
                                    ":" & strPort & "/schema/" & _
                                    strObjectType

For Each strAttribute in objObjectProperties.MandatoryProperties
    strValues = objObject.GetEx(strAttribute)
    For Each strItem in strValues
        Wscript.Echo strAttribute & " -- " & strItem
    Next
Next

For Each strAttribute in objObjectProperties.OptionalProperties
    strValues = objObject.GetEx(strAttribute)
    If Err = 0 Then
        For Each strItem in strValues
            Wscript.Echo strAttribute & " -- " & strItem
        Next
```

```
    Else
        Wscript.Echo strAttribute & " --  No value set"
        Err.Clear
    End If
Next

' the following code will update an attribute value
objObject.Put strAttributeName, strAttributeValue
objObject.SetInfo
```

Discussion

Just like in Active Directory, each ADAM instance possesses a schema that defines what types of objects you can create and what sorts of attributes those objects possess. One of the major advantages of working with ADAM is that you can make changes to the schema of an ADAM instance without affecting the AD schema, thus allowing for more flexible application development that doesn't run the risk of making permanent or far-reaching changes to an entire Active Directory forest. Similar to AD, object classes can have both *mandatory* and *optional* attributes that you can view.

See Also

MSDN: Active Directory Application Mode Schema [ADAM], MSDN: Extending the Active Directory Application Mode Schema [ADAM], and Chapter 18 of *Active Directory*, Third Edition, by Joe Richards et al. (O'Reilly)

19.16 Importing Data into an ADAM Instance

Problem

You want to perform a bulk import of object data into an ADAM instance.

Solution

Using a command-line interface

To import objects using the *ldifde* utility, you must first create an LDIF file with the objects to add, modify, or delete. Here is an example LDIF file that adds three users to an ADAM application partition:

```
dn: cn=Joe Smith,cn=users,ou=AdamUsers,o=rallencorp,c=us
changetype: add
objectClass: user
cn: Joe Smith
name: Joe Smith

dn: cn=Richard Mahler,cn=users,ou=AdamUsers,o=rallencorp,c=us
changetype: add
objectClass: user
cn: Richard Mahler
```

```
name: Richard Mahler

dn: cn=Doug Martin,cn=users,ou=AdamUsers,o=rallencorp,c=us
changetype: add
objectClass: user
cn: Doug Martin
name: Doug Martin
```

Once you've created the LDIF file, you just need to run *ldifde* to import the new objects:

```
> ldifde -i -f c:\import.ldf -s <servername>:<portnumber> -k -j
```

 Be sure to use the version of *ldifde* that came with R2, not one from a previous version of the Windows OS or ADAM.

Discussion

For more information on the LDIF format, check RFC 2849.

Using a command-line interface

To import with *ldifde*, simply specify the -i switch to turn on import mode and -f <filename> for the file. It can also be beneficial to use the -v switch to turn on verbose mode to get more information in case of errors.

See Also

Recipe 4.29 for information on importing data using LDIF files, RFC 2849 (The LDAP Data Interchange Format (LDIF)—Technical Specification), MS KB 237677 (Using LDIFDE to Import and Export Directory Objects to Active Directory), and Chapter 18 of *Active Directory*, Third Edition, by Joe Richards et al. (O'Reilly)

19.17 Configuring Intrasite Replication

Problem

You want to create a replication schedule for an ADAM application partition that is hosted on multiple computers within a single site.

Using a graphical user interface

1. Open ADAM ADSI Edit. If necessary, create and bind to a connection of your ADAM instance.
2. Navigate to the Sites container and the name of the site you need to modify.
3. Right-click on CN=NTDS Site Settings, and then click Schedule.

4. Select the block of time that should be available for replication; for every available block of time, you can configure the replication frequency to None, Once per Hour, Twice per Hour, or Four Times per Hour. Click OK when you're finished.

Discussion

Like Active Directory, ADAM uses multimaster replication to copy information between replicas of each ADAM configuration set. By default, all ADAM instances that you create will be placed within a single site, Default-First-Site-Name. Similar to AD, ADAM's intrasite replication takes place through *update notifications*, where replication partners are notified as changes occur. The replication frequency schedule that you're configuring here is concerned with how replication occurs when no update notifications have occurred within the specified timeframe.

See Also

MSDN: Active Directory Application Mode Schema [ADAM], MSDN: Using Application Directory Partitions [ADAM], and Chapter 18 of *Active Directory*, Third Edition, by Joe Richards et al. (O'Reilly)

19.18 Forcing ADAM Replication

Problem

You want to force immediate replication of an ADAM application partition.

Solution

Using a command-line interface

```
> repadmin /syncall <servername>:<port> <AppPartitionDN>
```

Discussion

The *repadmin* command-line tool that comes with both AD and ADAM is primarily used to display and manage the replication topology of multiple directory servers. But *repadmin* can do much more, such as allowing you to view object metadata, update Service Principal Names (SPNs), and display information on trust relationships. You can see all of the basic options that are available by typing repadmin /? at a command prompt. Once you've familiarized yourself with these switches, you can then start learning about the more advanced features available by typing repadmin /experthelp. *repadmin* is one of those indispensable tools for an AD or ADAM administrator; it's well worth the time to learn its ins and outs to help you monitor and troubleshoot your network.

See Also

MS KB 229896 (Using Repadmin.exe to Troubleshoot Active Directory Replication), MS KB 905739 (TechNet Support WebCast: Troubleshooting Active Directory replication using the Repadmin tool), and Chapter 18 of *Active Directory*, Third Edition, by Joe Richards et al. (O'Reilly)

19.19 Managing ADAM Permissions

Problem

You want to manage permissions within an ADAM instance.

Solution

Using a graphical user interface

1. Open the version of LDP that was installed with ADAM, either ADAM SP1 or the ADAM that is installed with Windows Server 2003 R2.

2. Connect and bind to the object or container that you wish to modify.

3. Right-click on the object or container and select Advanced → Security Descriptor. To display and edit auditing information in addition to the Discretionary Access Lists (DACLs) associated with the object, place a checkmark next to SACL.

4. Click OK.

5. To delete an Access Control Entry (ACE), highlight the entry and click Delete.

6. To add an entry, click Add.

7. In the Trustee text box, enter the name of the user or group object that you wish to apply permissions to. In the ACE mask section, select whether you are creating *Allow ACE* or *Deny ACE*.

8. In the Access mask section, place checkmarks next to the permissions that you are allowing or denying.

9. Click OK when you are finished.

Using a command-line interface

To view the effective permissions on an ADAM object, use the following syntax:

```
> dsacls \\<servername>:<port>\<ObjectDN>
```

To grant permissions on an ADAM object, use the following:

```
> dsacls "\\<servername>:<port>\<ObjectDN>" /G <User or Group Receiving Permissions>:
<Permission Statement>
```

To deny permissions on an ADAM object, use the following:

```
> dsacls "\\<servername>:<port>\<ObjectDN>" /D <User or Group Receiving Permissions>:
<Permission Statement>
```

Discussion

One of the great new features of ADAM is the new version of the LDP utility that is installed with it, which provides you the ability to modify both DACL and SACL entries at an extremely granular level. You also have the familiar *dsacls* utility that will allow you to delegate permissions from the command line. When delegating permissions, you must first determine whether you are delegating permission over an entire container and all objects contained therein, or whether you are only going to delegate control over specific child objects. (For example, you can delegate control over all ADAM user objects within an OU.) Once you've made this determination, you'll then specify the specific permissions that you're delegating; you can delegate anything from Full Control of the entire object down to granting read permissions on a single attribute.

Using a command-line interface

dsacls requires a specific syntax for the permission statement used to grant or deny permissions, formatted in this manner:

```
[PermissionBits];[{Object|Property}];[InheritedObjectType]
```

[PermissionBits] here refers to any of the values listed in Table 19-1; you can specify one or more together with no spaces between them.

Table 19-1. Description of the PermissionBits values

Value	Description
GR	Generic Read
GE	Generic Execute
GW	Generic Write
GA	Generic All (FULL CONTROL)
SD	Delete
DT	Delete an object and all its child objects (DELETE TREE)
RC	Read security information
WD	Change security information
WO	Change owner information
LC	List child objects
CC	Create child objects
DC	Delete child objects
WS	Write to self
RP	Read property

Table 19-1. Description of the PermissionBits values (continued)

Value	Description
WP	Write property
CA	Control access
LO	List object access

The [Object | Property] option allows you to delegate permissions for an entire object, or for only specific properties of that object. For example, you can delegate the Write Property permission for all properties of an object, or only one or two specific properties.

See Also

MS KB 310997 (Active Directory Services and Windows 2000 or Windows Server 2003 domains), MS KB 315676 (How to Delegate Administrative Authority in Windows 2000), MS KB 281146 (How to Use Dsacls.exe in Windows Server 2003 and Windows 2000), and Chapter 18 of *Active Directory*, Third Edition, by Joe Richards et al. (O'Reilly)

## CHAPTER 20

Interoperability and Integration

20.0 Introduction

Active Directory supports several important industry standards that allow other services and platforms to interoperate and integrate with it. The LDAP is the standards-based protocol used by all major directory service vendors for directory access and management. LDAP is platform neutral, which means that you can access and manage data in Active Directory from a variety of platforms. Active Directory uses DNS for its name resolution services, so you can use tools such as *nslookup* or *dig* to locate domain controllers by making DNS queries. Kerberos is one of the most widely used network authentication protocols in existence and is supported by Active Directory so that even non-Windows-based Kerberos-enabled clients can authenticate. These are just a few of the standards that Active Directory supports. Throughout this chapter we will cover how you can access, manage, and integrate Active Directory in ways that are not typically documented.

20.1 Accessing AD from a Non-Windows Platform

Problem

You want to access or manage AD from a non-Windows platform.

Solution

Using a graphical user interface

One of the best platform-neutral graphical user interfaces for managing an LDAP directory such as Active Directory is the LDAP Browser/Editor. It was written in Java and can run on virtually any machine that has Java 1.2.2 or greater installed. It can be downloaded from the following site: *http://www.iit.edu/~gawojar/ldap*.

Using a command-line interface

The original LDAP server produced at the University of Michigan included a set of command-line utilities that can query and update an LDAP directory. Over time these tools have become very popular on the Unix platforms, and they can even be used to query and update Active Directory. The OpenLDAP project took over maintenance of the University of Michigan's LDAP server, as well as the command-line tools. To download the latest version of the tools, go to the following site: *http://www.openldap.org*.

Using a programming language

Any programming language that supports LDAP can be used to programmatically access and manage Active Directory. See Recipes 20.4, 20.5, and 20.6 for examples using Perl, Python, Java, and PHP.

Discussion

Due to the fact that LDAP is an open standard, it has been adopted on many platforms and programming languages. While you can perform 90 percent of the things you would need to do from a non-Windows platform, some tasks do still require a Windows GUI, CLI, or API. For example, there is no easy way to manage ACLs in Active Directory from a non-Windows platform. You can, however, do virtually anything you need to do as far as adding, modifying, and removing objects in Active Directory with the basic LDAP-enabled tools.

See Also

Recipes 20.4, 20.5, and 20.6 for more on how to programmatically query and update Active Directory using Perl, Java, and Python

20.2   Programming with .NET

Problem

You want to programmatically access Active Directory using the .NET Framework.

Solution

The System.DirectoryServices namespace can be used to interface with Active Directory using the .NET Framework. The following code is a simple VB.NET program that prints the attributes of the RootDSE:

```
    Imports System.DirectoryServices

    Module Module1

        Sub Main( )

            Dim objRootDSE As New DirectoryEntry("LDAP://RootDSE")

            Dim strAttrName As String
            Dim objValue As Object

            For Each strAttrName In objRootDSE.Properties.PropertyNames
                For Each objValue In objRootDSE.Properties(strAttrName)
                    Console.WriteLine(strAttrName & " : " & objValue.ToString)
                Next objValue
            Next strAttrName

        End Sub

    End Module
```

Discussion

The System.DirectoryServices namespace is a generic directory service interface that
is works with ADSI to provide a rich set of properties and methods for accessing,
querying, and manipulating objects in Active Directory. Currently, there is no native
support for scripting languages such as VBScript and Perl, but you can use Microsoft's
version of JavaScript (i.e., JScript) with .NET to utilize System.DirectoryServices.

The System.DirectoryServices DirectorySearcher class is a simple interface for making LDAP queries. The DirectoryEntry class is used for instantiating existing objects
or creating new ones. In the Solution section, we used the DirectoryEntry class to
access the RootDSE. DirectorySearcher and DirectoryEntry are the two main classes
to become familiar with if you want to do Active Directory programming with .NET.
For more information and examples on using System.DirectoryServices, see Chapter 31 of *Active Directory*, Third Edition, by Joe Richards et al. (O'Reilly).

System.DirectoryServices does not currently provide interfaces for everything that
could be done with ADSI. Instead, you can use the NativeObject property on an
instantiated object to return an ADSI object, which you can then use to access any
ADSI properties or methods for the object.

See Also

Chapter 31 in *Active Directory*, Third Edition, by Joe Richards et al. (O'Reilly) and
reference information for System.DirectoryServices at *http://msdn.microsoft.com/
library/en-us/cpref/html/frlrfSystemDirectoryServices.asp*

20.3 Programming with DSML

Problem

You want to programmatically access Active Directory using the Directory Services Markup Language (DSML). DSML is the answer for programmers who have been longing for an XML-based interface to query and access a directory.

Solution

To use DSML with Active Directory, you have to install the Windows DSML client (DSFW) on a Windows 2000 or Windows Server 2003 computer that is running IIS. The DSML client can be downloaded from the following site: *http://www.microsoft. com/technet/downloads/winsrvr/featurepacks/default.mspx*. If you are installing the client on a Windows 2000 machine, you will also need to make sure that MSXML 3.0 SP2 is installed.

After the client is installed, you can perform DSML queries against that server, which will translate the calls into LDAP queries to Active Directory. No additional software needs to be installed on domain controllers to support DSML.

The following code shows a DSML request for the RootDSE:

```
<se:Envelope xmlns:se="http://schemas.xmlsoap.org/soap/envelope/">
        <se:Body xmlns="urn:oasis:names:tc:DSML:2:0:core">
                <batchRequest>
                        <searchRequest dn="" scope="baseObject">
                                <filter>
                                        <present name="objectclass"/>
                                </filter>
                        </searchRequest>
                </batchRequest>
        </se:Body>
    </se:Envelope>
```

Discussion

DSML is an XML alternative to using LDAP to access and manage a directory server. The OASIS standards body has driven the development of DSML (*http://www.oasis-open.org/committees/dsml*) and now most directory vendors support it as of version 2 (DSMLv2).

DSML encodes LDAP-like functions in XML messages and transmits them to a SOAP client that can sit directly on the directory server or a separate server. Currently, Active Directory domain controllers do not support DSML directly, thus a separate client must be installed. For more information including the DSML specification, see the OASIS web site.

See Also

The DSML home page: *http://www.microsoft.com/technet/downloads/winsrvr/featurepacks/default.mspx*

20.4 Programming with Perl

Problem

You want to programmatically access Active Directory using Perl.

Solution

There are two options for accessing Active Directory with Perl. You can use the Net::LDAP modules that are cross platform and use the LDAP protocol, or you can use the Win32::OLE module that gives you access to ADSI and must be run on a Windows machine. Both modules can be downloaded from the Comprehensive Perl Archive Network (CPAN) web site, *http://www.cpan.org*.

The following example shows how to use the Net::LDAP modules to query the RootDSE:

```
#!/usr/SD/perl/bin/perl

use strict;
use Net::LDAP;

my $ldap_server  = $ARGV[0] || 'dc1';
my $ldapobj = Net::LDAP->new($ldap_server) or die " Could not connect: $@";
my $rootdse = $ldapobj->search(
                    base   => '',
                    filter => '(objectclass=*)',
                    scope  => 'base',
);
die $rootdse->error if $rootdse->code;
foreach $entry($rootdse->entries) {
   foreach $attr(sort $entry->attributes) {
      foreach ($entry->get($attr)) {
         print "$attr: $_\n";
      }
   }
}
```

This next example uses the Win32::OLE module and ADSI to display the attributes of the RootDSE:

```
use strict;
use Win32::OLE 'in';

my $rootdse = Win32::OLE->GetObject("LDAP://RootDSE");
$rootdse->GetInfo;
```

```
for my $i ( 0 .. $rootdse->PropertyCount - 1) {
    my $prop = $rootdse->Item($i);
    print $prop->Name,"\n";
    foreach my $val (in $prop->Values) {
        print "   ",$val->CaseIgnoreString,"\n";
    }
}
```

It is worth noting that with Net::LDAP, you generally need to bind to the target domain controller before performing a search or any other operation. In the Net::LDAP example above, we didn't need to do that because we queried the RootDSE, which allows anonymous (i.e., unauthenticated) connections. A bind can be done using the following code:

```
$ldapobj->bind('administrator@rallencorp.com', password => 'galt');
```

In the second example where we used ADSI with Win32::OLE, the credentials of the user running the script are used by default, so you only need to do an explicit bind if you need to authenticate as a different user.

Discussion

The Net::LDAP modules are a robust set of modules for querying and modifying an LDAP directory. Net::LDAP also supports DSML, the abstract schema, and LDIF. Net::LDAP is a native Perl implementation, which means that it does not rely on an external LDAP SDK. Since it is a pure Perl implementation, you can write Net::LDAP-based scripts on a variety of platforms to interface with Active Directory or other LDAP-based directories. Graham Barr initially developed the Net::LDAP modules and more information can be found about the modules on the following web site: *http://perl-ldap.sourceforge.net*.

The Win32::OLE modules provide an interface into Microsoft's Component Object Model (COM). Most of the ADSI classes and methods are available from the COM automation interface, known as IDispatch. This allows you to combine the flexibility of Perl with the robustness of ADSI. Documentation for the Win32::OLE module can be found at *http://aspn.activestate.com/ASPN/Perl/Products/ActivePerl/site/lib/Win32/OLE.html*.

See Also

To download Perl modules, see *http://www.cpan.org/*, *http://perl-ldap.sourceforge.net*, and *http://aspn.activestate.com/ASPN/Perl/Products/ActivePerl/site/lib/Win32/OLE.html*

20.5   Programming with Java

Problem

You want to programmatically access Active Directory using Java.

Solution

The Java Naming and Directory Interface (JNDI) is a standard extension to Java that can be used to access a variety of naming and directory services including DNS and LDAP. JNDI is part of the Java Enterprise API set and is documented on the following site: *http://java.sun.com/products/jndi*. JNDI provides an object-oriented interface to programming with LDAP that is not based on the LDAP C API, unlike many other LDAP APIs.

The following code uses JNDI to print out the RootDSE for the host DC1:

```java
/**
 * Print the RootDSE for DC1
 * usage: java RootDSE
 */

import javax.naming.*;
import javax.naming.directory.*;

class RootDSE {
    public static void main(String[] args) {

        try {
            // Create initial context.
            DirContext ctx = new InitialDirContext( );

            // Read attributes from root DSE.
        Attributes attrs = ctx.getAttributes(
            "ldap://DC1", new String[]{"*"});

        // Get a list of the attributes.
        NamingEnumeration enums = attrs.getIDs( );

        // Print out each attribute and its values.
        while (enums != null && enums.hasMore( )) {
           String nextattr = (String)enums.next( );
                 System.out.println( attrs.get(nextattr) );
        }

            // Close the context.
            ctx.close( );

    } catch (NamingException e) {
        e.printStackTrace( );
    }
  }
}
```

Discussion

Any serious Java programmer should be familiar with JNDI. It is a generic interface that can be used with a variety of services, not least of which includes Active Directory. A good tutorial on JNDI is available on Sun's web site: *http://java.sun.com/products/jndi/tutorial*.

See Also

Sun's JNDI home page: *http://java.sun.com/products/jndi*

20.6   Programming with Python

Problem

You want to programmatically access Active Directory using Python.

Solution

As with Perl, you have two options for programming Active Directory with Python: the native LDAP-based approach and a COM interface, which allows you to use ADSI on computers that run a Windows operating system. The LDAP module can be downloaded from *http://python-ldap.sourceforge.net*. The COM interface is part of the standard ActivePython install available from ActiveState (*http://www.activestate.com/ActivePython*).

The following Python code sample prints out the RootDSE of DC1 using the LDAP interface:

```
import ldap

try:
    l = ldap.open("dc1")
except ldap.LDAPError, e:
    print e

baseDN = ""
searchScope = ldap.SCOPE_BASE
retrieveAttributes = None
searchFilter = "objectclass=*"

try:
    ldap_result_id = l.search(baseDN, searchScope, searchFilter,
                              retrieveAttributes)
    result_type, result_data = l.result(ldap_result_id, 0)
    if result_type == ldap.RES_SEARCH_ENTRY:
        print result_data

except ldap.LDAPError, e:
    print e
```

This next code sample uses the `win32com.client` module to access the RootDSE with ADSI:

```
import win32com.client

objRootDSE = win32com.client.GetObject('LDAP://RootDSE')
objRootDSE.GetInfo( )

for i in range( 0, objRootDSE.PropertyCount - 1):
    prop = objRootDSE.Item(i)
    print prop.Name
    for val in prop.Values:
        print "   ",val.CaseIgnoreString
```

Discussion

Python's home page: *http://www.python.org*

20.7   Integrating with MIT Kerberos

Problem

You want to integrate your existing MIT Kerberos infrastructure with Active Directory.

Solution

Integrating MIT Kerberos with Active Directory typically means setting up a trust between an Active Directory domain and your MIT Kerberos realm. Creating a trust between a domain and realm is the first step toward Kerberos interoperability. It will allow users to access resources in either the AD domain or Kerberos realm. Here are the steps to create the trust:

1. Create a trust to the Kerberos realm on a domain controller:

    ```
    > netdom trust AD.RALLENCORP.COM /Domain:MIT.RALLENCORP.COM /Add /Realm /\
    PasswordT:"Password"
    ```

2. Make the trust transitive (if necessary):

    ```
    > netdom trust AD.RALLENCORP.COM /Domain:MIT.RALLENCORP.COM /Transitive:yes
    ```

3. Add a KDC for the Kerberos realm on the domain controller(s):

    ```
    > ksetup /addkdc MIT.RALLENCORP.COM kdc01.mit.rallencorp.com
    ```

4. Add the AD domain principal to the Kerberos realm (on the Unix host):

    ```
    kadmin: addprinc -e des-cbc-crc:normal krbtgt/ad.rallencorp.com
    ```

Discussion

What we've shown here is just the tip of the iceberg. To accomplish full integration in your environment, you may need to: configure name resolution and time synchronization; create service principals, account mappings, and host principals; and tweak the *krb5.conf* configuration file on your MIT KDCs. Providing details on how to do all of that is beyond the scope of this book, but a great resource on Kerberos is *Kerberos: The Definitive Guide*, Jason Garman (O'Reilly), which covers all the ins and outs of the Kerberos protocol and interoperability with Active Directory. Also, there are some good resources on the Web, which are listed in the See Also section.

See Also

MIT Kerberos home page (*http://web.mit.edu/kerberos/www*), Microsoft's Step-by-Step Guide to MIT Kerberos Interoperability (*http://www.microsoft.com/windows2000/techinfo/planning/security/kerbsteps.asp*), Windows 2000-MIT Kerberos Interop Trip-ups (*http://calnetad.berkeley.edu/documentation/test_environment/kerb_interop_trip-ups.html*), MS KB 217098 (Basic Overview of Kerberos User Authentication Protocol in Windows 2000), MS KB 230476 (Description of Common Kerberos-Related Errors in Windows 2000), MS KB 248758 (Information About the Windows 2000 Kerberos Implementation), MS KB 324143 (How to Use the Kerberos Setup Tool (Ksetup.exe)), and MS KB 810755 (White Paper: Windows 2000 Kerberos Interoperability and Authentication)

20.8 Integrating with Samba

Problem

You want your Samba clients to authenticate against Active Directory and access Active Directory resources.

Solution

Samba 3.0, which is the current build of Samba at the time of this writing, provides client-side support of Active Directory. OpenLDAP and MIT Kerberos must also be installed on the client to provide full LDAP and Kerberos functionality.

Discussion

Samba has a rich history of providing Unix integration and interoperability solutions for the Windows NOS under Windows NT. Samba is typically deployed so that Windows-based clients can use Unix-based file and print services seamlessly. A Samba server can join a Windows 2000 or Windows Server 2003 domain as a member server.

See Also

The Samba project (*http://www.samba.org*)

20.9 Integrating with Apache

Problem

If your organization has Active Directory and Apache deployed, one way to reduce logins is to integrate the two by having HTTP authentication on Apache use Active Directory.

Solution

There are several Apache modules that support authentication to an LDAP store, and with the release of Apache 2.0, it is supported natively with the mod_auth_ldap module. The documentation for mod_auth_ldap can be found at the following site: *http://httpd.apache.org/docs-2.0/mod/mod_auth_ldap.html*.

The mod_auth_ldap module works in the following way:

1. Binds using preconfigured bind DN and bind password.
2. Searches the directory with the preconfigured search filter and username of the user that is authenticating.
3. If a match was found, it performs a bind attempt with the matching user's DN and password.

If you are still running Apache 1.x, the auth_ldap module is widely used and works in much the same way as mod_auth_ldap. For more information, visit the following site: *http://www.rudedog.org/auth_ldap/*.

Discussion

The mod_auth_ldap module isn't ideal from an Active Directory perspective. Typically, the second step (search for the user's DN) is completely unnecessary. If you have been configuring a UPN for all of your users, the search could be eliminated by attempting to authenticate the user with its UPN instead of the DN. Active Directory supports binding with either. That means mod_auth_ldap could instead just take the user name entered in the user name/password prompt and prepend it to a preconfigured UPN suffix (e.g., @rallencorp.com). (You can also use the domain\username syntax.) Hopefully, the developers of mod_auth_ldap will take this into consideration for a future enhancement.

Another issue to be aware of when using this module is that you will need to hard-code a domain controller name to query and bind against in the mod_auth_ldap configuration. Unless you are using some type of load balancing software or hardware, you will be placing a dependency on that domain controller's availability.

Both mod_auth_ldap and auth_ldap support SSL and TLS, and we highly recommend enabling that if you plan on using either of these modules. If you don't enable SSL/TLS support, passwords sent from the Apache server to a domain controller will be sent in clear text.

See Also

For more information on Apache, see *http://www.apache.org,* *http://httpd.apache.org/ docs-2.0/mod/mod_auth_ldap.html,* and *http://www.rudedog.org/auth_ldap/.*

20.10 Integrating with Novell Netware

Problem

You want to integrate your Microsoft Active Directory network with an existing Novell NetWare infrastructure, either with an eye toward migration or long-term co-existence.

Solution

Microsoft offers the Services for Netware (SFN) component as a free download from *http://www.microsoft.com/windowsserver2003/sfn/default.mspx.* The most recent version of SFN (version 5.03 Service Pack 2 as of this writing) offers a Directory Synchronization Service to synchronize user account information between Active Directory and Novell NetWare using either the Netware Directory Service (NDS) or the NetWare bindery. You can use the Directory Synchronization Service to perform two-way synchronization between your AD and Novell infrastructure, thus reducing the amount of effort required to administer it, or to facilitate the migration of user and group accounts from NetWare to Active Directory. SFN also provides a File Migration Utility to ease the process of migrating from NetWare file and print servers to Windows 2000 or Windows Server 2003 computers. Finally, you can deploy the Client Services for NetWare on a Windows Server 2003 or Windows XP machine to connect directly to NetWare servers and networks.

Gateway Services for NetWare, which was previously available with Windows 2000, is no longer included with Windows Server 2003.

See Also

http://www.microsoft.com/windowsserver2003/sfn/default.mspx, MS KB 274279 (How to Migrate or Deploy a Novell NetWare Environment to Windows), MS KB 310671 (How to Obtain the Latest Services for NetWare 5.0 Service Pack), and MS KB 300976 (How To Use Both NetWare Servers and Windows Servers in Windows 2000)

20.11 Integrating with Macintosh

Problem

You want to allow Macintosh clients to access resources on your Active Directory network.

Solution

To allow easy integration for Macintosh clients, Windows Server 2003 provides Services for Macintosh as a built-in feature. Installing this service enables the following on a 2003 server:

File Server for Macintosh
> Allows you to create Macintosh-accessible shares on any NTFS-formatted drive or a shared CD.

Microsoft User Authentication Module
> Enables stronger password encryption (NTLMv2) than the default Apple standard UAM.

Print Server for Macintosh
> Allows you to create shared printers that can be accessed by Macintosh clients.

AppleTalk networking and routing
> For those Macintosh clients that have not transitioned to using TCP/IP, you can enable the AppleTalk protocol to allow communication between Macintosh computers and your Active Directory network.

In addition, there are third-party vendors such as Vintela (now part of Quest Software) and Centrify who have made solutions available to leverage Group Policy Objects for Macintosh clients, a feature that is not available by default in any version of Active Directory.

See Also

MS KB 101747 (How to Install Microsoft Authentication on a Macintosh), MS KB 328417 (Cannot Log On from a Macintosh Client After You Change Your Password), and MS KB 897718 (Macintosh-Based Computers Stop Responding When You Try to Browse a Services for Macintosh Shared Folder on a Computer That Is Running Windows Server 2003 with Service Pack 1)

20.12 Replacing the Network Information Service

Problem

You want to replace all or part of your NIS infrastructure with Active Directory. NIS serves many of the same functions as Active Directory, and you can reduce costs by integrating both infrastructures.

Solution

Prior to Windows Server 2003 R2, the Microsoft Services for Unix (SFU) suite was the main tool that aided in integrating your Unix and Windows systems. SFU has an NIS server that can be used as a replacement for existing NIS servers and uses Active Directory as its data store. SFU comes with a set of schema extensions that the NIS server uses to structure the user, group, and host information that NIS clients require. SFU also includes an NFS server and client software if you are trying to interoperate with NFS. All of the SFU software runs on Windows operating systems. More information on SFU can be found on the following site: *http://www.microsoft. com/windows/sfu/default.asp*.

Another option for pre-R2 servers is the NIS/LDAP Gateway from PADL Software (*http://www.padl.com*). The PADL NIS/LDAP Gateway utilizes the SFU schema extensions to provide NIS services with an Active Directory backend. NIS clients can use the gateway to resolve user, group, and host information and works with SunONE Directory Server as well as Active Directory. The NIS/LDAP Gateway is supported on a host of Unix-based platforms including Solaris, FreeBSD, and Linux.

When you're ready to make the move to Windows Server 2003 R2, you'll find that it includes built-in tools for Unix integration, including the ability to allow a Windows DC to act as a master NIS server for one or more NIS domains, as well as services to allow users to synchronize their passwords between Windows and Unix systems.

See Also

http://www.microsoft.com/windows/sfu/default.asp, *http://www.padl.com*, *LDAP System Administration*, Gerald Carter (O'Reilly), MS KB 324083 (How to Install Server for NIS on Windows for Unix-to-Windows Migration), MS KB 262965 (How Unix Permissions Are Approximated by Server for NFS), MS KB 324541 (How to Configure Server for NIS for a Unix-to-Windows Migration), and MS KB 324543 (How to Migrate Existing NIS Maps to Server for NIS in a Unix-to-Windows Migration)

20.13 Using BIND for DNS

Problem

You've decided that you do not want to use Microsoft DNS for Active Directory and instead prefer to use BIND.

Solution

The two main requirements for supporting Active Directory DNS are SRV records and Dynamic DNS support. The first version of BIND to support SRV records was 8.2.2 patch 7. Hopefully you are running a much more recent version since that was released in 2000. You technically don't have to use DDNS with Active Directory DNS records, but if you don't, you end up doing a lot of work to manually maintain the Active Directory-related resource records.

Here is an example BIND 8 configuration to support the *ad.rallencorp.com* domain:

```
Options {
directory "/etc/namedb";
};
Zone "ad.rallencorp.com" IN {
type master;
file "db.ad.rallencorp.com";
allow-update { dc1.; dc2.; dc3.; };
check-names ignore;
};
```

The directory directive specifies where the zone files are stored. The type should be master, and the file directive is the name of the file to store the contents of the zone in. The allow-update directive indicates which servers (either by name or IP address) can dynamically update the zone. Finally, the check-names ignore directive tells BIND not to be restrictive about the names used in resource records. Without this setting, BIND would fail to respond to queries for records containing underscores used by Active Directory.

The BIND 9 configuration for the same zone would look exactly the same, except the check-names ignore line is not necessary. By default, BIND 9 allows underscores in resource records.

After your BIND servers are properly configured, be sure that the resolvers on your domain controllers point to at least one of the BIND name servers. This can be done by going into the Network Connections for each domain controller and right-clicking the active connection. Click on Properties, highlight Internet Protocol (TCP/IP), and select Properties. You can configure the resolvers under the General tab. This setting can also be configured through DHCP or Group Policy.

Discussion

At an absolutely minimum, any DNS implementation used to support Active Directory must be able to publish and resolve queries for Service Locator (SRV) records. For ease of administration it's also useful for dynamic updates to be supported. The most recent versions of BIND DNS support both of these features; however, certain features will still be unavailable to you unless you use Active Directory-integrated DNS that's housed on an AD domain controller. Most notably, this means that BIND DNS does not support secure dynamic updates, which can limit its usefulness in many Active Directory implementations.

See Recipe 14.16 for forcing a domain controller to reregister its records and Recipe 14.14 for verifying that a domain controller can register its records.

BIND documentation and source can be downloaded from the following ISC site: *http://www.isc.org/products/BIND*.

See Also

Recipe 4.14, Recipe 4.16, MS KB 255913 (Integrating Windows 2000 DNS into an Existing BIND or Windows NT 4.0-Based DNS Namespace), MS KB 323419 (How to Migrate an Existing DNS Infrastructure from a BIND-Based Server to a Windows Server 2003-Based DNS), and *http://www.isc.org/products/BIND*

20.14 Integrating Down-level Windows Clients

Problem

You want to allow down-level Windows clients such as those running Windows NT 4.0 to participate in Active Directory.

Solution

Integrating down-level clients into Windows 2000 Active Directory was a relatively straightforward process; however, many people noticed that installing Windows Server 2003 prevented their older clients from connecting to Active Directory. This was because the default installation of Windows Server 2003 enables SMB signing, a feature that is not available on older client operating systems. To enable this feature, you need to install the Directory Services Client Extensions for Windows 95/98 or Windows NT 4.0. In addition to SMB signing, the client extensions enable the following Active Directory features for your down-level clients:

Site awareness
> The Active Directory client extensions will allow your down-level clients to locate a DC within their local site to authenticate with. In addition, they will allow down-level clients to change their password on any available domain controllers, rather than just the PDC Emulator.

Active Directory Service Interfaces (ADSI)
    The DS client will allow you to perform ADSI scripting and provides a common programming API for your AD developers.

DFS fault tolerance client
    This feature provides access to fault-tolerant DFS shares, which allows for seamless access to DFS file shares even when the physical server hosting a particular share fails or is otherwise unavailable.

Windows Address Book (WAB)
    Computers with the client extensions installed can view and modify user objects through the Search function on the Start Menu.

NTLM version 2 authentication

Even with the Client Extensions installed, however, your down-level clients will still not have access to a number of AD-specific features that are only available to Windows 2000, XP, and 2003 clients and servers. These features include the following:

- Kerberos
- Group Policy
- Intellimirror
- IPSec/L2TP
- Service Principal Names
- Mutual authentication

See Also

MS KB 555038 (How to Enable Windows 98/ME/NT Clients to Logon to Windows 2003-Based Domains) and MS KB 147706 (How to Disable LM Authentication on Windows NT)

20.15 Using VMWare for Testing AD

Problem

One of the issues that developers and administrators commonly face when trying to do Active Directory testing is the limitation of being able to host only a single domain on a server, particularly because of the cost implications of requiring additional hardware to support each additional domain. You can use VMWare to work around this issue and host multiple domains on a single server.

Solution

VMWare (*http://www.vmware.com*) develops a very popular virtual machine technology that allows you to run multiple operating systems, even of different varieties, on a single machine. The VMWare Workstation product can be used on laptops and desktop servers and is great for running simulations. VMWare ESX Server is oriented for enterprise solutions so that you could even run production-grade services from VMWare virtual machines.

As far as Active Directory goes, you can create several virtual machines on a single host using either the Workstation or ESX Server products to simulate a forest. We've personally used VMWare to help facilitate schema extension testing. Since there is no supported schema deletion process, once you've extended the schema, you cannot extend the schema again with the same extensions (if you wanted to test the extension process again). VMWare stores each virtual machine as a collection of files. Once you've created a baseline domain controller virtual machine, you can copy the files that make up that virtual machine and create as many domain controllers as needed.

If you support multiple domains in a forest, it can be expensive in terms of both hardware and people to support multiple test environments that are similar to your production environment. For each domain in a forest, you need a separate server. If you have a four-domain forest and want to create three test environments, you'd need 12 servers total. With VMWare, you could use three servers and host all four domains on each server. It's possible that if you had a big enough server, you could even host all four test environments on the same server!

The new snapshot capability with VMWare 4.0 and later can make testing even easier. With it you can take a snapshot of a virtual machine and preserve its state at a specific moment in time. You can then revert to the saved snapshot at any time, irrespective of whether the machine is powered on or off. This is ideal for testing schema changes.

Discussion

One of the caveats with using VMWare is that Microsoft will not support any issues that arise while running Active Directory (or any other product) under VMWare. In our experience, Microsoft support will make a best effort to try and troubleshoot problems with VMWare, but they will not guarantee a resolution. For example, there is an issue with VMWare's *hgfs.sys* driver that's used for the Shared Folders feature. This causes problems, including an inability to create cross forest trusts. For more informationm, see *http://www.activedir.org/article.aspx?aid=75*.

See Also

http://www.vmware.com, MS KB 897615 (Support Policy for Microsoft Software Running in Non-Microsoft Hardware Virtualization Software), and MS KB 897613 (Microsoft Virtual Server Support Policy)

20.16 Using Virtual Server in an Active Directory Environment

Problem

You wish to use Microsoft's Virtual Server product to deploy Active Directory domain controllers.

Solution

Microsoft has two product offerings in the virtual technology space: Virtual PC and Virtual Server. Virtual PC is useful for test environments, such as when you are vetting operating system patches from Windows Update or testing Group Policy changes before deploying them into a production environment. To actually deploy virtual servers in a production environment, you should use Microsoft's Virtual Server product. Similar to the VMWare offerings, Virtual Server allows you to run multiple virtual server instances (called *guests*) on a single piece of physical hardware (called a *host*).

When you create a virtual server, it is represented on the hard drive of the host by a single *.vhd* file, which represents the entire hard drive of the virtual machine. It is therefore critical to handle these VHD files with care, as starting up an out-of-date instance of a virtual domain controller can cause replication issues similar to what would happen if you fired up a similarly out-of-date physical DC. Similarly, you should avoid using the Undo Disks feature of Virtual Server with a virtual domain controller, as you can also create replication issues by rolling Active Directory back to an earlier state in this manner.

See Also

MS KB 888794 (Things to Consider When a Windows Server 2003-Based Domain Controller or a Windows 2000-Based Domain Controller Runs In a Virtual Hosting Environment), MS KB 875495 (How to Detect and Recover from a USN Rollback in Windows Server 2003), and Running Domain Controllers in Virtual Server 2005 (*http://www.microsoft.com/downloads/details.aspx?FamilyID=64db845d-f7a3-4209-8ed2-e261a117fc6b&displaylang=en*)

## CHAPTER 21

Active Directory Federation Services

21.0 Introduction

Active Directory Federation Services (ADFS) is one of the new features available in Windows Server 2003 R2. It is used to allow single sign-on (SSO) capabilities to web applications hosted by multiple organizations without the need to configure an Active Directory trust relationship between them. This task is performed by using ADFS servers to separate the process of *authentication* (proving who a user *is*) from that of *authorization* (specifying what a user can *do*). ADFS allows this separation by configuring *account partners* to authenticate users and groups, and *resource partners* to control the actual access to resources.

This relationship between account partners and resource partners is called a *federated trust*. This verbiage can sometimes lead to confusion, since it seems to imply that ADFS requires an Active Directory trust relationship to exist between account and resource partners. In this case, the word *trust* merely refers to a business agreement between two organizations that have agreed to this type of distributed authentication and authorization arrangement, and a federated trust refers to a scenario in which the ADFS Federation Service has been properly configured by both the organization that performs user authentication and the organization that controls access to web resources.

You can, however, combine ADFS with an Active Directory forest trust to create a Federated Web SSO with Forest Trust configuration. This is typically used within a single organization that has one forest configured in a perimeter network or DMZ and a second forest configured on an internal network. In this case, ADFS allows users on the internal network to be able to access resources on the perimeter network without needing to maintain two separate accounts. The other ADFS configuration, Federated Web SSO, will be more commonly used by two separate organizations (most notably in a B2B relationship) for whom an Active Directory forest trust would create too much access for users on both sides of the equation or where Selective Authentication would require too much ongoing maintenance.

Using a graphical user interface

Because ADFS is such a new technology, you'll notice that most of the management options available to you are only those within a graphical user interface: either the ADFS MMC snap-in or the Internet Services Manager snap-in. In its current release, ADFS lacks the ability to perform many enterprise-level tasks such as managing remote servers or performing command-line administration. The version of ADFS that ships with the next version of Windows Server (currently code-named Longhorn) might show some improvement in this area.

21.1   Installing ADFS Prerequisites

Problem

You want to install the necessary prerequisites to configure ADFS on a Windows Server 2003 server.

Solution

Using a graphical user interface

To install IIS on a Windows Server 2003 R2 server, follow these steps:

1. Click Start → Control Panel → Add or Remove Programs.
2. Select Add/Remove Windows Components.
3. Click on the Application Server check box and select Details.
4. Place a check mark next to ASP.NET and Internet Information Service (IIS), then click OK.
5. Click Next to begin installing the necessary components, then click Finish.

To enable SSL for the Default Web Site, do the following:

1. Open the Internet Service Manager snap-in.
2. Navigate to the server that you want to manage, and click on Web Sites.
3. Right-click the Default Web site and select Properties.
4. On the Directory Security tab, select Server Certificate in the Secure Communications section. Click Next to begin the wizard.
5. Select "Create a new certificate" and click Next.
6. Select "Prepare the request now, but send it later" and then click Next.
7. Enter a name for the certificate, and the bit length of the certificate. Select Server Gated Cryptography if your users will be accessing your site from countries that have any sort of encryption restrictions.
8. Enter your organization name and organizational unit, and then click Next.
9. Enter the FQDN of the server name and click Next.

10. Enter your location information, and then click Next.

11. Enter the path and filename that you want to save the certificate information to, and then click Next to continue.

12. Click Next to create the certificate request.

Once you have submitted the certificate request to a Certification Authority, use these steps to install the certificate:

1. Right-click on the Default Web Site and select Properties.

2. On the Directory Security tab, click Server Certificate. Click Next to continue.

3. Select "Process the pending request," install the certificate, and click Next.

4. Browse to the location of the certificate that you received from the Certification Authority. Click Next twice, followed by Finish, to install the certificate.

Using a command-line interface

To perform an unattended install of IIS, you must create an answer file containing a [Components] section and an optional [InternetServer] section, similar to the following:

```
[Components]
iis_common = on
aspnet = on
complusnetwork = on

[InternetServer]
PathWWWServer = "d:\docs\webfiles"
```

Save the unattended file as *unattended.txt*, then run the following command:

```
> sysocmgr /i:sysoc.inf /u:<PathToUnattendedFile>
```

Using VBScript

```
' This code creates an unattended installation file,
' installs IIS, then configures the Default Web Site with
' an SSL certificate.

' ------ SCRIPT CONFIGURATION ------
strFile = "c:\iis_install.txt"
constForWriting = 2
strComputer = "<ServerName>"
strSiteID = "<SiteID>"     ' Use "1" for the Default Web Site

' Taken from AccessSSLFlags
'    8 = AccessSSL
'   256 = AccessSSL128
intFlag = 8 + 256
' ------ END CONFIGURATION ---------
```

```
' First install IIS
set objFSO = CreateObject("Scripting.FileSystemObject")
set objFile = objFSO.OpenTextFile(strFile, constForWriting, True)
objFile.WriteLine("[Components]")
objFile.WriteLine("iis_common = ON")
objFile.WriteLine("iis_doc = ON")
objFile.WriteLine("iis_www = ON")
objFile.WriteLine("iis_inetmgr = ON")
objFile.WriteLine("complusnetwork = ON")
objFile.WriteLine("aspnet = ON")
objFile.WriteLine("")
objFile.WriteLine("[InternetServer]")
objFile.WriteLine("SvcManualStart = www")
objFile.WriteLine("PathWWWRoot = C:\webstuff")
objFile.Close

set objWshShell = WScript.CreateObject("WScript.Shell")
intRC = objWshShell.Run("sysocmgr /i:%windir%\inf\sysoc.inf /u:" & _
                        strFile, 0, TRUE)
if intRC <> 0 then
   WScript.Echo "Error returned from sysocmgr command: " & intRC
else
   WScript.Echo "IIS installed"
end if

' Now enable SSL on the Default Web Site
set objWebSite = GetObject("IIS://" & strComputer & "/W3SVC/" & strSiteID)
objWebSite.AccessSSLFlags = intFlag
objWebSite.SetInfo
WScript.Echo "Successfully modified SSL settings for: " & _
            objWebSite.ServerComment
```

Discussion

Because ADFS is primarily used to enable web-based SSO solutions, ADFS requires the following components installed as a prerequisite:

- IIS
- ASP.NET
- COM+

These components can be installed during the initial operating system install or after the fact using Add/Remove Programs or the *sysocmgr* utility.

To improve the security of an ADFS installation, you will also need to install an SSL certificate on the Default Web Site before the ADFS install can continue. This can be a certificate purchased from a third-party CA such as VeriSign, or one issued by an internal Certificate Authority. For a test environment, you can also use the *SelfSSL.exe* utility from the IIS 6 Resource Kit to install a self-signed certificate; however, this option should never be used for a production application.

See Also

MS KB 309506 (How To Perform an Unattended Installation of IIS 6.0) and MS KB 299875 (How to Implement SSL in IIS)

21.2   Installing the Federation Service

Problem

You want to install the ADFS Federation Service on a Windows Server 2003 R2 computer.

Solution

Using a graphical user interface

1. Click Start → Control Panel → Add or Remove Programs.
2. Select Add/Remove Windows Components.
3. Click on the Active Directory Services checkbox, and select Details.
4. Click on Active Directory Federation Services (ADFS) and select Details.
5. Place a check mark next to Federation Service, then click OK.
6. If you have not enabled ASP.NET 2.0, you will receive a warning message asking if you want to enable it. Click Yes to continue.
7. Click OK twice and then Next to begin the installation.
8. In the token-signing certificate section, select either "Create a self-signed token-signing certificate" or "Select token-signing certificate" to browse for an existing one.
9. In the Trust policy section, select either "Create a new trust policy" or "Use an existing trust policy" to browse for an existing one.
10. Click Next and then Finish to complete the installation.

Using a command-line interface

To perform an unattended install of the ADFS Federation Services, you must create an answer file containing a [Components] section, an [ADFS] section, and an [ADFSFederationServer] section, similar to the following:

```
[Components]
ADFSFederationServer = On

[ADFS]
UseASPNet = 1

[ADFSFederationServer]
SignCertificateThumbprintFS = ""
TrustPolicyPath = "d:\ADFS\TrustPolicies\defaulttrust.xml"
```

Save the unattended file as *unattended.txt*, then run the following command:

```
> sysocmgr /i:sysoc.inf /u:<PathToUnattendedFile>
```

Using VBScript

See Recipe 21.1 for an example of simulating the *sysocmgr* command from a VBScript file.

Discussion

In an ADFS solution, *federation servers* are servers that have the Federation Service component installed on them. These servers are responsible for routing authentication requests between the different organizations involved in a federated trust, or from external (i.e., Internet) clients accessing a Web SSO application.

A federation server will perform slightly different tasks depending on whether your organization is an *account partner* (an organization that hosts user accounts that need access to resources) or the *resource partner* (the organization hosting the actual resources being accessed). When configured by an account partner, federation servers are used to validate users against an Active Directory or ADAM account store, and to issue the initial security tokens that those accounts can use to access applications hosted by the resource partner. Federation servers in the resource partner organization will then validate the security tokens that were issued by the federation servers for the account partner. Resource partner federation servers can also issue cookies to a user's web browser to enable single sign-on capabilities if they need to access multiple applications that are hosted by the resource partner.

See Also

Recipe 21.1 and Windows Server Tech Center: ADFS Server Roles

21.3 Configuring an Active Directory Account Store

Problem

You want to configure ADFS to use Active Directory for authentication.

Solution

Using a graphical user interface

1. Open the ADFS MMC snap-in. Navigate to Federation Service → Trust Policy → My Organization.
2. Right-click on Account Stores. Select New ▸ Account Store and click Next.
3. Select Active Directory for the type of account store and then click Next.
4. Click Finish to add the AD account store.

Discussion

ADFS relies on *account stores* to authenticate users and to retrieve whatever security claims those users are using to authenticate. You can configure one or multiple account stores for any Federation Service that you've configured, and you can define relative priorities between multiple stores. When you configure an Active Directory account store, ADFS can examine attributes of Active Directory user objects in addition to simply authenticating the user. AD logon requests can be in the UPN format, like *jsmith@rallencorp.com*, or in a domain\username format such as *RALLEN-CORP\jsmith*.

If you've configured multiple account stores, ADFS will attempt to process incoming authentication requests against each account store in order. You can modify this order by navigating to Federation Service → Trust Policy → My Organization. Right-click on Account Stores and select Store Priority, then use the Up or Down buttons to modify the priority order of the account stores.

 You can only configure one Active Directory account store per federation server, and this option is only available if the server hosting the Federation Service is joined to a domain.

See Also

Recipe 21.4 for information on Configuring an ADAM Account Store and MSDN: System.Web.Security.SingleSignOn

21.4   Configuring an ADAM Account Store

Problem

You want to configure ADFS to use an instance of ADAM for authentication.

Solution

Using a graphical user interface

1. Open the ADFS MMC snap-in. Navigate to Federation Service → Trust Policy → My Organization.
2. Right-click on the Account Stores node, then select New → Account Store. Click Next to bypass the initial Welcome screen.
3. Select Active Directory Application Mode (ADAM) for the Account Store Type, then click Next.
4. Enter a display name and a Uniform Resource Identifier (URI) for the ADAM account store and click Next.

---

5. Specify the FQDN or IP address of the ADAM server, and the TCP/IP port that this instance is listening on.

6. For "LDAP search base distinguished name," enter the search base that should be used for any LDAP queries made against this ADAM instance; for example, `dc=rallencorp,dc=us`.

7. Enter the name of the ADAM username attribute, i.e., `userPrincipalName`.

8. Click Next to continue.

9. On the Identity Claims page, place a check mark next to one or more of the following:

   UPN
   > Enter the LDAP attribute name that stores the UPN.

   Email
   > Enter the LDAP attribute name that stores the user's email address.

   Common name
   > Enter the LDAP attribute name that stores the user's CN.

10. Click Next and then Finish to enable the account store.

Discussion

ADAM account stores are configured quite similarly to Active Directory stores; but unlike an AD account store, you can configure multiple ADAM account stores on a given federation server. Configuring an ADAM account store requires the following configuration information:

- Server name/IP address of a server hosting the ADAM instance.
- Port number that the instance is using to communicate.
- LDAP search base, such as `dc=IntranetApp,dc=rallencorp,dc=com`.
- User name attribute, such as `userPrincipalName`. This is the attribute that ADFS will use to attempt to authenticate incoming requests.

You can also modify the default timeout period for searches; the default is five seconds. In addition, you can enable SSL/TLS to encrypt the connection between the federation server and the web server hosting the application.

See Also

Recipe 21.3 for information on configuring an Active Directory account store and Chapter 19 for more on configuring ADAM instances and application partitions

21.5 Configuring an Account Partner

Problem

You want to configure an account partner to allow them to access applications that are managed by an ADFS Federation Service.

Solution

Using a graphical user interface

1. Open the ADFS MMC snap-in. Navigate to Federation Service → Trust Policy → Partner Organizations.

2. Right-click on Account Partners, and select New → Account Partner.

3. To create an account partner manually, click No on the Import Policy File page and click Next.

4. On the Account Partner Details screen, enter the display name of the account partner, the Federation Service URI (such as *http://www.rallencorp.com/adfs*), and the Federation Service endpoint URL (such as *https://www.rallencorp.com/adfs/ls/clientlogon.aspx*). Click Next to continue.

5. On the Account Partner Verification Certificate screen, browse to or manually enter the path to the verification certificate and click Next.

6. For Federation Scenario, select one of the following:

   Federated Web SSO
   > Choose this for a scenario with an external organization or one where you're not using a forest trust. To use this option, simply click Next to continue.

   Federated Web SSO with Forest Trust
   > To configure this option, click Next, then select "All Active Directory domains and forests" to allow users from any domain in the organization to authenticate. To restrict the domains that can submit requests, click on "The following Active Directory domains and forests." Select the domain or forest that you want to accept logons from and click Add. Click Next to continue.

7. On the Account Partner Identity Claims screen, select one or more of the following:

   UPN Claim
   > This will take you to the Accepted UPN Suffixes page. From here you can select All UPN Suffixes, or else specify a suffix and click Add. Click Next to continue.

   E-Mail Claim
   > This will take you to the Accepted E-mail Suffixes page. From here you can select All E-mail Suffixes, or specify an accepted suffix and click Add. Click Next to continue.

Common Name Claim
> This option requires no additional configuration; simply click Next to continue.

8. Click Next and then Finish to create the Account Partner.

> The All UPN Suffixes and All E-Mail Suffixes options are only available when you are configuring a Federated Web SSO with Forest Trust.

Discussion

In an ADFS configuration, you'll configure account partners to represent the organization that houses user accounts, either in AD or ADAM, that require access to applications hosted by one or more resource partners. The ADFS Federation Server in the account partner's organization will create security tokens or claims that can be processed by the Federation Service in the resource partner and used to make authorization decisions.

> You can think of an account partner as being analogous to a trusted domain or forest in an Active Directory trust relationship; however, it is not absolutely necessary for an Active Directory trust relationship to be configured for ADFS to function in this manner.

You can configure an account partner in one of two AFDS scenarios: Federated Web SSO or Federated Web SSO with Forest Trust. In the Federated Web SSO scenario, there is no need for a forest trust to exist between the account partners and resource partners; this is typically used for two separate organizations that do not wish to create a forest trust between them. The Federated Web SSO with Forest Trust scenario is more typically used within a single organization to allow secure web access via the Internet.

> In the case of the Federated Web SSO with Forest Trust scenario, you can configure the account partner either to allow logon requests from any domain that is trusted by the account partner or to only accept logon requests from particular domains.

Once you've configured the ADFS scenario, you need to specify what types of claims will be sent by the account partner to the federation server hosted by the resource partner. You can send any combination of UPN, E-Mail, Common name, Group, or Custom claims. (Claims types are discussed further in Recipe 21.7.)

See Also

Recipe 21.7 for more on creating group or custom claims and Recipe 21.6 for information on configuring a resource partner

21.6   Configuring a Resource Partner

Problem

You want to configure a resource partner to allow access to a resource by users defined within an ADFS Federation Service account partner.

Solution

Using a graphical user interface

1. Open the ADFS MMC snap-in. Navigate to Federation Service → Trust Policy → Partner Organizations.

2. Right-click on Account Partners, and select New → Resource Partner.

3. To create a resource partner manually, click No on the Import Policy File page and click Next.

4. On the Resource Partner Details screen, enter the display name of the resource partner, the Federation Service URI (such as *http://www.rallencorp.com/adfs*), and the Federation Service endpoint URL (such as *https://www.rallencorp.com/adfs/ls/clientlogon.aspx*). Click Next to continue.

5. For Federation Scenario, select one of the following:

   Federated Web SSO
   > Choose this for a scenario with an external organization or one where you're not using a forest trust. To use this option, simply click Next to continue.

   Federated Web SSO with Forest Trust
   > Use this for federated trusts within the same organization.

6. Select one or more of the following on the Resource Partner Identity Claims screen:

   UPN Claim
   > This will bring up the Select UPN Suffixes screen. From here, either select "Pass all UPN Suffixes through unchanged" or "Replace all UPN suffixes with the following:," and specify the UPN suffix that you want to replace all incoming suffixes with. Click Next to continue.

   E-Mail Claim
   > This will bring up the Select E-Mail Suffixes screen. From here, either select "Pass all E-Mail Suffixes through unchanged" or "Replace all E-Mail Suffixes with the following:," and specify the email suffix that you want to replace all incoming suffixes with. Click Next to continue.

   Common Name Claim
   > This type of claim just denotes a string such as "Joe Smith" or "RAllenCorp Employees."

7. Click Next and then Finish to create the Resource Partner.

Discussion

A resource partner is the necessary second piece of the ADFS puzzle, and is the organization that is hosting the web resources that need to be accessed by the account partner. It's important to note that resource partners do not actually authenticate users from the account partner's organization; rather, they simply process the claims that are forwarded to them after the account partner has performed any necessary authentication. This process cuts very much to the heart of ADFS—the resource partner trusts the account partner to perform whatever authentication is needed, after which the resource partner performs the authorization portion of the process using the claims that were produced by the account partner.

 Each web server in the resource partner organization that needs to be protected by the ADFS Federation Service needs to be configured with the ADFS Web Agent.

See Also

Recipe 21.5 for more on creating an account partner, Recipe 21.7 for more on configuring a claim, and Recipe 21.8 for more on configuring an application

21.7 Creating a Claim Type

Problem

You want to add a new type of claim that can be used by ADFS applications

Solution

Using a graphical user interface

1. Open the ADFS MMC snap-in. Navigate to Federation Service → Trust Policy → My Organization.

2. Right-click on Organization Claims, then select New → Organizational Claim.

3. Enter a name for the claim, then select Group Claim or Custom Claim and click OK.

4. To map a Group Claim to an existing group, right-click on the claim you just created and select Properties. On the Resource Group tab, place a check mark next to "Map this claim to the following resource group." Manually enter the DN of the group or use the browse button to select it from the Active Directory tree. Click OK when you're done.

Discussion

ADFS *claims* are created by account partners to allow resource partners to authorize users in an ADFS federated trust relationship. There are three types of claims that are currently supported by the ADFS Federation Service: identity claims, group claims, and custom claims.

An *identity claim* refers to some type of identifier that's used to establish a user's identity within the account partner organization: this can be a UPN, an E-Mail address, or a Common Name. UPN and E-Mail claims are formatted in the familiar *user@rallencorp.com* format, while a Common Name claim is made up of an arbitrary string like RAllenCorp Employees or Joe Smith. For this reason, you should avoid using Common Name claims as identity claims unless UPN or E-Mail claims are unfeasible in your environment.

 Although you can send multiple claim types from an account partner to a resource partner, you can only send one UPN and one E-Mail claim at a time. You can use custom claims if you need to configure additional claim types using E-Mail or UPN information.

A *group claim*, as the name would suggest, indicates that the user is a member of a particular group or role in the account partner organization. The resource partner can then make authorization decisions based on this group membership claim. (Again, the resource partner will do nothing to verify that the user is actually a member of the group they claim to be; it is up to the account partner to perform this authorization process before submitting the claim to the resource partner.)

You can create a *custom claim* to allow users in the account partner organization to use additional information to submit claims to the resource partner; this can include information such as an employee ID number or some other unique identifier.

See Also

Recipe 21.5 for more on configuring an account partner and Recipe 21.6 for more on configuring a resource partner

21.8 Configuring an Application

Problem

You want to add a claims-based or token-based application to ADFS.

Solution

Using a graphical user interface

1. Open the ADFS MMC Snap-in. Browse to Federation Service → Trust Policy → My Organization.

2. Right-click on Applications and select New → Application. Click Next to continue.

3. On the Application Type screen, select either Claims-aware application or Windows NT token-based application and click Next.

4. On the Application details screen, enter the name of the application and the URL used to access the application. Click Next to continue.

5. On the Accepted Identity Claims page, place a check mark next to one or more of the following:

   - UPN
   - E-Mail
   - Common name (only available with a claims-aware application)

6. Click Next and then Finish to add the new application.

Discussion

You can use the ADFS Web Agent for two different types of web applications: *claims-aware applications* and *Windows NT token-based applications*. As the names imply, claims-aware applications can make authorization decisions based on claims submitted to it by the ADFS server in the account partner organization, while token-based applications can use only traditional Windows-based authorization mechanisms. Claims-aware applications can use a combination of identity claims, group claims, and custom claims to gain access to applications hosted by the resource partner. Windows NT token-based applications are not capable of handling ADFS claims, and instead use traditional Windows authorization. For a user to access a token-based application, the user needs to be a member of the resource web server's domain or any domain that is trusted by that domain. In other words, token-based applications are far less flexible and far more limiting than claims-aware applications when used in ADFS implementations.

See Also

Recipe 21.7 for more on configuring a claim and Recipe 21.11 for more on configuring the ADFS Web Agent

21.9 Configuring a Forest Trust

Problem

You want to create a forest trust to enable ADFS to use the Web SSO with Forest Trust configuration.

Solution

Using a graphical user interface

1. Open the Active Directory Domains and Trusts snap-in.
2. In the left pane, right click the forest root domain and select Properties.
3. Click on the Trusts tab.
4. Click the New Trust button.
5. After the New Trust Wizard opens, click Next.
6. Type the DNS name of the AD forest and click Next.
7. Select Forest trust and click Next.
8. Complete the wizard by stepping through the rest of the configuration screens.

Using a command-line interface

```
> netdom trust <Forest1DNSName> /Domain:<Forest2DNSName> /Twoway /Transitive /ADD
        [/UserD:<Forest2AdminUser> /PasswordD:*]
        [/UserO:<Forest1AdminUser> /PasswordO:*]
```

For example, to create a two-way forest trust from the AD forest *rallencorp.com* to the AD forest *othercorp.com*, use the following command:

```
> netdom trust rallencorp.com /Domain:othercorp.com /Twoway /Transitive /ADD
        /UserD:administrator@othercorp.com /PasswordD:*
        /UserO:administrator@rallencorp.com /PasswordO:*
```

Discussion

A new type of trust called a *forest trust* was introduced in Windows Server 2003. Under Windows 2000, if you wanted to create a fully trusted environment between two forests, you would have to set up individual external two-way trusts between every domain in both forests. If you have two Windows 2000 forests with three domains each and wanted to set up a fully trusted model, for example, you would need to set up nine individual one-way trusts.

With a forest trust, you can now define a single one-way or two-way transitive trust relationship that extends to all the domains in both forests. You may want to implement a forest trust if you merge or acquire a company and you want all of the new company's Active Directory resources to be accessible to users in your Active Directory environment and vice versa. To configure a forest trust, the forests on both sides of the trust need to be at the Windows Server 2003 Forest Functional Level; by default, forest trusts also have SID filtering enabled, as do external trusts that are created on Windows Server 2003 DCs or Windows 2000 DCs that are running 2000 Service Pack 4 or later. For ADFS, you can implement a forest trust to leverage the Federated Web SSO with Forest Trust scenario, which will allow you additional options when configuring an ADFS account partner.

See Also

Recipe 21.5 for more on configuring an account partner and Recipe 2.16 for more on trust transitivity in a Windows Server 2003 environment

21.10 Configuring an Alternate UPN Suffix

Problem

You want to modify or add a new UPN suffix for the users in an Active Directory forest.

Solution

Using a graphical user interface

1. Open the Active Directory Domains and Trusts snap-in.
2. In the left pane, right-click Active Directory Domains and Trusts and select Properties.
3. Under Alternate UPN suffixes, type the name of the suffix you want to add.
4. Click Add and OK.

Using a command-line interface

```
> admod -b cn=Partitions,cn=configuration,<ForestRootDN>
  uPNSuffixes:+:rallenhome.com
```

 The *attributeName*:+:*attributeValue* syntax will add an additional value to an existing list of values in a multivalued attribute. Using *attributeName*::*attributeValue* would add the value you specify and remove all other values.

Using VBScript

```
' This code adds a new UPN suffix.
' ------ SCRIPT CONFIGURATION ------
strNewSuffix = "<NewSuffix>"     ' e.g. othercorp.com
strDomain = "<DomainDNSName>"    ' e.g. rallencorp.com
' ------ END CONFIGURATION ---------
```

```
set objRootDSE = GetObject("LDAP://" & strDomain & "/RootDSE")
set objPartitions = GetObject("LDAP://cn=Partitions," & _
                             objRootDSE.Get("ConfigurationNamingContext"))
objPartitions.PutEx ADS_PROPERTY_APPEND, "uPNSuffixes", Array(strNewSuffix)
objPartitions.SetInfo
```

Discussion

The UPN allows users to log on with a friendly name that may or may not correspond to their email address. Also, UPN logons do not require the domain to be known, so that it can be abstracted away from the user. You may need to create an additional UPN suffix (e.g., *@rallencorp.com*) if you want UPNs to map to email addresses, but your AD forest is rooted at a different domain name (e.g., *ad. rallencorp.com*) than the domain name used in email addresses (e.g., *rallencorp.com*). In the case of ADFS identity claims, only one UPN claim can be used for a given application, so it may also be necessary to configure additional UPN suffixes to meet this requirement as well.

 Keep in mind that shared UPN suffixes are not supported in cross-forest trust environments. In other words, the UPN suffixes must be different in either forest.

Using a command-line interface

Like many command-line recipes in this guide, this recipe references the AdMod utility that can be downloaded from *http://www.joeware.net*.

Using VBScript

UPN suffixes are stored in the multivalued uPNSuffixes attribute on the Partitions container in the Configuration naming context. The default forest UPN suffix is assumed and not stored in that attribute.

See Also

MS KB 243280 (Users Can Log On Using User Name or User Principal Name), MS KB 243629 (How to Add UPN Suffixes to a Forest), and MS KB 269441 (How to Use ADSI to List the UPN Suffixes that Are Defined in Active Directory)

21.11 Configuring the ADFS Web Agent

Problem

You want to install and configure the ADFS Web Agent to allow or deny access to an ADFS-aware web application.

Solution

Using a graphical user interface

To install the ADFS Web Agent, do the following:

1. Click Start → Control Panel → Add or Remove Programs.
2. Select Add/Remove Windows Components.
3. Click on the Active Directory Services checkbox, and select Details.
4. Click on Active Directory Federation Services (ADFS) and select Details.
5. Place a check mark next to ADFS Web Agent, and then click OK.
6. Click OK twice and then Next to begin the installation.

To configure a web site to use Windows NT token-based authentication, do the following:

1. Open the Internet Service Manager MMC snap-in.
2. Right-click on the Web Sites folder and select Properties. On the ADFS Web Agent tab, specify the Federation Service URL, e.g., *http://www.rallencorp.com/adfs/service.asmx*.
3. Next, right-click on the specific web site you wish to configure and select Properties.
4. On the ADFS Web Agent tab, place a check mark next to "Enable the ADFS Web Agent for Windows NT token-based applications." If needed, specify the cookie path, cookie domain, and the return URL being used by the application.
5. Click Apply and then OK to save your changes.

> To configure claims-based applications, you'll need to modify the *web.config* file for the claims-aware application. You can see an example of this in Microsoft Knowledge Base article 911687.

Using a command-line interface

To perform an unattended install of the ADFS Web Agent, you must create an answer file containing a [Components] section, similar to the following:

```
[Components]
ADFSClaims = On
ADFSTraditional = On
```

Save the unattended file as *unattended.txt*, and then run the following command:

```
> sysocmgr /i:sysoc.inf /u:<PathToUnattendedFile>
```

Discussion

For a web application that's hosted by a resource partner to process ADFS claims, it must have the ADFS Web Agent installed on it. The Web Agent is a standalone component of ADFS; you do not need to install the Federation Service itself on individual web servers. Rather, you configure the web agent to point to a Federation Service in the resource partner organization so that it can refer to it as needed.

See Also

Recipe 21.8 for more on configuring an ADFS application, Recipe 21.12 to enable auditing on a resource web server, and MS KB 911687 (You Cannot Use IIS Manager to Configure the Logging Settings for the ADFS Web Agent in Windows Server 2003)

21.12 Enabling Logging for the ADFS Web Agent

Problem

You want to enable logging for an application running on a web server in a resource partner's organization.

Solution

Using the registry

To enable auditing for a Windows NT token-based application, create or modify the following Registry keys:

```
HKLM\System\CurrentControlSet\Control\Lsa\WebSSO\Parameters\DebugLevel
DWORD - "FFFFFFFF"

HKLM\System\CurrentControlSet\Control\Lsa\ifssvc\Parameters\DebugPrintLevel
DWORD - "FFFFFFFF"

HKLM\Software\Microsoft\ADFS\WebServerAgent\DebugPrintLevel
DWORD - "FFFFFFFF"
```

 To modify the auditing level for a claims-based application, you need to modify the appropriate *web.config* file.

Using VBScript

```
' The following script creates the necessary DWORD values to
' configure logging for a token-based application

'-------------SCRIPT CONFIGURATION-------------------------
```

```
Const HKEY_LOCAL_MACHINE = &H80000002
strComputer = "."
'-----------------------------------------------------------

Set oRegistry=GetObject("winmgmts:{impersonationLevel=impersonate}!\\" & _
    strComputer & "\root\default:StdRegProv")

strKeyPath = "System\CurrentControlSet\Control\Lsa\WebSSO\Parameters"

strValueName = "DebugLevel"
dwValue = FFFFFFFF
oReg.SetDWORDValue HKEY_LOCAL_MACHINE,strKeyPath,strValueName,dwValue

strKeyPath = "System\CurrentControlSet\Control\Lsa\ifssvc\Parameters"
strValueName = "DebugPrintLevel"
oReg.SetDWORDValue HKEY_LOCAL_MACHINE,strKeyPath,strValueName,dwValue

strKeyPath = "Software\Microsoft\ADFS\WebServerAgent"
oReg.SetDWORDValue HKEY_LOCAL_MACHINE,strKeyPath,strValueName,dwValue
```

Discussion

Unlike standard IIS logging, you cannot use the Internet Services Manager (ISM) MMC snap-in to configure logging for the ADFS Web Agent. Instead, you need to modify the Registry entries listed here in the case of a Windows NT token-based application. To configure logging for a claims-based application, you need to modify the contents of that application's *web.config* file.

See Also

MSDN: System.Web.Security.SingleSignOn and MSDN: StdRegProv.SetDWORD-Value method [WMI]

## CHAPTER 22

Exchange Server 2003

22.0 Introduction

Exchange Server 2003 is Microsoft's messaging and calendaring server application. It enables you to send and receive email and other interactive messages through computer networks. Exchange is designed to integrate directly with Microsoft Outlook and has a rich application programming interface (API) that can be utilized to integrate custom applications, making it a very flexible framework for business collaboration.

Although Windows Server 2003 has built-in SMTP and POP3 support, it isn't enough for serious corporate needs. If you like analogies, SMTP/POP3 services are to Exchange what the Model-T is to the modern automobile. You can certainly recognize the basic pieces but there have been notable extensions to those pieces to make the product more flexible and powerful for today's needs. Some additional features in the product are IMAP, web email support via Outlook Web Access (OWA), mobile client email synchronization, advanced message routing, distribution lists, public folders, spam filtering, and considerable functionality for controlling message flow and client experience.

Exchange was one of the first Active Directory-enabled applications. This is an unsurprising fact as Active Directory is based in great part on directory technology borrowed from Exchange 5.5 and earlier versions. It is probably also unsurprising that Exchange is a heavy consumer of Active Directory services, for the same reason, and entirely dependent upon Active Directory functioning correctly. Because of this tight integration, you should try to incorporate Exchange requirements into your overall Active Directory design as early as possible. Failure to do so can have significant impact on the quality of service of both Active Directory and Exchange. The integration of Exchange could require your Active Directory design to change considerably.

Exchange has an extensive feature-set, and several books have been written that cover designing, implementing, and running Exchange. What we present here is a small set of appetizer recipes covering some of the more basic functions, including installing a new instance of Exchange Server 2003 and some basic administration tasks. If you want the full seven-course meal, you should consider getting the *Exchange Server Cookbook* by Paul Robichaux et al. (O'Reilly).

Using a Graphical User Interface

Exchange has traditionally been administered exclusively from the GUI. There are two primary Microsoft GUI tools for administrating Exchange, both based on the MMC.

The first is a tool you probably already know: ADUC. Microsoft has extended the functionality of this Active Directory tool to manage many aspects of the users and groups used by Exchange. This makes sense since most Active Directory administrators are already familiar with this tool and the information being updated is primarily in Active Directory. If you are working only with managing users' Exchange information, you will most likely spend your time with this tool. It is a common misconception that installing Microsoft Exchange into an organization will present the Exchange tabs in ADUC to all Domain Controllers. You must install Exchange System Manager (ESM) on each and every server or workstation from which you intend to manage Exchange attributes on the user account.

The second tool is the ESM, which is used for configuring and monitoring the overall Exchange environment, including servers, policies, queues, routing connectors, and other configuration specific settings.

You can find these tools on any server running Exchange, and they can also be installed onto non-Exchange servers and clients for remote administration of Exchange. See Recipe 22.6 for more on this topic. All GUI-based solutions in this chapter require that the Exchange management tools be present on the workstation or server being used.

Using a Command-Line Interface

As previously mentioned, Exchange was traditionally managed from the GUI, so the availability of command-line tools for basic Exchange management functions is somewhat limited compared to the command-line tools available for Active Directory itself. The primary reason for this is the complexity of the Exchange system. Simply put, Exchange can do a lot of different things and needs specific customizations for each deployment. Using custom scripts tends to be the most efficient way for most organizations to handle Exchange functions from the command line.

If you really prefer nonscripted CLI though, most of the configuration information for Exchange is kept in Active Directory. This means you can use your usual Active Directory command-line tools to query and set Exchange information. You simply have to understand what specific attributes are used to control that specific functionality in Exchange. This may be less intuitive than one would hope, but with sufficient testing and research you can do a considerable amount with Exchange via Active

Directory command-line tools such as *csvde* and *ldifde*. The general process that most admins follow when trying to work this out is to use the GUI to do something, look at the resulting Active Directory object created or modified, and then trying to duplicate it via script or CLI. Of course, you will want to do this in a test lab before using your results in a production environment.

Unless otherwise noted, all command-line solutions require the Exchange management tools to be present on the workstation or server being used. See Recipe 22.6 for more on installing these tools.

Table 22-1 contains the list of command-line tools used in this chapter and the recipes they are used in.

Table 22-1. Command-line tools used in this chapter

Tool	Windows Server 2003	Windows 2000	Recipes
ldifde	%SystemRoot%\system32	%SystemRoot%\system32	22.9, 22.10, 22.12, 22.18, 22.19, 22.20, 22.21, 22.22, 22.24
ExchMbx	http://www.joeware.net	http://www.joeware.net	22.9, 22.10, 22.11, 22.12, 22.16, 22.18, 22.19, 22.20
dsadd	%SystemRoot%\system32	N/A	22.20

Using VBScript

Through the WMI, ADSI, and Collaboration Data Objects for Exchange Management (CDOEXM) scripting interfaces you have the capability to automate many Exchange tasks. Table 22-2 contains a list of all WMI classes used in this chapter. Unfortunately, the CDOEXM interface isn't available by default on Windows computers, so you will need to load the Exchange management tools on computers that run any scripts using that interface.

Table 22-2. WMI classes used in this chapter

WMI Class	Description	Recipes
Exchange_Mailbox	WMI class that represents Exchange mailboxes.	22.13, 22.14, 22.15, 22.17
Exchange_DSAccessDC	WMI Class that represents DSAccess.	22.26

Since CDOEXM is specific to Exchange programming, we'll cover it in more depth here. CDOEXM is a COM library supplied by Microsoft for developing messaging and administration applications for Exchange. You can find the documentation for CDOEXM in the Microsoft Online MSDN Library and the Exchange Server 2003 SDK. There are additional WMI classes available for Exchange that are not used for recipes in this chapter—see the Exchange SDK for more information.

Notes on Managing Exchange

Managing Exchange is a little different from managing most other Microsoft applications. The computer where you run the tools or scripts must be a member of a domain in the forest where the Exchange organization resides. This is true whether you are using a script or the GUI. Exchange doesn't allow you to select other organizations to manage. This can be troublesome for someone managing multiple Exchange organizations or a mobile worker who moves between sites or companies and likes to run her workstation in workgroup mode instead of being a member of any specific domain.

Permissions are very important and often misunderstood in Exchange. Permissions can be set up very simply or in a very complicated way; it is tough to find a middle ground. The simplest method is to give your Exchange administrators Domain Admin access. This is pretty standard in small companies where the Exchange admins are doing all aspects of administration. But this practice is usually unacceptable in larger companies where separation of duties and more security is required. Please see Recipe 22.7 for more discussion and details on permissions.

Exchange Server has several software prerequisites that must be installed prior to its installation. You must have these prerequisites in place prior to installing Exchange or Exchange will refuse to install. The prerequisites vary by operating system.

Windows 2000 SP3+ prerequisites:

- Windows Server 2003 Administration Tools Pack (*adminpak.msi*)
- Internet Information Services (IIS)
- World Wide Web (WWW) Publishing Service
- Simple Mail Transport Protocol (SMTP) Service
- Network News Transfer Protocol (NNTP) Service

Window Server 2003 requires the Windows 2000 prerequisites plus:

- .NET Framework
- ASP.NET

See *Windows Server Cookbook for Windows Server 2003 and Windows 2000* by Robbie Allen (O'Reilly) for more details on the installation of IIS.

It is preferable to run Exchange in Active Directory native mode (for Windows 2000) or at the Windows Server 2003 forest functional level. Running Exchange in an Active Directory mixed mode environment can be troublesome. If you must run in this mode, try to keep that time frame as short as possible and anticipate that things will not work exactly as expected during that time.

22.1 Preparing Active Directory for Exchange

Problem

You want to prepare your Active Directory forest and domains for installation of your first Exchange Server.

Solution

Using a graphical user interface

The first phase of the installation is *ForestPrep* and it needs to be run once on the Schema FSMO domain controller.

1. Log on to the Schema FSMO forest root domain controller with an account that has both Enterprise Admin and Schema Admin rights.

2. Prepare the domain controller for a schema update (see Recipe 11.6).

3. Per your corporate standards, create either a global or universal group for the initial Exchange administration delegation. Name the group in a descriptive way like *ExchangeRootAdmins*. See Chapter 7 for assistance on creating groups.

4. Insert the Exchange Server CD into the CD-ROM.

5. On the Start menu, click Run, and type:

   ```
   <driveletter>:\setup\i386\setup.exe /forestprep
   ```

   where `<driveletter>` is the drive letter of your CD-ROM drive. This path may vary for certain versions of Exchange Server such as MSDN or Select versions.

6. On the Welcome screen, click Next.

7. On the License Agreement screen, read through the agreement and if you agree, click "I agree" and click Next.

8. If the Product Identification screen is presented, enter your Exchange Server product key and click Next.

   > This screen may not appear for certain versions of Exchange Server, such as the MSDN or Select versions.

9. On the Component Selection screen, verify that the action specified is ForestPrep, and click Next.

10. On the Server Administrator Account screen, enter the group created in Step 3 and click Next.

11. On the Completing the Microsoft Exchange Wizard screen, click Finish.

The second phase is *DomainPrep* and it needs to be run once for the forest root domain and once for every domain in the forest that will contain mail-enabled objects. Preferably you will run this process on every domain in the forest. You will want to wait for the schema updates from the ForestPrep to replicate prior to starting DomainPrep.

1. Log on to a machine that is part of the domain with an account that is a member of the *Domain Admins* group.

2. Insert the Exchange Server CD into CD-ROM.

3. On the Start menu, click Run, and then type:

   ```
   <driveletter>:\setup\i386\setup.exe /domainprep
   ```

   where *<driveletter>* is the drive letter of your CD-ROM drive. This path may vary for certain versions of Exchange Server such as MSDN or Select versions.

4. On the Welcome screen, click Next.

5. On the License Agreement screen, read through the agreement and if you agree, click "I agree" and click Next.

6. If presented, on the Product Identification screen, enter your Exchange Server product key and click Next.

 This screen may not appear for certain versions of Exchange Server, such as the MSDN or Select versions.

7. On the Component Selection screen, verify that the action specified is Domain-Prep and click Next.

8. Depending on how your domain is configured for Pre-Windows 2000 Compatible Access, you may get a pop-up with a message saying "The domain "*<domainname>*" has been identified as an insecure domain for mail-enabled groups with hidden DL membership…." If you get this pop-up, click OK.

9. On the Completing the Microsoft Exchange Wizard screen, click Finish.

Using a command-line interface

You cannot run ForestPrep from the command-line. You can, however, run an unattended DomainPrep. You will need to create an unattended installation configuration file, which is described in "Creating Unattended Installation Files for Exchange and Exchange Service Pack Installations." For further details on this process, see the Exchange Server 2003 Deployment Guide.

You can load the Exchange schema extensions to your forest before running ForestPrep, allowing you to import the Exchange-specific schema modifications months in advance without needing to specify an organization name as you had to do in Exchange 2000.

Discussion

Microsoft Exchange will not run in an Active Directory forest unless the forest and the domains have been properly prepared. Microsoft did not make the assumption that everyone would use Exchange and therefore did not include all of the Exchange attributes and classes in the base Active Directory schema. The ability to dynamically extend the schema for Active Directory makes it possible for only those people running Exchange to install the Exchange infrastructure.

In addition to schema changes, you have to make security changes to Active Directory and the domain policy, as well as create some basic Exchange infrastructure objects. All of this is completed in the Exchange ForestPrep and DomainPrep processes. Do not confuse these with the Windows 2003 ForestPrep and DomainPrep processes (using the *adprep* command); the concept is the same but the specific changes are different.

You need to run the ForestPrep process once per forest to make the schema changes, create the Exchange organization structure in the Configuration container, and set up Exchange-specific permissions. The ForestPrep process is also responsible for the initial delegation of Exchange rights to a specific user or group for administrative control. We recommend that you create a security group in your root domain for this delegation. You could use a domain local group in a single domain forest in which you will never create another domain. In a multidomain forest, you must use a global group or a universal group. The group is used to assign rights to objects in the Configuration container. Whether you use a global or universal group is up to you— either will do the job. The ForestPrep process requires the person running the process to be part of both the *Enterprise Admins* and *Schema Admins* groups.

You need to run the DomainPrep process in the root domain of the forest and for every domain that will contain mail-enabled objects. Normally, DomainPrep is run on every domain in an Active Directory forest. The process creates Exchange security principals, modifies the domain security policy, creates some Exchange specific infrastructure objects, and assigns permissions to the domain's Active Directory partition. The DomainPrep process requires the person running the process to be a member of the *Domain Admins* group of the domain being prepared.

Depending on whether your domain has Pre-Windows 2000 Compatible Access enabled, you may get a scary looking message during the DomainPrep process that tells you your domain is insecure for mail-enabled groups with hidden distribution list membership. Instead of making quick changes to your domain that could break other applications, investigate whether you need that compatibility access. If you do not need the access, by all means lock down the Pre-Windows 2000 Compatible Access group as specified.

Just like any application, there are requirements for the installation of Exchange Server 2003. The requirements are split into forest requirements and machine requirements.

For ForestPrep and DomainPrep, there are no machine requirements. However, the requirements for the forest are:

- Domain controllers must be running Windows 2000 Server Service Pack 3 or Windows Server 2003.
- Global catalog servers must be running Windows 2000 Server Service Pack 3 or Windows Server 2003. You should have at least one global catalog server per site that you intend to install Exchange into.
- DNS and NetBIOS name resolution (typically using WINS) must be properly configured.

Due to the depth of changes made to the overall structure of Active Directory, the ForestPrep process requires Schema Admin and Enterprise Admin rights and the DomainPrep requires Domain Admin rights. This prevents anyone but the centralized administration group responsible for the overall Active Directory forest from initially installing Exchange into the forest.

For a more in-depth discussion of the Exchange Server 2003 deployment requirements, considerations, and the specifics of what the preparation processes do, please see the Exchange Server 2003 Deployment Guide. This is a free download from Microsoft and can be obtained by going to *http://www.microsoft.com/exchange/ library*. You should also review the Exchange Server 2003 Deployment Tools and the Exchange Best Practices Analyzer, available from the same site.

See Also

Chapters 7 and 11 for more on groups and the AD schema, *http://www.microsoft.com/ exchange/library*, MS KB 314649 (Windows Server 2003 adprep/forestprep Command Causes Mangled Attributes in Windows 2000 Forests that Contain Exchange 2000 Servers), MS KB 327757 (How to Extend the Active Directory Schema for Exchange Without Installing Exchange), and the Exchange Server 2003 Deployment Guide

22.2   Installing the First Exchange Server

Problem

You want to install the first Exchange Server of an Exchange organization.

Solution

Using a graphical user interface

1. Install and configure prerequisite services. See the "Discussion" section for more on these services.

2. Log on to a server that is a member of an Exchange-enabled domain with an account that is a member of the delegated group in Recipe 22.1. This account should also be a local administrator of the server.

3. Go to the Windows Update site and install any critical security patches, or use your organization's existing patch management solution such as WSUS. Click on Start → All Programs → Windows Update.

4. Insert the Exchange Server CD into CD-ROM.

5. On the Start menu, click Run, type *<driveletter>:\setup\i386\setup.exe*, and click OK. *<driveletter>* is the drive letter of your CD-ROM drive. The path to *setup.exe* may vary for certain versions of Exchange Server such as MSDN or Select versions.

6. On the Welcome screen, click Next.

7. On the License Agreement screen, read through the agreement and if you agree, click "I agree" and click Next.

8. If presented, on the Product Identification screen, enter your Exchange Server product key and click Next.

 This screen may not appear for certain versions of Exchange Server, such as the MSDN or Select versions.

9. On the Component Selection screen in the Action column, verify that the action selected is Typical. Verify the install path is correct for your installation and click Next. It is a common practice to load Exchange onto a drive other than the system drive.

10. On the Installation Type screen, verify Create a new Exchange Organization is selected, and click Next.

11. On the Organization Name screen, enter the name you want for your Exchange organization, and click Next. You can leave the default name of "First Organization" or name it something specific to your installation (e.g., "RALLENCORP-MAIL").

12. On the License Agreement screen, select "I agree" and then click Next.

13. Review the Installation Summary screen and click Next.

14. On the Completing the Microsoft Exchange Wizard screen, click Finish.

15. Stop and disable the NNTP service unless you specifically wish to use newsfeeds within your Messaging environment.

16. Download and install the latest Exchange 2003 service pack. (As of the time of this writing it is Service Pack 2.) See Recipe 22.4 for more on installing Exchange service packs.

17. Download and run the Exchange Best Practices Analyzer to determine its compliance with security and performance best practices.

Using a command-line interface

You cannot install the first Exchange Server of the Organization via the command line. However, you can install subsequent Exchange servers using an unattended installation, as we will discuss in Recipe 22.3.

Discussion

The first Exchange server you install is special. This is because in addition to installing the Exchange Server software on the server, the process is also creating Active Directory objects in the Configuration container for the Exchange organization. As such, the install is slightly different from any other Exchange Server installation you will do in the forest (see Recipe 22.3). The difference is in Steps 10 and 11, which will not be present for any other Exchange Server Installations within the Exchange organization. In these steps you will choose whether you want to create a new Exchange organization or join an existing Exchange 5.5 organization. The additional considerable amount of work involved in joining an existing Exchange 5.5 organization is outside the scope of this chapter. See the *Exchange Server Cookbook* by Paul Robichaux et al. (O'Reilly) for more information.

See Also

Recipe 22.1, Recipe 22.3, Recipe 22.4 for more on installing Exchange service packs, MS KB 822593 (Description of the /ChooseDC Switch in Exchange Server 2003), MS KB 822893 (Setup Options for Exchange Server 2003), and *Exchange Server Cookbook* by Paul Robichaux et al. (O'Reilly)

22.3   Installing Additional Exchange Servers

Problem

You want to install an additional Exchange Server.

Solution

Using a graphical user interface

1. Install and configure prerequisite services. See the "Discussion" section for more on these services.

2. Log on to a server that is member of an Exchange-enabled domain with an account that is a member of the group delegated in Recipe 22.1. This account should also be an administrator of the server.

3. Go to the Windows Update site and install any critical security patches. Click on Start → All Programs → Windows Update.

4. Insert the Exchange Server CD into CD-ROM.

5. On the Start menu, click Run, type *<driveletter>:\setup\i386\setup.exe*, and click OK. *<driveletter>* is the drive letter of your CD-ROM drive. This path may vary for certain versions of Exchange Server such as MSDN or Select versions.

6. On the Welcome screen, click Next.

7. On the License Agreement screen, read through the agreement and if you agree, select "I agree" and click Next.

8. If presented, on the Product Identification screen enter your Exchange Server product key and click Next.

 This screen may not appear for certain versions of Exchange Server such as the MSDN or Select versions.

9. On the Component Selection screen in the Action column, verify that the action specified is Typical. Verify that the install path is correct for your installation and click Next. It is a common practice is to load Exchange onto a drive other than the system drive.

10. Where additional Administration Groups have been created, you will be presented with a drop down list of which Administration Group you wish to install the Exchange Server into. Choose carefully here, because the server cannot be moved to another Administration Group after installation.

11. On the License Agreement screen, select "I agree" and click Next.

12. Review the Installation Summary screen and click Next.

13. On the Completing the Microsoft Exchange Wizard screen, click Finish.

14. Download and Install the latest Exchange 2003 service pack. (As of the time of this writing it is Service Pack 2.) See Recipe 22.4 for more on installing Exchange service packs.

15. Download and run the Exchange Best Practices Analyzer to determine its compliance with security and performance best practices.

Using a command-line interface

Any Exchange server installations after the initial Exchange server can be handled through the command-line with the unattended installation process. You will need to generate and use an unattended installation (INI) file. See Recipe 22.5 for more on the INI file creation process.

Once you have an unattended file, use the following command to install Exchange.

```
> <driveletter>:\setup\i386\setup.exe /unattendfile <unattendfile>
```

If there is an error during the install process, it will be recorded in the Exchange Server setup log, which by default will be located in the root of the system drive, generally *C:*.

Discussion

Exchange Server has several software prerequisites for its installation. You must have these prerequisites met prior to installing Exchange or else Exchange will not install. See Recipe 22.2 for more detail on the prerequisites.

Using a command-line interface

If you have only one or two Exchange servers, automating the Exchange Server installation will probably not appeal to you. However, if you have several Exchange Servers, using the unattended installation features of Exchange can certainly lead to time savings, efficiency, and consistency.

See Also

Recipe 22.1, Recipe 22.2, Recipe 22.4 for more on installing Exchange service packs, Recipe 22.5 for more on unattended installation, MS KB 822593 (Description of the /ChooseDC Switch in Exchange Server 2003), and MS KB 822893 (Setup Options for Exchange Server 2003)

22.4 Installing an Exchange Service Pack

Problem

You want to update your Exchange Server with the latest Exchange service pack.

Solution

Using a graphical user interface

1. Download the latest service pack from Microsoft. It can be found at *http://www.microsoft.com/exchange*. The current Exchange service pack at the time of this writing for Exchange 2003 is Service Pack 2.

2. On the Start menu, click Run, type the path to the service pack executable (e.g., *E3SP2ENG.exe*), and click OK.

3. When asked for a folder to extract the files to type *C:\Temp\Exchange2003* and click OK.

4. On the Extraction Complete screen, click OK.

5. On the Start menu, click Run, type the full path to *update.exe*, and click OK. This will vary by service pack and language version, but here is an example path: *C:\Temp\Exchange2003\E3SP2ENG\setup\i386\update.exe*.

6. On the Welcome screen, click Next.

7. On the License Agreement screen, read through the agreement and if you agree, select "I agree" and click Next.

8. On the Component Selection screen in the Action column, verify that the action specified is Update, and click Next. If an operating system update is required first, you will get a pop-up explaining what needs to be done. See the "Discussion" section for more information.

9. On the Installation Summary screen, verify actions and click Next.

10. On the Completing the Microsoft Exchange Wizard screen, click Finish.

Using a command-line interface

Service pack installations can be handled through unattended installations just as can regular Exchange server installations. You will need to generate and use the appropriate unattended install INI file. See Recipe 22.5 for more on INI file creation.

Once you have an unattended file, use the following command to update.

```
> <driveletter>:\<path_to_sp_files>\update.exe /unattendfile <unattendfile>
```

Note that if there is an error during the installation process, it will be recorded in the Exchange Server setup log, which by default will be located in the root of the system drive, generally *C:*.

Discussion

Installing service packs is very important for keeping secure and for having a well running system. This procedure needs to be followed both for servers running Exchange and any machines that have the Exchange administration tools loaded. When applying any service pack you may be prompted to install some other hot fix or service pack first for the operating system. For example, when installing Exchange SP1 on Windows Server 2003, you also needed to have the hot fix from MS KB 831464. (This hot fix is included in Windows Server 2003 Service Pack 1.) See the *Windows Server Cookbook for Windows Server 2003 and Windows 2000* by Robbie Allen (O'Reilly) for information on installing hot fixes.

If you have split your Exchange environment into frontend (FE) and backend (BE) servers, you must update any and all FE servers before updating the BE servers.

Using a command-line interface

If you have only one or two Exchange servers, automating the Exchange Server Service Pack installation will probably not appeal to you. However, if you have several Exchange Servers, using the unattended installation feature of Exchange can certainly lead to time savings, efficiency, and consistency.

See Also

Recipe 22.5 for more on unattended installation, MS KB 831464 (FIX: IIS 6.0 Compression Corruption Causes Access Violations), MS KB 822893 (Setup Options for Exchange Server 2003), and *Windows Server Cookbook for Windows Server 2003 and Windows 2000* by Robbie Allen (O'Reilly).

22.5 Creating Unattended Installation Files for Exchange and Exchange Service Pack Installations

Problem

You want to create an unattended installation file for command-line installations and upgrades of Exchange Server.

Solution

Using a graphical user Interface

1. Follow the procedures for Exchange Server installation (Recipe 22.3), Exchange Server Management Tools installation (Recipe 22.6), or Exchange Server service pack installation (Recipe 22.4) to the point where you enter the setup or update command.

2. Append to the run command the option /createunattend <driveletter>:\<path>\ <filename>.ini. Note that <filename> should be descriptive of the install or update. Examples include *e2k3-unattended-sp2-install.ini* and *e23k-tools-install.ini*.

3. Follow all of the screen prompts of the normal installation or upgrade.

4. On the Completing the Microsoft Exchange Wizard screen, click Finish.

   The unattended installation is in the location specified in the /createunattend option.

Discussion

Using unattended installation is a great way to install Exchange on many servers, deploy the Exchange tools to many admin workstations, update service packs for Exchange on many servers, or maintain consistency in installation configurations.

The basic process is simply to add the /createunattend switch to the command line for either the *setup* or *update* command. You can also, if you so choose, create an encrypted unattended installation file by using the /encryptedmode option. To see a complete list of options, run the *setup* or *update* executable with the /? option. After you create the file, you can use it to install Exchange as shown in the command-line solution in Recipe 22.3.

See Also

Recipe 22.3 for more on installing Exchange Server, Recipe 22.4 for more on installing Exchange service packs, Recipe 22.6 for more on installing the Exchange Management Tools, and MS KB 822893 (Setup Options for Exchange Server 2003)

22.6   Installing Exchange Management Tools

Problem

You want to install Exchange Management tools onto a workstation or server that isn't running Exchange.

Solution

Using a graphical user interface

1. Install and configure prerequisite services. See the "Discussion" section for the list of these services.
2. Go to the Windows Update site and install any critical security patches.
3. Load the Exchange Server CD into your CD-ROM.
4. On the Start menu, click Run and then type *<driveletter>:\setup\i386\setup.exe* and click OK. *<driveletter>* is the drive letter of your CD-ROM drive. This path may vary for certain versions of Exchange Server such as MSDN or Select versions.
5. On the Welcome screen, click Next.
6. On the License Agreement screen read through the agreement and if you agree, select "I agree" and click Next.
7. If the Product Identification screen is presented, enter your Exchange Server product key and click Next.

This screen may not appear for certain versions of Exchange Server such as the MSDN or Select versions.

8. On the Component Selection screen, select Custom in the top row of the Action column. Next to Microsoft Exchange System Management Tools, select Install. Verify that the install path is correct for your installation and click Next.

9. Review the Installation Summary screen and click Next.

10. On the Completing the Microsoft Exchange Wizard screen, click Finish.

11. Download and install latest Exchange 2003 service pack. As of the time of this writing it is Service Pack 2. See Recipe 22.4 for more information.

Using a command-line interface

Any Exchange Management Tool installations can be handled through the command line with the unattended installation process. You will need to generate and use the appropriate unattended install INI file. See Recipe 22.5 for more on creating an INI file.

Once you have an unattended file, use the following command to install:

```
> <driveletter>:\setup\i386\setup.exe /unattendfile <unattendfile>
```

Note that if there is an error during the install process it will be recorded in the Exchange Server setup log, which by default will be located in the root of the system drive, generally C:\.

Discussion

Exchange Server has several software prerequisites for the Exchange Management Tools software, without which they will refuse to install. You must have the Windows Server 2003 Administration Tools Pack (*adminpak.msi*) installed on Windows XP SP1+, Windows 2000 SP3+, or Windows Server 2003 along with the following services:

- IIS
- WWW Service
- SMTP Service

See the *Windows Server Cookbook for Windows Server 2003 and Windows 2000* by Robbie Allen (O'Reilly) for more details on installation of these prerequisites.

Microsoft has a recommendation against installing Exchange tools on a machine that runs Outlook. We haven't had an issue with loading the Exchange tools on a workstation that had Outlook, but it is a point that we must mention. See MS KB 266418 for more details.

You may or may not run into issues loading the Exchange management tools on a client computer that is running the Outlook email client, However, it is absolutely essential that you do not install Microsoft Outlook on the Exchange server itself.

Using a command-line interface

If you have only one or two machines you want to install the tools on, automating the Exchange Server Management Tools installation will probably not be any value to you. However, if you have several machines you need to load the tools on, using the unattended installation feature can certainly lead to time savings, efficiency, and consistency.

See Also

Recipe 22.4, Recipe 22.5 for more on unattended installation, MS KB 822593 (Description of the /ChooseDC Switch in Exchange Server 2003), MS KB 822893 (Setup Options for Exchange Server 2003), MS KB 266418 (Microsoft Does Not Recommend Installing Exchange Server and Outlook on the Same Computer), and *Windows Server Cookbook for Windows Server 2003 and Windows 2000* by Robbie Allen (O'Reilly)

22.7   Delegating Exchange for the First Time

Problem

You want to delegate permissions to manage Exchange. This recipe allows you to configure the basic delegation of the three Exchange roles to users or groups.

Solution

Using a graphical user interface

1. Log on to a machine with an account that is in the initially delegated Exchange Group from Recipe 22.2.

2. Per your corporate standards, create three groups called ExchangeViewAdmins, ExchangeAdmins, and ExchangeFullAdmins. The groups can be any scope. See Chapter 7 for assistance on creating groups and the ramifications of the different group scopes.

3. Open the Exchange System Manager (ESM) snap-in.

4. In the left pane, right-click on the Organization name (e.g., RALLENCORP-MAIL) and select Delegate Control.

5. On the Welcome screen, click Next.

6. On the Users and Groups screen, click Add.

7. On the Delegate Control screen, click Browse.

8. On the "Select Users, Computers, Or Groups" screen, type into the text box the name of the group to which you want to delegate Exchange View Admin rights (e.g., "RALLENCORP\ExchangeViewAdmins").

9. Back on the Delegate Control screen, verify that Exchange View Only Administrator is listed in the role drop-down menu and click OK.

10. Repeat Steps 6–9 for ExchangeAdmins and ExchangeFullAdmins, selecting the appropriate permissions in the role drop-down menu.

11. If you used a group in the root delegation in Recipe 22.2, you may still see one or more accounts listed in the Users and Groups box. Remove these from the list by selecting them and clicking Remove.

12. Review the list of Users and Groups and click Next. You should have the following groups and roles listed:
    - ExchangeAdmins with role Exchange Administrator
    - ExchangeFullAdmins with role Exchange Full Administrator
    - ExchangeViewAdmins with role Exchange View Only Administrator

13. On the Completed Wizard screen, click Finish.

14. Add the accounts of the administrators to the various groups with your favorite group management tool.

Discussion

Exchange delegation is a delicate and complicated topic. Most of the Exchange permissions are granted through ACLs on objects in Active Directory. These permissions in Active Directory can be delegated in a very granular way. Exchange consolidates the permissions into three main layers of delegation called *roles*:

Exchange View Only Administrator
 Allows you to look at the Exchange System.

Exchange Administrator
 Allows you to fully administer Exchange Server computer information.

Exchange Full Administrator
 Allows you to fully administer Exchange.

Be aware that none of these Exchange Roles give you access rights on user objects themselves. You can be an Exchange Full Administrator and not be able to mailbox-enable a single user. For that, you need to determine what rights you want the Exchange Admins to have on user objects and grant them separately.

Unfortunately, it is beyond the scope of this chapter to dig into all of the various ways to delegate rights to Active Directory objects. We'll assume for the remainder of this chapter that any administrator who needs to make changes to a user or group, such as mail-enabling or mailbox-enabling a user, mail-enabling a distribution group, creating a contact, etc. is a member of the Account Operators group with the additional permissions outlined in the next paragraph delegated in Active Directory.

By default, Account Operators have permissions to manage user objects, inetOrgPerson objects, and group objects. They do not have permissions to manage contacts or query-based distribution lists. For an Account Operator to be able to fully manage mail specific contents of Active Directory, permissions to create, delete, and manage contacts (i.e., objects with an object class of contact) and query-based distribution groups (i.e., objects with an object class of msExchDynamicDistributionList) have to be added separately. For details on Active Directory security and delegation, see Chapter 15.

In this security-aware world we now live in, we should discuss delegation best practices. Security best practices dictate for a separation of duties for different types of administrators. This is also known as the principle of least privileges. Exchange is definitely large enough to follow this type of model and has a couple of levels where these separations can most logically be made.

The first level involves the help desk or call center Exchange troubleshooters. These are people who you don't want making changes. You only want them to look at what is in place so they can properly escalate to the next level of support if the issue is truly an Exchange issue. These admins will need only view only access to Exchange and Active Directory. This would map to the Exchange View Only Admin Role.

The second level are the Exchange data administrators—administrators who are responsible for manipulating which users get mailboxes, and managing contacts and distribution lists. They will need to be able to manipulate users and other mail-enabled objects, but not manipulate the overall Exchange system configuration. This level is often automated and the functionality wrapped into some sort of provisioning system as the requests and responses should be standard. This level of permission will need Exchange view access and various create/delete/change permissions on the user, contact, and group objects in the forest. This would map to the Exchange View Only Admin Role coupled with the specially delegated Account Operator as specified earlier. The primary tool these admins use will be the ADUC snap-in.

This functionality, placed in a custom web-based application with a proper authentication and authorization system, could be pushed to the help desk or even out to the business users so that business management can directly manage who can and can't have email. Microsoft also helps in the automation of this level by distributing a tool in the Exchange Resource Kit called *AutoDL* for automatically handling distribution lists. This tool has the concept of distribution list subscriptions and managed distribution lists and has a web frontend for ease of use by nontechnical users.

The last level are Exchange service administrators; these are the main Exchange administrators who are actually managing the overall messaging environment. They need to be able to manipulate the servers and the system configuration but don't generally need to manipulate the mail objects, such as users, groups, and contacts. This level would map to Exchange Admin or Exchange Full Admin Roles. This level also requires local administrator rights on the Exchange servers. There could be times that these admins will need additional permissions in Active Directory on user objects, most notably if they are moving mailboxes, as discussed in Recipe 22.16, or reconnecting mailboxes, as discussed in Recipe 22.14. The primary tool these admins will use will be the ESM snap-in.

Depending on the size of your company and your security concerns, you may have none of these divisions, a subset of these divisions, or possibly even more divisions.

See Also

Recipe 22.14, Recipe 22.16, Chapters 7 and 15 for more on groups and security, MS KB 823018 (Overview of Exchange Administrative Role Permissions in Exchange 2003), MS KB 316792 (Minimum Permissions Necessary to Perform Exchange-Related Tasks), Active Directory Delegation Whitepaper and Appendix (*www.microsoft.com/downloads*), and *http://www.microsoft.com/technet/prodtechnol/ exchange/2003/library/ex2k3ad.mspx*

22.8   Stopping and Starting Exchange Server

Problem

You want to stop or start Exchange Server.

Solution

Stopping and starting Exchange consists of stopping and starting the Exchange-related services through the Services MMC snap-in or the net stop/net start command-line utilities. See the "Discussion" of this recipe for the list of Exchange services.

Using a graphical user interface

1. Open the Computer Management MMC snap-in (*compmgmt.msc*).
2. Scroll to the service that you wish to manage, and click Stop, Start, or Restart.

Using a command-line interface

The following command will stop a service:

```
> net stop <ServiceName>
```

The following command will start a service:

```
> net start <ServiceName>
```

The following will stop and start a service in a single command:

```
> net stop <ServiceName> && net start <ServiceName>
```

Using VBScript

```
'-------------SCRIPT CONFIGURATION---------------------
strComputer = "<ComputerName>"
strServiceName = "<ServiceName>"

Set objWMIService = GetObject("winmgmts:" _
    & "{impersonationLevel=impersonate}!\\" & strComputer _
    & "\root\cimv2")

Set colServiceList = objWMIService.ExecQuery _
    ("Select * from Win32_Service where Name='" & strServiceName _
    _ '")

' The following code will start a service

For Each objService in colServiceList
    errReturn = objService.StartService( )
Next

' The following code will stop a service

For Each objService in colServiceList
    errReturn = objService.StopService( )
Next
```

Discussion

There are several services involved with Exchange Server, and stopping different services will accomplish different things. The services are interdependent, so when you stop or start various services you may see a message about having to stop dependent services. If you do stop dependent services, don't forget to restart them again when you restart the service that you began with.

To shut down Exchange completely on a given machine, you need to stop all of the following services:

Microsoft Exchange Event (MSExchangeES)
    This service was used for launching event-based scripts in Exchange 5.5 when folder changes were detected. Exchange 2000 offered the ability to create Event Sinks directly, so this use of this service has decreased. This service is not started by default.

Microsoft Exchange IMAP4 (IMAP4Svc)

This service supplies IMAP4 protocol message server functionality. This service is disabled by default. To use IMAP4 you must enable this service, configure it to auto-start, and start the service.

Microsoft Exchange Information Store (MSExchangeIS)

This service is used to access the Exchange mail and public folder stores. If this service is not running, users will not be able to use Exchange. This service is started by default.

Microsoft Exchange Management (MSExchangeMGMT)

This service is responsible for various management functions available through WMI, such as message tracking. This service is started by default.

Microsoft Exchange MTA Stacks (MSExchangeMTA)

This service is used to transfer X.400 messages sent to and from foreign systems, including Exchange 5.5 Servers. This service was extremely important in Exchange 5.5, which used X.400 as the default message transfer protocol. Before stopping or disabling this service, review MS KB 810489. This service is started by default.

Microsoft Exchange POP3 (POP3Svc)

This service supplies POP3 protocol message server functionality. This service is disabled by default. To use POP3 you must enable this service, configure it to auto-start, and start the service.

Microsoft Exchange Routing Engine (RESvc)

This service is used for routing and topology information for routing SMTP-based messages. This service is started by default.

Microsoft Exchange System Attendant (MSExchangeSA)

This service handles various cleanup and monitoring functions. One of the most important functions of the System Attendant is the Recipient Update Service (RUS), which is responsible for mapping attributes in Active Directory to the Exchange subsystem and enforcing recipient policies. When you create a mailbox for a user, you simply set some attributes on a user object. The RUS takes that information and does all of the work in the background with Exchange to really make the mailbox. If you mailbox-enable or mail-enable objects and they don't seem to work, the RUS is one of the first places you will look for an issue. If you need to enable diagnostics for the RUS, the parameters are maintained in a separate service registry entry called MSExchangeAL. This isn't a real service; it is simply the supplied location to modify RUS functionality. This service is started by default.

Microsoft Exchange Site Replication Service (MSExchangeSRS)

This service is used in Organizations that have Exchange 5.5 combined with Exchange 2000/2003. This service is not started by default.

Network News Transfer Protocol (NntpSvc)

This service is responsible for supplying NNTP Protocol Server functionality. This service is started by default.

Simple Mail Transfer Protocol (SMTPSVC)

This service is responsible for supplying SMTP Protocol Server functionality. This service is started by default.

 Different servers could be running a combination of different services based on the complexity of the environment and the specific function of the server. Not all Exchange Servers will run all Exchange Services.

See Also

MS KB 810489 and MS KB 263094 (XADM: Internal Names of Exchange 2000 Server Services)

22.9   Mail-Enabling a User

Problem

You want to mail-enable a user.

Solution

Using a graphical user interface

1. Open the Users and Computers (ADUC) snap-in.

    This needs to be run on a workstation or server that has the Exchange Management Tools loaded (see Recipe 22.6).

2. If you need to change domains, right-click on Active Directory Users and Computers in the left pane, select Connect to Domain, enter the domain name, and click OK.

3. In the left pane, browse to the parent container of the user, right-click on the user, and select Exchange Tasks.

4. On the Welcome screen, click Next.

5. Select Establish E-mail Address and click Next.

6. Verify the mail alias is what you want.

7. Click Modify, select external email address type (generally SMTP Address), click OK, enter an external email address, and click OK.

There is an Advanced tab on the Internet Address Properties screen. On this tab, you have the option to override the default handling of email sent to this recipient (e.g., you can force all email to be delivered as HTML or plain text, etc.).

8. On the Completion screen, click Finish.

Using a command-line interface

```
> exchmbx -b "<User DN>" -me <smtp email address>
```

Replace *<User DN>* with the user's distinguished name and *<smtp email address>* with the user's external email address.

To mail enable the user joe with the email address *joe@unixmail.rallencorp.com*, execute the following command. The command should be contained on one line:

```
> exchmbx -b "cn=joe,cn=users,dc=rallencorp,dc=com" -me joe@unixmail.rallencorp.com
```

For an alternative Microsoft-native tool method, create an LDIF file called *mailenable_user.ldf* with the following contents:

```
dn: <User DN>
changetype: modify
replace: targetAddress
targetaddress: SMTP:<smtp email address>
-
replace: mailNickName
mailNickname: <mail nickname>
-
replace: mAPIRecipient
mAPIRecipient: FALSE
-
replace: legacyExchangeDN
legacyExchangeDN: <legacy exchange DN>
-
replace: internetEncoding
internetEncoding: 1310720
-
```

Replace *<User DN>* with the user's distinguished name, *<smtp email address>* with the user's external email address, and *<legacy exchange DN>* with the proper legacy exchange distinguished name value. Then run the following command:

```
>ldifde -i -f mailenable_user.ldf
```

Using VBScript

```
' This code mail enables a user.
' ------ SCRIPT CONFIGURATION ------
strUserDN = "<UserDN>"    ' e.g. cn=jsmith,cn=Users,dc=rallencorp,dc=com
strEmailAddr = "<EmailAddress>" 'e.g. jsmith234@freemail.net
' ------ END CONFIGURATION ---------
```

```
set objUser = GetObject("LDAP://" & strUserDN)
objUser.MailEnable strEmailAddr
objUser.Put "internetEncoding",1310720
objUser.SetInfo( )
Wscript.Echo "Successfully mail-enabled user."
```

Discussion

A mail-enabled user is a user object that has at least one email address defined within Exchange, but does not have a mailbox. This does not give any access rights to the user within the Exchange system; it simply allows Exchange users to select the mail-enabled user from the GAL and easily send email to them. You would use a mail-enabled user when you have a user who needs to log in to the domain, but has an email address external to the forest's Exchange organization. The email address could be external to the company or it could just be external to the Exchange organization of that forest. Examples would be users with mailboxes on external email systems or users with mailboxes on internal non-Exchange servers.

To mail-enable a user, you need to have permissions of Exchange View-Only Administrator or higher for the target administrative group. In addition, you need to have Read and Write permissions to the following object attributes:

- adminDisplayName
- autoReplyMessage (ILS Settings)
- displayName (Display Name)
- dLMemDefault
- homeMDB (Exchange Mailbox Store)
- homeMTA
- internetEncoding
- legacyExchangeDN
- mail (E-Mail Address)
- mailNickname (Alias)
- mAPIRecipient
- msExchADCGlobalNames
- msExchControllingZone
- msExchFBURL
- msExchHideFromAddressLists
- msExchHomeServerName (Exchange Home Server)
- msExchMailboxGuid
- msExchMailboxSecurityDescriptor
- msExchPoliciesExcluded

- msExchPoliciesIncluded
- msExchResourceGUID
- proxyAddresses (Proxy Addresses)
- showInAddressBook
- targetAddress
- textEncodedORAddress

When you create a mail-enabled user with ADUC or with VBScript, you call out to the CDOEXM interface, which is the Microsoft-supported method of managing Exchange attributes on users, groups, and contacts. The specific method in this case is MailEnable. In the background, the specific changes made by the MailEnable method are on the user object in Active Directory and include changes to the following attributes:

- targetAddress
- mailNickname
- mAPIRecipient
- legacyExchangeDN

In addition to those attributes, the internetEncoding attribute should also be set for proper message handling. This is the attribute that is updated if you go into the Advanced tab of the Internet Address Properties screen. The default value for this attribute is 1310720, which tells Exchange to use the default settings of the Internet Mail Service. You can specify other values to force email to be converted to various formats. Table 22-3 contains the list of alternate values for the internetEncoding attribute.

Table 22-3 internetEncoding attribute values

Value	Meaning
1310720	Use Internet Mail Service settings
917504	Allow plain text
1441792	Allow plain text or HTML
2228224	Allow plain text/uuencoding
131072	Allow plain text/uuencoding with BinHex

Once all of those attributes are in place, the RUS sets additional attributes on the user object to make it useable for Exchange.

Using a graphical user interface

Mail-enabling a user is a little more confusing if you are creating new users because you don't get prompted to mail-enable them. To create a mail-enabled user from scratch, create the user and, when prompted to create a mailbox, clear the Create an Exchange Mailbox checkbox. Once the user is created, follow the directions described in the solution.

Using a command-line interface

Command-line administration tools for Exchange are rather rare. Luckily, the ExchMbx tool is available as a free download from *http://www.joeware.net*. This tool can turn a difficult process into something quite simple. If you need to modify the `internetEncoding` attribute, add the `-internetencoding` option to the parameter list specifying the proper value from Table 22-3. For example:

```
> exchmbx -b <UserDN> -me <SmtpEmailAddress> -internetencoding 917504
```

If you prefer Microsoft-native solutions, the LDIF solution we described will work, but can be dangerous because there is the possibility of duplicating critical values within the Exchange organization. If you put duplicate `mailNickname` or `legacyExchangeDN` values into the system, you will have bad results in your Exchange organization that will almost certainly start producing nondelivery reports (NDR) for the mail objects involved.

The `mailNickname` attribute can generally be set to be the same as the `sAMAccountName`, which has to be unique in the domain. But what should you do you with `legacyExchangeDN`? If you aren't tied to a legacy 5.5 organization, you can follow the simple format the system currently uses. If you have a legacy 5.5 organization, you need to follow the structure for that organization. For assistance with this, contact Microsoft PSS or Microsoft Consulting Services.

The general format of `legacyExchangeDN` is:

```
/o=<Org>/ou=<AdministrativeGroup>/cn=<RecipientContainer>/cn=<mailnickname>
```

Assuming your `mailNickName` is unique (it had better be) and you know the values for the other variables, you can quickly construct a `legacyExchangeDN` like:

```
/o=CORPMAIL/ou=NORTHAMER/cn=Recipients/cn=NICOLEHANSKNECHT
```

You should always verify by searching Active Directory that the `legacyExchangeDN` you chose is not already used. The reason for this is that someone may have changed an existing user's `mailNickname` but, correctly, did not touch the `legacyExchangeDN` value. You could, of course, fix the `legacyExchangeDN` of that other user so that it properly fits the pattern, but you would impact the user's email functionality.

The attribute `legacyExchangeDN` is used in Exchange internally for addressing email. If you try to respond to an email sent to you by a user within the same Exchange organization who has had her `legacyExchangeDN` changed, you will get an NDR and the mail will not be delivered. So, if a user has a name change from Chris Smith to Chris Jones and her `sAMAccountName` and `mailNickname` both change from *csmith* to *cjones*, her `legacyExchangeDN` must remain the same so that anyone within the Exchange organization will be able to easily respond to emails she sent as *csmith*. The point is that you should always check that the legacyExchangeDN value you are setting is unique. The simple solution to follow if the value is already present is to append a -1, -2, or whatever dash value is required to get to a unique value.

You have the option of *not* specifying the legacyExchangeDN in the LDIF file. If the attribute is empty, Exchange will populate it for you. If there is already a value, Exchange will not change the attribute.

Unfortunately, if you are mail enabling an object that was previously mail- or mailbox-enabled, it could have an existing value for legacyExchangeDN; this value may or may not be unique. One very specific case is that some tools will set the legacyExchangeDN value to ADCDisabled when an object is mail or mailbox disabled to alert the ADC to the object's status.

You can modify the internetEncoding attribute value in the LDIF file to any value in Table 22-3.

If you want to mail enable multiple users at once, remove the -b option from the parameter list and pipe the distinguished names into ExchMbx from another tool or from a file. Run exchmbx /? for usage details.

Using VBScript

Creating a mail-enabled user from VBScript is quite simple; one call to the MailEnable method and the work is done. As we indicated in the CLI solution, you can modify the internetEncoding value to one of the other values in Table 22-3 depending on your needs.

See Also

Recipe 22.6, Recipe 22.10 for more on mail-disabling a user, MS KB 275636 (Creating Exchange Mailbox-Enabled and Mail-Enabled Objects in Active Directory), and MS KB 281740 (XCON: Internet Mail Service Settings Are Not Overridden for Custom Recipients in Distribution List) for the values of internetEncoding

22.10 Mail-Disabling a User

Problem

You want to mail-disable a user.

Solution

Using a graphical user interface

1. Open the Active Directory Users and Computers (ADUC) snap-in.

 This needs to be run on a workstation or server that has the Exchange Management Tools loaded (see Recipe 22.6).

2. If you need to change domains, right-click on Active Directory Users and Computers in the left pane, select Connect to Domain, enter the domain name, and click OK.

3. In the left pane, browse to the parent container of the user, right-click on the user, and select Exchange Tasks.

4. On the Welcome screen, click Next.

5. Select Remove Exchange Attributes and click Next.

6. Read the warning and click Next.

7. On the Completion screen, click Finish.

Using a command-line interface

```
> exchmbx -b "<User DN>" -clear
```

Replace *<User DN>* with the user's distinguished name.

For an alternative Microsoft-native tool method, create an LDIF file called *clearmailattribs.ldf* with the following contents:

```
dn: <UserDN>
changetype: modify
replace: altRecipient
altRecipient:
-
replace: authOrig
authOrig:
-
...
<SEE DISCUSSION, NOT A COMPLETE LDIF FILE>
...
```

Replace *<UserDN>* with the user's distinguished name. Note that this is not a complete LDIF file as there are many attributes that must be cleared; see the "Discussion" section for further details. Once you've created the LDIF file, run the following command:

```
> ldifde -i -f clearmailattribs.ldf
```

Using VBScript

```
' This code mail disables a user.
' ------ SCRIPT CONFIGURATION ------
strUserDN = "<UserDN>"   ' e.g. cn=jsmith,cn=Users,dc=rallencorp,dc=com
' ------ END CONFIGURATION ---------
set objUser = GetObject("LDAP://" & strUserDN)
objUser.MailDisable
objUser.SetInfo()
Wscript.Echo "Successfully mail-disabled user."
```

Discussion

This recipe removes the Active Directory Exchange attributes for a previously mail-enabled user. This is a simple process from ADUC and from VBScript, but behind the scenes several attributes are being updated. For a complete list of the attributes that are modified, see MS KB 307350.

Mail-disabling a user requires Exchange View-Only Administrator or higher permissions, as well as Read and Write permissions to a number of object attributes. See the Microsoft Exchange Tech Center on the Microsoft web site for a list of all necessary attributes.

Using a graphical user interface

This process is identical to the process for deleting a user's mailbox.

Using a command-line interface

The ExchMbx solution is simple and, unlike the VBScript solution, can be used on either mail-enabled or mailbox-enabled users.

 If you want to clear the Exchange mail attributes on several objects at once, remove the -b option from the parameter list and pipe the distinguished names into ExchMbx from another tool or from a file. Run exchmbx /? for usage details.

The LDIF solution requires some additional explanation. The LDIF file shown in the solution is not complete. You must clear many more attributes than listed. Check out MS KB 307350 for the current listing of attributes that should be cleared when removing Exchange attributes (there were about 90 at the time of this writing).

Using VBScript

The VBScript solution leverages the CDOEXM MailDisable method to mail-disable the user. Unfortunately, you cannot use this method to mailbox-disable a user. So, when you call this method, you should be sure that the user is mail-enabled versus mailbox-enabled. If you use this method on a mailbox-enabled user, you will get an error such as "E-mail addresses cannot be removed from this user because it has a mailbox." The quick way to ascertain whether a user has a mailbox or is simply mail-enabled is to check for the existence of the homeMDB attribute. If a user object has homeMDB populated, there is an associated mailbox for that account.

See Also

Recipe 22.6 and Recipe 22.9 for more on mail-enabling a user and MS KB 307350 (XGEN: Using the "Remove Exchange Attributes" Option)

22.11 Mailbox-Enabling a User

Problem

You want to create a mailbox for a user. This is also known as mailbox-enabling a user.

Solution

Using a graphical user interface

1. Open the Active Directory Users and Computers (ADUC) snap-in.

    This needs to be run on a workstation or server that has the Exchange Management Tools loaded (see Recipe 22.6).

2. If you need to change domains, right-click on Active Directory Users and Computers in the left pane, select Connect to Domain, enter the domain name, and click OK.

3. In the left pane, browse to the parent container of the user, right-click on the user, and select Exchange Tasks.

4. On the Welcome screen, click Next.

5. Select Create Mailbox and click Next.

6. Verify the mail alias is what you want, select the server you want the mailbox on, select which store you want the mailbox in, and click Next.

7. On the Completion screen, click Finish.

Using a command-line interface

```
> exchmbx -b "<UserDN>" -cr "<server>:<storage group>:<mail store>"
```

Or alternatively, run the following command:

```
> exchmbx -b <UserDN> -cr "<Home MDB URL>"
```

To mailbox enable the user *joe* with a mailbox on Exchange Server SRV1, Storage group SG1, and mailbox store DB1, execute the following command:

```
> exchmbx -b "cn=joe,cn=users,dc=rallencorp,dc=com" -cr "srv1:sg1:db1"
```

> We highly recommend that you keep your storage group and mailbox store names short, simple, and space free. Spaces are troublesome to deal with at the command prompt and have caused many administrators unneeded grief. If you do not use spaces and other special characters, you can dispense with the quotes in all of the command-line examples.

Replace *<UserDN>* with the user's distinguished name, *<server>* with the Exchange server name, *<storage group>* with the storage group, *<mail store>* with the mail store, and *<Home MDB URL>* with the full homeMDB URL for the desired mailbox store.

Using VBScript

```
' This code creates a mailbox for a user.
' ------  SCRIPT CONFIGURATION ------
strUserDN = "<UserDN>"    ' e.g. cn=jsmith,cn=Users,dc=rallencorp,dc=com
strHomeMDB = "<Home MDB DN>"
' e.g. CN=Mailbox Store (SERVER),CN=First Storage Group,CN=InformationStore,
' CN=SERVER,CN=Servers,CN=First Administrative Group,CN=Administrative Groups,
'       CN=RALLENCORPMAIL,CN=Microsoft Exchange,CN=Services,
'       CN-Configuration,DC=rallencorp,DC=com"
' ------ END CONFIGURATION ---------
set objUser = GetObject("LDAP://" & strUserDN)
objUser.CreateMailBox strHomeMDB
objUser.SetInfo( )
Wscript.Echo "Successfully mailbox-enabled user."
```

Discussion

A mailbox-enabled user is a user object that has a mailbox defined in the Exchange organization that the user object exists in. This is the most common object in an Exchange organization.

> Mailbox-enabling a user requires Exchange View-Only Administrator or higher permissions, as well as Read and Write permissions to a number of object attributes. See the Microsoft Exchange Tech Center on the Microsoft web site for a list of all necessary attributes.

When you create a mailbox for a user with the GUI or VBScript, you call out to the CreateMailbox CDOEXM interface. In the background, the specific changes made by the CreateMailbox method are on the user object in Active Directory and include changes to the following attributes:

- mDBUseDefaults
- msExchUserAccountControl

- homeMTA
- msExchHomeServerName
- homeMDB
- mailNickname
- msExchMailboxGuid
- msExchMailboxSecurityDescriptor
- legacyExchangeDN

Once all of those attributes are in place, the RUS sets additional attributes on the user object. The mailbox cannot be used nor receive email until the RUS has gone through this stamping process. It's also important to note that the mailbox will not be physically created until it is accessed for the first time or until it receives an item of mail.

Using a graphical user interface

Creating a mailbox when you create a new user is a trivial task with ADUC, because you simply need to specify the email alias and where in the Exchange organization the mailbox should reside. All of the guesswork on where the mailbox can go is removed because you have to select the location from the drop-down menu.

Using a command-line interface

Prior to the ExchMbx tool, there was no simple way to mailbox-enable a user from the command line. The LDIFDE method is not feasible because the msExchMailboxSecurityDescriptor attribute is a binary value and difficult to manipulate with LDIF files and text editors. For flexibility, ExchMbx allows you to specify the entire homeMDB URL, or you can specify the server, storage group, and mailbox store.

 If you want to mailbox enable multiple users at once, remove the -b option from the parameter list and pipe the distinguished names into ExchMbx from another tool or from a file. Run exchmbx /? for usage details.

Using VBScript

The trickiest part of creating a mailbox for a user with VBscript is to know what to use for the homeMDB attribute. If you use the wrong value you will get the error: "The server is not operational," which isn't helpful feedback. This is where the GUI method is nice, because it looks up all of the possible values for you and lets you select from the list.

We present an alternative scripting method in Recipe 22.16, which lets you specify three well-known pieces of information to locate the proper homeMDB value.

Another alternative would be to search Active Directory for all valid homeMDB values, display them, and have the person running the script select from the list just like ADUC does. This third method involves searching against the Configuration container of Active Directory with the following filter:

```
(objectcategory=msExchPrivateMDB)
```

See Also

Recipe 22.6, Recipe 22.16, MS KB 275636 (Creating Exchange Mailbox-Enabled and Mail-Enabled Objects in Active Directory) and MS KB 253770 (XADM: Tasks Performed by the Recipient Update Service)

22.12 Deleting a User's Mailbox

Problem

You want to delete a user's mailbox. This is also known as mailbox-disabling a user.

Solution

Using a graphical user interface

1. Open the Active Directory Users and Computers (ADUC) snap-in.

    This needs to be run on a workstation or server that has the Exchange Management Tools loaded (see Recipe 22.6).

2. If you need to change domains, right click on Active Directory Users and Computers in the left pane, select Connect to Domain, enter the domain name, and click OK.
3. In the left pane, browse to the parent container of the user, right-click on the user, and select Exchange Tasks.
4. On the Welcome screen, click Next.
5. Select Remove Exchange Attributes and click Next.
6. Read the warning and click Next.
7. On the Completion screen, click Finish.

Using a command-line interface

See the command-line example for Recipe 22.10.

Using VBScript

```
' This code mail disables a user.
' ------ SCRIPT CONFIGURATION ------
strUserDN = "<UserDN>"    ' e.g. cn=jsmith,cn=Users,dc=rallencorp,dc=com
' ------ END CONFIGURATION ---------
set objUser = GetObject("LDAP://" & strUserDN)
objUser.DeleteMailbox
objUser.SetInfo( )
Wscript.Echo "Successfully deleted user's mailbox."
```

Discussion

Although the recipe title is "Deleting a User's Mailbox," these solutions don't really delete the mailbox. They actually just clear the Exchange attributes from the user object and that disassociates the mailbox from the user; the mailbox itself will still exist in the Exchange store. The length of time it will exist depends on the mailbox retention period, which is 30 days by default. While the mailbox exists in that state, it can be reconnected to the same or a different user object.

 Deleting a user requires Exchange View-Only Administrator or higher permissions, as well as Read and Write permissions to a number of object attributes. See the Microsoft Exchange Tech Center on the Microsoft web site for a list of all necessary attributes.

Using a graphical user interface

This process in ADUC is identical to that of mail-disabling a user. See Recipe 22.20.

Using VBScript

The VBScript solution leverages the CDOEXM DeleteMailbox method to delete the mailbox for the user. Unfortunately, you cannot use this method to mail-disable a user. So when you call this method, you should be sure that the user is mailbox-enabled versus mail-enabled. If you use this method on a mail-enabled user, you will get an error such as "This user does not have a mailbox." The quick way to ascertain whether a user has a mailbox or is simply mail-enabled is to check for the existence of the homeMDB attribute. If a user object has homeMDB populated, there is an associated mailbox for that account.

See Also

Recipe 22.6, Recipe 22.10, Recipe 22.13, Recipe 22.14 for more on reconnecting mailboxes, Recipe 22.20 for more on purging mailboxes, MS KB 307350 (XGEN: Using the "Remove Exchange Attributes" Option), and MS KB 274343 (How to Recover a Deleted Mailbox in Exchange)

22.13 Purging a Deleted Mailbox

Problem

You want to purge a deleted mailbox from the Exchange Store.

Solution

Using a graphical user interface

1. Open the Exchange System Manager (ESM) snap-in.

2. In the left pane, browse to the mailboxes container of the server, storage group, and database you want to purge a mailbox from.

3. In the left pane, scroll down until you find the mailbox that you wish to purge. The mailbox should have a small red circle with a white X in it, indicating that it is disconnected.

4. Right-click the mailbox and select Purge.

5. When prompted if you are sure you want to continue click Yes.

Using VBScript

```
' This code purges a deleted mailbox.
' ------ SCRIPT CONFIGURATION ------
strComputer = "<Exchange Server>" 'e.g. ExchServer2
strMailbox = "<Mailbox Alias>"    'e.g. jsmith
' ------ END CONFIGURATION ---------

set objWMI = GetObject("winmgmts:\\" & strComputer & _
                       "\root\MicrosoftExchangeV2")
set objDiscMbx = objWMI.ExecQuery("Select * from Exchange_Mailbox WHERE " _
                        & "MailboxDisplayName-'" & strMailbox & "'",,48)
for each objMbx in objDiscMbx
  objMbx.Purge
next
Wscript.Echo "Successfully purged mailbox."
```

Discussion

A mailbox that has been deleted still has physical presence in the Exchange store. This recipe wipes that mailbox from the store completely. Once a mailbox has been purged, the only way to retrieve it is through restoring from a backup, which could be a lengthy process given the need to recover the entire store. In other words, don't do this unless you are sure of the consequences.

> Purging a mailbox requires Exchange Full Administrator permissions. See the "Discussion" for Recipe 22.7.

Using a graphical user interface

You may run into a case where ESM doesn't show you a mailbox is disconnected when in fact you know it is. This can happen if you delete the mailbox and immediately look at it in ESM. To clear that condition, you will need to right-click on the mailboxes container and select Run Cleanup Agent. This will cause some house cleaning to be done; the mailbox should then show up as disconnected.

Using VBScript

The Purge method is part of the Exchange_Mailbox class, which is new for Exchange 2003. In Exchange 2000, there was no method available to purge a mailbox via a script.

Be extremely careful with this script because it could easily remove all disconnected mailboxes on a given Exchange server. If the WHERE clause is removed in the SELECT statement of the WMI query, the purge loop below that would then clear every mailbox that was disconnected, so be careful.

 Because this script uses Exchange WMI extensions, it can be run from any machine that has WMI; the machine does not have to have the Exchange Management Tools loaded.

See Also

Recipe 22.7 and Exchange Server 2003 SDK: WMI Reference

22.14 Reconnecting a Deleted Mailbox

Problem

You want to reconnect a mailbox in the Exchange Store to a user object.

Solution

Using a graphical user interface

1. Open the Exchange System Manager (ESM) snap-in.
2. In the left pane, browse to the mailboxes container of the server, storage group, and database you want to reconnect a mailbox.
3. In the right pane, scroll down until you find the mailbox that you wish to reconnect. The mailbox should have a small red circle with a white X on it indicating it is disconnected.
4. Right-click the mailbox and select Reconnect.

5. Choose a user object in the directory you wish to reconnect this mailbox to.

6. A dialog box indicating the Reconnect Operation has completed successfully should pop up. Click OK.

Using VBScript

```
' This code reconnects a mailbox to a user.
' ------ SCRIPT CONFIGURATION ------
strComputer = "<Exchange Server>" ' e.g. ExchServer2
strUser = "<Userid>"              ' e.g. jsmith
strMailbox = "<Mailbox Alias>"    ' e.g. jsmith
' ------ END CONFIGURATION ---------

set objWMI = GetObject("winmgmts:\\" & strComputer & _
                       "\root\MicrosoftExchangeV2")
set objDiscMbx = objWMI.ExecQuery("Select * from Exchange_Mailbox WHERE " _
                       & "MailboxDisplayName='" & strMailbox & "'",,48)
for each objMbx in objDiscMbx
  objMbx.Reconnect strUser
next
Wscript.Echo "Successfully reconnected mailbox."
```

Discussion

When you tell the system to delete an Exchange mailbox, it isn't really deleted. It is simply disassociated or disconnected from the user object. These mailboxes are referred to as *orphaned* or *disconnected*. Deleted mailboxes stay in this disconnected state for a configurable period, by default 30 days, and can be recovered any time in that period. To truly remove a mailbox before that time, you must purge the mailbox after the deletion. This recipe shows how to reconnect that disconnected mailbox back to the original user object or to an alternate user object.

Reconnecting a mailbox requires Exchange Full Administrator permissions plus additional permissions on user objects. See the "Discussion" for Recipe 22.7 and MS KB 316792.

Using a graphical user interface

You may run into a case where the ESM doesn't show you a mailbox is disconnected when in fact you know it is. This can happen if you delete the mailbox and immediately look at it in ESM. To clear that condition, you will need to right-click on the mailboxes container and select Run Cleanup Agent. This will cause some house cleaning to be done. The mailbox should then show up as disconnected.

On the Exchange 2000 Server CD in the *Support\Utils* folder, there was a tool called *mbconn.exe*, which could also be used to reconnect mailboxes. This tool is not included on the Exchange 2003 Server CD. However, it still functions fine against Exchange 2003.

Using VBScript

The Reconnect method is part of the Exchange_Mailbox class, which is new for Exchange 2003. In Exchange 2000, there was no method available to reconnect a mailbox via a script. Unfortunately, there are some rather serious flaws with this implementation of the Reconnect method, which severely limits its usability in some environments.

The first flaw is that the WMI method must be run directly on the Exchange Server with the disconnected mailbox, so the script must run on the Exchange server. You can't, for instance, have a script that runs from a workstation that will reconnect mailboxes on any of your Exchange servers.

The second flaw is that you cannot specify the domain of the user you want to reconnect to the mailbox. In a single domain Exchange environment, this will be fine. Trying to reconnect a mailbox in a forest with the same username in multiple domains could give unexpected results.

See Also

Recipe 22.7, Recipe 22.15 for more on enumerating disconnected mailboxes, Exchange Server 2003 SDK, MS KB 274343 (How to Recover a Deleted Mailbox in Exchange), MS KB 316792 (Minimum Permissions Necessary to Perform Exchange-related Tasks), and Exchange Server 2003 SDK: WMI Reference

22.15 Enumerating Disconnected Mailboxes

Problem

You want to enumerate all disconnected mailboxes on a server.

Solution

Using a graphical user interface

1. Open the Exchange System Manager (ESM) snap-in.
2. In the left pane, browse to the mailboxes container of the server, storage group, and database for which you want to view disconnected mailboxes.
3. In the right pane, scroll down through the list, taking note of all mailboxes with a small red circle with an X.

Using VBScript

```
' This code enumerates disconnected mailboxes.
' ------ SCRIPT CONFIGURATION ------
strComputer = "<Exchange Server>" 'e.g. ExchServer2
' ------ END CONFIGURATION ---------
```

```
set objWMI = GetObject("winmgmts:\\" & strComputer & _
                       "\root\MicrosoftExchangeV2")

set objDiscMbx = objWMI.ExecQuery("Select * from Exchange_Mailbox",,48)
for each objMbx in objDiscMbx
  if (objMbx.DateDiscoveredAbsentInDS <> "") then
    Wscript.Echo objMbx.MailBoxDisplayName & " " & _
                 objMbx.DateDiscoveredAbsentInDS
  end if
next
Wscript.Echo "Successfully enumerated disconnected mailboxes."
```

Discussion

When you tell the system to delete an Exchange mailbox, it isn't really deleted. It is simply disassociated or disconnected from the user object. These mailboxes are referred to as *orphaned* or *disconnected*. This recipe shows you how to enumerate the disconnected mailboxes you have on a specified server.

> Viewing mailbox details in the ESM requires Exchange View Admin role access. However, to do this with a script, the WMI provider also requires local administrator permissions on the Exchange server. See the "Discussion" in Recipe 22.7.

Using VBScript

This is one of the occasions where a script is not only quicker than the corresponding GUI, but also much easier. There is no method to just enumerate disconnected mailboxes in ESM. You have to actually go down the list and look at every mailbox. If you have thousands of mailboxes, this could be quite tedious. If you have thousands of mailboxes across many servers, it can quickly become unmanageable.

The DateDiscoveredAbsentInDS property is part of the Exchange_Mailbox class, which is new for Exchange 2003.

> Since this script uses Exchange WMI extensions, it can be run from any machine that has WMI. The machine does not have to have the Exchange Management Tools loaded.

See Also

Recipe 22.7 and Exchange Server 2003 SDK: WMI Reference

22.16 Moving a Mailbox

Problem

You want to move a mailbox to a new database, storage group, or server.

Solution

Using a graphical user interface

1. Open the Users and Computers (ADUC) snap-in.

    This needs to be run on a workstation or server that has the Exchange
   Management Tools loaded (see Recipe 22.6).

2. If you need to change domains, right-click on Active Directory Users and Computers in the left pane, select Connect to Domain, enter the domain name, and
   click OK.

3. In the left pane, browse to the parent container of the user, right-click on the
   user, and select Exchange Tasks.

4. On the Welcome screen, click Next.

5. Select Move Mailbox and click Next.

6. Select new values for Server and Mailbox Store and click Next.

7. Select how you want to handle corrupted messages and click Next.

8. Specify when to start processing the move task and click Next.

9. When the Completed screen is shown click Finish. If there are errors, select the
   View Detailed Report checkbox to get a failure report.

Using a command-line interface

```
> exchmbx -b <UserDN> -move "<server>:<storage group>:<mail store>"
```

Or alternatively, run the following command:

```
> exchmbx -b <UserDN> -move "<Home MDB URL>"
```

Replace *<UserDN>* with the user's distinguished name, *<server>* with the Exchange
server name, *<storage group>* with the storage group, *<mail store>* with the mail
store, and *<Home MDB URL>* with the full homeMDB URL for the desired mailbox store.

To move an existing mailbox for the user *joe* to Exchange server Srv1, Storage group
SG1, and mailbox store DB1, execute the following command.

```
> exchmbx -b "cn=joe,cn=users,dc=rallencorp,dc=com" -move "srv1:sg1:db1"
```

Using VBScript

```
' This code moves a mailbox.
' ------ SCRIPT CONFIGURATION ------
strUserDN       = "<UserDN>" ' e.g. cn=jsmith,cn=Users,dc=rallencorp,dc=com
strServer       = "<Exchange Server>"       ' e.g. ExchServer2
strSGName       = "<Storage Group Name>"    ' e.g. SG1
strMailStoreName = "<MailBox Store Name>" ' e.g. DB1
' ------ END CONFIGURATION ---------
' Find Storage Group URL and Generate Mailbox Store URL
strSearch = "cn=" & strSGName  & ","
set objSrv = CreateObject("CDOEXM.ExchangeServer")
objSrv.DataSource.Open strServer
for each strSg in objSrv.StorageGroups
    if (instr(1,strSg,strSearch,1)>0) then
        strSGUrl = strSg
        exit for
    end if
next
strMBUrl = "LDAP://cn=" & strMailStoreName & "," & strSGUrl

' Attach to user and move mailbox
set objUser = GetObject("LDAP://" & strUserDN)
objUser.MoveMailbox(strMBUrl)
Wscript.Echo "Successfully moved mailbox."
```

Discussion

Mailbox moves are commonly done in many Exchange organizations due to servers getting upgraded, server hardware issues, users migrating from Exchange 5.5 to Exchange 2003, or the administrators want to readjust the mailbox location for load balancing.

Moving a mailbox requires Read and Write permissions to the following attributes:

- msexchhomeservername
- homemdb
- homeMTA
- msExchOmaAdminWirelessEnable
- msExchOmaAdminExtendedSettings
- targetAddress

A mailbox move is an odd operation in terms of permissions. Logically, moving a mailbox is basically a combination of create and delete operations, which is something an Exchange data administrator can do just fine. However, to actually move a mailbox you must have Exchange service administrator role permissions with a subset of the permissions Exchange data administrators have on users. See MS KB 842033 for details of the permissions needed.

If you don't handle user mailbox administration through an automated web site, we recommend that you delegate permissions to the attributes listed in the knowledge base articles to some Active Directory group. Once delegated, add the Exchange Service Administrator Role users to that group and have them handle all mailbox moves.

 You may also run into an error if the mailbox limits on the target store are lower than they were on the source store. For more details, go to *http://www.activedir.org/article.aspx?aid=58*.

Using a graphical user interface

The move mailbox wizard is the only Exchange wizard that allows you to schedule when the changes will be made. This is obviously a handy feature for mailbox moves because it isn't something you tend to want to do in the middle of the day. This allows Exchange administrators who like to sleep at night to schedule the work to be done, and then go home with everyone else.

Using a command-line interface

Prior to the ExchMbx tool, there was no simple way to move a mailbox from the command line. The command structure to move a mailbox is very similar to the command structure to create a mailbox, see command-line solution in Recipe 22.11.

 If you want to move multiple mailboxes at once, remove the -b option from the parameter list and pipe the distinguished names into ExchMbx from another tool or from a file. Run exchmbx /? for usage details.

Using VBScript

The trickiest part of moving a mailbox for a user is to know what the Home MDB URL is for the database you want to move the user to. The method used here allows you to specify three well-known components and arrive at the answer. In Recipe 22.11, we use another method to do this by entering the exact value for the mailbox store URL. A third alternative would be to search Active Directory for all valid homeMDB values, display them, and have the person running the script select from the list like ADUC does. To get the list of mailbox store URLs, search against the Configuration container in Active Directory (e.g., cn=Configuration,dc=rallencorp,dc=com) with the filter (objectCategory=msExchPrivateMDB).

See Also

Recipe 22.6, Recipe 22.11, MS KB 842033 ("Access Denied" Error Message When You Move Mailboxes by Using the Exchange Task Wizard in Exchange Server 2003), MS KB 316792 (Minimum Permissions Necessary to Perform Exchange-related Tasks), and MS KB 821829 (Moving Mailboxes in Exchange Server 2003)

22.17 Viewing Mailbox Sizes and Message Counts

Problem

You want to view the sizes and message counts of all mailboxes on a server.

Solution

Using a graphical user interface

1. Open the Exchange System Manager (ESM) snap-in.

2. In the left pane, browse to the mailboxes container of the server, storage group, and database you want to view mailboxes in.

3. In the right pane, scroll down through the list of mailboxes noting the Size and Total Items columns.

Using VBScript

```
' This code displays all mailboxes and their sizes
' ------ SCRIPT CONFIGURATION ------
strComputer = "<Exchange Server>" 'e.g. ExchServer2
' ------ END CONFIGURATION ---------

set objWMI = GetObject("winmgmts:\\" & strComputer & _
                    "\root\MicrosoftExchangeV2")
set objMbxs = objWMI.ExecQuery("Select * from Exchange_Mailbox",,48)
for each objMbx in objMbxs
  Wscript.Echo objMbx.MailBoxDisplayName & " " & objMbx.size & "KB  " _
            & objMbx.TotalItems & " items"
Next
Wscript.Echo "Script completed successfully."
```

Discussion

Mailbox sizes and message counts are items on Exchange systems that administrators routinely want to know about for the purposes of reporting and metrics. Administrators want to know if their mail system is balanced and if users are spread across the mailbox stores evenly. Knowing the number of users and the size of their mailboxes in each mailbox store, the administrator can make better decisions about where new user mailboxes should be placed or if some leveling of mailboxes is required.

Viewing mailbox details in the ESM requires Exchange View Admin role access. However, in order to do this with a script, the WMI provider requires local administrator permissions on the Exchange server. See the "Discussion" for Recipe 22.7.

Using a graphical user interface

Click on the header of each of the columns displayed in the right pane of the ESM to sort by that value.

Using VBScript

This script can be modified to show several things for mailboxes. Some of the more notable items besides Size and Items are LastLogonTime, LastLoggedOnUserAccount, and DateDiscoveredAbsentInDS. Please reference the Exchange 2003 SDK for a complete list of items available in the Exchange_Mailbox class.

 Since this script uses Exchange WMI extensions it can be run from any machine that has WMI—the machine does not have to have the Exchange Management Tools loaded.

See Also

Recipe 22.7 and Exchange Server 2003 SDK: WMI Reference

22.18 Configuring Mailbox Limits

Problem

You want to enable storage limits for user mailboxes on an Exchange server.

Solution

Using a graphical user interface

1. Open the Exchange System Manager (ESM) snap-in.
2. In the left pane, browse to the mailboxes container of the server, storage group, and database you want to configure a storage limit for.
3. Right-click the mailbox store. Select Properties, and then select the Limits tab.
4. Select one or more of the following checkboxes:

   Issue warning at
   > Warns users that they have exceeded the storage limit, but their mailbox will continue to function.

   Prohibit send at
   > Warns users that they have exceeded the storage limit and then prevents them from sending new messages until their mailboxes are brought back underneath the configured storage limit. Users can still receive messages.

Prohibit send and receive at

> Warns users that they have exceeded the storage limit and then prevents them from both sending and receiving messages until they have corrected the situation.

5. Specify the appropriate values for these settings in kilobytes (KB).

 The maximum value that you can configure for these items through the GUI is 2 GB (2,097,151 KB). To establish larger values than that, you need to use ADSI Edit or the command-line or script solutions listed next.

Using a command-line interface

To configure the size at which a warning will be issued, use the following syntax:

```
> adfind -config -rb "cn=<StorageGroup>,cn=InformationStore,cn=<ServerName,
cn=Servers,cn=<Administrative Group>,cn=Administrative Groups,cn=<ExchangeOrg,
cn=Microsoft Exchange,cn=Services" -dsq | admod mDBStorageQuota::<LimitinKB>
```

To configure the size at which a user can receive mail but not send, use the following:

```
> adfind -config -rb "cn=<StorageGroup>,cn=InformationStore,cn=<ServerName,
cn=Servers,cn=<Administrative Group>,cn=Administrative Groups,cn=<ExchangeOrg,
cn=Microsoft Exchange,cn=Services" -dsq | admod mDBOverQuotaLimit::<LimitinKB>
```

To configure the limit at which a user can neither send nor receive messages, use:

```
> adfind -config -rb "cn=<StorageGroup>,cn=InformationStore,cn=<ServerName,
cn=Servers,cn=<Administrative Group>,cn=Administrative Groups,cn=<ExchangeOrg,
cn=Microsoft Exchange,cn=Services" -dsq | admod mDBOverHardQuotaLimit::<LimitinKB>
```

You can set multiple attributes in a single command by specifying more than one attribute in the AdMod portion of the command syntax, as follows:

```
> adfind -config -rb "cn=<StorageGroup>,cn=InformationStore,cn=<ServerName,
cn=Servers,cn=<Administrative Group>,cn=Administrative Groups,cn=<ExchangeOrg,
cn=Microsoft Exchange,cn=Services" -dsq | admod mDBStorageQuota::<LimitinKB>
mDBOverQuotaLimit::<LimitinKB> mDBOverHardQuotaLimit::<LimitinKB>
```

Using VBScript

```
' The following script will update the Warning, OverQuota, and
' HardOverQuota attributes of a mailbox store
'-----------SCRIPT CONFIGURATION -----------------------------
' strLDAPString = "cn=<StorageGroup>,cn=InformationStore," & _
  "cn=<ServerName>,cn=Servers,cn=<AdministrativeGroup>," & _
  "cn=Administrative Groups,cn=<ExchangeOrg>,cn=Microsoft Exchange," & _
  "cn=Services,cn=Configuration,<ForestRootDN>"

strWarningLimit = "<WarningLimitinKB>"
strSoftQuotaLimit = "<ReceiveOnlyLimitinKB>"
strHardQuotaLimit = "<NoSendOrReceiveLimitinKB>"
```

```
'-------------------END CONFIGURATION---------------------

Set objMaiboxStore = GetObject _
    ("LDAP://" & strLDAPString)

objMailboxStore.Put "mdBStorageQuota", strWarningLimit
objMailboxStore.Put "mdBOverQuotaLimit", strSoftQuotaLimit
objMailboxStore.Put "mdBOverHardQuotaLimit", strHardQuotaLimit

objMailboxStore.SetInfo
```

Discussion

It's not uncommon for administrators to want to set reasonable size limits on individual users' mailboxes; you can configure this globally at the mailbox store level. Since you can have multiple stores on a single server, this can allow you to create multiple stores with multiple storage limits for departments or groups that have greater storage needs. You can also override the mailbox store defaults for individual user accounts by modifying the Exchange General tab within Active Directory Users and Computers for an individual user account, or else by programmatically modifying the same three attributes and then setting the mdBUseDefaults attribute to FALSE. You can also set mailbox limits using a System Policy, and then apply the same policy to multiple stores.

See Also

MS KB 822938 (How to Use System Policies to Configure Mailbox Storage Limits in Exchange Server 2003), MS KB 823144 (How to Configure Storage Limits on Public Folders in Exchange 2003), MS KB 235895 (How to Monitor Mailbox Storage Limits in Event Viewer)

22.19 Mail-Enabling a Contact

Problem

You want to mail-enable a contact.

Solution

Using a graphical user interface

1. Open the Active Directory Users and Computers (ADUC) snap-in.

> This needs to be run on a workstation or server that has the Exchange Management Tools loaded (see Recipe 22.6).

2. If you need to change domains, right-click on Active Directory Users and Computers in the left pane, select Connect to Domain, enter the domain name, and click OK.

3. In the left pane, browse to the parent container of the contact, right-click on the contact, and select Exchange Tasks.

4. On the Welcome screen, click Next.

5. Select Establish E-mail Address and click Next.

6. Verify the mail alias is what you want.

7. Click Modify, select external email address type (generally SMTP Address) and click OK, enter an external email address, and click OK.

8. Select the associated administrative group and click Next.

9. On the Completion screen, click Finish.

Using a command-line interface

```
> exchmbx -b "<ContactDN>" -me <smtp email address>
```

Replace <ContactDN> with the contact's distinguished name and the <smtp email address> with the contact's external email address.

For an alternative method, create an LDIF file called *mailenable_contact.ldf* with the following contents:

```
dn: CN=<ContactDN>
changetype: modify
replace: targetAddress
targetaddress: SMTP:<smtp email address>
-
replace: mailNickName
mailNickname: <mail nickname>
-
replace: mAPIRecipient
mAPIRecipient: FALSE
-
replace: legacyExchangeDN
legacyExchangeDN: <legacy exchange DN>
-
replace: internetEncoding
legacyExchangeDN: 1310720
-
```

Replace <ContactDN> with the contact's distinguished name, <smtp email address> with the contact's external email addresss, and <legacy exchange DN> with the proper legacy exchange distinguished name value. Then run the following command:

```
>ldifde -i -f mailenable_user.ldf
```

Using VBScript

```
' This code mail enables a contact.
' ------ SCRIPT CONFIGURATION ------
strContactDN = "<ContactDN>" ' e.g. cn=jsmith,ou=Contacts,dc=rallencorp,dc=com
strEmailAddr = "<EmailAddress>" 'e.g. jsmith234@freemail.net
' ------ END CONFIGURATION ---------
set objContact = GetObject("LDAP://" & strContactDN)
objContact.MailEnable strEmailAddr
objContact.Put "internetEncoding",1310720
objContact.SetInfo()
Wscript.Echo "Successfully mail-enabled contact."
```

Discussion

A mail-enabled contact is a contact that has at least one email address defined within Exchange. A contact cannot have a mailbox because it is not a security principal, so there is no way to safely authenticate the object. You use a mail-enabled contact when you have an email address external to the forest's Exchange organization that you want to be listed in your Global Address List (GAL). The email address could be external to the company or it could just be external to the Exchange organization of that forest. Examples would be people from other companies or users who do not use the Active Directory of the Exchange organization.

Mail-enabling a contact requires the Exchange View-Only Administrator permissions or higher on the target administrative group, as well as Read and Write permissions for a number of attributes. See the Microsoft Exchange Server Tech Center on the Microsoft web site for more information.

When you create a mail-enabled contact with the GUI or VBScript, you are using the CDOEXM interface library. The specific method called in this case is MailEnable. In the background, the specific changes made by the MailEnable method are on the contact object in Active Directory. They include changes to the following attributes:

- targetAddress
- mailNickname
- mAPIRecipient
- legacyExchangeDN

In addition to those attributes, the internetEncoding attribute also needs to be set for proper message handling. See the "Discussion" in Recipe 22.9 for details.

Once all of those attributes are in place, the RUS sets additional attributes on the contact object to make it useable for Exchange.

Using a graphical user interface

Creating a mail-enabled contact from scratch is very similar to mail-enabling an existing contact.

Using a command-line interface

Please see the command-line discussion in Recipe 22.9 for details.

Using VBScript

Please see the VBScript discussion in Recipe 22.9 for details.

See Also

Recipe 22.6, Recipe 22.9 for more on mail-enabling users, Recipe 22.20 for more on mail-disabling a contact, and MS KB 275636 (Creating Exchange Mailbox-Enabled and Mail-Enabled Objects in Active Directory)

22.20 Mail-Disabling a Contact

Problem

You want to mail-disable a contact.

Solution

Using a graphical user interface

1. Open the Active Directory Users and Computers (ADUC) snap-in.

    This needs to be run on a workstation or server that has the Exchange Management Tools loaded (see Recipe 22.6).

2. If you need to change domains, right-click on Active Directory Users and Computers in the left pane, select Connect to Domain, enter the domain name, and click OK.

3. In the left pane, browse to the parent container of the user, right-click on the user, and select Exchange Tasks.

4. On the Welcome screen, click Next.

5. Select Remove Exchange Attributes and click Next.

6. Read the warning and click Next.

7. On the Completion screen, click Finish.

Using a command-line interface

See the command-line example for Recipe 22.10.

Using VBScript

```
' This code mail disables a contact.
' ------ SCRIPT CONFIGURATION ------
strContactDN = "<ContactDN>"
'            e.g. cn=jsmith,ou=Contacts,dc=rallencorp,dc=com
' ------ END CONFIGURATION ---------
set objContact = GetObject("LDAP://" & strContactDN)
objContact.MailDisable
objContact.SetInfo( )
Wscript.Echo "Successfully mail-disabled contact."
```

Discussion

This recipe shows how to remove the Active Directory Exchange attributes for a previously mail-enabled contact. The solutions are identical to the solutions for mail-disabling users, shown in the "Discussion" for Recipe 22.10.

 Mail-enabling a contact requires Exchange Data Administrator permissions. See the "Discussion" for Recipe 22.7.

See Also

Recipe 22.6, Recipe 22.7, Recipe 22.10 for more on mail-disabling users and MS KB 307350 (XGEN: Using the "Remove Exchange Attributes" Option)

22.21 Creating a Mail-Enabled Distribution List

Problem

You want to create a mail-enabled distribution list.

Solution

Using a graphical user interface

1. Open the Active Directory Users and Computers (ADUC) snap-in.

 This needs to be run on a workstation or server that has the Exchange Management Tools loaded (see Recipe 22.6).

2. If you need to change domains, right click on Active Directory Users and Computers in the left pane, select Connect to Domain, enter the domain name, and click OK.

3. In the left pane, browse to the parent container of the new DL, right-click on it, and select New → Group.

4. Enter group name, select group scope, select group type, and click Next.

5. Verify that "Create an Exchange e-mail address" is selected, and click Next.

6. Click Finish.

Using a command-line interface

The following command creates a group:

```
> dsadd group "<GroupDN>" -scope <Group Scope> -secgrp yes|no
```

The following command mail-enables a group:

```
> exchmbx -b "<GroupDN>" -me
```

Replace *<GroupDN>* with the group's distinguished name, *<Group Scope>* with l, g, or u for local group, global group, or universal group, respectively. -secgrp should be set to yes if this is to be a security group, no otherwise.

To create and mail enable a distribution universal group named *UniDL*, execute the following commands:

```
> dsadd group "cn=UniDL,ou=grps,dc=rallencorp,dc=com" -scope u -secgrp no
> exchmbx -b "cn=UniDL,ou=grps,dc=rallencorp,dc=com" -me
```

For an alternative method, create an LDIF file called *create_dl.ldf* with the following contents:

```
dn: CN=<group name>,<Parent DN>
changetype: add
objectClass: group
cn: <group name>
sAMAccountName: <group name>
groupType: <group type>
mailNickname: <mail nickname>
legacyExchangeDN: <legacy exchange DN>
reportToOriginator: TRUE
```

Replace *<ParentDN>* with the distinguished name of the container you want the group created in, *<group name>* with the name you want the group to be called, *<group type>* with the group's scope and type value, *<mail nickname>* with the group's mail nickname, and *<legacy exchange DN>* with the proper legacy exchange distinguished name value. As mentioned in Recipe 22.9 you can skip specifying the legacyExchangeDN if you want Exchange to populate the value for you.

To create a Universal Distribution List group with an Exchange generated legacyExchangeDN, create the file with the following contents:

```
dn: CN=UniMailGroup,CN=groups,DC=rallencorp,DC=com
changetype: add
objectClass: group
cn: UniMailGroup
```

```
sAMAccountName: UniMailGroup
groupType: 8
mailNickname: UniMailGroup
reportToOriginator: TRUE
```

Then run the following command:

```
> ldifde -i -f create_dl.ldf
```

Using VBScript

```
' This code creates and mail enables a Distribution List
' ------ SCRIPT CONFIGURATION ------
strParentDN  = "<ParentDN>"    ' e.g. ou=groups,dc=rallencorp,dc=com
strGroupName = "<GroupName>"    ' e.g. JoewareUsers
' ------ END CONFIGURATION ---------
' Constants taken from ADS_GROUP_TYPE_ENUM
Const ADS_GROUP_TYPE_DOMAIN_LOCAL_GROUP = 1
Const ADS_GROUP_TYPE_GLOBAL_GROUP       = 2
Const ADS_GROUP_TYPE_LOCAL_GROUP        = 4
Const ADS_GROUP_TYPE_SECURITY_ENABLED   = -2147483648
Const ADS_GROUP_TYPE_UNIVERSAL_GROUP    = 8

set objOU = GetObject("LDAP://" & strParentDN)
set objGroup = objOU.Create("group","cn=" & strGroupName)
objGroup.Put "groupType", ADS_GROUP_TYPE_UNIVERSAL_GROUP
objGroup.Put "sAMAccountName", strGroupName
objGroup.MailEnable
objGroup.SetInfo
Wscript.Echo "Successfully created mail-enabled DL."
```

Discussion

Anyone who has used a distribution list knows how useful they can be. It is much easier to send email to a single email address than to tens or hundreds or even thousands of addresses. Exchange allows you to mail-enable any group object in Active Directory. Then, when someone sends email to that group, every mail-enabled or mailbox-enabled user in the group will receive a copy of the email.

> Creating a mail-enabled group requires Exchange View-Only Administrator permissions or higher, as well as Read and Write permissions on a number of additional attributes. See the "Discussion" for Recipe 22.7.

Active Directory groups can have a group type of security or distribution. While distribution lists are usually of type distribution, you can mail-enable security groups as well. In fact, if anyone in the Exchange organization uses a distribution group to grant permissions to anything in Exchange, whether it is a calendar or a folder or any other object, Exchange converts the distribution group to a mail-enabled security group. This is something to be aware of because more than one administrator has found himself in a position trying to explain why distribution groups had mysteriously changed into security groups.

A popular question we've often heard is: what scope should my distribution groups have? The official response is: whatever scope you need. If you have a multidomain environment, you should probably use a universal group. Mail-enabled groups have to be fully expandable on any global catalog that gets the request to expand the membership. The only group scope that qualifies in a normal multidomain environment is a universal group. If you have a single-domain environment, any group scope will work fine. See *Active Directory*, Third Edition, by Joe Richards et al. (O'Reilly) for a more detailed discussion of the different security group scopes and how to combine them effectively.

When you create a mail-enabled group with the GUI or VBScript, you are using the CDOEXM interface. This interface is the Microsoft supported method of managing Exchange attributes on users, groups, and contacts. The specific method called in this case is the MailEnable method. In the background, the specific changes made by the MailEnable method are on the group object in Active Directory and include changes to the following attributes:

```
reportToOriginator
mailNickname
legacyExchangeDN
```

Once those attributes have been set, the RUS sets additional attributes on the group object to make the group usable by Exchange.

Using a graphical user interface

Using the GUI to create distribution groups is straightforward. Mail-enabling an existing group is similar to mail-enabling a user or contact, except you don't have to specify an email address.

Using a command-line interface

The main things to be concerned with the command-line version of this recipe are the group scope, group type value, and, for the LDIF solution, the specifics concerning the mail attributes mailNickname and legacyExchangeDN mentioned in Recipe 22.9. The group type determines the scope of the group and whether it is also security enabled. See the constants defined in the VBScript example for the values to use. The email address cannot be specified for mail-enabled groups, since this attribute will be handled by the RUS.

Using VBScript

This script creates a universal distribution group. All of the constants are included for group scope and type, so you can modify the code to suit your needs. If you need to make a group a security group, simply or in the TYPE_SECURITY_ENABLED flag like so:

```
ADS_GROUP_TYPE_UNIVERSAL_GROUP or TYPE_SECURITY_ENABLED
```

See Also

Recipe 22.6, Recipe 22.9, Recipe 22.7 for more delegating Exchange rights, MS KB 839949 (Troubleshooting Mail Transport and Distribution Groups in Exchange 2000 Server and in Exchange Server 2003), MS KB 275636 (Creating Exchange Mailbox-Enabled and Mail-Enabled Objects in Active Directory), MS KB 251631 (XADM: How to Create Distribution Lists in Exchange 2000 Server), and *http://www.microsoft.com/technet/prodtechnol/exchange/2000/deploy/access.mspx*

22.22 Creating a Query-Based Distribution List

Problem

You want to create a query-based distribution list.

> Creating a mail-enabled query-based distribution list requires the Exchange organization be in Exchange Native Mode. See MS KB 829577.

Solution

Using a graphical user interface

1. Open the Active Directory Users and Computers (ADUC) snap-in.

> This needs to be run on a workstation or server that has the Exchange Management Tools loaded (see Recipe 22.6).

2. If you need to change domains, right-click on Active Directory Users and Computers in the left pane, select Connect to Domain, enter the domain name, and click OK.

3. In the left pane, browse to the parent container of the new object, right-click on it and select New → Query-based Distribution Group.

4. Enter the group name and mail alias and click Next.

5. Select the search base, enter the specifics of the filter, and then click Next.

> The filter should be a standard LDAP filter; for example, `(&(objectcategory=user)(homeMDB=*)(employeeType=FT))`.

6. Verify the summary and click Finish.

Using a command-line interface

First, you need to create an LDIF file called *add_qbdl.ldf* with the following contents:

```
dn: CN=<QB DL Name>,<ParentDN>
changetype: add
cn: <QB DL Name>
displayName: <QB DL Name>
objectClass: msExchDynamicDistributionList
mailNickname: <mail nickname>
legacyExchangeDN: <legacy Exchange DN>
msExchDynamicDLFilter: <LDAP Filter>
msExchDynamicDLBaseDN: <BaseDN>
reportToOriginator: TRUE
systemFlags: 1610612736
```

Replace *<QB DL Name>* with the name of the address list, *<mail nickname>* with the mail nickname, *<legacy Exchange DN>* with the appropriate legacy Exchange DN value, *<LDAP Filter>* with the specific LDAP filter you want to be used to determine group membership, *<BaseDN>* with the base distinguished name you want used in combination with the filter, and *<ParentDN>* with the distinguished name of the container you want the group created in. Then run the following command:

```
> ldifde -i -f add-qbdl.ldf
```

Using VBScript

```
' This code creates and mail enables a Query Based Distribution List.
' ------ SCRIPT CONFIGURATION ------
strParentDN  = "<Parent DN>"      ' e.g. ou=groups,dc=rallencorp,dc=com
strGroupName ="<DL Name>"         ' e.g. Sales Dept
strBaseDN = "<Base DN>"           ' e.g. ou=mail,dc=rallencorp,dc=com
strFilter = "<Filter>"            ' e.g. (&( department=sales)(homemdb=*))
strLegacyDN = "<Legacy DN of Recipients>" & "/cn=" & strGroupName
' e.g. /o=RALLENCORPMAIL/ou=First Administrative Group/cn=Recipients

' ------ END CONFIGURATION ---------
' Set Dynamic values
set objOU = GetObject("LDAP://" & strParentDN)
set objGroup = objOU.Create("msExchDynamicDistributionList","cn=" & _
                            strGroupName)
objGroup.Put "msExchDynamicDLBaseDN", strBaseDN
objGroup.Put "msExchDynamicDLFilter", strFilter
objGroup.Put "displayName", strGroupName
objGroup.Put "mailNickname", strGroupName
objGroup.Put "legacyExchangeDN",strLegacyDN

' Set static values
objGroup.Put "systemFlags",1610612736
objGroup.Put "reportToOriginator",TRUE

objGroup.SetInfo
Wscript.Echo "Successfully created query-based DL."
```

Discussion

Exchange Server 2003 has introduced a new type of distribution list: the query-based distribution list (DL). As implied by name, these are distribution lists that are built on the fly based on a query, specifically an LDAP query against Active Directory.

 Creating a mail-enabled query based distribution list requires Exchange Data Administrator permissions. See the "Discussion" for Recipe 22.7.

This is an extremely powerful addition for Exchange, but you have to be careful because you can get into trouble with it. Unlike address lists, the query-based DL is resolved each time it is used with an actual LDAP query against Active Directory; specifically, it requires access to a Global Catalog server. This means that the query needs to be efficient. Used enough, a poorly designed query for the DL could severely impact Exchange and Active Directory performance. You will want to use indexed attributes and avoid bitwise operators, the NOT operator, and medial search strings as per normal Active Directory efficient programming guidelines. A *medial search string* is a search string that has a wildcard somewhere other than at the end of the string (e.g., *llen or j*e). See MSDN: Creating More Efficient Microsoft Active Directory-Enabled Applications.

 For Windows Server 2003 Active Directory, Microsoft made an undocumented change concerning how the Query Processor (QP) worked with linked attributes. Linked attributes, due to how they are stored, are implicitly indexed but the Windows 2000 QP did not take advantage of these indexes. In Windows Server 2003 Active Directory, the QP will use the implicit indexes for all linked attributes and greatly speed up searches using those attributes. This has tremendous implications around attributes such as homeMDB and member and the speed at which you can search on those attributes.

Unlike every other object you can mail-enable, when you create a query-based DL you are *not* using the CDOEXM interface. However, when you create this object with ADUC, the Exchange Management tools must be loaded or the distribution list object will not be properly populated and will not function properly. When creating the object from a script or the command line, you actually set all of the Active Directory attributes of the msExchDynamicDistributionList object directly. The specific changes that need to be made are to the following attributes:

- displayName
- mailNickname
- reportToOriginator
- legacyExchangeDN

- `systemFlags`
- `msExchDynamicDLBaseDN`
- `msExchDynamicDLBaseFilter`

Using a graphical user interface

Using the GUI is probably the safest way to generate a query for these DLs unless you are very familiar with how to construct efficient Active Directory queries. The GUI is configured to help direct you to create queries that are more efficient. If you use ADUC to construct these distribution groups, you will not have to deal with the `legacyExchange` and `mailNickname` issues discussed below.

Using a command-line interface

This example follows the standard LDIF method of importing or modifying an object used in other examples. Please see the comments in the using a command-line interface discussion section of Recipe 22.9.

 In Recipe 22.9 there is discussion indicating that you can omit specifying the `legacyExchangeDN` attribute and Exchange will auto-generate a value for you. Unfortunately, this functionality is *not* extended to the Query-Based DLs at this time.

Using VBScript

This is the one and only script in this chapter for mail-enabling objects that doesn't have a nice simple interface. It seems when Microsoft came up with the query-based distribution list object, they totally forgot about people who script and use the command line. You would expect that you could use the CDOEXM `MailEnable` method, but unfortunately it doesn't work. This is the only script in this chapter that has no choice but to deal with the `legacyExchangeDN` and `mailNickname` attributes. Please see the notes on these two attributes in the command-line interface discussion section of Recipe 22.9.

See Also

Recipe 22.6, Recipe 22.7, Recipe 22.9, MS KB 251631 (XADM: How to Create Distribution Lists in Exchange 2000 Server), MS KB 822897 (How to Troubleshoot Query-Based Distribution Groups), MS KB 829577 (Mixed Mode vs. Native Mode in Exchange Server 2003), and MSDN: Creating More Efficient Microsoft Active Directory-Enabled Applications

22.23 Creating an Address List

Problem

You want to create an address list.

Solution

Using a graphical user interface

1. Open the Exchange System Manager (ESM) snap-in.
2. In the left pane, browse to the Recipients → All Address Lists container.
3. Right-click on the All Address Lists container and select New → Address List.
4. Enter the address list name.
5. Click on Filter Rules, configure the filter settings, and click OK.

 The filter should be a standard LDAP filter; for example, `(&(objectcategory=user)(homeMDB=*)(employeeType=FT))`.

6. Click Finish.

Using a command-line interface

First, create an LDIF file called *add_al.ldf* with the following contents:

```
dn: CN=<Address List Name>,<ParentDN>
changetype: add
cn: <Address List Name>
displayName: <Address List Name>
objectClass: addressBookContainer
purportedSearch: <LDAP Filter>
systemFlags: 1610612736
```

Replace *<Address list Name>* with the name of the address list and *<ParentDN>* with the distinguished name of the Address Lists container in Active Directory (e.g., cn=All Address Lists, cn=Address Lists Container, cn=RALLENCORPMAIL, cn=Microsoft Exchange, cn=Services, cn=Configuration, dc=rallencorp, dc=com). Then run the following command:

```
>ldifde -i -f add-al.ldf
```

Using VBScript

```
' This code creates an Address List.
' ------ SCRIPT CONFIGURATION ------
strParentDN  = "<DN to All Address Lists Container>"
' e.g CN=All Address Lists,CN=Address Lists Container,
' CN=RALLENCORPMAIL,CN=Microsoft Exchange,
```

```
' CN=Services,CN=Configuration,DC=rallencorp,DC=com"

strObjClass = "addressBookContainer"
strALName = "<Address List Name>"    ' e.g. Sales Dept
strFilterAttrib = "purportedSearch"
strFilter = "<LDAP Filter>"    ' e.g. (&(department=sales)(homemdb=*))"

' ------ END CONFIGURATION ---------
' Set Dynamic values
set objOU = GetObject("LDAP://" & strParentDN)
set objNewObj = objOU.Create(strObjClass,"cn=" & strALName)
objNewObj.Put "displayName",strALName
objNewObj.Put strFilterAttrib,strFilter

' Set static values
objNewObj.Put "systemFlags",1610612736

' Save object
objNewObj.SetInfo
Wscript.Echo "Successfully created address list."
```

Discussion

Address lists are special groupings of email accounts that allow users to quickly find specific email users that are part of some logical grouping in the GAL. The RUS is responsible for creating and maintaining the address list links to the mail-enabled objects. The RUS links an address list to mail-enabled objects by adding the address list's distinguished name to the object's showInAddressBook multivalue attribute. Once an address list has been created, it can take hours or days for the RUS to fully populate the list by stamping all related objects' showInAddressBook attributes, depending on the size of your organization.

 Managing address lists requires Exchange Full Administrator permissions. See the "Discussion" for Recipe 22.7.

A curious point about address lists is that even though an LDAP filter is used to specify who should and shouldn't be in the list, Exchange doesn't actually use the filter to do an LDAP lookup against Active Directory. Instead, the RUS does its own compare on objects one by one. This is why you can't specify a search base where the address list should start; it encompasses the entire forest including the configuration container. This means you need to be very careful with the filter so that it is limited to the objects you truly want displayed. A positive aspect of this implementation is that it doesn't matter if you select indexed attributes for the filter. Since the RUS isn't using LDAP to resolve the objects from the filter, performance is not affected by any indexes on the attributes. One final note: be careful if you use the preview button in the Exchange System Manager to verify the list's validity. That method will use an LDAP query against Active Directory to display the values, and has no bearing on whether the list is built yet or even what will end up in it. It is possible in certain cases that the preview will not match with what you actually get in the address list, for example if the RUS has not run or if the HideFromAddressBook property has been set for one or more members of the group.

Address lists are represented in Active Directory by the addressBookContainer class. This is a simple class. The main value, the address list filter, is stored in the purportedSearch attribute.

Using a graphical user interface

Using the GUI for this process is straightforward and is the most likely the way you'll want to create address lists unless you need to create a lot of them on the fly or you are importing them from a test lab.

Using a command-line interface

As mentioned previously, you need to be very careful with the filter you specify for the purportedSearch attribute. The slightest mistake can cause the filter to not produce any results or produce an incorrect or incomplete result set. A filter such as (!attrib=value) instead of (!(attrib=value)), while acceptable to Active Directory's LDAP parser, will cause undefined results when interpreted by the RUS. The only way to verify that the list has been properly built is to manually compare what the query should generate with what has been generated.

To do this comparison, first generate a list of distinguished names that are members of the address list. This is done by using LDAP to query for all mail-enabled objects that have the address list distinguished name listed in the showInAddressBook attribute, for example:

```
(&(mailNickname=*)( showinaddressbook=cn=All Users,cn=All Address Lists,cn=Address
Lists Container,cn=RALLENCORP,cn=Microsoft Exchange,cn=Services,
cn=Configuration,dc=rallencorp,dc=com))
```

Next, generate a list of distinguished names that are matched by the query you used for the address list. Finally, compare these lists.

Using VBScript

Using VBScript is very similar to using the command-line method. You simply set the same attributes on a newly created object. As in the command-line method, the single most important attribute is the purportedSearch attribute; see the command-line discussion in this recipe for more details.

See Also

Recipe 22.7, MS KB 319213 (How to Use Address Lists to Organize Recipients in Exchange 2003) and MS KB 253828 (How the Recipient Update Service Populates Address Lists)

22.24 Creating a Recipient Policy

Problem

You want to create a recipient policy to configure an additional email address or mailbox manager policy.

Solution

Using a graphical user interface

1. Open the Exchange System Manager (ESM) snap-in.
2. In the left pane, browse to the Recipients → Recipient Policies container.
3. Right-click on Recipient Policies and select New → Recipient Policy.
4. Select the property pages you a want on the recipient policy form and click OK.
5. Enter the recipient policy name.
6. Click on Filter Rules, click Modify, select the search criteria, click OK.
7. Read the warning message that is displayed and click OK.
8. Set the desired policies on the E-Mail Addresses (Policy) and Mailbox Manager Settings (Policy) tabs.
9. When you are done, click OK.

Discussion

Recipient policies are used for controlling how the RUS stamps mail-enabled objects. It is in charge of stamping objects with the correct email addresses as well as Mailbox Manager settings, such as automatically deleting and reporting on messages that exceed certain ages and sizes. Companies that have multiple divisions and want different email addresses for users in the different divisions use multiple recipient policies for configuring the email addresses. Each recipient policy has a filter that specifies the mailboxes it should configure with its rules.

Recipient policy is too involved to do simply from the command line or through VBScript. Several of the values in the Active Directory msExchRecipientPolicy class are binary types, which are not trivial to manipulate with LDIF or VBScript. If you wish to programmatically create recipient policies, you can do it, but you will need to use something a bit more involved such as Visual Basic or C++.

Managing recipient policies requires Exchange Full Administrator permissions. See the "Discussion" for Recipe 22.7.

One note of warning: do not test the manipulation of recipient policies in your production environment. Changes to recipient policies get stamped on many or possibly all mail-enabled objects in the directory, and you could unintentionally bring down entire sections of your mail delivery system. Due to its widespread effect, you could have great difficulty getting it all back up and running quickly. For example, one company that shall remain nameless went through a merger process and was trying to standardize some of their mail systems. Unfortunately, they unintentionally changed the primary email address of more than 100,000 employees with one small incorrect recipient policy change. Due to the type of mistake, this wasn't noticed internally. It took a couple of days for people outside of the company to notice and report the issue to the company before it got worked on and corrected. In the meanwhile, most email going into the company from the outside was not properly delivered.

See Also

Recipe 22.7, MS KB 249299 (How to Configure Recipient Policies in Exchange), MS KB 319201 (How to Use Recipient Policies to Control E-mail Addresses in Exchange 2000), MS KB 259381 (XADM: How to Create a Custom Recipient Policy Based on Routing Groups), MS KB 319188 (How to Use Recipient Policies to Control Mailboxes in Exchange 2000 and Exchange 2003), MS KB 325921 (How to Configure E-mail Addresses Based on Domain Membership), and MS KB 328738 (XADM: How the Recipient Update Service Applies Recipient Policies)

22.25 Creating a Storage Group

Problem

You want to create a new storage group to allow for more mailbox stores, faster backups, or a logical organization of mailboxes.

Solution

Using a graphical user interface

1. Open the Exchange System Manager (ESM) snap-in.
2. In the left pane, browse to the server that you want to create a new storage group for.

3. Right-click on the server and select New → Storage Group.

4. Enter a name, transaction log location, system path location for storage of temporary and recovered files and click OK.

Using a command-line interface

First create an LDIF file called *add_sg.ldf* with the following contents:

```
dn: CN=<Storage Group Name>,<ParentDN>
changetype: add
objectClass: msExchStorageGroup
cn: <Storage Group Name>
showInAdvancedViewOnly: TRUE
systemFlags: 1610612736
msExchESEParamEnableIndexChecking: TRUE
msExchESEParamEnableOnlineDefrag: TRUE
msExchESEParamSystemPath: <Path to store system files>
msExchESEParamPageFragment: 8
msExchESEParamPageTempDBMin: 0
msExchRecovery: TRUE
msExchESEParamZeroDatabaseDuringBackup: 0
msExchESEParamBaseName: E01
msExchESEParamCircularLog: 0
msExchESEParamEventSource: MsExchangeIS
msExchESEParamCheckpointDepthMax: 20971520
msExchESEParamCommitDefault: 0
msExchESEParamLogFilePath: <Path to log files>
msExchESEParamDbExtensionSize: 256
msExchESEParamLogFileSize: 5120
```

Replace `<Storage Group Name>` with the name of the storage group, `<ParentDN>` with the distinguished named for storage groups container for the appropriate server, `<Path to store system files>` with the filesystem path where you want system files (temporary and recovered files), and `<Path to log files>` with the filesystem path where you want exchange log files. Then run the following command:

```
>ldifde -i -f add-sg.ldf
```

Using VBScript

```
' This code creates a Storage Group.
' ------ SCRIPT CONFIGURATION ------
strServer = "<Exchange Server>"      ' e.g. ExchServer2
strName   = "<Storage Group Name>"   ' e.g. SG1
strPath   = "<File Path>" & strName  ' e.g. D:\Program Files\ExchSrvr
' ------ END CONFIGURATION ---------

' Create URL to Storage Group
Set objSrv = CreateObject("CDOEXM.ExchangeServer")
objSrv.DataSource.Open strServer

' This for loop is a bit of a hack to retrieve the first Storage Group
' in the collection. VBScript doesn't let you access specific elements
```

```
' of a collection the way Jscript can.
for each strSg in objSrv.StorageGroups
    strTemp = strSg
    exit for
next
strTemp = mid(strTemp,instr(2,strTemp,"cn",1))
strSGUrl = "LDAP://cn=" & strName & "," & strTemp

' Create/configure Storage Group and save it
set objSG = CreateObject("CDOEXM.StorageGroup")
objSG.MoveSystemFiles(strPath)
objSG.MoveLogFiles(strPath)
objSG.DataSource.SaveTo strSGUrl
Wscript.Echo "Successfully created storage group."
```

Discussion

Storage groups are used for physically breaking your databases up into smaller management groups. This is done for several reasons. Chief among them are so you will
have more numerous but smaller databases, a logical organization of mailboxes, or
faster Exchange backups and restores since the Exchange Server can run one simultaneous backup for each storage group. For example, if you have four mailbox databases in a single storage group, you can only have one backup running for that
storage group; if you spread those four mailbox databases across two storage
groups, you can run two simultaneous backups. For more detailed information on
Exchange backups and file structures, see the *Exchange Server Cookbook* by Paul
Robichaux et al. (O'Reilly).

 Managing storage groups requires Exchange Full Administrator permissions. See the "Discussion" for Recipe 22.7.

Depending on the version (Standard or Enterprise) of Exchange, you can have up to
four storage groups per server and up to five mailbox stores per storage group. ESM
enforces these limits, but it is possible to directly modify Active Directory to exceed
them. If you create more databases or storage groups than allowed by your version,
the additional databases will not mount. In Exchange 2003, Microsoft recommends
that you spread your mailboxes across as many stores and storage groups as possible; this is because of memory management improvements since Exchange 2000.

Storage groups are represented in Active Directory by the msExchStorageGroup class.
This class has several attributes that have fairly intuitive string values and names and
can be matched up to the options in ESM. Unfortunately, the raw Active Directory
objects and attributes and their valid values for Exchange are not well documented. You
can experiment with their settings, but you should do so only in a lab environment.

Using a command-line interface

One negative aspect of creating storage groups by direct Active Directory object manipulation is that you will not get warnings concerning the maximum number of storage groups allowed.

Using VBScript

The process of calling the CDOEXM interfaces to create storage groups is rather straightforward once you have the URL for the location of the object in Active Directory. In this solution, to get the distinguished name of the storage group container for the server, the script loops through all storage groups on the sever and sets strTemp to the URL value of the last storage group. This value is then parsed to get the parent container for the storage groups to build the new storage group URL.

See Also

Recipe 22.7, MS KB 821748 (How to Add New Mailbox Stores in Exchange Server 2003), MS KB 890699 (How to Configure Storage Groups in Exchange Server 2003), and *Exchange Server Cookbook* by Paul Robichaux et al. (O'Reilly)

22.26 Creating a Mailbox Store

Problem

You want to create a mailbox store. The primary reason for creating additional mailbox stores is to decrease the size of the individual stores while supporting many users on one server.

Solution

Using a graphical user interface

1. Open the Exchange System Manager (ESM) snap-in.
2. In the left pane, browse to the server and storage group that you want to create a new mailbox store on.
3. Right-click on the storage group and select New → Mailbox Store.
4. Enter a name for the store, configure the settings on each tab, and click OK.
5. When prompted to mount the store click Yes.

Using VBScript

```
' This code creates a Mailbox Store.
' ------ SCRIPT CONFIGURATION ------
strServer = "<Exchange Server>"        ' e.g. ExchServer2
strSGName = "<Storage Group Name>"     ' e.g. SG1
strMailStoreName = "<MailBox Store Name>"   ' e.g. DB1
```

```
' ------ END CONFIGURATION ---------

' Find Storage Group URL
strSearch = "CN=" & strSGName  & ","
set objSrv = CreateObject("CDOEXM.ExchangeServer")
objSrv.DataSource.Open strServer
for each strSg in objSrv.StorageGroups
    if (instr(1,strSg,strSearch,1)>0) then strSGUrl = strSg
next

' Generate Mailbox Store URL
strMBUrl = "LDAP://CN=" & strMailStoreName & "," & strSGUrl

' Create/configure Mailbox Store and save it
set objMb = CreateObject("CDOEXM.MailBoxStoreDB")
objMb.DataSource.SaveTo strMBUrl

' Mount DataBase
objMB.Mount
Wscript.Echo "Successfully created mailbox store."
```

Discussion

Mailbox stores, which are also called *mailbox databases*, are where mailboxes are located. There are quite a few configuration settings for mailbox stores which are beyond the scope of this chapter, but going through the ESM GUI when manually creating a mailbox store should give you an idea of what can be configured.

 Managing mailbox stores requires Exchange Full Administrator permissions. See the "Discussion" for Recipe 22.7.

Depending on the version (Standard or Enterprise) of Exchange, you can have up to four storage groups per server and up to five mailbox stores per storage group. ESM enforces these limits, but it is possible to directly modify Active Directory to exceed these limits. If you create more databases or storage groups than allowed, the additional databases will not mount.

Mailbox stores are represented in Active Directory by the msExchPrivateMDB class. This class is not as simple as some of the other classes used by Exchange. In addition, several of the attributes hold binary data, so working with these Active Directory objects directly can be difficult via VBScript or command-line methods. One of the more notable attributes of the mailbox store objects is back-link attribute called homeMDBBL. This is multivalued attribute linking back to all of the user objects that have mailboxes in this mailbox store.

If you are using Windows 2000 Active Directory you will find it is much faster to enumerate the mailboxes on an Exchange Server by comparing the homeMDBBL and homeMDB attributes on the users. In Windows Server 2003 Active Directory there was a change in how the Query Processor handles linked attributes resulting in minimal difference between using the homeMDB and homeMDBBL attributes.

Using a command-line interface

Due to the binary attributes the mailbox store objects contain, they are not good candidates for the LDIFDE command-line tool.

Using VBScript

The process of calling the CDOEXM interface is rather straightforward once you have the URL for the location of the object in Active Directory. As with the GUI, there are many properties that can be configured through VBScript. To get a complete list of the various methods and properties available for the `MailBoxStoreDB` interface, see the Exchange Server 2003 SDK.

See Also

Recipe 22.7, MS KB 821748 (How to Add New Mailbox Stores in Exchange Server 2003)

22.27 Moving the Exchange Transaction Logs

Problem

You want to move the Exchange transaction logs

Solution

Using a graphical user interface

1. Prepare the drive letter and directory path to accept the moved log files.
2. Open the Exchange System Manager (ESM) snap-in.
3. In the left pane, browse to the server and storage group that you wish to move.
4. Right-click the Storage Group and select Properties.
5. Next to the Transaction log location, select Browse.
6. Browse to the prepared directory path and select OK.
7. Select Apply.

After the move has successfully completed, you should conduct another full backup of the Exchange Server as soon as possible.

Using a command-line interface

First create an LDIF file called *move_sg.ldf* with the following contents:

```
dn: CN=<Storage Group Name>,<ParentDN>
changetype: modify
objectClass: msExchStorageGroup
cn: <Storage Group Name>
msExchESEParamSystemPath: <Path to store system files>
msExchESEParamLogFilePath: <Path to log files>
```

Replace *<Storage Group Name>* with the name of the storage group, *<ParentDN>* with the distinguished named for storage groups container for the appropriate server, *<Path to store system files>* with the filesystem path where you want system files (temporary and recovered files), and *<Path to log files>* with the filesystem path where you want exchange log files. Then run the following command:

```
>ldifde -i -f move-sg.ldf
```

You can also use AdMod as follows:

```
> admod –b <StorageGroupDN> msExchESEParamSystemPath::<Path to store system files>
msExchESEParamLogFilePath::<Path to log files>
```

Using VBScript

```
' This code modifies the location of a Storage Group or its log files.
' ------ SCRIPT CONFIGURATION ------
strConnectionDN = "<Storage Group Name><ParentDN>"
strLogPath = "<LogFilePath>" ' e.g. D:\Program Files\ExchangSrvr\Logs
' ------ END CONFIGURATION ---------

Set objStorageGroup = GetObject _
    ("LDAP://" & strConnectionDN)

objStorageGroup.Put "msExchESEParamLogFilePath", strLogPath
objStorageGroup.SetInfo
```

Discussion

When you initially install Exchange Server 2003, the First Storage Group, First Mailbox Store, and First Public Folder Store are created in the default installation path. This path is almost certainly not where you want the store to be located at for performance and fault tolerance reasons, since it places the information store and logfiles on the same physical drive letter. If you will be moving the transaction logs on an

Exchange server that is actively servicing users in your organization, you need to plan this move carefully; since the information stores will be dismounted when the logs are moved, this will involve a service outage for any mailbox users on that store.

See Also

MS KB 890669 (How to Configure Storage Groups in Exchange Server 2003) and MS KB 821815 (How to Move Exchange Databases and Logs in Exchange Server 2003)

22.28 Listing Domain Controllers and Global Catalog Servers Used by an Exchange Server

Problem

You want to list the domain controllers and global catalog servers currently being used by an Exchange Server.

Solution

Using a graphical user interface

1. Open the Exchange System Manager (ESM) snap-in.
2. In the left pane, browse to the Servers container.
3. Right-click on the target server and select Properties.
4. Click on the Directory Access tab and view the domain controllers being used.

Using VBScript

```
' This code enumerates domain controllers being used.
' ------ SCRIPT CONFIGURATION ------
strComputer = "<Exchange Server>" 'e.g. ExchServer2
' ------ END CONFIGURATION ---------

set objWMI = GetObject("winmgmts:\\" & strComputer & _
                       "\root\MicrosoftExchangeV2")

set objDCList = objWMI.ExecQuery("Select * from Exchange_DSAccessDC",,48)
for each objDc in objDCList
  Wscript.Echo "DCName: objDc.name"
  strTemp = "Automatic"
  if (dc.ConfigurationType=0) then strTemp="Manual"
  Wscript.Echo "  Selection: " & strTemp
  Wscript.Echo "  Is Fast  : " & objDc.IsFast
  Wscript.Echo "  In Sync  : " & objDc.IsInSync
  Wscript.Echo "  Is Up    : " & objDc.IsUp
  Wscript.Echo "  Ldap Port: " & objDc.LDAPPort
  strTemp = "Global Catalog"
  if (objDc.type=0) then strTemp = "Config"
  if (objDc.type=1) then strTemp = "Local Domain"
```

```
    Wscript.Echo "  Role     : " & strTemp
    Wscript.Echo "-----------"
Next
Wscript.Echo "Script completed successfully."
```

Discussion

Exchange is highly dependent upon Active Directory domain controllers. The list of domain controllers currently being used by a server is usually one of the first pieces of information you should gather when you encounter an Exchange issue. Although this can be done through the GUI, it is much easier to get the data through a script.

 Unfortunately, you must have at least local administrator rights on the Exchange Server being queried to get this information.

Although the GUI provides only a listing of the domain controllers and global catalog servers in use, the WMI provider offers considerably more information. You can also set DSAccess logging to record additional information in the Windows Event Viewer. This additional information can be extremely important during troubleshooting, so you should have this script or something similar available to your Exchange admins for troubleshooting purposes.

Using VBScript

Because this script uses Exchange WMI extensions, it can be run from any machine that has WMI. The machine does not have to have the Exchange Management Tools loaded.

See Also

Exchange Server 2003 SDK: WMI Reference and MS KB 316300 (Event ID 2080 from MSExchangeDSAccess)

22.29 Mounting and Dismounting Mailbox Stores

Problem

You want to mount or dismount a mailbox store.

Solution

Using a graphical user interface

1. Open the Exchange System Manager (ESM) snap-in.
2. In the left pane, browse to the server and storage group that contains the mailbox store you want to manipulate.

---

3. Right-click on the mailbox store and select Dismount Store.

4. Click Yes when prompted to continue.

Using VBScript

```
' This code mounts/dismounts a Mailbox Store.
' ------ SCRIPT CONFIGURATION ------
strServer = "<Exchange Server>"      ' e.g. ExchServer2
strSGName = "<Storage Group Name>"   ' e.g. SG1
strMailStoreName = "<Database Name>" ' e.g. DB1
' ------ END CONFIGURATION ---------

' Find Storage Group URL
strSearch = "CN=" & strSGName  & ","
set objSrv = CreateObject("CDOEXM.ExchangeServer")
objSrv.DataSource.Open strServer
for each sg in oSrv.StorageGroups
    if (instr(1,sg,strSearch,1)>0) then strSGUrl = sg
next

' Generate Mailbox Store URL
strMBUrl = "LDAP://CN=" & strMailStoreName & "," & strSGUrl

' Open Mailbox Store
set objMb = CreateObject("CDOEXM.MailBoxStoreDB")
objMb.DataSource.Open strMBUrl

if (objMb.Status = 0) then
    Wscript.Echo "Mailbox store is mounted, dismounting..."
    objMb.Dismount
else
    Wscript.Echo "Mailbox store is dismounted, mounting..."
    objMb.Mount
end if
Wscript.Echo "Script completed successfully."
```

Discussion

There will be times that you need to dismount a mailbox store on the fly. This could be for integrity checking, mailbox restorations, or to make email unavailable to some users for some reason. When you dismount a mailbox store, users with mailboxes in that store will be unable to retrieve their mail; users with mailboxes in other mailbox stores will be unaffected.

Managing mailbox stores requires Exchange Full Administrator permissions. See the "Discussion" for Recipe 22.7.

Using a graphical user interface

When a store is stopped, it has a white circle with a red downward pointing arrow over the normal mailbox store icon.

Using VBScript

The mailbox store mount/dismount script shows off three basic functions: how to check status of a mailbox store, how to mount, and how to dismount. Once again, the method to get the mailbox store URL can vary between the three methods mentioned in Recipe 22.11 and 22.16.

See Also

Recipes 22.7, 22.11, 22.16, MS KB 314211 (How to Make a Data Store Temporarily Inaccessible to Users in Exchange 2000 Server), and Exchange Server 2003 SDK: WMI Reference

22.30 Enabling Message Tracking

Problem

You want to enable Message Tracking on an Exchange Server 2003 computer.

Solution

Using a graphical user interface

1. Prepare a directory on the local hard drive (preferably on a separate physical disk from the Exchange stores) to accept the tracking log directory.
2. Open the Exchange System Manager (ESM) snap-in.
3. In the lefthand pane, browse to the server for which you wish to enable message tracking.
4. Right-click the Server object and select Properties.
5. On the General tab, place a check mark next to "Enable message tracking" and "Remove log files." Enter the number of days you wish to retain the logfiles for and click Apply.
6. Click OK once you've read the warning message.
7. Ensure that the process has created a share called *%servername%.log* and that the share is accessible to those users whose responsibilities involve running message traces.

Using a command-line interface

```
> adfind -config -b "<cn=ServerName>,cn=Servers,cn=<Administrative Group Name,
cn=Administrative Groups,cn=<Exchange Organization>,cn=Microsoft
Exchange,cn=Services" -dsq | admod messageTrackingEnabled::TRUE
msExchTrkLogCleaningInterval::<Cleanup Interval in Days>
```

Once you have enabled these two settings in Active Directory, you should modify the following registry key on the Exchange server in question to prevent the Message Tracking Logs from being stored in the same directory as the Information Store:

```
HKLM\System\CurrentControlSet\Services\MSExchangeSA\Parameters\<ServerName>]
LogDirectory - REG_SZ:<PathToLoggingDirectory>
```

VBScript

```
' This code enables Message Tracking for an Exchange Server.
' ------ SCRIPT CONFIGURATION ------
strConnectionDN = "<Server Name><ParentDN>"
strLogPath = "<LogFilePath>" ' e.g. D:\Program Files\ExchangSrvr\Logs
strCleanupInterval = "<CleanupInterval>" ' From 1 - 99
                                          ' Set to 0 to retain indefinitely

Const HKEY_LOCAL_MACHINE = &H80000002 ' For configuring the Registry
strComputer = "<ComputerName>" ' Use "." for the local computer
strKeyPath = "SYSTEM\CurrentControlSet\Services\" & _
             "MSExchangeSA\Parameters\<ServerName>"
strValueName = "LogDirectory"
strValue = "<PathToLoggingDirectory>"
' ------ END CONFIGURATION ---------

' First configure the relevant AD attributes

Set objServer = GetObject ("LDAP://" & strConnectionDN)

objServer.Put "messageTrackingEnabled", "TRUE"
objServer.Put "msExchTrkLogCleaningInterval", strCleanupInterval
objStorageGroup.SetInfo

' Now configure the relevant Registry key

Set oReg=GetObject("winmgmts:{impersonationLevel=impersonate}!\\" & _
    strComputer & "\root\default:StdRegProv")
oReg.SetStringValue HKEY_LOCAL_MACHINE,strKeyPath,strValueName,strValue
```

Discussion

Message Tracking Logs are an invaluable aid to troubleshooting message delivery in any Exchange Server environment. A message can be tracked from submission to the Information Store all the way through to its departure out of the Exchange environment. As long as the administrator doing the tracking has the rights to and can resolve the NetBIOS name of each server along the message path, the administrator will be able to see how a particular message traveled through the network and how long it took to go through each server.

 You can also configure Message Tracking using a System Policy, which will allow you to apply the same setting to multiple servers.

See Also

MS KB 246856 (How to Enable Message Tracking in Exchange 2000 Server and in Exchange Server 2003)

## CHAPTER 23

Microsoft Identity Integration Server

23.0   Introduction

Microsoft Identity Integration Server (MIIS) is a full-featured and very powerful metadirectory service that can synchronize identity, passwords, and other identity-related data between disparate data stores such as directories, databases, files, and application repositories. It is supplied with out-of-the-box connectors—known as *managements agents* (MAs)—for 22 popular systems, including flat files, AD, Lotus Notes, Novell eDirectory, Sun Java System Directory Server, IBM Directory Server, SQL Server, IBM DB2, and Oracle. There is also an SDK so you can build your own MAs. The rather clumsily named "Identity Integration Feature Pack 1a for Microsoft Windows Server Active Directory," colloquially known as IIFP, is the same as MIIS except that it only supports MAs for Active Directory, ADAM, and GALSync (used to create a common address book across different Exchange 2000/2003 organizations) and is available as a download from Microsoft's web site. MIIS forms the heart of Microsoft's Identity and Management Strategy.

The ADAM Synchronizer is another downloadable tool for synchronizing ADAM and AD together. It lacks the flexibility of MIIS or IIFP, and is therefore only suitable for simple synchronization scenarios, but is much easier to use because of this.

Requirements for MIIS and IIFP

MIIS and IIFP both require SQL Server 2000 SP3 or higher, either Standard or Enterprise editions. The SQL Server does not need to be co-resident on the same server as MIIS or IIFP. However, bear in mind that performance will be sub-optimal if the database is located on the other side of a slow network link. Also, if the database is operated by another division of your organization, there may be a different security and management regime which will need to be considered.

MIIS runs on Windows Server 2003 Enterprise Edition. Contrary to popular belief, MIIS and IIFP *do not* need AD. The store of data for MIIS is SQL Server and the MIIS Server can run in a workgroup; it does not need to be a domain-joined server.

To develop advanced rules to do custom MIIS synchronization, you will need Visual Studio.NET. In these recipes, we assume you have it installed on the same machine as MIIS. This is because when you create Visual Studio projects from within the MIIS UI, it configures projects correctly, and the resulting code is built in the correct folder in MIIS.

MIIS Overview

Since MIIS is a complex application and not something most AD administrators have experience with, we are going to discuss the basic features and terminology in more depth.

MIIS data

As a metadirectory, MIIS's primary function is to synchronize data between different data sources. To do this, MIIS maintains several namespaces that keep track of the synchronization process. MIIS data is stored in one of three places:

Connected Directory (CD)
> This is a system external to MIIS such as AD, Lotus Notes, or an Oracle database.

Connector Space (CS)
> This is a namespace inside MIIS that keeps a copy of the specified objects from the CD.

Metaverse (MV)
> This is the joined and aggregated namespace that joins the data from many connector spaces.

Figure 23-1 illustrates these relationships.

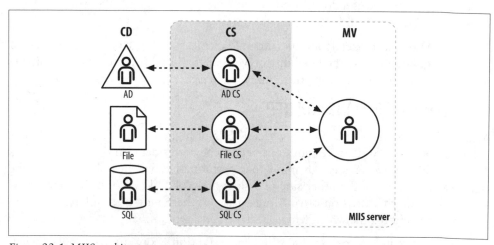

Figure 23-1. MIIS architecture

When the data moves from either the connector space to the metaverse or vice versa, it is controlled by MIIS software elements known as MAs. Each MA contains its own connector space. Thus there are MAs for AD, File, and SQL. The MAs can be configured with rules on how to process the data by using the MIIS UI. For more advanced rules, rule extensions can be created using any .NET-aware programming language. MIIS has native support for project creation of VB and C# rules extensions.

There are three types of MAs:

File-based
> These MAs deal with data in flat files such as DSML files, CSV files, LDIF files, and so on.

Call-based
> These MAs connect to systems using published APIs, for example, AD, NT4, SAP, Lotus Notes, and DB2.

Extensible connectivity
> An SDK that allows you to write your own MA to connect to a system for which MIIS does not already have a pre-built MA. This is especially useful for custom in-house developed applications.

MIIS also supports password management via a web-based application and password synchronization from AD to other systems. Many additional scenarios are covered in the Microsoft Identity and Access Management Series (see the "See Also" section).

The scenario

Figure 23-2 outlines the example scenario of synchronizing AD from an HR database, which is used throughout this chapter. The numbered points will be referenced in later recipes

We'll start with an employee database that runs on SQL Server, referred to from now on as the HR Database. You can download this database from *http://www.rallenhome.com/books/adcookbook2*.

Let's walk through how MIIS will synchronize the HR Database with Active Directory, and define some of the specialized terms Microsoft uses to describe the process. The numbers in brackets refer to the numbered points in the diagram.

First, we will *import* or *stage* (1) records from the HR Database into the HR Database MA connector space. The import process creates connector space objects (2).

Next, we will *synchronize* the data in the HR Database MA connector space. The first time we do this, and any time MIIS discovers a new user record in the MA connector space, MIIS will *project* (3) a new object (4) into the metaverse, and *join*, or link the HR Database MA object to the metaverse object. MIIS will then *flow* attribute data from the HR Database MA connector space object to the *joined* metaverse object through the MA's rules (5).

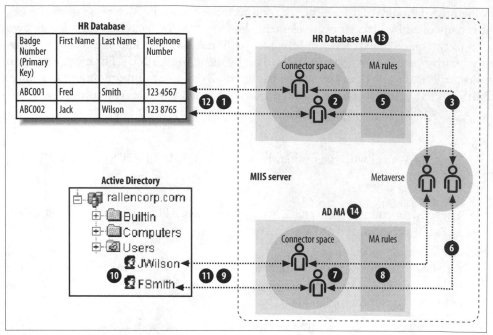

Figure 23-2. Example scenario

Synchronizing the HR Database MA will also *provision* (6) a new connector space object (7) in the Active Directory MA's connector space and join the new Active Directory connector space object to the metaverse object (4). MIIS will then flow the appropriate attribute information from the metaverse object (4) into the AD connector space object (7) through the Active Directory MA's rules (8).

We will *export* (9) objects (7) from the AD connector space into Active Directory itself to create Active Directory user objects (10).

We will also import (11) the telephoneNumber attribute from AD user objects (10) into the related AD connector space objects (7) and synchronize the AD management agent. This will flow attribute data through the ADMA rules (8) and into the joined metaverse object (4); from there, attribute data will flow through the HR Database MA's rules (5) to the joined HR Database MA connector space object (2). At this stage, the updated HR Database MA connector space object (2) will be exported (12) to the HR Database, resulting in the [telephoneNumber] column being updated.

De-provisioning will also be tested by deleting a row in the HR Database and then importing (1) objects from the HR Database in to the HR Database connector space. This will result in the related connector space object (2) being marked as deleted. Synchronizing the HR Database MA will cause the joined metaverse object (4) to be deleted. This will, in turn, cause the joined AD connector space object (7) to be deleted. Finally, the delete operation is exported to Active Directory, resulting in the deletion of an Active Directory user object (10).

See Also

Microsoft provides a great deal of useful documentation for MIIS on its web site. This section lists some of the most useful documents:

The MIIS Help Files
> MIIS comes with a very useful and complete help file. You can find it in the MIIS installation folder, typically at *C:\Program Files\Microsoft Identity Integration Server\UIShell\helpfiles*. There are two help files: *mms.chm* contains general help for configuring and running MIIS and *mmsdev.chm* contains information about programming rules extensions and interpreting MIIS XML files.

The MIIS Home Page
> The MIIS home page is the starting point for all the current information about MIIS, including recent releases and other MIIS news. The MIIS home page is at *http://www.microsoft.com/miis*.

Microsoft Identity and Access Management Series Overview
> This document provides an overview of MIIS and describes how MIIS fits into Microsoft's overall identity architecture. You can download it from: *http://www.microsoft.com/technet/security/topics/identitymanagement/idmanage/Overview.mspx*.

Identity Integration Feature Pack 1a for Microsoft Windows Server Active Directory
> This provides identity integration/directory synchronization, account provisioning/de-provisioning, and password synchronization between Active Directory directory service, ADAM, Microsoft Exchange Server 2000 or Exchange 2003 instances:
>> *http://www.microsoft.com/downloads/details.aspx?FamilyID=d9143610-c04d-41c4-b7ea-6f56819769d5&DisplayLang=en*

Microsoft Identity Integration Server 2003 Scenarios
> The MIIS Scenarios documents describe how to use MIIS to solve common identity management problems, including account provisioning, global address list synchronization, and password management. Download the scenarios from:
>> *http://www.microsoft.com/downloads/details.aspx?FamilyID=15032653-d78e-4d9d-9e48-6cf0ae0c369c&DisplayLang=en*

TechNet Virtual Lab: Microsoft Identity Integration Server 2003
> There is a virtual lab you can use to try out some of the recipes in this chapter before investing the effort to build a MIIS server. The labs are available at the following location: *http://www.microsoft.com/technet/traincert/virtuallab/miis.mspx*.

MIIS Users Group (MMSUG)
> There is an active user group on Yahoo that provides support and answers to common (and not-so-common) problems. You can join the group at: *http://groups.yahoo.com/group/mmsug*.

23.1   Creating the HR Database MA

Problem

You want to get employee records from the HR Database into MIIS so that they can be used as the source for new accounts in AD.

Solution

You need to start by creating an MA for the HR Database. Refer to **(12)** in Figure 23-2.

1. Open Identity Manager.
2. Click the Management Agents button on the toolbar.
3. In the Actions pane on the right, click Create.
4. In the Create Management Agent Designer, select SQL Server 7.0 or 2000 from the "Management Agent for" drop-down list.
5. Type HR Database into the Name text box.
6. Type a description in the Description field—this is where you can be creative.
7. Click Next.
8. In the Connect to Database pane on the right side:
    a. Type in the SQL server name in to the Server Name text box.
    b. Type the name of the database in the Database text box.
    c. Type the name of the table or view that contains the employee records in the Table/View text box.
    d. Leave the Delta View and Multivalue Table text boxes blank.
    e. Select the radio button for the type of authentication the SQL Server is set up to use.
    f. Fill in the User Name, Password, and Domain text boxes with the credentials of a user that has permissions to read and update the table we will read.
9. Click Next.
10. On the Configure Columns page:
    a. Click the Set Anchor button. This will display the Set Anchor dialog box.
    b. In the Set Anchor dialog box, select Badge Number and press the Add button.
    c. Click OK to save the anchor attribute definition.
11. On the Configure Connector Filter page, click Next.
12. On the Configure Join and Projection Rules, click Next.
13. On the Configure Attribute Flow page, click Next.

14. On the Configure Deprovisioning page, click the "Make them disconnectors" radio button in the lefthand pane.

15. Click Next.

16. In the Configure Extensions page, click Finish.

Discussion

Following these steps will create a SQL Server management agent. Associated with the MA is a namespace known as the *connector space*. MIIS will store the data from the relevant columns of the HR Database here and use them to provision, synchronize, and de-provision user accounts in Active Directory. Creating the HR Database MA is the first of several steps to get the data into MIIS. You should now see a Management Agent in the Management Agent pane of the Identity Manager with the name and comments displayed.

See Also

Recipe 23.2 for more on creating the HR database MA

23.2   Creating an Active Directory MA

Problem

You want to provision user accounts into Active Directory from the records in the HR Database.

Solution

The first step to accomplish this is to create an Active Directory management agent. In Recipe 23.1, see (**13**) on Figure 23-2.

1. Open Identity Manager.

2. Click the Management Agents button on the toolbar.

3. In the Actions pane on the right side, click Create.

4. In the Management Agent Designer, select Active Directory from the "Management Agent for" drop-down list.

5. In the Name box, type a name. The forest name is usually a good choice.

6. If you feel creative, type a meaningful description into the Description text box.

7. Click Next.

8. In the Connect to Active Directory Forest pane on the right side:

   a. Type the fully-qualified DNS name of the forest into the Forest Name text box.

b. Fill in the username, password, and domain name of an appropriate user account. The account must have sufficient access permissions. See the "Discussion" section for more details.

c. Click Next.

9. In the Configure Directory Partitions pane on the right side:

a. Select the domain(s) you wish to manage in the Select Directory Partitions field.

b. Click the Containers button in the lower-left portion of the dialog box.

c. In the Select Container dialog, select the containers you wish to manage.

d. Click OK.

e. Click Next.

10. In the Select Object Types pane on the right side, select user in the Object Types field and click Next.

> MIIS requires that the domainDNS, container, and organizationUnit object types always be selected. MIIS uses these objects to maintain the hierarchical structure of Active Directory in the MA's connector space.

11. In the Select Attributes pane on the right side, select the attributes you wish to manage from the Attributes field. You can check the Show All checkbox to display a full list of all attributes in the AD. Some AD attributes are mandatory; a typical minimal list would be: cn, displayName, employeeID, givenName, sAMAccountName, sn, userAccountControl, userPrincipalName, and unicodePwd (you need to select the Show All checkbox to see the unicodePwd attribute). Click Next to save the selected attributes.

12. On the Configure Connector Filter page, click Next.

13. On the Configure Join and Projection Rules page, click Next.

14. On the Configure Attribute Flow page, click Next.

15. On the Configure Deprovisioning page, click Stage a delete on the object for the next export run, then click Next.

16. On the Configure Extensions page, click Finish.

Discussion

The account used to connect to AD must have the following rights to the containers that you intend to write to:

- Standard
- Read

- Write
- Advanced
- Delete
- Replicate directory changes
- Create all child objects
- Delete all child objects
- List Contents
- Read all properties
- Write all properties
- Delete Subtree
- Read Permissions
- All Validated Writes

See Also

Recipe 23.1 for more on creating the HR database MA. This Active Directory MA will be further configured in Recipes 23.5 and 23.8

23.3   Setting Up a Metaverse Object Deletion Rule

Problem

You have decided on a single authoritative source for new employee: the HR Database. When a user record is deleted from it, you want MIIS to delete the corresponding Active Directory account.

Solution

One of the configuration options required to have deletions propagated from the HR Database to Active Directory is the metaverse object deletion rule:

1. Open Identity Manager.
2. Click the Metaverse Designer button on the toolbar.
3. In the Actions pane on the far right side, click Configure Object Deletion Rule.
4. Select the "Delete metaverse object when connector from this management agent is disconnected" radio button and ensure the HR Databse MA is selected in the drop-down list.
5. Click OK.

Discussion

The object deletion rule informs MIIS when to delete metaverse objects. Deleting a metaverse object does not necessarily cause anything to happen in the connected data source, but it *does* disconnect any connected objects in all of the connector spaces. This will cause the deprovisioning rule to fire for each disconnected object. The deprovisioning rule is configured for each management agent in the Configure Deprovisioning page for the management agent.

See Also

Recipe 23.1, Recipe 23.29 for deleting data in the connector space and metaverse, and Recipe 23.15 for the provisioning run profile

23.4 Setting Up Simple Import Attribute Flow—HR Database MA

Problem

You have already created the MAs needed, but you want to flow the column data from the HR Database to attributes in Active Directory.

Solution

You need to configure the ADMA's attribute flow rules page. In Recipe 23.1, refer to (5) in Figure 23-2.

1. Open Identity Manager.
2. Click the Management Agents button on the toolbar.
3. In the Management Agents pane, double-click the HR Database MA.
4. In the Management Agent Designer pane on the lefthand side, select Configure Attribute Flow.
5. Ensure "person" is selected in the data source object type drop-down list.
6. Ensure "person" is selected in the metaverse object type drop-down list.
7. In the data source attribute list, select the attribute whose data you wish to flow into the metaverse (see the "Discussion" section for some suggestions).
8. In the Metaverse attribute list, select the attribute you want the data to flow into (see the "Discussion" section for some suggestions).
9. In the Mapping Type section of the dialog, select Direct.
10. In the Flow Direction section of the dialog, select Import.
11. Click New. The new attribute mapping will appear in the attribute mapping list, with an arrow indicating that it is an import attribute flow.
12. Click OK.

Discussion

The MIIS has been configured to flow an attribute from the HR Database MA's connector space into the metaverse. In general, we can map any attribute from the connected system to any attribute in the metaverse. However, if a Mapping Type of Direct is issued, the attributes in the MA and the metaverse must be of the same data type (e.g., string or integer). To map from one data type to another, configure the advanced attribute flow (see Recipe 23.6).

Here are some typical simple mappings:

- FirstName → givenName
- LastName → sn
- Dept → department
- StaffNumber → employeeID
- TelNo → telephoneNumber

You need to make your own decisions about what data in the HR Database maps onto what data in the Metaverse attributes, but these are usually fairly obvious. If you want to construct a name—for example, you'd like the sAMAccountName to be derived from the first character of the first name prepended to the last name—you need an advanced flow.

See Also

Recipe 23.1, Recipe 23.5 shows simple export attribute flow to AD, Recipe 23.6 for more advanced attribute flow, and Recipe 23.7 for writing a rules extension to take the advanced flow even further; all these flows are eventually exported to AD.

23.5   Setting Up a Simple Export Attribute Flow to AD

Problem

You want to flow attributes in the metaverse to attributes in AD. For example, the givenName field in the metaverse needs to map to the givenName field in AD.

Solution

You need to configure the attribute flow pages on the ADMA. In Recipe 23.1, refer to (8) in Figure 23-2.

1. Open Identity Manager.
2. Click the Management Agents button on the toolbar.
3. In the Management Agents pane, double-click the ADMA.
4. In the Management Agent Designer pane on the lefthand side, select Configure Attribute Flow.

5. Ensure "user" is selected in the data source object type drop-down list.

6. Ensure "person" is selected in the metaverse object type drop-down list.

7. In the data source attribute list, select the connector space attribute you want to flow data into. See the "Discussion" section for some suggestions.

8. In the Metaverse attribute list, select the attribute you want to flow data from. See the "Discussion" section for some suggestions.

9. In the Mapping Type section of the dialog, select Direct.

10. In the Flow Direction section of the dialog, select Export.

11. Click New. The new attribute mapping will appear in the attribute mapping list, with an arrow indicating that it is an export attribute flow.

12. Click OK.

Discussion

This will configure a simple export attribute flow from the metaverse to the ADMA. You need to determine what attributes in the metaverse should flow to AD attributes.

Here are some typical simple mappings:

- givenName → givenName
- sn → sn
- department → department
- employeeID → employeeID
- telephoneNumber → telephoneNumber
- cn → displayName
- cn → cn
- uid → sAMAccountName

In many MIIS scenarios, data is manipulated on its way *in* to the metaverse, and then copied on its way out to other connected systems. In the above example, the cn comes from the displayName. This is because you will later create an advanced import flow which will write the first name followed by a space then the last name in to the displayName in the metaverse. Something similar will be done for uid, only you will take the first character of the first name and append the last name; e.g., Fred Smith gets a sAMAccountName of *FSmith*.

See Also

Recipes 23.1, 23.4, 23.6, and 23.7; these recipes are interesting because most of the data you are exporting to AD in this recipe was first imported from them

23.6 Defining an Advanced Import Attribute Flow— HR Database MA

Problem

You want to create an Active Directory username using the first and last name from the HR Database. Simple attribute to attribute mapping is not sufficient. You need to take partial strings from different attributes and combine them to form a new name.

Solution

This will involve writing some VB or C# for an advanced attribute flow, which is covered in Recipe 23.7. To start with, you must define the *flow rule*—an entity that connects the UI elements to the coding we will do later. In Recipe 23.1, refer to **(5)** in Figure 23-2.

1. Open Identity Manager.
2. Click the Management Agents button on the toolbar.
3. In the Management Agents pane, double-click the HR Database MA.
4. In the Management Agent Designer pane on the lefthand side, select Configure Attribute Flow.
5. Ensure "person" is selected in the data source object type drop-down list.
6. Ensure "person" is selected in the metaverse object type drop-down list.
7. In the Mapping Type section of the dialog, select Advanced.
8. In the Flow Direction section of the dialog, select Import.
9. Select FirstName and LastName from the data source attributes text box (to select multiple entries, hold down the control key).
10. Select cn from the Metaverse attribute list
11. Click New.
12. In the Advanced Attribute Flow Options dialog, delete the default name, type cn, and then click OK. The flow rule name you defined here will appear in the VB or C# you will write later. A convention among MIIS developers is to use the name of the destination attribute (in this case, cn).
13. Notice in the Type column in the upper pane, the newly created attribute mapping is detailed as Rules-Extension. A rules extension is a unit of managed .NET code.
14. Select First Name and Last Name from the Data source attribute mapping list (remember to use the control key to select multiple attributes).
15. Select uid from the Metaverse attribute mapping list.
16. Click New.

17. In the Advanced Import Attribute Flow Options dialog, type uid into the Flow rule name text box and click OK.

18. Notice in the Type column in the upper pane, the newly created attribute mapping is detailed as Rules-Extension.

19. Select Configure Extensions in the lefthand pane.

20. Type HR DatabaseExtension into the Rules Extension Name text box.

21. Click OK.

Discussion

In this recipe, an advanced attribute flow rule was defined. The rule extension is implemented in managed .NET code in Recipe 23.7.

There are two types of advanced attribute flow. One is where a constant is defined that will always be written to the selected attribute. No rules extension code is required for this type of advanced attribute flow. But if you need to manipulate the attributes being flowed using code, you must define an advanced attribute flow and provide a flow rule name. Even though you may not have created the DLL that will be used at this stage, you still have to put a name in the dialog to exit the MA designer.

See Also

Recipe 23.1, Recipe 23.4 for simple import attribute flow from the HR Database, Recipe 23.5, Recipe 23.7 for creating a rules extension to further extend advanced attribute flow, and Recipe 23.8 to export data to AD

23.7 Implementing an Advanced Attribute Flow Rules Extension—HR Database MA

Problem

You want to perform advanced attribute flow on the HR Database MA.

Solution

You've already defined an advanced attribute flow rule for the MA in the Identity Manager console. You now need to write the code and produce the DLL that implements that flow rule. See Recipe 23.1, refer to (5) in Figure 23-2.

1. Open Identity Manager.

2. Click the Management Agents button on the toolbar.

3. Select the HR Database MA in the Managements Agents pane.

4. Click Create Extension Project in the Action pane on the far right side.

---

5. Ensure the dialog box is filled in similar to Figure 23-3 (you can specify your own name and location).

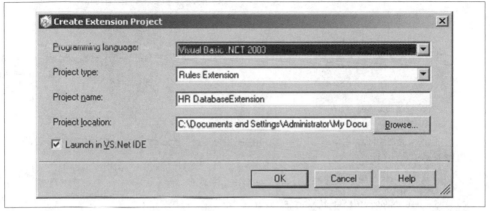

Figure 23-3. Create Extension Project dialog

6. Click OK. This will launch Visual Studio.NET.

This recipe assumes that you have already installed Visual Studio .NET 2003 on the machine running MIIS. If you are doing your development on another machine, you have two choices. You can map a drive to the MIIS server and modify the code through the mapped drive or you can copy the entire project to your development machine and work on it there. In any case, you will have to be sure to copy the resulting DLL back to the MIIS server any time you make a code change.

7. In the Solution Explorer in the far righthand pane in Visual Studio.NET and double-click the *HR DatabaseExtension.vb* node. This file contains the source code for your rules extension.

8. The main code window should show the automatically generated code (this auto code generation is provided for VB and C#). The first few lines of code should look like this:

```
Imports Microsoft.MetadirectoryServices
Public Class MAExtensionObject
    Implements IMASynchronization
```

9. Scroll to the code section that looks like this:

```
Public Sub MapAttributesForImport(ByVal FlowRuleName As String, ByVal csentry As
    CSEntry, ByVal mventry As MVEntry) Implements
    IMASynchronization.MapAttributesForImport
        ' TODO: write your import attribute flow code
        Select Case FlowRuleName
            Case "uid"
                ' TODO: remove the following statement and add your scripted
                ' import attribute flow here
                Throw New EntryPointNotImplementedException()
```

```
          Case "cn"
                ' TODO: remove the following statement and add your scripted
                  ' import attribute flow here
              Throw New EntryPointNotImplementedException( )

          Case Else
                ' TODO: remove the following statement and add your default
                  ' script here
              Throw New EntryPointNotImplementedException( )

        End Select
   End Sub
```

10. Edit this section to make the code look like this (the bold sections are new code that we typed in):

```
Select Case FlowRuleName
Case "uid"
If Not csentry("Last Name").IsPresent Then
        Throw New UnexpectedDataException("No Last Name!")
End If

If Not csentry("First Name").IsPresent Then
        Throw New UnexpectedDataException("No First Name!")
End If

mventry("uid").Value = csentry("First Name").StringValue.Substring(0, 1) + _
csentry("Last Name").Value

Case "cn"
   If Not csentry("Last Name").IsPresent Then
        Throw New UnexpectedDataException("No Last Name!")
   End If

   If Not csentry("First Name").IsPresent Then
        Throw New UnexpectedDataException("No First Name!")
   End If

   mventry("cn").Value = csentry("First Name").Value + " " + _
      csentry("Last Name").Value

Case Else
    ' TODO: remove the following statement and add your default script here
       Throw New EntryPointNotImplementedException

End Select
```

11. Go to the Build menu and select Build Solution. Ensure you see a message in the output panel at the bottom of the screen like this:

```
---------------------- Done ----------------------

     Build: 1 succeeded, 0 failed, 0 skipped
```

12. Close Visual Studio.NET.

13. Open Windows Explorer and browse to *C:\Program Files\Microsoft Identity Integration Server\Extensions* (this assumes you installed MIIS on the C: drive in the default location: if you didn't, substitute the relevant parts of the path), and ensure the DLL is present. In this case, the DLL will be called *HR DatabaseExtension.dll*.

14. To be absolutely sure you have the correct rules extension selected in MIIS, open Identity Manager.

15. Click the Management Agents button.

16. In the Management Agent pane, double-click the HR Database MA.

17. In the lefthand pane of the Management Agent Designer, click Configure Extensions.

18. Click the Select button.

19. Select HR DatabaseExtension.dll and click OK.

20. Click OK to close Management Agent properties.

21. Close Identity Manager.

Discussion

This code does some fairly simple string manipulation. This chapter doesn't venture into the world of advanced MIIS coding, but there are many examples in the Developer Reference off the help menu in Identity Manager.

The MIIS development environment is so flexible that human-driven digital identity business processes can be encapsulated in MIIS rules. However, there is no workflow engine, which means you may have to call workflow processes on another engine, such as BizTalk.

See Also

Recipes 23.1 and 23.8 for setting constants on certain attributes

23.8 Setting Up Advanced Export Attribute Flow in Active Directory

Problem

Simple attribute to attribute mapping is not flexible enough to create the attribute values you want. You want to set constant values on some attributes. In this case, there is a bit mask of great interest—the mask used to set properties for accounts, such as whether the account is disabled.

Solution

This will involve writing some VB or C# as the script for an advanced attribute flow that is covered in Recipe 23.9, but we must set up flow rule names for the code in this section. See Recipe 23.1, refer to **(8)** in Figure 23-2.

1. Open Identity Manager.
2. Click the Management Agents button on the toolbar.
3. In the Management Agents pane, double-click the ADMA.
4. In the Management Agent Designer pane on the lefthand side, select Configure Attribute Flow.
5. Ensure "user" is selected in the data source object type drop-down list.
6. Ensure "person" is selected n the metaverse object type drop-down list.
7. In the Mapping Type section of the dialog, select Advanced.
8. In the Flow Direction section of the dialog, select Export.
9. Select userAccountControl from the data source attributes list.
10. Click New.
11. In the Advanced Attribute Flow Options dialog, select Constant.
12. Type 512 into the Value text box, then click OK.
13. Notice in the Type column in the upper pane, the newly created attribute mapping is detailed as Constant, with an arrow indicating export attribute flow.
14. Click OK to close the Management Agent Designer.

Discussion

Active Directory requires a minimal set of attributes in order to create normal, usable, enabled accounts. In this recipe we have set the required attributes. We set the userAccountControl flag to 512 (bit 9 set), which indicates that this account is a normal account. In other cases we might use a rules extension and reset bit 9 to disable the account, e.g., if there was an employee status field in the HR Database that indicated the employee was inactive.

See Also

Recipes 23.1, 23.9, and 23.14 for writing a rules extension to provision user objects to the ADMA from objects in the HR Database MA. There are code examples in the "Simple Account Provisioning" walkthrough (Scenarios URL mentioned in the "Introduction" to this chapter) that show how to take an existing UserAccountControl flag and set the additional bits you require. For example, if the account is already disabled, it will remain disabled.

23.9 Configuring a Run Profile to Do an Initial Load of Data from the HR Database MA

Problem

You need to get the data from the HR Database to its connector space.

Solution

Before you can run a management agent, you must create a *run profile* for it. See Recipe 23.1, refer to **(9)** in Figure 23-2, which shows data being loaded from AD to the AD connector space.

1. Open Identity Manager.
2. Click the Management Agents button on the toolbar.
3. In the Management Agents pane, click the HR Database MA.
4. In the Actions pane on the far right side, click Configure Run Profiles.
5. In the Configure Run Profiles for HR Database, click New Profile.
6. In the Name text box type Full Import (Stage Only), then click Next.
7. Ensure Full Import (Stage Only) is selected in the Type drop-down list, then click Next.
8. Ensure default is showing in the Partition drop-down list, then click Finish.
9. Ensure the details in the Step Details field looks like Figure 23-4.
10. Click OK to create the run profile.

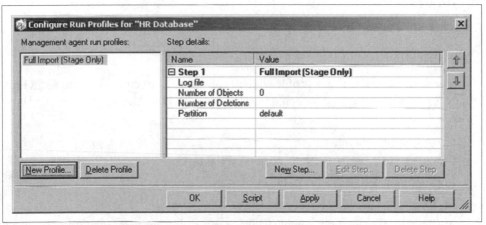

Figure 23-4. Configure Run Profiles dialog for the HR Database MA

Discussion

There are three steps required to get data into the HR Database MA connector space:

1. Create the MA.
2. Create a run profile to run the MA.
3. Execute the run profile. In this recipe you have created the run profile.

It is generally a good idea to give the run profiles exactly the same names as the step-type they represent. You will later create scripts that call run profiles. It is possible to give a run profile a name such as "Complete Cycle" and combine many steps in the run profile. However, when calling such entities from scripts, the calling script isn't self-documenting in that it hides what it is doing. It is also much easier to debug scripts when you know exactly what step is being called. Hence, you have created a run profile called Full Import (Stage Only), which consists of a single step of type Full Import (Stage Only). The one exception to this general rule is discussed in Recipe 23.17.

See Also

Recipe 23.1, Recipe 23.10 for more on how to use the run profile to load data, and Recipe 23.17

23.10 Loading Initial HR Database Data into MIIS Using a Run Profile

Problem

With the MA and run profile created, you now want to load the data in to MIIS.

Solution

You need to execute the run profile to load the data. In Recipe 23.1, refer to (1) in Figure 23-2, which shows data being loaded from the HR Database to the HR Database connector space.

1. Open Identity Manager.
2. Click the Management Agents button on the toolbar.
3. In the Management Agents pane, click the HR Database MA.
4. In the Actions pane on the far right side, click Run.
5. In the Run Management Agent dialog, select Full Import (Stage Only) and click OK.
6. You'll have to be quick if there is only a small amount of data in the database. Notice the MA says Running in the State column of the Management Agents pane.

7. In the Synchronization Statistics pane in the bottom lefthand corner, statistics show the number of adds is displayed. If you click the hyperlink, you can navigate the information that was loaded.

 The HR Database you are importing from must have records in it before MIIS can import any data.

Discussion

When designing a large system, work with a very small (maybe 10 records) representative set of data during development. This is because you will frequently find errors in your rules, and set about deleting everything in MIIS, re-configuring your rules, and starting again. It is much better to do these initial data loads with 10 or so records rather than 100,000 records, which will take a long time to load. When you are finally convinced your rules are good, start working with larger datasets.

See Also

Recipes 23.1 and 23.9 for how this run profile was configured

23.11 Configuring a Run Profile to Load the Container Structure from AD

Problem

Before you can provision and synchronize data in the AD connector space, you need to build the container structure in the connector space to reflect the container structure of Active Directory.

Solution

To do this, you have to create an appropriate run profile for the ADMA and import that AD container structure into the connector space.

 The fact that you have to separately import the container structure from AD into the MA's connector space is not obvious, and is frequently overlooked by even the most experienced MIIS developers. If you fail to perform this step, the synchronization process will fail when it tries to provision new objects into the AD connector space.

In Recipe 23.1, refer to **(9)** in Figure 23-2, which shows data being loaded from AD to the AD connector space:

1. Open Identity Manager.
2. Click the Management Agents button on the toolbar
3. In the Management Agents pane, click the ADMA.
4. In the Actions pane on the far right side, click Configure Run Profiles.
5. In the Configure Run Profiles dialog click New Profile.
6. In the Name text box type Full Import (Stage Only), then click Next.
7. Ensure Full Import (Stage Only) is selected in the Type drop-down list, then click Next.
8. Ensure the correct domain partition is showing in the Partition drop-down list, then click Finish.
9. Ensure the details in the Step Details field looks like Figure 23-5 (note: your partition name may be different).
10. Click OK.

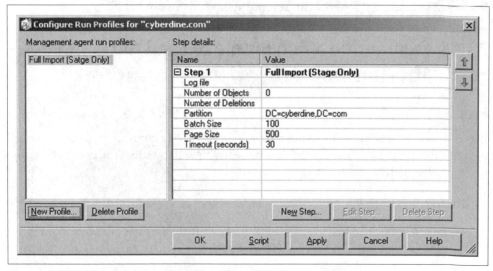

Figure 23-5. Configure Run Profiles dialog for the ADMA

Discussion

There are three steps required to get data into the ADMA connector space:

1. Create the MA.
2. Create the run profile.
3. Execute the run profile. In this recipe you create the run profile.

When you create an ADMA, you specify which partitions (naming contexts) you wish to synchronize. When creating a run profile you must be careful to select the correct partition (domain, typically) from which to load the container structure.

A common mistake among MIIS novices is to get "object does not have a parent" errors when running a synchronization step. This is because the container structure for Active Directory isn't loaded into the ADMA's connector space.

MIIS can create missing containers based on rules, but you need to configure and write those rules. That is beyond the scope of this book.

See Also

Recipe 23.1, Recipe 23.12 for more on how to use the run profile that was configured in this recipe, and the MIIS User Group has many discussion threads on programming techniques for the creation of missing containers (search for "OU creation" after you have joined the group at: *http://groups.yahoo.com/group/MMSUG*)

23.12 Loading the Initial AD Container Structure into MIIS Using a Run Profile

Problem

With the ADMA and run profile created, you need to get the data in to MIIS.

Solution

You now need to run the ADMA run profile to import the AD container structure. In Recipe 23.1, refer to **(9)** in Figure 23-2, which shows the data being loaded from AD into the AD connector space.

1. Open Identity Manager.
2. Click the Management Agents button on the toolbar.
3. In the Management Agents pane, click the ADMA.
4. In the Actions pane on the far right side, click Run.
5. In the Run Management Agent dialog, select Full Import (Stage Only) and click OK.
6. You'll have to be quick if there is only a small amount of data in AD. Notice the MA briefly says "Running" in the State column of the Management Agents pane.
7. Notice in the Synchronization Statistics pane in the bottom lefthand corner, statistics showing the number of adds is displayed. If you click the hyperlink, you can navigate the information that was loaded.

Discussion

The first time you load the container structure in to MIIS, you need to use a Full Import step. Once the container structure is loaded, subsequent imports can use Delta Import steps, which in normal daily operations will be considerably faster to execute, and will consume less resources on the MIIS server, the AD domain controller, and the network.

See Also

Recipes 23.1 and 23.11 for more on how to configure the run profile that was used in this recipe

23.13 Setting Up the HR Database MA to Project Objects to the Metaverse

Problem

The objects in the HR Database connector space now need to be projected into the metaverse. There are three steps:

1. Configuring the MA for projection.
2. Creating a synchronization run profile.
3. Executing the synchronization run profile.

Solution

In Recipe 23.1, refer to (3) in Figure 23-2, which shows objects being provisioned from the HR Database MA's connector space to the metaverse:

1. Open Identity Manager.
2. Click the Management Agents button on the toolbar.
3. In the Management Agents pane, double-click the HR Database MA.
4. In the Management Agent Designer pane on the lefthand side, select Configure Join and Projection Rules.
5. Click the New Projection Rule... button.
6. In the Projection dialog, ensure Declared is selected and that the drop-down list shows "person", and then click OK.
7. Notice in the "Join and Projection Rules for person" frame, the columns are detailed thus:
    - Mapping Group: 1

- Action: Project
- Metaverse Object Type: person

8. Click OK.

Discussion

The synchronization process *projects* (or creates) metaverse objects which are *joined* to objects in the HR Database MA connector space. When projected, MIIS can *provision* new objects to the ADMA's connector space. Hence it is *projection* that initiates *provisioning*. Novices often use the terms *project* and *provision* interchangeably, but they mean quite different things.

Table 23-1 clarifies this and introduces some new terminology: csentry for connector space objects and mventry for metaverse objects.

Table 23-1. Synchronization process

HR Database connector space	Action	Metaverse	Action	AD Connector space
csentry Objects →	Project to Metaverse →	mventry Objects →	Provision to Connector Space →	csentry Objects

See Also

Recipes 23.1 and 23.14 for more on provisioning

23.14 Writing a Rules Extension to Provision User Objects to the ADMA from Objects in the HR Database MA

Problem

You want MIIS to provision objects to the ADMA's connector space based on objects in the HR Database MA.

Solution

There are three steps to *provisioning*:

1. Writing a rules extension
2. Configuring a run profile
3. Executing the run profile

In this recipe you will write a Provisioning-Rules-Extension. MIIS will help you with the initial project creation. In Recipe 23.1, refer to **(6)** in Figure 23-2, which shows objects being provisioned from the metaverse to the AD connector space.

1. Open Identity Manager.
2. From the menu select Tools → Options.
3. In the Options dialog click the Create Rules Extension Project button.
4. Ensure the Create Extension Project dialog looks like Figure 23-6.

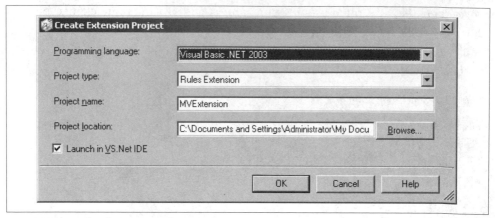

Figure 23-6. Dialog for creating the Metaverse Provisioning Rules Extension

5. Click OK.
6. In Visual Studio.NET, double-click *MVExtension* in the Solution Explorer.
7. The first few lines of the code pane should look like this:

```
Imports Microsoft.MetadirectoryServices

Public Class MVExtensionObject
    Implements IMVSynchronization
```

8. Navigate to the section that looks like this:

```
Public Sub Provision(ByVal mventry As MVEntry) Implements
IMVSynchronization.Provision
        ' TODO: Remove this throw statement if you implement this method
        Throw New EntryPointNotImplementedException( )
    End Sub
```

9. Modify it to contain the following code:

```
Public Sub Provision(ByVal mventry As MVEntry) Implements _
IMVSynchronization.Provision

    Dim container As String
    Dim rdn As String
    Dim ADMA As ConnectedMA
    Dim numConnectors As Integer
```

```
          Dim myConnector As CSEntry
          Dim csentry As CSEntry
          Dim dn As ReferenceValue

          ' Ensure that the cn attribute is present.
          If Not mventry("cn").IsPresent Then
              Throw New UnexpectedDataException("cn attribute is not present.")
          End It

          ' Calculate the container and RDN.
          container = "CN=users,DC=rallencorp,DC=com"
          rdn = "CN=" & mventry("cn").Value

          ADMA = mventry.ConnectedMAs("rallencorp.com")
          dn = ADMA.EscapeDNComponent(rdn).Concat(container)

          numConnectors = ADMA.Connectors.Count

          ' create a new connector.
          If numConnectors = 0 Then
              csentry = ADMA.Connectors.StartNewConnector("user")
              csentry.DN = dn
             csentry("unicodePwd").Value = "Password1"
              csentry.CommitNewConnector()

          ElseIf numConnectors = 1 Then
              ' If the connector has a different DN rename it.
              myConnector = ADMA.Connectors.ByIndex(0)
              myConnector.DN = dn
          Else
              Throw New UnexpectedDataException("Error: There are" + _
              numConnectors.ToString + " connectors")
          End If
       End Sub
```

10. Notice the highlighted entries "CN=users,DC=rallencorp,DC=com". You will need to enter your own domain and container information here.

11. Notice the highlighted entry mventry.ConnectedMAs("rallencorp.com"). You will need to modify this to your own ADMA name.

12. From the file menu select Build → Build Solution.

13. Open Identity Manager.

14. From the menu select Tools → Options.

15. In the Options dialog, click Browse.

16. Select *MVExtension.dll*, and click OK to close the Options dialog.

Discussion

Because you can use any .NET programming language, MIIS is very flexible in a multiteam environment. Like many modern systems, it is not great programming skills

---

that help you build good rules with MIIS, it is experience and familiarity with the object model. It is well worth getting to know the MIIS object model. Many novices spend hours or days coding a function only to find there is a method already on the object that already does the thing they have spent all their time on.

See Also

Recipe 23.1, Recipe 23.4 describes how the code in this recipe is triggered, and Recipe 23.13 for setting up the HR Database MA to project objects to the metaverse. Remember it is *projection* that triggers *provisioning*

23.15 Creating a Run Profile for Provisioning

Problem

You need to synchronize data using the management agent to provision new accounts in the AD connector space. Before you can run the MA, you have to create a run profile that will synchronize the MA's connector space with the metaverse.

Solution

You now need to create a provisioning run profile for the HR Database MA to synchronize user objects from it to the ADMA's connector space. The run profile step is of type *synchronization*.

1. Open Identity Manager.
2. Click the Management Agents button on the toolbar.
3. In the Management Agents pane, click the HR Database MA.
4. In the Actions pane on the far right side, click Configure Run Profiles.
5. In the Configure Run Profiles dialog, click New Profile.
6. In the Name text box type Full Synchronization, then click Next.
7. Ensure Full Synchronization is selected in the Type drop-down list, then click Next.
8. Ensure default is showing in the Partition drop-down list, then click Finish.
9. Ensure the details in the Step Details field looks like Figure 23-7.
10. Notice in the Management Agent run profiles list, the Full Import (Stage Only) profile you created earlier is still there.
11. Click OK.

Discussion

There are two types of synchronization run profile: full and delta. A *full synchronization* will process every object in the connector space. This is obviously necessary

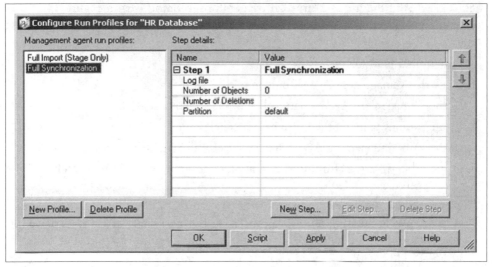

Figure 23-7. Dialog showing a Full Synchronization run profile added to the HR Database MA

when it is the very first synchronization on the data. But in normal daily operations you would only want to perform *delta synchronization* steps because they only process objects that have changed since the last synchronization.

Full synchronization is also used when you have made a change to management agent configuration, e.g., you have added a new attribute flow. Usually you will want to run the reconfigured MA against all of the objects in the connector space. A delta synchronization would only apply the rule to objects that had changed since the last synchronization.

See Also

Recipe 23.13 for setting up the HR Database MA to project objects to the metaverse, Recipe 23.14 for writing a rules extension to provision user objects to the ADMA from objects in the HR Database MA, and Recipe 23.16 for executing the run profile created in this recipe.

23.16 Executing the Provisioning Rule

Problem

You need to *provision* new objects to the AD connector space.

Solution

You need to run the provisioning run profile. The provisioning run profile triggers projection ((3) in Figure 23-2, in Recipe 23.1). The arrival of new objects in the metaverse ((**4**) in Figure 23-2) in turn triggers provisioning ((**6**) in Figure 23-2) and creates new objects ((**7**) in Figure 23-2) in the AD connector space. Follow these steps:

1. Open Identity Manager.
2. Click the Management Agents button on the toolbar.
3. In the Management Agents pane, click the HR Database MA.
4. In the Actions pane on the far right side, click Run.
5. In the Run Management Agent dialog, select Full Synchronization and click OK.
6. Notice the MA says "Running" in the State column of the Management Agents pane, and then says "Idle."
7. Notice in the Synchronization Statistics pane in the bottom lefthand corner, statistics showing the number of projections and provisioned entries is displayed. If you click one of the hyperlinks, you can navigate the information that was projected and provisioned.

Discussion

You have to be careful when executing synchronization run profiles. If you were to execute a synchronization run profile on the ADMA, nothing would happen because no projection is set up to move objects to the metaverse. No import attribute flow is yet set up to move attribute data from AD to the metaverse, and no provisioning is set up to create new objects in any MAs other than AD.

You will usually run a synchronization profile on the MA that you want new data to come from.

See Also

Recipe 23.1, Recipe 23.13 for setting up the HR Database MA to project objects to the metaverse, Recipe 23.14 for writing a rules extension to provision user objects to the ADMA from objects in the HR Database MA, and Recipe 23.15 for creating the run profile that was executed in this recipe

23.17 Creating a Run Profile to Export Objects from the ADMA to Active Directory

Problem

You want to create the new accounts in Active Directory.

Solution

There are two steps to get the data from an MA to a connected system: creating an *export* run profile and executing the profile. This is the first step (the second step is in Recipe 23.18):

1. Open Identity Manager.
2. Click the Management Agents button on the toolbar.
3. In the Management Agents pane, click the ADMA.
4. In the Actions pane on the far right side, click Configure Run Profiles.
5. In the "Configure Run Profiles for..." pane, click New Profile.
6. In the Name text box type Export, then click Next.
7. Ensure Export is selected in the Type drop-down list, then click Next.
8. Ensure the correct domain partition is showing in the Partition drop-down list, then click Finish.
9. Click New Step.
10. In the Configure Step dialog, ensure Delta Import (Stage Only) is selected in the Type drop-down list then click Next.
11. Ensure the correct domain is selected in the Partition drop-down list then click Finish.
12. Ensure the details in the Step Details field looks like Figure 23-8 (note: your partition name may be different).
13. Click OK.

Discussion

It was mentioned earlier that it is a good idea to name the run profiles you create exactly the same as the run profile steps; i.e., a run profile of type Full Import (Stage Only) is named Full Import (Stage Only). The one exception to this general rule applies to export run profiles. When an export is completed, the only way the MA can truly know the data was successfully written to the target data store is to re-import the changes and compare them with what it believes was written out. This is known as a *confirming import*. In AD for example, if we programmatically create a user account without a password, AD will automatically disable the user account by setting a flag in the userAccountControl attribute. For MIIS to maintain knowledge of this state, the confirming import brings this knowledge back in to MIIS. Therefore, exports need to include a confirming import stage. If the system we are exporting to supports some form of change logging (as AD does through USNs), then the type of confirming import can be a Delta Import (Stage Only). If the system doesn't expose any form of change logging (e.g., Novell eDirectory and NT4), a Full Import (Stage Only) step will be necessary.

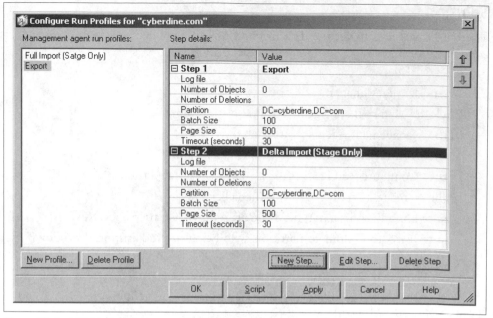

Figure 23-8. ADMA Export run profile showing an Export step followed by a Delta Import (Stage Only) step

MIIS's sync engine performs delta imports using the Active Directory Dirsync control. You need to assign the "Replicate Directory Changes" right to the user associated with the ADMA for delta imports to work (see MS KB 303972 for instructions).

See Also

Recipe 23.18 for more on how to use this run profile to export objects to AD and MS KB 303972 (How to Grant the "Replicating Directory Changes" Permission for the Microsoft Metadirectory Services ADMA Service Account)

23.18 Exporting Objects to AD Using an Export Run Profile

Problem

You need to execute the export run profile.

Solution

The second step is executing the export run profile to get the data in to AD (the first step is in Recipe 23.17. In Recipe 23.1, refer to (**9**) in Figure 23-2, which shows the objects being exported to AD. **(10)** in the same figure shows the objects created in AD. Follow these steps:

1. Open Identity Manager.
2. Click the Management Agents button on the toolbar.
3. In the Management Agents pane, click the ADMA.
4. In the Actions pane on the far right side, click Run.
5. In the Run Management Agent dialog, select Export and click OK.
6. You'll have to be quick if there is only a small amount of data in the ADMA. Notice the MA says "Running" in the State column of the Management Agents pane.
7. Notice in the Synchronization Statistics pane in the bottom lefthand corner, statistics showing the number of adds is displayed. If you click a hyperlink, you can navigate the information that was written to AD.
8. Open Active Directory Users and Computers.
9. Navigate to the Users container.
10. Ensure the user objects have been created.

Discussion

User accounts in Active Directory may be flagged as disabled even though you think they should be active. Assuming you set the `userAccountControl` attribute correctly, the usual reason for this is that some other attribute has not been set correctly and Active Directory has disabled the account. For example, if you do not set a password on an account, Active Directory will disable the account.

> If you do not set a password on a user object using the Active Directory Users and Computers MMC snap-in, you will receive a warning. If you do it programmatically, as MIIS does, the account will be disabled.

By performing all the previous recipes successfully, you have provisioned user accounts from employee records in the HR Database to AD.

See Also

Recipes 23.1 and 23.17 for how to configure the run profile that was used in this recipe

23.19 Testing Provisioning and De-Provisioning of User Accounts in AD

Problem

You want to test that new and deleted employee records in the HR Database propagate correctly to Active Directory.

Solution

You will add a new employee record and delete an existing employee record from the HR Database. You will then execute a series of run profiles that will perform the necessary operations.

1. Add and delete records from the HR Database.

    a. Open SQL Server Enterprise Manager.

    b. In the lefthand pane, drill down in to *Console Root\Microsoft SQL Servers\ SQL Server\SQL Server Group\(local)(Windows NT)\Databases\HR\Tables*.

    c. Right click the Employees table in the righthand pane, and select Open Table → Return all rows.

    d. Add a new row (you can type directly in to the table at the marker in the extreme lefthand column labeled *). Make sure you create a unique number in the Badge Number column.

    e. Delete a row by clicking one of the grey unlabelled buttons on the extreme lefthand edge of the table contents to select the row, and then pressing the Delete key. Note the name of the employee you deleted.

2. Execute the following run profiles in this order:

    a. HR Database MA's Full Import (Stage Only) run profile. For details on how to execute this run profile, see Recipe 23.10.

    b. The HR Database's Full Synchronization run profile. See Recipe 23.16 on executing the provisioning run profile.

    c. AD's Export run profile. See Recipe 23.18 on exporting objects using an export run profile.

3. To check if the add and remove were successful, open Active Directory Users and Computers.

4. Navigate to the Users container.

5. Ensure the user objects you modified in the HR Database have been created and deleted correctly.

Discussion

As the HR Database is modified, MIIS makes corresponding modifications to Active Directory. The order in which the MAs are run is important: import, synchronization, export. Synchronization is executed on the MA that imported data.

Delta imports are lightweight operations because MIIS requests only changes since the last time it connected to the data source. Delta synchronization only processes changed objects. Export run profiles only export changes.

Performing full imports and full synchronizations places a significant processing requirement on MIIS and its connected systems. If the system you are connecting to exposes a delta mechanism, you should use delta import and delta synchronization steps in normal daily operations. Database MAs connect to a delta-view or delta-table on the database server, which you will need to create before you can perform delta imports.

See Also

Recipes 23.10, 23.16, 23.18, and the Design and Planning Collection (*http://www. microsoft.com/downloads/details.aspx?familyid=DADC5021-222B-4AF7-8C58-2227C358756F&displaylang=en*)

23.20 Creating a Run Profile Script

Problem

It is impractical to continually use the UI every time you wish to execute a run profile. You want to automate the process, by calling MIIS run profiles to perform the required actions.

Solution

You need to create a run profile script:

1. Open Identity Manager.
2. Click the Management Agents button on the toolbar.
3. In the Management Agents pane, click the HR Database MA.
4. In the Actions pane on the far right side, click Configure Run Profiles.
5. In the Configure Run Profiles dialog, select the Export run profile.
6. Click the Script button.
7. In the File name text box, type HR Database MA Export.

8. In the Save as type text box, select VB Script.

9. Click the Save button.

10. Repeat Steps 3–9 for the other run profiles in the HR Database MA and the ADMA. Follow the same file naming convention.

Discussion

The scripts free you from the UI and can also form the building blocks of an MIIS implementation that runs unattended. You have several options, including:

1. Submit the scripts to the Windows Task Scheduler Service to run on a specified daily schedule. To do this, open the Task Scheduler, double-click Add Scheduled Task, and follow the steps in the wizard.

2. Create a Windows service that calls the scripts according to your own criteria. Perhaps submitting them to the task scheduler using its APIs.

3. If you already have a script execution environment, incorporate the new scripts.

See Also

Recipe 23.21 to create a controlling script, MSDN walkthrough about creating a Windows Service Application (*http://msdn.microsoft.com/library/en-us/vbcon/html/vbwlkwalkthroughcreatingwindowsserviceapplication.asp*), and the Task Scheduler API reference (*http://msdn.microsoft.com/library/en-us/taskschd/taskschd/task_scheduler_reference.asp*)

23.21 Creating a Controlling Script

Problem

Many times, you want to have a self-contained script that controls an entire sequence of operations, e.g., import the HR Database, synchronize, and then export to AD.

Solution

1. Open Notepad.

2. Type this script (or copy and paste the contents of the *GroupPopulatorSync.cmd* file from the MIIS Scenarios, referenced in the "See Also" section):

```
@echo off
rem
rem Copyright (c) Microsoft Corporation.  All rights reserved.
rem

setlocal
set zworkdir=%~dp0
pushd %zworkdir%
```

```
set madata="C:\Program Files\Microsoft Identity Integration Server\MaData"


rem Full Import of HR Dzatabase Employee Records
rem --------------------------------------------
cscript runMA.vbs /m:"HR Database" /p:"Full Import (Stage Only)"
if {%errorlevel%} NEQ {0} (echo Error[%errorlevel%]: command file failed) _
& (goto exit_script)

rem Full Sync of HR Database Employee Records
rem ------------------------------------------
cscript runMA.vbs /m:"HR Database" /p:"Full Sync"
if {%errorlevel%} NEQ {0} (echo Error[%errorlevel%]: command file failed) _
& (goto exit_script)

rem Export users in to AD
rem ---------------------
cscript runMA.vbs /m:"rallencorp.com" /p:"Export"
if {%errorlevel%} NEQ {0} (echo Error[%errorlevel%]: command file failed) _
& (goto exit_script)

:exit_script
popd
endlocal
```

3. In this case, HR Database is the name of the MA and Full Import (Stage Only) is the name of the run profile.

4. It is the same for the highlighted entries on the other two lines.

5. Save the file with a *.cmd* file extension.

6. Close Notepad.

7. Open Notepad.

8. Type the following script (or copy and past the contents of the *RunMA.vbs* file in the MIIS Scenarios, referenced in the "See Also" section):

```
option explicit
on error resume next


'=-=-=-=-=-=-=-=-=-=-=-=-=-=-=-=-=-=-=-=-=-=-=-=-=-=-=-=-=-=-=-=-=-=
'SCRIPT:      runMA.vbs
'DATE:        2003-02-05
'=-=-=-=-=-=-=-=-=-=-=-=-=-=-=-=-=-=-=-=-=-=-=-=-=-=-=-=-=-=-=-=-=-=
'= Copyright (C) 2003 Microsoft Corporation. All rights reserved.
'=
'*******************************************************************
'* Function: DisplayUsage
'*
'* Purpose:  Displays the usage of the script and exits the script
'*
'*******************************************************************
Sub DisplayUsage( )
        WScript.Echo ""
        WScript.Echo "Usage: runMa </m:ma-name> </p:profile-name>"
```

```
            WScript.Echo "                    [/s:mms-server-name]"
            WScript.Echo "                    [/u:user-name]"
            WScript.Echo "                    [/a:password]"
            WScript.Echo "                    [/v] Switch on Verbose mode"
            WScript.Echo "                    [/?] Show the Usage of the script"
            WScript.Echo ""
            WScript.Echo "Example 1: runMa /m:adma1 /p:fullimport"
            WScript.Echo "Example 2: runMa /m:adma1 /p:fullimport /u:domain\user
/a:mysecret /v"
            WScript.Quit (-1)
End Sub


'****************************************************************************
' Script Main Execution Starts Here
'****************************************************************************
'--Used Variables--------------------------
dim s
dim runResult
dim rescode
dim managementagentName
dim profile
dim verbosemode
dim wmiLocator
dim wmiService
dim managementagent
dim server
dim username
dim password
'-----------------------------------------

rescode = ParamExists("/?")
if rescode = true then call DisplayUsage
verbosemode = ParamExists("/v")

managementagentName = ParamValue("/m")
if managementagentName = "" then call DisplayUsage

profile = ParamValue("/p")
if profile = "" then call DisplayUsage

if verbosemode then wscript.echo "%Info: Management Agent and Profile is _
<"& managementagentName &":"& profile &">"
if verbosemode then wscript.Echo "%Info: Getting WMI Locator object"

set wmiLocator = CreateObject("WbemScripting.SWbemLocator")
if err.number <> 0 then
        wscript.echo "%Error: Cannot get WMI Locator object"
        wscript.quit(-1)
end if

server = ParamValue("/s")
password = ParamValue("/a")
username = ParamValue("/u")
```

```
if server = "" then server = "." ' connect to WMI on local machine

if verbosemode then
        wscript.Echo "%Info: Connecting to MMS WMI Service on <" & server &">"
        if username <> "" then wscript.Echo _
        "%Info: Accessing MMS WMI Service as <"& username &">"
end if

if username = "" then
        set wmiService = wmiLocator.ConnectServer _
        (server, "root/MicrosoftIdentityIntegrationServer")
else
        set wmiService = wmiLocator.ConnectServer_
        (server, "root/MicrosoftIdentityIntegrationServer", username, password)
end if

if err.number <> 0 then
        wscript.echo "%Error: Cannot connect to MMS WMI Service <" _
        & err.Description & ">"
        wscript.quit(-1)
end if

if verbosemode then wscript.Echo "%Info: Getting MMS Management Agent via WMI"

Set managementagent = wmiService.Get( "MIIS_ManagementAgent.Name='" & _
managementagentName & "'")
if err.number <> 0 then
        wscript.echo _
        "%Error: Cannot get Management Agent with specified WMI Service <" & _
        err.Description & ">"
        wscript.quit(-1)
end if

wscript.echo "%Info: Starting Management Agent with Profile <"& _
managementagent.name &":"& profile &">"
runResult = managementagent.Execute(profile)
if err.number <> 0 then
        wscript.Echo "%Error: Running MA <"& err.Description & _
        ">. Make sure the correct profile name is specified."
        wscript.quit(-1)
end if

wscript.Echo "%Info: Finish Running Management Agent"
wscript.Echo "%Result: <" & CStr(runResult) & ">"
wscript.quit(0)

'*****************************************************************************
'* Function: ParamValue
'*
'* Purpose:  Parses the command line for an argument and
'*           returns the value of the argument to the caller
'*           Argument and value must be seperated by a colon
'*
'* Arguments:
```

```
'* [in]      parametername      name of the parameter
'*
'* Returns:
'*          STRING     Parameter found in commandline
'*          ""         Parameter NOT found in commandline
'*
'******************************************************************************
Function ParamValue(ParameterName)

        Dim i                       '* Counter
        Dim Arguments               '* Arguments from the command-line command
        Dim NumberofArguments       '* Number of arguments from the command-line
        Dim ArgumentArray           '* Array to store arguments from command-line
        Dim TemporaryString         '* Utility string

        '* Initialize Return Value to e the Empty String
        ParamValue = ""

        '* If no ParameterName is passed into the function exit
        if ParameterName = "" then exit function

        '* Check if Parameter is in the Arguments and return the value
        Set Arguments = WScript.Arguments
        NumberofArguments = Arguments.Count - 1

        For i=0 to NumberofArguments
                TemporaryString = Arguments(i)
                ArgumentArray = Split(TemporaryString,":",-1,vbTextCompare)

                If ArgumentArray(0) = ParameterName Then
                        ParamValue = ArgumentArray(1)
                        exit function
                End If
        Next
end Function

'******************************************************************************
'* Function: ParamExists
'*
'* Purpose:  Parses the command line for an argument and
'*           returns the true if argument is present
'*
'* Arguments:
'* [in]      parametername      name of the paramenter
'*
'* Returns:
'*          true       Parameter found in commandline
'*          false      Parameter NOT found in commandline
'*
'******************************************************************************

Function ParamExists(ParameterName)

        Dim i                       '* Counter
```

```
Dim Arguments          '* Arguments from the command-line command
Dim NumberofArguments  '* Number of arguments from the command-line
Dim ArgumentArray      '* Array to store arguments from command-line
Dim TemporaryString    '* Utility string

'* Initialize Return Value to e the Empty String
ParamExists = false

'* If no ParameterName is passed into the function exit
if ParameterName = "" then exit function

'* Check if Parameter is in the Arguments and return the value
Set Arguments = WScript.Arguments
NumberofArguments = Arguments.Count - 1

For i=0 to NumberofArguments
        TemporaryString = Arguments(i)
        If TemporaryString = ParameterName Then
              ParamExists = true
              exit function
        End If
Next
end Function
```

9. Save the file in to the same folder as the previous script we created and name it *runMA.vbs*.

10. Close Notepad.

Discussion

A script to control these operations, known as a *controlling script*, is required. You could simply create a script that called each of your other scripts in turn, but managing large numbers of scripts as the solution gets more complex becomes a problem. Before you start this recipe, you may want to make sure you have the *GroupPopulatorSync.cmd* and *RunMA.vbs* files available. Refer to the "See Also" section for the URLs.

See Also

In Developer Help, navigate to *Microsoft Identity Integration Server 2003 Developer Reference/WMI Provider/Using the WMI Provider/Creating Scripts*; the *runMA.vbs* and *GroupPopulatorSync.cmd* script files can be obtained from the Group Management folder in the MIIS scenarios: *http://www.microsoft.com/downloads/details. aspx?FamilyID=15032653-d78e-4d9d-9e18-6cf0ae0c369c&DisplayLang=en*

23.22 Enabling Directory Synchronization from AD to the HR Database

Problem

You want AD to become the authoritative source for `telephoneNumber` attribute of Active Directory users.

Solution

You need to configure both the import attribute flow from the ADMA connector space to the metaverse, as well as the export attribute flow from the metaverse to the HR Database MA connector space. In Recipe 23.1, refer to (5) and (8) in Figure 23-2, which shows where the rules will be configured.

1. Open Identity Manager.
2. Click the Management Agents button on the toolbar.
3. In the Management Agents pane, double-click the ADMA.
4. In the Management Agent Designer pane on the lefthand side, highlight Select Attributes.
5. In the Attributes pane on the right side, select "telephoneNumber."
6. In the Management Agent Designer pane on the lefthand side, highlight Configure Attribute Flow.
7. In the Mapping Type section of the dialog, select Direct.
8. In the Flow Direction section of the dialog, select Import.
9. Ensure "user" is selected in the data source object type drop-down list.
10. Ensure "person" is selected in the metaverse object type drop-down list.
11. In the data source object type drop-down list, select "telephoneNumber."
12. In the metaverse object type drop-down list, select "telephoneNumber."
13. Click New.
14. Notice in the Attribute Flow pane, the arrow for this mapping indicates an import attribute flow. Click OK.
15. In the Management Agents pane, double-click the HR Database MA.
16. In the Management Agent Designer pane on the lefthand side, highlight Configure Attribute Flow.
17. In the Mapping Type section of the dialog, select Direct.
18. In the Flow Direction section of the dialog, select Export.
19. Ensure "person" is selected in the data source object type drop-down list.
20. Ensure "person" is selected in the metaverse object type drop-down list.

21. In the data source object type drop-down list, select "telephoneNumber."

22. In the metaverse object type drop-down list, select "telephoneNumber."

23. Click New.

24. Notice in the Attribute Flow pane, the arrow for this mapping indicates an export attribute flow. Click OK.

Discussion

You configured import attribute flow (IAF) from the ADMA to the metaverse and export attribute flow (EAF) to the HR Database MA. Notice these flows only dealt with attribute data. The object-level operations of projection and provisioning were not required because the objects already exist.

To put the new configuration to work you will need to configure run profiles to import, synchronize, and export the data. These steps are covered in Recipe 23.23.

See Also

Recipes 23.1, 23.23, and MIIS 2003 Design Concepts for Correlating Digital Identities, which is found in the MIIS 2003 Design Concepts download documents (*http://www.microsoft.com/downloads/details.aspx?familyid=40A52201-A297-4C35-82E9-F0B4CA05DAEB&displaylang=en*)

23.23 Configuring a Run Profile to Load the telephoneNumber from AD

Problem

You need to get the AD `telephoneNumber` attribute into MIIS and synchronize it.

Solution

Configure a run profile that combines import and synchronization (this recipe), then execute it (see Recipe 23.24):

1. Open Identity Manager.

2. Click the Management Agents button on the toolbar.

3. In the Management Agents pane, click the ADMA.

4. In the Actions pane on the far right side, click Configure Run Profiles.

5. In the Configure Run Profiles for "rallencorp.com" (the name in quotes will reflect the name you chose when creating the ADMA), click New Profile.

6. In the Name text box type Delta Import and Delta Synchronization, then click Next.

7. Ensure Delta Import and Delta Synchronization is selected in the Type drop-down list and then click Next.

8. Ensure the correct domain partition is showing in the Partition drop-down list, and then click Finish.

9. Ensure the details in the Step Details field looks like Figure 23-9 (note: your partition name may be different and the assumption is that you have completed the previous recipes).

10. Click OK.

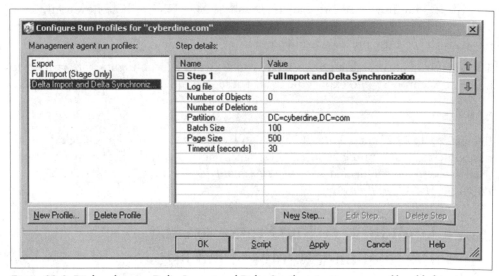

Figure 23-9. Dialog showing Delta Import and Delta Synchronization run profile added to the existing ADMA run profiles

Discussion

Because a previous import step was completed in an earlier recipe, you can use the combined Delta Import and Delta Synchronization step so that MIIS imports and synchronizes changes that have occurred in AD since the last time it connected. You can use this run profile from now on since it keeps track of changes internally using the DirSync control.

The Delta Import (Stage Only) step in the AD Export run profile (the confirming import from Recipe 23.17) also imports changes, which suggests you could simply configure a delta synchronization run profile to process those changes in this recipe. Such an approach will work. The decision on which approach to use will depend on the service-level agreements you make. If it is two hours since the last AD import, your service-level agreement might force you to import and synchronize the changes that have occurred over the last two hours and feed them to the HR Database; however, you may only need to export to AD every four hours. If you only rely on the changes detected in the confirming import step, you will only be able to update the HR Database with changes every four hours.

See Also

Recipes 23.17 and 23.24 for how to use the run profile configured in this recipe

23.24 Loading telephoneNumber Changes from AD into MIIS Using a Delta Import and Delta Synchronization Run Profile

Problem

You now need to pull the data from AD into MIIS.

Solution

With the MA and Run Profile created, you can now load telephoneNumber attribute data into MIIS by executing the run profile.

In Recipe 23.1, (**11**) in Figure 23-2 shows the telephoneNumber data being loaded into the AD connector space. The synchronization process then flows the data to the metaverse ((**6**) in Figure 23-2) and from there to the AD connector space ((**3**) in Figure 23-2).

1. Open Active Directory Users and Computers.
2. Navigate to a user in the container you are managing with MIIS.
3. Double-click the user object.
4. Ensure the General tab is selected and then type a telephone number in to the Telephone Number text box and click OK.
5. Open Identity Manager.
6. Click the Management Agents button on the toolbar.
7. In the Management Agents pane, click the ADMA.
8. In the Actions pane on the far right side, click Run.
9. In the Run Management Agent dialog, select Delta Import and Delta Synchronization and click OK.
10. Because you have changed the rules but not yet run a Full Synchronization on all the existing objects, a Run Step Warning dialog appears as shown in Figure 23-10. Click No.
11. Notice the MA briefly says Running in the State column of the Management Agents pane.

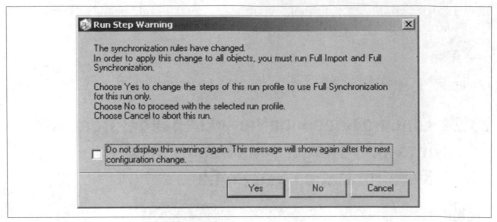

Figure 23-10. Run Step Warning dialog box

12. Notice the Synchronization Statistics pane in the bottom lefthand corner displays statistics showing the number of updates and connectors with flow updates. If you click one of the hyperlinks, you can navigate the information that was loaded.

Discussion

The Run Step Warning dialog says that you already have objects in the AD connector space, but you changed the attribute flow rules and then performed a delta synchronization. Therefore, the new attribute flow rules will only apply to new changes. All the telephoneNumber data that already exists in the connector space won't be subjected to those new rules. The warning is asking if you'd like to apply the new rules to the existing objects. Essentially you ignored the warning because if you have followed these recipes exactly, you should have only one new object in the ADMA's connector space with a telephone number, and that is the only one that will be synchronized anyway.

See Also

Recipes 23.1 and 23.18 for exporting objects to AD using an export run profile, which contains information about the confirming import (which is a Delta Import (Stage Only) step type)

23.25 Exporting telephoneNumber Data to the HR Database

Problem

You need to export the data from the HR Database MA connector space into the HR Database.

Solution

You need to configure and execute an export run profile. First, create the run profile:

1. Open Identity Manager.
2. Click the Management Agents button on the toolbar.
3. In the Management Agents pane, click the HR Database MA.
4. In the Actions pane on the far right side, click Configure Run Profiles.
5. In the Configure Run Profiles for HR Database pane, click New Profile.
6. In the Name text box type Export and then click Next.
7. Ensure Export is selected in the Type drop-down list and then click Next.
8. Ensure default is showing in the Partition drop-down list and then click Finish.
9. Click New Step.
10. In the Configure Step dialog, ensure Full Import (Stage Only) is selected in the Type drop-down list and then click Next.
11. Ensure default is selected in the Partition drop-down list and then click Finish.
12. Ensure the details in the Step Details field looks like Figure 23-11.
13. Click OK.

Discussion

You had to select Full Import (Stage Only) for the confirming import step in this run profile because the HR Database hasn't been configured to provide deltas.

See Also

Recipe 23.17 for similarities in how a run profile is configured to export objects to AD

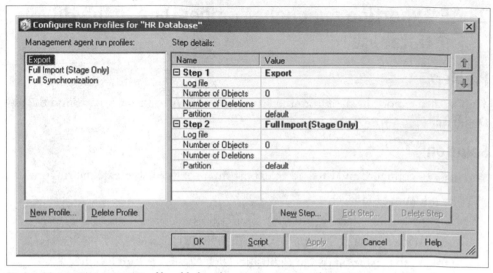

Figure 23-11. Export Run Profile added to the existing HR Database MA run profiles

23.26 Using the HR Database MA Export Run Profile to Export the Telephone Number to the HR Database

Problem

The run profile is configured, but you need to actually move the data from MIIS to the HR Database.

Solution

You need to execute the run profile. In Recipe 23.1, refer to (12) in Figure 23-2, which shows the telephoneNumber data being exported to the HR Database.

1. Open Identity Manager.
2. Click the Management Agents button on the toolbar.
3. In the Management Agents pane, click the HR Database MA.
4. In the Actions pane on the far right side, click Run.
5. In the Run Management Agent dialog, select Export and click OK.
6. Notice the MA briefly says Running in the State column of the Management Agents pane.
7. Notice that in the Synchronization Statistics pane in the bottom lefthand corner, statistics showing the number of updates is displayed. If you click the hyperlink, you can navigate the information that was written to the HR Database.

8. Open SQL Enterprise Manager.

9. In the lefthand pane, drill down to *Console Root\Microsoft SQL Servers\SQL Server\SQL Server Group\(local)(Windows NT)\Databases\HR\Tables*.

10. Right click the Employees table in the righthand pane, and select Open Table → Return all rows.

11. Find the record of the user you added the telephoneNumber to in AD and ensure the [telephoneNumber] column has been updated.

Discussion

Now would be a good time to add the last two run profiles you created to the controlling script from Recipe 23.21. Then we can make multiple changes to AD and the HR Database and watch the effects by simply running the script. We could even put a simple loop into the script so that it is executing continuously and watch new users, deleted users, and telephoneNumber changes as they propagate around the systems.

See Also

Recipe 23.1, Recipe 23.18 for similarities in how a run profile is used to export objects to AD, and Recipe 23.21

23.27 Searching Data in the Connector Space

Problem

You have started to use MIIS, but things aren't going according to plan. You want to see if the changes you made to either the HR Database or AD have made it into the associated connector space.

Solution

1. Open Identity Manager.

2. Click the Management Agents button on the toolbar.

3. In the Management Agents pane, click the MA you wish to search.

4. In the Actions pane on the far right side, click Search Connector Space.

5. In the Search Connector Space dialog, click the Search button.

6. You will notice records returned in the main search pane.

7. If this is the HR Database MA, the DN of each record will be the Badge Number—the primary key in the database that ensures uniqueness in the recordset. If this is the ADMA, the DN will be the object's DN in LDAP format (e.g., CN=Steve Plank,OU=oreilly,DC=rallencorp,DC=com).

8. Record the RDN of a record from the step above. If it's the HR Database MA, the RDN is the same as the DN. If it's the ADMA, it's the element that contains the least-significant object in the DN (e.g., CN=Steve Plank).

9. Select RDN in the Scope drop-down list.

10. Type the RDN you have recorded into the text box (e.g., CN=Steve Plank).

11. Click Search.

12. You will notice a single record returned, which matches the RDN you have specified.

13. If you double-click any of the returned records, you can examine the object in detail.

Discussion

You will see in the Scope drop-down list that there are more entries than just Sub-Tree and RDN. The error collections are useful when trying to debug records that give errors from a large connector space with many thousands of objects in it.

Also, once you have double-clicked a record and are viewing its properties, you will notice a Lineage tab at the top of the page. On it, there is a Metaverse Object Properties button. This will show you the properties held on the related metaverse object.

See Also

Recipe 23.28 for searching data in the metaverse and the MIIS 2003 help file section *Microsoft Identity Integration Server 2003/How To.../Manage a Connector Space/ Search a Connector Space*

23.28 Searching Data in the Metaverse

Problem

You are troubleshooting and want to view a metaverse object.

Solution

You need to search the metaverse:

1. Open Identity Manager.

2. Click the Metaverse Search button on the toolbar.

3. Click the Search button.

4. Records from the metaverse are returned in the Search Results pane.

5. Double-click a record in the Search Results pane.

6. You can see which MA contributed data to this metaverse object. If you double-clicked the object that you added a `telephoneNumber` to in AD, you should see its attributes detailed in the pane below the Attributes tab.

7. Click the Connectors tab.

8. You can see which MAs this metaverse object is joined to.

Discussion

The connectors tab highlights the difference between projection and provisioning. You should see that the link between the metaverse object and the connector space entries was created because of projection rules for the HR Database MA and provisioning rules for the ADMA. That is because you configure the HR Database MA to project objects to the metaverse, and then you wrote a rules extension to provision objects from the metaverse to the AD connector space.

See Also

Recipe 23.27 for searching data in the connector space and the MIIS 2003 help file section *Microsoft Identity Integration Server 2003/Concepts/Using Microsoft Identity Integration Server 2003/Using Management Agents/Using Metaverse Search*

23.29 Deleting Data in the Connector Space and Metaverse

Problem

You want to clear out the connector space or the metaverse, perhaps so you can perform a complete run through again of all these recipes to consolidate learning.

Solution

1. Open Identity Manager.

2. Click the Metaverse Designer button on the toolbar.

3. In the Actions pane on the far right side, click Configure Object Deletion Rule.

4. Ensure the "Delete metaverse object when connector from this management agent is disconnected" radio button is selected.

5. Select the HR Database MA from the drop-down list, then click OK.

6. Click the Management Agents button on the toolbar.

7. In the Management Agents pane, click the MA you wish to delete objects from—do the ADMA first.

8. In the Actions pane on the far right side, click Delete.

This is important: you risk deleting the whole MA if you do not perform the following step correctly.

9. Ensure the "Delete connector space only" radio button is selected.

10. When prompted that you are sure you want to delete the connector space, click Yes.

11. A message box appears with details of how many records were deleted. Click OK.

12. Perform Steps 7–11 again on the HR Database MA.

Discussion

You configured the metaverse object deletion rule so that when objects from the HR Database MA were deleted, the related metaverse objects would also be deleted. That is why you deleted objects from the ADMA first. When you performed Steps 7–10 the second time, the metaverse objects were also deleted. You can prove this by searching the metaverse in between delete operations.

There is no metaverse delete. MIIS ensures that objects in the metaverse *always* have a join to at least one object in a connector space from at least one MA. The object deletion rule is the configuration that tells MIIS what to do with metaverse objects when connector space objects get deleted.

To give more control, you can specify that a rules extension should be used to make the decision for you.

It is impossible to end up in the situation where MIIS has an object in the metaverse, but no corresponding object in any connector space.

See Also

To delete both the connector space and the MA, use the MIIS 2003 help file and navigate to *Microsoft Identity Integration Server 2003/How To…/Work with Management Agents/Create and Edit Management Agent Run Profiles/Delete a Management Agent and Connector Space*. To understand more about writing rules extensions to make deletion decisions, open the MIIS 2003 Developer Reference help and navigate to *Microsoft Identity Integration Server 2003 Developer Reference/ Microsoft Identity Integration Server 2003 Reference/Microsoft.MetadirectoryServices Namespace/Interfaces/IMVSynchronization/IMVSynchronization.ShouldDeleteFromMV* and to *Microsoft Identity Integration Server 2003 Developer Reference/ Microsoft Identity Integration Server 2003 Reference/Microsoft.MetadirectoryServices Namespace/Interfaces/IMASynchronization/ IMASynchronization.Deprovision*

Index

We'd like to hear your suggestions for improving our indexes. Send email to *index@oreilly.com*.

911

M

About the Authors

Robbie Allen is a technical leader at Cisco Systems, where he has been involved in the deployment of Active Directory, DNS, DHCP, and several network management solutions. He enjoys working on Unix and Windows, and his favorite programming language is Perl. Robbie was named a Windows Server MVP in 2004 and 2005 for his contributions to the Windows community and the publication of several popular O'Reilly books. Robbie is currently studying at MIT in the system design and management program. For more information, see Robbie's web site at *www.rallenhome.com*.

Laura E. Hunter is a Microsoft MVP for Windows Server Networking and holds the following certifications: CISSP, MCSE:Security, and MCDBA. She is a senior IT specialist with the University of Pennsylvania. She is also the author of several fine books on MCSE and security topics.

Colophon

The animal on the cover of *Active Directory Cookbook*, Second Edition, is a bluefin tuna (*Thunnus thynnus*), also known as a horse mackerel. It inhabits both the Atlantic and Pacific Oceans in temperate and subtropical waters. The body of a bluefin tuna is a metallic, deep blue on top, while the undersides and belly are silvery white. The first dorsal fin is yellow or blue; the second is red or brown. The rear fin and finlets are yellow, edged with black. The central caudal keel is black.

The bluefin tuna is one of the largest and fastest species of marine fish. An adult can weigh as much as 1,500 pounds (680 kilograms) and can swim up to speeds of 55 miles per hour (88.5 kilometers per hour). A bluefin tuna can swim across the Atlantic Ocean in 40 days. Recent pop-up satellite tracking has revealed that the bluefin tuna can dive to depths greater than 3,000 feet in a matter of minutes and still maintain a body temperature of 77 degrees Fahrenheit (25 degrees Celsius), even in near-freezing water.

Commercial fishing has reduced the stock of bluefin tuna to the extent that a single fish, once caught, can be worth up to $40,000. However, the situation is reversible, and the numbers of tuna could increase if the guidelines of the International Commission for the Conservation of Atlantic Tuna (ICCAT), an intergovernmental fishing organization that oversees tuna, are followed.

The cover image is from *Dover Pictorial Archive*. The cover font is Adobe ITC Garamond. The text font is Linotype Birka; the heading font is Adobe Myriad Condensed; and the code font is LucasFont's TheSans Mono Condensed.

Better than e-books

Buy *Active Directory Cookbook*, 2nd Edition, and access the digital edition FREE on Safari for 45 days.

Go to www.oreilly.com/go/safarienabled
and type in coupon code X5MW-Z7EL-7KL3-R5MP-C88Y

Search
thousands of
top tech books

Download
whole chapters

Cut and Paste
code examples

Find
answers fast

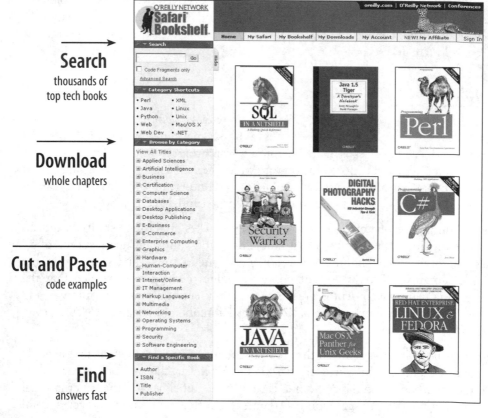

Search Safari! The premier electronic reference
library for programmers and IT professionals.